HIGHER EDUCATION:
Handbook of Theory and Research

Volume IV

Associate Editors

Philip G. Altbach, *State University of New York at Buffalo*
(comparative higher education)
Alan E. Bayer, *Virginia Polytechnic Institute and State University*
(faculty)
Kim S. Cameron, *University of Michigan*
(organizational theory and behavior)
Clifton F. Conrad, *University of Wisconsin*
(graduate and professional education)
David D. Dill, *University of North Carolina*
(governance and planning)
Cameron Fincher, *University of Georgia*
(curriculum and instruction)
Larry L. Leslie, *University of Arizona*
(finance and resource allocations)
Ernest T. Pascarella, *University of Illinois at Chicago*
(research methodology)
Patrick T. Terenzini, *University of Georgia*
(students)
John R. Thelin, *College of William and Mary*
(history and philosophy)

HIGHER EDUCATION:
Handbook of Theory and Research

Volume IV

Edited by

John C. Smart
University of Illinois at Chicago

Published under the sponsorship of
The Association for Institutional Research (AIR)
and
The Association for the Study of Higher Education (ASHE)

AGATHON PRESS, INC.
New York

EE

© 1988 Agathon Press, Inc.
111 Eighth Avenue
New York, NY 10011

ISBN: 0-87586-086-9
ISSN: 0882-4126

LCCN: 86-642109

Printed in the United States

7-10-89

Contents

The Contributors

LEONARD L. BAIRD has over 20 years experience assessing students and institutions in higher education, first as a researcher at the American College Testing Program and then at the Educational Testing Service, conducting studies on a variety of aspects of higher education. He is currently professor of Educational Policy Studies and Evaluation at the University of Kentucky. The author of numerous articles and books, his chief research interests are in the impact of college on students, college quality, and the social psychology of higher education.

KIM S. CAMERON is Associate Professor of Organizational Behavior and Industrial Relations in the Graduate School of Business Administration and Associate Professor of Higher Education in the College of Education at the University of Michigan. His research is concerned with various aspects of organizations, such as decline, effectiveness, downsizing, and redesign. His work has appeared in a variety of management and higher education journals. Books of which he is the author or coauthor include works on organizational effectiveness, management skills, strategic adaptation, and most recently, on organizational decline and the management of paradox and transformation.

SHIRLEY M. CLARK is Professor of Education and Sociology at the University of Minnesota. She also chairs the Department of Educational Policy and Administration and is active in campus governance. Her research and teaching interests are in the sociology of education, including higher education with a focus on faculty studies. Recently she co-edited *Faculty Vitality and Institutional Productivity: Critical Perspectives for Higher Education* with Darrell R. Lewis.

DAVID D. DILL is Assistant to the Chancellor and Associate Professor of Education at the University of North Carolina at Chapel Hill. His research has focused on issues of governance, organizational behavior and research performance in academic settings. He is currently editor of the journal *Planning*.

DEBORAH R. ETTINGTON is a doctoral student of Organizational Behavior in the University of Michigan Business School. Her research interests include organizational change, the impact of organizational change on individual careers, and management education.

PETER T. EWELL is Senior Associate at the National Center for Higher Education Management Systems (NCHEMS). His research and writing concentrate on the impact of college on students and the use of information in decision making.

JAMES C. HEARN is Associate Professor of Higher Education at the University of Minnesota. His research focuses mainly upon processes of organizational change in higher educational institutions and upon factors affecting students' postsecondary educational attainments.

vii

KAREN PETERSON HELM is Director of University Planning at North Carolina State University. Her responsibilities include strategic planning and administering a campus-wide planning complement to budget development. Previously, Ms. Helm served as Executive Assistant to the Chancellor at NCSU and Assistant to the Chancellor for Academic Affairs at the University System of New Hampshire.

DARRELL R. LEWIS is Professor of Educational Policy and Administration and Coordinator of the Higher Education Program at the University of Minnesota. An economist of education, his research and publications have focused on economics of education, reward systems, issues of productivity, and evaluation in education. With Shirley M. Clark he is co-editor of *Faculty Vitality and Institutional Productivity: Critical Perspectives for Higher Education.* His forthcoming book is *Assessing Outcomes, Costs and Benefits of Special Education Programs.*

GARY D. MALANEY is Director of the Student Affairs Research and Evaluation Office at the University of Massachusetts at Amherst. Previously, he was a postdoctoral research fellow at the Graduate School of The Ohio State University, where he wrote his chapter on research in graduate education. He has also served as Research Administrator in the Department of Political Science and as Assistant Director of the School of Public Administration, both at Ohio State. His recent research has focused on various aspects of graduate education, and his publications have appeared in several higher education journals.

ULRICH TEICHLER is Professor of Higher Education and Work at the Comprehensive University of Kassel (Federal Republic of Germany) and Professor of Education and Social Policy at Northwestern University. He served for seven years as Director of the Center for Research on Higher Education and Work in Kassel. His research interests and publications include education and social selection, causes and impacts of higher education expansion, access to higher education, patterns of the higher education system, curricula, placement and recruitment of graduates, and graduate employment.

JOHN R. THELIN is Chancellor Professor at The College of William and Mary in Virginia. He serves as Director of the Higher Education Doctoral Program and also is a member of the American Studies Program and Public Policy Studies Program faculties. In 1986 he received the university's Phi Beta Kappa Faculty Award for the Advancement of Scholarship.

BARBARA K. TOWNSEND is Assistant Professor in the Higher Education Program at Loyola University of Chicago. Her research on such topics as the community college heritage, students in higher education, and organizational policy has been published in *Research in Higher Education, The Review of Higher Education, Community College Review, Educational Studies,* and *The Chronicle of Higher Education.* Professor Townsend is a member of the Editorial Board for *The Review of Higher Education.*

The College Environment Revisited: A Review of Research and Theory

Leonard L. Baird
University of Kentucky

Researchers' interest in the important, but extremely complex and slippery topic of the college environment has waxed and waned over the last 30 years. Beginning with Pace and Stern's (1958) development of the College Character-istics Index to measure perceptions of environmental press, a great variety of approaches and instruments were developed to assess the psychological climates of colleges (Baird and Hartnett, 1980). The availability of these instruments, joined with an increased interest in college student development, led to a great deal of research on the perceptions of the environment by different groups and the effects of different environments in the 1960s and early 1970s (Feldman and Newcomb, 1969; Pascarella, 1985). From the mid-1970s to recent years, the focus seems to have turned to relatively specific aspects of the environment or of subgroups, perhaps because these aspects are more subject to intervention and manipulation, and because they may impinge more directly on students' lives than the global environment (Baird and Hartnett, 1980; Moos, 1979). Although the listings in *Higher Education Abstracts* suggest that researchers' interest in the college environment has remained at about the same level in recent years, it has not regained its popularity of the 1960s.

However, several recent developments have renewed interest in the college environment. First is the call for increased quality in the undergraduate *experience* (e.g., Boyer, 1986), which entails the environment. For example, the recommendations of several national reports recommend changes in the *process* of education as the pathway to excellence (e.g., Study Group on the Conditions of Excellence in American Higher Education, 1984). Second is the interest of researchers in finding better theoretical concepts to explain the ways in which the colleges affect students, as reflected in the development of models of student-environment interaction to account for student attrition (e.g., Pascarella and Terenzini, 1983; Tinto, 1987). These models use concepts which refer, at least partly, to the faculty and peer environments of colleges. A third is the "ecological" approach to guidance and counseling that has emerged in the last few years, which attempts to analyze information about students and their

1

environments and to identify matches and mismatches for the purposes of intervention (e.g., Huebner, 1980).

The purpose of this chapter is to examine the various conceptions of the college environment and to suggest appropriate assessment strategies. In so doing, I will discuss the history of problems in conceptualizing and assessing the environment, evidence from studies of college impact on students, criteria for theories, the issues of the level of analysis, and the validity of different kinds of measures. Finally, potentially useful conceptions from research into organizational behavior will be discussed.

A HISTORY OF APPROACHES
TO THE COLLEGE ENVIRONMENT

Approaches to studying the college environment can be categorized as demographic, perceptual, behavioral, and multimethod approaches (Menne, 1967; Feldman, 1972; Huebner, 1980). Demographic methods are primarily descriptive and are based on data of record such as enrollment, distribution of majors, and library books per student. The perceptual approach relies on students', faculty's, and administrators' responses to items and scales designed to assess their perceptions of their institutions. The behavioral approach attempts to assess the environment by measuring detailed observable behavioral regularities of students, faculty, and staff. The multimethod approach combines the other three into a single assessment. Probably the best way to understand these approaches is to examine them in their context in the history of research on college students and their institutions. In general, this history seems to have followed two main streams: one stream focused on understanding and assessing the environment per se, or environmental description, and a second stream assessed the environment as a part of research that focused on other concerns, such as the development of talent, the course of vocational choices, or attrition. Eventually these streams merged.

The First Stream: Environmental Description

The approaches that developed in this stream are mainly organized around specific instruments which are the operational definitions of various approaches to the environment. For this reason, this section of the chapter will describe these measures in some detail. Although there were many implicit theoretical approaches to the college environment, with attendant assessment procedures, reviewed by Barton (1960), the first formal proposal for measuring the college environment lies in the work of Pace and Stern (1958). During the 1950s at Syracuse University, Pace and Stern began to work with the idea that a student's behavior depends not only on personality but also on the demands of the college and the interaction between the student's personality and the college. For example, a rigid student may do well in a formal, structured college but poorly in an informal, unstructured one. Specifically, Pace and Stern attempted to implement the ideas of Harvard psychologist Henry Murray about the personality "needs" of an individual and the "presses" of the environment that influence the individual's behavior. *Needs* are manifested by a tendency to perform actions of a certain kind; for example, a "need for achievement" might be manifested by working hard for grades. A *press* is a property or attribute of an environment which encourages or discourages the individual to behave in particular ways (Stern, 1970).

Presses are of two types, first as they exist in reality or an objective inquiry discloses them to be (alpha press), and second as they are perceived or interpreted by the individual (beta press). The beta press is further composed of a *private press* based on the unique and personal view each person holds about his or her experience and a *consensual press,* which is the common or mutual interpretation of experiences shared by people participating in events. For example, a course in calculus could be judged as relatively difficult or easy by an external expert in mathematics who also had some information about the prior mathematics training and performance of the students. This would be the alpha press. An individual student could feel that the work was easy or difficult (private beta press) but could sense the class's collective view of its difficulty (consensual or aggregated beta press). Thus, an individual's perception of the environment is based partly on his or her own interpretation of experience and partly on the interpretations of important reference groups.

It is this perceived environment that Pace and Stern attempted to assess with the College Characteristics Index (CCI), designed to parallel the measure of needs tapped in the Activities Index (AI). Although Murray's theories did not require that needs and presses be conceived of as parallel, for the purpose of exploring the potential value of the CCI Pace and Stern included scales to parallel those of the AI. The scales were derived from Murray's list of "needs" (1938) and included such variables as affiliation, autonomy, order, and understanding. In other words, the 30 scales of the CCI were part of a strategy to find environmental presses that bore directly on the satisfaction or frustration of a psychological need. In some cases, this strategy had face validity; for example, the AI need-for-change scale was paralleled by the CCI change-press scale, which included items on whether course and procedures were frequently revised and whether the student body was diverse in background, opinions, and behavior. Other scales seemed to be stretching to find environmental parallels of needs. For example, "harm avoidance" included items on fire drills, health campaigns, housing requirements, and the absence of such "rough" activities as intramural sports. The parallelism, not intended by Murray in any case, seems strained and even misleading as a guide to the environment. In any case, the approach seemed to focus on the individual's perceptions of the environment.

Stern (1970) subsequently argued that these individual perceptions of the environment from the CCI could be aggregated and averaged to yield a portrait of the collective environment.

Empirical studies showed that the CCI did indeed differentiate among colleges; for example, the profiles for Bennington and Syracuse differed. However, the original hope that the parallelism would reveal a person-environment "fit" which would affect academic performance and student satisfaction was not realized. Although one would expect, for example, students with needs for affiliation to get better grades and to be more satisfied in colleges with high average scores on the CCI affiliation scale, most studies showed no effect of congruence on satisfaction or achievement and have shown negative effects as often as positive effects (see Walsh, 1973, and Huebner, 1980, for summaries of evidence). Further, little has been written to show how the CCI could be used to improve the student-college fit, even if it were shown to make a difference, and less has been written on how CCI results could be specifically used to improve "congruence" on campuses.

These negative results are partly due to the multiple scales on the CCI (i.e., there are 30 possible "fit" scores), and to the fact that the psychometric strategy used to develop the CCI was to examine the variance between individuals, rather than the differences among colleges. That is, differences in CCI scores were based on differences in how different students saw colleges, some portion of which were due to their personalities, attitudes, and so on, and on another indeterminant portion which was due to differences among the colleges they were attending. This was because Stern used the student as the unit of analysis rather than the college. These limitations led Pace (1969), who had moved to UCLA at this time, to use a different strategy. Pace abandoned the press-need parallelism, used the average scores of colleges as the unit of analysis, and selected items that seemed directly relevant to the college experience. Pace used the statistical techniques of cluster analysis and factor analysis and used the college as the unit of analysis to reduce the number of scales to reflect only the major ways *colleges* differed from one another. Finally, for the final selection of items, Pace used a scoring system that was designed to reflect "consensus." An item is counted toward a score in a scale only if two thirds of the respondents agree (or disagree) in the scored direction. For example, if 69% agreed that "students are encouraged to take an active part in social reforms or political programs," it would count for one point for a college on the awareness scale; if only 62% agreed, it would not count.

The outcome of Pace's analyses was the College and University Environment Scales (CUES). CUES originally consisted of 150 items drawn from the CCI and provided 30-item scales on five dimensions: pragmatism, reflecting the college's emphasis on practicality, status, and college fun; community, reflecting the friendliness and warmth of the campus; awareness, reflecting an active cultural and intellectual life; propriety, reflecting properness and conventionality; and scholarship, reflecting the academic rigor of the college. Eventually, CUES also included a 22-item scale of campus morale, and an 11-item scale of quality of teaching (faculty-student relationships). Pace (1969) related these scales to a variety of other information about colleges to establish their validity. For example, among colleges with high scholarship scores, a greater proportion of the faculty held doctorates. Small colleges were more likely than large colleges to have high community scores.

In a subsequent study with CUES, Pace (1974) compared the activities of upperclassmen and alumni of 100 institutions. Pace found that these eight types of institutions, selected to reflect the diversity of American higher education, had quite different patterns of CUES scores. For example, selective universities, engineering schools, and selective liberal arts colleges had similar high scores on the scholarship dimension, but engineering schools had very low awareness scores, while the other two had very high scores; less selective liberal arts colleges had community scores as high as selective liberal arts colleges but had lower scholarship and awareness scores. The other types of colleges—general comprehensive universities, strongly denominational colleges, and teacher's colleges—also showed distinctive patterns on CUES.

However, the most important results of Pace's study for questions of validity were the correlations between CUES scores and the activities and attitudes of students and alumni. For example, the art-activity scale measured whether students and alumni read about art, talk about it, went to galleries and museums to see it, bought it, and expressed themselves through it. The art-activity scale correlated .67 among upperclassmen and .62 among alumni with their college's score on the CUES awareness scale. A college scoring high on this scale would have "an environment that encourages concern about social and political problems, individuality and expressiveness through the arts, and tolerance of criticism" (Pace, 1974). Although one would expect people who experience an environment that encourages expressiveness through the arts to be active in art, colleges that score high on the CUES awareness scale are seldom art schools; usually they are private liberal arts colleges, many of which do not consider themselves to place an extraordinary emphasis on art education. And they are not necessarily highly selective, so the high scores on art activity received by these schools' upperclassmen and alumni cannot be explained simply by the caliber of students that the college attracts. Thus, the art activity of these students and alumni may be a result of the lively intellectual atmospheres of their colleges.

This study also found many other relationships between CUES scores and student and alumni sense of educational progress on a variety of areas, such as writing, understanding science, and critical thinking. In general, students or alumni reported stronger evaluations of their progress in colleges with high CUES scores in areas related to the area of progress. Although not nearly as strong as evidence from studies of student change, these self-reports of amount of progress suggest that the aspects of the environment measured by CUES may be related to the impact of colleges; at least, they are related to satisfaction.

CUES has also been used to compare the perceptions of different campus subgroups, with results indicating that most groups perceive the overall environment in approximately the same way (e.g., Berdie, 1967), although administrators often have a much more positive view of their colleges than do students (Pascarella, 1974). Pace (1972) also showed that the CUES scores of 80 protestant colleges were related to the strength of their legal ties to their denominations: "The more firmly and zealously a college is related to a church the more clearly it emerges as a distinctive college environment. And this distinctiveness is defined by uniformly high scores on the characteristics labeled community, propriety, and practicality" (p. 37).

CUES was also used in a great many studies that compared the scores of incoming freshmen with those of upperclassmen (Feldman and Newcomb, 1969, reviewed many of these studies). In general, incoming freshmen seemed to share a general idealized image of college as friendly, stimulating, and vigorous, regardless of the description provided by students who had actually experienced the environment. Stern (1970) called this the "freshman myth." Some studies suggested that students quickly formed a less idealistic view of their college, sometimes within a few weeks. However, there is little evidence that this "disillusion" has any long-lasting effects.

CUES has also been used by other researchers to examine other topics. For example, Chickering, McDowell, and Campagna (1969) studied institutional differences and student development. Although, like other researchers, they found little relationship between environmental scores and changes in personality, measured in this study by the Omnibus Personality Inventory, they did find relationships with college "orientations." Specifically, students in colleges with high practicality scores tended to shift out of the "nonconformist" orientation, and students in colleges with high community or scholarship scales tended to shift away from the vocational orientation, intellectual students moved into academic orientations, and practical students shifted into vocational and collegiate orientations. All of this suggests some interactions between student characteristics and college environments. Unfortunately, there are very few other studies examining the influence of the variables measured by CUES and change in students. Thus, the main evidence for the influence of the environment as measured by CUES is correlational.

The development of CUES suggests several issues that apply to all measures of the environment and that will be considered again in the concluding section of the chapter. These problems include finding an appropriate theoretical scheme to conceptualize the environment, generalizing from *individual* perceptions or characteristics to a group or total environment, finding conceptually and statistically sound units of analysis and methods of scoring, and establishing the validity of the environmental measure.

Stern (1970) attempted to deal with one of the limitations of the CCI approach: its large number of *a priori* variables and scales. Stern factor-analyzed the CCI, using individual students' responses as the unit of analysis. Technically, this meant he had analyzed the variance between students' perceptions of colleges in general, rather than the variance between colleges per se. The dimensions identified are therefore the dimensions of how different students view their colleges, as well as the dimensions of how colleges differ from one another as reflected in the perceptions of their students. Stern has reported second-order factor analyses of the CCI and has developed versions for use in high schools, evening colleges, and organizations. Stern has also attempted to describe the "culture" of colleges by factor-analyzing the Activities Index and the CCI together, and then describing colleges in joint terms of the characteristics of their students and the students' perceptions of the environment. This procedure seems to finesse another question about the college environment: Is it due more to the characteristics of the people in the college, or is it due more to the characteristics of the institution independent of its students?

Although Stern (1970) does not provide a satisfactory definition of college "culture" or give a convincing rationale for his analyses, the idea of simultaneously analyzing average individual characteristics and aggregate perceptions of the environment appears to have merit. Stern used institutions as the unit of analysis, and he used average scores on the AI need factors and CCI press factors as variables. The second-order factor analysis recorded five "culture" factors: the expressive, a non-work-oriented, nonconforming climate peopled by students with nonapplied interests, who do not value orderliness; the intellectual, characterized by intellectually demanding courses and faculty, opportunities for expressiveness, little bureaucratic control, peopled by students with high levels of interest in academic achievement and ideas; the protective, characterized by a highly organized, supportive environment and a relatively dependent, submissive student body; the vocational, characterized by heavily applied programs, conventionality, and authoritarianism, with students who tend to be selfish and manipulative; and the collegiate, characterized by extensive facilities for student recreation and amusement, ambiguous standards of achievement, and uncertain administrative practices, with friendly and assertive students.

Stern also proposed three additional indexes: dispersion, deviancy, and dissonance. The dispersion index is the average variation around the college or group mean. For example, a college with a small dispersion index score would presumably have a high degree of consensus on desirable behavior and characteristics; a college with a large dispersion index would have little such consensus. The deviancy index is simply the *individual's* distance from the college mean. The dissonance index is the discrepancy between the need component and the press component of each culture score. This index can be calculated for individuals for assessing intraindividual dissonance or for groups, to assess what Stern calls "cultural dissonance." As intriguing as these indexes are, they, like the "culture" idea, have not been used systematically in subsequent work.

Other Environmental Measures

The interest in the environment *per se* and student characteristics in the mid-1960s led to a variety of additional measures, most of which were developed at the Educational Testing Service. The first of these was the College Student Questionnaire (CSQ; Peterson, 1968), a lengthy survey which was designed to do two things: first, to assess student characteristics that presumably will affect their adjustment to college or could be affected by their college experiences, and second, to assess aspects of the environment that could influence that adjustment or development. Obviously, the questionnaire mixes student and institutional characteristics. However, one of its chief values has been its utility in studying *changes* in groups on variables that one would hope would be affected by college study. It consists of two parts.

Part I, covering students' backgrounds, attitudes, and plans, was designed to be used with entering students; Part II, which obtains information about students' educational and vocational plans, college activities, and attitudes toward their college, is designed to be used with students who have had one or more years of college. Each questionnaire consists of 200 multiple-choice questions, some of which are fairly complex. Part I can be scored for 7 scales: Family Independence, Peer Independence, Liberalism, Social Conscience, Cultural Sophistication, Motivation for Grades, and Family Social Status. Part II can be scored for 11 scales: the first five described for Part I plus Satisfaction with Faculty, Satisfaction with Administration, Satisfaction with Major, Satisfaction with Students, Study Habits, and Extracurricular Involvement. Although the CSQ was developed atheoretically, there is an *implicit* theory of college impact in these scales; that is, one would hope that as students move through college, they would become independent of their families and independent of peer pressures, would develop greater social consciousness, would become more culturally sophisticated, and, depending on one's political views, would become more liberal in their attitudes. One might also hope that students would be satisfied with their professors, their majors, their peers, and the administrative policies and procedures, which, together, would reflect satisfaction with the environment. That is, again implicitly, the CSQ assumes that the most salient feature of the environment is whether students feel satisfied that it is meeting their educational needs.

Because its format is designed to study change, the CSQ has been used in a wide variety of studies of student groups, particularly residence groups such as those in fraternities and sororities and residence halls (Longino and Kart, 1974). Wilder et al. (1986), for example, studied three cohorts of students at Bucknell, with data gathered when they were freshmen and upperclassmen in the 1960s, the 1970s, and the 1980s. In each time period, "Greek" students tended to score lower than independent or former Greek students on the scales assessing family and peer independence, cultural sophistication, social conscience, and liberalism. The Greeks also gained less on these scales during college. However, the most intriguing finding was that the students of the 1980s *also* scored lower on these measures and gained less. This result belies the belief that today's students start college at a higher level of maturity than students in the past.

The CSQ was also used in a great many studies of the "subcultures" in the Clark and Trow (1966) typology, consisting of the academic, nonconformist, collegiate, and vocational subcultures. Although the CSQ actually measures the "orientation" that a student prefers among those described in four paragraphs, it has, nevertheless, been the operational definition used in studies which find a number of differences among the four groups of students (e.g., Terenzini and Pascarella, 1977; Doucet, 1977).

The next environmental approach measure, the Institutional Functioning Inventory (IFI), was developed in the "environmental description" tradition with a project to assess "institutional vitality," that is, to identify the characteristics of colleges that seemed to have strong, individual atmospheres. This effort changed to one of identifying the major dimensions of how colleges *function* (Peterson et al., 1970). In addition, the authors realized that, in order to understand how colleges function, they would need to assess the perceptions of faculty and administrators, as well as students. The 11 scales in the IFI thus represent the aspects that the authors considered the most important for institutional functioning: Intellectual-Aesthetic Curriculum; Freedom; Human Diversity; Concern for the Improvement of Society; Concern for Undergraduate Learning; Democratic Governance; Meeting Local Needs; Self-Study and Planning; Concern for Advancing Knowledge; Concern for Innovation; and Intellectual Esprit. Although a factor analysis of average faculty scores on these scales suggested that they could be more parsimoniously described by only four factors (liberal atmosphere, sense of community, intellectual climate, and ivory tower outlook), the authors contend that the conceptual distinctions among the scales warrant their retention.

The "validity" of the scales was suggested by correlating them with data of record, CUES scores, and a study of student protest (Sasajima, Davis, and Peterson, 1968). The correlations seemed plausible; for example, library size and research funds were correlated with the Advancement of Knowledge Scale (.77 and .72, respectively), the Concern for the Improvement of Society Scale correlated with the CUES awareness scale (.68), and the Concern for Undergraduate Learning Scale was negatively correlated with the incidence of student complaints and demonstrations about the quality of teaching. In addition, a multigroup-multiscale analysis showed that faculty, administrators, and students generally described their campuses the same way, with the interesting exception of the Democratic Governance Scale. On this scale, students often perceived much less democracy than did their professors and administrators.

The IFI seems to be sensitive to the actual differences among colleges. For example, although there is a positive correlation between the Institutional Esprit and Democratic Governance scores across all colleges, the profile of one of the armed service academies shows a very high score on Institutional Esprit and a very low score on Democratic Governance; in contrast, a selective liberal arts college renowned for its flexibility had a very high score on Democratic Governance and a very low score on Institutional Esprit.

One of the most extensive studies using the IFI was conducted by Anderson (1983), who compared the "functioning" of a number of colleges, defined by scores on the IFI obtained between 1968 and 1972 and scores obtained between 1979 and 1981, and related these scores to the financial conditions of the colleges. Overall, colleges' scores on the IFI suggested greater human diversity and less democratic governance in the later period. However, state-supported institutions reported gains on all 11 scales, while community colleges declined on 4 scales. Most important, Anderson found little relationship between changes in finances and changes in the IFI. For example, faculty morale was less affected by salaries and institutional finances than by participation in governance. As this study illustrates, the IFI assesses perceptions of components of the environment that are important to faculty, as well as components that are important to students. In that sense, it involves an implicit recognition that there are multiple environments that are based on the experiences of the respondents. For example, faculty would generally have little knowledge of student social life or groups, and students would have little knowledge of the institution's policies on publication and tenure, although these are extremely important to the groups that can report on them. However, it is unlikely that most people who are knowledgeable about college affairs would agree that the IFI adequately describes how colleges actually work, or how their daily activities are carried out.

Another approach to the environment was taken from the literature on organizational theory and behavior. One consistent theme in that literature is that it is critical to understand the *goals* of an organization in order to understand how it functions (e.g., Georgion, 1973). This idea has been applied to universities by sociologists Gross and Grambsch (1968, 1974), who studied the goals of 68 Ph.D.-granting universities as seen by faculty and administrators in two different time periods. The results were basically that the universities in both periods were heavily committed to research and scholarly pursuits, with much less attention given to students and their needs. Peterson and Uhl (1977) adapted the Gross and

Grambsch strategy by designing an Institutional Goal Inventory (IGI) so that respondents can rate each of 90 statements of goals both according to how those goals are currently emphasized at the college and according to how they believe the goals should be emphasized. The differences between these "is" and "should be" ratings show how closely present campus goals match the goals that people prefer, and they identify areas where changes may be needed. Furthermore, differences among groups of respondents on their preferred goals show how much agreement exists about institutional purposes and objectives.

The IGI consists of 20 scales. Most of the goal statements form scales that comprise 13 *outcomes,* or substantive objectives, that a college may seek to achieve: Academic Development, Intellectual Orientation, Individual Personal Development, Humanism/Altruism, Cultural/Esthetic Awareness, Traditional Religiousness, Vocational Preparation, Advanced Training, Research, Meeting Local Needs, Public Service, Social Egalitarianism, and Social Criticism/ Activism. The remaining statements form 7 scales relating to educational or institutional *process* goals: Freedom, Democratic Governance, Community, Intellectual/Esthetic Environment, Innovation, Off-Campus Learning, and Accountability/Efficiency.

These scales are based on the perceptions of respondents in response to items concerning their institution's goals. For example, in the Academic Development Scale, respondents report their perceptions of the importance their institution currently gives to such goals as "to help students acquire depth of knowledge in at least one academic discipline" and "to hold students throughout the institution to high standards of intellectual performance."

Although IGI scores correlated with such published institutional data as proportion of faculty with doctorates and sectarian control, the most interesting study was an analysis of the views of faculty, students, administrators, and other members of the institution's community, such as residents and legislators, which showed that different types of institutions differed dramatically on the IGI, reflecting their sharply different missions. In a study of 105 California colleges, Peterson and Uhl (1977) reported that differences were especially large on the scales of Research, (universities high, community colleges low), Vocational Preparation and Social Egalitarianism (community colleges high, private institutions low).

It is striking that for all institutions combined, the "should be" scores were higher than the "is" scores on every scale, suggesting that few institutions are currently meeting their goals, according to their constituencies. The discrepancy was particularly large for the scales of Community, Intellectual Orientation, Individual Personal Development, and Vocational Preparation. In addition, a study comparing the IGI scores of the students, faculty, administrators, chancellors, regents, and residents of local communities of the University of California revealed some large differences *within* the institutions.

As with the IFI, factor analysis revealed a much simpler structure:

> In summary, five factors were identified in the analyses of present importance ratings: (1) humanistic development, which emphasized the personal and ethical development of the student; (2) a liberal, flexible environment characterized by freedom in many activities; (3) service to society; (4) research and graduate training; and (5) academic and intellectual development of students and the associated academic and intellectual climate. With only two minor exceptions, these factors were consistent for each participating group.
>
> The results of the analyses of preferred importance ratings are very similar to the analyses of present importance ratings with two exceptions: (1) the academic and intellectual development factor was not isolated as a separate factor; and (2) for the faculty and administrator groups only, an ivory-tower factor was identified, which included Factor 3 (service to society) at one pole and Factor 4 (research and graduate training) at the other pole. (Peterson and Uhl, 1977, p. 55)

Although an analysis of institutional goals is commonly considered critical in order to understand a college's policies and procedures, most goals are specifically tied to the history, the clientele, and the particular programs of the colleges. Therefore, it may not appear to be especially fruitful to many observers to examine *general* goals as the approach of the IGI does (Lunneborg, 1978). A better strategy would be a consideration of *detailed* goals. However, for research purposes, this general approach may allow for comparisons among institutions that would not be possible in the clutter of particular institutions' goals.

Despite its "goal" rationale, it should be obvious that the IGI, at least in the "is" section, is basically a perceptual measure, and thus, it is not surprising that the factors found in the factor analysis are fairly similar to those found in analyses of other perceptual measures. And these factors tend to reflect the general ways in which perceptions of colleges differ from one another, which do not necessarily correspond to other information about colleges or the people in them.

A Shift in Environmental Assessment Research

The possible limitations of the perceptual approach led to two strategies: the first was to use multiple sources of information about colleges, and the second was to make environmental assessments more specific and practical. The first strategy was used by Centra (1970, 1973) in the development of the Questionnaire on Student and College Characteristics (QSCC) to describe the college environment accurately by including information on students' perceptions of their institutions, their behavior during college, and their personal backgrounds and characteristics. After an initial tryout in 8 colleges, Centra (1970) obtained data from a sample of students in 214 colleges, which were subjected to a variety of factor analyses. First, the 77 items that asked for students' perceptions were analyzed separately. (These items asked students either to indicate whether statements were true or false or to rate their agreement with statements on a 4-point scale.) A typical item was "Faculty members tend to be aloof and somewhat formal with students." The factors obtained were termed Restrictiveness, Faculty-Student Interaction, Activism, Nonacademic Emphasis, Curriculum Flexibility, Challenge (academic), Laboratory Facilities, and Cultural Facilities. From these analyses, factor scores based on two to nine items per factor were computed. The median coefficient alpha reliabilities of the scales were .86, and six of the eight scales had reliabilities of .84 or higher.

In a second analysis, the eight factor scores just described were included with 34 student self-report items about their behavior in college (for example, the extent of their involvement in intramural athletics or dramatic productions), plus objective information about the colleges (such as the percentage of students in residence halls, the number of books in the library per student, and student SAT scores). A factor analysis yielded six factors: athletic emphasis versus cultural activities, size and cliquishness, academic elitism, activism and flexibility, students' satisfaction with their college, and social life. A second, multimethod factor analysis yielded 10 factors. The first 4 were similar to those obtained in the standard factor analysis, supporting the meaning and stability of those factors. The remaining 6 factors were regulation, fraternity and sorority emphasis, emphasis on science, and three other factors with unclear meanings. The variety of these factor solutions suggests the dependence of the description of the environment on the methods used in analysis.

In an interesting precursor to the student consumerism movement, the colleges that had participated in the administration of the QSCC had been encouraged to use the results in their self-descriptions for the "College Life" section of the College Board's *College Handbook*. Interestingly, 53% did not use the results at all, 9% used them for only one to three sentences, 13% used them for as much as a short paragraph, and only 25% used them extensively.

However, the key finding, again, is that the dimensions of the environment that are found are considerably dependent on the methods used to assess them. The point was also made by Chickering (1972), who found that "Colleges which are bedfellows on CUES, where students give their general impressions, may not even be roommates on an instrument like the ECQ [Experience of College Questionnaire], where they report their daily experiences and behaviors, although they may remain in the same dormitory. Conversely, strangers on one instrument may find themselves friends or acquaintances on another" (p. 141). This point will be discussed in greater detail later in the chapter.

The second strategy for increasing the value of environmental measures was to make them more specific and practical. As Baird (1974) pointed out, most measures were so "global as to be unrelated to concepts suggesting practical actions" (p. 307). This is partly due to the fact that most have been perceptual measures, relying on generalizations, and that they were designed to reflect interinstitutional variance, or how colleges as units vary from one another. This means that local or specifically important concerns may not be reflected in the measures in any useful detail. For this reason, some researchers attempted to develop more detailed measures or techniques.

For example, Warren and Roelfs (1972) developed the Student Reactions to College questionnaire for colleges to use in identifying students' views of institutional strengths and weaknesses. To maximize the instrument's usefulness to staff members and its relevance to students, Warren and Roelfs did not simply develop their own questions; instead, they interviewed students, faculty members, and administrators about what they thought was important to know about their colleges. And on a pretest version of the form, students were asked to write in issues of importance to them that were not covered in the questionnaire. Its first 150 items cover such areas as instruction, grading, faculty and staff contact with students, registration and class scheduling, student activities, financial problems, housing, food services, and transportation. In addition, the questionnaire includes 9 background questions about the student and space for 20 questions that the college can develop itself. The items ask students if they feel their needs are being met.

Betz, Klingensmith, and Menne (1970) reviewed industrial research on job satisfaction for its insights into students' satisfaction with their colleges, and after a variety of analyses, they developed the College Student Satisfaction Questionnaire, which assesses satisfaction with fairly specific areas: (1) Policies and Procedures (for example, choice of classes); (2) Working Conditions (for example, comfort of residence); (3) Compensation (for example, amount of study required to attain good grades); (4) Quality of Education (for example, making friends); and (6) Recognition (for example, faculty acceptance of the student as worthwhile).

An even more specific technique, the Environmental Referent, has been developed by Huebner and Corrazini (1978), which asks respondents to provide written descriptions of the factors that caused them to experience a particular situation as stressful and incongruent or enhancing and congruent. When common themes appear, the concrete situation is analyzed so that corrective actions can be taken.

In general, then, in recent years, the "environmental description" stream of research has seemed to focus more on relatively specific aspects of the environment that are related to student satisfaction. What began with the rather abstract theoretical concept of need-press congruence, across colleges, has come to emphasize the concrete practical details of specific local conditions.

The Second Stream: Approaches to the College Environment Developed as Part of Other Research Questions

A variety of approaches to the college environment are the result of research projects which attempted to understand an issue in higher education where the environment was of secondary importance. For example, one of the major concerns of research in the late 1950s and the 1960s was the development of "talent," which usually meant some form of academic achievement. Knapp and Goodrich (1952) and Knapp and Greenbaum (1953) conducted some of the earliest of these studies that touched on the college environment. Knapp and Goodrich calculated the *rate* at which colleges' baccalaureates were later listed in *American Men of Science,* and Knapp and Greenbaum examined the rate at which they later won graduate fellowships or earned doctorate degrees. Knapp and Goodrich correlated various factual characteristics of the colleges with the rate of "success" and found that the most productive institutions had moderate rather than high costs, were often small liberal arts colleges, and drew many students from semirural areas. For example, the 10 most productive institutions in this study were, in descending order, Reed, Cal Tech, Kalamazoo, Earlham, Oberlin, University of Massachusetts, Hope, DePauw, Nebraska Wesleyan, and Iowa Wesleyan. Intrigued that these colleges outperformed such institutions as Harvard, Yale, Princeton, Berkeley, Michigan, and Columbia, none of which were in the top 50 in the production of scientists, Knapp and Goodrich did case studies of the institutions to attempt to understand why some colleges were so unexpectedly productive. They examined their histories, finances, students, faculty, and curricula. Although each institution was unique, in general, they were characterized by "a student body in which the scholar is the hero rather than the athlete or socialite" (p. 94). They also did a study of ratings of faculty and found that "productive" colleges had faculty characterized as "masterful," as exemplified by rigorous standards of grading and a high level of energy; as "warm," as illustrated by the use of humor and concern for students; and as having "intellectual distinction," as manifested in intellectual mastery of the field and scholarly production.

As the Cold War progressed in the 1950s, the concern about America's "talent resources" increased greatly (e.g., Wolfle, 1954). One of the consequences was the founding of the National Merit Scholarship Corporation (NMSC) in 1955. The Merit Corporation was founded with the purpose of identifying the nation's most talented high school students and providing financial assistance for their college education. Supported by funds from the Ford Foundation and the National Science Foundation, the NMSC tested several million high school students each year. After a number of studies of the predictors of the academic accomplishment of the very bright students who received scholarships, the NMSC research staff began to explore the conditions in colleges that were associated with the educational attainments of the Merit Scholars, particularly plans to attend graduate or professional school, and to obtain the Ph.D.

One group of these studies stemmed directly from the work of Knapp and his associates. Thistlethwaite (1960, 1963) and Thistlethwaite and Wheeler (1966) conducted a series of analyses using samples of current students, all of whom had taken the NMSC examination in high school. The criteria in the last of these studies were degree aspirations and plans for entry into graduate school of the students as seniors. Statistical controls for initial aspirations, sex, test scores, social class, finances, and initial major were used. Thistlethwaite developed a perceptual measure designed to assess the environmental factors that might influence educational aspirations. There were 14 lower division scales (9 for faculty press and 5 for student press) and 20 upper division scales (12 for faculty press and 8 for student press). Factor analysis of the press scales suggested six factors: excellence of faculty in major field, lower division humanistic and intellectual press, upper division student intellectualism, lower division faculty supportiveness and enthusiasm (all these factors were positively related to plans and aspirations for advanced study), student camaraderie and playfulness, and faculty press for vocationalism and compliance (both negatively related to plans and aspirations). However, it should be noted that none of these variables was as strongly related to plans after the controls were applied as were undergraduate grade-point average and the proportion of the students' friends who were entering graduate school immediately after college. In any case, Thistle-thwaite's measures were another perceptually based attempt to analyze the subtleties of the environment, which resulted in dimensions that were quite similar to those found by Pace and other researchers, although the research question was quite different.

The next development at the National Merit Scholarship Corporation was a fairly direct extension of John Holland's (1962, 1966) theory of vocational choice. Holland theorizes that there are six types of vocational choices corresponding to six personality groupings (the Realistic, Scientific, Artistic, Social, Conventional, and Enterprising), and that there are six corresponding types of environments. The environments are consistent with the interests, needs, habits, and interpersonal styles of the personalities. When personality and environment type match, this congruence leads to satisfaction and reinforcement of the individual's characteristics. When they are incongruent, the result is dissatisfaction and dissonance. (A formal statement of the theory will be discussed later in the chapter.) Therefore, in order to study this theory of vocational choice among college students, Astin and Holland (1961) developed the Environmental Assessment Technique (EAT), which is based on the assumption that

> the college environment depends on the personal characteristics of the students, faculty, administration and staff of the institution. Since the undergraduate's personal contacts are chiefly with fellow students, it is further assumed that the major portion of the student's environment is determined by the characteristics of his fellow students. Accordingly the environment was defined in terms of eight characteristics of the student body; average intelligence, size, and six personal orientations based on the proportions of the students in six broad areas of study. (p. 308)

The "orientations" were based on Holland's theory of vocational choice and were estimated by the percentage of students majoring in realistic (or technical) fields, scientific fields, social fields, conventional (or clerical) fields, enterprising (or business and sales) fields, and artistic fields. How did this relatively simple system work? Astin and Holland first found that the EAT variables correlated with the perceptual CCI scores. For example, the average intelligence of students was strongly related to the CCI Understanding Scale, and the Realistic Scale had a highly negative relation with the CCI Humanism Scale.

Astin (1963b) later showed that the EAT correlated with seniors' ratings of their colleges at 82 colleges. For example, he reported that size correlated .57 with the percentage of students reporting that "many of the social groups on campus have a definite snob appeal." Intelligence level correlated .63 with the percentage reporting that "The typical student spends a lot of time in the library"; the realistic orientation correlated .57 with students' reports that their attitudes toward fraternities and sororities had become more positive; intellectual (or scientific) orientation was correlated −.58 with the percentage who agreed that "Many of the students are interested primarily in getting married and raising families"; the social orientation was correlated .41 with the percentage who agreed that "A student who is not very skilled in etiquette or social graces would probably feel out of place on the campus"; the conventional orientation was correlated .56 with the percentage who agreed that "Faculty members usually don't like the student to question their judgment or point of view"; the enterprising orientation correlated .42 with the percentage who agreed that "Students are always ready to argue or debate almost any issue"; and the artistic orientation correlated −.47 with the percentage who felt that their interest in sports had increased during college. Most of the relations were both sizable and plausible. Altogether, Astin and Holland martialed substantial evidence that the characteristics of the student body have a considerable influence on the total environment.

Richards, Seligman, and Jones (1970) provided evidence that the characteristics of the faculty and the curriculum, as well as the students, have an influence on the environment. These researchers modified the EAT strategy to derive measurements of school environments by counting the number of courses, the numbers of degrees, and the number of faculty members rather than using the proportions of students in the six types of fields derived from Holland's theory.

These three measures correlated with each other, but at a lower level than one might expect, so that scores based on one data source would provide a different "environment" score than scores based on another. For example, faculty and student scores correlated .53 for enterprising and −.18 for conventional. Perhaps more important, the faculty scores correlated only moderately with CUES scores; the highest correlation was −.43 between faculty intellectual (scientific) scores and CUES practicality scores. Correlations between faculty scores and CUES scores that one would predict to be higher often were not. For example, faculty social scores correlated .12 with CUES community scores, faculty artistic scores correlated .19 with CUES awareness scores, and faculty realistic scores correlated .04 with CUES practicality scores. Perhaps a perceptual measure for faculty, like the IFI, would correlate more highly. However, it is plausible to think that if one were studying faculty, these faculty measures might be of value, and if one were studying curriculum, the curricular measures could be used.

Astin (1962) was subsequently motivated by a researcher's desire to provide other researchers "with a more limited set of empirical dimensions which account for the major variations among institutions" for use as independent variables in their studies. Astin's strategy was to factor-analyze the factual information that can be obtained from college directories and fact books such as tuition and number of books in the library. Astin did this for 33 variables concerning four-year colleges and obtained six dimensions that accounted for many of the differences on these variables between colleges (80% of the variance). He called the six dimensions affluence or wealth, size, private versus public control, proportion of males in the student body, technical emphasis, and homogeneity of curriculum and EAT scores. Astin (1963a) then used these measures to show that very bright students were less likely to aspire to the Ph.D. degree in large colleges, predominantly male colleges, and colleges emphasizing clerical curricula. Astin (1965) showed that these scores correlated with student characteristics (e.g., degree aspirations and high school accomplishments) and differed by college types (e.g., technological institutions and liberal arts colleges). He also reported scores for most individual four-year colleges for the purpose of guiding students in their choice of college.

Astin's strategy was subsequently used with junior colleges by Richards, Rand, and Rand (1966), who found six factors: cultural affluence, technological specialization, size, age, transfer emphasis, and business orientation. Richards and Braskamp (1969) showed that these factors were related to a wide variety of average student characteristics. The junior college factors had a few similarities with the four-year college factors. Subsequently, Richards, Rand, and Rand (1968) used the same strategy with medical schools and found four factors: affluence, Canadian versus United States admissions practice, size, and hospital training emphasis. The limitations of these various factual approaches will be discussed later in the chapter.

After moving to the American Council on Education, Astin (1968, 1972) decided that the perceptual approach was too ambiguous, and that what he called the "student characteristics" approach provided too little information about the educational process to be adequate for assessing the college environment. He proposed another approach to the environment, which he called a "stimulus" approach. His idea was that the actual behavior of students and faculty and specific features of the college represent stimuli that have an impact on each student's perceptions of the college as well as on his or her own behavior. An environmental stimulus is "any behavior, event, or other observable character-istic of the institution capable of changing the student's sensory input, the existence of which can be confirmed by independent observation" (p. 5). Astin asked students to respond to 275 relatively specific items concerning their own behaviors and the characteristics of their peers, classrooms, college rules, and so on. In addition, students responded to 75 items that were similar to CUES items to analyze their "image" of their college. Astin separately analyzed the items referring to the "peer," "classroom," "administrative" and "physical" environments and found 27 dimensions on which colleges differed from one another. Analysis of the "image" items produced eight additional factors, resulting in 35 dimensions to describe the college environment.

The content of the factors was clearly dependent on the particular items Astin had used. For example, the "peer environment" factors ranged from the general factor "competitiveness versus cooperativeness" to "regularity of sleeping habits." All of the "administrative" environment scales consisted of factors whose names began with "severity of administrative policy against . . ." since all the original items referred to rules. Although some students may be strongly affected by rules and their enforcement, most students are affected in more areas of their behavior by such administrative decisions as tuition, registration, and degree requirements. And, of course, students are also influenced, albeit indirectly, by administrative policies that are usually beyond their knowledge, such as requirements for hiring and promotion of faculty and the allocation of the budget. Thus, Astin's description, in spite of its 35 dimensions, seems quite limited in some areas, even if we accept Astin's "stimulus" idea. There are other aspects of the college that serve as unperceived or indirect "stimuli."

In addition, although the interpretations of original factors are based on all the loadings in a factor analysis, the actual "scales" used in the Inventory of College Activities are amazingly short. Of the 25 "stimulus" scales, 12 are three items long, six are two items long, and seven consist of one item. Sometimes the content is peculiar, as often happens in studies based on the factor analysis of a hodge-podge of variables. For example, the percentages of students who said that in the past year they had gambled with cards or dice, had *not* participated in an informal group sing, and had *not* voted in a student election are weighted and summed to measure "competitiveness versus cooperativeness." "Informal dating" was measured solely by the percentage of students who said they had fallen in love in the past year.

Furthermore, many of the items seemed problematical; some seemed as "perceptual" as other instruments, for example, the three items that composed the "Extraversion of the Instructor" scale: "The instructor was enthusiastic," "The instructor had a good sense of humor," and (scored negatively), "The instructor was often dull and uninteresting." More generally, it is hard to see how many of the items which refer to private behavior that is usually unobservable by other people could be "stimuli" for other students in the aggregate, for example, "I had a blind date," "I took weight-reducing or dietary formula," and "I overslept and missed a class or appointment." In sum, although the general *idea* of examining the physical, social, intellectual, and organizational stimuli that impinge upon students for keys to the environment seems to have considerable potential, this particular attempt does not seem to fulfill that potential. An approach that is based more on theoretically, or even intuitively, based ideas and less on a shotgun approach would be much better. I shall return to this point later in the chapter.

Creager and Astin (1968) factor-analyzed ICA scores from the research just described as well as variables from earlier factual analyses: the colleges' affluence, size, and so on, and such "commonsense" variables as type of control and region of the country. Most of the resulting dimensions placed great weight on the commonsense and factual data. This suggests the possibility that we may be able to infer a good deal about a college from a few basic facts without a much more extensive investigation. For example, the first factor, Drinking versus Religiousness, has high negative loadings on selectivity, status, and private nonsectarian control as well as high positive loadings on severity of the policies against drinking, sex, and aggression. Thus, if we knew that a college was private, nonsectarian, highly selective, and prestigious, we could make a pretty good guess that it would be a free and open campus with regard to drinking, sex, and so on. The greatest weight on the second factor was given to the proportion of males at the school, the third factor to the size of the student body, the fourth to the presence of Roman Catholic colleges in the sample, and the fifth to technical institutes. The rest of the weights on these factors were consistent with general expectations about such institutions and consisted of the "stimulus" and "image" factors as well as other commonsense variables. In general, many of the differences between colleges were associated with commonsense distinctions, suggesting that some typology of institutions could be developed that would provide us with a great deal of information about colleges. For example, we know a lot about a college just by knowing that it is a selective engineering college in the Northeast or an unselective womens' Catholic college in the Midwest.

In contrast, when Astin and Panos (1969) studied the influence of college environments on the vocational and educational plans and achievements of college students, the stimulus and image measures had a considerable influence, independent of and sometimes larger than the commonsense or factual variables. In predicting 28 criteria after controlling for input, commonsense and factual environmental variables appeared in the equations 88 times, while "stimulus" and "image" factors appeared 68 times. Although the stimulus and image factors seemed to have more powerful influences on educational aspirations and plans than upon career choices, which were influenced by the composition of the student body, they seemed to be getting at something unique in college environments that influence students' development. Thus, while we may know a good deal just by knowing the facts about a college, we still need to know more to really understand its environment.

RECENT RESEARCH ON THE COLLEGE ENVIRONMENT

Interest in the topic of the general college environment seemed to subside in the 1970s. Instead, researchers began to focus on subenvironments and more specific aspects of the college experience, which more directly impinge upon the behavior of students. The two major research efforts in these areas were conducted by Moos, who concentrated on subenvironments, and Pace, who concentrated on student experiences.

Moos (1979), who began his career studying therapeutic milieus, turned his attention to residence units in colleges. The eventual product of his research was the University Residential Environment Scales (URES). Partly from his psychiatric background, Moos proposed that environments can be seen as having three domains of social climate and their related dimensions: *relationship* dimensions, which assess the extent to which people are involved in the setting, the extent to which they support and help one another, and the extent to which they express themselves freely and openly; *personal growth* or goal orientation dimensions, which measure the basic goals of the setting, that is, the areas in which personal developmental self-enchancement tends to occur; and *system maintenance and change* dimensions, which measure the extent to which the environment is orderly and clear in its expectations, maintains control, and responds to change.

The URES designed to measure these constructs consist of 9–10 items each and measure 10 dimensions, which are grouped into "domains." These 10 scales, with typical items, are as follows:

Relationship Domain

1. Involvement ("There is a feeling of unity and cohesion here").

2. Emotional Support ("People here are concerned with helping and supporting one another").

Personal Growth Domain

3. Independence ("People here pretty much act and think freely without too much regard for social opinion").

4. Traditional Social Orientation ("Dating is a recurring topic of conversation around here").

5. Competition ("Around here, discussions frequently turn into verbal duels").

6. Academic Achievement ("People here work hard to get top grades").

7. Intellectuality ("People around here talk a lot about political and social issues").

System Maintenance and Change Domain

8. Order and Organization ("House activities are pretty carefully planned here").

9. Student Influence ("The students formulate almost all the rules here").

10. Innovation ("New approaches to things are often tried here").

The validity of the URES approach was suggested by a series of studies. Some correlated URES data about dormitories with other information about dormitories (Gerst and Sweetwood, 1973); others used the URES to construct a typology of student living groups (Moos et al., 1975); some related URES scores to the influence of living groups on students' vocational choices (Hearn and Moos, 1976); and still others studied the effects of "megadorms" (Wilcox and Holahan, 1976).

Moos (1979) also developed a College Experiences Questionnaire, which was designed to assess the consequences of college attendance in four general areas: styles of coping with college life; personal interests and values; self-concept, mood, and health-related behaviors; and aspiration and achievement levels. Moos and his associates administered this instrument to students in 52 living groups on two campuses at the beginning and at the end of their freshman year. Moos also administered the URES. Moos first identified clusters of living groups based on the similarity of their URES profiles. These clusters include relationship-oriented groups, traditionally socially oriented groups, supportive achievement-oriented groups, competitive groups, independence-oriented groups, and intellectually oriented groups. When Moos compared the changes in group scores using a comparison of residuals (actual versus predicted scores), there were distinctive impacts of each grouping, with the interesting exception that competitive groups had no significant effects on any outcome. Residence groups had no influence on any of the measures of self-concept and mood, or on the coping style of "hostile interaction", but had a considerable effect on "student body involvement" (such as attending a school political rally and voting in a student election); academic orientation (participating in a science contest or being a member of a scholastic honor society); and achievement level (grade-point average). Other research examined the influence of the groups on students' health. Moos and Van Dort (1977), for example, found that groups with low social and emotional support and high competition had higher than average reports of stress and physical complaints.

Additional evidence about the idea of the importance of the environment of living groups comes from a variety of studies. For example, Winston, Hutson, and McCaffry (1980) found that while the fraternities with the highest grades on one campus had no higher average SAT scores than the fraternities with the lowest grades, their URES scores showed that the high-achieving fraternities scored significantly higher on the Academic Achievement and Intellectuality scales and lower on the Independence scale. However, occasional negative results, at least those using Moos's approach, cast doubt upon the idea that the residence group environment influences grades. For example, Ballou (1985) found numerous differences among types of residence halls on the URES, but the type of residence was unrelated to grades, student participation in campus activities, and health habits. These inconsistent or complex, even muddled, results are much like those in a good deal of the research on residential units.

However, Moos's strategy can be seen as a fairly direct continuation of Astin and Panos's (1969) comment on their extensive analyses of the influences on the vocational and educational development of a large sample of students and institutions:

> Since most of the environmental effects of our 246 institutions appeared to be mediated through the peer environment rather than the classroom, administrative, or physical environments, further study of the nature and influence of undergraduate peer groups is clearly indicated. At the same time, a greater effort should be devoted to the identification of other effective environmental variables which are more directly manipulatable and not so highly dependent on the characteristics of the entering students. (p. 158)

Residence groups are clearly a major force in the peer environment, and one that can often be manipulated to have rather different characteristics. More generally, Moos's strategy represents a move away from interest in the global or distal environment and toward a concern with the local or proximal environment and the use of important subgroups rather than the institution as a whole as the unit of analysis, which may be a more fruitful research approach.

Pace's attempt to assess students' quality of effort, while not designed to provide a measure of the environment, does, in fact, demonstrate large differences among types of colleges not only in the average "level of effort," but in the specific incidence of particular experiences of students, some of which must be due as much to the type of college they attend as to their own effort.

The instrument Pace developed to assess these ideas was the College Student Experiences questionnaire (CSEQ), a standardized self-report survey of how students spend their time and the nature and quality of their activities (Pace, 1987). Students respond by checking "never," "occasionally," "often," or "very often" for activities in 14 clusters of mostly 10 items: Library Experiences; Course Learning: Art, Music, and Theater; Science Lab Activities; Student Union; Athletic and Recreation Facilities; Dormitory or Fraternity/

Sorority; Experiences with Faculty; Clubs and Organizations; Experiences in Writing; Personal Experiences; Student Acquaintances; Topics of Conversation; and Information in Conversation. The items are arranged in a hierarchy so that participation in a high-level activity is qualitatively different from participation in a lower level activity.

Although not designed to measure environments, the norm group information by type of college suggests major differences in the experiences of students among types of institutions which, if the "aggregate behavior" approach is used, would play a larger role than the characteristics of the students in defining the character of the environment. Baird (1987) compared CSEQ scores of doctoral universities, comprehensive colleges and universities, selective liberal arts colleges, general liberal arts colleges, and community colleges and found fairly sizable differences. Although the community college students understandably reported a lower rate of activity and involvement in many out-of-classroom areas, especially in athletics and recreation, clubs and organizations, art, music and theatre, and student acquaintances, they reported an activity rate equal to other types of colleges in the areas of library usage, writing, and interactions with faculty. Thus, the *academic* side of the college experience was strong in community colleges, but the nonacademic side was not, probably due to the high rate of commuting. In contrast, doctoral universities were below average in library usage, writing, and interactions with faculty. Comprehensive colleges and universities were below average in athletics and recreation, clubs and organizations, and student acquaintances. General liberal arts colleges' students reported a high rate of activity in interactions with faculty, use of the student union, athletics and reaction, and clubs and organizations. Selective liberal arts college students reported the highest levels of activity of all groups in the areas of use of the library; interaction with faculty; art, music, and theater; student union; athletics and recreation; clubs and organizations; and student acquaintances.

More specifically, students at doctoral universities reported the lowest frequency of any type of college of "working on a paper or project where you had to integrate ideas from various sources," "talked with a professor," "asked your instructor for information related to a course you were taking (grades, make-up work, assignments, etc.)," "visited informally and briefly with an instructor after class," and "made friends with students whose age was very different from yours."

The comparison of doctoral universities, which were only average in most areas, and which were below average in several, with selective liberal arts colleges, which were superior to other colleges in a variety of areas, suggests several points. First, these differences held, although these two types of colleges are fairly comparable in quality of facilities and faculty. Thus, it is not so much the *presence* of facilities, funding, and staff, but the uses to which they are put that determines their educational impact. The second point is the importance of the emphasis that different types of colleges place on undergraduate education in the quality of the experience for students. Both of these points illustrate how different environments can influence behavior.

An interesting demonstration of the interaction of environment and "effort" is shown in some results provided by Pace (1984) in which the the predictors of student satisfaction and students' sense of gain in five areas were studied. The independent variables were the "quality of effort" scales, student background characteristics, a brief student assessment of the college environment (nine items for nine characteristics), and college status. The brief environment scores were the best predictors of the criterion of satisfaction in every type of college. Turning to sense of gain, college status variables (class, major, degree plans, grades, residence, and hours employed) accounted for the largest amount of variance (increases in R^2 ranged from .19 to .33), but the environment items made the next largest contribution to prediction in three of five areas (ranging from .11 to .14). Quality-of-effort scales were next in these three areas and were next to background in the other two areas.

In sum, current work in college environments seems to be concentrating on subenvironments or is concerned with more specific aspects of the environment that can be used for particular research projects. Examples of the latter include types of student-faculty interaction (Pascarella and Terenzini, 1978, 1980); academic alienation and political climate (Long, 1976, 1977); student perceptions of cheating and attitude toward cheating of other students (Haines et al., 1986); minority students' feelings about the level of discrimination and the quality of peer relations (Nettles, Thoeny, and Gosman, 1986); and compatibility of the work environment among graduate faculty (Baird, 1986). Additional measures of environment have been developed in secondary analyses of existing data sets. For example, Pascarella (1984) reanalyzed data from a longitudinal sample of college students and developed three very brief scales of "academic or intellectual competition," "impersonalism and inaccessible faculty," and "conventional or conformist press." These variables had modest effects on students' aspirations. Although these variables are much more appropriate to the research problems involved in the studies than global measures of the environments, they do not in themselves further our understanding of how the overall college operates and how it influences students and faculty.

Criticisms of Currently Available Approaches to the Environment

Although there is a long research history devoted to the college environment, there are many problems in the area. These can be divided into the technical-logical and the theoretical.

Technical-Logical Criticisms

Many of the approaches to the college environment are based on an assessment of the perceptions of students, faculty, administrators, and sometimes others. Measures of student and faculty perceptions of the environment have several difficulties. The first is the ambiguity of what an aggregate perception of an environment means. A person's perceptions of a social situation depend on many things, as Feldman (1972) and Chickering (1972) have pointed out. Students' interests and characteristics help determine the colleges they choose to attend. Students' characteristics then form part of the total environment. For example, the presence of many bright, intellectual students may lead an individual student to perceive the whole college as intellectual. In addition, students select subgroups, major fields, courses, and activities consistent with their interests and characteristics. Professors and administrators likewise have different patterns of experiences. These experiences compose their sampling of the total physical and interpersonal environment and thus the way in which they perceive the environment. And even these perceptions are influenced by their personal characteristics and social position. For example, students who think of their college may think first of their classes, a president may have uppermost in his or her thoughts the budget, a professor his or her research, and a dean his or her work with curriculum reform.

This problem may be particularly difficult when there are distinct subenvironments in the campus, since the scoring of most instruments sums across the subenvironments. For example, at a highly politicized college, the disparate perceptions of a leftist subgroup and a conservative subgroup may cancel each other out, and the college would appear to be nonpolitical on the environmental measure. Having said this, we should note that the evidence about the influence of personal characteristics on perceptions of the college environment is limited. For example, Pace (1966), Hartnett and Centra (1974), and Moos and Bromet (1978) have provided evidence that personal characteristics have little influence on environmental perceptions, and that environmental scores for subgroups are seldom different from the scores of the majority. Although subgroups may have different college experiences, they seem to describe the total environment in much the same way (e.g., Berdie, 1967).

It is also clear that the accuracy of perceptions depends on the knowledge of the respondent, a factor which varies from person to person and from area to area. For example, most students know very little about some aspects of faculty life, and commuting students have little to say about life in the dormitories. Furthermore, some respondents may report stereotypes or rumors, particularly when an item refers to activities that are not publicly visible, for example, when a student believes that other students do not study very much, just because he or she cannot see them study.

A major limitation of the perceptual approach is that a person can describe only those aspects of the college covered by the items in the instrument and only in the particular way the items allow. This difficulty is increased since the items in environmental instruments, of necessity, tend to be general and without precise referents. The items must refer to things that are common to all or most colleges and then must be phrased in such a way that they can be answered by people from any subgroup of the college.

Since many of the important aspects of the atmosphere of a college tend to be elusive and can be captured only by items that ask for the respondent's overall impressions, even the most skillfully prepared items will appear vague or ambiguous. This ambiguity can lead to descriptions of environments that may bear little relationship to the realities of campus life. For example, Chickering (1972) found extremely large differences among four colleges in their students' reports of the percentage of their classroom time they spent in different behaviors (e.g., listening and taking notes primarily to remember, thinking about the ideas presented); studying outside of class (memorizing, synthesizing ideas); or using information (applying concepts or principles to new problems, interpreting). The colleges also differed greatly in descriptions of specific instructor behaviors, students' reasons for studying, feelings about courses, and patterns of academic work (pace and promptness). However, on the CUES Quality of Teaching and Faculty Student Relationship scale, the colleges were very similar. In contrast, at the two colleges with the highest CUES scholarship scores, students spent the least time thinking about ideas in class and spent the least amount of studying time synthesizing, applying, and interpreting their assignments. In short, this study raises the possibility that general impressions may not correspond to specific behaviors.

Of course, there are the ambiguities that arise when the responses of individuals to each item are combined with those of the other respondents. These combined responses thus reflect the degree of consensus among the reporters as well as the intensity of the environment. For example, when half the students only moderately agree that "the college encourages individual freedom," it is quite different from when half strongly agree and half strongly disagree with the item. The items are also typically summed on a scale, the meaning of which has been decided by the authors of the instrument. In many cases, the items have been selected for strictly statistical reasons and may have slight coherent meaning. For example, the Inventory of College Activities "Cohesiveness" scale consists of the items "I discussed how to make money with other students" and "Freshmen have to take orders from upperclassmen for a period of time."

Because of the generality and ambiguity of perceptual measures, they are not very useful to people who want to evaluate or change their colleges. For example, what can an administrator do with the finding that his or her college scored at the 50th percentile on a scale of "friendliness"? The administrator finds nothing in the score to serve as a guide to action; doesn't know if the 50th percentile is good or bad; and is not sure what the "friendliness" scale really measures. However, an unexpectedly high or low score can be a "red flag" that can identify potential problem areas that can be the subject of more pointed, detailed investigation. A student choosing a college may find perceptual scores more useful.

Perhaps the most fundamental problem with the perceptual approach is its assumption that reports of individual perceptions in fact represent some kind of agreed-upon reality. That is, how can we logically move from the level of an individual's view of an institution to the level of a characteristic of the entire institution for everyone? As Feldman and Newcomb (1969) pointed out:

> To know whether the "is" of the environment represents pressures on students, one needs to know such things as the degree to which there is shared awareness about the desirability of certain attitudes and behaviors, the structural arrangements and systems of rewards and punishments that implement and ensure conformity to norms, and the degree to which individuals accept these norms. (p. 72)

A central problem for the perceptual approach, then, is to find procedures to determine "shared awareness," and to determine how "shared awareness" and individual perceptions interact to form an environment. Even more important is what the "environment" really represents, and whether and how it influences behavior.

Factual Approaches

Demographic, financial, and other "objective" information about institutions can tell us a good deal about institutions and can also be quite misleading. For example, one might make many assumptions about the character of small Roman Catholic liberal arts colleges for women that are located in large cities. However, this category includes Alverno College in Milwaukee, Mundelein College in Chicago, and Mount Vernon College in the District of Columbia, which are very different institutions. Size, a variable found in many studies, and used as evidence of "validity" in others, has rather problematical significance. For example, Ohio State, with the largest enrollment in the United States on one campus, actually spends a larger *proportion* of its budget on instruction than many smaller institutions. Michigan State, another extremely large campus, has made great efforts to create separate "subcolleges" within the university.

More generally, the problem with size, as with "objective" measures, is that it is, in reality, no more objective than any other piece of information. That is, to be objectively valid, a piece of information must lead to accurate and meaningful interpretations of current phenomena and have logical and empirical connections to, or predictions of, other phenomena (Cronbach, 1969). What does an enrollment of a certain size mean? What are its psychological and sociological implications? Do the students at a college with an enrollment of 1,000 feel they are in an institution that is twice as "large" as one with an enrollment of 500? What about an enrollment of 40,000 compared to one of 20,000? The point is, without theories and evidence about the measuring of such factual variables, such as Barker's behavior-setting theory (1968), we are using them based only on vague intuitions. In addition, "objective" data can vary to a much greater extent than is sometimes assumed. For example, there are many ways to calculate enrollment, based on varying definitions of students—full-time equivalents, etc.—and these can be calculated in different ways. For example, an institution may report one figure on enrollment to the legislature if an enrollment-driven budget system is used but may use quite another figure when it is calculating its average student-faculty ratio for reporting in recruiting literature.

Another example of the problematical meaning of factual measures is "affluence" or the wealth of the institution per student. Although one might assume that larger endowments and operating budgets would make life more pleasant for students, the monies may be spent in very different ways. In some calculations prepared by Charles Elton (1987) comparing the budgets of institutions with the highest rated graduate programs, the dollar amounts and the percentages of the budget spent on instruction, research, and service varied dramatically, even though all the institutions were relatively wealthy. Detailed analyses of the budgets of these institutions may reveal even greater differences in how funds are actually spent, which may indicate that interpretations of the categories based on their face value are based on erroneous assumptions. For example, much of the money spent on instruction may actually go to support some "stars" on the faculty, who may see very few students, or the funds spent for minority student affairs may chiefly go to administrators and their staffs, not to students. To illustrate the point another way, no one would confuse New York University and Dartmouth. However, the values of their endowments are very similar. In short, to properly use "factual" information to understand institutions, we need to examine it in considerable detail just to see if the data represent what we think they do. However, the most fundamental problem with "factual" information is that it is, in itself, *not* the environment. Factors such as size or affluence create the conditions for the environment but should be kept distinctly separate in our thinking about the environment. They are probably best considered contextual variables.

THEORETICAL CRITICISMS OF CURRENT APPROACHES TO THE COLLEGE ENVIRONMENT

There are many approaches to the college environment, but few of them provide comprehensive accounts of how colleges and universities operate and influence students. To some extent this is understandable, since colleges and universities are very complex social institutions. Although the research efforts just reviewed are based on various notions of what is important to attend to in the college environment (e.g., needs and press, "fit," institutional "functioning," goals, the characteristics of people in the institution), they have, in fact, very few theoretical propositions that can be tested unambiguously—and fewer conceptions of *mechanisms* to explain how colleges operate and affect the people in them.

For example, the needs-press approach has essentially one proposition: that when students' personal characteristics "fit" or are "congruent" with the environment, the students are more satisfied, perform at a higher level, and have greater commitment to the institution. Why and how these consequences follow is not really explained; that is, there is no mechanism to explain the operations and effects of "congruence" except for a vague idea of needs being "met." Further, one might argue with the basic concept, based on the ideas of Feldman and Newcomb (1969), Chickering (1969), and such theorists as Loevinger (Wethersby, 1981) and Perry (1981), who emphasize the critical role of challenge in promoting change and growth in college students. That is, it is not *congruency* that is conducive to growth, achievement, and, eventually, satisfaction, but *incongruity*, that is, a challenging, if supportive, environment.

The approach used by Astin and Holland in the EAT, quoted earlier, and by Richards in subsequent work (Richards et al., 1970) is that characteristics of individuals compose the environment operationally (the basic assumption of the EAT is that "students make the college," according to Richards et al.). The sheer number of people in a given category of occupational or major choice therefore defines the environment. Holland's (1985) explanation is that, since people in a given vocational or major group tend to have similar personalities, they will respond to many situations and problems in similar ways and will therefore create characteristic interpersonal environments. Again, it is unclear why this is supposed to be the case; that is, there is no mechanism other than an equally general idea of "reinforcement" to explain the contention. In other words, *how* do people with similar personalities create environments? Do they agree on goals? Do they create contingencies or rewards and punishments that promote certain behaviors and attitudes just by being together? How does reinforcement work?

Beyond the contention that the personal characteristics of the members define the environment, the remaining proposition of Holland's theory is, in structure, the same as in need-press theory: congruence. Holland (1985) does expand upon the concepts:

> People find environments reinforcing and satisfying when environmental patterns resemble their personality patterns. This situation makes for stability of behavior because persons receive a good deal of selective reinforcement of their behavior. The greater the discrepancy between people's personality patterns and environmental

patterns, the more dissatisfying, uncomfortable, and destructive these interactions become. . . .

Incongruent interactions stimulate change in human behavior; conversely, congruent interactions encourage stability of behavior. Persons tend to change or become like the dominant persons in the environment. This tendency is greater, the greater the degree of congruence is between person and environment. Those persons who are most incongruent will be changed least. Or, the closer a person is to the core of an environment, the greater the influence of the environment.

A person resolves incongruence by seeking a new and congruent environment, by remaking the present environment, or by changing personal behavior and perceptions.

A. Differentiation and consistency of personality pattern as well as identity usually make for a change of environment in the face of an incongruent environment.
B. Persons with differentiated and consistent personality patterns and clear identity are more apt to remake the environment itself, if they cannot leave it, to achieve greater congruence. For example, people usually hire people whom they like or see as congenial.
C. Persons with undifferentiated and inconsistent personality patterns and diffuse identity tend to adapt to incongruence by changing their own behavior and personality pattern to achieve greater congruence with their environment.
D. A person's tendency to leave an environment increases as the incongruity of the interaction increases. (pp. 53–54)

Although there are some inconsistent propositions in this statement, the key *mechanism* lies in the phrase "reinforcing and satisfying" and "selective reinforcement," and in the idea that people who are sure of themselves will change their environments, while people who are unsure of themselves will be changed by their environments, although there is little explication of how this works.

The remainder of the approaches to the environment are chiefly atheoretical, although they sometimes have implicit theories, as have been noted when these approaches were described. Perhaps this atheoretical quality is due to the difficulty in conceptualizing something as complex as colleges' environments, as suggested in the following section.

THE ROAD AHEAD: NEEDED
THEORETICAL AND EMPIRICAL WORK

The review of the majority of the work in analyzing and understanding the college environment covered a great deal of research activity through the 1960s that continued into the early 1970s. This work raised many fundamental issues, suggested in the description of the research, which seemed to have resulted in some very difficult questions, such as the following:

1. Is there such a phenomenon as a "college environment" that somehow

includes and also exists beyond the perceptions and characteristics of the individuals in it?

2. How, specifically, can we logically and empirically deduce the characteristics of a group or an overall environment from the perceptions and characteristics of its members?

3. How, specifically, can we relate financial and organizational conditions to the characteristics of the overall environment?

4. What are the most salient and potent aspects of the environment? For which criteria?

5. How can we best conceive of these aspects and their interaction?

6. How, specifically, do environments influence the individuals in them?

7. What are the "subenvironments" on campuses (which may not correspond to traditional groupings at all)?

8. How do "subenvironments" interact with the overall environment?

9. How do we deal, conceptually and technically, with the multiple overlap among subenvironments? For example, a student may be a sophomore, an English major, a member of a fraternity, enrolled in ROTC, a member of an intramural team, and work part time in the book store. How can we assess the influence of these different possible subenvironments, let alone others which may escape our categorizations, as, for example, students who are fervent fans of a particular rock group?

It is easy to recognize the difficulty, perhaps even the intractability, of these questions about the overall environment, but we should note that many of them apply equally well to assessments of parts or details of colleges that are only apparently more easily conceptualized and assessed. However that may be, the key tasks seem to be to develop better theories of college environments and to deal with the problems of interrelating individual perceptions or characteristics to those of the global environment.

THEORIES: THEIR REQUIREMENTS
AND THEIR ADVANTAGES

Colleges and universities are complex social institutions. Given their importance, it is surprising that this review has found so few theoretical ideas about how colleges operate or theories of how to implement change in them. Walsh (1973) has reviewed the approaches of several writers on colleges and has gone to considerable lengths to show that each approach is based on some theory of person-environment interaction, and Huebner (1980) and Williams (1986) have

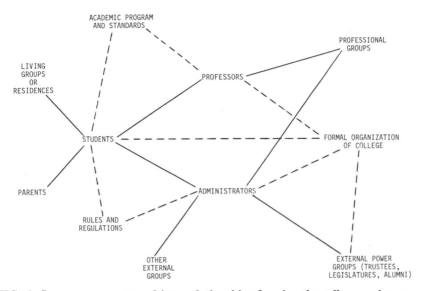

FIG. 1. Some components and interrelationships forming the college environment.

extolled the virtues of the idea of matching students and environments for counseling and guidance. However, except for Barker's (1968) behavioral setting propositions, which explain why students in small schools participate in more activities than students in large schools, and Holland's (1973) work on the consistency between an individual's vocational preferences and the distribution of those preferences in the student body, there are almost no theoretical propositions in the current approaches beyond the vague idea that students are better off if their characteristics are congruent with those of the college.

What other theories can be used or developed to understand the college environment and therefore to serve as the basis for meaningful and useful measures of that environment? There is no simple answer to this question. The range of applicable theories varies with the level of analysis and the focal person whose environment we are examining. The range varies depending on whether we concentrate on the environments of the students, the professors, or the administrators or if we concentrate on the person's relations with his or her immediate group, other groups, peripheral members of his or her own group, the organization, the total community, other colleges, and the external society.

For example, Figure 1 shows some of the major groups that research has suggested may help form the college environment and some of the social mechanisms that may affect group relationships. (There are, of course, many other groups and relationships. Figure 1 is intended to illustrate only some of the applications of theories.) The solid lines indicate relationships among groups of people, and the dashed lines indicate some social mechanisms that influence their behavior.

For example, students and professors are related, and one of the mechanisms is academic programs and standards. A variety of theoretical approaches could be applied to the relationships of any of these groups. The academic relationship between professors and students might by analyzed by learning theory and congitive psychology, the relationship of professors with professional groups by reference group theory, and the influence of the formal structure of the college on professors by organizational sociology. As potentially useful as these applications might be, they still apply to *segments* of the college environment rather than to the environment as a whole. Are there theories that can encompass the complexity of the college environment as a whole? Put another way, how can we decide which theories can best provide an understanding of the college environment?

One possible basis for choice are the criteria suggested by Nadler (1980) and Walsh (1973): comprehensiveness, clarity and explicitness, operational adequacy in measuring persons and the environment, the inclusion of empirical findings, the empirical research generated, and face validity. These are all helpful criteria, but two more should be added that seem to be required elements of all theories: the production of testable theoretical predictions and the existence of an internal theoretical logic. As Deutch and Krauss (1965) put it:

> It is evident that a theory will be fruitful to the extent that it contains constructs that meet the requirements of (1) logical fertility (such constructs enable logical inferences to be made), (2) multiple connections (the constructs are not isolated from one another but, rather, are so richly interconnected that it is possible to go from one to another by various routes), and (3) empirical extensibility (some of the constructs can be related to empirical observables in such a way that a variety of equivalent empirical definitions can be given to any specific construct). . . . without rules of correspondence to link some of the constructs in a theory to observables, there is no way of ascertaining or testing its empirical consequences. (pp. 8–9)

Which theories or sets of theories best fit these criteria? Which theories are comprehensive enough to encompass the complexity of the college environment? Which suggest ways to measure meaningful or comparable aspects of the college environment? Which have been tested empirically? Which have relatively clear and parsimonious constructs? Which have clear internal logic interrelating concepts in orderly ways? Most important, which lead to testable hypotheses?

Where can we find such theories? A reasonable argument can be made that we still need to develop comprehensive theories that describe the unusual features of the *college* environment, as distinct from other environments. However, it seems clear that there are many potentially useful ideas on and insights into the college environment in the work on organizational assessment.

ORGANIZATIONAL RESEARCH CONTRIBUTIONS TO UNDERSTANDING AND ASSESSING THE ENVIRONMENT

Defining Organizational Climate

One of the most important contributions of organizational research to the study of college environments is its general analysis of the components of organizational climate (e.g. Ashforth, 1985; Guion, 1973; James and Jones, 1974; Johannesson, 1973; Schneider, 1975, 1983). One example is the schema developed by Naylor, Pritchard, and Ilgen (1980), who consider the individual's perceptions of the climate as a judgmental process "involved in attributing a class of humanlike traits to an entity outside the individual where this entity may be a work-group or even an entire organization" (p. 254). This schema is shown in Figure 2. Although the actual flow of influence is from left to right, Naylor, Pritchard, and Ilgen find it advantageous to consider the schema from right to left, that is, to begin with the individual's psychological climate construct, in this case "friendliness."

These general constructs represent anthropomorphic characteristics that the individual attributes to the organization and are the most fundamental aspect of "climate." In the schema, they are at "Level Three Climate." It is important to emphasize that these perceptions are affect-free; that is, it is important to keep the distinction between perceptions of the degree to which an attribute is present in an organization and the positive or negative affect that the individual has due to that perception. For example, an individual might perceive his or her organization as having middling friendliness but could be quite happy or sad about that perception. These global constructs are based on contingencies or weights that the individual gives to various categories of cues, or on the relationships that the individual sees between a construct and the cues shown in the Figure as $Cx_1'F$, $Cx_2'F$, and so on. For example, one person might consider "friendliness' to be based on the number of times each day people say hello, another person might consider being greeted with a smile *and* a verbal greeting to be required, and another might consider the number of parties important. The point is, that each person may have his or her own *set* of contingencies or types of cues that represent a construct. (This suggests that one approach to the college environment is to examine the referents or types of cues that individuals use to define difficult constructs such as "scholarship" and "sense of community." If most people use the same cues, then one would have good evidence that the bases for their judgments of environments—that is, the ways they define environments—are the same.) The contingencies are related to the individual's perception that the required cues actually exist, that is, that they perceive that people say hello to them a certain number of times a day, or that there are so

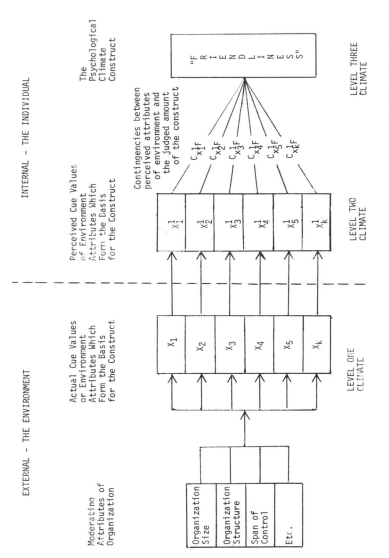

FIG. 2. A schematic representation of organizational climate. From Naylor, Pritchard, and Ilgen (1980).

many parties each week. This is the "Level Two Climate" described in the figure as "Perceived Cue Values of Environmental Attributes Which Form the Basis for the Construct." (Studying the extent of variability in people's reports of the rate or incidence of the various behaviors or cues that define their constructs would provide additional evidence of a "shared" environment.) Up to this point, the figure has referred to the internal, psychological perceptions of environment.

Moving across the boundary separating the internal from the external world, we move to the "Level One Climate," which is the "Actual Cue Values or Environmental Attributes Which Form the Basis for the Construct" in the figure. These are the *actual* cue values associated with the cue values that are *perceived* by the individual, for example, the *actual* number of times people say hello in a day. It would be theoretically possible for external observers to provide measures of these various cues or behaviors, although it would be almost impossible in practice.

Finally, on the far left of the figure are the "Moderating Attributes of the Organization," such as organizational size and organizational structure, that influence the incidence of the cues that influence the individuals' perceptions. For example, at a small college, there is a high probability that a student will meet many other students whom he or she knows many times a day, and who will therefore say hello frequently. At a very large college, given the physical space and the numbers of other students and classes, it is less probable that a student would encounter very many people he or she knows and, therefore, may report a lower frequency of hellos. It is a mistake, in this view, to regard such moderating attributes as a form of climate, as has sometimes been done; rather, they should be regarded as important influences *on* climate.

Naylor et al. (1980) conclude:

> In summary, in our opinion, it is not wise to approach the environmental influence by the question "what are the critical or basic characteristics (or dimensions) of the environment?" We would argue that a richer and more productive perspective on environmental influence is provided by working within the context provided by the question "What are the critical or basic processes by which environmental characteristics influence individual behavior?" (p. 12)

A similar, if somewhat more elaborate, schema has been developed by Lord (1985). Lord proposes an information-processing approach to social perceptions, which begins with an assumed behavioral style or trait of the observed person or group. This leads to stimulus behaviors, which are then subject to the selective attention of the perceiver. This information is encoded or comprehended by the perceiver via various internal schemas, the most important of which are *person* schemas, based on abstractions or exemplars of categories of people, and *event* schemas or scripts, which are coherent sequences of actions associated with a particular setting. This encoded information is then stored and retained in memory, where it may be recategorized or reevaluated. This processed information about events or people is later retrieved from memory. Its salience is then subject to the respondent's judgment, which leads to inferences about the style or trait.

Lord notes that there are several important aspects of this process. One is that "much of the information required for accurate, unbiased social judgment is likely to be filtered before reaching attention. What is noticed depends on the schema guiding perceptions and a few salient stimulus properties," and "retrieval is guided by the point of view espoused during retrieval, which may result in substantial distortions of information" As complex as this model may be, it suggests that the usual methods of asking respondents to make judgments via questionnaires neglects the processes of selective attention, memory, and the reorganization and simplification due to the schema used. Thus, the covariances and factors that a researcher may find in responses to a questionnaire may be due more to the simplification and/or inferential processes used by the respondents than to the underlying structure of the social situation. For example, a scale based on a factor analysis of questionnaire responses may be as much a reflection of how people commonly think about social situations as of how behaviors or events are actually related. In sum, the Naylor, Pritchard, and Ilgen model and the Lord model (greatly simplified in this discussion) provide a much more analytical and carefully reasoned approach to the use of perceptual data, which researchers in the area of college environments could use to their advantage (Peterson et al., 1986).

Contributions of Organizational Research
to Considerations of the Level of Analysis

One of the recurring problems in research on the college environment is the level of analysis. That is, how do we relate the levels of the individual, the subgroup, and the overall environment? Researchers in organizational behavior, particularly organizational climate, have attempted to deal with this issue in considerable detail. Rousseau (1985) described some of the complexities and distinctions. The object of the research (individual, subgroup, or total institution) is the *focal unit*. Research on the focal unit involves two kinds of levels: *level of measurement,* which refers to the unit to which data are directly attached (for example, self-reports of personal behaviors are usually at the individual level, the number of people is measured at the group level, the and degree of bureaucracy at the organizational level). The *level of analysis* is the unit to which data are assigned for hypothesis testing and statistical analysis.

However, Rousseau points out that, in practice, the level of measurment and the level of analysis may not correspond, and that neither may be the level to which generalizations are made. This leads to the error of misspecification which "occurs when we attribute an observed relationship other than the actual behavioral or responsive unit." For example, if faculty's scores on the IFI Democratic Governance Scale at a particular college were correlated with the number of articles they published, it would be a mistake to conclude that democratic governance leads to research productivity; that is, we risk misspecification. Another common error lies in the aggregation of data based on homogeneous groups which, when correlated, yield higher results than when individual data are used, or are actually artifacts due to other factors. For example, the correlation between college mean SAT scores and the percentage of seniors planning to go to graduate school is higher than the correlation between SAT scores and graduate school plans based on individuals. A related error is the cross-level fallacy, which exists when the same construct is used inappropriately to characterize phenomena at different levels. For example, *colleges* don't behave; *individuals* behave.

The contribution made by organizational researchers is to compose models and logical rules that provide for careful reasoning about evidence of the influence of one level on another. For example, the overall college culture may create group norms that influence individual behavior. The task for researchers is to assess each of these kinds of variables, (i.e., culture, group norms, and individual behaviors) and to analyze how they influence each other. As Burstein (1980) has pointed out, different variables may enter a model at different levels and may mean different things at different levels. For example, in the international mathematics study, the perceptions of the teachers' friendliness may mean something quite different when the individual student, the classroom, the school, the school system, or the country is the unit of analysis. Burstein (1980) and others have developed statistical procedures for giving the proper weight to these different levels in the prediction of achievement; that is, they have partitioned the variance.

Some of the models that organizational researchers have developed to deal with multiple levels include composition models, which relate nondependent variables across levels; cross-level models, which relate independent and dependent variables at different levels; and multilevel models, which relate independent and dependent variables generalizing across two or more levels (see Rousseau, 1985, for an explication of these models). An example of a composition model is provided by James (1982), who argues that when the definitions of organizational "climate," are the same at the individual and the unit levels, then psychological and organizational climate represent the same construct. For example, when professors' academic rigor means the same thing at the level of the individual student and at the level of the classroom as a whole, then it is the same construct. The criterion for equivalent definitions is perceptual agreement, according to James. When unit members perceive the unit in the same way, they share psychological meaning, perceptual agreement exists, and therefore, psychological and organizational climate represent the same construct. However, it is important to keep the levels distinct and carefully in mind when we study a particular criterion.

For example, Hulin and Rousseau (1980) report a series of studies that demonstrate these differences. Studying a phenomenon that is comparable to attrition among college students, employee turnover, they found that while economic factors explain 70% of the variance in unit-level turnover rates, individual attitudes and behavioral intentions explain 70% of the variance in *individual* turnover rates.

Cross-level models would include studies of such phenomena as the influence of college environmental characteristics, such as CUES community scores, on individual behavior, such as the individual's satisfaction with the social life of the college, and would use contextual moderators, such as a college's location or private-public status, that affect these relationships.

The third type of model, the multilevel model, examines phenomena and their consequences at individual, group, and organizational levels. For example, Staw, Sandelands, and Dutton (1981) examined the parallel processes by which individuals, groups, and organizations cope with adversity. The general process that was common across levels was that threat produced rigidity, a process that the behavior and the decisions at each level reinforced and solidified.

There are many other examples of these models in organizational research, but the lesson for researchers in higher education is that fellow researchers have wrestled with the same issues and types of constructs that concern researchers studying the college environment. Organizational researchers provide guidelines and techniques for careful reasoning about relating data, variables, and constructs from one level to another (see Roberts and Burstein, 1980, for discussions of statistical methods). One possible application would be to study in a single model the individual, peer-group, and college influences on students' aspirations toward graduate school.

INSIGHTS AND POSSIBILITIES FROM ORGANIZATIONAL THEORY

In organizational research, there are many potential contributions of theory to the understanding and assessment of college environments. First is the variety of theories that have been considered (Benson, 1983; Hauser, 1980; Lawler, Nadler, and Cammann, 1980). Some of the more recent of these theorists include, at one extreme, the demythologizers, who argue that the idea that organizations are rationally articulated structures organized to meet specific goals is a myth, especially as it applies to educational institutions (e.g., Meyer and Rowan, 1978; Weick, 1976). What is important, according to this view, is to keep a particular coalition in power. Rituals and symbolism are used to convince others of the legitimacy and rationality of the organization. For example, a university has a variety of rituals to assume legitimacy among other people, including hiring a ritually approved staff, offering a conventional curriculum, granting credentials, and satisfying accrediting agencies and professional associations. However, the university goes to great lengths to be sure that the core of the teaching and learning process is not evaluated by external groups. Given that the goal is simply the perpetuation of the organization, not the rational meeting of goals, the organization can allow opposing interests to exist and can use multiple nonaccountable administrative structures. However, this very nonrational structure allows the organization to be quite adaptable to changing conditions. The demythologizers would have us look less at organizational structures in colleges and more at rituals, symbols, and their functions, and at how colleges construct our views of reality.

Another class of recent theorists are termed the "politicizers" by Benson (1983), because they argue that power considerations, particularly the control of resources, are the key to organizations. For example, organizational decisions may be made as much to maintain or enhance the control of a power coalition as to enhance efficiency and effectiveness. Even technical decisions may be largely based on political considerations (Pfeffer, 1981). This group of theorists would argue that in order to understand why environments have the characteristics they do, we need to examine the underlying power coalitions in colleges at universities and how their relations affect decisions, rather than the colleges' purported educational goals.

Another group, the "ecologizers" (Aldrich, 1979; Hanf and Scharpf, 1978), go beyond the single organization to focus on interorganizational power-dependence relations. These theorists would have us concentrate on the relations between colleges, state legislatures, major economic groups, and professional agencies and examine how those relations influence the environment. For example, part of the growing environmental press for "vocationalism" on many campuses may stem from the demands of professional organizations and state or federal agencies.

Another group of innovative theorists are the "totalizers," who examine how organizations are entangled in the economic and political structure of the total society, as well as their role in the reproduction or maintenance of that structure. The totalizers concentrate on the place of organizations, networks of organizations, and populations of organizations in the total social structure. Thus, they would have us examine how colleges and universities have been and are linked to technological and economic developments. They would then have us examine how these developments influence the internal structure of colleges, following a Weberian analysis (McNeil, 1978) or how they are part of a capitalistic domination, following a Marxian analysis (Clegg and Dunkerley, 1980). The view of colleges and universities in Collins's *The Credential Society* (1979) and the views of the true purpose of liberal education by Rossides (1984) can be considered in this category.

Other theorists have studied a variety of additional concepts, including that of organizational evolution (Tushman and Romanelli, 1985), focusing on considerations of forces for stability and forces for fundamental change, and identifying the reasons for periods of relative calm or convergence and periods of reorientation or divergence. These are associated with internal requirements for coordinated action and external demands or challenges for the organization. This research has led some even to propose institutional "life cycles," although this concept is controversial (Cameron and Whetten, 1983). In any case, this approach suggests determining where an organization is in its evolution in order to understand its priorities, structure, and functioning. Kimberly (1980) provides an example of this kind of analysis in a study of an innovative medical school.

Another approach, developed by Albert and Whetten (1985), is that of "extended metaphor analysis" in which the organization being analyzed is compared to a set of alternative organizations. Albert and Whetten developed this method when they attempted to define organizational identity, that is, how an organization answers the questions "Who are we?" and "What do we want to be?" They proposed that organizational identity is composed of a claimed central character, claimed distinctiveness from other organizations, and claimed continuity and consistency over time. However, these authors found that institutions can often have dual, even multiple, identities, illustrating this idea with the modern research university. To explicate the dual identity of the university, these authors used the metaphors of the church and the business organization. They compared these organizations in terms of their ideological claims, their socialization procedures, their organizational pattern, and, most important, their normative versus utilitarian functions. These have implications for decisions during times of retrenchment, attitudes toward leadership, and attitudes toward marketing the organization. The method of extended metaphor analysis, then, also suggests different ways of viewing the college environment.

Another potentially useful approach is the study of organizational demography (Pfeffer, 1983). Particularly appropriate for the faculty environment, this approach examines the demographic characteristics of the staff, such as age, sex, ethnicity, SES, and especially length of service. These characteristics influence such variables as acceptance of innovation and adaptability, the form of control employed and the size of the administrative staff, cohort identity, and mobility aspirations. The effects of organizational demography in colleges can be seen in such areas as the "graying of the professoriate" and the increasing numbers of "new students" and "returning students." Although these factors have been discussed on a national level, the effects of the demographics of the student body, the professors, and the administrators on individual college environments

TABLE 1. Definitions of Fits

Fit	The issues
Individual-organization	To what extent individual needs are met by the organizational arrangements, to what extent individuals hold clear or distorted perceptions of organizational structures, and the convergence of individual and organizational goals
Individual-task	To what extent the needs of individuals are met by the tasks, to what extent individuals have skills and abilities to meet task demands
Individual-informal organization	To what extent individual needs are met by the informal organization, to what extent the informal organization makes use of individual resources, consistent with informal goals
Task-organization	Whether the organizational arrangements are adequate to meet the demands of the task, whether organizational arrangements tend to motivate behavior consistent with task demands
Task-informal organization	Whether the informal organization structure facilitates task performance, whether it hinders or promotes meeting the demands of the task
Organization-informal organization	Whether the goals, rewards, and structures of the informal organization are consistent with those of the formal organization

Source: Nadler and Tushman (1980).

have not been explored systematically. However, it seems very plausible that the environments of colleges with a high proportion of returning or older students would be different from colleges with low proportions. These possibilities are worth exploring.

One significant contribution of organizational behavior research is the explication of the idea of *fit*. As described by Nadler and Tushman (1980), there are at least six definitions of *fit*, as shown in Table 1.

The drawback of this delineation of the varieties of fit, or congruence, is that it does not show how to deal with multiple fits. For example, a student may fit quite well in a residence group which has an antiacademic, social orientation, which does not fit with the college's academic orientation. When the residence group is involved in a "task" that has an academic purpose, there may be a further lack of fit. Situations like this may explain why studies of congruence have obtained such disappointing results. That is, a student can be congruent with some aspects of a college and incongruent with others. It may be the total *level* of congruency, or his or her degree of congruency with the elements of the environment, that is most *important* to him or her, or congruence with the areas that are most *salient* to a particular criterion that will play the largest role. Although it is extremely difficult to distinguish among these multiple interactions in our research, it is important to attempt to assess their influence.

In sum, organizational behavior research includes many concepts that can be applied to several of the problems in the study of the college environment that were identified in the review of research. These include clarification of the meaning of perceptions, clarity concerning the level of analysis, and recognition of the multiple meanings of *fit*. In addition, organizational theory provides many useful perspectives on the college environment, suggesting reconceptualizations of their structure and functioning.

CONCLUSION

This review of research on the college environment has discussed a wide variety of concepts and assessment techniques. This variety might be expected. The "environment" can be an elusive concept, since it includes such components as campus mores and traditions; standards of achievement; political atmosphere; physical facilities and architecture; values and priorities; organizational structure; and long-standing issues and controversies (Dressell, 1976). In addition, each of these components affects members of the environment through other people, so that the characteristics of the individual members of the environment help determine its overiding features. For example, a college could have stringent academic standards, but the environment for learning would be very different if these standards were upheld by friendly, supportive faculty or by martinets. Although it is important to analyze the separate components and to distinguish between general characteristics and individual behaviors, it is an even more important and difficult task to analyze the ways in which they interact to form an overall "evironment" (Glick, 1985). A related conceptual problem is whether it is the local or "proximal" environment or subenvironment or the total or "distal" environment or "climate" that is most important (Pace and Baird, 1966; Moran and Volkwein, 1987).

Another issue with far-reaching consequences is whether we conceive of the environment as an individual psychological variable or a group of organizational variables. In addition to the problems in analysis and statistics that this issue creates, it leads to very different consequences for our research methods. If we consider the environment a psychological issue, we might attempt to examine each individual's ideas about the environment by assessing the person's "construct space," akin to semantic space. We would be less concerned with the "objectivity" of the descriptions of the environment than with the consequences for the individual's behavior. We would examine the individual's coping mechanisms and other psychological reactions to the environment. (Moos, 1979, has proposed something along this line.) We would also turn to environmental psychology for insights and methods (e.g., Holahan, 1986). If we consider the environment as a sociological or social psychological issue, we would concentrate on identifying norms, sanctions, controls for deviancy, patterns of affiliation, power relations, and so on, using the group or the organization as the unit of analysis.

Since the interaction of the individual with his or her environments involves many complexities and subtleties, consideration should be given to qualitative research methods (Jacob, 1987). These methods include cognitive anthropology, symbolic interaction, and ethnography. Ethnography seems particularly appropriate to the analysis of the environment. Originally developed in anthropology, ethnography is today an "extended family" of techniques, but its key focus is on analyzing the cultural patterns of a defined group and on describing the culture as it is seen by participants in the culture (Hammersley and Atkinson, 1983). Therefore, it involves participation, observation, interviewing, and documentation of behaviors and attitudes (Clammer, 1984). Although it has rarely been applied to higher education, ethnography has been profitably used to study medical education (Atkinson, 1981) and such educational units as high schools (e.g., Peshkin, 1978).

The problem is, of course, that the "environment" is where the individual mind, the social group, and the organizational structure meet and interact. And these interactions create many conceptual and statistical difficulties. However, it seems that, in order to understand how colleges educate and influence their students, we will have to deal with these difficulties. The recent research in organizational behavior offers some very helpful insights and techniques. However, the greatest need is for comprehensive theories that will allow us to deal with the complexities of the person-environment interaction in all its richness.

More specifically, my opinion is that future research will be more fruitful if it moves in certain directions. The first is to continue the trend of movement away from analyses of specific measures and toward the identification of the psychological and social *processes* that create the environment. That is, it would be profitable to concentrate on understanding how students are attracted to one another, how informal groups form, how cohesiveness operates, how peers influence one another, how norms are formed and enforced, how people become identified with their group and college, how social judgments are formed, and how the social roles on campuses conflict with or reinforce each other. It would also be very useful to have better ways of identifying the real subgroups on campuses. That is, almost all research involving college subgroups uses nominal groups, such as the residence group, the major field, and student organizations, which may not have any true social interaction and cohesiveness. Research projects that could identify the real norm and peer groups of students would be very valuable. A related advance in research methodology would be a technique for assessing students' degree of *involvement* in different groups and methods of assessing their *saliency* in different areas. For example, a student might base his or her ideas of the right number of hours to study on interactions with the members of an informal study group in a math class but might base his or her drinking behavior upon a group of friends in his or her residence hall. Different groups are salient for different behaviors.

A more general issue is that of the general level of involvement in campus life. Many students today experience little of the college. Nationally, 42% of students are enrolled part time. Of freshmen, 40% do not live on campus, and this percentage increases as students progress toward their degrees. As commuting and working students, they come to college only to attend classes or to do required assignments. What is the "environment" for these students? Clearly, our usual conceptions of the environment, which are based on the fully involved student, are inadequate for understanding how the college affects such students.

Whatever the topic pursued, researchers should keep the distinctions between *levels* of measurement in mind and should develop measures that are appropriate for the individual psychological environment, the group social-psychological environment, and the global or college culture environment. Likewise, researchers should use statistical methods that properly link data at different levels.

Finally, progress can be made if we recognize that a good deal of research bears on the analysis of the college environment, even if it is concerned with another topic. For example, a recent study of the characteristics of productive research departments included a variety of measure of the environments of graduate programs (Baird, 1986). These kinds of research should be brought into our thinking about the environment. Likewise, I hope this review will encourage researchers working on a variety of topics in higher education to include assessments of environments in their designs.

In summary, this review of the extensive history of research efforts to understand and assess the college environment indicates that the general concept is alive and well and is living in the minds of more than a few researchers.

REFERENCES

Albert, S., and Whetten, D. A. (1985). Organizational identity. In Cummings and Staw, *Research in Organizational Behavior,* Vol. 7.

Aldrich, H. E. (1979). *Organizations and Environments.* Englewood Cliffs, NJ: Prentice-Hall.

Anderson, R. E. (1983). *Finance and Effectiveness: A Study of College Environments.* Princeton, NJ: Educational Testing Service.

Ashforth, B. E. (1985). Climate formation: issues and extensions. *Academy of Management Review* 10: 837–847.

Astin, A. W. (1962). An empirical characterization of higher educational institutions. *Journal of Educational Psychology* 53: 224–229.

Astin, A. W. (1963a). Differential effects on the motivation of talented students to pursue the Ph.D. degree. *Journal of Educational Psychology* 54: 63–71.

Astin, A. W. (1963b). Further validation of the environmental assessment technique. *Journal of Educational Psychology* 54: 217–226.

Astin, A. W. (1965). *Who Goes Where to College?* Chicago: Science Research Associates.

Astin, A. W. (1968). *The College Environment*. Washington, DC: American Council on Education.

Astin, A. W. (1972). *Manual for the Inventory of College Activities*. Minneapolis: National Computer Systems.

Astin, A. W., and Holland, J. (1961). The environmental assessment technique: a way to measure college environments. *Journal of Educational Psychology* 52: 308–316.

Astin, A. W., and Panos, R. J. (1969). *The Educational and Vocational Development of College Students*. Washington, DC: American Council on Education.

Atkinson, P. (1981). *The Clinical Experience*. Farnsborough, U.K.: Gower.

Baird, L. L. (1974). The practical utility of measures of college environments. *Review of Educational Research* 44(3): 307–329.

Baird, L. L. (1986). What characterizes a productive research department? *Research in Higher Education* 25(3): 211–225.

Baird, L. L. (1987). The undergraduate experience: commonalities and differences among colleges. Paper presented at 1987 Meetings of the Association for the Study of Higher Education, February, San Diego.

Baird, L. L., and Hartnett, R. T. (1980). *Understanding Student and Faculty Life*. San Francisco: Jossey-Bass.

Ballou, R. A. (1985). An analysis of freshman students perceptions of the living environment, behavior, and academic achievement in the residence hall systems of twelve colleges and universities. Paper read at National Association of Student Personnel Administrators Meetings.

Barker, R. G. (1968). *Ecological Psychology: Concepts and Methods for Studying the Environment of Human Behavior*. Stanford, CA: Stanford University Press.

Barton, A. H. (1960). Organizational measurement and its bearing on the study of college environments. *Research Monograph No. 2*. New York: College Entrance Examination Board.

Benson, J. K. (1983). Paradigm and praxis in organizational analysis. In Cummings and Staw, *Research in Organizational Behavior*, Vol. 5.

Berdie, R. F. (1967). A university is a many-faceted thing. *Personnel and Guidance Journal* 45: 269–277.

Betz, E. L., Klingensmith, J. E., and Menne, J. W. (1970). The measurement and analysis of college student satisfaction. *Measurement and Evaluation in Guidance* 3: 110–118.

Boyer, E. L. (1987). *College: The Undergraduate Experience in America*. New York: Harper & Row.

Burstein, L. (1980). The analysis of multilevel data in educational research and evaluation. In D. E. Berliner (ed.), *Review of Research in Education*, Vol. 8. Washington, DC: American Educational Research Association.

Cameron, K. S., and Whetten, D. A. (1983). Models of the organizational life cycle: applications to higher education. *Review of Higher Education* 6: 269–299.

Centra, J. A. (1970). The college environment revisited: current descriptions and a comparison of three methods of assessment. *Research Bulletin 70-44*. Princeton, NJ: Educational Testing Service.

Centra, J. A. (1973). Comparison of three methods of assessing college environments. *Journal of Educational Psychology* 63: 56–62.

Chickering, A. W. (1969). *Education and Identity*. San Francisco: Jossey-Bass.

Chickering, A. W. (1972). Undergraduate academic experience. *Journal of Educational Psychology* 63(2): 134–143.

Chickering, A. W., McDowell, J., and Campagna, D. (1969). Institutional differences and student development. *Journal of Educational Psychology* 60: 315–326.

Clammer, J. (1984). Approaches to ethnographic research. In R. F. Ellen (ed.), *Ethnographic Research: A Guide to General Conduct*. London: Academic Press.

Clark, B. R., and Trow, M. (1966). The organizational context. In T. M. Newcomb and E. K. Wilson (eds.), *College Peer Groups: Problems and Prospects for Research*. Chicago: Aldine.

Clegg, S., and Dunkerley, D., eds. (1980). *Organization, Class and Control*. Boston: Routledge & Kegan Paul.

Collins, R. (1979). *The Credential Society*. New York: Academic Press.

Creager, J. A., and Astin, A. W. (1968). Alternative methods of describing characteristics of colleges and universities. *Educational and Psychological Measurement* 28: 719–734.

Cronbach, L. J. (1969). *Essentials of Psychological Testing*. New York: Harper & Row.

Cummings, L. L., and Staw, B. M., eds. (annual, 1978–). *Research in Organizational Behavior*. Greenwich, CT: JAI Press.

Deutch, M., and Krauss, R. M. (1965). *Theories in Social Psychology*. New York: Basic Books.

Doucet, J. A. (1977). The implications of rank-ordering on the Clark-Trow typology. *Journal of College Student Personnel* 18(1): 25–31.

Dressell, P. L. (1976). *Handbook of Academic Evaluation*. San Francisco: Jossey-Bass.

Elton, C. F. (1987). Unpublished analyses, University of Kentucky.

Feldman, K. A. (1972). Measuring college environments: some uses of path analysis. *American Educational Research Journal* 8: 51–70.

Feldman, K. A., and Newcomb, T. M. (1969). *The Impact of College on Students*. San Francisco: Jossey-Bass.

Georgion, P. (1973). The goal paradigm and notes toward a counter paradigm. *Administrative Science Quarterly* 18: 291–310.

Gerst, M. S., and Sweetwood, H. (1973). Correlates of dormitory social climate. *Environment and Behavior* 5: 440–464.

Glick, W. H. (1985). Conceptualizing and measuring organizational and psychological climate: pitfalls in multilevel research. *Academy of Management Review* 10: 601–616.

Gross, E., and Grambsch, P. V. (1968). *University Goals and Academic Power*. Washington, DC: American Council on Education.

Gross, E., and Grambsch, P. V. (1974). *Changes in University Organization, 1964–1971*. New York: McGraw-Hill.

Guion, R. M. (1973). A note on organizational climate. *Organizational Behavior and Human Performance* 9: 120–125.

Haines, V. J., Deifhoff, G. M., LaBeff, E. G., and Clark, R. E. (1986). College cheating: immaturity, lack of commitment and the neutralizing attitudes. *Research in Higher Education* 25(4): 342–354.

Hammersley, M., and Atkinson, P. (1983). *Ethnography: Principles in Practice*. New York: Tavistock.

Hanf, K., and Scharpf, F., eds. (1978). *Interorganizational Policy Making, Limits to Coordination and Central Control*. Beverly Hills: Sage.

Hartnett, R. T., and Centra, J. A. (1974). Faculty views of the academic environment: Situational vs. institutional perspectives. *Sociology of Education* 47: 159–169.

Hauser, D. L. (1980). Comparison of different models for organizational analysis. In Lawler et al., *Organizational Assessment.*

Hearn, J. C., and Moos, R. H. (1976). Social climate and major choice: A test of Holland's theory in university student living groups. *Journal of Vocational Behavior* 8: 293–305.

Holahan, C. J. (1986). Environmental psychology. *Annual Review of Psychology, 1986* 37: 381–407.

Holland, J. L. (1962). Some explorations of a theory of vocational choice: one-and two year longitudinal studies. *Psychological Monographs* 76(26): entire issue.

Holland, J. L. (1966). *The Psychology of Vocational Choice: A Theory of Personality Types and Model Environments.* Waltham, MA: Blaisdell.

Holland, J. L. (1973). *Making Vocational Choices: A Theory of Careers.* Englewood Cliffs, NJ: Prentice-Hall.

Holland, J. L. (1985). *Making Vocational Choices* (2nd ed.). Englewood Cliffs, NJ: Prentice-Hall.

Huebner, L. A. (1980). Interaction of student and campus. In U. Delworth and G. R. Hanson (eds.), *Student Services: A Handbook for the Profession.* San Francisco: Jossey-Bass.

Huebner, L. A., and Corrazini, J. G. (1978). Ecomapping: a dynamic model for intentional campus design. *Journal Supplement Abstract Service.* Am. Psychol. Assn.

Hulin, C. L., and Rousseau, D. M. (1980). Analyzing infrequent events: once you find them your troubles begin. In R. H. Roberts and L. Burstein (eds.), *Issues in Aggregation: New Directions for Methodology of Social and Behavioral Science,* Vol. 6. San Francisco: Jossey-Bass.

Jacob, E. (1987). Qualitative research traditions: a review. *Review of Educational Research* 57(1): 1–50.

James, L. R. (1982). Aggregation bias in estimates of perceptual agreement. *Journal of Applied Psychology* 67: 219–229.

James, L. R., and Jones, A. P. (1974). Organizational climate: a review of theory and research. *Psychological Bulletin* 81: 1096–1112.

Johannesson, R. E. (1973). Some problems in the measurement of organizational climate. *Organizational Behavior and Human Performance* 10: 118–144.

Kimberly, J. R. (1980). Initiation, innovation, and institutionalization in the creation process. In J. R. Kimberly and R. H. Miles (eds.), *The Organizational Life Cycle.* San Francisco: Jossey-Bass.

Knapp, R. H., and Goodrich, H. B. (1952). *Origins of American Scientists.* Chicago: University of Chicago Press.

Knapp, R. H., and Greenbaum, J. J. (1953). *The Younger American Scholar.* Chicago: University of Chicago Press.

Lawler, E. E., Nadler, D. A., and Cammann, C., eds. (1980). *Organizational Assessment.* New York: Wiley.

Long, S. (1976). Sociopolitical ideology as a determinant of students' perceptions of the university. *Higher Education* 5: 423–435.

Long, S. (1977). Dimensions of student academic alienation. *Educational Administration Quarterly* 13: 16–20.

Longino, C. F., and Kart, C. S. (1974). The college fraternity: an assessment of theory and research. *Journal of College Student Personnel* 14: 118–125.

Lord, R. G. (1985). An information processing approach to social perceptions, leadership, and behavioral measurement in organizations. In Cummings and Staw, *Research in Organizational Behavior,* Vol. 7.

Lunneborg, C. E. (1978). Review of the institutional goals inventory. In O. K. Buros (ed.), *The Eighth Mental Measurements Yearbook*. Highland Park, NJ: Gryphon Press.

McNeil, K. (1978). Understanding organizational power: building on the Weberian legacy. *Administrative Science Quarterly* 23: 65–90.

Menne, J. W. (1967). Techniques for evaluating the college environment. *Journal of Educational Measurement* 4: 219–225.

Meyer, J. W., and Rowan, B. (1978). The structure of educational organizations. In W. Meyer and Associates (eds.), *Environments and Organizations*. San Francisco: Jossey-Bass.

Moos, R. H. (1979). *Evaluating Educational Environments*. San Francisco: Jossey-Bass.

Moos, R. H., et al. (1975). A typology of university student living groups. *Journal of Educational Psychology* 67: 359–367.

Moos, R. H., and Bromet, E. (1978). Relation of patient attributes to perceptions of the treatment environment. *Journal of Consulting and Clinical Psychology* 46: 350–351.

Moos, R. H., and Van Dort, B. (1977). Physical and emotional symptoms and campus health center utilization. *Social Psychiatry* 12: 107–115.

Moran, E. T., and Volkwein, I. (1987). Organizational climate of institutions of higher education: construct determination and relationship to organizational effectiveness criteria. Paper presented at Association for the Study of Higher Education meetings, San Diego.

Murray, H. A. (1938). *Explorations in Personality*. New York: Oxford University Press.

Nadler, D. A. (1980). Role of models in organizational assessment. In Lawler et al., *Organizational Assessment*.

Nadler, D. A., and Tushman, M. L. (1980). A congruence model for organizational assessment. In Lawler et al., *Organizational Assessment*.

Naylor, J. P., Pritchard, R. D., and Ilgen, D. R. (1980). *A Theory of Behavior in Organizations*. New York: Academic Press.

Nettles, M. T., Thoeny, A. R., and Gosman, E. F. (1986). Comparative and predictive analyses of black and white students' college achievement and experiences. *Journal of Higher Education* 57: 289–318.

Pace, C. R. (1966). *Comparisons of CUES Results from Different Groups of Reporters*. (College Entrance Examination Board Report No. 1.) Los Angeles: University of California.

Pace, C. R. (1969). *College and University Environment Scales: Technical Manual* (2nd ed.). Princeton, NJ: Educational Testing Service.

Pace, C. R. (1972). *Education and Evangelism: A Profile of Protestant Colleges*. New York: McGraw-Hill.

Pace, C. R. (1974). *The Demise of Diversity? A Comparative Profile of Eight Types of Institutions*. New York: McGraw-Hill.

Pace, C. R. (1984). *Measuring the Quality of College Student Experiences*. Los Angeles: UCLA-Higher Education Research Institute.

Pace, C. R. (1987). *CSEQ: Test Manual and Norms: College Student Experiences Questionnaire*. Los Angeles: The Center for the Study of Evaluation, Graduate School of Education, University of California, Los Angeles.

Pace, C. R., and Baird, L. L. (1966). Attainment patterns in the environmental press of college subcultures. In T. M. Newcomb and E. K. Wilson (eds.), *College Peer Groups*. Chicago: Aldine.

Pace, C. R., and Stern, G. G. (1958). An approach to the measurement of psychological characteristics of college environments. *Journal of Educational Psychology* 49: 269–277.

Pascarella, E. T. (1974). Students' perceptions of the college environment: how well are they understood by administrators? *Journal of College Student Personnel* 15: 370–375.

Pascarella, E. T. (1984). College environmental influences on students' educational aspirations. *Journal of Higher Education* 55: 751–771.

Pascarella, E. T. (1985). College influences on learning and cognitive development. In J. Smart (ed.), *Higher Education: Handbook of Theory and Research*, Vol. 1. New York: Agathon Press.

Pascarella, E., and Terenzini, P. (1978). Student-faculty informal relationships and freshman-year educational outcomes. *Journal of Educational Research* 71: 183–189.

Pascarella, E., and Terenzini, P. (1980). Student-faculty and student-peer relationships as mediators of the structural effects of undergraduate residence arrangement. *Journal of Educational Research* 73: 344–353.

Pascarella, E., and Terenzini, P. (1983). Predicting voluntary freshmen-year persistence/withdrawal behavior in a residential university: a path analytic validation of Tinto's model. *Journal of Educational Psychology* 75: 215–226.

Perry, W. G. (1981). Cognitive and ethical growth: the making of meaning. In A. W. Chickering and Associates (eds.), *The Modern American College*. San Francisco: Jossey-Bass.

Peshkin, A. (1978). *Growing Up American: Schooling and the Survival of Community*. Chicago: University of Chicago Press.

Peterson, M. W., Cameron, K. S., Mets, L. A., Jones, P., and Ettington, D. (1986). *The Organizational Context for Teaching and Learning: A Review of the Research Literature*. Ann Arbor, MI: National Center for Research to Improve Postsecondary Teaching and Learning.

Peterson, R. E. (1968). *College Student Questionnaire: Technical Manual*. Princeton: Educational Testing Service.

Peterson, R. E., et al. (1970). *Institutional Functioning Inventory: Preliminary Technical Manual*. Princeton: Educational Testing Service.

Peterson, R. E., and Uhl, N. P. (1977). *Formulating College and University Goals: A Guide for Using the IGI*. Princeton: Educational Testing Service.

Pfeffer, J. (1981). *Power in Organizations*. Marshfield, MA: Pittman.

Pfeffer, J. (1982). *Organizations and Organization Theory*. Boston: Pittman.

Pfeffer, J. (1983). Organizational demography. In Cummings and Staw, *Research in Organizational Behavior*, Vol. 5.

Richards, J. M., Jr., and Braskamp, L. A. (1969). Who goes where to junior college. In L. A. Munday (ed.), *The Two-Year College and Its Students: An Empirical Report*. Iowa City: American College Testing Program.

Richards, J. M., Jr., Rand, L. M., and Rand, L. P. (1966). Description of junior colleges. *Journal of Educational Psychology* 57: 207–214.

Richards, J. M., Jr., Rand, L. M., and Rand, L. P. (1968). A description of medical college environments. *American Educational Research Journal* 5: 647–658.

Richards, J. M., Jr., Seligman, R., and Jones, P. K. (1970). Faculty and curriculum as measures of college environment. *Journal of Educational Psychology* 61: 324–332.

Roberts, K. H., and Burstein, K., eds. (1980). *Issues in Aggregation: New Directions for Methodology of Social and Behavioral Science*, Vol. 6. San Francisco: Jossey-Bass.

Rossides, D. W. (1984). What is the purpose of education: the worthless debate continues. *Change* 16(3): 14–46.

Rousseau, D. M. (1985). Issues of level in organizational research: multi-level and cross-level perspectives. In Cummings and Staw, *Research in Organizational Behavior*, Vol. 7.

Sasajima, M., Davis, J. A., and Peterson, R. E. (1968). Organized student protest and institutional climate. *American Educational Research Journal* 5: 291–304.

Schneider, B. (1975). Organizational climates: an essay. *Personnel Psychology* 28: 447–479.

Schneider, B. (1983). Work climates: an interactionist perspective. In N. W. Feimer and E. S. Geller (eds.), *Environmental Psychology: Directions and Perspectives*. New York: Praeger.

Staw, B., Sandelands, L. E., and Dutton, J. E. (1981). Threat-rigidity effects in organizational behavior: a multi-level analysis. *Administrative Science Quarterly* 26: 501–524.

Stern, G. G. (1970). *People in Context*. New York: Wiley.

Study Group on the Conditions of Excellence in American Higher Education. (1984). *Involvement in Learning*. Washington, DC: U.S. Department of Education.

Terenzini, P. T., and Pascarella, E. T. (1977). An assessment of the construct validity of the Clark-Trow typology of college student subcultures. *American Educational Research Journal* 14: 225–248.

Thistlethwaite, D. T. (1960). College press and changes in study plans of talented students. *Journal of Educational Psychology* 51: 222–234.

Thistlethwaite, D. T. (1963). Rival hypotheses for explaining the effects of different learning environments. *Journal of Educational Psychology* 53: 310–315.

Thistlethwaite, D. T., and Wheeler, N. (1966). Effects of teaching and peer subcultures upon student aspirations. *Journal of Educational Psychology* 57: 35–47.

Tinto, V. (1987). *Leaving College*. Chicago: University of Chicago Press.

Tushman, M. L., and Romanelli, E. (1985). Organizational evolution: a metamorphosis model of convergence and reorientation. In Cummings and Staw, *Research in Organizational Behavior*, Vol. 7.

Van deVen, A. H., and Drayin, R. (1985). The concept of fit in contingency theory. In Cummings and Staw, *Research in Organizational Behavior*, Vol. 7.

Walsh, W. B. (1973). *Theories of Person-Environment Interaction: Implications for the College Student*. Iowa City: American College Testing Program.

Warren, J. R., and Roelfs, P. J. (1972). Student reactions to college: the development of a questionnaire through which junior college students describe their college experiences. *Research Project Report 72-23*. Princeton: Educational Testing Service.

Weick, K. (1976). Educational organizations as loosely coupled systems. *Administrative Science Quarterly* 21: 1–19.

Weick, K. (1977). Repunctuating the problem. In P. S. Goodman and J. M. Pennings (eds.), *New Perspectives on Organizational Effectiveness*. San Francisco: Jossey-Bass.

Wethersby, R. P. (1981). Ego development. In A. W. Chickering and Associates (eds.), *The Modern American College*. San Francisco: Jossey-Bass.

Wilcox, B., and Holahan, C. J. (1976). Social ecology of the megadorm in university student housing. *Journal of Educational Psychology* 68: 453–458.

Wilder, D. H., Hoyt, A. K., Surbeck, B. S., Wilder, J. C., and Carney, P. I. (1986). Greek affiliation and attitude change in college students. *Journal of College Student Personnel* 27(6): 510–518.

Williams, T. E. (1986). Optimizing student-institution fit: an interactionist perspective. *College and University* 61: 141–152.

Winston, R. B., Jr., Hutson, G. S., and McCaffry, S. S. (1980). Environmental influences on fraternity academic achievement. *Journal of College Student Personnel* 21: 449–455.

Wolfle, D. (1954). *America's Resources of Specialized Talent*. New York: Harper Bros.

Outcomes, Assessment, and Academic Improvement: In Search of Usable Knowledge

Peter T. Ewell

National Center for
Higher Education Management Systems

Assessing and improving the outcomes of undergraduate instruction have recently taken on a new urgency in public dialogue. National reports such as *Involvement in Learning* (NIE, 1984), *Integrity in the College Curriculum* (AAC, 1985), and *To Reclaim a Legacy* (Bennett, 1984) have not only directed attention toward the effectiveness of undergraduate instruction but have also raised many questions about how "effectiveness" is to be defined and attained.

Such attention, of course, is not new. Indeed, it is one of the features of American higher education to periodically raise and wrestle with such questions. But a key aspect of the current discussion is its claim to be empirically rather than normatively grounded. First, most recommendations are advanced and justified on the basis of a considerable body of findings about the impact of college on students. Recommendations for heavy investment of instructional resources in the first two years of college and for learning technologies that increase the amount of direct contact between students and faculty, for example, are advanced on grounds of past research on retention and student involvement (NIE, 1984; Astin, 1985). But a second "empirical" element is equally apparent in recent calls for reform. In addition to identifying problems and remedies, research on student learning and development is seen as part of the solution itself. Ongoing "assessment" of both students and institutions is proposed as a permanent mechanism to attain and maintain quality.

Both claims raise thorny questions about the adequacy of our existing knowledge base with respect to student outcomes. While a great deal has indeed been written about college impact, how much of the knowledge that has been gained is "usable knowledge" in the sense of informing academic policy? And given the knowledge to correctly determine policy, what is in fact known about our ability to effectively implement it—particularly in the area of assessing student learning and development at the campus level? The tenor of reports from outside the academy (for example, National Governors' Association, 1986), and an emerging pattern of state initiatives on undergraduate assessment (Boyer et al., 1987) suggest that action will likely not wait until these questions are fully answered.

The purpose of this chapter is therefore dual. One requirement is to reexamine the research literature on college impact from the perspective of academic policy. Of necessity, this will be a selective exercise. Excellent summaries of this literature in its own right already exist (Pascarella, 1985a; Pace, 1979; Bowen, 1977a; Feldman and Newcomb, 1969), and need little amplification beyond sharpening their policy focus. But a focused review may help administrators to begin to determine which of a myriad of distinct findings provides sufficient "leverage" on improvement to be worth pursuing in practice. A second requirement is more complex. If information on student outcomes is to be used to inform practice, research on the utilization of evaluation results and emerging institutional experience with assessment suggest that it must be of a particular kind and character. By examining the much more fragmentary literature on recent information-based change efforts, lessons can be drawn not only about the most fruitful lines of inquiry for future research, but also about the forms, methods, and types of studies that will probably yield the greatest policy dividends.

It is important to stress that much past work on the impact of college was originally intended as action research. Pace (1979) documents the establishment of numerous offices at major universities in the mid-thirties charged with local educational research. Their activities included, among others, evaluating alternative curricular forms, assessing student development and achievement, and comparing teaching methods. Among these offices were the "Bureau of Institutional Research" at the University of Minnesota and the "Division of Educational Reference" at Purdue. Resnick and Goulden (1987) argue that this surge of applied educational research emerged out of a need to reevaluate basic curricular questions in a period of enrollment consolidation. In the great expansion of higher education in the postwar period, Pace contends, this original conception of "institutional research" was lost, and the function of such offices shifted toward questions of cost, efficiency, and internal management. The history of college impact research that Pascarella (1985a) recounts, beginning with the "Jacobs Report" in the mid-fifties, is therefore largely a history of scholarly, rather than of policy-oriented work.

Changes in the notion of "institutional research," however, did not mean abandonment of the notion of investigating impact from the point of view of action. Indeed, it is in the mid-sixties that the term "student outcomes" becomes explicitly visible in discussions of higher education management. Documenting "outcomes" was an integral part (though admittedly the most difficult part) of implementing increasingly fashionable new systems of "Planning, Management, and Evaluation'' imported from other public sectors. A prime example of this line of inquiry was a multiyear, federally-funded effort at the National Center for Higher Education Management Systems (NCHEMS) in the mid-seventies (Lenning et al., 1977). Though never fully carried out, the major intent of this project was to ''standardize'' discussions of postsecondary effectiveness through construction of a common taxonomy and suggested procedures for gathering information on higher education outcomes. The promise of these activities seemed considerable in a period yet to experience the limits of ''scientific management.'' But large-scale implementation of such concepts foundered on questions of operationalization and utility, and was generally dropped as higher education suffered increasing retrenchment.

Current reemergence of the outcomes issue in the guise of ''assessment'' partakes of both these earlier action research traditions. First, assessment aims at recreating the kinds of campus-based applied research offices that were typical five decades ago. It is no coincidence that a surviving office of this type, the Learning Research Center at the University of Tennessee, Knoxville, played a significant role in shaping the state of Tennessee's experiment in outcomes-based ''performance funding'' (Branscomb et al., 1977) in the late seventies, or that this office currently is considered a leader in campus-based assessment for purposes of local program improvement. Secondly, consistent with the tenets of ''scientific management,'' there has been an increasing tendency to formally incorporate information on student outcomes into decision making. For example, Ewell (1985b) notes rising utilization in two areas—budget making and program review—at the institutional level. Similar trends have been observed in statewide program review (Shapiro, 1986; Barak, 1982), and in institutional and program accreditation (Thrash, 1984).

What is needed to sustain these developments? If their central intent is to inform actions designed to improve the undergraduate product, three kinds of questions need to be posed. First, what in fact *is* the ''product?'' Recent confusions about use of the term ''assessment'' (e.g., Edgerton, 1987) only echo myriad earlier definitions of the term ''outcome.'' Reviewing some of these many definitions and understanding their commonalities and differences is thus a critical prerequisite for both effective action and for directed research. Second, given an adequate description of the ''product,'' is it possible to specify the ''production function'' that produced it? This is a much more difficult question, and answers will necessarily be incomplete. At the very least, however, a review of past research can suggest some fruitful lines of action and can point out some critical gaps in our knowledge. Finally, can we in fact intervene in the ''production function'' in ways that have the potential to actually change outcomes? Critical questions here are both the manipulability and range of variation of some available management levers, and particularly the degree to which assessment-based improvements can actually be implemented in complex institutional settings. Again, a review of emerging experience, though fragmentary, can both suggest immediate direction and can note places where more systematic inquiry is needed.

STRUCTURING INQUIRY: OUTCOMES TAXONOMIES AS A POINT OF DEPARTURE

A major challenge in reviewing the outcomes literature is to determine exactly what is meant by an "outcome." Surveying the literature on outcomes taxonomies a decade ago, Lenning identified and described 89 distinct classifications (Lenning, 1977). Since that review, several dozen additional examples have emerged—mostly for purposes of curriculum planning at individual institutions. In examining this considerable array, four rough categories emerge. Some classifications, like Astin's fourfold typology of college outcomes, were developed to support particular research efforts (Astin, Panos, and Creager, 1967). Others, like Harshman's taxonomy of student outcomes (1979), Bloom's taxonomy of cognitive objectives (1956), and Chickering's "vectors of identity" (1969), were primarily constructed to summarize and structure the results of past research in a particular area of impact. Still others, like Lenning's own "Outcomes Structures for Postsecondary Education" (Lenning et al., 1977), or Ewell's "Classification of Outcomes Dimensions" (1984), result from attempts to build a common language for policy making, institutional comparison, or data exchange. Finally, a substantial number of taxonomies, for example, the classic Harvard List of General Educational Behavioral Goals, the Clapp Commission Classification of College Outcomes, or the Association of American College's "Nine Criteria Defining Undergraduate Learning" (AAC, 1985), were primarily intended to establish goals for curriculum planning.

The characteristics of each of these major types reflects its intended purpose. Therefore each possesses important limitations when applied outside its original conceptual environment. In examining the literature on outcomes taxonomies, therefore, two approaches are useful. First, it is important to briefly discuss a few of the most commonly used and broadly representative outcomes classification schemes. Intended for different purposes, each constructs the universe of inquiry in a somewhat different way. Collectively, however, they raise a series of definitional and operational issues that are applicable to all such efforts. More importantly, discussion of these common taxonomic issues provides an excellent point of departure for reviewing findings of the outcomes literature itself.

Probably the most widely used taxonomy of educational outcomes is Bloom's (1956). Originally designed to inform curriculum building and evaluation at the elementary and secondary level, the taxonomy has also been widely used as a basis for discussion and evaluation of higher education outcomes. The Bloom taxonomy is confined to the cognitive domain, and consists of six types of learning arranged in a hierarchical order—knowledge, comprehension, application, analysis, synthesis, and evaluation. The presumed cognitive progression implied by this hierarchy is of two types: from simple to complex mental operations, and from concrete to abstract applications. In its distinction among types of cognitive process and in its hierarchical organization, the Bloom taxonomy resembles other more recent schemes for describing outcomes. For example, Perry's (1970) widely discussed framework for student development is also hierarchical. Students progress through nine "positions" in this hierarchy ranging from "dualistic" judgments of right and wrong, through "relativistic" positions in which many analytic frames of reference are recognized, to "commitment" in which a personal affirmation or choice of perspective is accomplished. "Staging" of cognitive processes is also recognized in such operational documents as a recent proposal to evaluate "general intellectual skills" in New Jersey (COEP, 1987). Here, three independent cognitive operations are identified—getting information, manipulating information, and presenting information. Each of these operations is intended to define a distinct focus for collecting statewide performance information at the freshman, sophomore, and senior years.

The most heavily cited classification of student outcomes in higher education is probably the fourfold conceptual scheme developed by Astin and his associates at UCLA (Astin et al., 1967). Originally designed to organize and report findings of the Cooperative Institutional Research Program (CIRP) in the mid-sixties, this typology classifies outcomes on two dimensions. The first, "type of outcome," distinguishes cognitive from noncognitive outcomes. The second, "type of data," distinguishes outcomes that are observable in overt student behaviors from those that must be detected and measured psychometrically. The resulting four cells— psychological/cognitive, psychological/affective, behavioral/cognitive, and behavioral/affective—have been used both to summarize research results and to identify broad classes of inquiry. For example, Pascarella (1985a) chooses Astin's psychological/cognitive cell to delimit his review of college impact. In later formulations, Astin adds a time dimension (for example, 1975, 1977) that is treated as a continuous variable. Using these three dimensions, Ewell (1985a) identifies three methodologically distinct "clusters" of research activity that have dominated recent assessment efforts: (1) cognitive/psychological/within-college based largely on cognitive testing, (2) affective/psychological/within- and after-college based largely on survey methods, and (3) behavioral/within-college based on student tracking and "trace data" methods.

In his comprehensive review of the benefits of higher education, Bowen (1977a) uses a somewhat similar classification of individual outcomes. His "goals for individual students" include three major headings: cognitive learning, emotional and moral development, and "practical competence" (the last including such traits as "need for achievement, adaptability, citizenship, and consumer efficiency"). Three additional types of outcomes—personal self-discovery, career choice and placement, and satisfaction/enjoyment—are identified as "by-products" of the educational experience. In a more recent formulation, Astin recognizes this latter category by referring to such outcomes as "fringe" and "existential" benefits (1985). Moreover, Bowen's classification involves a further distinction between "dispositions" and "behaviors" quite similar to Astin's psychological/behavioral dimension, but not quite so tied to data collection. Speaking as an economist, Bowen asserts that behaviors are the ultimate goal of instruction, and that each individual outcome of experience can be described in terms of both a disposition to act and an actual behavioral manifestation. More importantly, Bowen's classification moves beyond the individual to include an explicit catalogue of "societal" outcomes ranging from the satisfactions and enjoyments of an educated population to enhanced economic efficiency and growth due to increases in trained manpower. Several of these categories have spawned highly specialized research literatures of their own, for example, the "rate of return" on economic investments in higher education (Douglass, 1977; Leslie and Brinkman, 1986).

Probably the most comprehensive single classification of outcomes is that of Lenning and his associates at NCHEMS (Lenning et al., 1977). Reflecting Bowen's shift of perspective from the individual to society, early formulations of this scheme noted three types of outcome: individual student benefits, "private" (or in economic terms "separable") postgraduate benefits, and "societal" (or nonseparable) benefits (Lenning, 1974). The complete taxonomy, intended to classify all forms of postsecondary outcomes as a basis for common data collection, is organized around three major dimensions. A "Type of Outcome" dimension identifies the particular "entity" that is intended to be changed or maintained through higher education. Examples included economic outcomes; human characteristic outcomes such as aspirations, satisfactions, and competence in particular skill areas; knowledge, technology and art form outcomes; and resource and service provision outcomes. An "Audience" dimension identifies particular types of beneficiaries that receive or are affected by a particular outcome. These range from individuals, through various types of defined "communities" to society at large. Finally, a "Time" dimension identifies the particular point at which specified benefits are realized by a particular beneficiary.

These four examples suffice to raise most of the issues involved in building and using an outcomes taxonomy, and are representative of the wider classification literature. What are their real commonalities and differences? Two observations are appropriate to begin this discussion. First, it is apparent that most architects of outcomes taxonomies are viewing the same landscape. Most recognize core phenomena of cognitive and affective development during instruction; most define and describe these core phenomena in roughly similar ways. On the other hand, considerable diversity occurs when additional conceptual dimensions are added to amplify or constrain descriptions of these core phenomena. In some cases, additional dimensions are intended to further break down distinct elements within the cognitive or affective arena. Bloom's framework consists of such an attempt within the cognitive realm that is representative of a wide body of taxonomic work (e.g., Gagne, 1977; Guilford, 1967). Such formulations as Chickering (1969) and Perry (1970) extend discussion to the affective area, though many of the categories used in these classifications represent combinations of cognitive and affective traits. In most cases, however, additional conceptual dimensions are constructed in order to describe ways in which core phenomena are located, constrained, or observed. These include the temporal occurrence and duration of the phenomenon, the unit of analysis or entity experiencing it, the manner in which the outcome is made manifest, and the kinds of observations or measurements necessary to detect it.

A primary difficulty with most of these formulations, however, is that modifying dimensions of this kind are not clearly distinguished from those that describe core phenomena. More importantly, different value perspectives on the conceptual or empirical importance of such ancillary dimensions often lead to subtle but substantial disagreements. Bowen's (1977a) and Astin's (1985) treatment of personal development and satisfaction outcomes as "externalities" is thus strongly at variance with the tradition of Chickering (1969) and Heath (1968) who see such results as primary intended outcomes of the college experience. Such differences are of relatively little importance so long as each tradition pursues an independent line of inquiry. But they become important when the issue is one of informed intervention. Here a somewhat different approach to conceptualization is needed. Figure 1 represents one attempt to address this need. Like all such schemes, it emanates from a particular phenomenal and value perspective—that of the administrator or manager concerned with understanding the system with a view toward manipulating it. Rather than constructing an additional taxonomy, however, the intent is to advance a series of analytical and operational questions that are driven by the salient features of past classification schemes, and that can be posed of any particular set of higher education outcomes. This, in itself, can be a valid and valuable planning exercise. At the same time, these analytical questions serve as a useful frame for organizing a discussion of relevant findings from the college impact literature.

The heart of this scheme is a definition of "outcome" consisting of three distinct components. Each component frames a series of questions that in turn uncover a set of concrete research and measurement issues. First, an "outcome" is a *result*. It is of primary interest less as a phenomenon than as a product—one that action and intervention can at least hope to influence. Moreover, it is a *specifiable* result. It is (or ideally can be made to be) concrete enough to

FIG. 1. Analytical questions for constructing or evaluating statements of higher education outcomes.

"An *outcome* is. . .	Analytical Questions	Particular Research issues
● A specifiable *result*	● Of What Kind?	Classification/Taxonomy
Identification and Assessment →	● In What Direction and Magnitude?	"Value-Added" Assessment
		Subgroup Disaggregation
	● For Whom?	Behavioral/Psychometric Evidence
	● Manifested in What Manner?	
		Timing/Sequencing of Observation
	● At What Time?	
● . . . of a constructed *experience*	● Of What Kinds?	Documenting Environment
	● At What Level of Aggregation?	Unit of Analysis
		Observation/Experimental Design
Attribution →	● Involving What Particular Activities or Settings?	
		Incentives/"Quality of Effort"
	● Requiring Investments on Whose Part?	
● . . . viewed from a particular *goal perspective.*"	● Whose Perspective?	Intentions Analysis
	● With What Values?	Views of "Effectiveness"
Valuation →	● With What Stake in the Result?	Cost-Benefit/Rate of Return

determine its direction and degree, and it may be of many particular kinds. Primary analytical questions raised at this point are questions of identification and assessment. To what degree can we in fact specify the result with respect to magnitude, location, and particularity? Secondly, an "outcome" is the result of an *experience*. Like the result itself, the experience must be specifiable. If it cannot be minimally specified, there is little hope of influencing the result. More importantly, the experience is "constructed." That is, it takes place in a particular setting (Sarason, 1972) or environment whose elements are not only organized, but are *intentional*. Here the primary analytical questions are those of attribution: To what extent can particular aspects of the experience be isolated and linked to particular attributes of the result? Finally, because it is intentional, an "outcome" is never value-neutral. The same result may be viewed by different constituencies in quite different ways, depending on their goals and levels of investment in the process (Ewell, 1984). Thus a final set of analytical questions, though beyond the scope of the outcomes literature, has to do with valuation. Once a demonstrated link between result and experience is established, how critical is the need for action, and what will be its likely payoff given current goals and investments? Each of these areas frames a wide field for discussion of prior research.

More importantly, each frames a distinct arena for management action. In specifying intended results through formal planning and goal-setting, management action both articulates and constrains institutional activity. Moreover, in its consistency and its explicit reference to established goals, management action helps to determine the degree to which such goals are internalized throughout the institution or remain artificial or vestigal. In allocating and manipulating the flow of resources, management action provides and shapes the institutional environment within which instructional experiences are "constructed." While the actual construction is done by others, their actions are directly conditioned by both the current content of management action and its past accumulation. Finally, a crucial role of management—formal or informal—is evaluation, to review accomplished results from the perspective of intended goals and of broader organizational interests. Prominent among the latter may be the satisfaction of key external constituencies critical to the institution's future survival.

DEFINING THE PRODUCT:
OUTCOMES AS GOAL SPECIFICATIONS

In response to the impetus of such reports as *Involvement in Learning* and *Integrity in the College Curriculum*, many institutions are currently engaged in the process more concretely describing the goals of their undergraduate curricula. In doing so, they pose questions of identifying and assessing educational results that have been raised and discussed in the outcomes literature many times before. Such questions generally involve, as a prerequisite for actual investigation or for effective planning, further specification of the nature of impact, of the types of students involved, and of the ways in which evidence of attainment is exhibited and assembled. Following the logic of figure 1, these may be discussed in terms of a set of explicit questions about "result."

Outcomes of What Kind?

A first issue is that of explicitly specifying the intended core phenomenon, and this generally involves making a number of typological distinctions. Virtually all outcomes taxonomies recognize a distinction between cognitive and affective outcomes, a distinction rooted firmly in psychology, which constitutes the grounding discipline of most outcomes work. In general, more research has been directed toward affective than toward cognitive outcomes, partly because they appear somewhat easier to define and detect (Bowen, 1977a). Apparent ease of definition, however, also leads to a profusion of operational measures. Feldman and Newcomb (1969), for example, report freshman-to-senior gains on such diverse attributes as "open-mindedness" and "independence," "decreased conservatism," and "sensitivity to aesthetic and inner experiences," based on studies that operationalize these traits in vastly different ways. Astin's (1977) research notes broad changes in all types of students at all types of institutions in such attributes as "social and intellectual competence," "increased liberalism," decreased "religiosity," and "need for status." Most of these trends, however, obscure considerable variations among particular student subgroups and among different institutional environments.

Cognitive outcomes are more difficult to definitively detect, but again a wide range of gains have been reported. Bowen's (1977a) review of this literature notes typical gains in the range of half to a full standard deviation between the freshman and senior years on most measures of verbal and quantitative skill, and of two-thirds to a full standard deviation on substantive knowledge measures. Studies based on student self-reports of cognitive gain (for example, Spaeth and Greely, 1970) tend to confirm these findings. One significant exception to general gain, however, appears to be in quantitative skill areas, where regressions have been widely reported (Robertshaw and Wolfle, 1982; Lenning, Munday, and Maxey, 1969). As with affective development, however, general population findings obscure considerable differences among particular subpopulations and environments. More importantly, many fewer cognitive than affective studies are able to credibly link changes in outcome measures with particular aspects of the institutional environment (Pascarella, 1985a), or with such "exogenous" policy variables as selectivity (Astin, 1968) or resources per student invested (Bowen 1980, 1981).

Major difficulties with the cognitive/affective distinction only occur in such areas as intellectual persistence, aesthetic awareness and enjoyment, and value neutrality when applied to inquiry. For example, McKeachie and his colleagues (1986) include in their "taxonomy of learning strategies" a set of attributes labelled "resource management strategies." Together with skills like scheduling and goal-setting, this category includes such partially attitudinal elements as attribution of result to effort, mood, and self-reinforcement. At the same time, a prominent element of the literature on critical thinking emphasizes "relativism" or value neutrality with respect to content as part of the process of cognitive development (e.g., Perry, 1970). Similarly, Bowen (1977a) lists "intellectual tolerance" as a "cognitive" goal of higher education. Findings at Alverno College on such traits as "self-sustaining learning" or "attributions about the value of experience in learning" are equally difficult to fully classify in terms of the cognitive/affective distinction (Mentkowski and Doherty, 1984). For most observers most of the time, however, this distinction remains solid, and provides a reasonable guide for specification.

Typical outcomes taxonomies further differentiate "knowledge" from "skills" within the cognitive domain, a distinction based upon perceived differences between raw cognitive content and the ability to perform explicit tasks. While this distinction appears to work well for so-called "basic skills" (reading, writing, and computation) that have a considerable history of independent assessment, there remains considerable controversy about the degree to which such "higher-order" skills as critical thinking and problem-solving are separable from a particular knowledge base (e.g., Campione and Armbruster, 1985). Proponents of "metacognition" argue that such attributes as the general awareness of and control of individual cognition on the part of individual learners can be taught, and many current assessment models (see, e.g., Alverno College Faculty, 1979) are founded upon the generalizability of higher-order skills. On the other hand, there is some experimental evidence that these distinctions are not as clear in practice as they might be. For example, based on a series of experiments involving textual learning, Marton (1979) argued that most "skills" are acquired, processed, and manipulated in the same ways as more traditional content elements.

The actual specification of such higher-order skills as critical thinking also remains a problem. In reviewing 27 studies on determinants of critical thinking ability in college, McMillan (1987) found little pattern of impact for particular instructional methods or approaches; he did, however, indicate a general positive trend as a result of college attendance. Part of the explanation was felt to be the lack of a good definition of critical thinking with appropriate instrumentation to support it. Bowen (1977a) and Pascarella (1985a) also report generally positive results between critical thinking and college attendance, but both note that the magnitude of change in such higher-order skills attributes is considerably less than for basic skills or substantive knowledge outcomes.

A final definitional difficulty is specifying the nature of the experience itself. Some outcomes models (among them the popular "value-added" construct) rest on what might be termed a "mechanistic" view of instruction. Under this view, student characteristics are seen largely as input conditions to a process supplied and managed by the institution. Quite different are conceptions that conceive of the learning process as "organic"—involving equally important actions and investments on the part of the learner. In choosing the word "impact" to circumscribe their comprehensive review of learner outcomes, Feldman and Newcomb (1969) wished particularly to call attention to the interactive aspect of the experience. Going somewhat farther, Pace throughout his work uses the term "impress" rather than "impact" to describe the influence of educational environments; his explicit object is to suggest the importance of "content-provision" rather than "production" aspects of a given educational environment

(Pace, 1974, 1979). Probably the most vivid example of this distinction is Marton's portrayal of two kinds of learning from the student's perspective: learning is "something that you do" as opposed to "something that happens to you" (Marton, 1979).

In What Direction and Magnitude?

A more compelling definitional question is that of the direction and magnitude of change. Here there has been considerable debate in the outcomes literature on the appropriateness and technological difficulty of assessing growth. Much of the former has revolved around the terms "value-added" or "talent development" made current by Astin (1974, 1977, 1985). The essence of this position is that institutional quality or effectiveness is best assessed in terms of the changes in student outcomes that can be observed from entry to exit, and that can be attributed to institutional action.

Clearly, there is little real disagreement in the research literature about the importance of assessing development. As Pascarella points out, the entire "value-added" controversy can be readily subsumed under the traditional researcher's question: To what degree can observed developmental outcomes be ascribed to the college experience? (See Pascarella, 1987.) From a policy perspective, however, the issue can be real and concrete: Are institutions and programs to be judged primarily in terms of the degree to which they "develop talent" or in terms of the degree to which their ultimate products meet accepted standards? This issue is more than theoretical, as documented by recent debates about the use of assessment evidence in state policy in Tennessee and New Jersey. Ewell (1984) notes that while these are different questions, both answers are important for policy.

Moreover, from a planning perspective, it may be important for an institution to explicitly determine those particular dimensions on which it expects to induce considerable change from those where the instructional objective is to maintain skills at an acceptable level (Ewell, 1983). Determinations of this kind may appropriately vary from program to program depending on the particular content and value perspectives of each. In the absence of such distinctions, use of a "value-added" model may be actively misleading because it fails to distinguish arenas where gains are not intended from those where producing gain is critical for meeting established instructional goals. Furthermore, value-added models may fail to detect situations, again consistent with instructional objectives, where instruction has been effective in maintaining skills that would otherwise have eroded (Pascarella, 1987).

Far more difficult than determining the appropriateness of such concepts are the technical issues involved in documenting change in the first place. Most large-scale operational uses of the "value-added" construct rely on a pre-test/

post-test design using a single instrument (see, for example, McClain, 1984; Dumont and Troelstrup, 1981; Banta, 1986). As discussed by Hanson, however, such designs are vulnerable to a range of measurement and attribution problems including sample attrition, regression effects, and compound measurement error (Hanson, 1982).

Outcomes For Whom?

A third major analytical question involves specifying the entity experiencing the outcome. Operationally, this is a question of both determining appropriate levels of aggregation, and of selecting appropriate variables to be used in differentiating among particular subpopulations. As Pascarella points out, there is powerful evidence that different kinds of students experience college in different ways (Pascarella, 1985a); many problems in interpreting findings in the impact literature are therefore due to the fact that a high level of aggregation may obscure quite real subgroup differences. Bowen (1977b) makes a similar point in observing that research on outcomes is based upon analytical groups, and that a finding of "no effect" may be the joint product of many individuals experiencing significant positive and negative impacts. Both these observations call for considerable care in disaggregating student study populations, both when specifying intended outcomes and when assessing effects.

A first set of differences among student subpopulations concerns aptitude and learning style. Though most examinations of such differences have been in elementary and secondary education, there appear to be substantial grounds for generalizing findings to postsecondary classrooms and environments (McKeachie et al., 1986). In a major review of the literature on individual learning styles, Messick (1976) summarizes the effects on learning styles of such factors as sex and cultural background, and concludes that different types of students learn best using idiosyncratic styles, modes, and strategies. Examining the literature on individual learner differences some ten years later, Corno and Snow (1986) concluded that major differences involved (1) intellectual abilities—"enabling cognitive abilities and skills"; (2) personality characteristics—"motivational and affective traits"; and (3) cognitive styles—"predispositions for processing information".

Viewing such differences from a broader frame of reference, Feldman and Newcomb (1969) suggest that overall college impact is mediated by the relative degrees of "openness" with which students approach the experience of college. Moreover, they view differences on "openness" on two independent dimensions—openness to new experiences and stimuli, and openness to the influence of others (peers and faculty). A major research question, however, is the degree to which such differences have a direct effect on outcomes, or are mediated by different types of experiences and instruction. Cronbach and Snow (1977) provide many examples of the way important interactions among student characteristics and particular classroom learning situations can condition cognitive outcomes. Pascarella (1985a) further cites a range of postsecondary studies that document differential effects of this kind, including such factors as race, career aspiration, and mode of instruction.

A major difficulty with this line of inquiry in higher education, however, is the fact that the "learning environment" often goes far beyond the individual classroom. One of the most fruitful types of analytical disaggregation, therefore, involves distinguishing among student subcultures. For example, Clark and Trow's classic typology of student subcultures specified four types (academic, nonconformist, collegiate, and vocational) based on the intersection of two orientation dimensions, amount of involvement with ideas, and amount of identification with the institution (Clark and Trow, 1966). Although largely dated, research experience with the Clark/Trow typology has indicated substantial differences among student goals for students subscribing to each type (Kees, 1974). A more recent attempt at classification was attempted by Katchadourian and Boli at Stanford (1985). Also using a two-dimensional classification scheme (constructed on scales of "intellectualism" and "careerism"), they distinguished four student types: careerist, intellectual, striver, and unconnected. Based on longitudinal interviews over a five year period, a major finding was the distinctiveness of self-intended outcomes among these populations. Indeed, students in each category tended to ascribe to the institution as a whole their own distinctive outcomes goals. Differences were also noted in such important in-college behaviors as amount and initiation of out-of-class contact with faculty members.

Differences in the environmental perceptions of different types of students may also substantially influence patterns of outcomes and experience. In an early study involving both public and private institutions, Pace and Baird (1966) attempted to relate student-reported institutional outcomes with identified characteristics of the college environment as assessed by the College Characteristics Index, and with individual personality characteristics. They found both significant, though student perceptions of the environment appeared more powerful. Pace (1963) makes a similar point in reviewing development of the College and University Environment Scales (CUES) instrument: pilot research revealed many instances where the same physical and social environment was viewed differently by students in different programs, at different levels, and who exhibited different amounts of involvement with the campus. Examining student perceptions of institutional "effectiveness domains" at three state universities, Kleemann and Richardson (1985) report significant differences in perceived outcomes for different types of students. Moreover, they observed that perceived outcomes were considerably more positive for students whose own goals appeared congruent with those of the institution.

Among other conclusions, these studies suggest the importance of ascertaining differences in student goals and motivations as a prerequisite to specifying or explaining outcomes. This conclusion is particularly salient when applied to "nontraditional" students, or in multiclientele settings such as urban public universities or community colleges. In a three-year statewide longitudinal study of 6,550 community college students in California, for example, Sheldon (1981) distinguished among eighteen distinct student subpopulations, based upon expressed goals and revealed enrollment behavior. These groups showed markedly different patterns of persistence and success. Walleri and Japely (1986), studying a different population of community college students, found significant differences in persistence and outcomes based on initial intent. Examining patterns of academic integration among commuting students in a four-year institution, Iverson and associates (Iverson, Pascarella, and Terenzini, 1984) found markedly different patterns of faculty/student interactions than those typical of resident students. A most important finding was the salience of motivation; students with high aspirations initiated contacts with faculty and experienced levels of academic integration on a par with resident students. Similar evidence on motivation is suggested by a study by Erwin (1986). Using such outcome measures as the Scale of Intellectual Development, Erwin's findings indicated that students who financed at least 75% of their own postsecondary education showed higher gains than their peers in such areas as sense of personal direction and the ability to express thoughts and values.

In What Manner Are Outcomes Manifested?

A fourth and analytical question concerns the ways in which a given core outcome is exhibited. Consistent with Bowen's notion of "disposition" and Astin's "psychological/behavioral" distinction, a particular cognitive or affective state may manifest itself in action, or may it remain latent. The importance of this distinction in practice depends largely upon an institution's or program's identification of particular behaviors as explicit instructional goals. For example, job and graduate school placements are both commonly used as indicators of undergraduate major program effectiveness. It makes a considerable difference, however, whether the basic reason for the program's existence—as in a community college occupational program—is to *produce* placements, or whether placements are interpreted as manifestations of the attainment of more basic instructional goals.

To what degree does research evidence indicate that psychological and behavioral outcomes are really different manifestations of the same core result? Concrete evidence is scarce because most studies of behavioral outcomes have tended to be postcollege, while those involving direct assessment of cognition and affect have been within-college. Nevertheless, some suggestive parallels can be drawn. Astin's findings (1977) that postgraduate income and professional success is related to undergraduate performance, and that early and continuous exposure to the major field results in more consistent attainment of career objectives, resonate well with Pace's (1979) summary of cognitive impact that indicates the greatest growth in areas of greatest exposure. Results reported by Bowen (1977a) under the heading of "practical competence" indicate roughly similar parallels between dispositions and actions. While hardly startling, these parallels point toward some consistency between the correlates of psychological and behavioral outcomes. More compelling are the results of attempts to use theories of college attrition to also explain changes in cognition and affect. For example, a series of recent studies using Tinto's (1975) concepts of academic and social integration as mediating variables has convincingly demonstrated the efficacy of employing these concepts in explanations of such outcomes as self-reported personal growth (Terenzini and Wright, 1987), goal development in "liberal education" (Theophilides, Terenzini, and Lorang, 1984), grade performance and academic growth (Terenzini, Pascarella, and Lorang, 1982), satisfaction with college (Pascarella, 1984), and intellectual self-concept and educational aspiration (Pascarella, 1985b).

The Timing of Outcomes

The timing and sequencing of particular outcomes raise similar questions of specification. Indeed, it is possible to maintain that the time dimension represents a special case of "manifestation" discussed above. Just as Bowen argues that an individual may have learned a "disposition" to act without actually having done so, certain outcomes of college may be consistently present, but latent. Part of this may be due to the individual's inability to recognize their presence and thus offer them to researchers in the form of self-reports (Ewell, 1983).

Virtually all major outcomes taxonomies recognize the importance of time, though they model it differently. As noted by Lenning and associates (1977), time may be important in a number of ways. First, certain bodies of content or particular learning experiences may have little effect until they are "triggered" by a need or opportunity for use. Other outcomes will differ in how long they persist. Most long-term research on postcollege cognitive results, for example, notes considerable atrophy in such skills as computation and quantitative reasoning that are rarely practiced (Pace, 1979).

Staged learning models such as Perry (1970) or those employed at Alverno College (Alverno College Faculty, 1979), as well as developmental models such as those of Chickering (1969) or Heath (1968), are time-dependent in a different sense. Here the importance of time is ordinal: to array expected and achieved outcomes in terms of a stepwise or prerequisite pattern. Research focusing on student development from year to year raises similar issues of sequencing. Summarizing a considerable body of early work on student development, Feldman and Newcomb (1969) report considerable differences in the perceptions of entering and continuing students at different stages of progress. In their study of Stanford students, Katchadourian and Boli (1985) characterize each year of a four-year undergraduate sequence as a somewhat different arena of experience. At the same time, Terenzini and Wright (1987) found identifiable differences in the factors responsible for self-reported outcomes among freshmen and sophomores, based upon changes in the mediating effects of academic and social integration. Confirming findings reported by Feldman and Newcomb (1969) that entering freshmen tended to overestimate the ''academic'' aspects of the college experience, Terenzini and Wright noted that academic integration was considerably more important for freshmen than for sophomores in explaining self-assessments of personal development. Year-to-year variations of this kind are also consistent with findings on the differences in retention correlates between freshmen and later year (Lenning, Beal, and Sauer 1980).

Finally, from a policy or action perspective the time categories of particular interest to different types of decision makers may themselves be different. As noted by Lenning (1977) and Pace (1985), those focusing on the effects of a particular course or sequence will appropriately use a quite different time frame from those whose interest is campuswide. It may also be extremely difficult in practice to link long-term outcomes to actual changes that might be made in institutional policy or practice, both because of difficulties in attribution and because during the time elapsed between a graduate's report and his actual experience, many shifts in institutional practices, environment, and clientele may have occurred.

LINKING OUTCOMES AND
EXPERIENCE: ATTRIBUTION AS POTENTIAL ACTION

Questions of identification and assessment raise numerous issues for the design and conduct of ''action research'' on student outcomes. But far more complex are questions having to do with attribution—the degree to which a specifiable result can credibly be linked to identifiable elements of ''constructed experience.''

Many methodological difficulties are associated with studies of this kind. First, lack of appropriate control groups means that it is extremely difficult to unambiguously attribute observed changes to actual college attendance (Astin 1970a,b). Furthermore, if multi-institutional samples are used, there are substantial differences in aptitude, motivation, and background among student populations at different institutions due to self-selection (Astin 1970a, 1977). The same observation can generally be applied to studies that attempt to document the differential effects of different departments and instructional experiences. Finally, few true longitudinal studies exist, and those that do are subject to such difficulties as panel attrition and regression effects (Astin, 1977; Pascarella, 1987).

Methodological challenges of these kinds have made it difficult for past research to unambiguously establish cause. Reviewing the literature on cognitive impact, Pascarella (1985a) cites considerable disappointing early evidence of links between institutional characteristics and achievement, once entering student attributes were statistically controlled (for example, Astin and Panos, 1969; Nichols, 1964). Though somewhat better evidence of differential effect was reported when the institution rather than the student was used as the unit of analysis (for example, Centra and Rock, 1971), findings remain inconclusive. Pascarella attributes these results to four possible difficulties, including (1) lack of sufficient variation in the types of institutions studied, (2) insufficient specification and definition of differences in institutional characteristics, (3) too high a level of aggregation in analysis that obscures real effects among subpopulations, and (4) insufficient specificity and precision in the way cognitive outcomes are measured. He then proposes a number of methodological remedies to counter these conditions, among them greater attention to causal modeling and multilevel analysis. Evidence of progress in this regard is provided by Kuh and associates (1986). Based on a review of 1,189 studies of college students appearing in eleven selected journals since 1969, they found a decrease in the absolute number of impact studies, but an increase in their methodological sophistication as indicated by such features as the use of true longitudinal designs and multivariate statistical techniques. Reflecting the difficulty of definitionally specifying and operationalizing outcomes measures, however, they also found an increasing trend toward nonstandardization and institution-specific measures.

Despite methodological difficulties, considerable weight of evidence about particular impacts exists. One useful way of assembling such evidence is to structure discussion around a further set of analytical questions noted in Figure 1, this time dealing with specific aspects of "constructed experience."

What Particular Kinds of Experience?

As a guide to action, answers to the researcher's question "Does college make a difference?" are clearly insufficient. It is also necessary to provide evidence of reliable linkages between desired outcomes and particular, manipulable aspects of the "constructed experience" provided at each institution. The question of specifying experience first calls attention to a need to thoroughly *describe* particular patterns of student behavior. For example, Shapiro (1986) notes that concern in higher education evaluation is currently as much focused on specifying "stimuli" as in cataloging results. The use of carefully constructed cross-sectional studies applied to carefully selected student subpopulations as advocated by Pascarella (1985a, 1987), or "trace-data" approaches such as transcript analyses or documentation of aggregate student course-taking patterns to determine the "behavioral curriculum" (Terenzini, 1987; Grose, 1976) represent proven methods for beginning to meet this need. But the use of such approaches remains uncommon. Based on the extant literature, what are some of the dimensions of experience that seem most fruitful for further exploration as foci for intervention?

One appears to be the sheer magnitude of exposure. Studies of cognitive development dating back to the thirties indicate the importance of "time-on-task" to the gain achieved (e.g., Learned and Wood, 1938). In general, the greater a given student's exposure to a body of material, as indicated by the number of courses taken or the student's choice of major field, the higher the established gains (Pace, 1979). Moreover, there are suggestions that performance in class may not be as important in the long term as simple exposure to and interaction with a particular body of material. In a study using the CLEP battery on freshmen and sophomore students, Harris (1970) found that students' course-grade performance did not generally affect their level of subsequent knowledge; students failing the course achieved scores not markedly different from those who did well, while both scored significantly above those who were not exposed to the material.

A second body of findings involves the impact of specific aspects of the institutional environment. Despite problems of attribution due to self-selection, numerous studies have documented differences in affective and in certain behavioral outcomes by institutional type. Particularly prominent have been findings linking institutional characteristics such as size and type (liberal arts curriculum, private control, or religious affiliation), with a range of noncognitive outcomes including authoritarianism (Trent and Medsker, 1968), liberalism and personal adjustment (Clark et al., 1972), aesthetic and religious orientation (Pace, 1972, 1974; Astin, 1977), and altruism/interpersonal self-esteem (Astin, 1977). The distinctive environments provided by single-sex institutions has also been linked to particular outcomes, for example, increased ambition and success among women in entering male-dominated fields (Bressler and Wendell, 1980). Moreover, findings summarized by Feldman and Newcomb (1969) indicate that initial noncognitive differences among students in different institutions tend to be amplified rather than decreased, and that students appear to internalize learning goals consistent with those that the institution publicly espouses (Winter, McClelland, and Stewart, 1981). These results suggest that careful attention to maintaining distinctiveness in both instructional goals and in ensuring provision of an institutional environment consistent with these goals may be a policy consideration with considerable payoff.

Such findings have not been without exception. For example, in a study of twelve small liberal arts colleges, Chickering (1970) documented considerable similarities among patterns of student development, despite what he saw as substantial differences in institutional characteristics. A partial explanation of this result is the consistent emergence in most multi-institutional studies of the small liberal arts college as a distinctive environment in its own right. For example, Astin's work with the CIRP (1968, 1977; Astin and Lee, 1972) yields few differences in noncognitive or "existential" benefits due to selectivity, but it does show significant differences associated with private control and small size. Moreover, in a summary of CUES results on 247 institutions, Pace notes a particular environmental emphasis on the "community" dimension at private liberal arts colleges, regardless of level of selectivity (Pace, 1979). Small private liberal arts institutions also achieve the highest ratings on ten of fourteen scales on involvement and "quality of student effort" in research using Pace's more recent College Student Experiences Questionnaire (Pace, 1984; Friedlander, 1980).

Findings on exposure and distinctiveness provide important clues about the particular elements of "constructed experience" that appear linked to desirable outcomes. Many of these can be conveniently summarized in terms of Astin's concept of "involvement." Originally developed to synthesize results of research on student persistence (Astin, 1975), the theory of involvement is considerably elaborated in Astin's later work on the differential effects of institutional characteristics on affective and behavioral outcomes (1977). In discussing the positive impact of such characteristics as small size, student residence on campus, on-campus employment, and time spent in academic, research, and athletic pursuits, Astin noted that all these factors tended to increase students' "involvement" with the campus. Moreover, such factors appeared to be much more powerful in explaining outcomes than either student or institutional characteristics. Moving the discussion to a policy perspective, Astin has recently advocated a number of actions intended to promote involvement (Astin, 1979, 1985). Among these are better monitoring of student time and on-campus activities, greater attention to promoting faculty/student interaction in the first two years of enrollment, and the establishment of "learning communities" within larger institutions.

Somewhat similar are the concepts of "academic and social integration" proposed by Tinto (1975). Also developed originally to summarize research on student retention, Tinto's construct has fruitfully been applied in broader work on student outcomes. Unlike Astin's more general concept of involvement, academic and social integration are held to be reasonably independent, and indeed, most work that has operationalized these constructs as scaled sets of questionnaire items has established their empirical distinctiveness (e.g., Terenzini and Pascarella, 1977). Specifically, Tinto's definition of integration follows Durkheim's classic investigation of suicide behavior. As such, the concept involves specific psychological elements relating to identification with and positive affect toward the institution's academic and social environment, and a range of behaviors that both sustain and reveal these traits. Following this logic, academic integration is generally operationalized using questionnaire items that deal with such areas as faculty/student interaction, time spent in academic pursuits, and faculty concern for student development and teaching. Social integration is similarly operationalized by means of such items as the number of hours per week spent in organized extracurricular activities, extent and quality of peer interaction, and quality of nonacademic contacts with faculty.

Though already cited as aspects of both involvement and academic integration, student/faculty interaction is also worth noting as a salient aspect of environment in its own right. Both in and out of the classroom, contact with faculty emerges in a wide range of studies as a factor significantly associated with a wide range of outcomes. Investigating the impact of various institutional characteristics on GRE scores at 27 liberal arts colleges, for example, Centra and Rock (1971) determined that student perceptions of faculty/student interactions were clearly associated with gains in the humanities and natural sciences. Gaff (1973) found involvement with faculty an important predictive variable in all eight institutions studied, using perceived cognitive gain as a dependent variable.

Similarly, in a single-institution study of freshmen, Terenzini et al. (1982) established important relationships between the frequency and quality of faculty contact, and dependent variables such as grade performance and perceptions of academic and personal growth. Factors also identified as important in this study included student perceptions of their level of involvement in the classroom and their own goal commitments. Parallel studies have noted strong relationships between the extent and quality of student/faculty contact and such outcomes as student perceptions of "liberal education" goal development (Theophilides et al., 1984), student retention (Pascarella and Terenzini, 1980), and a range of personal development goals (Terenzini and Wright, 1987). Finally, in his ongoing analysis of the CIRP database, Astin has repeatedly identified faculty/student interaction as the strongest single variable associated with overall student satisfaction with the college experience (Astin, 1977, 1979, 1985).

Concepts such as involvement and integration are helpful both in summarizing a wide range of effects and in emphasizing that the impact of such institutional factors as size, instructional emphasis, instructional delivery, or residence arrangements, may be indirect. As emphasized in the discussions that follow, the indirect nature of these relationships has profound implications for management intervention.

At What Level of Aggregation?

Pascarella (1985a) indicates that one reason why the results of many attempts to specify linkages between environmental factors and cognitive outcomes are disappointing is because analysis takes place at too great a level of aggregation. Baird (1976) echoes this concern from an action perspective by noting that changes in curriculum or policy may have no observable effect on outcomes because "everyday life" in the classroom or residence hall remains the same. Most institutions are sufficiently large that they themselves do not constitute an "environment"; rather they represent collections of quite distinctive but overlapping microenvironments, each of which may operate differently. Addressing this condition requires much more finely focused research approaches and models of college impact (Korn, 1986). A related issue involves the need to carefully match particular outcomes measures with the level of analysis at which they may legitimately be expected to emerge. Many popular institutional outcomes measures— for example, the ACT College Outcomes Measures Project (COMP)—have proven ambiguous in their ability to isolate particular curricular effects (Banta et al., 1987). As Pace puts it, "if you choose to think big about the scope and significance of outcomes, then you must also think big about the magnitude of college experiences when you seek explanations" (Pace, 1985, p. 17).

One of the most comprehensive treatments of disaggregated educational environments is that of Moos (1979). Reporting on a range of studies and experiments conducted in university residence hall settings and in elementary/secondary classrooms, Moos concludes that many aspects of these quite different environments operate in similar ways. A critical factor, however, is to isolate and observe student experiences in particular "microsettings" where peer interactions take place. Furthermore, once identified, Moos argues that such microsettings must be treated holistically. To investigate the effects of student living arrangements, for example, Moos used the University Residential Environment Scales to build a typology of residence environments. Included were living groups characterized as relationship oriented, traditionally socially oriented, supportive achievement oriented, competition oriented, independence oriented, and intellectually oriented. Using his own instrument to assess student activity and involvement, he then investigated the effects of microsettings in several different institutions. Results were summarized in three ways. First, microsettings exerted notable impact on students' development of such characteristics as autonomy and identity, and on their patterns of social relationships. Secondly, most of the differences in such settings were attributable to the differing characteristics of the students who inhabited them. Finally, reflecting earlier work reported by Feldman and Newcomb (1969), there was a "press to conformity" in most microsettings; not only did students "select themselves" into different environments, but the environments appeared to act back on them, accentuating many of the characteristics that initially distinguished the students who chose them.

One prime candidate for analysis as a microsetting is the academic department. Not only do departments provide an increasing source of identification for students as they progress, but they also structure patterns of peer and faculty interaction. Considerable work on departmental culture confirms (though it does not completely specify) marked differences in values and perceptions (e.g., Biglan, 1973), and in several dimensions of personality (e.g., Smart, 1982) on the part of faculty in different disciplines. Similarly, students of different backgrounds and abilities tend to select themselves into different undergraduate fields of study (Astin, 1977). Feldman and Newcomb (1969) summarize a range of early studies documenting both differences in student attributes across major fields and differences in the interactive and values environments provided by different departments. Although considerable shifts in student demand for particular major programs over two decades render the particulars of these results problematic, evidence that the same phenomenon may be currently occurring is provided by the Stanford students studied by Katchadourian and Boli (1985). Not only did different student types tend to major in different fields, but they also tended to ascribe to the entire institution the kinds of instructional goals and intellectual values characteristic of their chosen fields.

Probably of more enduring validity are studies on departmental environments reported by Feldman and Newcomb (1969), using variants of the College and University Environment Scales and the College Characteristics Index. Not only did the majority of these studies show that environments among departments differed, but that like residence groupings their diversity tended to accentuate initial student differences on a range of intellectual values. It remains unclear from the results of these studies whether established differences were due to distinct curricula or simply to continuing exposure to a particular body of peers. Also unclear is whether it is possible to generalize any detected "discipline cultures" across institutions, as hoped by early researchers (e.g., Pace, 1963). The latter point is amplified in the cognitive domain by Hartnett and Centra (1977). Using results of the UAP Field examinations as a measure of cognitive attainment, Hartnett and Centra found significantly greater variance in impact when departments rather than institutions were used as the unit of analysis.

In What Particular Institutional Activities and Settings?

Certainly the most relevant and potentially manipulable "microsettings" in colleges and universities are provided by individual classrooms. Less, however, is known about the impact of instructional mode and curricular design in higher education settings than in elementary and secondary classrooms. Recent reviews of college curriculum (Stark and Lowther, 1986) and of postsecondary teaching and learning (McKeachie et al., 1986) both turn frequently to comparable K-12 literature in making important points. While it is beyond the purposes of this chapter to provide an in-depth review of this topic, a number of consistent findings from the instructional literature are of considerable relevance.

One set of findings concerns the relative effectiveness of different instructional modes. Reviewing the literature on classroom process, Schalock (1976) found few consistent differences in mode on students' ability to recall content. Indeed, many of the studies cited by McKeachie and associates report lecture modes slightly superior to discussions or student-centered strategies for producing factual recall. Discussion appears better for fostering higher-order skills and for enhancing student motivation. Evidence of the impact of class size within instructional mode is mixed. Size appears to have more effect within discussion-oriented classrooms than in lectures, but of much more importance than size is the quality of interaction or engagement taking place (McKeachie et al.) Strategies attempting to maximize such interaction, for example, peer-tutoring, learning "cells," and "student-centered teaching," show few consistent cognitive effects across studies, beyond clear increases in student motivation. Partly this is because these strategies appear to be experienced differently by different kinds of students.

McKeachie and associates conclude that student-centered approaches appear better for developing higher-order skills than do other methods, and that such methods are at least as good as traditional approaches in developing knowledge of content and basic skills. Moreover, they argue that student-centered methods also teach important social functioning skills, including leadership and appropriate group membership behavior. More extensive claims are made for individualized but often highly structured instructional modes, such as mastery learning. Studies cited in Schalock (1976) and Astin (1985) show significant gains in effectiveness for these methods over more traditional approaches, particularly in building such higher-order skills as critical thinking.

A second issue has to do with structure and level of difficulty. Citing a range of impact studies, Feldman and Newcomb argue that students learn best when they experience "a continuing series of not-too-threatening discontinuities" (1969, p. 295). The policy implication is to promote experiences that highlight discontinuity while maintaining a careful balance between novelty and familiarity. Classroom research indicates that creating structure may be important in managing discontinuity, particularly when the object is to communicate content. Examining literature on interactions between student aptitudes and instructional modes, for example, McKeachie et al. (1986) report that logical, externally imposed structures appear superior to "learner-controlled" sequencing of instruction for students without prior knowledge of course material at all aptitude levels. Similarly, they make the salient observation that all aspects of structure within the environment must remain consistent. This is particularly important with respect to testing, as students will quite rightly focus their energy on learning strategies most appropriate to good test performance.

A final set of findings concerns the nature of interaction within the classroom. Prominent among these is the importance of frequent and consistent feedback on student performance. Citing numerous studies of cognitive gain in elementary and secondary classrooms, Gagne (1977) stresses the importance of "knowledge of results" as a causal factor. Similarly, Wilson and associates (1975) reported results of two multi-institutional studies focused on identifying and specifying the attributes of "effective" instructors. They found that the most effective faculty members were those who regarded students as partners in a common learning enterprise, as manifested by high levels of interaction both in and outside the classroom, and by attempts to relate class material to other situations.

Summarizing much of the research in this tradition, Cross (1976) stresses the importance of differences among students and the consequent need to "individualize" the curriculum. The "design criteria" that she proposes for instruction serve as an excellent summary of the issues raised above. They include (1) active rather than passive modes of instruction, (2) clear and explicitly presented goals for instruction, (3) small lesson units each organized around a single concept, (4) frequent feedback and evaluation, and (5) self-pacing to reflect different learning styles. These criteria serve as a useful template in terms of which to review extant curricula and classroom practices.

Requiring Investments on Whose Part?

Constructing "microsettings" that meet the kinds of criteria noted by Cross in both the classroom and in the wider institutional environment requires "investments" of many kinds. Most important, however, are those required of faculty and of students. Given the repeated finding that the extent and quality of peer and faculty interaction is associated with valued outcomes, a fundamental focus of institutional policy becomes the manner in which explicit structures and incentives can be designed to encourage and maintain such investments.

Certainly for faculty, a primary factor is willingness to devote scarce time and attention to instruction. Strongly conditioning this decision, of course, is the existence of competing interests such as research and scholarship that in most institutional settings (and perhaps more importantly, in most disciplinary cultures) remain highly rewarded. Astin (1985) and Gamson et al. (1984) thus see a major challenge to improving outcomes in providing institutional structures that promote faculty/student interaction and visible incentives that reward teaching innovation and sheer time-on-task.

A much deeper issue is one of relative values. In a discussion that remains compelling, Feldman and Newcomb (1969) described the challenge as one of bridging "two cultures"—one associated with faculty and one with students. Summarizing a number of studies comparing faculty and student views about the relative importance of instrumental, aesthetic, and intellectual values, they noted that these perceptions often differed. Moreover, faculty themselves may differ considerably in these values, both by discipline and by type. Smart (1982), for example, used the Holland personality classification scheme in a study of undergraduate teaching goals to demonstrate that particular personalities are both drawn to particular disciplines and teach them in particular ways. Similarly, a range of studies cited by Feldman and Newcomb (1969) demonstrate that students seem to desire different qualities of instructors in different disciplines. Most marked in this respect were the natural sciences, where qualities of organization and clarity were generally ranked higher than involvement and dynamism.

As noted by Wilson and associates (1975), those faculty identified as being good teachers also engage in certain recognizable activities such as out-of-class contact with students and making frequent connections between their disciplines and broader issues and concerns. Certainly these findings suggest important areas to pursue in faculty development and recognition. But it is important not to view any of these results as mechanistic or uniform. In the realm of student/ faculty contact, for example, evidence is strong that students are less interested in and benefit less from sheer personal interaction with individual faculty members, than they do from encounters with clear intellectual or professional content (Baird, 1976).

Equally important, though often neglected, are the investments made by students. As noted by Astin (1979, 1985) and Bloom (1974), probably the most relevant disposable resource for students is time. As a result, how student time is spent, how it is organized, and how its disposal might be profitably channeled become important elements of what Astin terms "student-oriented manage-ment." A considerable body of learning research highlights these observations. Thomas and Rohwer (1986), for example, note that internalization of time-management strategies on the part of students is a critical factor in cognitive development. Other identified "resource management strategies" for learning (McKeachie et al., 1986) include constructing and managing a congenial study environment, managing the support of others, and managing students' own motivations and attitudes toward learning. Combinations of such strategies are often deemed of greater importance than any one of them. Sternberg (1985), for example, subsumes such elements under the notion of "practical intelligence," and stresses particularly the ability of students to know where and from whom they can seek assistance upon encountering difficulty. Similarly, Corno and Rohrkemper (1985) use the term "self-regulating learners" to describe students who practice effective combinations of resource management and cognitive learning strategies.

One of the most powerful constructs describing student resource investment is Pace's notion of "quality of student effort." Using the College Student Experiences Questionnaire (CSEQ), an instrument designed to assess student involvement with various aspects of the institutional environment based on self-reported behavior, Pace and his associates have examined both the impact of quality of effort on achievement and the levels of involvement characteristic of different types of institutions. For example, in studies involving more than 10,000 students at over 40 institutions, quality of effort has been demonstrated to make independent and large contributions toward explaining student achievement using both self-reports of cognitive gain and actual grades received (Pace, 1984). At the same time, particular types of institutions—notably small private liberal arts colleges—appear particularly to be characterized by high "quality of effort" as assessed by the CSEQ (Porter, 1982). Because it focuses on actual student behavior, the notion of "quality of effort" combines elements of resource management and motivation. By focusing on the actual content rather than simply the extent of student investment, however, this line of inquiry avoids many pitfalls. Based on CSEQ results from thirty institutions, for example, Friedlander (1980) demonstrated that simple time-on-task is powerfully mediated by quality of effort. Students who spend a great deal of time at below average levels of effort make considerably less progress than those investing less time at higher levels of effort.

Specifying the "Production Function"

The above review highlights two important characteristics of the literature on outcomes correlates. First, causality is complex and is difficult to firmly establish. Associations between particular outcomes and a bewildering array of structural and process characteristics have been demonstrated, but there is often no clear evidence of the degree to which particular elements of environment are substitutable or act in concert. Second, the effects that have been identified often vary considerably across different types of students and different types of settings. There appear to be very few mechanisms that work for all students or that apply to all types of institutional environments. Together, these two characteristics constitute a major challenge to improvement. Though generalizations can assuredly be made, they must be advanced with appropriate caution and with due regard for variations in local conditions and clienteles. More importantly, these findings suggest that a critical policy need is for appropriate local studies to establish the manner in which the kinds of relationships noted in the research literature operate in practice on each campus.

One attempt to systematize these generalizations is presented in Figure 2. The purpose of this conceptual scheme is twofold. First, it attempts to array the primary factors that appear associated with positive outcomes in the research literature in rough order of conceptual priority. Though not a "causal model" in the formal sense, the intent is to organize findings so that their conceptual flow is intelligible. This leads to a second purpose: to identify some explicit points in this body of findings that appear able to be influenced through administrative action. While it is beyond the scope of this discussion to treat each potential point

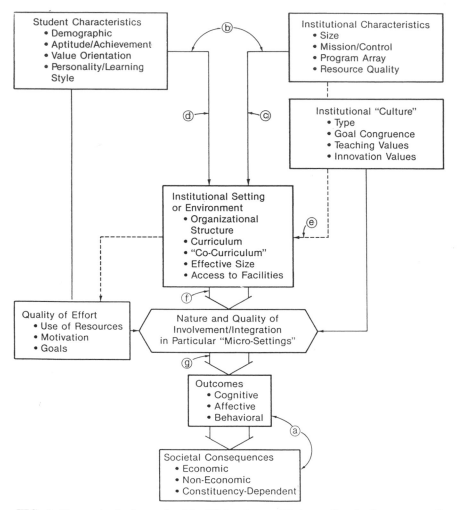

FIG. 2. Conceptual scheme for identifying types of intervention in the process of producing outcomes.

Key. Intervention points for managerial action: (a) planning/goal-setting; (b) selectivity/enrollment management; (c) curriculum/academic policy; (d) person/environment fit; (e) academic leadership; (f) instructional/faculty development; (g) assessment/evaluation.

of intervention in detail, the presentation should be sufficient both to note connections with other bodies of research that shed light on the potential efficacy of such action, and to suggest fruitful areas for additional inquiry.

The scheme proposed is roughly based on similar models advanced by Bowen (1977a), Pace (1979), Peterson et al. (1986), and Pascarella (1985a). Given a particular focus on administrative and academic policy, several of its features are worth noting. First, its heart is the nature and quality of involvement/integration in particular "microsettings" such as the classroom, residence hall, student organization, or informal peer group. This is the factor ascribed primarily responsible for the "production" of outcomes, with all prior elements modifying its operation. Critical for policy is to recognize that this central factor, and not the outcomes themselves, constitutes the primary dependent variable for action. Second, with the addition of Bowen's concern with societal impacts, the focus of attention is not exclusively intrainstitutional. Policy must also specify and take account of the ways in which outcomes are consistent with and influence a range of wider societal purposes—particularly as they are embodied in the perceptions and values of critical constituencies.

Finally, the impact of such concrete factors as student characteristics and institutional structure is relatively far removed from the outcomes themselves. Both operate indirectly through such intermediate mechanisms as student quality of effort and institutional culture (which also may have their own unique impacts), and the particular institutional setting or environment. While well-designed research on the causal linkage between institutional or student characteristics and outcomes remains rare (Pascarella, 1985a), those few studies that do employ and estimate causal models strongly suggest that the impact of institutional and student characteristics on both cognitive and affective outcomes is indirect, mediated by such factors as student involvement, motivation, and integration (e.g., Pascarella, 1984, 1985b; Pascarella, Terenzini, and Wolfle, 1986; Lacy, 1978).

Relationships described by this scheme suggest a number of points of attack for institutional policy.

Planning and Goal Setting

One important point of leverage for institutional action is the specification and definition of outcomes themselves. Though most extant planning processes begin with goal setting, goals are rarely of sufficient specificity to adequately encompass expected educational outcomes. Outcomes-oriented planning, however, has considerable potential for focusing and redirecting institutional discussions about mission. First, particularly when planning discussions are curricular or programmatic, an outcomes focus has the benefit of rendering such discussions concrete enough that concerted action is possible (Banta and Fisher, 1984). Second, an outcomes focus in strategic planning raises important questions both about the kinds of external constituency needs that are most salient to the institution, and about the areas in which the institution is distinctive enough to possess a strategic advantage (e.g., Caruthers and Lott, 1981). Both processes are often able to mobilize and manipulate scarce channels of institutional attention.

Enrollment Management

Most discussions of enrollment management tend to focus relatively narrowly on recruitment (Hossler, 1984, 1986). An important aspect of the concept, however, emphasizes achievement of a careful match between student characteristics and institutional environments in order to ensure later retention and student success. By treating student attributes and attainments as a critical institutional resource, those in charge of enrollment management policies should first recognize that their primary goal is to help *create* specific kinds of environments that are consistent with institutional goals and values. Even if an institution is nonselective, it can nevertheless in certain areas be distinctive, and can therefore devote attention to obtaining and retaining students whose values and aspirations are consistent with its educational vision. And in so far as the institution serves many constituencies, it should be minimally aware of the characteristics and experiences of each of its various student bodies, and the fact that each may experience the institutional environment in a different way.

Curricular and Academic Policy

As emphasized by Stark and Lowther (1986), from a policy perspective the curriculum is an "academic plan." As such, it is subject to the canons of good planning including the need to carefully specify both outcomes and the means to achieve them. Conrad and Pratt (1986) note that there is very little systematic research that provides evidence of clear linkages between curricular structure and particular outcomes, though a large body of emerging case material strongly suggests that such linkages may eventually be established for alternative curricular forms (e.g., Gamson et al., 1984, Mentkowski and Doherty, 1984). Moreover, the notion of "academic policy" goes beyond curriculum design to include planning additional concrete aspects of the institutional environment. Among these are organizational issues encompassing the existence and influence of units responsible for undergraduate instruction or for instructional development, policies governing a range of "cocurricular" activities including cultural programming and student activities, policies directly affecting the way institutional environments are configured such as learning/residence groupings or thematic learning communities, and policies affecting student access to campus resources such as the library, laboratory facilities, and cultural facilities. Rarely, however, are the myriad factors shaping academic policy in this sense treated in a coherent fashion. A strong implication of the research literature, in contrast, is that institutions should view such environments as students see them—in a holistic and relatively undifferentiated fashion.

Person/Environment Fit

While enrollment management highlights the need for policy intended to carefully match potential students and institutions, an additional fruitful arena for intervention is to develop programs that carefully match existing students with particular elements of environment. In the area of curriculum and classroom practice, notions of individualized or "tailored" instruction advocated by Cross (1976) and Astin (1985) are of particular relevance. Learning/residence communities that attempt to foster interaction among students and faculty around particular ongoing topics or interests represent a similar approach at a different level of aggregation (e.g., Gamson et al., 1984). For other aspects of the environment, suggestive experiments have been undertaken using a range of assessment instruments to help determine residence groupings or to similarly establish parameters for peer interaction (Moos, 1979). As in curriculum design, little systematic work as yet exists documenting the effectiveness of such practices on particular outcomes. Given evidence of considerable diversity among institutions, however, a primary requirement is again the need for each to determine through local research the kinds of "subject/treatment interactions" experienced on its own campus.

Academic Leadership

If the research literature on linkages between outcomes and such factors as curricular structure and person/environment fit is limited, that establishing linkages between outcomes and institutional culture is almost nonexistent (Peterson et al., 1986). Partially this is due to lack of agreement on what institutional culture really means. In an attempt to meet this difficulty, the conceptual scheme in Figure 2 restricts the term to (1) perceived patterns of action, communication, and decision making as embodied in such classifications as Cameron's (1978) typology of institutional cultures—clan, hierarchy, market, and emergent; (2) goal congruence as embodied in both the content and degree of internalization of commonly held institutional goals; and (3) specific values about the importance of teaching and receptivity to innovation.

With this more restricted definition, some evidence of the importance of "culture" can be cited. Most important is probably work by Pace and Baird (1966) with the College and University Environment Scales (CUES), suggesting that agreement about the importance of teaching as a value is an important element in accounting for outcomes. Examining institutional culture more directly, Ewell (1985b) used results from the Assessment of the Performance of

Colleges and Universities (ACPU) survey administered to faculty and staff at 320 four-year institutions; findings indicated that linkages between institutional characteristics and perceived outcomes were strongly mediated by variables such as mission direction and specification, reward for recognition and achievement, and a "clanlike" institutional culture.

Managing this "mediation" seems clearly a task for academic leadership. As March (1984) points out, managerial action can always be viewed on two planes—active and interpretative—and the latter may well be the more decisive. By articulating centrally held values, and by ensuring their visibility through a range of symbolic actions intended to "manage meaning" (Dill, 1982), an important role of leadership is to monitor and challenge the consistency between articulated values and the structure of the institutional environment. Where such values are academic, symbolic action of this sort involves both explicit references to tradition and concrete structures for providing recognition and nonmaterial rewards for exemplary faculty, students, and support personnel.

Instructional/Faculty Development

The specific ways in which aspects of the institution's environment are made manifest in particular "microsettings" is largely a function of how faculty, staff, and students behave, and of the ways in which classroom and other immediate experiences are structured. The effects of administrative action will therefore necessarily be indirect. Nevertheless, such actions may facilitate other more direct processes. Examples include support and encouragement for faculty development aimed at fostering a range of classroom and assessment skills, or for instructional development efforts intended to improve or supplement classroom practices. The linkages between environment and behavior in particular "microsettings" may also be positively influenced by a number of changes in institutional incentives. These include increased attention to teaching in promotion and tenure decisions, visible recognition and reward for effective changes in classroom practice, and the use of discretionary funds for unit-level experiments or pilot programs. Again, the nonmaterial dimension of such incentives should not be overlooked; as Dill (1982) puts it, incentives of this sort might emphasize the "selection, canonization, and celebration of faculty exemplars."

Assessment and Evaluation

Considerable emerging evidence indicates that the presence and use of explicit information on instructional performance is among the most powerful administrative levers for inducing institutional action along any of the above lines. Some evidence of this kind will be examined in the following section. At this point it is sufficient to emphasize that powerful though it appears to be, assessment represents an approach to change that is indirect in a compound manner. First, its role is to support, direct, and induce other kinds of administrative actions. Administrative actions themselves then operate indirectly to influence the actual practice of teaching and learning. Current claims for the assessment movement now popular in higher education should be tempered by this observation. More importantly, the potential value of assessment and evaluation in improving outcomes should not be obscured by research that fails to properly specify the indirect nature of these activities with respect to the production of observable outcomes.

GETTING THERE: USING
OUTCOMES INFORMATION AS A CHANGE AGENT

While assessment and evaluation represents but one of many potential management levers to improve outcomes, the emerging literature on its potential is worth further exploration for at least three reasons. First, the issue of assessment is prominent in public discussion, and constitutes a major focus of current policy concern. Second, many of the issues of implementation and use raised by discussions of assessment are equally applicable to any type of management intervention. Finally, because of the strong "action research" tradition in the outcomes literature, discussions of implementation form an integral part of any comprehensive review.

Some Evidence from the Field

Knowledge about the utilization of outcomes information is currently based largely on participant observation in particular field settings. A great deal of this has taken place in multi-institutional demonstration projects exploring the impact of outcomes information on curriculum and management practice (e.g., Astin, 1976; Baldridge and Tierney, 1979; Kemerer, Baldridge, and Green, 1982; Ewell, 1984; Kinnick, 1985; AASCU, 1986). Additional observations have been generated by attempts to design and implement local assessment programs on the part of individual institutions (e.g., Mentkowski and Doherty, 1984; Mentkowski and Loacker, 1985; McClain, 1984; McClain and Krueger, 1985, Banta, 1985, 1986; Banta and Fisher, 1984; Dumont and Troelstrup, 1980; Palola, 1981; Palola and Lehman, 1976). Useful lessons also arise from related efforts to use information to affect academic decision making through such areas as program evaluation and review, teacher evaluation, and student retention or enrollment management programs.

One of the first multi-institutional attempts to systematically incorporate outcomes information in decision making was Astin's ACE/CIRP Dissemination Project (Astin, 1976). Using a sample of 20 institutions in the early 1970s, the structure of the project involved providing institutions with data packages containing summary comparative information based on CIRP surveys. Each campus was expected to convene a local committee on data utilization charged with examining the data, drawing conclusions, and making recommendations on program change. Regression-based methods were used to compute "expected" results profiles based on institutional characteristics (Astin, 1977). These profiles were then compared to actual results in order to stimulate discussion.

The impact of the project was mixed at best, as a total of eight of the twenty original participants failed to complete the task. (Similarly disappointing results were reported by Baird in 1976 for a project attempting to "feed back" results of a multi-institutional survey of student and college characteristics.) Indeed, Astin's report on the ACE/CIRP project (Astin, 1976) is much more useful for its perceptive analysis of the functioning of faculty committees, and for its "theory of institutional conservatism" than for its positive evidence of the effectiveness of information-based improvement. Nevertheless, important lessons emerged, including the need to involve faculty thoroughly in planning and implementation, the need for clear (but not constant) top administrative support, and the need for flexibility in the ways information is packaged and communicated.

A related effort, though not confined to student outcomes, was the Exxon/ RAMP project on management training (Baldridge and Tierney, 1979). Involving a total of 49 institutions in a set of local projects directed toward database development and implementation of MBO-based planning approaches, this project too met with mixed success. Baldridge and Tierney provide an estimate of 50% success based on actual changes made, but it is interesting to note that participants themselves rated the impact of the project much higher. Lessons learned parallel Astin's and include the need for top administrative support, for consistent involvement, and for clear links between information and the institution's regular incentive structure. The Exxon/RAMP project also reiterated the need to communicate policy information in different formats for different audiences, and Baldridge and Tierney noted such now familiar phenomena as "information glut" and "the tyranny of numbers" as typical of participating institutions.

A somewhat later large scale multi-institutional effort was the NCHEMS/ Kellogg Student Outcomes Project (Ewell, 1984, 1985a; Kinnick, 1985). Eventually involving 22 public and private institutions, the intent of the project was to demonstrate the use of existing information on student outcomes in institutional planning and decision making. Rather than using a common approach, each participating institution undertook a local project intended to address a particular problem on campus. Like the ACE/CIRP project, substantial responsibility was placed on local committees for implementation, but perceived success rates were higher largely because these committees were able to deal with strictly local problems of high salience. Results of the project strongly confirmed earlier lessons about top management support, the need for broad-based involvement and participation, and the need to carefully tailor data-based communications to local needs. In addition, the project demonstrated the existence of substantial bodies of underutilized information on most campuses, highlighted the need for considerable disaggregation in data analysis and interpretation, and emphasized a need to decentralize implementation to the departmental and unit level.

Other recent multi-institutional projects provide additional evidence in support of these basic lessons. For example, the AASCU Academic Program Evaluation Project (APEP) involved 10 institutions in a multiyear project to identify and assess "generic intellectual skills" associated with a baccalaureate degree (AASCU, 1986). Among the skills agreed upon were communication, quantification, analysis, synthesis, and valuing. Each participating institution undertook a locally defined and implemented project to further specify and assess these skills, though by the end of the project most had not yet used the resulting information in decision making. Nevertheless, many institutions reported that reviewing curricula from an outcomes perspective and carefully thinking about sources of evidence in themselves helped to induce needed curricular improvements. This last observation echoes a range of emerging institutional experience. Reporting on the design of a comprehensive assessment program at the University of Tennessee, Knoxville, Banta (1985, 1986) notes that a significant impact of efforts to design major field examinations was that it forced faculty to rethink the structure and intended outcomes of their curricula. As a result, changes in curriculum occurred even before outcomes data were collected and disseminated.

Institutional experience also highlights the importance of multiple methods and broad participation in assessing outcomes. For example, guided by a Master Question—"What kinds of students working with what kinds of faculty in what kinds of learning programs change in what ways at what cost?"—the Program Effectiveness and Related Costs (PERC) model at Empire State College employs such methods as goal inventories, standardized tests, evaluation of student portfolios, and interviews to build a comprehensive picture of student experience (Palola and Lehman, 1976). Assessment programs at the University of Tennessee, Knoxville (Banta, 1985, 1986), Northeast Missouri State University (McClain and Krueger, 1985), and other institutions currently experimenting with assessment (Ewell, 1985c) generally involve at least three distinct kinds of instruments: standardized national examinations, locally designed examinations, and assessments (generally in the major field), and student surveys. One of the most comprehensive evaluation efforts of this kind is at Alverno College, where the Office of Research and Evaluation regularly conducts research on student development using quantitative and qualitative measures, and employing both nationally recognized and locally developed instruments (Mentkowski and Doherty, 1984). Among the latter are the Kolb Learning Styles Inventory, McBer's Behavioral Event Interview, the Watson-Glaser Critical Thinking Appraisal, and a range of measures of moral, ego, and intellectual development as described by Kohlberg, Loevinger, Piaget, and Perry.

Another important attribute of these programs is their stress on communicating the results of outcomes information in a manner designed to stimulate a "dialogue" about implications. Describing the PERC project at Empire State, Palola (1981) noted that participation was increased when individual departments were given a chance to generate their own information to "correct" centrally provided statistics. Similar results are reported by Kinnick (1985) in describing data communications formats designed to induce local responses on the part of faculty and unit-level administrators. In the NCHEMS/Kellogg Project, information-based "dialogue" of this kind was considerably enhanced when the kinds of results communicated centered visibly on an institutional problem of clear salience to most parties (Ewell, 1984). A risk in this situation, however, is that once the identified problem was successfully addressed, many of informal mechanisms supporting information-based improvement tended to atrophy if not intentionally institutionalized.

Emerging institutional experience also emphasizes that "utilization of information" with respect to outcomes should not be constructed too narrowly. Reviewing the literature on the utilization of evaluation results in higher education generally, Shapiro (1986) notes that a major line of recent inquiry centers around changes in the notion of "use." While a few studies show that evaluation information has a direct impact on the content of particular decisions, evaluation results can nevertheless influence policy through such mechanisms as "conceptual use" where information is used to help set context and formulate problems, and "symbolic use," where it is used to justify or legitimize action.

Such alternative uses of information emerge strongly in the literature on developing and implementing outcomes programs. Forrest (1981), for example, reports that a major feature of early utilization of the ACT-COMP was to "sell" nontraditional programs to external constituencies who doubted their effectiveness. Similarly, in examining a range of cases where institutions attempted to use information on effectiveness for improvement, Ewell and Chaffee (1984) identified four different types of information utilization beyond the "rational decision making" paradigm. These included the use of information to (1) identify the existence of problems or decision alternatives, (2) set context for informing broad classes of decisions, (3) induce action and end discussion, and (4) legitimize action previously decided on other grounds. Kinnick (1985) reports similar results on the basis of the NCHEMS/Kellogg Project, and notes that patterns of utilization may differ depending upon whether intended audiences are internal or external.

FIG. 3. Issues and themes of outcomes-based improvement projects.

	Issues/Concerns	Themes of Successful Efforts
Philosophical	Threats to institutional autonomy/academic freedom	
	Narrowing curriculum/ "teaching to the test"	Curriculum specificity
	Problems in defining "quality"	Link to goals/priorities
	Impact on minority access	
Organizational	Lack of commitment/incentives	Visibility link to incentives
	Fragmented responsibilities	Create forum for discussion/ center for coordination
	Fear of abuse	
		Maximize involvement/ participation
Practical	Excessive cost	Build on strength
	Few channels of communication	Create an information "dialogue"
	Lack of action focus	
		Focus on recognized problems
Technical	Imprecision/measurement error	Multiple methods/ "triangulation"
	Credibility/"face validity"	Keep it simple
	Interpretation/dissemination	Tailored reporting around audiences/issues

A Classification of Issues and Lessons

Based on experiences such as these, most observers exhibit a consistent view of both the major obstacles and issues surrounding successful use of assessment as an agent of change, and the primary lessons that ought to guide such an effort. Figure 3 represents one attempt to identify these commonalities in general terms. Appendix A provides a detailed presentation of selected comments on assessment by source.

Philosophical issues generally begin with reservations about assessing the "ineffable" consequences of a complex educational experience. Although most such difficulties can ultimately be reduced to a series of more concrete concerns, many faculty objections to assessment-based improvement are initially voiced in philosophical language (Ewell, 1986b). One set of issues has to do with anticipated consequences of allowing concrete evaluation processes—possibly designed and implemented by those outside the academy—to provide evidence of the effectiveness of higher education (e.g., Smith, 1986). Another manifestation of this point of view is that assessment violates tenets of individual academic freedom. As Adelman (1986) points out, assessment may symbolically raise the question of whether or not we trust our faculty. A second set of issues has to do with anticipated effects on curriculum and classroom practice. "Teaching to the test" and narrowed curricula covering only those areas to be assessed are topics commonly raised in this regard (e.g., Smith, 1986). A third set of issues revolves around the difficulties of defining broad qualitative outcomes. Not a measurement objection, this position concentrates on the difficulty of even specifying outcomes in such a way that they are not rendered mechanical and meaningless (e.g., Hanson, 1982; Warren, 1984). Related topics center around defining outcomes in ways that go beyond traditional litanies of basic skills and minimal behaviors (e.g., Hartle, 1986; Adelman, 1986b; Nettles, 1987). A final set of concerns addresses possible negative impacts on student access, particularly for minority students who may be victims of assessment approaches that are culturally biased, or that attempt to control access through setting minimum qualifications (Hartle, 1986; Nettles, 1987).

Noted characteristics of successful change efforts that partially address these concerns include ensuring that all assessment is tailored to the curriculum as taught at each institution, and ensuring that the goals to be assessed are truly important goals for the institution (Bowen, 1977b; Hartle, 1986; Nettles, 1987). An important ingredient of success, therefore, is likely to be disaggregation. Bess (1979), for example, lists six distinct institutional decision areas, each of which requires a different "tailored" approach to information-gathering and utilization. Like philosophical issues, many of the ingredients of these two admonitions are contained in other, more concrete, observations. Particularly relevant, however, is Bowen's observation that "whole persons" should be the primary focus of all assessment (1977b).

Organizational issues raised by outcomes assessment programs are particularly generalizable to other attempts at management-initiated instructional improvement. A first set of issues centers around incentives and commitment. As Baldridge and Tierney (1979) observe from the Exxon/RAMP project, little change can be expected unless information is directly tied to unit or individual reward. Most attempts at curriculum change, moreover, are merely that (Stark and Lowther, 1986); they do not involve changes in the priority given undergraduate instruction at the institution or the reward structure that surrounds it. As a result, many of the attributes of successful change efforts involve changes in incentives. For example, a number of observers note the importance of pilot programs and department-specific initiatives that make discretionary funds available for units to experiment with assessment or improvement efforts (e.g., Banta, 1985; Banta and Fisher, 1984; Ewell, 1984). Attempts at "performance funding" as practiced by Tennessee also fall within this category (e.g., Bogue and Brown, 1982). An observation shared by most observers, however, is that reform approaches that concentrate on modifying incentive structures are at their best when they are marginal; entire reconstructions of familiar reward systems are simply too threatening to have a long-term impact (Levy, 1986; Ewell, 1986b).

A second set of organizational issues focuses on the fact that undergraduate education is rarely centrally coordinated—particularly in the arena of general education. Attributes of successful efforts generally cited in response to this condition involve the creation of central offices responsible for assessment and improvement activities—generally reporting to a high administrative level. Such offices generally span many functions, but three appear critical. First, they serve as visible embodiments of the institution's commitment to change (Ewell, 1987). Second, they are proactive in assisting faculty in individual departments to undertake their own assessment efforts (Banta, 1986; Mentkowski and Doherty, 1984; Palola and Lehman, 1976). Finally, they are changed with coordinating, maintaining, and enhancing, and helping to interpret information about student learning and development (Astin, 1985; Baldridge and Tierney, 1979; Gamson, 1984). Each of these functions can also to a lesser extent be played by institutionwide committees (e.g., Ewell, 1984; Banta, 1985). Here a chief function is to create a legitimate forum for discussing implications and new ideas.

Fear of abuse also constitutes a formidable organizational issue mentioned by most observers. In many cases the locus of concern is the anticipated use of outcomes information by state authorities and others outside the academy (e.g., Smith, 1986). Within institutions, the locus of concern is most likely to be anticipated use in faculty evaluation (Ewell, 1987). In both cases, substantial involvement of interested parties throughout the development process is seen as an attribute of success (e.g., Palola, 1981; Braskamp, 1982). Moreover, it is important to recognize that achieving broad-based involvement is likely to take considerable time, and that successful assessment-based change efforts have evolved over many years (Ewell, 1984, 1985a).

Practical issues cover a range of topics, but the most frequently mentioned is probably cost. Even the most ardent proponents of assessment recognize that substantial investments are likely to be involved, so most discussions of this issue attempt to frame the issue in "cost/benefit" terms (e.g., Ewell, 1986b; Nettles, 1987; Bowen, 1977b). Nevertheless, observers of successful change efforts note that they are founded on considerable existing information, and consequently involve sustained activities that build on data-gathering mechanisms already in place (e.g., McClain and Krueger, 1985; Palola, 1981; AASCU, 1986; Ewell, 1985a). Astin (1979, 1985) observes, for example, that most institutions invest substantially in "assessment" data collection, but that these data are rarely integrated and used for program improvement. Incremental costs of information-based programs are thus likely to be less than initially anticipated (Ewell and Jones, 1986). Other practical issues include the fact that outcomes information is rarely "decision- specific" information (e.g., Kinnick, 1985), and that few opportunities exist to discuss its implications with those who are affected.

Observations focused on overcoming these difficulties include the benefits of focusing investigation and discussion on recognized problems at the unit level, or that command sufficient attention that institutionwide committees can legitimately address them. Also prominent are observations stressing the need for constant dialogue about the possible implications of assessment findings. Enthoven's (1970) early observation that a good way to induce change using information about results is to engage in "analysis to stimulate 'counteranalysis'" is particularly appropriate in this context. The results of field experience as reported by Palola (1981), Lindquist (1981b), and Kinnick (1985) emphasize the importance of communicating information in formats that encourage or provoke active responses of this kind.

Technical issues cover both questions of the adequacy of particular measurement approaches and techniques, and of the unique challenges associated with communicating complex information to a diverse audience of users and affected parties. Most measurement issues are identical to those raised earlier by the research community. They include problems of validity and reliability associated with particular instruments or techniques (e.g., Banta et al., 1987), observations about the difficulties of adequately assessing change (e.g., Hanson, 1982; Pascarella, 1987), and problems of attribution and control. Observers of successful programs for the most part concede that considerable methodological difficulties are apparent, but that the use of multiple methods and such techniques as sensitivity analysis in particular decision contexts allows them to be in practice overcome (e.g., Mentkowski and Loacker, 1985; Ewell, 1985a).

A final set of practical issues concerns the communication of assessment results in such a way that they will be used to effect change. As such observers in Guba (1969), Shapiro (1986), and Newman, Brown, and Braskamp (1980) point out, this is an old problem in educational evaluation. A particular challenge in using outcomes results, however, is that the kinds of research designs necessary to establish reliable findings are complex; communicating them simply therefore constitutes a considerable challenge (e.g., Ewell, 1983). Techniques reported by Kinnick (1985) or Palola (1981) involving heavy use of graphics and tailored reports for identified audiences, or the use of innovative qualitative techniques to supplement more traditional measurement (e.g., Lindquist, 1981b; Mentkowski and Doherty, 1984) constitute excellent examples of attempts to overcome such difficulties.

TOWARD AN AGENDA FOR ACTION RESEARCH

Emerging lessons from assessment-based improvement projects serve as a reminder that research intended to inform administrative action is constrained in multiple ways. First, it must be conceptually sound and methodologically well-founded. Second, it must focus on arenas where management action can actually expect to influence outcomes. Finally, it must be credible, accessible, and usable in an often political and value-laden operational context. Each of these constraints helps determine the shape and content of needed research. Furthermore, inquiry useful for policy direction has always appropriately proceeded on two planes. Large-scale, methodologically rigorous, and primarily "discipline-based" studies are needed to establish generalizable findings. But at least as important are multiple local research efforts intended to specify and describe how these general mechanisms operate for particular students in particular environments on particular campuses.

Some Implications for the Study of College Impact

Without doubt, informed action requires further developments in scholarly research on college impact. But the major emphasis of such studies should increasingly be focused upon establishing specific causal sequences among the many factors that have in the past been bilaterally associated with particular outcomes. Research on student learning and development that allows patterns of causality to be meaningfully identified remains distressingly infrequent, and certainly the technical requirements for executing such studies are daunting. But balancing this observation is the fact that powerful methods and appropriate multi-institutional datasets to ground research of this kind are increasingly available.

Most of the requisites for improving such research are familiar and echo the concerns of prior observers (e.g., Pascarella, 1985a). First, more and better longitudinal studies are needed. While a great deal can be learned from well-designed cross-sectional studies of selected student populations (Pace, 1979), longitudinal studies are still required to unambiguously specify the nature and sequence of different types of college impact. Secondly, more and better multi-institutional studies are needed. Available databases based on student self-reports such as the CIRP are increasingly being supplemented by newer multi-institutional counterparts such as the CSEQ. At the same time, the rising salience of assessment as an issue has meant heavy institutional use of such cognitive instruments as the ACT-COMP, CLEP, and a range of standardized basic skills examinations. Though institutional representation in such databases is uneven due to self-selection, they constitute a rich potential resource for undertaking multi-institutional studies. Finally, more studies are needed that are driven by clear theoretical frameworks and that employ appropriate statistical procedures to estimate causal priorities and isolate indirect effects. LISREL, path analysis and causal modelling, and a range of other multiple regression-based techniques are becoming widely available through statistical packages. Furthermore, the upgraded file handling capabilities of such packages as SPSS-X and SAS mean that it is now a manageable procedure to assemble for use in a common analysis variables of quite different sources and types.

Given these methodological imperatives, what particular topics might such studies address? A first requirement is to more fully document student behavior. In most choice-based curricula, for example, there is little likelihood that students in the same program will have taken the same pattern and sequence of courses. And there is even less likelihood that their patterns of interaction outside the curriculum are standard. Without further specification, then, studies attempting to isolate the effects of students in different curricula are extremely problematic. Approaches to documenting behavior based on self-reports such as the CSEQ represent one way to approach this problem. But equally important may be the use of "trace data" drawn from student records or other unobtrusive methods (e.g., Terenzini, 1987). A second requirement is to more fully describe "environment." Specifications of the "nonmaterial" aspects of environment such as institutional culture or perceived patterns of institutional values and reward are in their infancy. Proven instruments such as the CUES need to be updated to reflect a heavily nontraditional student population. More importantly, instruments that examine a wider arena of faculty and staff perceptions of institutional culture and values might be beneficially included in research investigating instructional outcomes.

Finally, past studies of student impact have been disappointingly noncumulative. Primarily this has been because studies operationalize outcomes concepts in quite different ways. This condition limits attempts to meaningfully generalize findings across studies. Techniques such as metaanalysis that have proven useful for summarizing knowledge in other fields are largely inapplicable for this reason. But as syntheses such as those of Bowen (1977a) and Pascarella (1985a) illustrate, it is possible to use "effect sizes" to support generalization, provided that the studies included supply requisite baseline information about the type and range of variation of the measures employed. It is also helpful for generalization if information on study contexts (for example, important characteristics of the student clientele and institutional environment) and on the conceptual framework employed is also clearly presented. Consequently, an important directive to individual researchers is to report all results with more general uses of this kind explicitly in mind.

A Call for Local Action Research

At least as important as scholarly work is a need to undertake more locally based action research on student outcomes. In contrast to basic research on impact, however, the proper emphasis of local studies is diversity. Guided by more general findings concerning causal sequence and priority, the prime focus of work of this kind should be to investigate linkages between particular observed patterns of student experience and locally valued outcomes. Following this logic, effective studies will disaggregate student experience in at least two ways. One involves using units of analysis that correspond to the actual levels at which such experiences take place: programs and curricula, classrooms, living units, and other identifiable "microsettings." A good example is a recent proposal by Cross (1987) that faculty themselves engage in informal research on student learning and development in their own classrooms. Another form of disaggregation involves carefully specifying student subpopulations in terms of their characteristics, their aptitudes and values, and their actual behavior. It is important to recognize here that the particular kinds of analytical disaggregations needed will appropriately vary across institutions. Indeed, a critical task for the local researcher is to carefully select variables to guide disaggregation that are appropriate to both the distinctive structure of the institutional environment and the developmental goals that the institution purports to achieve.

A second important point is that local action research of this kind need be no less rigorous than its more scholarly counterpart. Indeed, most of the admonitions on method noted above are equally applicable to both types of studies. But local research also involves considerable opportunities for methodological innovation. For example, the need to isolate experiences in "microsettings" raises excellent opportunities for qualitative or ethnographic investigation. Though published as part of the wider literature, for example, Katchadourian and Boli's (1985) in-depth study of Stanford students began as a local evaluation effort. Similar longitudinal efforts involving participant observation and in-depth interviewing are often of particular value in isolating promising avenues for action and intervention (Lindquist, 1981b). Even such "quick and dirty" methods as transcript studies and teaching evaluations can be rendered rigorous if part of a more general, mutually reinforcing local research program. Finally, it is important to recognize that studies intended primarily to inform local policy can also make significant contributions to wider knowledge if they are approached in the light of a common guiding policy framework or research question. Palola's work at Empire State (1981), Banta's at the University of Tennessee, Knoxville (Banta, 1985, 1986); and Mentkowski's at Alverno College (Mentkowski and Doherty, 1984); are all instructive in this regard.

An Emerging Need for Implementation Research

A final important research question goes beyond the immediate scope of outcomes investigation. As greater numbers of institutions initiate activities intended to improve instruction, a significant knowledge gap is emerging about the factors responsible for the successful implementation of such efforts. Emerging institutional assessment programs represent only one of many possible objects of inquiry within this arena. Nevertheless, they present an excellent available research opportunity. In several states (for example, Virginia, Missouri, and Colorado) all public institutions are being required to undertake identifiable assessment programs, and most are in the earliest stages of development. Such states constitute a universe of "natural experiments" for investigating the impact of a specified innovation across a range of institutional settings. Second, assessment programs usually fuse a variety of mechanisms for change, and their implementation raises a number of issues that are typical of any intervention. Among these are organizational and political issues such as the location of responsibility, the nature and extent of faculty involvement, and the consequences of action. Such programs also raise issues of institutional culture including the symbolic value of information and the degree of agreement on and internalization of goals. Most importantly, they involve direct examination of goals themselves, and consequently have the potential to raise latent conflicts about appropriate values. Finally, assessment programs are usually directly linked to a range of additional types of intervention, among them new structures for curricula, of incentives, and of faculty and staff development. Because of these linkages, research focused on the organizational implementation of such programs constitutes an excellent point of departure for more focused investigations of the fielding and impact of additional undergraduate reforms.

Certainly, considerably greater knowledge is needed about such interventions in themselves. As Conrad and Pratt (1986) and Stark and Lowther (1986) point out, very little is known about the consequences or about the factors associated with successful implementation of various approaches to curriculum design. McKeachie and associates (1986) identify parallel needs to further specify the outcomes consequences of particular types of teaching modality and classroom activity. Investigations of the precise forms of incentives capable of inducing different kinds of faculty to alter classroom practices constitutes yet another promising line of inquiry. As Blackburn and associates (1986) note, very little research has been able to link extrinsic reward structures with effective teaching, and very few have explicitly explored the nature and impact of intrinsic reward. Pointing out such needs, however, comes perilously close to posing a classic academic dilemma: the requirement to know everything before attempting anything. The most important demand, therefore, remains the resolution to act on what has already been determined. Posed as a challenge to outcomes research almost two decades ago, Enthoven's observation remains germane: "Because there is no agreement on purposes or on relative values, there is no 'optimum' program for the university. There are only better and worse programs. Avoiding bad programs is a sufficiently ambitious goal to keep us all occupied for many years" (1970, p. 53).

REFERENCES

Adelman, Clifford, ed. (1986a). *Assessment in American Higher Education: Issues and Contexts.* Washington, DC: OERI, Department of Education.

Adelman, C. (1986b). To imagine an adverb. In Adelman, *Assessment in American Higher Education,* pp. 73–82.

Alverno College Faculty (1979). *Assessments at Alverno College.* Milwaukee: Alverno Publications.

American Association of State Colleges and Universities (1986). *Defining and Assessing Baccalaureate Skills.* Washington, DC.

Association of American Colleges (1985). *Integrity in the College Curriculum: A Report to the Academic Community.* Washington, DC: Association of American Colleges.

Astin, A. W. (1985). *Achieving Educational Excellence.* San Francisco: Jossey-Bass.

Astin, A. W. (1979). Student-oriented management: a proposal for change. In *Evaluating Educational Quality: A Conference Summary.* Washington, DC: Council on Postsecondary Accreditation (COPA).

Astin, A. W. (1977). *Four Critical Years: Effects of College on Beliefs, Values, and Knowledge.* San Francisco: Jossey-Bass.

Astin, A. W. (1976). *Academic Gamesmanship: Student-Oriented Change in Higher Education.* New York: Praeger.

Astin, A. W. (1975). *Preventing Students from Dropping Out.* San Francisco: Jossey-Bass.

Astin, A. W. (1974). Measuring the outcomes of higher education. In H. W. Bowen (ed.), *Evaluating Institutions for Accountability,* New Directions for Institutional Research. San Francisco: Jossey-Bass.

Astin, A. W. (1970a). The methodology of research on college impact (I). *Sociology of Education* 43: 223–254.

Astin, A. W. (1970b). The methodology of research on college impact (II). *Sociology of Education* 43: 437–450.

Astin, A. W. (1968). Undergraduate achievement and institutional excellence. *Science* 161: 661–668.

Astin, A. W. and Lee, C. B. T. (1972). *The Invisible Colleges.* New York: McGraw-Hill.

Astin, A. W. and Panos, R. (1969). *The Educational and Vocational Development of College Students.* Washington, DC: ACE, 1969.

Astin, A. W., Panos, R. J., and Creager, J. A. (1967). *National Norms for Entering College Freshmen—Fall 1966.* Washington, DC: AE.

Baird, L. (1976). Structuring the environment to improve outcomes. In O. T. Lenning (ed.), *Improving Educational Outcomes.* New Directions for Higher Education, No. 16, pp. 1–23.

Baird, L. (1974). The practical utility of measures of college environments. *Review of Educational Research* 44: 307–329.

Baldridge, J. V.,and Tierney, M. L. (1979). *New Approaches to Management: Creative, Practical Systems of Management Information and Management by Objective.* San Francisco: Jossey-Bass.

Banta, T. W. (1986). *Performance Funding in Higher Education: A Critical Analysis of Tennessee's Experience.* Boulder, CO: National Center for Higher Education Management Systems [NCHEMS].

Banta, T. W. (1985). Use of outcomes information at the University of Tennessee, Knoxville. In Ewell, *Assessing Educational Outcomes,* pp. 19–32.

Banta, T. W., and Fisher, H. S. (1984). Performance funding: Tennessee's experiment.

In J. Folger (ed.), *Financial Incentives for Academic Quality.* New Directions for Higher Education, No. 48, pp. 29–41. San Francisco: Jossey-Bass.

Banta, T. W., Lambert, E. W., Pike, G. R., Schmidhammer, J. L., and Schneider, J. A. (1987). Estimated score gain on the ACT COMP exam: valid tool for institutional assessment? Paper presented at the annual meeting of the American Educational Research Association, Washington, D.C., April.

Barak, R. (1982). *Program Review in Higher Education: Within and Without.* Boulder, CO: NCHEMS.

Bennett, W. J. (1984). *To Reclaim a Legacy: A Report on the Humanities in Higher Education.* Washington, DC: National Endowment for the Humanities.

Bess, J. L. (1979). Classroom and management decisions using student data. *Journal of Higher Education* 5: 256–279.

Biglan, A. (1973). Relationships between subject matter characteristics and the structure and output of university departments. *Journal of Applied Psychology* 57: 204–213.

Blackburn, R. T., Lawrence, J. H., Ross, S., Okoloko, V. P., Meiland, R., Bieber, J., and Street, T. (1986). *Faculty as a Key Resource: A Review of the Research Literature.* Ann Arbor: NCRIPTAL, University of Michigan.

Bloom, B. S. (1974). Time and learning. *American Psychologist,* 1974, 683–688.

Bloom, B. S., ed. (1956). *Taxonomy of Educational Objectives, Handbook 1: Cognitive Domain.* New York: David McKay.

Bogue, E. G., and Brown, W. (1982). Performance incentives for state colleges. *Harvard Business Review,* Nov./Dec., 123–128.

Bowen, H. R. (1981). Cost differences: the amazing disparity among institutions of higher education in educational costs per student. *Change,* Jan./Feb., 21–27.

Bowen, H. R. (1980). *The Costs of Higher Education: How Much Do Colleges and Universities Spend per Student and How Much Should They Spend?* San Francisco: Jossey-Bass.

Bowen, H. R. (1978). Outcomes planning: solution or dream? In *Planning, Managing and Financing in the 1980s: Proceedings of the NCHEMS 1977 National Assembly,* pp. 41–51. Boulder, CO: NCHEMS.

Bowen, H. R. (1977a). *Investment in Learning.* San Francisco: Jossey-Bass.

Bowen, H. R. (1977b). Outcome data and educational decisionmaking. In Carl R. Adams (ed.), *Appraising Information Needs of Decisionmakers.* New Directions for Institutional Research, No. 15. San Francisco: Jossey-Bass.

Boyer, C. M., Ewell, P. T., Finney, J. E., and Mingle, J. R. (1987). Assessment and outcomes measurement: a view from the states. *AAHE Bulletin,* March, pp. 8–12.

Branscomb, H., Milton, O., Richardson, J., and Spivey, H. (1977). *The Competent College Student: An Essay on the Objectives and Quality of Higher Education.* Nashville: Tennessee Higher Education Commission.

Braskamp, L. A. (1982). Evaluation systems are more than information systems. In R. Wilson (ed.), *Designing Academic Program Reviews.* New Directions for Higher Education, No. 37, pp. 55–66. San Francisco: Jossey-Bass.

Bressler, M., and Wendell, P. (1980). The sex composition of selective colleges and gender differences in career aspirations. *Journal of Higher Education* 51: 651–663.

Cameron, K. S. (1978). Measuring organizational effectiveness in institutions of higher education. *Administrative Science Quarterly* 23: 604–632.

Campione, J. C., and Armbruster, B. B. (1985). Acquiring information from texts: an analysis of four approaches. In J. W. Segal, S. F. Chipman, and R. Glaser (eds.), *Thinking and Learning Skills VI,* pp. 317–362. Hillsdale, NJ: Lawrence Erlbaum Associates.

Caruthers, J. K., and Lott, G. B. (1981). *Mission Review: Foundation for Strategic Planning*. Boulder, CO: NCHEMS.

Centra, J., and Rock, D. (1971). College environments and student academic achievement. *American Educational Research Journal* 8: 623–634.

Chickering, A. W. (1970). College experience and student development. Paper delivered at Annual Meeting of the American Association for the Advancement of Science, December.

Chickering, A. W. (1969). *Education and Identity*. San Francisco: Jossey-Bass.

Clark, B., Heist, P., McConnell, T., Trow, M., and Yonge, G. (1972). *Students and Colleges: Interaction and Change*. Berkeley: Center for Research and Development in Higher Education, University of California-Berkeley.

Clark, B. R., and Trow, M. (1966). The organizational context. In T. M. Newcomb and E. K. Wilson (eds.), *College Peer Groups: Problems and Prospects for Research*, pp. 17–70. Chicago: Aldine.

College Outcomes Evaluation Program (COEP), State of New Jersey Department of Higher Education (1987). *Fifth Progress Report of the Student Learning Outcomes Subcommittee*. Trenton: Department of Higher Education.

Conrad, C. F., and Pratt, A. M. (1986). Research on academic programs: an inquiry into an emerging field. In J. C. Smart (ed.), *Higher Education: Handbook of Theory and Research*, Vol. II, pp. 235–273. New York: Agathon Press.

Corno, L., and Rohrkemper, M. M. (1985). The intrinsic motivation to learn in classrooms. In C. Ames and R. Ames (eds.), *Research on Motivation in Education*. New York: Academic Press.

Corno, L., and Snow, R. E. (1986). Adapting teaching to individual differences among learnings. In M. Wittrack (ed.), *Handbook of Research on Teaching*. New York: Macmillan.

Cronbach, L., and Snow, R. (1977). *Aptitudes and Instructional Methods: A Handbook for Research on Interactions*. New York: Irvington.

Cross, K. P. (1987). Teaching for learning. *AAHE Bulletin* 39 (April): 3–7.

Cross, K. P. (1976). *Accent on Learning: Improving Instruction and Reshaping the Curriculum*. San Francisco: Jossey-Bass.

Dill, D. D. (1982). The management of academic culture: notes on the management of meaning and social integration. *Higher Education* 11: 303–320.

Douglass, G. K. (1977). Economic returns on investments in higher education. In Bowen, *Investment in Learning*, pp. 359–387.

Dumont, R. G., and Troelstrup, R. L. (1981). Measures and predictors of educational growth with four years of college. *Research in Higher Education* 14: 31–47.

Dumont, R. G., and Troelstrup, R. L. (1980). Exploring relationships between objective and subjective measures of instructional outcomes. *Research in Higher Education* 12: 37–51.

Edgerton, R. (1987). An assessment of assessment. In ETS, *Assessing the Outcomes of Higher Education*, pp. 93–110.

Educational Testing Service (1987). *Assessing the Outcomes of Higher Education*. Proceedings of the 1986 ETS Invitational Conference, Princeton, NJ.

Enthoven, A. C. (1970). Measures of the outputs of higher education: some practical suggestions for their development and use. In G. B. Lawrence, G. Weathersby, and V. W. Patterson (eds.), *Outputs of Higher Education: Their Identification, Measurement, and Evaluation*, pp. 51–58. Boulder, CO: WICHE.

Erwin, T. D. (1986). Students' contributions to their college costs and intellectual development. *Research in Higher Education* 25: 194–203.

Ewell, P. T. (1987). Establishing a campus-based assessment program: a framework for choice. In D. Halpern (ed.), *Student Outcomes Assessment: A Tool for Improving Teaching and Learning*. New Directions in Higher Education. San Francisco: Jossey-Bass.

Ewell, P. T. (1986a). Transformational leadership for improving student outcomes. In M. D. Waggoner, R. L. Alfred, M. C. Francis, M. W. Peterson (eds.), *Academic Effectiveness: Transforming Colleges and Universities for the 1990s*, pp. 25–30. Ann Arbor: University of Michigan.

Ewell, P. T. (1986b). The state role in assessing college outcomes: policy choices and probable impacts. In *Time for Results: The Governors' 1991 Report on Education—Task Force on College Quality: Supporting Works*, pp. 43–73. Washington, DC: National Governors Association.

Ewell, P. T., ed. (1985a). *Assessing Educational Outcomes*. New Directions for Institutional Research, No. 47. San Francisco: Jossey-Bass.

Ewell, P. T. (1985b). Linking outcomes and institutional characteristics: the importance of looking deeper. Boulder, CO: NCHEMS.

Ewell, P. T. (1985c). Assessment: what's it all about? *Change*, Nov./Dec., 32–36.

Ewell, P. T. (1984). *The Self-Regarding Institution: Information for Excellence*. Boulder, CO: NCHEMS.

Ewell, P. T. (1983). *Information on Student Outcomes: How to Get It and How to Use It*. Boulder, CO: NCHEMS.

Ewell, P. T., and Chaffee, E. E. (1984). Promoting the effective use of information in decisionmaking. Boulder, CO: NCHEMS.

Ewell, P. T., and Jones, D. P. (1986). The costs of assessment. In Adelman, *Assessment in American Higher Education*, pp. 33–46.

Feldman, K. A., and Newcomb, T. M. (1969). *The Impact of College on Students*. San Francisco: Jossey-Bass.

Forrest, A. W. (1981). Outcome evaluation for revitalizing general education. In Lindquist, *Increasing the Use of Institutional Research*, pp. 59–71.

Friedlander, J. H. (1980). The importance of quality of effort in predicting college student attainment. Ph.D. dissertation, Graduate School of Education, University of California at Los Angeles.

Gaff, J. G. (1973). Making a difference: the impacts of faculty. *Journal of Higher Education*, Nov., 605–622.

Gagne, R. M. (1977). *The Conditions of Learning*, 3rd ed. New York: Holt, Rinehart, & Winston.

Gamson, Z. F. and associates (1984). *Liberating Education*. San Francisco: Jossey-Bass. (Cited in the text as Gamson.)

Grose, R. F. (1976). The use of academic histories in decisionmaking. Paper presented at the Third Annual Meeting of the Northeast Association of Institutional Research.

Guba, E. G. (1969). The failure of educational evaluation. *Educational Technology* 9: 29–38.

Guilford, J. P. (1967). *The Nature of Human Intelligence*. New York: McGraw-Hill.

Hanson, G. R. (1982). Critical issues in the assessment of student development. In G. R. Hanson (ed.), *Measuring Student Development*. New Directions for Student Services, No. 20. San Francisco: Jossey-Bass.

Harris, J. (1986). Assessing outcomes in higher education. In Adelman, *Assessment in American Higher Education*, pp. 13–31.

Harris, J. (1970). Gain scores on the CLEP general examination and an overview of research. Paper presented at the annual meeting of AERA, Minneapolis.

Harshman, C. L. (1979). *A Model for Assessing the Quality of Non-Traditional Programs in Higher Education*. St. Louis: Metropolitan College, St. Louis University.

Hartle, T. W. (1986). The growing interest in measuring the educational achievement of students. In Adelman, *Assessment in American Higher Education*, pp. 1–11.

Hartnett, R., and Centra, J. (1977). The effects of academic departments on student learning. *Journal of Higher Education* 48: 491–507.

Heath, D. (1968). *Growing Up in College*. San Francisco: Jossey-Bass.

Hossler, D. (1986). *Creating Effective Enrollment Management Systems*. New York: College Entrance Examination Board.

Hossler, D. (1984). *Enrollment Management: An Integrated Approach*. New York: College Entrance Examination Board.

Iverson, B. K., Pascarella, E. T., and Terenzini, P. T. (1984). Informal faculty-student contact and commuter college freshmen. *Research in Higher Education* 21: 123–136.

Katchadourian, H. A., and Boli, J. (1985). *Careerism and Intellectualism Among College Students*. San Francisco: Jossey-Bass.

Kees, D. J. (1974). The Clark-Trow typology revisited. *Journal of College Student Personnel* 15: 140–144.

Kemerer, F. R., Baldridge, J. V., and Green, K. C. (1982). *Strategies for Effective Enrollment Management*. Washington, DC: AASCU.

Kinnick, M. K. (1985). Increasing the use of student outcomes information. In Ewell, *Assessing Educational Outcomes*, pp. 93–110.

Kleemann, G. L., and Richardson, R. C., Jr. (1985). Student characteristics and perceptions of university effectiveness. *Review of Higher Education* 9: 5–20.

Korn, H. A. (1986). Psychological models explaining the impact of college on students. Ann Arbor: NCRIPTAL at University of Michigan.

Kuh, G. D., Bean, J. P., Bradley, R. K., Coomes, M. D., and Hunter, D. E. (1986). Changes in research on college students published in selected journals between 1969 and 1983. *Review of Higher Education* 9: 177–192.

Lacy, W. (1978). Interpersonal relationships as mediators of structural effects: college student socialization in a traditional and an experimental university environment. *Sociology of Education* 51: 201–211.

Learned, W. S., and Wood, B. D. (1938). *The Student and His Knowledge: A Report to the Carnegie Foundation on the Results of the High School and College Examinations of 1928, 1930, and 1932*. New York: Carnegie Foundation for the Advancement of Teaching.

Lenning, O. T. (1977). *Previous Attempts to Structure Educational Outcomes and Outcome-Related Concepts: A Compilation and Review of the Literature*. Boulder, CO: NCHEMS.

Lenning, O. T. (1974). *The Benefits Crisis in Higher Education*. Washington, DC: American Association of Higher Education.

Lenning, O. T., Beal, P. E., and Sauer, K. (1980). *Retention and Attrition: Evidence for Action and Research*. Boulder, CO: NCHEMS.

Lenning, O. T., Lee, Y. S., Micek, S. S., and Service, A. L. (1977). *A Structure for the Outcomes and Outcome-Related Concepts: A Compilation and Review of the Literature*. Boulder, CO: NCHEMS.

Lenning, O., Munday, L., and Maxey, J. (1969). Student educational growth during the first two years of college. *College and University* 44: 145–153.

Leslie, L. L., and Brinkman, P. T. (1986). Rates of return to higher education: an intensive examination. In J. C. Smart (ed.), *Higher Education: Handbook of Theory and Research*, Vol. II, pp. 207–234. New York: Agathon Press.

Levy, R. A. (1986). Development of performance funding criteria by the Tennessee Higher Education Commission: a chronology and evaluation. In Banta, *Performance Funding in Higher Education,* pp. 13–26.

Lindquist, J., ed. (1981a). *Increasing the Use of Institutional Research.* New Directions for Institutional Research, No. 32. San Francisco: Jossey-Bass.

Lindquist, J. (1981b). Quick, dirty, and useful. In J. Lindquist (ed.), *Increasing the Use of Institutional Research.* New Directions for Institutional Research, No. 32, pp. 87–97. San Francisco: Jossey-Bass.

March, J. G. (1984). How we talk and how we act: administrative theory and administrative life. In T. J. Sergiovanni and J. E. Corbally (eds.), *Leadership and Organizational Culture.* Urbana, IL: University of Illinois Press.

Marton, F. (1979). Skill as an aspect of knowledge. *Journal of Higher Education* 50 (Sept./Oct.): 602–614.

McClain, C. J. (1984). *In Pursuit of Degrees with Integrity: A Value-Added Approach to Undergraduate Assessment.* Washington, DC: AASCU.

McClain, C. J., and Krueger, D. W. (1985). Using outcomes assessment: a case study in institutional change. In Ewell, Assessing Educational Outcomes, pp. 33–46.

McKeachie, W. J., Pintrich, P. R., Lin, Y., and Smith, D. A. F. (1986). *Teaching and Learning in the College Classroom: A Review of the Research Literature.* Ann Arbor: NCRIPTAL at University of Michigan, 1986.

McMillan, J. H. (1987). Enhancing college students' critical thinking: a review of studies. *Research in Higher Education* 26: 3–29.

Mentkowski, M., and Doherty, A. (1984). *Careering After College: Establishing the Validity of Abilities Learned in College for Later Careering and Performance.* Milwaukee: Alverno Productions.

Mentkowski, M., and Loacker, G. (1985). Assessing and validating the outcomes of college. In Ewell, *Assessing Educational Outcomes,* pp. 47–64.

Messick, S., and associates (1976). *Individuality in Learning.* San Francisco: Jossey-Bass.

Moos, R. H. (1979). *Evaluating Educational Environments.* San Francisco: Jossey-Bass.

National Governors' Association (1986). *Time for Results: The Governors' 1991 Report on Education.* Washington, D.C.: NGA.

National Institute of Education, Study Group on the Conditions of Excellence in American Higher Education (1984). *Involvement in Learning: Realizing the Potential of American Higher Education.* Washington, DC: U.S. Government Printing Office.

Nettles, M. T. (1987). The emergence of college outcome assessments: prospects for enhancing state colleges and universities. Trenton: New Jersey State College Governing Boards Association.

Newman, D. L., Brown, R. D., and Braskamp, L. A. (1980). Communication theory and the utilization of evaluation. In L. Braskamp and R. D. Brown (eds.), *Utilization of Evaluative Information.* New Directions for Program Evaluation, No. 5, pp. 29–35. San Francisco: Jossey-Bass.

Nichols, R. (1964). Effects of various college characteristics on student aptitude test scores. *Journal of Educational Psychology* 55: 45–54.

Pace, C. R. Perspectives and problems in student outcomes research. In Ewell, *Assessing Educational Outcomes,* pp. 7–18.

Pace, C. R. (1984). *Measuring the Quality of College Student Experiences.* Los Angeles: Higher Education Research Institute at the University of California, Los Angeles.

Pace, C. R. (1979). *Measuring the Outcomes of College.* San Francisco: Jossey-Bass.

Pace, C. R. (1974). *The Demise of Diversity: A Comparative Profile of Eight Types of Institutions.* Berkeley: The Carnegie Commission on Higher Education.

Pace, C. R. (1972). *Education and Evangelism.* New York: McGraw-Hill.

Pace, C. R. (1963). *Preliminary Technical Manual: College and University Environment Scales.* Princeton, NJ: Educational Testing Service.

Pace, C. R., and Baird, L. (1966). Attainment parameters in the environmental press of college subcultures. In T. Newcomb and E. Wilson (eds.), *College Peer Groups.* Chicago: Aldine.

Palola, E. G. (1981). Multiple perspectives, multiple channels. In Lindquist, *Increasing the Use of Institutional Research,* pp. 45–58.

Palola, E. G., and Lehmann, T. (1976). Improving student outcomes and institutional decisionmaking with PERC. In O. T. Lenning (ed.), *Improving Educational Outcomes,* New Directions for Higher Education, No. 16, pp. 73–92.

Pascarella, E. T. (1987). Are value-added analyses valuable? In ETS, *Assessing the Outcomes of Higher Education,* pp. 71–91.

Pascarella, E. T. (1985a). College environmental influences on learning and cognitive development: a critical review and synthesis. In J. C. Smart (ed.), *Higher Education: Handbook of Theory and Research,* Vol. I, pp. 1–61. New York: Agathon Press.

Pascarella, E. T. (1985b). Students' affective development within the college environment. *Journal of Higher Education* 56(Nov./Dec.): 640–663.

Pascarella, E. T. (1984). Reassessing the effects of living on-campus versus commuting to college: a causal modelling approach. *Review of Higher Education* 7: 247–260.

Pascarella, E. T., and Terenzini, P. T. (1980). Predicting freshman persistence and voluntary dropout decisions from a theoretical model. *Journal of Higher Education* 51 (Jan./Feb.): 60–75.

Pascarella, E. T., Terenzini, P. T., and Wolfle, L. M. (1986). Orientation to college and freshman year persistence/withdrawal decisions. *Journal of Higher Education* 57 (Mar./Apr.).

Perry, W. J., Jr. (1970). *Forms of Intellectual and Ethical Development in the College Years: A Schema.* New York: Holt, Rinehart, & Winston.

Peterson, M. W., Cameron, K. S., Mets, L. A., Jones, P., and Ettington, D. (1986). *The Organizational Context for Teaching and Learning: A Review of the Research Literature.* Ann Arbor: NCRIPTAL, University of Michigan.

Porter, O. (1982). The role of quality of effort in defining institutional environments: An attempt to understand college uniqueness. Ph.D. dissertation, Graduate School of Education, University of California at Los Angeles.

Resnick, D., and Goulden, M. (1987). Assessment, curriculum and expansion in American higher education: a historical perspective. In Diane Halpern (ed.), *Student Assessment: A Tool for Improving Teaching and Learning.* San Francisco: Jossey-Bass.

Robertshaw, D., and Wolfle, L. (1982). The cognitive value of two-year colleges for whites and blacks. *Integrated Education* 19: 68–71.

Romney, L. C., Bogen, G., and Micek, S. S. (1979). Assessing institutional performance: the importance of being *careful. International Journal of Institutional Management in Higher Education* 3 (May): 79–89.

Sarason, S. B. (1972). *The Creation of Settings and the Future Societies.* San Francisco: Jossey-Bass.

Schalock, H. D. (1976). Structuring process to improve student outcomes. In O. T. Lenning (ed.), *Improving Educational Outcomes.* New Directions for Higher Education, No. 16. San Francisco: Jossey-Bass.

Shapiro, J. Z. (1986). Evaluation research and educational decisionmaking. In J. C.

Smart (ed.), *Higher Education: Handbook of Theory and Research*, Vol. II, pp. 163–206. New York: Agathon Press.

Sheldon, M. S. (1981). *Statewide Longitudinal Study: 1978–81 Final Report*. Los Angeles: Los Angeles Pierce College.

Smart, J. C. (1982). Faculty teaching goals: a test of Holland's theory. *Journal of Educational Psychology* 74: 180–188.

Smith, H. L. (1986). Testimony for the National Governors' Association task force on college quality on behalf of the American Association of State Colleges and Universities. Washington, D.C.

Spaeth, J., and Greely, A. (1970). *Recent Alumni and Higher Education: A Survey of College Graduates*. New York: McGraw-Hill.

Stark, J. S., and Lowther, M. (1986). *Designing the Learning Plan: A Review of Research and Theory Related to College Curricula*. Ann Arbor: NCRIPTAL at University of Michigan.

Sternberg, R. J. (1985). *Beyond IQ: A Triarchic Theory of Human Intelligence*. Cambridge: Cambridge University Press.

Terenzini, P. T. The case for unobtrusive measures. In ETS, *Assessing the Outcomes of Higher Education*, pp. 47–61.

Terenzini, P. T., and Pascarella, E. T. (1977). Voluntary freshman attrition and patterns of social and academic integration in a university: a test of a conceptual model. *Research in Higher Education* 6: 25–43.

Terenzini, P. T., Pascarella, E. T., and Lorang, W. (1982). An assessment of the academic and social influences on freshman year educational outcomes. *Review of Higher Education* 5: 86–109.

Terenzini, P. T., and Wright, T. M. (1987). Students' personal growth during the first two years of college. Paper presented at the annual meeting of the Association for the Study of Higher Education, San Diego.

Theophilides, C., Terenzini, P. T., and Lorang, W. (1984). Relation between freshman year experience and perceived importance of four major educational goals. *Research in Higher Education* 20: 235–252.

Thomas, J. W., and Rohwer, W. D., Jr. (1986). Academic studying: the role of learning strategies. *Educational Psychologist* 21: 19–41.

Thrash, P. R. (1984). Accreditation and the evaluation of educational outcomes. Paper presented at a professional development session sponsored by the Council of Specialized Accrediting Agencies (CSAA) and the Council on Postsecondary Accreditation (COPA).

Tinto, V. (1975). Dropout from higher education: a theoretical synthesis of recent research. *Review of Educational Research* 45 (Winter): 89–125.

Trent, J. W., and Medsker, L. (1968). *Beyond High School: A Psychosociological Study of 10,000 High School Graduates*. San Francisco: Jossey-Bass.

Walleri, R. D., and Japely, S. M. (1986). Student intent, persistence, and outcomes. Paper delivered at the 26th Annual Forum of the Association for Institutional Research, Orlando, Fla.

Warren, J. (1984). The blind alley of value-added. *AAHE Bulletin*, Sept., pp. 10–13.

Wilson, R. C., Gaff, J. G., Dienst, E. R., Wood, L., and Barry, J. L. (1975). *College Professors and Their Impact on Students*. New York: Wiley.

Winter, D. G., McClelland, D. C., and Stewart, A. J. (1981). *A New Case for the Liberal Arts*. San Francisco: Jossey-Bass.

APPENDIX A. Diagnostic Summary of Recent Observations About the Implementation of Assessment Programs

Philosophical	Organizational	Practical	Technical
		Issues	
		Adelman (1986b)	
Faculty resistence to "third-party assessment		Investment/cost	
Promises to students			
Effects on minorities			
Problem if confined to basic skills			
		Ewell (1985)	
Faculty resistance	Lack of incentive	Excessive cost	
		Ewell (1986a)	
Unmeasurability of certain outcomes	Lack of visible commitment	Data don't automatically indicate what actions to take	Measurement complexity
Uncertainty over what to measure	Lack of incentives		
		Ewell (1986b)	
Threatens institutional autonomy/academic freedom		Excessive cost/ technical infeasibility	
Narrows curriculum			
Promotes "teaching to the test"			
		Guba (1969)	
Lack of theoretical framework and adequate definitions	Lack of knowledge about decision processes	Lack of adequate criteria for judgment	Lack of mechanisms for organizing/ reporting data
		Hanson (1982)	
Multiple definitions of student development	Competing priorities within the institution	Failure to identify possible uses before assessment	Complex administration and scoring
Multidimensional nature of development		Lack of planning	Different methods produce different results
		Inability to use results	Consistency/accuracy of response
		Hartle (1986)	
Definition of "quality"	Link to funding	Costs of improvement	
Achievement and access		Legal issues	
Impact on institutional autonomy			

APPENDIX A. (*Continued*)

Philosophical	Organizational	Practical	Technical
	Kinnick (1985)		
	Cost of access to information		Lack of data integrity
	Organizational structure		Lack of face validity
	Limited or no incentives		Information arrives late
	Lack of linkage between data users, developers and managers		Excessive bulk
			Limited interpretability
	McClain (1984)		
Teaching to the test	Controlling blame and taking credit	Student motivation	Analyzing and interpreting data
	Maintaining open communications		
	Dealing with fear of data abuse		
	Romney, Bogen, and Micek (1979)		
Philosophical Caveats —Autonomy —Flexibility	Political liabilities	Economic concerns	Methodological cautions
	Smith (1986)		
Concern about the way goals of assessment will be established	Data rarely approximately made available to relevant decision makers	Problems of "the politics of the single figure"	
Assessment may "freeze" innovation		Insufficient financial support available	
	Themes of Successful Practice		
	Bowen (1977b)		
Avoid confusing inputs and outputs	Should be "bottom-up"	Keep it simple	Study *after* as well as during college
Link to *all* goals			Study *change*
Relate to development of whole persons			
	Braskamp (1982)		
		Center investigation on recognized issues and concerns	
		Concentrate on building communications	

APPENDIX A. (*Continued*)

Philosophical	Organizational	Practical	Technical
	Enthoven (1970)		
	Use appropriate incentives	Engage in analysis to stimulate "counteranalysis"	Use external examinations and observers
	Ewell (1983)		
	Assess needs of decision makers Create forums for discussion Create attitude that improvement can be accomplished and will be rewarded	Focus on recognized problems	Use "tailored reports" Use comparative formats Integrate outcomes information with other decision information
	Ewell (1984)		
Focus on the curriculum	Maximize involvement/ participation		Choose correct unit of analysis Use comparisons
	Ewell (1985)		
Make sure the shoe fits (tailor assessment to curriculum) Object is to learn		Look before you leap (examine existing data)	There's more than one way (methodological "triangulation")
	Ewell (1986a)		
Concentrate on actual level of student experience	Create visible centers for improvement Create concrete incentives for improvement	Use external requirements as opportunities for action	Insist on concrete information about student learning and development
	Ewell (1987)		
	Create a visible center for assessment activity	Capitalize on existing information Experiment with pilot programs Discover and critically evaluate "model" programs	Use results in identifiable ways
	Forrest (1981)		
Focus on specific outcomes Focus on important outcomes Phrase outcomes clearly	Involve decision makers throughout	Encourage decision makers to communicate need for action	Test student ability to apply learning Use objective techniques

APPENDIX A. (*Continued*)

Philosophical	Organizational	Practical	Technical
		Harris (1986)	
Stress linkage to specific institutional goals			Reviews/critiques available instruments
		Hanson (1982)	
		Simplify the assessment process Reduce the cost of assessment	Assess multiple dimensions of student development Encourage longitudinal studies Require analysts with appropriate research skills
		Kinnick (1985)	
	Focus utilization on regular institutional decision making and evaluation processes	Focus utilization on recognized institutional issues and problems	Reviews innovative data communication formats
		Lindquist (1981)	
	"Involve, involve . . ."	Be systematic but flexible Learn to be a "change agent"	Vary and compare
		Nettles (1987)	
Should exceed goal of minimum competency Should include provisions for analyzing the effects of assessment (on minorities)		Should yield dividends that are worth (the substantial) investment	Assessment policies should be multidimensional
		Palola (1981)	
	Involve users throughout Get to the powerful Fit data to interests	Seek small "cross-group" or one-to-one interactions Encourage "follow-up structures" Provide "contract assistance" after initial dissemination	Fit data to learning Underwhelm Study your own dissemination and use

Higher Education and Work in Europe

Ulrich Teichler

Gesamthochschule Kassel, Kassel, FRG
and
Northwestern University

Any attempt to describe and analyze developments in the relationships between higher education and employment or work in Europe as well as related research has to address two seemingly contradicting problems. On the one hand, any overview on Europe will be discouraged by the diversity of higher education and employment systems, by language barriers, and by problems regarding the accessibility of documents. On the other hand, we observe such a homogeneity of emergence and change of paradigms both in political debates and research as regards what are conceived to be the major issues in the relationships between higher education and work, that we either might conclude that the diversity between European countries is small or that the paradigms oversimplify. Therefore, these problems will be briefly described at the beginning.

Subsequently, a brief overview on the research scene as well as major topics of research will be provided. This approach allows us to put in perspective the selection made in this analysis: It focuses on three topics which became popular during the debates in the 1970s about what was termed *overeducation, overqualification,* and so on. The topics are (1) problems in transition from studies to work and in graduate employment in general; (2) the issue of "appropriateness" of graduate employment and work; and (3) employers' expectations as regards higher education and graduates' competences. This selection was made because experts' debates in Europe still address these issues strongly—whether they continue to adhere to views of "overqualification" or whether they claim the need for new foci of emphasis.

The research findings presented will emphasize the relationships between higher education and employment or work in Europe since the mid-1970s. One has to keep in mind that most summarizing reports on such themes will have a time lag of about five years. Therefore, two synthesis reports of the early 1980s will be summarized beforehand: They may explain what the situation had been at the beginning of the period under observation and what interpretations developed as regards changes emerging in the late 1970s. It should be added that this report does not cover all European countries in detail; rather, it focuses (in alphabetical order) on Austria, France, the Federal Republic of Germany, the Netherlands, Poland, Sweden, Switzerland, and the United Kingdom, with some additional information on other European countries as well. The countries selected belong to those in which the statistics and the research available provided more in-depth information than in most other European countries. The analysis, of course, will be influenced by the author's familiarity with his home country, the Federal Republic of Germany.

A brief explanation of the terminology might be appropriate at the beginning. Words such as *employment, occupations, professions, career,* and *work* vary in their meaning and carry diverse meanings in different countries. A substantial number of the research issues presented here could well fit the term *employment,* that is, the formal conditions of work, for example employment status, employment conditions, status, income, career, and mobility. What we observe though, in the literature and research in this context since the 1970s is a shift of emphasis from *employment* to *work* (see Little, 1984, p. 7, in a trend report referring to both industrial and developing societies): Issues of the content and character of learning and their relationships to the content and character of work became an important issue in analyzing the relationships between higher education and the employment system—obviously a response to the insight that narrow specializations of research and expertise on higher education and employment or work were not appropriate anymore for understanding their changing relationships.

AIMS AND LIMITATIONS OF THE ANALYSIS

Diversity of European Systems and Problems of Accessibility of Information

Efforts to summarize the current knowledge about recent developments in the relationships between higher education and work in Europe face almost insurmountable difficulties. Five major obstacles have to be named.

First, higher education systems in Europe, as well as the character and conditions of graduate employment and work, vary from one European country to the other. Contrary to many publications in the United States, which often discuss a comparative view of higher education in "Europe" as if Europe was quite homogeneous, the European experts in this field emphasize variety much more strongly than any commonality among European countries. Certainly, medieval universities were not "national" ones; also, certain concepts of universities became popular internationally and had considerable impacts on higher education systems in other countries (see for example Briggs, 1985; Perkin, 1984). Also, one can name a few similarities among European countries in comparison to the United States and Japan, for example, some quantitative and structural elements such as enrollment quotas of less than 30% or even less than 20% of the corresponding age group; a share of still less than 10% of college-trained persons among the total labor force in most European countries; and a stronger role of government in the coordination of higher education, at least some emphasis on higher education planning, as well as low tuition or no tuition at all. But if one takes into consideration types of institutions and the role played by nonuniversity higher education, major approaches of planning and administration of higher education, curricular concepts, and graduate employment and its economic and societal conditions, any in-depth analysis of the topic under consideration is confronted with a bewildering diversity among European countries (cf. de Moor, 1978; Vedel, 1981; Goldschmidt, 1981; UNESCO, 1982; Neave, 1986; Teichler and Lanzendoerfer, 1986).

Second, attempts to provide overviews of Europe face the variety of languages in Europe as one major obstacle. Contrary to the United States, where many scholars do not read publications in foreign languages at all, European experts in this area might read documents in two or three languages. But the knowledge of about 20 languages would be needed in order to get an in-depth knowledge of higher education systems in Europe. As a consequence, we find many reports on Europe covering very few European countries, which are more easily accessible either because their language is widely used internationally or because politicians and scholars of that country tend to publish frequently in foreign languages. Or reports on Europe are based primarily on country reports commissioned by international organizations (see for example Fulton, Gordon, and Williams, 1982; OECD, 1983a; Council of Europe, 1984; W. Taylor, 1986). Such country reports are usually available in English and sometimes in French or in Russian and thus limit the language barriers, but they are unlikely to cover just the topics one likes to address and the breadth needed.

Third, documents on higher education and work in Europe are not easily accessible (see Altbach, 1985, pp. 43–44), in part because of the "linkage" between areas that might be considered "subsystems" or branches of government activities. Whereas information on issues which fit into such boxes is readily available, information on cross-cutting issues is sparse. In addition, documentation is select: There are about a dozen international documentation centers in Europe relevant to the topic under consideration, but they focus primarily either on work or on education; also, they are established by international organizations emphasizing specific programs, and they mostly cover certain political subregions of Europe. Besides, contrary to national systems of documentation, which are well established in a few countries, such international documentation centers do not have many resources and do not aim to be comprehensive in their coverage; rather, they hope that both active search for the most "important" documents and a growing international awareness in dissemination policies may secure appropriate stocks of documents.

Fourth, international organizations provide considerable information on the relationships between higher education and work in European countries, but the information provided tends to be far from what one would consider comprehensive. If, for example, one wants to be informed on the relationships between higher education and work in the Federal Republic of Germany, reports published by OECD, ILO, UNESCO, International Institute for Educational Planning (UNESCO), the European Centre for Higher Education (CEPES/ UNESCO), Council of Europe, and the Commission of the European Communities (EC) will be useful. Also, information provided by the International Association of Universities and by CRE, the rectors' conference of European universities, will be of help. One has to bear in mind, though, that the coverage of topics and the ways the reports are written are likely to reflect (1) the specific programs of the international organizations: For example, publications by the EC emphasize issues of mobility between European countries; (2) issues important to the activities of governments rather than of institutions of higher education or of students (i.e., an emphasis on quantitative, structural, and financial issues rather than on content-related issues or those of teaching and learning or issues of educational and occupational biographies); and (3) the prevailing political sentiments of governments, both in their selection of the most "important" issues to cross-national communication and in their moderate ways of presenting "problems."

This does not mean, however, that analyses conducted or commissioned by international organizations are closely confined. On the contrary, they are obviously regarded by governments and scholars as very interesting heuristic activities in exploring new issues, getting to know alternative solutions, and so on; thus, some analyses of that kind are based on excellent country reports, and some synthesis reports demonstrate an impressive quality. However, this does not preclude select emphasis.

In addition, one has to take into consideration that most studies are based on quite limited resources. Country reports vary substantially according to the efforts implied in analyzing the available information; for many issues, an appropriate knowledge base will not be available in all countries; many comparative reports of experts which the international organizations consult predominantly refer to very few European countries, partly due to the limits in foreign language expertise on the part of the authors.

Fifth, academic research and expertise play only a limited role in counterbalancing such limitations. Most research funds are available for national rather than comparative projects. Most scholars specializing in higher education or in the relationships between higher education and work see their topics primarily from a national perspective. Most comparative activities are likely to be secondary analyses commissioned in the context of activities of government-based international organizations.

Dominant Paradigms

The difficulties of gathering and analyzing information from different European countries, as well as the diversity of higher education systems, obviously do not prevent experts from drawing general conclusions about major commonalities of higher education or of the relationships between higher education and employment in "industrial societies," "market economy systems," "Europe," "continental Europe," "Western Europe," or similar political or geographical entities. On the contrary, we observe notions that since the early 1960s all Western industrial societies have been challenged with more-or-less similar problems in the relationships between higher education and work (see the summaries in Teichler, Hartung, and Nuthmann, 1980; Sobel, 1982; Huefner, 1984a; Williams, 1984; OECD, 1985; Windolf, 1986).

In a first stage, many experts in industrial societies came to the conclusion, around 1960, that expansion of higher education was needed in order to stimulate economic growth and that efforts to reduce inequalities in the educational opportunity would be instrumental both in providing the supply needed by the economy and in establishing a modern, democratic society. In a second stage, this optimistic view of the desirable function of the expansion of higher education was somewhat modified in the debates in the late 1960s and the early 1970s about the need to restructure the higher education system in response to the growing diversity of students and their talents, motives, and job prospects (see Watts, 1972; OECD, 1973; Trow, 1974; Hermanns, Teichler, and Wasser, 1983; Teichler, 1986b). In a third stage, the optimism of the 1960s was finally replaced in the 1970s by a dramatic pessimism or criticism of the higher education expansion (see Freeman, 1976; Carnoy, 1977; Husén, 1979; Rumberger, 1981; Vincens, 1985): The expansion of higher education seemed to have led to "overeducation" or "overqualification," and efforts to reduce inequality of educational opportunities seemed to have fueled educational "inflation" without having been very successful in making success easier for the hitherto disadvantaged.

During these three stages, a strikingly far-reaching commonality of views could be observed in most Western industrial societies about the major current problems, about the desirable model of higher education and its relationships to the employment system, and about the reforms needed. Shortages of personnel, responses to a diverse student body, and problems due to overeducation were viewed similarly in societies that differed by a ratio of more than 3:1 in their enrollment quotas of the corresponding age groups or in the number of college-trained persons in their labor force (see OECD, 1981, 1984). Thus, a far-reaching consensus could be observed among politicians and scholars. Whereas, in many other educational areas, there were major gaps in communication and mutual influences (Husén and Kogan, 1984), many politicians and planners who emphasized the need of modernizing society in order to promote economic developments and many scholars, especially adherents to the human capital or personnel requirement approaches, communicated closely and were influenced each other. The notion of *overeducation* certainly led to an erosion of the common belief in the suitability of certain theories and policies, but at least at the beginning, this belief was shared by those with a very broad spectrum of political views (see Husén, 1979).

One might, of course, raise the question whether such a far-reaching consensus of views in a given period across countries, politicians and scholars, and different philosophies and political views rested to a certain extent on the mood of the time rather than on detailed insight, that is, on simplification in the face of complexity rather than on appropriate analysis. The paradigmatic force, however, has turned out to be so strong that most dissenting views were also compelled to define their position vis-à-vis those prevailing notions.

The basic questions emerging in the third stage of debates on the relationships between higher education and employment, which are well addressed by such value-laden terms as *overeducation* and *overqualification,* remained the most important focus of political debates and of research, even when a shift of mood took place during the late 1970s and the 1980s. As will be pointed out later, in Europe we no longer see such a single issue dominating the scene. The qualitative links between the content of education and learning, the impact of unemployment and the reduction of overall work time on the relationships between higher education and employment, the challenge of new technologies, and merely adjustments in the relationships between higher education and work, which challenge any dramatic interpretations—all of these issues have become the points of emphasis. There is no longer a single issue shaping the mood of the times. These changes notwithstanding, the tension between the expansion of higher education and the limits on the presumed demands of the employment system have continued in Europe to be—more than any other issue—a common point of departure for a substantial share of research.

Obviously, this debate, which ranges from assumptions that higher education expansion has turned out to be superfluous or even detrimental to emphases on the changing rationales of highly-educated societies, became much more similar in Eastern and Western Europe. In spite of different rationales for economic and social planning as well as differences in employment policies, the issue (what graduates' competences beyond the immediate "demands" of the economy mean) has become increasingly important in Eastern Europe as well (see Sanyal and Jozefowicz, 1978; Ivanov, 1982; Hegedues, von Kopp, and Schmidt, 1982; Buttler, Kluczynski, and Teichler, 1984; Avakov et al., 1984; Korn et al., 1984).

THREE MAJOR TOPICS

This chapter addresses three topics, which play a considerable role in the research conducted in Europe on the relationships between higher education and work:

1. *Changes in the labor market for graduates.* How do the employment opportunities of graduates change in terms of employment or unemployment, the economic and occupational sectors of employment, income and positions, employment conditions, and so on? Research refers to college-trained labor in general as well as to recent graduates in particular; in the latter case, emphasis is also placed on the process of transition from higher education to employment.

2. *Changes in the link between education and work.* Whereas the first theme refers to the typical quantitative and structural descriptors of employment and frequently implies the normative issues of unemployment, employment conditions, and so on, the research addressed here asks for closer ties between the character of education and the character of the employment: To what extent do studies in certain fields lead to "corresponding" jobs? Do higher levels of educational attainment continue to promise similar levels in the occupational hierarchy? To what extent are jobs given to persons who have acquired the suitable competences, or to what extent is their knowledge utilized? Whether strict normative positions regarding "appropriate" employment and work guide the interpretation or whether a looser concepts of acceptable allocation are used, the question in this kind of research is whether a loss of the traditional ties between higher education and work has taken place and how the newly emerging situation can be interpreted.

3. *Expectations by the employment system regarding the competences of graduates.* What kinds of training are in demand? How do persons having a say in the employment and careers of graduates assess certain elements of learning or their formalized results, that is, the credentials? Instead of inferring the rationale of the market actors from labor market processes and instead of taking fields of study or occupational categories as suitable descriptors of sets of knowledge and their utilization, such research is based on the assumption that the relationship between job requirements, on the one hand, and the competences provided by the education system, on the other, are more likely to explain the dynamics of the relationships between higher education and employment.

All three topics have been frequently addressed in many European countries since the mid-1970s, and all three are related to the "overeducation" or "overqualification" debate, which continues to have a substantial impact on research in spite of the increasingly diversified political and scholarly debate in the 1980s. Last but not least, information on basic statistics and on research in these areas is more easily accessible and comparable than research in some other areas.

Whereas the first topic addressed the most obvious indicators of quantitative and structural changes, the two other topics, which had already become popular in the late 1970s, reflect the "qualitative" changes between higher education and work. When it became obvious that the employment systems had absorbed the increased number of graduates more easily than the first dramatic reactions had predicted, the debate began to focus on the latter topics: Do education and employment "decouple" in terms of links between educational level and occupational status and in terms of the utilization of knowledge, or what kind of new links emerge? What kind of competences are most likely to promise satisfactory employment under these conditions of generally worsening employment prospects for the average graduate? A brief overview of two reports written on higher education and employment around 1980 might explain the mood of that time and the role that such issues play in research. One might add, though, that the range of experts' interpretations in Europe at that time certainly was broader than these two examples might show; this question is addressed in the last section, where recent debates are described.

Prevailing Views in Europe Around 1980 on Higher Education and Employment

Two efforts were made around 1980 to summarize the state of knowledge and the prevailing views on higher education and employment in Europe. First, in a comparative analysis of various country reports commissioned by the International Labour Office and by the UNESCO European Centre for Higher Education (CEPES), the British scholars Fulton et al. (1982) addressed commonalities and differences in higher education and manpower planning in "centrally planned and market economies" in Europe. Their report is based on studies of the German Democratic Republic, Hungary, Poland, and Rumania, on the one hand, and of the Federal Republic of Germany, the Netherlands, and Sweden, on the other each provided by scholars from their respective countries. Second, in 1981, the OECD summarized trends and possible future solutions in the relationships between higher education and work for OECD countries (which, in addition to most Western European countries, include Canada, the United States, Japan, Australia, and New Zealand, as well as Yugoslavia). This was done in the context of the conference "Policies for Higher Education in the 1980s" (OECD, 1983b), which also addressed access to higher education, "patterns of authority" as well as financing, and other resources as major policy issues of that time.

Fulton et al. argue that higher education policies in both Western and Eastern Europe address problems caused by "imbalances between demand and supply." Although the expansion of higher education had slowed down, the experts saw a "widening gap between the aspirations and expectations of students and graduates and the job opportunities open to them" (Fulton et al., 1982, p. 1).

Although policies in relating higher education to economic and social needs differ substantially, the authors note a certain degree of convergence in actual developments and problems. In centrally planned economies, "the basic criterion determining the size and structure of higher education is the expected needs of the economy for specific categories of qualified manpower. However, this manpower planning criterion is tempered to some extent by the two alternative aims of encouraging an orientation towards social equality in the provision of higher education and of allowing a measure of individual choice" (ibid., p. 121). In market economies in Europe, "the starting point in planning the future size and structure of higher education is the expected demand for places by individual school-leavers and, increasingly other adults. . . . This basic criterion, however, of planning on the basis of social demand is also somewhat modified in practice, to take account of manpower need in particular areas" (ibid., p. 121).

It might be added at this point that most scholars who have compared higher education policies in the Western industrial societies agree that most Western European countries differ substantially from the United States in putting an emphasis on educational "planning" (see, for example, OECD, 1983a). The German scholar Huefner (1984b, pp. 186–188), for example, suggests placing "higher education and employment systems" in industrialized societies on a "continuum which links the two extremes of the perfect market system on the one side, and the central planning planning system on the other . . ." Huefner considers the United States as being close to the former extreme, because higher education in that country operates "under the rules of market economies"; on the other hand, higher education systems of the socialist countries in Eastern Europe "function as integral part within the context of planned national economies . . ." Several European countries, such as the Federal Republic of Germany, could be considered as a third, a "mixed" type, in which a certain degree of educational planning is considered appropriate in order to provide competences for the somewhat more "fuzzy" needs of a society shaped by a market economy.

Obviously, the Western European countries had experienced a supply of graduates which considerably surpassed the demands in terms of the number of positions offered or, as Fulton et al. (1982, p. 25) phrase it, "employers are willing to hire at certain wage rates." (They suggest using the term *demand* rather than the term *needs,* which ought to be used to describe the number of persons "considered desirable to achieve policy objectives," or the term *requirements,* which refers to skills or the number of persons "technically necessary to achieve certain objectives.") This state of affairs led to the increasing popularity of policies in favor of moderating educational expansion according to manpower demand. On the other hand, Eastern European countries had gradually accepted a broader range of aims guiding educational planning. In the 1970s, these countries faced a problematic process of adjustment to increased manpower supply as well as a need to reconsider methods of projection and planning that take into consideration this broadened range of aims.

Whereas the problems of graduate employment seemed to have renewed an interest in manpower planning both in Eastern and Western Europe, strong criticism was voiced in all the countries analyzed in this comparative study regarding the utility of manpower projections for higher education planning (on forecasting, see Ahamad and Blaug, 1973; Arbeitsgruppen, 1976; Teichler et al., 1980; Clement, 1982; Ivanov, 1982; Huefner, 1984a; Youdi and Hinchliffe, 1985). Diverse conclusions were drawn about either disregarding manpower planning in general, applying broader and more flexible approaches, or establishing more refined and detailed models. According to Fulton et al. (1982) the critics especially emphasized the weakness of traditional manpower approaches in paying "insufficient attention to the precise content and knowledge and skills which are implied by the possession of high-level qualifications" (p. 102).

The British experts share the view that manpower planning has to take into consideration the content of education without, however, suggesting what curricular strategies would fit most easily with the labor market strategies. Whereas, for example, the German labor market expert Mertens (1974) considered emphasis on the promotion of "key qualifications" rather than specific knowledge as essential for easing the absorption of the growing number of graduates, Fulton et al. (1982, pp. 105–106) point at divergent pressures by the employing organizations: partly for general learning and competence, and partly for a more specific and vocational emphasis in higher education.

In their conclusion, the British scholars discuss the appropriate role of higher education planning. They argue that manpower considerations play a considerable role in both Eastern and Western Europe, notwithstanding the limitations of the projections and planning techniques applied; the major difference rests in the extent to which efforts are made to plan the development of higher education. The consequences of both rigid planning and lack of planning suggest, according to their views, the need to implement new, flexible planning approaches: "In the 1970s we are discovering that unplanned expansion can lead to all sorts of social and economic imbalances; while too rigid planning can result in excessive limitation of individual choice. However much the social and economic values underlying the use of these techniques continue to differ, there are increasing pressures leading to a convergence of the technical aspects of alternative planning approaches" (ibid., p. 123).

The OECD report also saw a substantial deterioration of employment prospects for young graduates during the 1970s in most OECD countries. On the one hand, the increased enrollment in higher education, although levelling off somewhat in the 1970s, had led to a much higher supply of new graduates than in the past. On the other hand, the declining economic growth, further drastic measures to keep public expenditures in bounds (thereby reducing job openings in the public sector), and finally, the declining employment opportunities for teachers caused, in many Western industrialized countries, a stagnation or reduction of the job vacancies traditionally filled by graduates. According to the

OECD (1983b, p. 32), this state of affairs required an increasing number of graduates to seek employment in "nontraditional, lower level jobs."

Obviously, the consequences of the oversupply of graduates—if traditional graduate employment is taken as a yardstick—varied substantially from one industrial society to the next: "Whilst in some countries, among which [are] Japan and the United States, such imbalances seem to have been absorbed, in others the size of the gap and the numbers affected may become a matter of concern" (OECD, 1983b, p. 34). The high unemployment among recent graduates in Italy was considered the most striking example of the visible problems.

In deliberating about the possible solutions in the framework of the conference convened on Policies for Higher Education in the 1980s, the OECD did not recommend a contraction of higher education systems. Apart from a general attitude of favoring market-oriented or moderate steering mechanisms rather than strong interventionist policies, fear was expressed that innovation in higher education, which had been encouraged under conditions of growth in the past, might come to a halt. On the other hand, the OECD assumed that a laissez-faire policy (i.e., just hoping for adjustments in terms either of decreasing individual demand for higher education or of absorbing graduates in lower level jobs) was not acceptable for most OECD countries, given the state of the visible problems and the public concern. Rather, suggestions were made to enhance "the employment relevance of higher education studies" (OECD, 1983b, p. 35) in various ways: guiding students toward "more occupationally-relevant courses," "encouraging institutions to be more sensitive to employment problems and to give priority to courses that respond to the requirements of working life," "placing more emphasis on technology and applied subjects," reforming the content and structure of studies and thereby "imparting a more practical orientation of studies," and finally, promoting a "new partnership between higher education and the world of work."

The OECD document refrains, however, from recommending any specific curricular strategy in pursuing "employment relevance" in higher education studies. Among other difficulties, the different traditions in the countries and their higher education systems in emphasizing the pursuit of knowledge, training the mind, or stressing cultural or vocational objectives; the varied preferences of employers for general abilities or specific skills; and finally, the different emphases of higher education systems on preparation for employment, on the one hand, and other spheres of life, on the other hand—all of these differences make it impossible to recommend any "best" solution (OECD, 1983b, p. 36). Rather, the OECD suggested raising the students' and the institutions' awareness of employment requirements, as well as a closer communication between higher education and the world of work, in order to develop varied ways of "enhancing the employment relevance."

Other Research Topics
on Higher Education and Employment

The three major research topics discussed in the following sections obviously do not cover the whole range of research on higher education and work in Europe (some general research overviews on higher education and work, mostly in individual countries, are provided in Anckar, 1985; Archer, 1982; Bjoerklund, 1984; Bodenhoefer, 1981; Bundesministerium fuer Wissenschaft und Forschung, 1985; Huefner, 1984a; Kaiser, 1986; Kluczynski, Szarras, and Teichler, 1986; Lindley, 1981; Teichler, 1979, 1984; Williams, 1984). There is no established convention of categorizing such research areas; one might name the research topics as follows (although they overlap with the three topics discussed in the following sections).

1. *Studies on quantitative and structural demand and supply of graduates.* Forecasts, based on traditions of the manpower requirement approach and similar concepts played an important role in Eastern Europe and several Western European countries as well in the 1960s and the early 1970s. Both criticisms of the methodological and planning implications of such studies and the shift of the dominant notion from *shortage* to *oversupply* of graduates decreased the role that such studies played. Altogether, the number of such studies declined; at the same time, however, more flexible approaches had already developed in the early 1970s (see Youdi and Hinchliffe, 1985).

2. *Studies on returns for educational investments.* This core approach in the human capital theory did not become in Europe at all as popular as it has been in the United States. Some economists emphasized this approach (see Psacharopoulos, 1978, 1986), but the basic rationales—that income differentials explain educational choices and that "social returns" are important indicators of the shortage or oversupply of graduates—were obviously seen in Europe as being too unrealistic.

3. *Theories and studies on the economic, technological, managerial, societal, and cultural determinants of qualification requirements.* A major domain of research on education and work in many European countries addresses the development of the economy and occupational structures and the personnel structure and job requirements in employing organizations; in this approach, one tries to explore to what extent sociopolitical conditions and policies, technological requirements, firm strategies of utilizing the competences of their staff, and so on explain the presumed "requirements" or reactions to the supply of qualifications (see Hegelheimer, 1974; Teichler and Sanyal, 1982). Frequently, detailed analyses of jobs tasks and qualification requirements are included (see van Hoof and Dronkers, 1980; Baethge and Teichler, 1984; Baethge and Overbeck, 1986); another major topic in this area is the rationales of higher education policies and planning (for example, Premfors, 1981; OECD, 1983a;

Teichler, 1983b; "New Forms of Planning in Higher Education," 1984; Oehler et al., 1986; Wolter, 1986; Kellermann, 1986b). These important areas of research are not treated in this overview, because their discussion would require the inclusion of a much broader spectrum of educational levels, as well as of issues of educational policy.

4. *Studies on curricula, teaching, and learning.* As curricular reform was conceived to be one of the major needed responses to the increased employment problems of graduates in the 1970s, it is not surprising to find, that research on teaching and learning, as well as on curricula, more frequently directly addressed the relationship between higher education and work (cf. the overview in Teichler, 1985).

5. *Studies on students.* In research on students' values, orientation, studies, and life emphasis obviously shifted during the 1970s from academic or political values to job prospects and their implications for orientation and study behavior. Views differ about the extent to which students' ways of thinking and acting have changed in the process of educational expansion and in anticipation of changing graduate employment and work (see for example the comparative research presented in Framhein and Langer, 1984; for further examples, see Bargel et al., 1984; Ciucci, 1984; Liebau, 1984; Huber, 1987).

6. *Studies on professions and careers.* Many studies focus on various elements of careers and professions well beyond the labor-market and transition issues already mentioned. Some address single, a few, or a large range of professions and provide information in careers, job assignments, professional values, living and working conditions, and so on (for example Busch et al., 1981; Langer, 1981; Lindley, 1981; Suda, 1981; Holtkamp and Teichler, 1983; Buelow, 1984; Haeyrynen, 1985; Kluczynski and Sanyal, 1985). Some studies focus on special issues of careers and professions, such as the role that credentials play (Dore, 1976; Girod de l'Ain, 1981; Oxenham, 1984); professional control (Goodlad, 1984); or graduates' not getting positions in typical graduate careers (Holtkamp and Teichler, 1981; Sommer, 1986; cf. also Herlyn and Weymann, 1987).

7. *The relationships between higher education and social mobility.* This topic is frequently addressed within the framework of other prime emphases of research, but, except in the U.S., it is not a major theme of research projects per se (see Kaiser, Kolosi, and Robert, 1984).

8. In addition, many further issues have been addressed here and there in research in Europe related to the relationships between higher education and work, for example, credentials and international mobility, the lifelong education of graduates, and part-time study by adults.

A detailed overview of this broad range of research topics in higher education and work in Europe would require improved documentation as well as specific research projects analyzing the research trends.

The Institutional Basis and Resources of Research

Research on higher education in most European countries cannot be claimed to be very well established and well supported (see Altbach, 1985). In several Eastern European countries, large central institutes—notably those in Moscow, Warsaw, and East Berlin—play a leading role. Research on higher education is fairly decentralized in Western Europe; it is predominantly based at institutions of higher education, but government-sponsored research institutes, as well research directly sponsored by government, plays a considerable role (see European Centre for Higher Education, 1981). The major topics of research range widely, as they do in the United States as well; but it is justifiable to generalize that whereas a larger share of higher education research in the U.S. focuses on the inner life of higher education, the links between education and society (including the relationships between higher education and work) are a relatively strong domain of research on higher education in many European countries.

CHANGING EMPLOYMENT OPPORTUNITIES
FOR GRADUATES

Increasing Numbers of Graduates

As pointed out in many studies on the quantitative and structural developments in higher education (Cerych, Colton, and Jallade, 1981; OECD, 1981, 1984; UNESCO-CEPES, 1983; Wolter, 1986; Oehler et al., 1986), enrollment quotas continued to grow in the 1970s and 1980s, though there had been a short-term stagnation or decline in some countries, as well as a general leveling off of growth in most Western and some Eastern European countries. Thus, it is not surprising to find that the number of graduates continues to increase in many European countries, as the following data show.

1. The number of university first-degree graduates in the United Kingdom rose from 53,000 in 1976 to 68,800 in 1983 and declined thereafter to 67,400 in 1985; the number of polytechnic graduates increased from 11,600 to 28,500 in 1985. The overall increase in nine years was 25% in the case of universities and 146% in the case of polytechnics. The number of graduates from other colleges increased from 2,700 in 1980 to 7,600 in 1985 (Harrison and Gretton, 1987, p. 51).

2. The number of graduates from all French institutions of higher education increased by 21%, from 132,700 in 1972–1973 to 216,700 in 1979–1980 (Vincens, 1986, p. 10). As for universities only, the number of graduates in 1983 was 18% higher than in 1975 (Neave, 1986, p. 72).

3. The number of all final examinations passed at institutions of higher

education in the Federal Republic of Germany rose by 21% from 117,300 in 1975 to 141,500 in 1984 (Federal Ministry of Education and Science, 1986, p. 76).

4. In Sweden, the number of graduates from all institutions of higher education was 31,800 in 1977–1978 and increased by 14% to 36,100 in 1983–1984. In the subsequent year, the absolute number declined to 33,900 (Statistiska centralbyran, 1986b, p. 2).

5. The number of Dutch university graduates increased by 50% in eight years from 9,900 in 1975–1976 to 14,900 in 1983–1984 (Neave, 1986, p. 92).

6. A comparative study of higher education in eight higher education systems in Western Europe shows that the number of university graduates (excluding graduates from other institutions of higher education) from 1975 to 1983 increased from 10% to 40% in all cases except in Spain, where there was an increase of 88%—from 39,300 to 73,700 university graduates—during that period (Neave, 1986, pp. 17 and 44).

7. During the 1970s (contrary to the development in the 1960s), the absolute number of graduates increased in most Eastern European countries in faster rates than in Western Europe. The relative increase from 1970 to 1982 was highest in Czechoslovakia (from 18,400 to 31,000) and Poland (from 47,100 to 75,900) and lowest in the German Democratic Republic (from 22,300 to 25,000). In the USSR, the number of graduates rose by 33% from 631,000 in 1970 to 841,000 in 1982 (Wolter, 1986, p. 53).

In some Western European countries, large-scale representative surveys are conducted annually or biannually describing the situation of new graduates about half a year or one year after graduation. In some countries, regular unemployment statistics are available on college-trained labor or specifically on new graduates. In almost all countries, we find, at least, surveys, which are not regularly conducted, on all graduates or on graduates from individual fields of study or on specific sectors of the higher education system. Such surveys may provide information on (1) employment status (employed/unemployed/continued education, etc.); (2) employment conditions (regular/temporary/partial employment, income, etc.); (3) occupation (economic sector, occupational group, and relatedness of employment to education); and (4) differences of employment opportunities by type of higher education (institution, field of study, etc.). Comparative secondary analyses were been conducted the 1970s (Tessaring and Werner, 1975, 1981) but have not been available since then.

In this section, we provide only selected findings of surveys which are representative of all graduates or of major sectors (from certain institutions or fields) of the country under consideration; the emphasis is on data which allow one to examine changes over time. This presentation of the findings and interpretation is aimed at answering the question of how graduate employment, especially the employment of recent graduates, in Western European countries has changed since the mid-1970s. We focus here on issues of employment status (i.e., unemployment, period of job search, and employment conditions) whereas information regarding the "appropriateness" of employment is treated in the next section.

Examples of Information Available for Selected Countries

In the United Kingdom, the Careers Advisory Service of each university conducts, at the end of each year, a survey of the status of those persons who graduated that year (see Tarsh, 1985; J. Taylor, 1986); similar surveys are conducted on graduates from other institutions of higher education in England and Wales as well. The data show that the unemployment of recent university graduates increased from about 5% in the latter half of the 1970s to 10% or more in the 1980s (J. Taylor, 1986, p. 18). The rate of unemployed recent graduates from polytechnical institutions was continuously somewhat higher than that of recent university graduates and shows the same historical trend. Both curves reflect the overall unemployment in Britain, which increased from 3% in 1974 to 6% in 1980 and 12% in 1983 (see Tarsh, 1985, p. 272). In most overviews on the findings of these regular surveys, "unemployment" includes graduates in "short-term" employment; according to this definition, the "unemployment" rate of recent university graduates increased from 7% in 1979 to 17% in 1983, and that of recent polytechnic graduates from 10% to 20%. The unemployment rate of female graduates was somewhat higher than that of their male colleagues in the 1970s, but it has been more-or-less identical since 1980 (ibid.).

The share of graduates from British institutions of higher education opting for further education and training upon the completion of a degree decreased substantially, from 34% in 1976 to 25% in 1983 (J. Taylor, 1986, p. 28). As regards type of employment, short-term employment decreased compared with regular employment. By and large, the gap of job opportunities between most science, engineering, and business fields and most other fields seems to have widened over time (Burns, 1980; Tarsh, 1985). In 1985, the percentage of recent male university graduates who were either unemployed or short-term employed ranged from 4% in accountancy, 6%–8% in engineering fields, and 8% in business to more than 30% in most humanities and social science fields and even to 42% in botany and 47% in zoology (Harrison and Gretton, 1987, p. 56). As regards sectors of employment the percentage of recent graduates employed in public service (excluding education) declined: among male graduates, from 25% in 1976 to 21% in 1985, and among females, from 42% to 31%. A major relative increase could be observed in commerce, however: the percentage of recent male graduates employed there rose during that period from 20% to 28%, and of recent female graduates, from 19% to 32% (ibid., p. 59).

In Switzerland, biannual surveys conducted since 1977 provide an overview of the employment of new graduates from all Swiss universities about one year after graduation (see Morgenthaler, 1986). The percentage of unemployed recent graduates in 1983 and 1985 (5.1% and 4.4%) turned out to be higher than in the preceding surveys (2.2%–2.6%). As in Britain, the percentage of graduates declined who did not seek employment but who opted instead for further learning and other activities. As regards the kind of employment, the Swiss surveys indicate an increase in part-time employment, a growing transition of graduates to the private sector of the economy, and a growing number of graduates reporting having taken positions not requiring a degree. Altogether, the gap between good employment opportunities in most fields clearly linked to certain employment sectors and shaky employment opportunities in fields not clearly linked as well as in teacher training has widened over time. In 1985, the unemployment rate for graduates in chemistry and economics was less than 2%, whereas it was higher than 10% for psychology and social science graduates. It might be added that the unemployment of graduates from mechanical engineering (6.7%) was clearly above average.

In the Federal Republic of Germany, no regular surveys on recent graduates are available. The number of college-trained unemployed persons increased from between 30,000 and 40,000 during the latter half of the 1970s to 60,000 in 1981 and to 117,000 in 1985 (114,000 in 1986). This development is, by and large, in tune with growing unemployment in general: the ratio of the graduate employment rate to the total unemployment rate increased only slightly and not in a continuous process. In 1975, the unemployment rate of university-trained labor was 1.5%, that of graduates from other institutions of higher education 3.2%, and that of the total labor force was 4.4%; the corresponding figures were 2.1%, 2.0%, and 3.4% in 1980, and 4.8%, 4.9%, and 8.6% in 1984 (Teichler, 1986a, pp. 77–78). A detailed analysis of the unemployment statistics shows that the unemployment of graduates searching for their first job increased more than proportionally, and that female graduates in general and graduates of teacher training and some humanities and social science, as well as architecture, have been most strongly affected (Baethge et al., 1986, 115–126). The available statistics indicate an increase in college-trained labor of about 50% from 1970 to 1982. Whereas the absolute numbers stagnated among scientists and artists, the number of graduates working as (middle-level) technicians, office workers, and sales workers, as well as those working in knowledge and cultural occupations others than education, more than duplicated during that period (ibid., pp. 24–25). There are obvious changes of employment according to economic sectors, but not—as expected by some experts—along the public-private sector division: graduate employment increased strongly in some private and some public sectors while being more or less stagnant in some private as well as in some public sectors; thus, private services other than trade and commerce turn out to be the fastest growing employment sector for graduates (Hegelheimer, 1984; Baethge et al., 1986).

These examples should suffice to demonstrate the different kinds of data bases in Western European countries on graduate employment. Data from other countries will be included in some later comparative discussions of graduate employment.

Development of Graduate Unemployment

In many Western European countries, the unemployment of recent graduates, as well as unemployment among college-trained labor has become an issue of increasing concern. Graduate unemployment in the 1980s has become much higher than it was in the late 1970s. The cases of the three countries discussed in detail above show a great similarity. An additional country might be mentioned: In the Netherlands, the absolute numbers of unemployed university-trained persons and of unemployed persons having completed nonuniversity higher education (*hoger beroepsonderwijs*) tripled from 1979 to 1983; the unemployment rates rose from about 3% to about 8% and 10%, respectively (Netherlands Ministry of Education and Science, 1985, pp. 27–31). According to the changed registration system introduced in the mid-1980s, the absolute number of university-trained persons being unemployed increased by 32% from 12,100 in 1983 to 16,000 in 1986 (Ministerie van Onderwijs en Wetenschappen, 1986, p. 2); almost half the unemployed university-trained persons had graduated recently and were waiting for their first regular job after graduation (Schut, 1987, p. 2). Even in Austria, where unemployment in the latter half of the 1970s was lower than in most other Western European countries, the registered unemployment of university-trained labor quadrupled from 1978 to 1983 (Lassnigg, 1985, p. 24).

The increase in graduate unemployment is not an isolated phenomenon; rather, it reflects an overall rise of unemployment in most Western European countries since the late 1970s. As a rule, the unemployment rate for college-trained labor has remained substantially lower than that of the total labor force. In the Netherlands, for example, the unemployment rate for college-trained persons was 8%–10% in 1983, but the overall rate was registered as 17%; or in the summer of 1986, the rate of unemployed university-trained persons in the Netherlands was, according to the changed registration system of unemployment, 6.5%, as compared to the overall unemployment rate of 12.5% (Ministerie van Onderwijs en Wetenschappen, 1986, p. 2). The corresponding ratios were somewhat more than 1% and 4% in Sweden (Swedish Ministry of Education and Cultural Affairs, 1985, p. 34) and 5% as compared to 9% in the Federal Republic Germany (Teichler, 1986a, p. 78).

Italy turns out to be an exception to the above-stated dominant trends. In 1978, the unemployment rate of university-trained persons (7.4%) was slightly higher than of the total labor force (7.2%). During the subsequent years, graduate unemployment declined to 6.2% in 1983, whereas overall unemployment increased to 9.9% (Jarousse and de Francesco, 1984, p. 216).

The data differ in the Western European countries regarding the ratios of graduate unemployment to unemployment among the total labor force. Whereas in some countries, such as the Federal Republic of Germany and the Netherlands, the advantages of graduates in this respect seem to have declined slightly over time (or even substantially, in Austria), statistics from some other countries show the reverse trend. In France, the unemployment of graduates increased much less during the 1970s than the unemployment of youth without a degree from an institution of higher education (Jarousse and de Francesco, 1984, p. 96). In Italy, the unemployment of young graduates, which is traditionally high and reflects a long period of search for appropriate jobs, remained on the same level from 1978 to 1983, whereas the unemployment of young people who had not completed academic secondary school substantially increased (ibid., p. 216). As regards the total Italian labor force, the unemployment of university-trained labor decreased, whereas the overall unemployment rate increased during that period, as already mentioned above.

The data available hardly allow any exact comparative conclusion about the difficulties of graduates in various European countries in finding a job. Certainly, Swedish or Swiss graduates seem to face fewer problems than graduates from the other countries referred to above, but any more detailed comparisons face considerable difficulties. First, the methods of registering unemployment in these countries differ substantially (Hitz, 1986). This was demonstrated strikingly when a decision was made by the Netherlands in 1986 to change its system of registration and thereby to reduce the number of registered unemployed by more a third. As another example, Austrian data show that the unemployment rate among university-trained labor is more than three times as high when established by microcensus data (2.7% in 1983), than if calculated on the basis of registered unemployment (0.8%; see Lassnigg, 1985, p. 24). Second, it is difficult to assess to what extent a certain rate of graduate unemployment is considered a serious issue per se, or to what extent it may be considered low, because a comparison of this rate with the overall employment rate in that country shapes the minds of those concerned. Third, the rate of unemployment may be strongly influenced by the timing of the survey. In addition, there are different customs as regards the timing and periods of job search; nine months of job search for a graduate may be considered typical in one country, whereas it may be considered a serious problem in another country.

Job Search Period

Many surveys on recent graduates provide data on the duration of the period needed after graduation to find a job. For example, among Swiss graduates of 1984 employed in 1985, 47% reported that they had either continued in the jobs they had held while being enrolled or had started working immediately on graduation. The transition period lasted up to 3 months for 30% of graduates, 4–6 months for 15%, and more than 6 months for 8% (Morgenthaler, 1986, p. 55).

Among Swedish graduates in 1984–85 who were employed one year after graduation, three quarters had been employed immediately after graduation or after less than 1 month of additional search. A further 19% had got jobs within 4 months after graduation. Only 4% took more than 4 months to find employment (Statistiska centralbyran, 1986a, p. 20).

Various German surveys indicate that a job search period of almost 6 months is now the average for graduates (see Kaiser, Nuthmann, and Stegmann, 1986). One has to keep in mind, though, that such data do not tell the complete story because they do not include those who remain unemployed for a long period.

As has already pointed pointed out, job searches tend to be extraordinarily long in Italy. In 1983, 28% of university-trained persons younger than 30 were reported as being unemployed. Once regular employment is found, the risk of again being unemployed hardly exists: Among university-trained Italians 30 years old and older, the unemployment rate is only 2% (Jarousse and de Francesco, 1984, p. 216).

In France, too, search periods tend to be long. According to a survey in the early 1980s, 13.7% of university graduates (10.7% of men and 16.5% of women) were unemployed 9 months after graduation (Ministère de l'Education Nationale, 1985, p. 30).

Altogether, the data available suggest that in those countries in which the unemployment of college-trained persons increased in the 1980s over that in the late 1970s, the average search period also became longer for those who succeeded in getting a job during the year after graduation.

Unstable Employment and Prolonged Learning

The unemployment rates and the length of job search are by no means the only indicators of problems in the transition from studies to employment. Students may also prolong their studies before graduation or continue study after graduation because of problems they anticipate or have experienced in the job search; they may accept employment considered to be transitory or shaky employment conditions. Such problems are additionally addressed in many surveys and form (in addition to employment-nonemployment, already discussed, and to the issue of the appropriateness of employment as regards status, utilization of knowledge, etc., which will be discussed later) a third group of indicators of problems in graduate employment.

One has to bear in mind, though, that prolonged study, part-time work, a contract for a limited time span, and so on are not per se indicators of employment problems. Most surveys addressing large numbers of graduates with the help of short questionnaires usually do not provide any information about whether such phenomena are "involuntary" or not.

As regards employment indicators of that kind, the British surveys examine the percentage of recent graduates who are in short-term employment. Since the definition changed at the end of 1970s, a decrease of that share from about 6%–7% in the latter half of the 1970s to about 3% in the 1980s (J. Taylor, 1986, p. 28) may be an artifact. The regular Swiss surveys showed that the number of recent graduates regularly employed (i.e., whose contract does not name any fixed time span) was 42% in 1981, 37% in 1983, and 42% in 1985 (Morgenthaler, 1985, p. 231; 1986, p. 62). The Swedish surveys ask similarly about regular employment: The 1985 rate was 53% among recent graduates (Statistiska centralbyran, 1986a, p. 24).

As regards continued education after graduation, both the Swiss and the British surveys show a decline in recent years. In the Federal Republic of Germany, the percentage of students enrolled at institutions of higher education who had been already obtained a degree remained constant at a level of 12%–13% from 1973 to 1983 (Bundesminister fuer Bildung und Wissenschaft, 1985, pp. 144–5); the increase in the length of time taken to complete a first degree, which can be observed during that period, has to be attributed primarily to a more frequent choice of long courses rather than to a deliberate prolonging of the time in school (Reissert, 1983). Thus, the data do not confirm the argument frequently put forward in Germany that universities are graduately becoming "waiting rooms" (see the criticism of that argument in Baethge et al., 1986, pp. 140–142ff.).

The few data available on change over time, such as those reported in the preceding paragraphs, challenge the widespread assumption that both general employment problems and the growing proportion of graduates among new-job seekers has led to the increased involuntary study and the deteriorating employment conditions among graduates. The data base certainly is too weak to clearly "falsify" such views, but there is obviously a need to reconsider the conventional wisdom. One explanation may be found in the increasing polarization of employment opportunities for graduates from different fields and sectors; detailed studies might well show that the increased "involuntary" additional studies and the increased deterioration of employment conditions for the graduates in some sectors are "balanced" statistically by corresponding decreases in other sectors. Another explanation could be that dim employment prospects lead many graduates to seek quick employment and stable positions by lowering their expectations regarding income, status, and utilization of knowledge.

The findings underscore the difficulty in inferring the problems in job searches for graduates on the basis of data such as partial and short-term employment, further learning, and so on. This difficulty reveals the need of a more direct approach in analyzing problems in the transition from studies to employment. Among the regular large-scale surveys conducted in European countries, only the Swiss surveys provide such direct information.

First, the graduates are asked: "Due to changes in the labor market which have been observed for a few years, problems might occur in the search for employment. Did you face such problems?" Of the 1984 graduates, 46% replied affirmatively in 1985. This percentage differed substantially according to field of study: from 6% (theology) to 89% (forestry). By and large, problems are more frequently reported by graduates in fields in which both employment per se and appropriate employment are hard to find. There are, however, notable exceptions: graduates in medicine frequently stress problems in finding a job (77%) (see Morgenthaler, 1986, pp. 43–45).

Second, the Swiss graduates were asked what kind of solutions they had chosen, if they had faced such problems. This approach had been developed in some surveys conducted in the Federal Republic of Germany (Hochschul-Informations-System, 1980; Kaiser et al., 1981). About 15% of the graduates reported that they had tried to solve such problems by accepting a smaller income in order to secure a job related their competencies, by being geographically mobile, and by acquiring additional qualifications. About 11% stated that they had accepted up to half a year of unemployment. Only very few graduates (2–3% in each category) had tried to find a solution by accepting jobs not related to their education, by working abroad, or by choosing "alternative" ways of living and working (see Morgenthaler, 1986, p. 49).

Third, the graduates not working full time were asked whether their working part time work was voluntary or not. Altogether, of all graduates working, 72% did so full time, 22% voluntarily part time, and only 6% "involuntarily" part-time (ibid., pp. 64–67).

Fourth, graduates were asked to compare their present position with their long-term occupational goals; 7% considered their employment one year after graduation as just an interim solution which was not related to their long-term goals (ibid., p. 78).

Not surprisingly, the Swiss researchers showed that the different types of problems are cumulative. Their data allow the conclusion that about a tenth of all Swiss graduates who are employed one year after graduation have faced serious problems in looking for a job.

Different Employment Opportunities by Field of Study

All surveys which allow an analysis of change over time and all experts' assessments agree in observing a widening gap of employment opportunities by field of studies in Western European countries. The problems for graduates in some fields were substantially aggravated in the 1980s, as far as the length of the search, regular employment, status and income, or getting jobs at all after some period is concerned, whereas recent graduates from other fields continue, as their fellow graduates in the late 1970s did, to face many fewer problems. In most countries, there is a shortage of graduates in a few fields.

The trend toward the widening of this gap can be observed for at least a decade. There are no indicators that market mechanisms will solve the problem. Certainly, the number of students opting for "marketable" fields seems to have increased over time in many European countries (see, for example, the overview in Williams, 1985), but those adjustments remain small in comparison to the differences in employment perspectives. In the country reports provided to the OECD in the framework of the project "The Role and Functions of the Universities" in the mid-1980s, only the U.S. report indicates a dramatic shift of students' options toward "marketable" fields of study.

As regards those fields whose graduates face severe problems, and those fields whose graduates seem to be in demand, W. Taylor (1986) summarizes in the general report of that OECD study: "Any attempt to compare the relative success in the labor market of graduates from different disciplines is vitiated by lack of common categorisation. In general terms, graduates in physics, chemistry, earth sciences and technology have less problems in obtaining employment than those in languages, letters and social sciences" (p. 79).

A detailed analysis of the data available from different countries leads to doubts even about such cautious generalizations. Some examples follow.

In France, a survey conducted in 1983 on university graduates nine month after graduation showed that the unemployment rate of the graduates from most science fields was relatively low; for graduates of chemistry and earth sciences, however, the unemployment rate was substantially higher than that for all graduates (18.3% as compared to 13.7%). On the other hand, the unemployment rate for humanities graduates (12.0%) was below the average (Ministère de l'Education Nationale, 1985, p. 30).

In Austria, employment in the late 1970s and the early 1980s was relatively high for university-trained persons in the humanities and the social sciences who had not been prepared for the teaching profession, and it was also high for those in the natural science fields, except for mathematics and physics (Lassnigg and Schramm, 1985, pp. 100–103).

In Sweden, the highest unemployment rates for 1984–1985 graduates one year after graduation were observed in general humanities (19%), biology (9%), and mechanical engineering (8%), as compared to 3% for all recent graduates. If we take long duration of job search as a yardstick, employment problems seem to be grave for graduates in the fine arts, library science, and chemistry (Statistiska centralbyran, 1986a, pp. 16, 20).

In the United Kingdom, the unemployment rates for recent male university graduates were in 1985, as already reported, especially high for graduates in zoology and botany and also above average in most humanities and social science fields, whereas low rates could be observed in accountancy, business, and most engineering fields. As regards all (male and female) polytechnic graduates, the highest rates of "unemployment" (including short-term employment) were reported for graduates in the humanities, except for foreign languages; there was a very high rate, too, for graduates in the fine arts, sociology, and a few science areas (Harrison and Gretton, 1987, p. 56).

In the Federal Republic of Germany, the statistics on registered unemployment indicate a very high unemployment rate for university-trained labor in the fields of psychology, sociology, and political science. In addition, unemployment is very high among architects, but this rate is not visible in the official statistics, which put architects and civil engineers into one category. Finally, among young university-trained persons, the unemployment of teachers is increasing rapidly in the 1980s (see Tessaring, 1982; Teichler, 1983b, pp. 100–101; Baethge et al., 1986, pp. 115–126). Among graduates from other institutions of higher education, social workers are most strongly affected by unemployment (Kaiser et al., 1981).

In Switzerland, too, the highest unemployment rates for recent graduates surveyed in 1985 were reported in the social sciences and psychology, whereas the unemployment rates for graduates in business and electrical engineering were low; the unemployment rate in mechanical engineering was higher than average. Involuntary part-time employment was relatively frequent among graduates in the humanities, in all science fields except chemistry, in education, and in psychology (Morgenthaler, 1986, pp. 34, 65).

In the Netherlands, higher unemployment rates for university-trained persons in 1986 were reported in the humanities, the social sciences, and biology (15%–20%), whereas as unemployment in the medical, legal, and economic fields was below the average of graduate unemployment. Dutch government publications provide two indicators: First, the ratio of the number of unemployed university-trained persons to the number of recent graduates was, in 1986, highest in the social sciences, followed by the humanities and the natural sciences (between 1.6:1 and 1.3:1); it was somewhat lower in the medical fields and considerably lower in engineering, law, and economics (between 0.6:1 and 0.3:1). Second, the ratio of the long-term unemployed to all unemployed ranged, in 1986, from more than 59%–53% in the former fields of studies to 42%–45% in the latter fields of studies and, finally, 35% in medical fields (Ministerie van Onderwijs en Wetenschappen, 1986, pp. 2–3). Thus, the two indicators substantially differ in their ranking of employment problems by fields only in the cases of persons in the medical fields: They face unemployment almost as frequently as the average graduate, but the unemployment periods seem to be the shortest.

In summarizing the findings from various Western European countries, we find relatively few problems in getting jobs for graduates in most economic and engineering fields. Also, most graduates in the medical and legal fields do not face serious problems, in spite of increasing complaints in some countries about deteriorating prospects. As for the sciences, some fields seem to be in high demand and others face serious problems, but the fields whose graduates face large employment problems vary substantially from one country to the other. In most Western European countries, graduates in the social sciences and the humanities face more employment difficulties than average. In some countries, they face the most serious problems, and in others fewer problems than graduates in some science fields; in all countries, we observe a broad range in the degree of problems that graduates in various humanities and social science fields face. Generalizations in this respect can hardly be made for various reasons: The proportions of students studying in those fields vary substantially from one European country to another. Also, the recruitment strategies of employers in those fields are quite diverse. Finally, the link of those fields to teacher training varies substantially: In some Western European countries, teacher training courses are provided for persons who have completed a first degree (for example, in France, except for primary-school teachers, and in the United Kingdom), whereas in other countries all or at least major sectors of teacher training are part of the studies for the first degree (i.e., in most German-speaking countries, except for primary education, and in most Scandinavian countries); thus, the declining job opportunities for teachers lead to completely different employment problems for recent graduates.

Different Employment
Opportunities by Type of Institution

The various studies discussed above shed very little light on differences by types of institutions of higher education. In Sweden, the statistics on graduation and employment do not provide such information because all institutions of higher education have been called *hoegskolan* since 1977. Most surveys quoted from France, Italy, Austria, Switzerland, and the Federal Republic of Germany address either the universities only or do not provide the same kind of data for both universities and other institutions of higher education.

As far as data are available, they do not show a common pattern in Western Europe. For example, surveys conducted in Britain suggest that opportunities of getting employment without substantial difficulty and more-or-less in the range of acceptable positions are more favorable for university graduates than for graduates from polytechnical and other institutions of higher education: the rate of recent university graduates who were unemployed or short-term employed continued to be lower than that of the polytechnical graduates from the mid-1970s to the mid-1980s (Harrison and Gretton, 1987, pp. 54–6).

In the Federal Republic of Germany, the unemployment rate of university-trained persons was lower than that of persons having graduated from *Fachhochschulen* during the late 1960s, but since about 1980, the rates for persons at both degree levels have been more or less the same. If one follows the public debates, the most serious unemployment problems seem to be those of graduates from teacher training, political science, sociology, and psychology, that is, fields provided only in the university sector. There are, however, similar employment problems for graduates in social work as well, who are predominantly trained by *Fachhochschulen* and comprise a large share of graduates from this type of nonuniversity higher-education institutions.

In France, graduates from *instituts universitaires de technologie* (IUTs) and *grandes écoles* are generally believed to have much more favorable labor market prospects than graduates from universities. This is in part due to the fact that IUTs predominantly provide courses in engineering and that *grandes écoles* train most of their students in engineering, business, and public administration (i.e., fields which, in general, lead clearly to certain occupational areas).

Altogether, it might be justified to argue that differences by field of study are more important than differences by institutions of higher education, as far as problems in transition from studies to work are concerned. In this respect, the situation has not changed during the 1980s from the pattern that had already emerged during the 1970s (Furth, 1982). In order to avoid misunderstandings, we should stress that the data discussed here do not say anything about differences in status, income, and so on between university graduates and graduates of other institutions of higher education.

Employment Opportunities for Male and Female Graduates

The data provided by the surveys discussed above indicate, as could be expected from other research available on women in education and employment (see the overview in OECD, 1986), more problems for women than for men in the transition process from education to employment.

In Britain in 1976, the percentage of female graduates being either unemployed or short-term employed six months after graduation was 4%–5% higher than that of men (21% as compared to 17% in the case of universities, and 25% and 21% in the case of polytechnics); in 1985, this difference was only 2%–3% (17%/ 15% and 24%/21%; see Harrison and Gresson, 1987, p. 55). This remaining difference has to be attributed to a higher share of short-term employment and not, however, to unemployment (see Tarsh, 1985). As already mentioned, the increasing shift from graduate employment in public service to employment in commerce has affected women more strongly than men. In 1984, the percentage of recent female university graduates taking over secretarial, clerical, and manual positions was twice as high as that of male graduates (8% and 4%; see Harrison and Gretton, 1987, p. 58).

A survey conducted in 1983 of graduates from French universities nine months after graduation shows that 16.5% of women were still unemployed at that time, as compared to 10.7% of men. A survey conducted in 1982 on graduates from selected universities about a year after graduation indicates somewhat smaller, but still considerable, differences according to sex within the same fields of study (Jarousse and de Francesco, 1984, p. 104).

In Switzerland, the percentage of recent female graduates who were unemployed in 1985 was twice as high as that of male graduates (6.9% and 3.4%, respectively). The survey also shows that women more frequently face unfavorable employment conditions and inappropriate employment. If one compares men and women within major disciplinary groups, the disadvantages for women are stronger for those in the humanities and the social sciences than in other fields (Morgenthaler, 1986, pp. 89–91).

In the Federal Republic of Germany, the unemployment rate of university-trained women was 5.7% in September 1983 as compared to 3.8% of men. In the case of persons having graduated from nonuniversity higher-education institutions, the unemployment rate for women was 8.9%, as compared to 4.0% for men. Data are not available for differences in the same fields of study.

According to the Austrian microcensus of 1983, the percentage of university-trained women who were unemployed was 8.3%, whereas the corresponding rate for men was only 0.5% (Lassnigg, 1985, pp. 24–25). One can assume that these figures also include some persons who are not seeking employment.

As far as the data are available, they indicate more frequent and more serious employment problems for female than for male graduates. Obviously this difference can be explained only in part by the fact that women traditionally opt more frequently for those fields in which graduates have faced relatively serious problems in the 1980s. There are also obvious differences among Western European countries in the degree to which female graduates face more serious problems than male graduates.

"APPROPRIATE" EMPLOYMENT AND "UTILIZATION OF KNOWLEDGE"

One of the most popular and at the same time most controversial topics both in higher education policy and in research on higher education and work in Europe is "adequate" or "appropriate" employment. The unemployment of graduates might seem to be a more obvious indicator of the problems a graduate faces, but it turns out not to be the most frequent problem. Critics of educational expansion, especially, many of whom predicted substantial unemployment of graduates, began to emphasize overeducation, overqualification, the displacement of nongraduates by graduates, misallocation, underutilization, and so on, once it became obvious that in all European countries, graduate unemployment remained substantially lower than average unemployment. In addition, in Eastern European countries, underutilization of competences or dissatisfaction with jobs or salaries also became a potential indicator of oversupply (see Sanyal and Jozefowicz, 1978; Chuprunov, Avakov, and Jiltsov, 1984, pp. 72–77).

This section provides an overview of the diversity of methods used in Europe to measure how many graduates are inappropriately employed and how many graduates make little use of the knowledge they have acquired. For each of the studies introduced, we summarize the major findings. This analysis does not cover the extent to which "appropriate" employment and limited utilization of knowledge may have increased since the mid-1970s, because most of the relevant surveys do not allow an examination of such changes. "Cross-sectional" approaches (i.e., efforts to infer historical changes from differences by age group) are inappropriate: For example, in one survey conducted in the Federal Republic of Germany, elder college-trained persons considered their work more complex and satisfying than young college-trained persons (Stooss, 1979), but this effect is more likely to be the result of career patterns than of historical changes in employment opportunities. In addition, the following analysis shows that the degree to which the presumed overeducation occurs in the results of surveys is due to a large extent to the concepts of the researchers and the methods used in their surveys.

Occupational Categories

Employment statistics frequently serve as a basis for assessing the percentage of graduates being inappropriately employed. This approach has also been frequently taken by U.S. and Japanese experts to prove that a growing proportion of graduates are employed in administrative middle-level occupations, sales occupations, and manual work. For example, one can show that the proportion of college-trained persons in such categories in increased in the United States from 15.4% in 1970 to 27.9% in 1982 (Sargent, 1984, p. 4). Similarly, the percentage of recent Japanese university graduates (bachelor level) employed in such occupational groups increased from 49.7% in 1975 to 58.4% in 1985 (Monbushô , 1986, pp. 94–97; see also Ushiogi, 1984). Similar approaches have been taken in many European studies as well.

For example, Vincens (1986, p. 55) considers those graduates to be most downgraded whose jobs are categorized as *employés* and *ouvriers*. In 1985, 2.5% of university-trained men and 7.7% of women (as well as 8.1% of men and 21.9% of women having completed short-cycle higher education) were registered in those categories.

Similarly, one can show that 5% of recent graduates from British universities in 1985 entered secretarial, clerical, and manual occupations. The corresponding figure for graduates from polytechnical institutions was 6%, and for those from other colleges, 14% (Harrison and Gretton, 1987, p. 57).

Analyses based on this approach certainly provide more-or-less clear evidence that an increasing number of graduates have taken office or sales positions in the last two decades, whereas the percentage of graduates employed in blue-collar occupations has not consistently increased (see, for example, Vincens, 1986). The data are frequently criticized for not being adequate to assess inappropriate employment. On the one hand, they are misleading in suggesting that "inappropriate employment" is more likely for graduates in the humanities and social science fields than for those in the science and engineering fields; this, however, might be a statistical artifact, because employment statistics in many countries put engineers and middle-level technicians in one occupational category (such as "technical professions") but differentiate administrative personnel (e.g., management may be differentiated from other office and sales occupations); thus, "vertical substitution," i.e., a process whereby jobs are filled by persons with higher education levels than their predecessors, seems to take place only in the latter areas and is bound to be overlooked in the former areas. For example, if one disaggregates the census and microcensus data available in the Federal Republic of Germany, the proportion of university-trained persons working as "technicians" among all university-trained persons in higher technical and scientific positions seems to have increased from 5% in 1970 to 9% in 1982, a finding that tends to be overlooked in most studies; however, the corresponding figure of university-trained persons in middle-level office occupations among all university-trained persons in administrative occupations (the figure usually presented in various statistical overviews) remained constant at 30% during the same period (see Baethge et al., 1986, pp. 24–25). On the other hand, some occupations categorized as "middle-level occupations" may be more demanding than the occupational category suggests, as was found, for example, in surveys in the United States that examined differences in self-ratings of the utilization of education by occupational groups (see Solmon, Bisconti, and Ochsner, 1977).

General Assessment of the Relationship
Between Studies and Work

Many surveys ask graduates to assess how they view the relationship between their studies and their work. A very general assessment is used in annual surveys of recent graduates in Sweden one year after graduation. Graduates are asked whether the training, which they had completed in the previous year, was completely, somewhat, or not at all suitable to their present work assignment. Altogether, 70% of the 1984 graduates reported in 1985 that their education was (completely) suitable to their jobs; about 60% of science and engineering, social science, and arts graduates; 73% of teacher-training graduates; and 83% of graduates in medical fields. Altogether, 24% perceived a partially suitable relationship, and 5% replied that their education did not fit their work assignment at all (Statistiska centralbyran, 1986a, pp. 9, 28).

Other studies that also used a single question related to that topic have addressed the degree to which the knowledge acquired during study was utilized at work. Among university-trained persons in the Federal Republic of Germany questioned in 1979 in a representative survey, 57% reported that they did use the knowledge acquired during their studies. This share varied considerably according to subjects: It was especially high among graduates in the medical fields and in law (83% and 81%), about average among graduates in the humanities, engineering, and science (59%, 57%, and 56%), and below average for graduates in economics and the social sciences (50%), as well as for those in teacher training (44%); the latter percentage was as low as the average one obtained from graduates of nonuniversity institutions of higher education (*Akademiker in Deutschland,* 1980, p. 177).

Predecessors and Suitable Successors

In several surveys in Western European countries, graduates were asked about the educational attainment of their predecessors, an approach that was first used in the late 1960s in a German study on the employment of political science graduates (Hartung, Nuthmann, and Winterhager, 1970). For example, 7% of the recent Swiss graduates surveyed in 1985 reported that they had taken positions previously held by nongraduates (Morgenthaler, 1986, p. 75). This approach describes the process of vertical substitution in more detail than the above-mentioned approach, but it does not provide any evidence about "overeducation": vertical substitution may take place, in some cases, because a higher level of education is considered desirable for proper job performance and, in other cases, merely as a consequence of an increased supply of graduates, professional pressures for upgrading, and so on. The substitution itself does not provide any explanation.

One survey, however, shows directly that graduates who have taken positions previously held by nongraduates frequently do not consider a degree essential to their job. Of university-trained Austrian engineers surveyed in the early 1980s who had taken positions previously held by nongraduates, 61% said that their work could have been done by nongraduates. The corresponding figure for engineers who had taken positions from graduates was 31%, and for engineers whose positions had been newly established, 21% (Bodenhoefer and Ofner, 1986, p. 43).

Several studies have taken another approach introduced by Hartung et al. (1970) in asking graduates to assess globally the suitable relationships between education and employment; that is, they asked graduates what, according to their view, the most suitable education would be for their successors. According to a survey conducted in Poland in 1979 addressing graduates one year after graduation, 55% of the respondents considered the same educational level appropriate for their potential successors; 11% suggested a higher level (i.e., advanced higher education); and 33% considered a lower level (no degree) to be appropriate. The percentage that considered the same educational level appropriate ranged from 61% of graduates in physics to as low as 27% in the economic fields (Buttler, 1984, pp. 178–179). Similarly, some surveys asked respondents to name the most suitable educational level for their current job. As an example, the representative survey on college-trained persons in the Federal Republic of Germany conducted in 1979, which has already been referred to above, showed that 3% of the respondents did not see any necessity for college education in the accomplishment of their tasks (Stooss, 1979, p. 616).

Credentials as Indispensable Prerequisites

At the next stage of complexity, replies to two or three general questions are used to create an index of appropriate employment. For example, in a comparative study in the winter of 1981–1982, persons graduating in 1980 from some Italian and French universities had been asked to assess the correspondence between higher education and work in two ways. First, rather than being asked, like Swedish graduates, whether their education was suitable to their jobs, these French and Italian graduates were asked whether the job fit their education: "Does your current job correspond to your university training?" The authors categorized those replying "no" as being "misallocated." In addition, the graduates were asked, "Do you know of people without degrees who do the same job as yourself?" Those replying affirmatively were categorized as "underutilized" by the authors. Replies to both questions were combined into one index of "adequately utilized"; "partially utilized," if only "misallocation" was observed; and "underutilized," if the second question was replied to affirmatively (no matter what the reply was to the former question; see Jarousse and de Francesco, 1984, p. 50; the English preview of the survey in de Francesco and Jarousse, 1983, pp. 69–70, is somewhat misleading).

According to this definition, the authors came to the conclusion that 58% of Italian graduates were adequately utilized [sic!], 8% were partially utilized, and 34% were underutilized. The corresponding percentages in France were 44%, 22%, and 34%. Both surveys included graduates in a few subjects only. The percentage of adequately employed Italian graduates was 71% in law, 66% in economics and business, and 43% in the humanities. The corresponding figures were 52% for French business and economics graduates and 34% for French humanities graduates (Jarousse and de Francesco, 1984, pp. 108 and 227). The data suggest that in both countries, the competences of humanities graduates are more likely to be underutilized than those of graduates in the economic fields. In addition, one can conclude that in both fields, the Italian graduates surveyed reported more frequent utilization than French graduates.

If we compare the findings of the surveys discussed above to the results in this study, we could conclude, for example, that Swedish arts graduates have a far better chance of utilizing their competences in their job role than their French and Italian colleagues, and that French and Italian graduates in the economic and law fields have a comparatively limited chance of finding appropriate employment. One might argue, though, that the somewhat more complex questions asked in the French-Italian survey are misleading: If nongraduates do jobs similar to those of graduates, this does not necessarily prove underutilization of the graduates' competences; rather, it may indicate a flexible and permeable employment sector that makes allowances for experience gained on the job instead of being controlled by credentials. The definition of underutilization chosen by Jarousse and de Francesco seems to be inappropriately strict and thus inflates the findings of "inappropriate" employment.

Acceptance of Jobs Clearly Unrelated to Training

Another approach in creating an index of "inadequate" employment based on very few questions was taken in a Swiss survey conducted in 1985. First, the graduates were asked whether their employers had required a degree for their position. Of the 1984 graduates, 17% replied that their employers had not required a degree—an increase over the 13% of 1982 graduates surveyed in 1983. The percentages differed dramatically according to the field of study: from 1% in medicine and 9% in science, on the one hand, to 44% in the social sciences, 30% in the humanities, and 27% in the economic fields, on the other hand (1985 data). Among those reporting that their employers had not necessarily required a degree, only those were categorized as being inadequately employed who reported additionally that they had faced difficulties in finding a job and had either "accepted a job hardly related to their training for financial reasons" or "turned instead to a job hardly related to their training and not matching their monetary expectations." Only 3% of Swiss graduates are "inadequately employed" according to this definition (Morgenthaler, 1986, pp. 74–79), among them hardly any medical and engineering graduates, but about 10% of the humanities graduates.

As opposed to the authors of the French-Italian study, the Swiss researchers assumed that a position for which a degree was not necessarily required could nevertheless be appropriate: The graduates might make use of their knowledge as they would have in positions where a degree was formally required or where most persons in similar positions were degree-holders. One might argue, however, that the additional criterion used by the Swiss researchers in order to define the "inadequately employed" graduates was relatively strict; compared to other studies, the Swiss study may have belittled the problem of inadequate employment because of the method chosen.

Appropriate Level, Relationship Between Field and Occupation, and Utilization of Knowledge

One interesting example of a complex model used to assess the utilization of competences with the help of a very small set of questions is provided by a study conducted in Poland in 1979 (Kluczynski and Sanyal, 1985) on university-trained economists. The researchers combined the replies to three questions to yield a typology of "match between qualifications and job": (1) whether the job corresponded to the profession and its specifications (relevant, partly relevant, or irrelevant); (2) whether higher education was necessary for the job the graduate was performing or whether lower levels of education would do; and (3) to what extent knowledge acquired in higher studies was utilized (full, to a high degree, partial, to a low degree, or not utilized). The researchers (ibid., p. 144) called the types:

1. Good match (28% of women, 42% of men).
2. Surplus of qualifications (15%/22%).
3. Lack of qualification (16%/8%).
4. Partial match (16%/8%).
5. Waste of qualifications (14%/9%).
6. Loss of qualification (8%/5%).
7. Bad match (3%/5%).

There is one component in the typology (Type 3) that the other surveys completely overlooked or at least did not address directly: The graduate might take over a position typically held by nongraduates because he or she was not as well qualified as a typical degree-holder should be. It might be added here that the (frequently made) simplistic inference about the amount of "overeducation" in society, which is made on the basis of the percentage of graduates considering themselves inadequately employed, may also overlook the possibility of a reverse "mismatch"; that is, positions requiring a degree may be held by nongraduates. Thus, graduates' surveys will not suffice. An employers' survey conducted in the Federal Republic of Germany in the late 1970s showed that, according to employers' assessments, the number of positions held by nongraduates that would have been better held by graduates was as large as the number of positions held by graduates that could have been held by nongraduates (see Stooss, 1979).

In addition, the Polish researchers combined answers to a list of job characteristics ("Makes me to decide on my own," "Requires managing other workers and giving instructions," "Is boring," etc.) into an index of work complexity. Not surprisingly, the need of a higher education and the complexity of a job thus defined were closely related: 83% of the economists surveyed, whose work seemed to be highly complex, considered a higher education degree necessary for their job; if, however, the work seemed to be of low complexity, only 25% considered a degree necessary (Kluczynski and Sanyal, 1985, p. 139).

Varied Dimensions of "Appropriateness"

Other studies cast doubt on efforts to establish a single index of appropriate graduate employment at all, because the dimensions of appropriateness turn out to be quite heterogeneous. A job might be considered appropriate as regards one dimension (for example, the degree of knowledge utilized) and might, at the same time, be considered inappropriate as regards another dimension (for example, the position held). This heterogeneity can be demonstrated by means of a comparison between fields of study in a survey on graduates two years after graduation conducted in 1985–1986 in the Federal Republic of Germany.

According to this survey, graduates in mechanical engineering (71%) and economic fields (64%) much more frequently considered their income appropriate than graduates in social work (37%). The average income of the graduates in mechanical engineering turned out to be 64% and that of the graduates in economic fields to be 57% higher than that of the graduates in social work. The same order of fields, but much smaller differences, is visible in replies to a question about whether the graduates considered their position appropriate (61%, 56%, and 52%, respectively).

On the other hand, graduates in social work (85%) more frequently considered their field to be suitable to their assignment than those in the engineering (78%) and economic fields (73%). They also utilized, according to their own view, their skills and knowledge more frequently, either predominantly (29%) or partially (58%), than graduates in economic fields (26% and 53%) and those in engineering (21% and 57%).

As regards the necessity of a college education for the job, graduates in the economic fields (as in some of the other surveys previously mentioned) more frequently raised doubts than one would expect on the basis of other indicators of "inappropriate" employment. Of graduates in those fields, 24% considered a college degree not to be necessary for their job as compared to 13% of the graduates in each of the other fields of study surveyed (*Kasseler Hochschulabsolventenv-verlaufsstudie,* 1986, pp. 108–114).

Three dimensions are addressed in these examples: (1) status; (2) content of education and work; and (3) a clear versus a blurred borderline between the functions of graduates and nongraduates in the corresponding employment areas.

In criticizing restrictive concepts on "inappropriate employment," Teichler (1978) suggested taking into consideration at least the following dimensions: income; social benefits; nonmonetary income; prestige; power and influence; leisure and communication networks; utilization of skills; interesting and satisfying work; complex job tasks; the disposition of time, personnel, and material resources; and career and training opportunities. This approach is based on the observation that in the process of the expansion of higher education, an increasing number of graduates consider positions of lesser status to be acceptable if the work is complex and interesting, and that graduates have become more and more diverse in their occupational values (see also Baethge et al., 1986).

One way of following such an approach is just to ask graduates about the different dimensions of status, utilization of knowledge, complexity of assignment, autonomy, and so on, without aggregating the findings—that is, just to demonstrate the diversity. In a survey conducted in the southwestern state of Baden-Wuerttemberg of the Federal Republic in 1979, only 4% of persons having graduated four or five years earlier from institutions of higher education considered their jobs monotonous; 6% had hardly any say about the rhythm of their work; 16% could not determine their assignment in a cooperative manner with their superiors and colleagues; and 4% did not have any chance to realize their ideas and views on the job (Kaiser et al., 1981, pp. 100–104).

One has to note, though, that such an approach is not suitable for comparing the degree of "appropriate" employment between graduates and nongraduates. For example, the number of college-trained persons in the Federal Republic of Germany reporting that they were not continuously supervised hardly surpassed the corresponding share of all the labour force not being continuously supervised (50% and 47%; see *Akademiker in Deutschland,* 1980, p. 32); this does not mean, however, that graduates and nongraduates are supervised in the same way.

The authors of a survey on education graduates (Diplom-Paedagogen) conducted in the late 1970s in the Federal Republic of Germany (Busch and Hommerich, 1981; see also Hommerich, 1986) went a step further. They examined the correlation between a general notion of an "appropriate job" and various dimensions typically addressed in surveys on job satisfaction, such as the characteristics of the job, the colleagues, the employing organization, the supervisors, the working conditions in general, and the income and the opportunities for promotion. Thus, they provided evidence that the "appropriateness" of a job seems to be, at least for graduates in that field, closely linked to elements of the organization of the work and the working conditions (i.e., "open" organization, nonbureaucratic organization, limited supervision, and high decision-making power).

The Diversity of Criteria for "Appropriateness"

Obviously, a broad range of indicators has to be taken into consideration in any analysis of the relationships between studies and work that tries to establish how many graduates do not have "appropriate work." A comparison of various research approaches does not allow the conclusion that certain criteria are the most suitable ones. This result does not mean, however, that complex research models have turned out to be unsatisfactory. On the contrary, they have been important in demonstrating the preoccupations underlying many simple research approaches and many arguments in the political debate on the consequences of higher education expansion. Rather, the difficulties in choosing a limited set of clear criteria for analyzing what work is "appropriate" to one's studies reflect the diversity of the links existing between higher education and work.

First, the differences between occupational sectors are striking as regards the typical distinctions between traditional graduate jobs and lower-level positions and whether the borderlines between levels of positions have traditionally been very clear or vague. For example, vertical distinctions between job roles may be more clearly established in public employing organizations than in private ones, in large organizations than in small ones, in production sectors than in administrative sectors, and in typical professional organizations (e.g., law firms and schools) than in occupational areas comprising a continuous vertical job structure.

Second, there are obviously distinct cultures in various disciplines and in various occupations as regards values and perceptions, what a desirable high-level job is and what a proper link between education and work means. Income, status, complex and demanding work, disposition and autonomy, job security, utilization of knowledge, and so on, are differently evaluated in different sectors.

Third, it is generally assumed that students' and graduates' values regarding employment and work and regarding the relationships between education and employment have changed in the 1970s and 1980s. Interesting, demanding, relevant, and relatively autonomous work seems to be highly appreciated by a growing number of students and graduates. This suggests that absorption in jobs not outstanding in status terms may be more frequently considered appropriately than in the past. In any event, changes in appropriate employment according to set criteria can hardly be measured exactly, if most of the research in this area relies on graduates' views, and if those views change over time.

This does not mean, however, that the issue of "inappropriate" employment has become obsolete. There are indicators, on the one hand, that a growing number of graduates take positions that lack some elements of the jobs traditionally considered typical for graduates in general or considered typical for graduates in a particular field of study. On the other hand, the number of graduates in European countries taking jobs that are strikingly inappropriate by all standards for appropriate graduate employment has increased much less in the 1970s and 1980s than pessimistic statements widespread in the 1970s had predicted (see, for example, the analysis of Teichler, 1988). In addition, the values of students and graduates have seemed to change with regard to desirable jobs. Most research in this area in European countries does not suggest that graduates have just adapted their views to the changing job prospects, although, according to many experts' views, this may have been the case in the United States and in Japan. Rather, many graduates in Europe seem to have upheld certain expectations about work and the relationships between their studies and their work. The reactions to changed relations between higher education and work differ: adaptation, disappointment, an emphasis on the value of certain dimensions of jobs, an active shaping of the job that underscores the utilization of knowledge and that may change the job in accordance with the expectations held, and so on. Many of these responses to changing employment opportunities are obviously based on a vision of appropriateness—a vision, however, that is not in all cases as static and defensive as the "overeducation" approach suggests.

EMPLOYERS' EXPECTATIONS AND RECRUITMENT CRITERIA

Employers' Views: A New Major Research Emphasis

Most research on the relationships between higher education and work is based on higher-education or labor-market statistics or on surveys addressing students or graduates. The views and actions of the employing organizations are not, in most cases, analyzed at all or are analyzed only indirectly: in several surveys, graduates have been asked about the recruitment and personnel policies they experienced during their job search or thereafter; also data on job offerings frequently serve as a starting point for speculations on "demand" and employers' rationales.

Two major reasons can be given that have led to an increasing curiosity about the employers' views of the relationships between higher education and work:

First, the "overeducation" debate speculated to such an extent about the rationales of both the students and graduates and the employers that direct evidence had to be sought for. Most concepts that were put forward by economists on education and employment and that gained popularity in the 1960s, especially human capital concepts and, to some extent, the manpower requirement approach, analyzed numbers of graduates, positions, employed persons, educational expenditures, income, and other "objective" data; their interpretations were based on stereotyped model assumptions about the motives and rationales of the actors: if the *Homo oeconomicus* happens to be a student, he or she will opt for higher education if the return for educational investment is more profitable than the corresponding capital investment; the *Homo oeconomicus* on the other side of the market (the employer) is assumed to change salaries constantly according to productivity and market conditions and employs as many graduates as are clearly required by technological and economic needs. When, however, in the 1970s almost everybody concerned believed that the number of graduates surpassed the presumed "demand" substantially, employers continued to employ more graduates, and students continued to opt for higher education in larger numbers than seemed to be appropriate on the basis of such assumptions, these concepts could obviously not claim clear proof. Subsequently, many additional assumptions were introduced about the employers' rationales in order to save or modify the explanatory models.

For example, employers might reward higher credentials as indicators of a higher level of ability and might thus reinforce the screening processes taking place in the education system, even though the competences acquired at university were superfluous; or the private employers might have to pay higher salaries for graduates than were justified in terms of the utility of their knowledge in order to lure some talented graduates away from the public employers, who, according to such claims, provided substantial income advantages for graduates because of bureaucratic routine. Or students might continue to attend college in spite of deteriorating employment opportunities because they disregarded information, hoped to be exceptions to the rule, took study as a consumption good, appreciated the nonmonetary benefits of graduate employment, or even substituted the economic rationale by "postindustrial" values. No matter which speculation could claim most plausibility, it became obvious that the "objective" data analyzed so far could not provide anymore evidence by itself and needed to be supplemented by research on the rationales of all the major actors, including those of the employers.

Second, most experts agreed in the 1970s that the higher education policies of the past had overemphasized the quantitative relationships between higher education and employment and had not sufficiently taken into consideration the institutional patterns of the higher educational system and other structural aspects, as well as the content of learning and of job tasks. This argument was put forward in many connections, for example, in criticisms of educational expansion as diluting the quality of competences or in criticisms of manpower requirement forecasts for ignoring the possible differences in competences between persons formally holding the same degree, and also in criticisms that emphasized the importance of employers' expectations: As the employment prospects for graduates deteriorated and the employers' position in the labor market became stronger, the kind of structures of institutions and curricular approaches that were likely to be rewarded in the employment system became one of the most important or even the most important criterion in many debates on higher education reform in the 1970s.

Approaches of a British and a German Research Project

From among the various research projects conducted on employers' expectations of higher education and on employers' ways of recruiting graduates, personnel policies, and so on, two projects are summarized here because they addressed almost the same topics, chose almost the same methods, and were conducted simultaneously in 1981–1982 in Britain and in the Federal Republic of Germany. Both the British project (Roizen and Jepson, 1985; see also Kogan, 1984) and the German project (Teichler, Buttgereit, and Holtkamp, 1984; see also Buttgereit, 1983, 1984) analyzed the processes and criteria used in recruiting new graduates by conducting interviews with the heads of personnel offices or other persons in charge of recruiting graduates.

As these publications show, both projects analyzed in detail the stages of the recruitment process; the criteria and methods applied during those stages; the role that personnel officers played in the recruitment process; the relative weight placed on various types of competences and skills, on certain fields of study, on graduating from certain institutions of higher education, and on other kinds of information associated with credentials; and finally, the critical views of the employing organizations regarding the competences of graduates as well as their expectations and recommendations about innovation and reform in higher education. Also, the presentation of findings in the two projects is quite similar in their use of extensive quotation and their interpretation of these complex statements; the main thrust of the reports is to demonstrate and interpret the reasoning of the interviewees.

Some differences between the two research projects have to be mentioned: The British study intended to provide a fairly representative overview of all employing organizations; the 139 organizations that were finally included comprise small and large firms, some government agencies, and so on but also includes a very large, possibly overproportionate, share of commerce and other private services. The German study includes 47 of the 100 largest industry and private services firms, more than two thirds of them industrial firms; employers of large numbers of graduates were selected based on the assumption that these employing organizations were more likely to acquire a systematic basis of knowledge of the relationships between higher education and work and were also more likely to act or react strategically on changes in technology or economy and on changes in the supply of graduates. The British study focused on the employers' views, expectations and policies; in this framework, the researchers put an emphasis on such issues as the expected competences, preferences for certain institutions of higher education, the "shortages" felt, and suggestions put forward by the interviewees for higher education reforms. The German study emphasized more strongly the details of the recruitment process. This "procedural" approach was based on the assumption that otherwise the representatives of the employing organizations might reply in a stereotypical way, rather than providing valid information on the criteria really shaping the decisions implied in the recruitment process. Also, the German study tried to elicit detailed information on the role played by various aspects of the information provided by credentials, such as grades and marks and the courses chosen; further, the German study discussed recruitment in the context of initial training and early career stages. Finally, it might be pointed out that the German study (cautiously) quantified the findings, in addition to presenting of many examples, whereas the British study provided information about the frequency of certain views in a more general way ("many," "few," "generally," "typical for" certain branches, etc.).

There is a considerable number of surveys available on recruitment criteria or qualification requirements as viewed by representatives of the employment system, which have chosen written questionnaires for the collection of information. Teichler et al. (1984) criticized such approaches as being methodologically inappropriate. According to their view, the standardized questionnaires on recruitment criteria are, as a rule, misleading in three ways.

First, they put together in the same list of items two incomparable categories: competences (knowledge of mathematics, problem-solving ability, etc.), on the one hand, and sources of information (grades, institution of higher education, etc.), on the other. A certain source of information, such as the institution that a candidate comes from, may be considered by the respondents as an indicator of certain competences, but the relative weight of such an indicator cannot be compared directly to the weight placed on individual competence criteria.

Second, such standardized surveys do not recognize that the weight of certain sources cannot be established because the sources are frequently not independent. For example, those personnel officers who do not consider grades or the institutions of higher education separately but weigh the grades according their assumptions about the differences of standards between institutions of higher education (for example consider an "A" at Institution X to be equivalent to a "B" at Institution Y) cannot disentangle the different weights they place on grades and on the institutions.

Finally, the authors of the German study argue that personnel officers might, at most, be able to provide information on what they are looking for in a certain stage of the recruitment process, but they do not know what the aggregate weight of certain criteria is for the total recruitment process, in which, for example, academic competences may play an important role in the first selection stages, and general attitudes and social skills may play an important role in the final selection. The authors claim that many personnel officers overestimate the weight placed on the different criteria that play an important role at the most time-consuming stages of the recruitment and selection process.

Diversity of Employers' Views

The authors of both the British and the German studies emphasize one finding very strongly in all parts of their reports: a great variety in the employing organizations in terms of both recruitment procedures and selection criteria and expectations regarding the graduates' competences in general. This finding of extraordinarily diverse rationales and recruitment exercises is strongly emphasized by the authors of both studies because it contrasts with the popular notions of the requirements of *the* employers or *the* employment system. The various types of procedures used by the employing organizations surveyed, as well as the major emphases on criteria, do not seem to be closely related to certain economic sectors, types of firms, and so on, apart from certain procedural preferences of large firms and apart from the somewhat different priorities in the criteria for technical positions and for administrative or commercial positions. This variety leads, first, to the conclusion that individual employing organizations develop their own styles and strategies of recruitment, rather than being predominantly driven by a logic of technology or economy that determines qualification requirements. Second, as is strongly pointed out in the German study, the institutions of higher education and the students are under much less pressure to strive for the single best set of curricula and competences in order to secure employability than popular debates tend to suggest.

The Recruitment Process

The descriptions of recruitment procedures differ in the two studies: Whereas the British study explains in detail the degree of centralization or decentralization of recruitment in large firms, the German study puts an emphasis on the different roles of management, personnel officers, and supervisors of the prospective new employees in the recruitment process. A comparison of the reports suggests that personnel officers in both countries play an important role in the early stages of recruitment, as well as in securing a certain degree of homogeneity of recruitment in a firm. In the later stages of final decision, however, they hardly seem to have any say in Britain, whereas several German respondents reported an important advisory or participatory role for personnel officers in this final stage or, in some cases, even in the final decision, especially if persons are being hired for administrative or commercial positions.

As regards the search and selection process, one difference between the two countries is worth mentioning. Most British firms employing a considerable number of graduates conduct a "milk round"; the personnel officers make a tour of institutions of higher education in order to conduct preselection interviewees. Many employing organizations invite only a small number of promising candidates to the firm for a second interview. The German firms, on the other hand, do no on-campus interviewing; they are more likely to invite a larger number of graduates for interviews and, in some cases, for tests at the firm. On average, one in six applicants will be invited to the employing organizations, and one in seven persons invited will be offered a position. These figures are certainly not representative of the employment opportunities or of the difficulties that German graduates experience in the job search process. Instead, they are indicative of the strong market positions of the large employing organizations that were surveyed in the German study; however, they do indicate that a relatively high number of applicants are invited for interviews to these firms. The typical procedures in both Britain and Germany have specific strengths and weaknesses, which are discussed below. The pattern popular in Germany creates some frustration on the part of the personnel officers: their position in selecting candidates is strong as regards screening the files, when the information base is limited anyway, but relatively weak when it comes to interviews, that is, when their competence in discovering talents—from their point of view certainly much superior to that of the supervisors of the prospective new employees—could be utilized most effectively. However, German personnel officers have put all their professional pride in increasing their say in the final selection process, and this policy seems to have been successful in a substantial number of firms.

Institutions of Higher Education Given Preference

As regards selection criteria, the two studies differ because of the differences on the higher education systems of Britain and the Federal Republic of Germany. In Britain (this generalized description does not take fully into account all the characteristics of Scottish higher education), the universities differ substantially according to prestige, quality, and attractiveness to students, although the quality differences are considered much narrower than, for example, in Japan or in the United States. In addition, the British nonuniversity sector (i.e., the polytechnics and colleges of higher education) is unique in neither differing from the universities in the length of prior schooling required for admission nor in their duration of course programs and or the degrees granted; British higher education policies have aimed at emphasizing a similar level of competences as well as a more practical curricular approach in the former institutions (see Becher, Embling, and Kogan, 1977).

Roizen and Jepson (1985) confirmed the view that employers perceive a considerable hierarchy of quality differences among universities and strive for a large share of new graduates from the more prestigious universities. In their presentation of interviewees' replies and their interpretations, these authors emphasized another finding as being most striking: a strong preference of most employing organizations for university graduates rather than for graduates from "public" institutions (i.e., polytechnics and other colleges). The authors came to the conclusion that most employers differentiate much more clearly between universities and other institutions of higher education in their preferences and their perception of quality than British public policies emphasize. The authors even went so far as to conclude that market forces in Britain affecting both higher education and employment proved to be dominant and demonstrated "the impotence of government policy makers" (Roizen and Jepson, 1985, p. 97).

One has to add, though, that many British experts doubt whether employers' preferences clearly confirm the popular views about institutional prestige and quality hierarchies. As regards differences among universities, J. Taylor (1986) shows that differences in the unemployment rate and in the permanent employment rate by university, as shown by regular surveys of recent graduates, can be attributed primarily to the instability of the market over time and to a mix of subjects that may be found at various universities. As regards differences between universities and other institutions of higher education, some experts have criticized Roizen and Jepson's findings as being somewhat exaggerated. Certainly, the study itself shows that many employing organizations try to overcome the uncertainties of recruitment by employing a substantial number of persons on the basis of experience gained through "sandwich programs" and "sponsorships," which allow the firms to get to know candidates on the job rather than only on the basis of "paper" and interviews; this approach to selection gives some edge to students in polytechnics and thus may counterbalance, to some extent, the general preference of many employers for university graduates.

In the Federal Republic of Germany, the universities were fairly homogeneous in quality, and most students enroll in the university of their region. *Fachhochschulen* differ from universities not only in taking a more vocational approach, but also in the length and type of schooling required for admission and in the shorter duration of study (see Peisert and Framhein, 1978). The German survey addressed the question of whether representatives of employing organizations perceive substantial differences of quality among universities, as some experts have recently claimed in Germany (cf. the overview on the literature and the diverse interpretations in Framhein, 1983; Rau, 1984; Teichler, 1986c). Teichler et al. (1984, p. 91) rated only 7 firms as strongly emphasizing the individual institution of higher education, whereas 24 weighed the institution somewhat, and 14 did not even have a recruitment policy based on university quality, contrary to widespread rumors regarding differences in quality between universities. On the basis of their findings, the authors concluded that employers emphasize institutional hierarchies much less that they are believed to do in public debates on higher education and employment in the Federal Republic of Germany. In most cases in which the interviewees talked about "good" universities during the interviews, they were referring to specific programs and to training in special production techniques used by the firm, rather than to the quality of a department or a university as a whole; on the other hand, several interviewees criticized two universities, combining their reservations about these universities' left-wing political environments with claims that these institutions were too lenient in their standards and thereby did not guarantee a minimum standard for acquiring a degree. The authors admitted, however, that employers might place more emphasis on differences between individual institutions of higher education than was visible in the study's findings, for some interviewees might have been reluctant to be candid with the interviewers.

On the other hand, the German study addressed the employers' views about the relationships between the universities and other institutions of higher education. The authors showed that about half of the firms foresee different career paths for graduates of the two kinds of institutions, with some overlap in the long run; although almost half of the employing organizations did not recruit the graduates of these two types of institutions separately, they were more likely to put the majority of university graduates in somewhat higher entry positions. Hardly any of the large firms surveyed provided the same career opportunities for graduates from both types of institutions. The authors concluded that many employers like to claim in debates on higher education and employment that these career opportunities are the same in order discourage a further increase of enrollment at the universities.

It might be added at this point that many interviewees seemed to regret somewhat the role that grades or the institution that the applicants came from played in the recruitment process. Some interviewees deemphasized the role of these criteria, although it was obvious that they played a considerable role in the early stages of the recruitment process. Some personnel officers blamed their colleagues in the firm for being too stereotyped regarding these criteria. Some respondents expressed their regret that the limited information available on the candidates in the application files or the pressure to economize in recruitment procedures might force them not to be completely fair to all candidates or might lead them to overlook some talents. Whether British recruiters select some institutions on their "milk round" and exclude others, or whether German recruiters screen the limited information available in the application files, the procedure still enforces a more generalized judgment about the information associated with credentials, whether it is the grades, the institutions, or anything else, than many persons, especially those in charge of recruitment, would ideally consider appropriate.

Weight Placed on Grades

As regards marks or grades, the majority of British and German employers seem to agree that, on the whole, better grades indicate better candidates. In the Federal Republic of Germany, several surveys confirm that employers stress grades (in most cases, only the grades on the final exam at college) as the most important information provided by the education system on the graduates' competence (von Landsberg, 1985; see the overview on various studies in Teichler, 1986c). On the other hand, many British interviewees also considered grades at the completion of high school (number of A-levels and marks) as fairly valid indicators. Preferences for graduates from certain universities or for university graduates in general, as compared to graduates of polytechnics, were frequently explained in terms of the differences in the high school credentials of their student body.

This does not mean, however, that employing organizations rely heavily on college grades in their recruitment. The authors of the German study, for example, rated 5 firms analyzed as emphasizing grades very strongly, 11 strongly, 12 moderately, and 10 marginally or not at all (Teichler et al., 1984, p. 56). Again, many preferences may be due to the specific style of recruitment of the individual firm, but some qualifications were mentioned frequently in both studies and seem to indicate general patterns, as follows.

The employers consider grades important in their recruitment of "specialists." It is interesting to note in this context that views seem to differ from one country to another regarding the graduates of which fields are be considered specialists in this respect: Whereas the British employers emphasized grades for graduates in accountancy, law, and science, many German employers considered engineers high-level experts whose diploma thesis, for example, might be an important predictor of achievement on the job. On the other hand, many employers considered differences between grades as weak predictors or even as meaningless, as long as a certain minimum level of qualification was given, for job performance in many areas of administration, sales, and so on. In this context, a survey conducted in Poland provides interesting findings: Representatives of employing organizations rated 66% of those graduates as being well prepared for their jobs by their studies who had the highest marks ("very good") at university. The corresponding figures were 58% in the case of graduates with good marks and 55% in the case of students who had just passed. The author took this finding as striking evidence how much the views of the universities and the employers differ as regards a good graduate (Buttler, 1983, pp. 104–105).

Some interviewees in both countries emphasized that they were reluctant to recruit very high achievers because they might not fit into the world of work and might become disappointed if they were not constantly provided with challenging tasks.

If the value of grades as criteria for recruitment is put into question, the arguments vary substantially. In addition to the above-mentioned point of view (that the employing organizations and the universities might differ in their view of what competences are needed and should be rewarded), three other arguments put forward by some interviewees challenge the validity of grades in terms of the goals and criteria of the higher education institutions themselves: First, grades conferred in exams may be accidental in some cases and may not represent the student's level of competence adequately. Second, standards in grading differ and may be balanced only in part if the differences in grading of different institutions of higher education are known. Finally, some teaching staff—and especially teaching staff at lower-ranking institutions—may be too lenient in their grading. A comparison of the two studies suggests that German employers more frequently question the validity of grading at German institutions of higher education than their British colleagues do.

Again, as discussed in the previous section on the role that the institution of higher education plays in the recruitment criteria, one has to keep in mind that grades may be more important selection criteria than personnel officers admit because they play a considerable role in the first stage of selection, which tends to be underestimated in comparison to the final stage. Even some German interviewees who reported that those who conduct interviews deliberately remain ignorant of the candidates' grades in order to avoid any "bias" regard the overall role of grades as being inevitably important given the limited information available in the first stage of hiring.

Weight Placed on General Versus Specific Competences and on Social Skills

The two studies discussed here show that both British and German employers vary substantially in their preferences for very specific skills or more general competences as well as in the role that values, attitudes, social skills, and so on play in recruiting graduates; also in both countries, specific skills and cognitive competences are more likely to play a role in positions requiring scientific, technical, legal, and accounting knowledge than in other positions. On the whole, a comparison of the two studies confirms the view that German employers continue to put more emphasis on the knowledge acquired, on specific qualifications, and on cognitive competences in general as a basis of problem solving, whereas British employers are more likely, even in many technical areas, to search for the trained mind in general and are also more likely to put a substantial weight on attitudes and social skills. These different findings fit the statistical data from the 1970s showing that German industry and trade firms hired less than half a percent of graduates from fields of study not considered related to the private economy (e.g., the humanities, sociology, and political science), whereas more than 5% of graduates employed in private firms in Britain were arts-degree holders (see for example Butler, 1978; Holtkamp and Teichler, 1981). Apart from the different traditions regarding the relationships between education and work, a second difference is worth mentioning in this respect: It is not surprising that German employers expect a higher level of specific competences after the nineteen or so years of learning that the German graduates are likely to have completed when they graduate (German universities do not award any degree commensurate with the baccalaureate) than British employers expect of graduates who have mostly been awarded a baccalaureate.

Both studies confirm the conventional wisdom that a very important rationale in recruitment interviews and other assessment techniques is to explore the attitudes and the social skills of the candidates. Complaints are widespread in employing organizations that there is a shortage graduates considered to be well prepared for the job in those respects. The British and German studies also confirm that such characteristics are more strongly emphasized in recruitment for administrative and commercial positions, and that they also frequently play a role in the recruitment of engineers and scientists as well. In this respect, the findings are by and large in tune with those of other studies that have aimed at providing more detailed lists of the most frequently preferred characteristics. For example, a German survey conducted in 1985 names as the most frequent ''nonspecific'' requirements for highly qualified personnel in the technical sector (1) effort, achievement orientation, and so on; (2) leadership potentials; (3) creativity; (4) ability to cooperate; (5) ability to carry things out and follow them through; and (6) problem-solving abilities (von Landsberg, 1986, p. 16). Both of the surveys discussed show, however, that the relative weight placed on these characteristics differ among employing organizations. The authors of the German study argued that such criteria may play a lesser role in most firms than the public debate or many less complex surveys on employers' expectations suggest.

In the above-mentioned general report of an OECD project on ''The Role and Functions of the Universities,'' W. Taylor (1986, pp. 77–78) pointed out three types of ''attempts to strengthen the linkages between the content of higher education courses and occupational performance''; first, courses ''closely tailored'' to specific job requirements; second, ''to build curricula round a core of skills and knowledge deemed to be relevant in a wide variety of tasks and occupational contexts''; third, relying ''on developing the powers of the mind and strengthening dispositions favorable to subsequent success'' (i.e., working hard, team work, and responsibility). W. Taylor suggested not only that the British survey discussed here indicates exactly that the third approach is dominant, but also that this approach is the one rightly preferred by employers in general, given the labor market imperfections, the difficulties in predicting performance and future requirements, and finally, the difficulties in dismissing employees later on. The findings of the two surveys discussed here, however, suggest that Taylor's summary overgeneralizes the views held by some employers (more frequently represented in Britain than in Germany) and held about certain graduates. Certainly, most employers criticize "narrow specialization" and lack of the attitudes and the social skills preferred in the employment system, but many employers view either very specific skills or a somewhat broader range of firm knowledge to be the indispensable preparation for a job, which higher education has to provide; many employers also believe that professional socialization on the job may make up for some of the deficiencies in attitudes and social skills that they observe among recent graduates.

Employers' Views on Higher Education

The two studies indicate some similarities between the employers in Britain and in the Federal Republic of Germany in their way of assessing higher education systems and of recommending changes. First, most personnel officers or other persons in charge of graduate recruitment are much less concerned about the details of the structure of the higher education system, the content of courses, and so on than representatives of the higher education system tend to believe. Second, many employers in both countries expressed their concern about a superfluous expansion of higher education, although when it came to recruitment, they strove to pick the talents believed to be scarce and, in several instances, complained about a lack of quality of higher education and the deplorable lack of competence of some graduates. Finally, the surveys show that employers in both countries suggested that the institutions of higher education and the students be more practical-minded and business-oriented than academic cultures tend to be, but their suggestions were varied and sometimes inconsistent when it came to specific curricular strategies.

In one respect, however, the two studies suggest an obvious difference between the countries under consideration: A higher share of those German representatives of the employment system questioned tended to be critical of the higher education system than their British colleagues. Many of the British interviewees seemed to be fairly impressed by the quality of British higher education and did not suggest any major changes. As was shown in a workshop of British scholars and government representatives, which was arranged by the Society for Research into Higher Education and which addressed the two studies discussed here, this distinction of dominant moods allows for varied interpretations: It might just reflect the different historical academic cultures and a stronger historical antinomy between government and business in Germany. It might be taken as in indicator that British universities are functioning fairly well, whereas German universities are in a state of crisis. Finally, it might suggest—as some participants in that workshop concluded—that British industry misses chances of innovation because the industrial and business elite happily accept the traditions of higher education.

The results of those surveys cannot be expected to provide convincing answers about the causes of such a difference in attitudes toward the present higher education systems in the two countries; also, the surveys cannot be expected to suggest the single best curricular response. They show what employers miss and suggest. In this way, they provide information similar to the surveys that ask graduates what knowledge they acquired at college they can utilize on the job and what job tasks they have not been prepared for. Such research provides a data base for a range of possible curricular solutions, but it does not legitimize a single best curricular strategy, because although both the employers and the graduates can state single arguments, neither can present a comprehensive view based on all the expertise needed to assess, for example, what would be lost if the present emphases in courses were replaced by new ones, what competences beyond the obviously useful ones might be overlooked, or how certain types of competences would be promoted (see Holtkamp and Teichler, 1983, pp. 13–21).

Employers' Responses to the Expansion of Higher Education

As already mentioned at the beginning of this section, many surveys on employers' expectations in the 1980s in Europe have intended to explore whether employers perceive an "overeducation" or "over-qualification" as a consequence of the rapid expansion of higher education, which has not been matched by changes in the structure of occupations. The findings relevant to this question deserve special emphasis in our analysis here, because they link recruitment criteria with the previously discussed issues of graduates' problems in their transition from studies to employment and with the issue of "inappropriate" employment and work.

If one summarizes the different direct and indirect answers provided in the two surveys discussed here, the two studies indicate, at first glance, an ambivalence on the part of many employers regarding the increase in the number of graduates. On the one hand, a substantial share of interviewees in Britain and in the Federal Republic of Germany regarded the rapid expansion of higher education during the 1970s as superfluous or undesirable, notwithstanding some criticism on the part of British employers that the financial cuts in funding for British institutions of higher education in the early 1980s may have been too harsh. A few opinions that some graduates now are not better prepared for their jobs than were qualified nongraduates before the development of mass higher education can be seen in this context as well. On the other hand, the same interviewees might indicate quantitative shortages in certain areas (as some of them did regarding various fields of engineering), lack of certain skills, or a general low level of competences among most graduates. This might confirm the view that most employers are inconsistent in their assessment of higher education expansion and that they tend to stress "overeducation" when issues of education policies are addressed, and to stress "undereducation" when they are considering their own recruitment policies (see Teichler, 1983a).

The two surveys discussed here also allow another interpretation, if we consider the possible implications of the research methods used. Most of the information collected on the recruitment criteria is not relevant to employers' positions regarding educational expansion because (and this has been frequently overlooked in the past) the relationship between the overall demand and supply of graduates is addressed to only a limited extent in the recruitment process. The issue of vertical substitution might be decided on before the recruitment process by fixing the numbers of graduates to be hired in advance; therefore, during the recruitment process, one will notice only relative deficiencies of graduates for the jobs that graduates are typically recruited for. Changes in the ratio between the number of job applicants and the number of positions offered might indicate the popularity of the individual employing agency among graduates rather than the labor market situation in general, or these changes might reflect cyclical differences in recruitment more strongly than long-term trends. For example, the British employers seemed to ascribe the decline in the number of positions offered in 1981–1982 to recent economic problems rather than to long-term changes. Altogether, the recruitment process makes the actors aware primarily of their relative role as competing units striving for the best "match," and not of the macrostructures shaping the likelihood of certain kinds of matches. Thus, the averages of the perceptions of the actors do not represent such macrostructures. It would be interesting in this context to speculate to what extent the differences in the debate on educational expansion and employment between the United States and many European countries are due to the fact that a lesser share of the relevant U.S. research addresses the macrostructures in this relationship: Does this explain why the recent debates in the United States focus on problems of lack of quality of teaching and learning in higher education and of the competence of students, whereas projections by the U.S. Bureau of Labor Statistics continue to project much higher numbers of graduates than numbers of corresponding jobs?

In the German study on recruitment processes and criteria, the consequences of educational expansion are more directly addressed in two contexts. First, the representatives of the employing organizations were asked to what extent the positions were open to both graduates of *Fachhochschulen* (at least 15 1/2 and, on average, about 16 1/2 years of education) and graduates of universities (at least 17 and, on average, 19 years of education) or were offered for certain types of higher education only. Second, the interviewees were asked to assess the changes in their personnel and recruitment policies regarding graduate employment in the past five years. The answers given, which are similar to the findings in additional surveys conducted by institutions closely linked to German employers' associations (Kemmet, Linke, and Wolf, 1982; Ferring, von Landsberg, and Staufenbiel, 1984), seem to be inconsistent at first glance: The number of graduates recruited increased more rapidly than expected; at the same time, however, the jobs offered did not seem to have become much more demanding in recent years. Notwithstanding these two perceptions, most employers were convinced that they had not hired more graduates just because the supply had increased.

These findings do not fit any major explanatory model, neither the "over-education" assumption nor the assumptions that employers just recruit according to demand, that demand might have increased corresponding to increased recruitment, nor finally to the assumption that absorption is determined by supply. The authors of the German study discussed here (see also Teichler, 1988) argue instead that less dramatic shifts occur concurrently: A small increase in the level of job requirements, a small decline in the average competences of graduates in the process of educational expansion, a small response to increased supply, a gradual change of perceptions of the appropriate relationships between education and work and so on have contributed jointly to an increase in positions offered to graduates.

CHANGES IN THE RELATIONSHIPS BETWEEN HIGHER EDUCATION AND WORK: FACTS AND INTERPRETATIONS

In spite of the diversity of higher education systems and their economic and societal contexts in Europe, research on the relationships between higher education and work in most European countries was shaped for more than a decade by the assumption that the tensions caused by expansion of students' and graduates' numbers beyond the presumed demand were the major issues to be addressed. The research was aimed at providing an account of that discrepancy and of subsequent developments, for example, possible "solutions" in terms of leveling off the discrepancy, new adjustments between educational attainments and careers, changes in aspirations and expectations, and new curriculum approaches. Research was obviously strongly involved in the normative issue, that is, what relationships between higher education, on the one hand, and employment and work, on the other, would be "desirable" or "acceptable," once a "shortage" of highly qualified persons was not a major issue anymore and the high supply of graduates was a more-or-less irreversible fact. This is true for both Western and Eastern European countries even though the Eastern European countries more strongly emphasize quantitative planning of higher education and full employment policies.

Three research areas that have played a substantial role in this debate are the focus of this chapter: (1) changes in graduate employment and in the transition from school to employment in terms of employment status, period of job search, employment conditions, and so on; (2) changes in the "link" (or the nonlink) between higher education and work; that is, how "appropriate" the relationships between the studies completed and the work are in terms of a correspondence between field of study and occupation, utilization of knowledge, and the levels of employment of graduates; and (3) changes in the quality of requirements, as expressed in the expectations of the representatives of the employment system, the recruitment criteria, and so on.

In this concluding section, first, major findings as regarding these three themes are summarized. Then various interpretations by European experts regarding the changing relationships between higher education and work are described and discussed. These interpretations may help to show explain how differently the research findings and other information available are interpreted, to what extent views have changed since the 1970s, and what role other issues, such as the general rise of unemployment and new technologies, play in efforts to understand the causes and trends in the relationships between higher education and work.

A Summary of Research Findings

Since the early 1970s, the view has become widespread in most European countries that higher education has expanded beyond the demand for highly qualified labor. This discrepancy seems to be the consequence of both rapid educational expansion and a slower increase in the number of positions considered to require college-trained persons. The economic problems following the "oil crisis" of 1973 aggravated the problems frequently termed *mismatch, over-education, overqualification,* and so on. Nevertheless, the number of graduates has continued to increase, partly because many students who had enrolled because of optimistic interpretations of educational expansion, finally graduated, after the public mood and the labor market indicators had changed, and partly, because the enrollments in institutions of higher education continued to increase, though at a lower rate in several countries and after a period of stagnation in some countries. Demographic factors played an additional role. Altogether, the increase in the number of graduates from the early 1970s to the early 1980s varied among European countries from less than 20% (for example, in the German Democratic Republic) to about a duplication (for example, in Spain).

The unemployment of college-trained persons was not at all a frequent phenomenon in the Western European countries before the "oil crisis" in 1973. In most countries, we observe the first signs of considerable graduate unemployment after 1973 and an obvious increase again in the early 1980s. The latter increase reflects primarily an increase in overall unemployment. In almost all Western European countries, the unemployment rate for college-trained labor is substantially lower than overall unemployment rate. This has held true in the late

1970s and in the 1980s; in some countries, the difference between graduate unemployment and the overall unemployment rate has tended to become somewhat smaller; in others, it has remained constant or has even increased.

In many countries, we observe other signs of increased problems in graduate employment, for example, extended job search periods, increased part-time and short-term employment, and an increased number of graduates holding temporary positions. The developments, however, have been less consistent and homogeneous in Western Europe, than some experts' generalizations suggest. We have observed in some countries a decline in the students opting for prolonged education or a decline in the persons being employed short-term. In addition, surveys in some countries suggest that only a very limited number of persons are involuntarily employed part-time or short-term. Finally, it is frequently overlooked that some phenomena now interpreted as indicators of crisis were already widespread before the general concern about "overeducation" emerged; for example, long transition periods from graduation to regular employment had been common in some European countries.

In all Western European countries, the gap has obviously widened over the last ten years in employment opportunities for graduates in different fields of study. Graduates in some fields of study face increasing unemployment as well as various problems in their employment once they have found it, such as the employment conditions, the income, and access to work related to their education. On the other hand, graduates in other fields face few problems or even improved prospects. A detailed analysis shows, however, that there are substantial differences among the Western European countries in the fields of study that present the most problems and the fewest problems. Graduates in various natural science disciplines have very unfavorable labor market prospects in one country, whereas they are sought for in another country. Also, the employment prospects for humanities and social science graduates may be somewhat below average in some countries and extraordinarily grave in other countries. The labor market is not bright in all Western European countries for graduates in medicine, law, civil engineering, or mechanical engineering. Only graduates in economic fields seem to fare well in all countries.

It is not possible not to make any generalized statement about the employment opportunities of graduates from nonuniversity institutions of higher education as compared to university graduates in Europe. The roles of the nonuniversity sector and the university sector, as well as the fields of study represented in both sectors, differ substantially among the European countries. As regards gender, the degree to which females face more employment problems than men and the trends in this respect during the last ten years vary considerably.

Experts in Europe seem to agree that a reasonable link between studies completed and subsequent work assignments is the most crucial issue in analyzing the relationship between expanded higher education systems and employment, careers, and work. This is true both in the market economies and in the planned economies in Europe. The norms underlying this research, as well as the public debates, however, are extraordinarily diverse as regards what the proper links are and what methods should be used to measure these links.

Regarding occupational categories, it is generally assumed that the number of graduates continues to increase in middle-level administrative, office, and sales jobs. Weaknesses in the provision or the analysis of data prevent us from knowing to what extent the number of graduates has risen in middle-level technical positions, new types of private services, small establishments, the "alternative" sector, and blue-collar work—areas frequently mentioned in this context.

The available research suggests that the number of graduates who, one or two years after graduation, are in positions that are completely unrelated to their higher education is relatively small in all European countries. On the basis of the available research, this number might be estimated at even less than 5% of the employed graduates (not including those unemployed or those who do not reply to surveys on graduate employment). In some countries, notably Italy, the percentage may be higher, but such countries generally report longer periods between graduation and regular employment.

There is, however, a substantial number of graduates who are neither unfavorably employed nor do they seem to have jobs which fulfill all the standards of a "typical" graduate's career. Depending primarily on the concepts and methods employed, surveys have provided very varied results: Findings that about 10% of humanities graduates in one country and 60% in another are inappropriately employed one year after graduation explain more about the research concepts than about the differences among European countries regarding the employment prospects for graduates.

The ways of analyzing the links between higher education and work in Europe are manifold. They range from broad self-assessments by graduates in one or two questions in large surveys to very detailed surveys about many dimensions of such links. In many cases, the underlying concepts and the methods used are undoubtedly very sophisticated. However, we can observe various conceptual weaknesses in research that indicates very high amounts of inappropriate employment; for example, a complete neglect of possible underqualification, the unrealistic assumption that less-than-perfect links also existed two decades ago, and the variety of the possible links between higher education and work. On the other hand, research on this issue validly indicates that many graduates in European countries perceive a discrepancy between their expectations and the reality of their jobs that cannot be discounted as just being the typical tension between "dreams" and reality.

According to research on the criteria and procedures used in the recruitment of graduates and on the expectations of the representatives of the employment system regarding the competences of graduates, the requirements of the employment system are much more diverse than public debates tend to suggest. In addition, employers seem to be less interested in the structure and content of higher education and in innovations in higher education than many of those in higher education seem to believe. Finally, the complexity of the process of recruiting graduates hardly allows any sweeping statements about the relative weight of specific criteria.

A comparison of two similar surveys conducted in the early 1980s in the United Kingdom and in the Federal Republic of Germany on the criteria and procedures used in the recruitment of recent graduates shows some further commonalities, such as a stronger emphasis on attitudes and social skills and a smaller concern about good grades in recruitment for general administrative and sales positions than for "specialists'" positions, as well as a complaint about the generally low level of competence of some applicants. On the other hand, some findings seem to be specific to one country and, again, suggest caution in making generalizations about the typical views of *the* employers. The majority of British employers seem to be more-or-less satisfied with the higher education system, consider graduates of the universities to be superior to those of other institutions of higher education, and favor broad education and a "trained mind" in many cases, whereas the German employers consider grades to be, on average, more important than differences in reputation among universities, more frequently stress discrepancies between the aims of the education system and the recruitment criteria, and are more likely to appreciate specific competences.

Finally, the expansion of higher education beyond the traditional notions of demand seems to be less a concern in the context of the recruitment of graduates than the political debates suggest, partly, perhaps, because quantitative discrepancies, when they exist, become only partly visible in the recruitment process. In addition, the German survey shows that representatives of the employment system neither see a need to recruit considerably larger numbers of graduates nor conceive of the recruitment of increasing numbers, when it takes place, as an adaptive response to the increased supply. Obviously, a change of views regarding the demand for graduates and the utilization of their supply takes place in a gradual way not clearly perceived or strategically handled by the employment system.

The Range of Experts' Interpretations of the Changing Relationships Between Higher Education and Work

As already noted, research in Europe specifically on the relationship between higher education and work tends to be discussed very broadly: What do the individual phenomena mean in explaining the overall relationship between higher education and work? Thus, the experts' debate is closely related to macrostructural policy and planning.

Those experts' assessments are very diverse in their perceptions of trends since the 1970s, in their projections of future developments, and in their recommendations, as will be shown below. However, in looking back to the range of arguments discussed in the 1970s—that is, early in the development of the pessimistic mood about the consequences of higher education expansion (see the overview in Teichler et al., 1980)—we note that certain "extreme" interpretations have vanished in the course of events. Thus, the lesser diversity of current interpretations indicates a certain degree of commonality of developments existing in European countries.

First, the view vanished that the expansion of higher education leads to a "proletariat" of the college-trained. The current problems of graduates seem to be less severe, in comparison to those of persons with lower qualifications, than they were in the earlier stages of the "oversupply" of graduates (see the overviews in Triebel, 1986; Windolf, 1986). Instead of an *akademisches Proletariat,* as it was called in Germany, which faced very high unemployment, jobs far distant from one's education, and extreme dissatisfaction and radical political inclinations, current graduates face, on average, only some problems and, in only some countries, have lost some of their privileges as compared to nongraduates.

Second, the opposite extreme of interpretation plays no significant role in either scholarly or political debates in European countries. Nobody claims seriously that a new balance is emerging between the supply of graduates and the current "demand" of the employment system. An oversupply of the number of graduates is generally assumed, as long as the current job opportunities are taken as a yardstick. Interpretations vary only concerning to what extent we find shortages in some areas; to what extent dynamic and long-term views of economic, technological, and social needs might justify an expansion beyond the current demand for graduates; to what extent uncertainties about the future demand an "overeducation" risk policy; and to what extent rationales other than labor market demand should be taken into consideration as well. Also, the claims by many employers and many representatives of the higher education system that an increasing number of graduates lack the desirable competences have not led to any serious claim that a new equilibrium between demand and supply has been achieved by inflating credentials or watering down standards. At most, it is argued that the increased absorption of graduates into the employment system can be explained in some part by the employers' assumption that some graduates nowadays are no more competent than the most capable nongraduates of prior generations. In addition, there is a certain commonality in controversial interpretations of students' behavior and of rationales of higher education policies, which will be addressed in later sections.

Third, experts agree that growing employment problems have not had the expected result of deterring youth from going to college and from choosing fields in which there are low employment opportunities.

Fourth, it is generally assumed that political ground has been lost by those who advocate restoring a balance between the demand for graduates and their supply by regulating higher education on the basis of the presumed demand. Rather, we can observe a general shift of emphasis in the debate on the changing relationships between higher education and work as stated below.

Fifth, observers agree that past debates put too much emphasis on the relationships between level of education and level of job position and thereby underestimated the qualitative dimensions of particular fields of study and specific competences (see Williams, 1985).

Sixth, experts agree that the changes in the relationship between higher education and employment can be explained only partly by the oversupply of graduates and the various responses to this oversupply and must take into consideration other technological, economic, and social changes (in this respect, debates on education and employment in the developing countries seem to have changed similarly, as Little, 1984, p. 7, suggests).

Deferred Crisis or Gradual Adaptation?

As opposed to the assumption that the quantitative "mismatch" between the supply of graduates and the positions offered to them was bound to lead to serious employment problems, the experts seem to agree that the consequences of this quantitative discrepancy turned out to be dispersed. As, for example, Vincens (1985) and Teichler (1987) argue, we find a broad range of responses: Some youth qualified to enroll decide not to proceed to higher education, some are deterred by fading financial support for students, some postpone graduation because of unfavorable job prospects and the length of the job search period, some graduates accept temporary jobs, some graduates face long-term unemployment, some graduates are absorbed by the employment system by means of vertical substitution, and so on.

This state of affairs might be interpreted differently in a long-term perspective. Historically, according to Vincens, major problems have been deferred, and an aggravation is likely to occur. This might turn out to be true in the Federal Republic of Germany: because of changes in birth rates, the percentage of new graduates in the labor force more-or-less stagnated in the 1970s but has grown rapidly since the early 1980s. On the whole, however, declines in graduate unemployment, in short-term employment, or in the percentage of graduates opting for further education in some countries do not suggest that the problems have just been deferred and continue to grow; there are also signs of adjustments as well.

Changes Affecting Demand for Graduates

Obviously, the employment prospects of graduates depend on both discrepancies and adjustments between the education and the employment systems. But the long-term trends in technology, the economy, and society have played a more important role recently in explaining the relationship between higher education and the employment system. The finding that graduate unemployment in many Western European countries is twice as high in the 1980s than it was in the late 1970s but continues to remain substantially below the overall unemployment rate can be interpreted as a continued sign of the adjustment of the employment system to a high supply of graduates, because the "oversupply" of labor would easily allow the employers to uphold their traditional recruitment policies (for example, see Teichler, 1987). Or, as some experts assume, increased graduate unemployment can be viewed as one component of a continuous change in society that is due to a decline in organized work and that is thus due to a general crisis of the "work society" (see Beck, 1986).

On the other hand, some scenarios point out new and increasing demands in some areas. In many Western and Eastern European countries, a growing need is expected for highly qualified labor to promote new technologies and a society based on new technologies (see for example Avakov et al., 1984; Klevard and Sternerup, 1986; Neave, 1985; Williams, 1985; Wolter, 1986; *Zukunftsperspektiven*, 1983). This view has spread rapidly in the 1980s. Up to the present, it has had a stronger impact, though, on research priorities and on cooperation between higher education and the community or industry than on new concepts regarding the demand for college-trained labor. It might be added at this point that in some countries, the major increase in the demand for graduates is not in the area of science engineering. In the USSR, for example, higher education planning is based on the assumption that managerial improvements are equally important and quantitatively more far-reaching; highest increase of graduates to be called for in higher education planning, therefore, is in the economic fields of study (see Avakov et al., 1984).

Obviously, the scenarios are instructive in showing the possible implications of major changes in society as compared to the traditional manpower requirement forecasts, which tended to be very conservative in usually assuming marginal modifications in technological, economic, and societal developments as well as in the education system. Depending on whether we head for a technological society, an ecological society, or a society no longer shaped by the centrality of work, we have to expect completely different demands for graduates (see Weber, Arend, and Weiss, 1985). Up to the present, we have not seen any obviously dominant major trends or policies that would allow us to predict the future of graduates' work.

"Decoupling" or Continued Reward of Educational Attainment?

In debates during the 1970s on the causes and consequences of educational expansion, many experts considered a routinized reward of credentials not in tune with job requirements to be one of the major causes of the "mismatches" in the labor market (see for example Dore, 1976); also, policies were recommended of intentionally "decoupling" educational attainments from rewards in the employment system. Although such policies were not implemented in any significant way, some experts claim that a gradual process of "decoupling" has taken place since then: Education continues to sell tickets for careers, but the trains don't leave the stations anymore, as Beck (1986) drastically put it in his discussion of a presumed continuous reduction in paid work time.

A loss of rewards for educational attainment can be claimed now only in certain fields of study. If the labor market splits into a modern technological sector, a sector in charge of the coordination of society, and a sector continuously threatened by a loss of work, as Kellermann (1986a) suggests, this crisis in some sectors could be accompanied by improving job prospects in other sectors. Many experts (see for example Stooss, 1985) have raised doubts, however, about whether the increased unemployment in Western Europe in the 1980s is going to have as far-reaching consequences as are suggested by those who foresee a crisis in the "work society" and a loss of the "centrality" of work in society. Also, a substantial deterioration in the job prospects of graduates in certain fields of study does not necessarily indicate a "decoupling" of the education and the employment systems; rather, it may indicate a changing pattern of the labor market value of different sectors of higher education (see Furth, 1982; OECD, 1983b).

Changing Options of Students and Changing Higher Education Policies

As has already been pointed out, most experts seem to agree that the increased problems in graduate employment in the 1970s did not lead to a lowering of educational aspirations. There is obviously substantial variation in the interpretations of the changes in students' views and "strategies." On the other hand, some experts consider a growing preference for fields of study providing "employable" skills as an indicator of market-oriented behavior, thereby assuming that growing vocationalism reflects rewards for education more accurately than the emphasis on educational levels in the past (Williams, 1985). On the other hand, the shift in the choice of fields of study is interpreted by some authors as being surprisingly small in comparison with the substantially widening gap in employment opportunities; some students may have changed their values so that they are willing to accept some loss of privileges, as long as they can expect studies and work that they consider interesting and meaningful (Baethge et al., 1986).

Surveys of students' views obviously do not allow any firm conclusions. In the Federal Republic of Germany, the available surveys of students are interpreted by some scholars as indicating a historical continuity of academic values among students (Bargel et al., 1984). A second interpretation points out a substantial change of the students' role in the last decades: "Today for a relevant part of the students the studies, the fact of being a student, is [sic] losing its central place in life" (Huber, 1987, p. 276). Finally, interpretations of students' and graduates' career aspirations, job expectations, and so on emphasize that a substantial number of students and graduates favor interesting and meaningful studies and work, even if the occupational status turns out to be somewhat less attractive than the traditional view of appropriate employment for graduates (for example, see Minks and Reissert, 1985).

As regards quantitative and structural higher education policies and their labor market rationales, we observe quite diverse interpretations. Some authors claimed around 1980 that the educational system is expected to take over a "custodial function," that is, keeping an increasing number of graduates out of both employment and visible unemployment (see, for example, Kellermann and Lenhardt, 1980). It is not surprising, that this view did not become popular. We note, in European countries generally, an increased reservation regarding the utility of traditional manpower forecasts as well as regarding a demand-oriented steering of the overall numbers of graduates, but notions of demand have kept a strong influence on access policies, at least in certain fields of studies (notably the medical fields) and in certain types of institutions (for example, the universities in the United Kingdom). Also, higher education policies in several European countries in the 1980s have aimed to reduce the actual period of study by means of new regulations regarding the existing course programs (for example, in the Netherlands), by upgrading the interim exams to some kinds of terminal degrees (as in France and Belgium), or by extending the share of short-course programs and nonuniversity higher education (as intended rather than realized in the Federal Republic of Germany). If a generalization on structural and quantitative higher education across European countries is at all appropriate, we seem to frequently observe an acceptance of increasing admissions quota alongside efforts to diversify structures and programs, as well as to reduce the average duration of studies (Teichler, 1986c).

Absorption of Superfluous Educational Expansion or New Directions of a Highly Educated Society?

Graduates' transitions to employment continue to be considered more a problem in Europe than in the United States and in Japan. This reflects, in part, differences in obvious problems in the labor market. In part, however, reservations in Europe remain strong, even when the absorption of the growing number of graduates turns out to be relatively smooth. These reservations are attributable to different notions about the function of higher education. Whereas in the United States and Japan we observe much steeper hierarchies of quality and reputation of higher education institutions and programs than in most European countries, as well as more popularity of the concept of "postsecondary" rather than "higher" education, the view persists in Europe that a certain level of competence defines the character of higher education and that certain expectations are appropriate regarding the character and content of graduate employment; the expansion of higher education is frequently considered superfluous or detrimental if that character of higher education and of graduates' work is diluted.

A substantial share of the research available is shaped by that view, because many research designs allow the investigators to trace information only about to what extent such problems occur. We must also note, however, some European scholars who do not share such pessimistics notions about the possible consequences of higher education expansion. For example, research on changes in the division of labor, job assignments, and so on that are due to an expanded supply of graduates provides information about more far-reaching consequences of educational expansion. Certainly, findings based on such kinds of research are sometimes interpreted as an infringement of the autonomy and the responsibility of manual workers and middle-level employees (for example, see Lutz, 1981); on the other hand, some scholars see indicators that an increased number of persons might share responsibilities and interesting job roles (for example, see Baethge and Overbeck, 1986). Also, some experts have suggested changing both higher education and the employment system so that better use can be made of the competences supplied by the expansion of higher education; some gradual change seems to be taking place toward a highly educated society anyway (see, for interpretation, Teichler, 1988), but active policies are recommended based on a rethinking of the potentials of a highly educated society (Kluczynski and Opolski, 1984; Baethge et al., 1986).

Conclusion

In addressing the relationship between higher education and work, both the public and the scholarly debates continue to put a substantial emphasis on the issue frequently termed *overeducation, overqualification,* or *mismatch.* The question continues to be raised whether the expansion of higher education has led to problems in getting jobs, and in being assigned to "inappropriate" positions and work, or whether an absorption takes place independently of policies of higher education expansion, or whether expanded higher education serves new purposes or hitherto latent needs. The debate has become more complex because we now envisage possible technological, economic, and societal changes that could have far-reaching consequences for higher education and work, but it cannot yet be established what kinds of trends are most likely to occur or what kinds of long-term policies are likely to be implemented. Also, we note that some research is indicating new ways of learning in higher education and new kinds of employment in highly educated societies, which may considerably change our ways of perceiving the links between higher education and work. Both the commonalities and the controversies in the analyses of higher education and work in Europe since about 1975 suggest that higher education has remained important in the process of status distribution and that the concern about expansion beyond the traditional requirements has not disappeared. There are various—though heterogeneous and rather vague—indicators that both the needs for graduates' competence and the concept about the function of higher education may change in a way that would challenge those notions fundamentally. However, it would be premature at present to predict for European countries a rapid change of concepts regarding higher education and work.

REFERENCES

Ahamad, B., and Blaug, M., eds. (1973). *The Practice of Manpower Forecasting.* Amsterdam: Elsevier.

Akademiker in Deutschland. (1980). Hamburg: Spiegel-Verlag.

Altbach, P. G. (1985). *Perspectives on Comparative Higher Education: A Survey of Research and Literature.* New York: International Council for Educational Development.

Altrichter, H. (1982). Austrian graduates in education and their jobs: an empirical analysis of the occupational distribution of university graduates. *Higher Education* 11(5): 499–510.

Ambrosio, T., Avakov, R., and Tiburcio, L., eds. (1983). *Structures industrielles, changements technologiques et enseignement supérieur au Portugal.* Paris: UNESCO, International Institute for Educational Planning.

Anckar, O. (1985). Research on the economics of higher education in Finland. In R. Maekinen, M. Panhelainen, and M. Parjanen (eds.), *Recent Finnish Research in Higher Education.* Jyvoeskylae: University of Jyvoeskylae, Institute for Educational Research, 25–39.

Arbeitsgruppen des Instituts fuer Arbeitsmarkt- und Berufsforschung und des Max-Planck-Instituts fuer Bildungsforschung, eds. (1976). *Bedarfsprognostische Forschung in der Diskussion.* Frankfurt a.M.: Aspekte.

Arbeitskreis Berufsforschung et al., eds. (1983). *Hochschulexpansion und Arbeitsmarkt.* Nuernberg: Institut fuer Arbeitsmarkt- und Berufsforschung der Bundesanstalt fuer Arbeit (Beitraege, 77).

Archer, M., ed. (1982). *The Sociology of Educational Expansion.* Beverly Hills, CA: Sage.

Avakov, R., Chuprunov, D., and Jiltsov, E. (1982). *Enseignement supérieur, emploi et progrès technique en URSS.* Paris: UNESCO, International Institute for Educational Planning.

Avakov, R., et al., eds. (1984). *Higher Education and Employment in the USSR and in the Federal Republic of Germany*. Paris: UNESCO, International Institute for Educational Planning.

Baethge, M., et al. (1986). *Studium und Beruf*. Freiburg i.Br.: Dreisam.

Baethge, M., and Overbeck, H. (1986). *Zukunft der Angestellten*. Frankfurt a.M./New York: Campus.

Baethge, M., and Teichler, U. (1984). Bildungssystem und Beschaeftigungssystem. In *Enzyklopaedie Erziehungswissenschaft* (Vol. 5). Stuttgart: Klett-Cotta, 206–225.

Bargel, T., et al. (1984). Ist die These vom Wandel der Sozialisation haltbar? *Hochschulausbildung* 2(3): 137–147.

Baudelot, C., Benoliel, R., Cucrowicz, H., and Establet, R. (1981). *Les étudiants, l'emploi, la crise*. Paris: Maspero.

Becher, T., Embling, J., and Kogan, M. (1977). *Systems of Higher Education: United Kingdom*. New York: International Council for Educational Development.

Beck, U. (1986). *Risikogesellschaft*. Frankfurt a.M.: Suhrkamp.

Bergendahl, G. (1977). *Higher Education and Manpower Planning in Sweden*. Stockholm: National Swedish Board of Universities and Colleges.

Bjoerklund, E. (1984). The research on higher education program. *Swedish Research on Higher Education* 5: 1–27.

Bodenhoefer, H.-J., ed. (1981). *Hochschulexpansion und Beschaeftigung*. Wien: Boehlau.

Bodenhoefer, H.-J., and Ofner, F. (1985): Universitaet und Arbeitsmarkt fuer Akademiker. In G. Burkart (ed.), *Maturanden, Studenten, Akademiker*. Klagenfurt: Kaertner Druck- und Verlagsgesellschaft, 225–274.

Bodenhoefer, H.-J., and Ofner, F. (1986). "Akademisierung" in der Wirtschaft— Ingenieure in der oesterreichischen Industrie. In G. Von Landsberg, et al., *Ingenieure in der Wirtschaft*. Koeln: Deutscher Instituts-Verlag, 24–45.

Bollinger, E. (1986). Les jeunes universitaires et le march d'emploi. *Berufsberatung und Berufsbildung* 71(5); 270–272.

Bowen, H. (1978). Measurements of efficiency. In C. Kerr, et al., *12 Systems of Higher Education: 6 Decisive Issues*. New York: International Council for Educational Development.

Boys, C., Brennan, J., and McGeevor, P. (1986). *Higher Education and the Labour Market*. Reading: CNAA Development Services Unit, Bulmershe College of Higher Education (working paper, 1).

Brennan, J. (1985). Preparing students for employment. *Studies in Higher Education* 10(2): 151–162.

Briggs, A. (1985). Study abroad: A European perspective. In A. Briggs and B. Burn, *Study Abroad: A European and an American Perspective*. Paris: European Institute of Education and Social Policy, 1–31.

Buelow, H. (1981). De langvarigt uddanedes arbejdsmarked tre ar efter eksamen. *Satistiske Efterretninger*, 73: A 35.

Buelow, M., ed. (1984). *Akademikerbeschaeftigung im Wandel*. Frankfurt a.M./New York: Campus.

Bundesminister fuer Bildung und Wissenschaft. (1985). *Grund- und Strukturdaten 1985/86*. Bonn: BMBW.

Bundesministerium fuer Wissenschaft und Forschung. (1985). *Berufliche Situation und soziale Stellung von Akademikern*. Wien: Bundesministerium fuer Wissenschaft und Forschung.

Bundesministerium fuer Wissenschaft und Forschung, Bundesministerium fuer soziale

Verwaltung, und Oesterreichische Hochschuelerschaft (1986). *Studium und Beruf: Universitaeten, Hochschule.* Wien: Jugend und Volk.

Burkart, G., ed. (1985). *Maturanden, Studenten, Akademiker: Studien zur Entwicklung von Bildungs- und Berufsverlaeufen in Oesterreich.* Klagenfurt: Kaertner Druck- und Verlagsgesellschaft.

Burkart, G. (1986). *Maturandenkarrieren.* Klagenfurt: Universitaet fuer Bildungswissenschaften, mimeo.

Burns, T. (1980). Science and arts: The job gap widens. *Employment Gazette* 88(11): 1182–1184.

Busch, D. W., and Hommerich, Chr. (1981). Arbeitsmarktspaltung und Probleme der Adaequanz von Ausbildung und Beruf am Beispiel eines neuen sozialwissenschaftlichen Qualifikationsprofils (Diplom-Paedagogen). In H.-J. Bodenhoefer (ed.), *Hochschulexpansion und Beschaeftigung.* Wien: Boehlau, 355–378.

Busch, D., et al. (1981). *Taetigkeitsfelder und Qualifikationen von Wirtschafts-, Sozial-, Ingenieur- und Naturwissenschaftlern.* Frankfurt/New York: Campus.

Butler, R. (1978). *Employment of the Highly Qualified 1971–1986.* London: Department of Employment.

Buttgereit, M. (1983). The relevance of certificates in recruitment. In W. Rieck (ed.), *Higher Education by the Year 2000: Congress Preparatory Papers (Vol. 3).* Frankfurt a.M.: EARDHE, 94–108.

Buttgereit, M. (1984). Certificates and recruitment. In R. Avakov et al. (eds.), *Higher Education and Employment in the USSR and in the Federal Republic of Germany.* Paris: UNESCO, International Institute for Educational Planning, 217–230.

Buttler, A. (1983). Qualifikationen der Hochschulabsolventen und Anforderungen der beruflichen Praxis. In J. Kluczynski, U. Teichler, and Chr. Tkocz (eds.), *Hochschule und Beruf in Polen und in der Bundesrepublik Deutschland.* Kassel: Stauda, 102–107.

Buttler, A. (1984). Probleme von Hochschulabsolventen im ersten Jahr der Berufstaetigkeit. In J. Klcuzynski, A. Neusel, and U. Teichler (eds.), *Forschung zu Hochschule und Beruf in Polen und in der Bundesrepublik Deutschland.* Kassel: Stauda, 176–184.

Buttler, A., Kluczynski, J., and Teichler, U., eds. (1984). *Szkolnictwo wyzsze i praca zawodana w Republice Federalneij Niemiec i w Polsce Ludowej. Czesc 1.* Warszawa/Lodz: PWN.

Carnoy, M. (1977). *Education and Employment: A Critical Appraisal.* Paris: UNESCO, International Institute for Educational Planning (Fundamentals of Educational Planning, 26).

Centre d'Études et de Recherches sur les Qualifications (ed.). (1982a). *L'entrée dans la vie active des étudiants en droit et sciences économiques à la sortie des universitiés.* Paris: CEREQ.

Centre d'Études et de Recherches sur les Qualifications. (1982b). Les universités et la crise: Evolution de l'éntrée sur le marche du travail des étudiants scientifiques entre 1975 et 1980. *Note d'Information (CEREQ)* 73.

Cerych, L., Colton, S., and Jallade, J. P. (1981). *Student Flows and Expenditure in Higher Education.* Paris: Institute of Education, European Cultural Foundation.

Cerych, L., and Sabatier, P. (1986). *Great Expectations and Mixed Performance: The Implementation of Higher Education Reforms in Europe.* Stoke-on-Trent: Trentham.

Chuprunov, D., Avakov, R., and Jiltsov, E. (1984). Higher education, employment and technological progress in the USSR. In R. Avakov, M. Buttgereit, B.C. Sanyal, and U. Teichler (eds.), *Higher Education and Employment in the USSR and in the Federal*

Republic of Germany. Paris: UNESCO, International Institute for Educational Planning.

Ciucci, R. (1984). Studying in 1984: A part-time activity along with other jobs? Illustrations from Italy. *European Journal of Education* 19(3): 299–308.

Clement, W. (1982). *Educational and Labour Market Forecasting Activities in the Federal Republic of Germany and Austria*. Paris: UNESCO, International Institute for Educational Planning, mimeo.

Coleman, J. S., and Husén, T. (1985). *Becoming Adult in a Changing Society*. Paris: OECD.

Council of Europe. (1984). *U 2000: Higher Education and Research Policies in Europe Approaching the Year 2000*. Strasbourg: Council of Europe.

Dean, T. E. (1983). Degrees of success into the nineties. *Employment Gazette* 91(1): 24–28.

De Francesco, C., and Jarousse, J.-P. (1983). Under-utilisation and market value of university degrees: Findings of a survey in France and Italy. *European Journal of Education* 18(1): 65–79.

De Moor, R. A., ed. (1978). *Changing Tertiary Education in Modern European Society*. Strasbourg: Council of Europe.

Dore, R. (1976). *The Diploma Disease*. London: Allen & Unwin.

European Centre for Higher Education (CEPES). (1981). *International Directory of Higher Education Research Institutions*. Paris: UNESCO.

Federal Ministry of Education and Science. (1986). *Basic and Structural Data 1986/87*. Bonn: BMBW.

Ferring, K., von Landsberg, G., and Staufenbiel, J. E. (1984). *Hochschulexpansion und betriebliche Personalpolitik*. Koeln: Deutscher Industrie-Verlag.

Framhein, G. (1983). *Alte und neue Universitaeten*. Bad Honnef: Bock.

Framhein, G., and Langer, J., eds. (1984). *Student und Studium im interkulturellen Vergleich: Student Worlds in Europe*. Klagenfurt: Kaertner Druck- und Verlagsgesellschaft.

Freeman, R. B. (1976). *The Over-Educated American*. New York: Academic Press.

Fulton, O., Gordon, A., and Williams, G. (1982). *Higher Education and Manpower Planning: A Comparative Study of Planned and Market Economies*. Geneva: International Labour Office.

Furth, D. (1982). New hierarchies in higher education. *European Journal of Education* 17(2): 145–151.

Galley, F., Joye, D., Sauer, J.-J., and Bassand, M. (1986). L'entrée dans la vie professionelle. *Politique de la science* 35: 1–122.

Gesser, B. (1985). *Utbildning-jaemlikhet-arbetsdelning*. Lund: Arkivs.

Girod de l'Ain, B. (1981). Certifying effect and consumer effect: Some remarks on strategies employed by higher education institutions. *Higher Education* 10(1): 55–73.

Goldschmidt, D. (1981). Tendenzen der internationalen Hochschulentwicklung. *Zeitschrift fuer Sozialisationsforschung und Erziehungssoziologie* 1(2): 173–186.

Goodlad, S., ed. (1984). *Education for the Professions: Quis custodiet . . . ?* Guilford: Society for Research into Education & NFER-Nelson.

Gordon, A. (1983). Attitudes of employers to the recruitment of graduates. *Educational Studies* 9(1): 45–64.

Gordon, A. (1986). Education and training for information technology. *Studies in Higher Education* 11(2): 189–198.

Gruson, P., and Markiewicz-Lagneau, J. (1983). *L'enseignement superieur et son efficacité—France, États-Unis, URSS, Pologne*. Paris: La Documentation Francaise.

Haeyrynen, Y.-P. (1985). Academic careers study 1965–83: Account of life course. In R. Maekinen, M. Panhalainen, and M. Parjanen (eds.), *Recent Finnish Research on Higher Education*. Jyvaeskylae: University of Jyvaeskylae, Institute for Educational Research, 43–74.

Harrison, A., and Gretton, J., eds. (1987). *Education and Training UK 1987: An Economic, Social and Policy Audit*. London: Policy Journals.

Hartong, J. (1985). Overscholing? *Economisch-Statistische Berichten* 13(2): 152–156.

Hartung, D. (1984). Some manifestations and implications of underemployment of college graduates: The case of the Federal Republic of Germany. In R. Avakov et al. (eds.), *Higher Education and Employment in the USSR and in the Federal Republic of Germany*. Paris: UNESCO, International Institute for Educational Planning, 212–216.

Hartung, D., Nuthmann, R., and Teichler, U. (1981). *Bildung und Beschaeftigung*. Muenchen: Saur.

Hartung, D., Nuthmann, R., and Winterhager, W. D. (1970). *Politologen im Beruf*. Stuttgart: Klett.

Hegedues, L., von Kopp, B., and Schmidt, G. (1982). *Hochschulstudium und Berufseingliederung in sozialistischen Staaten*. Koeln: Boehlau.

Hegelheimer, A., ed. (1974). *Texte zur Bildungsoekonomie*. Frankfurt a.M.: Ullstein.

Hegelheimer, A. (1984). *Strukturwandel der Akademikerbeschaeftigung*. Bielefeld: Universitaet Bielefeld.

Heimgartner, E. (1983). Die Beschaeftigungssituation der Neuabsolventen der Schweizer Hochschulen 1981. *Berufsberatung und Berufsbildung*, 68(1): 25–32.

Herlyn, I., and Weymann, A., eds. (1987). *Bildung ohne Berufsperspektive?* Frankfurt a.M./New York: Campus.

Hermanns, H., Teichler, U., and Wasser, H., eds. (1983). *The Compleat University: Break from Tradition in Germany, Sweden and the U.S.A.* Cambridge, MA: Schenkman.

Higher education, the state and the economy: An Anglo-German symposium (1985). *Oxford Review of Education* 11: 3.

Hitz, H. (1986). *Erwerbsstatistische Praxis und die Ermittlung von Arbeitslosenquoten im internationalen Vergleich*. Nuernberg: Institut fuer Arbeitsmarkt- und Berufsforschung der Bundesanstalt fuer Arbeit (Beitraege, 97).

Hochschul-Informations-System. (1980). *Studenten zwischen Hochschule und Arbeitsmarkt*. Muenchen: Saur.

Holtkamp, R., and Teichler, U. (1981). *Ausserschulische Taetigkeitsbereiche fuer Absolventen sprach- und literaturwissenschaftlicher Studiengaenge*. Kassel: Wissenschaftliches Zentrum fuer Berufs- und Hochschulforschung der Gesamthochschule Kassel.

Holtkamp, R., and Teichler, U., eds. (1983). *Berufstaetigkeit von Hochschulabsolventen*. Frankfurt a.M./New York: Campus.

Hommerich, Chr. (1984). *Der Diplompaedagoge—ein ungeliebtes Kind der Bildungsreform*. Frankfurt a.M./New York: Campus.

Huber, L. (1987). Changes of the student role. In H. Roehrs (ed.), *Tradition and Reform of the University under an International Perspective*. Frankfurt a.M.: Lang, 267–282.

Huefner, K. (1984a). Forschung zur Oekonomie der Hochschule. In D. Goldschmidt, U. Teichler, and W.-D. Webler (eds.), *Forschungsgegenstand Hochschule*. Frankfurt a.M./New York: Campus.

Huefner, K. (1984b). Higher education in the Federal Republic of Germany: A planned or market system? Or a third way? In R. Avakov, et al. (eds.), *Higher Education and*

Employment in the USSR and in the Federal Republic of Germany. Paris: UNESCO, International Institute for Educational Planning, 185–196.

Huefner, K., Hummel, Th., and Rau, E. (1986). *Efficiency in Higher Education: An Annotated Bibliography.* Berlin: Freie Universitaet Berlin, Zentralinstitut fuer sozialwissenschaftliche Forschung.

Husén, T. (1979). *The School in Question.* Oxford: Oxford University Press.

Husén, T., and Kogan, M., eds. (1984). *Educational Research and Policy: How Do They Relate?* Oxford: Pergamon.

Hutt, R., Parsons, D., and Pearson, R., eds. (1980). *Education and Employment 1980.* Brighton: Institute of Manpower Studies.

Ivanov, I. V. (1982). *Skilled Manpower Planning, Forecasting and Training in the USSR.* Paris: UNESCO, International Institute for Educational Planning, mimeo.

Jarousse, J.-P., and de Francesco, C. (1984). *L'enseignement supérieur contre le chômage.* Paris: European Institute of Education and Social Policy.

Kaiser, M. (1986). Arbeitsgruppe: Hochschulabsolventen beim Übergang in den Beruf. *Beitraege zur Arbeitsmarkt- und Berufsforschung* 90(4): 71–137.

Kaiser, M., Kolosi, T., and Robert, P. (1984). Bildungsexpansion, Beschaeftigung und Mobilitaet: Ein empirischer Vergleich zwischen der Bundesrepublik Deutschland und Ungarn. *Mitteilungen aus der Arbeitsmarkt- und Berufsforschung* 17(3): 388–406.

Kaiser, M., Nuthmann, R., and Stegmann, H., eds. (1986). *Berufliche Verbeibsforschung in der Diskussion: Hochschulabsolventen beim Uebergang in den Beruf.* Nuernberg: Institut fuer Arbeitsmarkt- und Berufsforschung der Bundesanstalt fuer Arbeit (Beitrage, 90.3).

Kaiser, M., et al. (1981). *Fachhochschulabsolventen beim Uebergang vom Studium in den Beruf.* Nuernberg: Institut fuer Arbeitsmarkt- und Berufsforschung der Bundesanstalt fuer Arbeit (Beitraege, 24).

Kasseler Hochschulabsolventenverlaufsstudie: Erste Kurzauswertung: Hochschulabsolventen auf dem Weg in den Beruf. (1986). Kassel: Wissenschaftliches Zentrum fuer Berufs- und Hochschulforschung der Gesamthochschule Kassel, mimeo.

Kellermann, P. (1981). *Arbeit und Bildung II.* Klagenfurt: Kaertner Druck- und Verlagsgesellschaft.

Kellermann, P. (1986a). *Arbeit und Bildung III.* Klagenfurt: Kaertner Druck- und Verlagsgesellschaft.

Kellermann, P., ed. (1986b). *Universitaet und Hochschulpolitik.* Wien: Boehlau.

Kellermann, P., and Lenhardt, G. (1980). Erfahrung, Schule, Lohnarbeit: Zusammenhang zwischen Arbeitsmarkt und Bildungssystem. In U. Beck et al. (eds.), *Bildungsexpansion und betriebliche Beschaeftigungspolitik.* Frankfurt a.M./New York: Campus, 98–114.

Kemmet, C., Linke, H., and Wolf, R. (1982). *Studium und Berufschancen.* Herford: Maximilian.

Klevard, A., and Sternerup, Chr. (1986). Technikermangel und Technikerausbildung— was tut man in Schweden. *Aktuelle Informationen aus Schweden* 346:1–9.

Kluczynski, J. (1983). Das Hochschulwesen in Polen—Probleme und Perspektiven. In J. Kluczynski, U. Teichler, and Chr. Tkocz (eds.), *Hochschule und Beruf in Polen und in der Bundesrepublik Deutschland.* Kassel: Stauda, 10–24.

Kluczynski, J., and Opolski, K. (1984). Probleme der Ausbildung und Absorption qualifizierter Arbeitskraefte. In J. Kluczynski, A. Neusel, and U. Teichler (eds.), *Forschung zu Hochschule und Beruf in Polen und in der Bundesrepublik Deutschland.* Kassel: Stauda, 11–26.

Kluczynski, J., and Sanyal, B. C., eds. (1985). *Education and Work on Poland.* Warsaw: PWN/UNESCO.

Kluczynski, J., Szarras, H., and Teichler, U., eds. (1986). *Szkolnictwo wyzsze i praca zawodana w Republice Federalneij Niemic i w Polsce Ludowej. Czesc 2.* Warszawa/ Lodz: PWN.

Kogan, M. (1984). Expectations of higher education. In D. Jacques and J. Richardson (eds.), *The Future of Higher Education.* Windsor: NFER/Nelson.

Korn, K., et al. (1984). *Education, Employment and Development in the German Democratic Republic.* Paris: UNESCO, International Institute for Educational Planning.

Lamoure, J. (1981). *Les instituts universitaires de technologie en France.* Paris: Institute of Education, European Cultural Foundation.

Langer, J. (1981). *Ingenieure und Kaufleute.* Klagenfurt: Kaertner Druck- und Verlagsgesellschaft, 1981.

Lassnigg, L. (1985). Entwicklung der Akademikerbeschaeftigung. In *Berufliche Situation und soziale Stellung von Akademikern.* Wien: Bundesministerium fuer Wissenschaft und Forschung, 16–41.

Lassnigg, L., and Schramm, B. (1985). Einige Aspekte des Berufseinstiegs von Hochschulabsolventen in der zweiten Haelfte der siebziger Jahre. In *Berufliche Situation und soziale Stellung von Akademikern.* Wien: Bundesministerium fuer Wissenschaft und Forschung, 89–107.

Liebau, E. (1984). Expansion of higher education and crisis of employment: A chance for education? *European Journal of Education* 19(3): 269–282.

Lindley, R. M. (ed.). (1981). *Higher Education and the Labour Market.* Guilford: SRHE.

Little, A. (1984). *The Coordination of Education Policy and Planning and Employment Policy and Planning. Vol. 1: A State of the Art Review.* Paris: UNESCO, Division of Educational Policy and Planning.

Lutz, B. (1981). Education and employment: Contrasting evidence from France and the Federal Republic of Germany. *European Journal of Education* 16(1): 73–86.

Magnussen, O. (1979). A survey of various aspects of the education-employment relationship. *European Journal of Education* 14(1): 75–80.

Mertens, D. (1974). Schlüsselqualifikationen: Thesen zur Schulung fuer eine moderne Gesellschaft. *Mitteilungen aus der Arbeitsmarkt- und Berufsforschung* 7(1): 36–43.

Mignat, A., and Eicher, J.-C. (1982). Higher education and employment markets in France. *Higher Education* 11(2): 211–220.

Ministère de l'Education Nationale. (1985). *Le rôle et les fonctions des universités: Rapport de la France.* Paris: OECD, mimeo.

Ministerie van Onderwijs en Wetenschappen. (1986). Conceptbeleidsvoornemens groei en krimp universiteiten en academische ziekenhuizen 1987–1991. *Extra uitleg* 2(64): 1–8.

Minks, K.-H., and Reissert, R. (1985). Der Uebergang vom Studium in den Beruf. *HIS-Kurzinformationen* A 1/85: 1–40.

Monbushô. (1986). *Monbu tôkei yoran: Shôwa 61 nenban.* Tokyo: Monbushô.

Morgenthaler, B. (1985). Die Beschaeftigungssituation der Auabsolventen der Schweizer Hochschulen: Ergebnisse der Befragung des Examensjahrgangs 1982. *Beitraege zur Arbeitsmarkt- und Berufsforschung* 90(3): 229–246.

Morgenthaler, B. (1986). Die Beschaeftigungssituation der Neuabsolventen der Schweizer Hochschulen 1985. *Wissenschaftspolitik* 34(Beiheft): 1–106.

Neave, G. (1981). On the road to Silicon Valley? The changing relationship between higher education and government in Western Europe. *European Journal of Education* 19(2): 116–136.

Neave, G. (1985). Higher education and economic change: France. Paper presented to Fifth International Conference of Europeanists. Washington, DC: October 18–20, mimeo.

Neave, G., ed. (1986). European university systems. Part 1. *CRE-Information* 3: 3–142.

Netherland Ministry of Education. (1985). *The Role and Functions of the Universities: Country Report: The Netherlands.* Paris: OECD, mimeo.

New forms of planning in higher education (special issue). (1984). *Higher Education in Europe* 7(1): 3–53.

Niessen, M., and Peschar, J., eds. (1982). *Comparative Research on Education.* Oxford/Budapest: Pergamon/Akadémiai Kiadó.

OECD. (1973). *Short-Cycle Higher Education: A Search for Identity.* Paris: OECD.

OECD. (1977). *Selection and Certification in Education and Employment.* Paris: OECD.

OECD. (1981). *Educational Statistics in OECD Countries.* Paris: OECD.

OECD. (1983a). *Educational Planning: A Reappraisal.* Paris: OECD.

OECD. (1983b). *Policies for Higher Education in the 1980s.* Paris: OECD.

OECD. (1983c). *The University and the Community.* Paris: OECD.

OECD. (1984). *Educational Trends in the 1970s: A Quantitative Analysis.* Paris: OECD.

OECD. (1985). *Education in Modern Society.* Paris: OECD.

OECD. (1986). *Girls and Women in Education.* Paris: OECD.

Oehler, Ch., and Teichler, U. (1984). Changing approaches to planning in higher education in the Federal Republic of Germany. *Higher Education in Europe* 9(1): 13–21.

Oehler, Ch., Teichler, U., and Hornbostel, St. (1986). Aspects of higher education planning in market economy systems. In *Planning in Higher Education.* Bucharest: European Centre for Higher Education, 59–116.

Orzack, L. H. (1980). Educators, practitioners and politicians in the European Common Market. *Higher Education* 9(3): 307–323.

Oxenham, J., ed. (1984). *Education versus Qualifications?* London: Allen & Unwin.

Parsons, D., and Hutt, R. (1981). *The Mobility of Young Graduates.* Brighton: Institute of Manpower Studies (IMS report, 26).

Paul, J.-J. (1981). Education and employment: A survey of French research. *European Journal of Education* 16(1): 95–119.

Paul, J.-J. (1985). Basic concepts and methods used in forecasting skilled-manpower requirements in France. In R. V. Youdi and K. Hinchliffe (eds.), *Forecasting Manpower Needs: The Experience of Eleven Countries.* Paris: UNESCO, International Institute for Educational Planning, 35–56.

Payne, J. (1983). The Open University and unemployment. In *Teaching at a Distance.* Milton Keynes: The Open University, 54–56.

Peisert, H., and Framhein, G. (1978). *Systems of Higher Education: Federal Republic of Germany.* New York: International Council for Educational Development.

Perkin, H. (1984). The historical perspective. In B. R. Clark (ed.), *Perspectives on Higher Education.* Berkeley: University of California Press, 17–55.

Pigelet, J.-L., and Pottier, F. (1983). Populations universitaires et accès à l'emploi. *Formation-Emploi (CEREQ)* 3.

Pottier, F. (1985). L'avenir des diplômés de l'enseignement supérieur scientifique. *Formation-Emploi (CEREQ)* 10.

Premfors, R. (1981). National policy styles and higher education in France, Sweden and the United Kingdom. *European Journal of Education* 16(1): 3–8.

Psacharopoulos, G. (1978). *Education and Work: An Evaluation, and Inventory and Current Research*. Paris: UNESCO, International Institute for Educational Planning.

Psacharopoulos, G. (1986). The planning of education: Where do we stand? *Comparative Education Review* 30(4): 560–573.

Rau, E. (1984). Mal diese, mal jene an der Spitze. *Deutsche Universitaetszeitung* 40(19): 15–20.

Reissert, R. (1983). Studienzeiten—Entwicklungen und Ursachen. *HIS Kurzinformationen* A5.

Ritzen, J. (1981). Education and employment: The Dutch situation. *European Journal of Education* 16(1): 59–71.

Roizen, J., and Jepson, M. (1985). *Degrees for Jobs: Employer Expectations for Higher Education*. Guilford: SHRE and NFER/Nelson.

Rudolf, H., and Husemann, R. (1984). *Hochschulpolitik zwischen Expansion und Restriktion: Ein Vergleich der Entwicklung in der Bundesrepublik Deutschland und der Deutschen Demokratischen Republik*. Frankfurt a.M./New York: Campus.

Rumberger, R. W. (1981). *Overeducation in the U.S. Labor Market*. New York: Praeger.

Sanyal, B. C., and Jozefowicz, A., eds. (1978). *Graduate Employment and Planning of Higher Education in Poland*. Paris: UNESCO, International Institute for Educational Planning.

Sargent, J. (1984). The job outlook for college graduates through the mid-1990's. *Occupational Outlook Quarterly* 28(2): 2–7.

Schelzky, M. (1985). Entsprechung der beruflichen Befaehigungsnachweise zwischen Mitgliedsstaaten der Europaeischen Gemeinschaft: Dokumentation zentraler Texte der EG. *Berufsbildung* 19.

Schut, W. W. (1987). *Werkloosheidcijfers academici, November 1986*. Zoetemeer: Ministerie van Onderwijs en Wetenschappen, Directoraat-General Hoger Onderwijs en Wetenschappelijk Onderzoek.

Schweizerischer Wissenschaftsrat. (1981). Hochschulbildung–Arbeitsmarkt–Beschaeftigung. *Wissenschaftspolitik* 26.

Secretary of State for Education and Science et al. (1985). *The Development of Higher Education into the 1990s*. London: HMSO.

La situation de l'emploi des jeunes universitaires suissess—Résultats de l'enquete effectué en 1983. (1984). *Politique de la Science* 1: 53–74.

Sobel, I. (1982). The human capital revolution in economic development. In P. G. Altbach, R. F. Arnove, and G. P. Kelly (eds.), *Comparative Education*. New York: Macmillan, 54–77.

Sohlman, A. (1981). *Education, Labour Market and Human Capital Models*. Stockholm: Nationalekonomiska institutionen.

Solmon, L. C., Bisconti, A. S., and Ochsner, N. L. (1977). *College as a Training Ground for Jobs*. New York: Praeger.

Sommer, M., ed. (1986). *Lehrerarbeitslosigkeit und Lehrerausbildung*. Opladen: Westdeutscher Verlag.

Statistiska centralbyran. (1986a). *Hoegskolan 1984/85: Elevuppföljningar 1985*. Oerebro: Statistiska centralbyran (Statistiska meddelanden, U 25 SM 8601).

Statistiska centralybyran. (1986b). *Hoegskolan 1984/85: Grundutbildning och pabyggnadsutbildning: Examina laesaret 1984/85*. Oerebro: Statiskiska centralbyran (Statistiksa meddelanden, U 20 SM 8601).

Steedman, H. (1982). Recent developments in higher education in the United Kingdom. *European Journal of Education* 17(2): 192–205.

Stooss, F. (1979). Ausgewaehlte Befunde zur Situation der Hochschulabsolventen in der

Bundesrepublik Deutschland im Jahre 1979. *Mitteilungen aus der Arbeitsmarkt- und Berufsforschung* 12(4): 607–624.

Stooss, F. (1985). Verliert der "Beruf" seine Leitfunktion fuer die Integration der Jugend in die Gesellschaft? *Mitteilungen aus der Arbeitsmarkt- und Berufsforschung* 18(2): 198–208.

Suda, Z. (1981). *Occupational Satisfaction of Graduates under Conditions of "Over-Qualification"*. Maastricht: European Centre for Work and Society.

Swedish Ministry of Education and Cultural Affairs. (1985). The role and functions of universities: Country report: Sweden. Paris: OECD, mimeo.

Tarsh, J. (1982). The labour market for new graduates. *Employment Gazette* 90(5): 205–215.

Tarsh, J. (1985). Trends in the graduate labour market. *Employment Gazette* 93(7): 269–273.

Tarsh, J. (1986). The labour market for new graduates. *Employment Gazette* 94(9): 427–436.

Taylor, J. (1984). The unemployment of university graduates. *Research in Education* 31:11–24.

Taylor, J. (1986). The employability of graduates: Differences between universities. *Studies in Higher Education* 11(1): 17–27.

Taylor, W. (1986). *The Role and Functions of the Universities: General Report*. Paris: OECD, mimeo.

Teichler, U. (1978). Der *Wandel der Beziehungen von Bildungs- und Beschaeftigungssystem und die Entwicklung der beruflich-sozialen Lebensperspektiven Jugendlicher*. Kassel: Wissenschaftliches Zentrum fuer Berufs- und Hochschulforschung der Gesamthochschule Kassel (Arbeitspapiere, 2).

Teichler, U., ed. (1979). *Hochschule und Beruf: Problemlage und Aufgaben der Forschung*. Frankfurt a.M./New York: Campus.

Teichler, U. (1980). *A Challenge to the German Higher Education System*. London: London Association for Comparative Educationists (Occasional Papers, 1).

Teichler, U. (1981a). Hochschule und Beruf in Rumaenien. *Paedagogik und Schule in Ost und West* 29(3): 57–62.

Teichler, U. (1981b). Zur Einfuehrung: Hochschulexpansion. *Zeitschrift fuer Sozialisationsforschung und Erziehungssoziologie* 1(2): 159–172.

Teichler, U. (1983a). Conflicts between employers' demands, societal pressures and individual choices. *International Journal for the Advancement of Counselling* 6(1), 39–45.

Teichler, U. (1983b). *"Oeffnung der Hochschulen"—auch eine Politik fuer die achtziger Jahre?* Bremen: Senator fuer Wissenschaft und Kunst.

Teichler, U. (1984). Forschung ueber Hochschule und Beruf. In D. Goldschmidt, U. Teichler, and W.-D. Webler (eds.), *Forschungsgegenstand Hochschule*. Frankfurt a.M./New York: Campus, 193–216.

Teichler, U. (1985). Higher education: Curriculum. In T. Husén and T. N. Postlethwaite (eds.), *The International Encyclopedia of Education*. Oxford: Pergamon, 2196–2208.

Teichler, U. (1986a). *Higher Education in the Federal Republic of Germany*. New York/Kassel: Center for European Studies, Graduate School and University Center of the City University of New York/Wissenschaftliches Zentrum fuer Berufs- und Hochschulforschung der Gesamthochschule Kassel.

Teichler, U. (1986b). Hochschulpolitik im internationalen Vergleich. In P. Kellermann (ed.), *Universitaet und Hochschulpolitik*. Wien: Boehlau, 24–47.

Teichler, U. (1986c). Strukturentwicklung des Hochschulwesens. In A. Neusel and U.

Teichler (eds.), *Hochschulentwicklung seit den sechziger Jahren*. Weinheim/Basel: Beltz, 93–143.

Teichler, U. (1988). Beziehungen von Bildungs- und Beschaeftigungssystem—Erfordern die Entwicklungen der achtziger Jahre neue Erklaerungsansaetze? *Soziale Welt* 38: 27–57.

Teichler, U. (1987). Higher education and new challenges of the occupation system. In H. Roehrs (ed.), *Tradition and Reform of the University under an International Perspective*. Frankfurt a.M.: Lang, 293–307.

Teichler, U., et al. (1987). *Hochschule-Studium-Berufsvorstellungen*. Bad Honnef: Bock.

Teichler, U., Buttgereit, M., and Holtkamp, R. (1984). *Hochschulzertifikate in der betrieblichen Einstellungspraxis*. Bad Honnef: Bock.

Teichler, U., Hartung, D., and Nuthmann, R. (1980). *Higher Education and the Needs of Society*. Windsor: NFER Publishing.

Teichler, U., and Lanzendoerfer, M. (1986). *European Diploma Handbook: A Feasibility Study*. Kassel: Wissenschaftliches Zentrum fuer Berufs- und Hochschulforschung der Gesamthochschule Kassel, mimeo.

Teichler, U., and Sanyal, B. C. (1982). *Higher Education and the Labour Market in the Federal Republic of Germany*. Paris: UNESCO Press.

Teichler, U., and Sanyal, B. C. (1984). Higher education and the labour market. In R. Avakov et al. (eds.), *Higher Education and Employment in the USSR and in the Federal Republic of Germany*. Paris: UNESCO, International Institute for Educational Planning, 89–184.

Tessaring, M. (1982). Beschaeftigungsmoeglichkeiten und Arbeitsmarktrisiken hochqualifizierter Arbeitskraefte. *Aus Politik und Zeitgeschichte: Beilage zur Wochenzeitschrift Das Parlament* Sep. 25.

Tessaring, M. (1985). An evaluation of labour-market and educational forecasts in the Federal Republic of Germany. In R. V. Youdi and K. Hinchliffe (eds.), *Forecasting Skilled Manpower Needs: The Experience of Eleven Countries*. Paris: UNESCO, International Institute for Educational Planning, 57–74.

Tessaring, M., and Werner, H. (1975). *Beschaeftigungsprobleme von Hochschulabsolventen im internationalen Vergleich*. Goettingen: Schwartz.

Tessaring, M., and Werner, H. (1981). *Beschaeftigung und Arbeitsmarkt fuer Hochschulabsolventen in den Laendern der Europaeischen Gemeinschaft*. Nuernberg: Institut fuer Arbeitsmarkt- und Berufsforschung der Bundesanstalt fuer Arbeit (Beitraege, 46).

Timár, J. (1983). *L'enseignement supérieur et le dévelopment économique et technique en Hongrie*. Paris: UNESCO, International Institute for Educational Planning.

Triebel, A. (1986). 200 Jahre Wachstumsforschung der tertiaeren Bildung. In *Bevoelkerungsentwicklung, Studienverhalten und Hochschulpolitik*. Berlin: Freie Universitaet Berlin, Zentralinstitut fuer sozialwissenschaftliche Forschung, 1–109.

Trow, M. (1974). Problems in the transition from elite to mass higher education. In OECD (ed.), *Policies for Higher Education*. Paris: OECD, 51–101.

Unemployment among graduates will rise still further. (1981). *Higher Education and Research in the Netherlands* 25(3–4): 32–36.

UNESCO. (1982). *World Guide to Higher Education*. Paris: UNESCO Press.

UNESCO-CEPES. (1983). *Higher Education and Economic Development in Europe 1975–1980: A Statistical and Economic Study* (2 vols). Bucharest: UNESCO-CEPES.

Ushiogi, M. (1984). *Job Perspectives of College Graduates in Japan*. Kassel: Wissenschaftliches Zentrum fuer Berufs- und Hochschulforschung der Gesamthochschule Kassel (Arbeitspapiere, 14).

Utbildnings-Department, eds. (1986). *Engine or Train? The Role of Education in Economic and Regional Development*. Stockholm: Liber.

Valli, P.-P. (1985). Accès à l'emploi, monopole et concurrence à la sortie des universitiés. In A. Bienaymé, L. Cerych, and G. Neave (eds.), *La professionalisation de l'enseignement supérieur*. Paris: Institute of Education and Social Policy, 45–65.

Van Hoof, J. J. (1986). *Aansluiting tussen onderwijs en arbeid: Recente ontwikkelingen en uitgaangspunkten voor beleid*. 's-Gravenhage: Organisatie voor Strategisch Arbeidsmarktonderzoek (OSA-werkdocument, W 28).

Van Hoof, J. J., and Dronkers, J. (1980). *Onderwijs en arbeitsmarkt*. Deventer: Van Loghum Slaterus.

Vedel, G., ed. (1981). *Reform and Development of Tertiary (Post-Secondary) Education in Southern Europe*. Strasbourg: Council of Europe.

Vincens, J. (1981). Post-secondary education and employment: The French case. *European Journal of Education* 16(1): 29–57.

Vincens, J. (1982). Insertion professionelle et marche du travail. In Centre National de la Recherche Scientifique and Centre Régional de Publications de Toulouse Sciences Sociales (eds.), *Formation et Emploi: Colloque de Toulouse*. Paris: Éditions du CNRS, 111–124.

Vincens, J. (1985). Formation universitaire et emploi vus dans une perspective internationale. *Politique de la science* 32: 45–61.

Vincens, J. (1986). Enseignement supérieur et marche du travail, unpubl. manuscript.

Vincens, J., et al. (1985). L'insertion des diplomes de l'enseignement supérieur. In Centre National de la Recherche Scientifique and Centre Régional de Publications de Toulouse Sciences Sociales (eds.), *Formation et Emploi: Colloque de Toulouse*. Paris: Éditions du CNRS, 125–161.

Von Landsberg, G. (1985). Fachhochschulabsolventen als Bewerber—die Auswahlkriterian der Privatwirtschaft. In M. Buttgereit, et al. *Betriebliche Personalpolitik*. Koeln: Deutschler Instituts-Verlag, 43–58.

Von Landsberg, G. (1986). Qualifikation und Berufserfolg. In H.-J. Bodenhoefer, et al., *Ingenieure in der Wirtschaft*. Koeln: Deutschler Instituts-Verlag, 6–23.

Von Recum, H. (1984). The identity crisis of educational planning. *International Review of Education* 30(2): 155–161.

Watts, A. G. (1972). *Diversity and Choice in Higher Education*. London: Routledge & Kegan Paul.

Weber, K. (1984). Konstanz und Wandel der Akademikerbeschaeftigung. *Bulletin der Vereinigung Schweizerischer Hochschuldozenten* 3: 18–32.

Weber, K., Arend, M., and Weiss, P. (1985). Arbeit 2000: Bestimmungsgroessen, Wirkungszusammenhaenge, Szenarien der akademischen Beschaeftigung. *Wissenschaftspolitik* 32: 67–126.

Weiler, H. N., ed. (1980). *Educational Planning and Social Change*. Paris: UNESCO, International Institute for Educational Planning.

Westergard-Nielsen, N. C. (1981). A Study of a professional labor market. *Studies in Labor Market Dynamics: Working Papers* 2: 1–69.

Williams, G. (1980). Educational planning—past, present and future. *Higher Education in Europe* 5(1): 12–19.

Williams, G. (1984). The economic approach. In B. R. Clark (ed.), *Perspectives on Higher Education*. Berkeley: University of California Press, 79–105.

Williams, G. (1985). Graduate employment and vocationalism in higher education. *European Journal of Education* 20: 2–3.

Williamson, P. (1981). Flow of new graduates into employment. *Employment Gazette* 89(2): 71–75.

Windolf, P. (1982). *Formale Bildungsabschlüsse als Selektionskriterium am Arbeitsmarkt: Eine vergleichende Analyse zwischen Frankreich, der Bundesrepublik Deutschland und Grossbritaninnen.* Berlin: Wissenschaftszentrum Berlin, IIMV (Discussion papers, IIM/LMP 82–21a).

Windolf, P. (1986). *Bildungsexpansion und Arbeitsmarkt.* Marburg: Universitaet Marburg, Habilitationsschrift.

Wolter, W. (1986). Aspects of planning in higher education under socialist conditions. In *Planning in Higher Education.* Bucharest: European Centre for Higher Education, 11–58.

Youdi, R. V., and Hinchliffe, K., eds. (1985). *Forecasting Skilled Manpower Needs: The Experience of Eleven Countries.* Paris: UNESCO, International Institute for Educational Planning.

Zomer, H. (1982). Graduate unemployment: making sense of a problem. *Higher Education and Research in the Netherlands* 26: 1–2.

Zukunftsperspektiven gesellschaftlicher Entwicklungen. (1983). Stuttgart: Kommission "Zukunftsperspektiven gesellschaftlicher Entwicklungen."

Fiction to Fact: College Novels and the Study of Higher Education

John R. Thelin
The College of William and Mary
and
Barbara K. Townsend
Loyola University of Chicago

"Keeping up with the literature in the field" usually means the task of reading articles in scholarly journals. For those committed to the understanding and study of higher education, however, there is another connotation: the opportunity, even the obligation, to read the fiction which uses colleges and universities as subject and setting. We are heirs to a rich legacy of "college novels"—yet, unfortunately, it has had little incorporation or acknowledgment in the formal study of higher education. Our aim is to correct this imbalance, to anticipate both the problems and the prospects which come with using fiction as a source of information and insights about colleges and universities.

Failure to do so is a grave sin of omission. The sheer bulk, popularity, and longevity of the college novel genre warrant attention. One historic anecdote which illustrates its potency is the popularity of the "Frank Merriwell" stories in shaping the popular juvenile image of college life. Between 1896 and 1915, this fictional college hero appeared in 986 consecutive weekly stories and in 415 paperback novels—with an estimated weekly readership of close to 3 million! At the peak of the Merriwell publications, a total of 123 million copies of his stories were sold in one year. Confirmation of the American public's insatiable appetite for college adventure stories was that the author of the "Frank Merriwell" series (who himself had never attended college) used a second pseudonym during the same years to write a best-selling series of "Boltwood of Yale" boys' novels (Cain, 1927, p. 129; O'Donnell, 1969, p. 61; Thelin, 1976b, p. 11).

Even if one discounts juvenile stories and mystery novels, the college remains integral to American literature. It has at one time or another attracted outstanding authors, including Sinclair Lewis, Willa Cather, E. B. White, Robert Penn Warren, Mary McCarthy, George Santayana, John P. Marquand, James Thurber, F. Scott Fitzgerald, Henry Seidel Canby, Bernard DeVoto, Joyce Carol Oates,

Allison Lurie, Philip Roth, Vladimir Nabokov, Saul Bellow, Bernard Malamud, and John Barth (Spectorsky, 1958). According to John E. Kramer's comprehensive annotated bibliography, *The American College Novel* (1981), in the century between 1880 and 1980 over 425 "serious" American college novels were published.

Our intent is to make a case for the serious and systematic analysis of college fiction as part of the study of higher education. At very least, such an analysis suggests an alternative or supplement to overreliance on questionnaire data which has characterized the bulk of the research effort on the college experience and on behavior within organizations (Webb et al., 1966; Thelin, 1976a). For example, Hodgkinson's analysis (1967) of the impact of college on undergraduates, Alexander Astin's *Four Critical Years* (1978), and Astin's annual survey of college student attitudes and values document changes over time and within the college experience—but it is the detailed and sharp eye of the participant observer who may best tell us how such changes actually take place within the campus walls.

We hope our study will encourage triangulation as a research strategy, in which fiction can serve as one important source to be checked and confirmed by tests for validity, accuracy, and significance in concert with a variety of other kinds of data, including institutional records, archival materials, and student and alumni memoirs and biographies. Our approach to fiction is twofold: on the one hand, we have read and analyzed the novels about college life; on the other, we ultimately intend to connect our findings to the strand of scholarship in such fields as literary analysis, social history, and American studies for models and inspiration as to how these different disciplines have respectively treated the college novel (e.g., Bail, 1958; Boys, 1946; Carpenter, 1960; DeMott, 1962; Hall, 1931; Randel, 1947). Implicit is our contention that most mainstream higher education research projects have given scant attention to these scholarly methods or traditions.

Ironically, in the course of our research project, we have come across an interesting phenomenon: the initial response of many researchers is to be skeptical about the approach; then, later, in a more informal setting, the same skeptic says, "By the way, have you read *The Paper Chase?* It really captures the pressure and trauma of Harvard Law School" (Osborn, 1971). There are some strange gaps. Journalist Tom Wolfe, whose articles probe virtually every dimension of American popular culture, received his Ph.D. in American studies from Yale but has had little to say about the graduate school experience. On the contrary, he observed over a decade ago that there has been no great American novel about graduate school due to a conspiracy of silence among its participants (Wolfe, 1976, p. 1; Thelin, 1982, p. 165). Apparently, few of the victims/ survivors can bring themselves to reconstruct its peculiar combination of boredom, pain, and servitude. This social fact of organizational life alone ought usher in wholesale educational reforms within the academic profession.

David Riesman contends that George Weller's *Not to Eat, Not for Love* (1933) is an excellent profile of the complexities of Harvard's growing pains, internal schisms, and diverse, disconnected constituencies as it evolved into a national university in the late 1920s (the era when Riesman himself was an undergraduate and editor of *The Crimson* newspaper) (Gwynn, 1949, p. 388; Bail, 1958). Or as one colleague and reviewer advised, "If you want to understand the Political Science department at Yale, you ought to read *Tell the Time to None*" (Hudson, 1966). From time to time, specific focus on fiction for the study of colleges and universities surfaces as a special-topics seminar in graduate programs (Clifford, 1983). And one well-known contemporary researcher who emphasizes experimental design studies based on questionnaire data is justifiably proud of the list of college novels he uses for readings in his graduate course on "The College and University Professor" (Blackburn, 1983).

Novels, then, can be a fertile, intriguing source about colleges if handled carefully. They are not a neat, obvious solution to the information problem about describing college life. Rather, they stand as a puzzle in which the researcher's task is to decode the images, events, and symbols. They are to be connected to other sources of information and ultimately are to generate insights and interpretations. We heed well historian W. L. Burn's warning, "Art mirrors life. The problem is that mirrors have the power to distort" (1964, p. 85).

PROBLEMS

Our topic and approach faces some predictable criticisms. We acknowledge these problems but see them as interesting complications rather than as an order to cease and desist.

Complaint 1: "The genre of college novels is amorphous and unwieldy, not legitimate as a source of serious or systematic analysis. At worst, it is leisure reading masquerading as empirical research."

This need not be so. Thanks in large measure to two superb annotated bibliographies (Kramer, 1981; Lyons, 1962), along with our own categorization, we can bring a measure of order and coherence to the 425 American college novels. For example, we have "sliced" and cross-listed works within the genre into the following categories:

Faculty-staff versus student-centered plots

Private versus public institutions as settings

Decade-by-decade chronology

Land-grant college novels

Novels about women's colleges

Novels by authors who actually attended the depicted college

Since one can isolate themes, eras, and settings with great precision, one thus has an antidote to vague impressions and blurring over time and place. Our study, for example, focuses on the eighty student-centered campus novels written by authors who actually attended the depicted college.

Complaint 2: "College novels are skewed to portray only a few campuses."

Imbalance is neither good nor bad, but it is important and intriguing as a social fact. This limit is hardly license to dismiss the novels. As Berton Braley wrote in the 1930s:

It's general knowledge that many a college
That's not very socially smart
Has teams that can crush dear old Harvard to mush
And take Yale and Princeton apart
But gridiron heroes exclusively hail
(In stories) from Harvard, or Princeton, or Yale!
(Quoted in Thelin, 1976b, p. 46)

Our own statistical analysis confirms Braley's lyrical observation. Within a cluster of eighty novels about students at specific institutions, the tally is as follows: 27 for Harvard, 12 for Yale, 7 for Princeton, 4 for Columbia (including Barnard), 5 for the University of Chicago, 13 for various large state universities, and the remainder scattered among assorted campuses. At the same time, we offer the remainder that coverage by *Newsweek, Time,* and the national press is equally skewed. A comparable trend holds as well among researchers in higher education. Institutional case studies by social and behavioral scientists also tend to focus on a relative handful of prestigious institutions.

Rather than use "imbalance" as an excuse to ignore the genre, why not try to figure out the reason for the imbalance? We have already alluded to Tom Wolfe's contention about the absence of novels dealing with graduate students. A good puzzle for the 1980s might be "Why hasn't the community college as a distinctive American institution spawned the Great American Novel?" Also worth consideration is that novels deal with generic campuses and universal themes. The scholar is left with the interesting task of continually weighing between induction and deduction in the research act, distinguishing between specific and perennial features of undergraduate life.

Complaint 3: "Novels are not intended necessarily to provide accuracy or facts. They are a very dubious source of information about colleges and universities."

Part of the attraction that college novels hold is that they may *unwittingly* provide information and insights, thus fulfilling one of the favorable characteristics of "unobtrusive measures" outlined by Eugene Webb and other social scientists in their 1966 manifesto. There are some good ways to gauge the plausibility of a novel; namely, by checking the author's background and by triangulation with myriad other sources for signs of authenticity, accuracy, and significance. Historians accept this responsibility as a matter of course when they analyze the tone and context of any document.

Indeed, we are vigilant to ferret out "hack" authors who have contrived a formula for "college novels." Our screening criterion is indebted to the editors of the *Harvard Lampoon,* who in 1906 compiled advice for outsiders attempting to write superficial best-sellers about Fair Harvard:

> It is well to begin by spending at least half a day at the University, jotting down the names of streets and buildings. You will depend on these for local color.
>
> Make your characters extravagant, financially and otherwise. Make them appear several times stretched in lounging robes before a blazing fire while the rain patters on the window panes—and at least once in the front row at the Tremont.
>
> Make them drink frequently and variously, and smoke on every possible pretext. Put a bull pup in each chapter and a Morris chair on every page. Talk familiarly of the Regent, Gore Hall, and clubs. . . . Introduce a girl who is innocuous and one or two who are not. (Quoted in Bentinck-Smith, 1953, pp. 13–14)

More serious is the charge that a student author presents a distorted view of campus life. This is known as the "$n = 1$" indictment of fiction (along with memoirs and biographies) as sources of institutional information. This "complaint" is a *non sequitur* which ought not to halt inquiry. The fact that a distinctive point of view is neither pervasive nor representative does not diminish its significance. Indeed, this is the very point of view which we need to leaven the tendency of aggregate studies to cut the sharp edges off depictions of life within organizations. By this standard, college novels by former students represent "tales out of school," potentially valuable as a lens which literally turns the campus inside out (Thelin, 1979, pp. 295–298). In those works which are institutional exposés, a student author may have an axe to grind; but here the analyst's problem is to decipher this tone, not merely to discard the account. And there is the fascinating possibility that the atypical point of view has something important to say about issues that most fellow students either overlooked or were silent about.

PROSPECTS

Our resolution is that the preceding criticisms, which some see as insurmountable obstacles, are actually healthy caveats—warnings which complicate and sophisticate the analysis of college life. Having briefly responded to major reservations, let us shift to positive ways in which college novels can be used. Here we draw first from the tradition of literary analysis and finally from the historian's craft.

LITERARY APPROACHES TO THE COLLEGE NOVELS

When we use the literary tradition, college novels can be examined from a number of approaches (Rohrberger, Woods, and Dukore, 1968, pp 6–16). A major approach used in this study is the "biographical" analysis, whereby knowledge of the author's life is fundamental to understanding and appreciating the text. For this reason, we have concentrated upon campus novels written by persons who actually attended the colleges or universities depicted in the novels. An author's attendance at the institution used as the setting for the college experience tends to add legitimacy to the portrayal of the institution's customs and values. It also renders the portrayal of college as an interpretation of the author's experiences therein, particularly important if the novels are to be considered as pertinent sources of alumni opinion about college. Thus, when we read F. Scott Fitzgerald's *This Side of Paradise* (1920), we assume that his portrayal of Amory Blaine's years at Princeton before World War I reflects some of Fitzgerald's experiences during his own sporadic attendance at Princeton from 1913 through 1917. And Percy Marks's best-selling novel about undergraduate life, *The Plastic Age* (1924), draws from his firsthand observations at Brown. Likewise, James T. Farrell draws from his off-again, on-again enrollment at the University of Chicago from 1925 to 1929 in his novels *My Days of Anger* (1943) and *The Silence of History* (1963), both of which depict the experiences of a working-class Irish Catholic commuter student who finds writing to be an outlet for his intelligence and emotions.

College novels can also be approached from a sociocultural perspective whereby they are seen as reflections of the social milieu in which they were created. From this perspective, they are particularly useful for illustrating facets of the prevailing national culture and their ultimate diffusion to campus life. This does not imply a facile one-to-one correlation between school and society; on the contrary, one enduring question for higher education researchers is whether campus values are ahead, behind, or congruent with those of the dominant national or regional culture (Stone, 1971). A college may be a vanguard for social change; yet it is equally plausible that it can be a reactionary stronghold for some beliefs, or it may merely ratify existing values held outside campus walls.

For example, college novels often reflect the anti-Semitism once widely accepted in large segments of American society, including its colleges and universities. Worth note is the historical fact that official admissions policies and practices were often far ahead of tolerance and assimilation within the student body, where exclusion persisted. Typical is a conversation in Robert Nathan's *Peter Kindred* (1920), set at Harvard around 1920, in which Peter's friendship with a Jewish student is discussed by two of Peter's friends:

> "It hurts Peter to be seen around with him."
> "Because he's a Jew?"

"Yes, rather. . . . Oh, I'm not down on Jews as a race. There's something . . . a rather pathetic and wistful sweetness about Jewish women . . . some Jewish women. And some Jewish men have a lot of fire. But this chap David doesn't seem to have found himself. . . . And then, of course, he's a Jew, and Peter simply can't take him around with him, Don, because the men who might like Peter, don't like Jews. I don't blame them . . . they've been brought up that way." (Nathan, 1920, pp. 83–84)

College novels also illustrate the social customs of their times. Changing patterns of dating and attitudes toward sex between unmarried partners are clearly seen in these novels. At the turn of the century, sex between unmarried people was viewed as sinful for both men and women—and undergraduates ascribed to this belief, even if they sometimes failed to live up to the code. In Reginald Kaufman's *Jarvis of Harvard* (1901), much of the story is about Jarvis's efforts to come to terms with his having slept with a woman. Eventually he falls in love with a "pure" woman who, after much anguished soul-searching, finds herself able to forgive his error and is willing to marry him. By the 1930s, student sexual mores had changed considerably as "nice" women necked and even petted with "socially acceptable" men. In the college novels of this period, a college woman occasionally uses her sexuality "to get what she wants," for example, Lee Drayton, a 1930s Vassar student in Gertrude Carrick's *Consider the Daisies* (1941), but such promiscuity is exceptional. Then, as in the 1950s and part of the 1960s, college women were hesitant to "go too far too soon." A comment by a Smith College student in Nora Johnson's *A Step Beyond Innocence* (1961) reflects well the sexual mores of the 1950s as two friends discuss whether one of them should have let her date take off her blouse: "I wanted to let him, but I was afraid if I did, the first time he tried, he'd think I ran around taking my blouse off all the time" (p. 125). After the so-called sexual revolution in the 1960s, characters usually couple with minimal concern about reputation or morals, as in Perdita Buchan's *Girl with a Zebra* (1966), set at Radcliffe and Harvard in the 1960s.

Perhaps the most useful literary approach to college novels is that which focuses upon the text itself. Setting aside such matters as the author's biography or the sociocultural milieu in which the work was created, we can focus upon the novel as an art form. By this standard, college novels project distinctive images of undergraduate life (or of faculty life), images which influence those who read the novels and later attend college. The novels provide a kind of "anticipatory socialization" (Jencks and Riesman, 1968), an engendered set of expectations about what life at college will be like—or ought to be like. If the expectations spawned by the novels are not met, students must somehow reconcile the gap. Students may feel they have attended the wrong college—perhaps the experience would have been different (and more like the novels) elsewhere. Or they may feel that "college ain't what it's cracked up to be." In both cases, the art of the college novel is influencing the life and expectations of applicants and students.

A graphic illustration comes from F. Scott Fitzgerald's fictional Amory Blaine, who explains the rationale he used as a high school senior in the early 1900s to choose Princeton:

> "I want to go to Princeton," said Amory, "I don't know why, but I think of all Harvard men as sissies, like I used to be, and all Yale men as wearing big blue sweaters and smoking pipes. . . . I think of Princeton as being lazy and good-looking and aristocratic—you know, like a Spring Day. Harvard seems sort of indoors—"
>
> "And Yale is November, crisp and energetic," finished Monsignor.
>
> "That's it." (Fitzgerald, 1920, p. 8)

A half century later, college selection as a ritual in American adolescent life and as a theme in American fiction seems amazingly familiar; for example, in Bruce Jay Friedman's novel *A Mother's Kisses* (1964), Joseph, a high school student from New York City, recollects how his campus images were shaped:

> He had finished high school and sent out applications to two colleges for the fall, Columbia and Bates, the latter because he liked the name. Once at a summer resort, he had watched a short scrappy fellow with heavy thighs play basketball, staying all over his man, hollering out catcalls, giving his opponent no quarter. The fellow said he went to Bates and Joseph had come to think of the school as a scrappy little heavy-thighed college full of fast little fellows who pressed their opponents. He chose Columbia in case the out-of-town school rejected him for not being scrappy enough. (pp. 9–10)

So, although art imitates life, this situation coexists with the prospect that life sometimes imitates art. In either case, the residual question is "What *are* the images of undergraduate life projected by novels?" A salient finding is that the bulk of student-centered novels project a world in which extracurricular activities dominate while the formal curriculum and faculty are peripheral. It is a campus world at wide variance with that projected in most higher education reform reports and commission studies—reports which emphasize formal studies, with scant attention to the extracurriculum. In this respect, the novels are in harmony with historian Laurence Veysey's analysis (1965) of student life during the period 1870–1910, the era of the "emergence of the American university"—a study which found evidence of a persistent "gulf between students and faculty," an intricate, self-contained undergraduate world which ascribed to the motto, "Don't let your studies interfere with your education" (pp. 268–301).

Precisely which aspects of the extracurriculum emerge as important from the novels? Not surprisingly, intercollegiate athletics (especially football) are conspicuous. Numerous novels depict football games as a potent source of student spirit which provides not only entertainment as an event to watch and to which to bring a date, but also as an outlet for energy and as a focal point for loyalty to one's alma mater. And this inspirational power continues when students become alumni. Membership on a varsity team can also be central to a fictional student's institutional involvement and growth in character. We see this in

Dorothy Canfield's *Rough-Hewn* (1922), in which the protagonist, Neale Crittenden, a student at Columbia, class of 1904, finds that being a member of the football team gives meaning to his college experience. After the freshman season ends, Neale thinks, ". . . what a vacuum! Nothing in life but classes! . . . What did the fellows do who hadn't anything but classes? How could they stand it?" (p. 216). Indeed, football has become a "collegiate religion" to Neale, as we learn in his senior year:

> The end of the football season was a door slammed in Neale's face forever. He had given four years of his life to football, flung them joyfully and proudly to feed the sacred flame. Now for the rest of his life, he was to be shut out from the temple of the only religion which had as yet been offered him . . . he woke to the knowledge that the aim of his life had been taken away . . . (p. 262)

Courses have little influence on Neale; in fact, he mentions only one course ("General European History") as stimulating or influential. Football connects him to college and develops his sense of maturity and responsibility. And although Neale initially has only minimal involvement in college life apart from football, eventually he is recruited into a fraternity and becomes a big man on campus—as abbreviated in the collegiate argot, a "BMOC."

A comparable pattern holds in numerous novels: stature as a college athlete almost guarantees that a student will become a "big man on campus." This was true for Dink Stover at Yale in 1910 (Johnson, 1912), as well as for Oliver Barrett IV at Harvard in the 1960s, as depicted in *Love Story* (Segal, 1970). In a humorous vein, the character of Eino Effllukkinnenn at the University of Minnesota of the 1930s illustrates the athlete as both "BMOC" and "dumb jock." Author Max Shulman describes Eino's transformation and elevation in campus life as follows in *Barefoot Boy with Cheek* (1943):

> Four years go he was an unknown boy roaming around the North Woods precariously keeping body and soul together by stealing bait from bear traps. Then a Minnesota football scout saw him, lassoed him, put shoes on him, taught him to sign his name, and brought him to the university to play football. And last year Eino was an All-American! All-American! (p. 42)

Although written over forty years ago, Shulman's description of athletic recruitment comes perilously close to recent revelations of excesses in college recruiting practices—with allowance for historical changes in the ethnic groups who disproportionately rely on sports as an avenue of social mobility and educational opportunity. Whereas in 1930 it was the immigrant son of Scandinavian, Irish, or Eastern European stock who was the object of college recruiters, since the 1970s it has been the black athlete who commands attention and exploitation.

Large state universities were not the only place where "dumb jocks" were found in college novels. A description of a football player at Yale in the early

1920s sounds remarkably like that of Eino: "Hank O'Day from out of the backwoods somewhere, as good-natured a boob as ever lived, gets by big because he is a good athlete"; Hank has "the body of a giant and the mind of a child," according to novelist John Wiley in *The Education of Peter* (1924, pp. 235, 241). In *My Days of Anger* (Farrell, 1943), a fictional student offers the following profile of the captain-elect of the University of Chicago's football team in the mid-1920s:

> He's taking a geology course. They pass rocks round for the students to examine, and Mike doesn't know what to make of the rocks. So he tosses them out of the window. The Geology Department has lost all its stones and is in a dither. Dr. Shafton is reorganizing a field expedition for geology students to hunt for his rocks on campus. (p. 382)

The paradox is that athletes are portrayed as highly visible, influential campus figures yet are simultaneously ridiculed as "dumb jocks" in a peculiar mixture of admiration and derision by fellow students, perhaps indicative of conflicting values and tensions within the American campus culture. Those most admired on campus are often those least equipped for classroom success. Their popularity is consistent with the picture and proportions of successful college life depicted in the novels: three-fourths extracurricular and one-fourth academic.

Another important part of extracurricular life is dating and thoughts about the opposite sex, whether the fictional college is a coeducational campus or a single-sex institution. Jocks and other "BMOCs," such as *Love Story*'s Oliver Barrett IV, are popular with women and date frequently. Undergraduates who do not date are usually portrayed as very shy or socially ill at ease with their college fellows.

Fraternities and sororities—the Greeks—constitute a third important group in extracurricular life which emerges from the college novels. Membership signals popularity and a necessary passport to full social standing on campus among the traditional-age full-time college students who are neither "grinds" nor "townies." Those who are not Greeks are usually viewed by themselves, as well as by others, as social misfits. For example, in Charles Thompson's 1957 *Halfway Down the Stairs*, David Pope (a 1950s Cornell student) is acutely aware of the social gap between himself and the fraternity men and sorority women. At those Greek parties he attends because his popular, socially savvy girlfriend has been invited, David is awkward and unsure of himself; he commits social blunders that clearly stigmatize him as an outsider, a non-Greek.

Not every college or university has Panhellenic groups, though. Some institutions, including Harvard, Princeton, and Yale, have their own indigenous clubs and societies, which are like the Greeks in that they are exclusive groups which self-determine the "right" students to be selected for membership. Rarely are the "right" students those who concentrate upon the formal curriculum. Especially in novels set in Princeton and Yale, much of the action deals with student efforts to "make" a secret society or eating club. According to F. Scott Fitzgerald's *This Side of Paradise* (1920), Princeton students of the pre-World War I era devoted their first two years to doing so "until at club elections . . . every one should be sewed up in some bag for the rest of his college career" (p. 48). Yale men were on trial through their junior year, when "tapping" for membership in the hallowed Skull and Bones, Key, and Wolf's Head societies occurs (Johnson, 1912).

Few novels question the rationale for or the legitimacy of the fraternities, clubs, and exclusive sororities. From time to time, a novel will focus on how exclusion from these organizations can damage students' self-esteem or will critically analyze their conformist character. The Greeks are indicted in several novels set at large state universities. In Mildred Evans Gilman's *Fig Leaves* (1925), Lydia Carter, of the class of 1917, at the University of Wisconsin is initially unhappy in her life as a sorority sister, but the stress of a romance and an impending world war lead her to participate in an antisorority movement. Criticizing the sorority system as "undemocratic," Lydia says:

> It's a *rotten* system. . . . It's terrible. The autocratic manner of the sororities, the way they run everything, elections and social events. They *make* a girl, and for every girl they make, they reduce seven or eight to social nothingness. (p. 277)

Fraternities are also criticized in the novel, albeit indirectly. When a fraternity man speaks to Lydia about her view of sororities, he says:

> Fraternities are different. Men don't bother about the little things that women do, the way a person looks and all that. Of course, he's got to look respectable, but they don't make such a big fuss over appearance. If a man has a good record behind him, comes of a decent family and seems to be clean-minded—and isn't a Jew—that's all that's necessary, if the fellows like him. Fraternities aren't like sororities. (p. 295)

Sororities and fraternities are the object of criticism in Keith Winthur's *Beyond the Garden Gate* (1947), in which a brother and sister are Greeks at the University of Oregon. In Forrest's senior year as fraternity president, he fights with a pledge who is making crude sexual comments about Forrest's girlfriend. When Forrest resigns from the fraternity, his freshman sister, Alice, is dropped from the sorority pledge list. She later tells her brother she is glad of what has happened because the incident has made her see the insincerity of the sororities' so-called sisterhood: "Those girls know I hadn't done anything wrong. They told me they were sisters and that we should always be loyal, and a hundred other things; and then, just because you quarreled with the boys at your house, or something, they dropped me" (p. 232). A more recent novel (and also a movie), *Breaking Away* (Howard, 1979), presents the Greeks from the townies' perspective. Its members are seen as wealthy: the men own Mercedes and Jaguars, wear LaCoste shirts and cashmere sweaters, and live in huge houses on Fraternity Row. Sorority women are incredibly good-looking and well-built. Larger than life in their wealth and physical attractiveness, they are also presented as one-dimensional in character: shallow and arrogant.

Clubs and secret societies also are criticized occasionally, particularly in Fitzgerald's *This Side of Paradise* (1920) and Johnson's *Stover at Yale* (1912). Fitzgerald's Amory Blaine senses the closed social system created by the clubs almost as soon as he enters Princeton, but at first he doesn't mind "the glittering caste system" because he just wants "to be one of them" (p. 48). In his junior year, several juniors and seniors resign from their eating clubs for reasons cavalierly listed by one student as follows: "Oh, clubs are injurious to Princeton democracy: cost a lot, draw social lines, take time; the regular line you get sometimes from disappointed sophomores. Woodrow Wilson thought they should be abolished and all that" (p. 114). Since the student who spearheaded the mass resignation is admired by Amory, the legitimacy of the criticism is established for the reader in spite of the above snide, flippant dismissal.

An even more telling indictment of secret societies appears in *Stover at Yale* (Johnson, 1912), where Dink Stover, headed for BMOC status, begins to question "the struggle for position" (p. 18), the fervent contest in which classmates compete for honors so that each will eventually be "tapped" for one of three secret societies in their junior year. When Dink's mentor counsels him how to behave during his first days at Yale, Dink finds his belief in "spontaneous democracy" (p. 231) inhibited. Contrary to the image of fraternities and sororities as an easy, idyllic life, Dink discovers that the Yale system and societies demand energy, even though formal studies are accepted as a necessary, albeit incidental, evil. Success in the extracurricular student life at Yale turns college into a "three years grind" characterized by "discipline" and "fatigue" (p. 212) to gain election to a society. When his friendship with social outsiders in his class is criticized by society members, Dink resigns in anger and disgust from his sophomore society to go his own way and to make friends with *all* Yale students. Dink and the prestigious secret societies ultimately reach a mutual agreement (and mutual admiration). The illustrious Skull and Bones Society acknowledges Stover's spirit by tapping him—even though (or possibly because?) he dared to criticize its secrecy as "un-American, undemocratic, and stultifying" (p. 375). Stover, in turn, admits to himself that despite his criticism and rebellion, he does want the rewards and fellowship of the society, which is at the heart of historic Yale. The happy ending is that the reader is left both with criticism and conformity, perhaps an indication of accommodation as a dimension of internal reform (Thelin, 1976b, pp. 11–13).

The formal curriculum intrudes upon college life only in the form of individual courses or examinations, as exemplified by the elaborate defiance and academic gamesmanship of Owen Wister's *Philosophy 4* (1903). When mentioned at all, courses are dismissed as "unimportant" in content or simply "a detail," as in the classic, *The Diary of a Freshman* (Flandrau, 1901, pp. 58, 126) or as not relevant to "real" learning. For example, in *Boys and Men: A Story of Life at Yale* (Holbrook, 1900), a "cheeky" callow youth named Budson begins to change for the better due to the positive influence of his roommate and friends, illustrative of "some of the deepest lessons that a man learns in college not being set down in the catalogue" (p. 63). In *The Education of Peter* (Wiley, 1924), Peter Carey reflects as he is about to graduate from Yale in the 1920s:

> In just a short time now he would have gone. His education was almost completed. He was still a little hazy concerning the use of specific gravity and the binomial theory was rapidly becoming a myth, but the other things he had learned had sunk much deeper. *Things not included in the curriculum.* Here in this mimic world were crowded in four years the desires and ambitions of a lifetime . . . the iron conventions, the struggles to predominate, the success of some, jealousy, idealism, work, the call of the glittering heights. He had come among them unknown and blindly struggled with each. It was over now, but somewhere beneath the elms he had found knowledge. (p. 293; italics added)

Although the curriculum and individual courses are seldom influential, a particular professor may be pivotal to a student in a college novel. In *The Diary of a Freshman* (Flandrau, 1901), the curriculum is depicted as classes to be cut or slept through, exams to be passed, and papers to be written. Despite these obligatory chores, the students do see one friendly professor as influential: Fleetwood, an unmarried English professor. Like Harvard's Charles T. Copeland, upon whom the character is based, Fleetwood keeps open house for students one evening per week and from time to time joins the boys for dinner. But such friendliness among faculty and students is rare, both in fiction and in reality.

Students at Columbia in *Bachelor—of Arts* (Erskine, 1933) concentrate on the extracurriculum of sports and fraternities and also experience the friendliness of a Professor Barth and his wife, for whom the students even babysit. As a Yale freshman, Philip Sellaby of Stephen Vincent Benet's *The Beginning of Wisdom* (1921) is impressed by his professors—especially one who he describes as follows:

> an affable and interesting 1911 man, enabled by means of a private fortune to accept the poverty's pence of a freshman-instructorship—he gave Philip much kindness and advice, tea and scones from the hands of a delightful wife, and the highest mark Philip ever received in college. (p. 57)

Another professor is influential from a curricular perspective, for he is remembered by Philip

> as one of the few, rare, lucently forceful intellects that can vivisect the smallest nerve or joint of a subject without ever losing its place and importance in the general anatomical scheme. . . . In *his* classes men neither yawned, wrote surreptitious letters, nor tried to bluff. (p. 57)

In *Consider the Daisies* (Carrick, 1941), Vassar student Flip Flippen develops a friendship with an English professor who encourages her writing aspirations. Although she develops a serious "crush" on him, he never takes advantage of her feelings for him and gently discourages these feelings at the novel's end.

Not all professors behave so well nor are presented so positively. In Clarkson Crane's *The Western Shore* (1916), a young English instructor is friendly with his male students, even inviting one of them to live in his home. Unfortunately, his friendliness has homosexual overtones. Yet such deviant behavior is unusual, as professors typically are criticized in novels for activities related to the classroom. In *Wild Asses* (Dunton, 1925), Harvard instructors are viewed as unfair in their grading: students believe they give the same paper different grades depending upon whose paper it is. *Bachelor—of Arts* presents two stereotypical views of professors. About one professor a student says, "He wasn't the sort you could fool easily; that is, he didn't look like a professor at all" (Erskine, 1933, p. 129). Another professor is accused by a student, "Professor Woolsey, you don't understand my case at all. That's the way college is. The professors don't understand!" (p. 129). Perhap the ultimate academic stereotype is presented in *Barefoot Boy with Cheek,* an admittedly satirical novel:

> A great deal of nonsense has been written about college professors. It has been averred that they live cloistered lives, protected by their ivy-covered, academic walls from the harsh realities of the world. They are supposed to be concerned only with hairsplitting and niceties. They are said to look upon the grimness of our age with loathing. I know different. Professors are just folks. They are fully as realistic, as informed, and as eager to participate in the affairs of the world as anyone else. I found that out at our Alpha Cholera faculty dinner, a gala annual event to which each member of Alpha Cholera invites a professor. I wish that the critics of professors could have been there. The conversation at the dinner table would have knocked that sheltered-life concept into a cocked hat. So heated were the discussions of burning issues at dinner that one could scarcely get a bite of food into his mouth. Many times I feared they would come to blows over such pertinent arguments as the dates of Pliny the Elder, the construction of anenthymemem, and the influence of El Greco on Kate Douglas Wiggin. (Shulman, 1944, pp. 119–120)

Shulman's satire reflects and reinforces the prevalent image of college professors as "eggheads," unconcerned with "real world" issues. Similarly, the image of the curriculum is also one of irrevelance to the real doings of college life: the extracurriculum, consisting largely of athletics, dating, and exclusionary social organizations.

These images of college life raise an important research question: "Is undergraduate life portrayed in this way because things are this way, or is undergraduate life like this because it has been portrayed this way in novels and movies?" In other words, are students acting out their expectations fostered by art forms? One novel, Milton White's *A Yale Man* (1966), directly addresses the issue "Does campus life imitate art?" An undergraduate, Dave Miller, thinks about his arrival at Yale in the 1930s. He decides he does not want his family to accompany him on that day because:

> I had received my impression of college from the movies I had seen. I knew that complete independence was a requisite for the young man entering college. In the movies, the fellow whose family brought him to school always turned out to be some sort of fool. (p. 12)

These images of college life also demand an important warning: they come from novels about institutions whose constituency is traditional college students, that is, full-time, white undergraduates between eighteen and twenty-two years old. Hence, many of the campus images would seem to be irrelevant to the "new learners" who do not fit the traditional student profile. But is this always so? We contend that despite demographic changes in who goes to college, even today students are influenced by and aware of the traditional fictional images, exemplified in the recent Rodney Dangerfield movie *Back to College* (1986). Most contemporary undergraduates have been conditioned by the media to believe that college life is (and, therefore, ought to be) overwhelmingly extracurricular in emphasis. Those who attend commuter institutions as part-time students with little time for campus activities often feel "cheated" of the "true" college experience and vow their children will have the "real thing." As faculty and administrators, we would be remiss if we ignored the existence and power of these fictional images in which the "side show" of the extracurriculum is valued by prospective students as the main event of the college experience.

COLLEGE NOVELS AS A GENRE: DISCERNING THE IMPACT OF COLLEGE ON STUDENTS

As a literary genre college novels can be classified according to the degree to which the college experience is the focal point of the story. From this perspective, there are three main categories: (1) those which use a campus setting to illustrate the main character's socioeconomic position; (2) those in which attendance at college is but one part of the main character's life depicted in the novel; and (3) those whose central focus is the collegiate experience.

Novels which rely upon characters' college attendance to indicate their socioeconomic position usually tell little about college life. Illustrative of this type is Erich Segal's *Love Story* (1970), the popular story of a Harvard student's love for a Cliffie who later dies at a young age. Since the Radcliffe library is the scene of their first meeting, we learn that Harvard students go there to get books already checked out from Harvard's Widener Library—but otherwise there is little about the two institutions. The university is used for its image of meritocracy: as places where the very bright and/or very wealthy go to college.

Where else could a gifted woman from a financially modest, immigrant family meet and captivate someone as wealthy and patrician as Oliver Barrett IV?

In this kind of college novel, most of the story takes place off campus. The central character's college attendance is peripheral, often just a prelude to forming romantic relations—an academic version of the "boy meets girl" theme. Thus we have Crane Stuart, a wealthy Harvard student in the 1930s, whose efforts to gain sexual experience at various locales off campus consume most of his energies as well as the pages of Lewis Wells's 1939 novel with the self-explanatory title, *They Still Say No*. Similarly there is B. H. Lehman's *Wild Marriage* (1925), in which Elam Dunston, sophisticated son of a Harvard professor, fills his one year at Harvard with his relationship with a young married woman.

More frequently a character's college years are but one part of his or her life, albeit an important part mainly because the friendships formed at college have lifelong consequences. In Frederick Wadsworth Loring's *Two College Friends* (1871), Ned and Tom meet at Harvard and become such strong friends that after they leave college to enlist in the Civil War, Ned ultimately sacrifices his life to save Tom's. Similarly, John Ward Leggett's *Who Took the Gold Away* (1969) depicts the friendship of Pierce Jay and Ben Mosely, which begins at Yale in the 1930s and continues (with twists and turns) until Pierce's death some twenty years later.

Occasionally emphasis is less upon friendships and more upon the central character's emotional and intellectual development while a college student and in later life, for example, the case of Princetonian Amory Blaine in Fitzgerald's *This Side of Paradise* (1920) or James Farrell's treatment of University of Chicago students: Danny O'Neill in *My Days of Anger* (1943) and Eddie Ryan in *The Silence of History* (1963). Although the Farrell novels cover only one or two years in the lives of the main characters, the college experience is peripheral because protagonists O'Neill and Ryan are commuter students who live at home with their parents and who balance their studies at the University of Chicago with full-time jobs. Thus concerns about economic survival, menial jobs, and family tensions fill many pages—along with a treatment of Danny's and Eddie's academic efforts and intellectual development. As Danny reflects on the stimulus of attending college:

> the three quarters at the University had awakened my memory and stimulated it into alertness. My personal past was becoming more rich than I could have believed possible or understood a year before. I was beginning to draw upon it for understanding, and to find in any experience, thought which helped me to learn, and which added to the basis of much understanding. (Farrell, 1943, p. 267)

Rarely do fictional college students achieve so much intellectual development as does Danny O'Neill. This is particularly evident in the third cluster of novels:

those whose central focus is the collegiate experience. As suggested in earlier sections, these novels illustrate well the hegemony of the extracurriculum. Virtual omission of the classroom does not mean that students are not receiving an education of sorts. Unless they have to "work their way through college," students have time and money to indulge their interests, whether these be sports, college journalism, or the opposite sex. Sometimes even intellectual activities compete successfully for attention! In Shirley Everton Johnson's 1902 novel, several Harvard undergraduates of the 1890s found a society known as "The Cult of the Purple Rose," whose purpose is "the advancement of art" (p. 90) manifested in a publication called, *The Pink Mule.*

Since many main characters are English majors, it is not surprising to find substantial student preoccupation with reading. The intriguing finding is that much of what students read is not required texts or class materials but works suggested by friends or books discovered by chance in the library stacks. Granted, this is not a universal occurrence, but it is conspicuous in such campus novels as *The Paragon* (Knowles, 1971); *The Shortest, Gladdest Years; This Side of Paradise; The Education of Peter; Peter Kindred; Not to Eat, Not for Love;* and *Who Took the Gold Away.* Here students delve into multitudinous works on topics that interest them, thus receiving an education independent of (and potentially equal to) the formal curriculum.

This reinforces the novels' message that education can and does occur, but that it may not be the formal instruction to which the curriculum addresses itself. Consider the feelings expressed by the young fictional graduate of Columbia in the 1930s, as portrayed in John Erskine's *Bachelor—of Arts* (1933):

> So here he was, educated! Or if not educated, at least well-shaken up. No question which seemed important had been solved and where one problem had befogged him, at least two others now thickened the darkness. He had mastered nothing, and he had learned of life chiefly this, that it is confused. (p. 331)

Advocates of "content-based" testing for seniors to determine the "value-added" dimension of the college experience might decry such an effect. After all, it cannot be readily measured, tested, or linked to a particular course syllabus. And by the "value-added" criterion, the student's college experience might be considered a failure because he apparently "learned little." On the other hand, this highly personal reflection provides college officials with a caveat to avoid an educational fallacy: simplistic reduction of the college experience to the literal knowledge acquired. Those who view an educated person as one who knows how little he or she knows would applaud the student's self-appraisal—and conclude that the student had been "educated," signaling that the undergraduate experience was, indeed, a success.

A theme which pervades most college novels is the student as "outsider," the person who feels that he or she does not belong in either the college world or the world at large. The drama, then, is the consequent search for acceptance and place. Usually the student outsider feels removed due to a lack of the money or the social background necessary for success in that microcosm of the real world: college. Thus we have Helen McKenna, a bright but impoverished student at Smith in Marion G. Champagne's *The Cauliflower Heart* (1944). Helen is on the fringes of a popular student clique, but she always feels awkward and physically unattractive in comparison to the other young women. Farrell's Danny O'Neill is also an outsider, happy only inside the classroom, not outside it—as illustrated by his thoughts about his history class:

> Every day after Professor Dorfman's class he experienced this same feeling of letdown. In class, he lived in history and ideas. Then he came outside to a scene like this, and he became an unimportant atom on the edge of campus life. Lost in the crowd of students, he felt like an interloper. The club girls, the frat men, the athletes, all seemed to belong here, and they acted as if students like himself were intruding on their rights. (Farrell, 1943, p. 145)

"Students like himself"—students who are socially inept, working-class Irish Catholic commuter students who thrive on intellectual discourse—are outsiders even in institutions like the University of Chicago, known for intellectual rigor. Occasionally a student will feel like an outsider even though she or he is accepted socially. In Oakley Hall's *Corpus of Joe Bailey* (1953), Joe, a financially poor student at Berkeley in the 1930s, is a member of the varsity football team who is eventually elected fraternity president—yet continues to feel alone and lonely because of his constant worry over lack of money.

Characters like Joe, Danny, and Helen are unusual in college novels, though, in that the standard formula is for a character to feel alienated initially, but eventually to "find happiness" through acceptance and even elevation to "BMOC" status. Illustrative of this "happy ending" type are Giles Dabney in Rollo Walter Brown's *The Hilliken* (1935) and "Hart" in James Barnes's *A Princetonian* (1896). Both men are initially outsiders because they are not wealthy easterners: Giles, attending Harvard, is a socially awkward provincial from the hills of Ohio; Hart is a slightly older student from Nebraska. Giles never becomes a BMOC as does Hart, yet both gain acceptance by fellow students—and as alumni achieve successful careers and romantic happiness, confirming the notion of "bright college years."

Obviously novels dealing with late adolescence tend to deal with issues of conformity and peer acceptance. Nonetheless, higher education faculty and administrators ought not take lightly this recurring theme. The desire to be accepted by one's college peers may well be the influence behind these novels' emphasis on the collegiate extracurricular life and the corollary deemphasis of formal studies. To excel on the athletic field or as part of the college newspaper staff is acceptable, whereas outstanding performance in the classroom brings unfavorable notice as a "ratebuster," "curvebreaker," or "grind." This strong message from the student culture dramatized in the campus novels is confirmed, for example, by Henry Seidel Canby's actual accounts of classroom conduct and undergraduate life at Yale in *Alma Mater: The Gothic Age of the American College* (1936).

Furthermore, academic success requires time devoted to study, time which otherwise could be spent on extracurricular activities among friends and as part of college groups. As Martin Smith realizes in *The Shortest Gladdest Years* (Sullivan, 1962) he has been so busy at Yale working on *The Daily*, being with his girlfriend, and socializing that he "hadn't been studying." He reflects:

> I was a good scholar and I like school work. The dream of myself at the University that I lived on during my last years at high school featured a brilliant thesis and a Phi Beta Kappa key. But instead, I'd done no more than skim for over a year now. My grades weren't bad, but they were far from satisfying me. I was enough of a realist to accept the unlikelihood of my ever fulfilling my scholarly ambitions. I was still enough of a dreamer, though, to regret them. (pp. 199–200)

A rite of passage for even conscientious students, then, is that there simply is not enough time to do everything; and usually the desire to be socially successful triumphs over the will to excel academically. College novels can alert us to these kinds of student dilemmas and sensitize us to student concerns.

Several novels in our study make explicit statements about the effect of "going to college" and the essence of a college education. Here are graphic testimonies to the potential of the college experience—both its academic and extracurricular sides—which provide an interesting accompaniment to such social and behavioral studies as Nevitt Sanford's *The American College* (1962), Hodgkinson's comprehensive review of the college influence (1967), or Alexander Astin's *Four Critical Years* (1978). In these examples, the fictional students' memoirs indicate that going to college has made a difference in their thinking. College novels, then, alert us to these kinds of transformations without providing final answers about the phenomenon. It is left to us as social and behavioral researchers to determine the extent of such differences.

Thus the genre of college novels is interesting not only to those who study literature, but also to those who study higher education. It provides a valuable tool for gleaning fresh insights into the college experience as seen through the eyes of students. Important to keep in mind in the search for answers about the impact of "going to college" is that fact, like fiction, is ultimately only an interpretation of reality.

HISTORICAL CONTEXT AND ORGANIZATIONAL ETHNOGRAPHY: CONNECTIONS WITH THE SOCIAL AND BEHAVIORAL SCIENCES

College novels are also useful for alerting us to historical innovations and episodes which otherwise might be overlooked or ignored. One such episode is indicated in the publisher's foreword to the 1925 Harvard novel *Wild Asses* by James Dunton. According to the foreword, the federal government provided some funds for college students who were World War I veterans; the novel describes the college careers of a few of them. Certainly the GI Bill of the post–World War II college era is familiar and celebrated—but when have we heard about precedents from World War I? Thus the novel may serve as a memory of policies and practices which official accounts have overlooked.

Customs, rituals, jargon, fashions, and rounds of life within the American campus can also be gleaned from the novels. For example, two novels set at Yale depict the student penchant for yelling, "Fire!" from dormitory windows. In the early 1900s, freshmen would do so when Italians driving hacks passed en route to a wedding. Then "the whole Freshmen class, not otherwise engaged, would be at its windows swelling the chorus, 'Fi-er—fi-er!'" (Minnigerode, 1921, p. 74). In the early 1930s Yale students were still yelling from their windows but for a different reason. As one student explained to his father, "Whenever a girl walks through the Oval, all the fellows lean out the windows and yell 'Fire!' It's a tradition." Why the word "Fire"? The student tells his father that according to Yale legend, it was "an imitation of the sex-crazed onga-onga crying for its mate" (Milton White, *A Yale Man,* 1966, pp. 34–35), but more likely it was a carryover from the earlier custom of yelling at Italians in open hacks!

One of the finest dissections of the anatomy of a college's distinctive "inner life" comes from Owen Johnson's *Stover at Yale* (1912), a seemingly innocent saga which critically probes the structure and ethos of the famous "Yale system." In addition to describing the traditions and ideals of Yale College student life, the novel focuses on incidents which suggest that the high-pressure system of reward had been subject to erosion and abuse. In fact, careful checking of primary sources, presidential reports, and trustee investigations in the Yale archives suggests that the student-as-novelist was on the mark. The episodes were both historically accurate and significant.

Novels hint at institutional practices often overlooked in official reports. For example, several novels indicate that long before women were formally admitted to Harvard as degree candidates, they were permitted to attend some classes and could even enroll in the summer school. At the same time, we learn that "regular" Harvard students looked askance at (and avoided) the summer session. Distinctions within the curriculum also spring to life in novels. George Santayana's *The Last Puritan* (1936) provides readers with hints about the lore of prestige within Harvard: in the 1880s, the medical school was viewed as a "last chance" haven for socially prominent students who could not pass the college's entrance examination, in marked contrast to the status accorded admission to graduate professional schools in recent decades.

Indeed, several novelists open the lid on Harvard's underworld of academic deficiency by describing the elaborate network of tutoring schools which flourished in Cambridge at the turn of the century. Apparently the "knowledge industry" included an enterprise which for a substantial price could salvage the "Gentleman C" from tumbling to the "Dunce F." Owen Wister's *Philosophy 4* (1903) tells of two wealthy Harvard undergraduates in the early 1880s who pay the princely sum of five dollars per hour to be tutored in order to pass their Philosophy 4 examination. In Holworthy Hall's *Pepper* (1915), we learn about catch-up seminars offered at a tutoring school known as "The Widow's." One fictional student comments:

> Now what is a seminar? Absolutely nothing but the Widow giving a complete resume of a course in three or four hours, and if you want to brace up on all your courses, you've got to spend the best part of a week in the Widow's joint and hand him bout thirty dollars. (pp. 272–273)

According to the novels, only the wealthier students could afford such assistance, while the university itself provided few academic support services.

In a similar vein, we learn from novels about social class schisms with the controversial appearance of university-operated dining halls and dormitories. The "student union" becomes the haven for "greasy grind" commuter students. The student novelists are the chroniclers of these landmark events and structures which altered the chemistry of undergraduate life. If one wishes to find evidence of the consequences of altered admissions policies and institutional priorities along with demographic change, some campus novels are a fertile, candid source. George Anthony Weller's *Not to Eat, Not for Love* (1933) endures as a classic collection of vignettes about university change and organizational complexity, reviewed as follows:

> The size and diversity of the campus was perceptively described by George Anthony Weller in his novel, *Not to Eat, Not for Love*. Weller, Class of 1929, captures the sense of "Several Harvards" in which the social register of *The University Blue Book* coexists with large numbers of "grinds" who wear white socks. (Thelin, 1976b, p. 34)

Thanks to the novelist, higher education researchers have vivid, contemporary descriptions of new additions to student life. Here, for example, is Weller's presentation of how one bemused patrician undergraduate at Harvard views the "nontraditional" students of the 1930s—academically oriented commuter students:

> The commuting students, carrying briefcases, many wearing tortoise shell glasses with extra lenses of power, are coming up out of the subway, talking examinations. Unlike those who live in the dormitories, who are now ordering breakfast in the restaurants in the Square, they will be too early for nine o'clock lectures. . . . While they wait they put the time to advantage by rereading their notes. (Weller, 1933, p. 6; Thelin, 1976b, pp. 34–35)

Policy changes, of course, are sources of social tension within the campus.

Here the utility of college novels is their power to describe the diffusion and impact of policy on the mores and customs of their times. Certainly this is true in depictions of dating, social behavior, and etiquette. Although most formal institutional histories have little to say about exclusion and discrimination, numerous novels provide graphic and subtle accounts of anti-Catholicism, anti-Semitism, gender discrimination, tracking, social snobbery, and other variants of the differentiation which takes place within the campus, usually outside public scrutiny.

Louise Blecher Rose illustrates this sequential relation between the student as novelist and as institutional historian. And her own experiences show how the sociocultural and biographical approaches may intertwine, as is the case with an examination of her college novel *The Launching of Barbara Fabrikant* (1974). In "real life," Rose was an undergraduate in the 1960s at Sarah Lawrence College—an experience which provided the basis for her 1974 novel about aspects of being a Jew at a socially prestigious women's college. Shifting back from fiction to reality, in the 1980s author Rose taught at Sarah Lawrence College and was commissioned by the board to write that institution's fiftieth anniversary official history. In the course of her research, she came across files which showed evidence of Jewish quotas at Sarah Lawrence in the 1930s—quotas which college officials had publicly denied; her refusal to omit such materials from her college history led her to be fired from her teaching position and to lose her commission as institutional historian. Such episodes suggest how far novelists have been ahead of social and behavioral scientists in focusing on the "dirty little secrets" of organizational subcultures (Rose, 1983; Biemiller, 1983).

College novels at best complicate rather than simplify our notions of the college experience, often supplying an antidote to nostalgia and superficial memory. For example, a familiar feature of institutional research for years has been for alumni to fill out questionnaires for a tenth or twenty-fifth annual reunion. Such questionnaires become the basis for how we assess the college experience. John Marquand's award-winning novel *H. M. Pulham, Esq.* (1940) uses the incident of a Harvard alumnus filling out his class report to illustrate the misleading limits of questionnaires. The first obstacle is that most alumni do not relish writing thoughtfully and critically about the college years, as H. M. Pulham, Harvard class of 1913, complains:

> It still looked a good deal like something on a tombstone, but I should have to get on with it. The main thing was not to give the impression of writing a lot in the book and of showing off. It was easy enough to think about my life, but now that I was face to face with a piece of paper it was quite a puzzle. I never did like writing. I turned on the radio for a while just to get myself in the proper mood. (p. 431)

The alumni survey format shapes and reduces Pulham's responses into predictable phrases which trivialize the memory of the college experience, as he dutifully fills out the form from the perspective of 1935:

Like all my other classmates, I look back upon my years at School and college as the happiest of my life. Among the activities the one I enjoy the most is being on the Alumni Board of St. Swithin's School. Being thus intimately thrown with the youth of today, I can not share with my classmates the discouragement and pessimism which has been engendered by the New Deal. It seems to me only a phase and that matters will be better soon in business and in national life. I do not believe that either Mr. Roosevelt or Germany can hold out much longer and I confidently look forward to seeing a sensible Republican in the White House. We spend our winters in town and our summers in North Harbor, Maine. In either place the latchstring is always out for any member of our Class. (pp. 430–432)

Meanwhile, alumnus Pulham drifts off to recall not only his college days but also his ensuing adult life. His detailed memories, queries, and insights have ironically been triggered by the college questionnaire but never come to be articulated or expressed on the reply sheet. The lesson is that higher education researchers must not be so naive as to accept superficial replies as the whole or significant story about the college years. This is the riddle of recall and reconstruction which we must acknowledge, especially in analyzing such nostalgic documents as photographs and class albums (Jensen, 1974). And often it is the college novel which provides the elaboration which is neither captured nor conveyed in the format of the yearbook, the class notes, and alumni questionnaires.

In sum, then, perhaps one of the most useful functions of the college novel is its service as a "distant early-warning" system to higher education officials and policy analysts about life within a complex organization. The quasi-autobiographical novels are especially useful when analyzed in conjunction with campus memoirs—lines which are often blurred, as illustrated by such diverse works as Benchley's "What College Did for Me" (1927), James Thurber's account of mass education at Ohio State University (Thurber, 1933), or Susan Allen Toth's recollection of Smith College in the 1950s (Toth, 1984; Thelin, 1979, 1983). Some of the major concepts and themes in the social and behavioral study of colleges and universities were preceded by graphic, thoughtful depictions in college novels. Here we have in mind such themes as the "hidden curriculum" (Snyder, 1971), status differences between the liberal arts and professional schools (Cheit, 1974), the "cooling out function" (Clark, 1960a), the notion of tracking and discrimination within an institution, sexual harrassment, cleavages and subcultures within colleges (Clark and Trow, 1967), and the distinctions between academic "nationalism and localism" (Jencks and Riesman, 1968).

CONCLUSION

Even though many of the novels we have analyzed deal with historically distant eras and institutions, there is no reason why our research strategies cannot be incorporated into understanding the recent past and the present. Two recent conspicuous episodes attest to the vitality of college novels due to the persistent circular relation between college fiction and college fact.

In November 1986, the national press featured stories about hazing and charges of racial discrimination toward a black cadet, Kevin Nesmith, at The Citadel in Charleston, South Carolina (Associated Press, 1 November 1986). Among the Citadel students, alumni, and faculty, the episode quickly worked its way into the institutional saga to be known as "The Incident." The ironic touch was that the controversial event of 1986 mirrored closely the fictional event in a "college novel" based on The Citadel, circa 1960, namely, Pat Conroy's *The Lords of Discipline* (1982). As Michael Hirschorn noted in *The Chronicle of Higher Education* (1987), the institution faced a severe public relations problem in which history, fiction, and symbolism coincided to compound a distinctive image in its difficulties to recruit and enroll black students:

> The [low Black] enrollment figures were reinforced in the public's mind by *The Lords of Discipline,* a novel by Pat Conroy, a Citadel graduate, that was turned into a movie in 1983. The book and the movie, in part about attempts by a secret society to scare the Citadel's first black cadet into leaving the college, have served as an ironic commentary on the current controversy, many say.

> "The Class of '87 came in the summer the movie was released and are leaving with the Nesmith incident," notes Darin L. Brockington, a black senior. (p. 25)

A second recent episode worth comment comes from Wisconsin to provide testimony of sorts to the lively and volatile character of campus fiction. Our comments have dealt primarily with undergraduate life. There is, however, an equally rich tradition of college novels which focus on the organizational life of faculty members, administrators, and board members. According to John E. Kramer's annotated records (1981), between 1900 and 1979 there were at least 208 bona fide novels which center on American faculty and staff; over half of these works had been published since 1960. Furthermore, Kramer himself has provided thoughtful analyses of these works, with particular attention to the place of college and university presidents in fiction (John Kramer, 1981), subsequently followed by other scholars' systematic dissection of portrayals of higher education administrators (Pittman and Theilmann, 1986, pp. 405–418; Altbach, 1986). A timely contribution to this tradition is Warren Carrier's *Death of a Chancellor* (1986), a novel which has kindled controversy at the University of Wisconsin at Platteville.

Members of the campus community claim that former Chancellor Carrier's fictional campus town of "Silverville" is a thinly veiled disguise for Platteville and its branch campus of the University of Wisconsin. Furthermore, Platteville faculty and administrators claim that the former chancellor-turned-author unfairly maligned their institution, leaving them "smarting over what they consider a mean-spirited depiction of their community in Mr. Carrier's book" (Heller,

1986, pp. 1, 15). The author, in turn, denies having presented a specific profile of the University of Wisconsin at Platteville, contending instead, "I held a shallow mirror up to typical small-university life. . . . If some people see pieces of themselves in it, that's their judgement" (Heller, p. 1). Thus, we inherit in 1986 yet another classic problem in decoding fiction and fact in the depiction of college and university life.

For skeptics who still distrust "college novels" as vague, light reading unsuited to critical research, let us shift momentarily from college fiction to the ultimate realities of death and taxes. Specifically, we bring your attention to a key volume in every professor's working library (at least between January and April), Allen Bernstein's *1987 Tax Guide for College Teachers* (1986), which notes:

> College teaching is one of the most misunderstood professions that exists today. Most people do not understand the difference between the job of teaching elementary or high school and that of teaching college. They do not understand that many college teachers must do more than just teach their classes, consult with students, and serve on administrative committees. College teachers are expected to keep abreast of advances in their field by reading journals, attending seminars, traveling to conventions, etc. Furthermore, in many colleges and universities, faculty members are required to be scholars in their own right. They must do original research and communicate their results by publishing articles in journals, writing books, giving colloquium and seminar talks, corresponding with colleagues, discussing topics with their fellow teachers and graduate students, etc. . . . College teachers often incur expenses in doing their research. They may spend money on attending meetings in their specialty, subscribing to journals, buying books, buying equipment or supplies, etc. . . . Fortunately, the tax regulations now specifically recognize the integral part that research plays in the duties of many professors. This was not always the case . . . (p. 381)

And fortunately, thoughtful novelists in their respective roles as student, as faculty member, or as administrator have used fiction as the vehicle to describe and interpret what it means to have gone to college or to have been a member of the academic profession. Novels remain an excellent source for glimpses at behavior within a presidential search committee, or for snapshots of a departmental tenure review. One adage in higher education is that academic politics are especially sinister because the stakes involved are so low. Novels about faculty and administration expand, elaborate, and interpret this theme so as to bring the observation to life.

When Gertrude Stein was on her death bed, she asked her friend Alice B. Toklas, with urgency and finality, "What is the answer?" When Alice gestured that she did not know "the answer," Gertrude Stein was prompted to sit up and respond, "In that case, what is the question?" (Stein, 1946, as quoted in Mellow, 1974). And so it is with thoughtful college novels. Certainly they provide no final answers about the character and content of higher education, but at the very least, they prompt us as scholars and professionals who study colleges and universities to ask in an interesting, significant way, "What is the question?"

Acknowledgments. The two coauthors contributed equally to the research and writing of this chapter. They thank Michael Wiese, doctoral student in higher education at Loyola University of Chicago, for his work on the study as graduate assistant and Allen Chamberlain, Head Reference Librarian, Williamsburg (Virginia) Regional Library, for assistance on key sources and citations. Research for this project was made possible in part by a faculty grant from The College of William and Mary.

REFERENCES

Altbach, Philip G. (1986). Reflections on the jet set: review essay. *Journal of Higher Education* 57 (3): 321–323.

Associated Press. (1986). Cadets to be punished for hazing. Hampton Roads, Virginia *Daily Press/ The Times-Herald,* 1 Nov., p. B10.

Astin, Alexander. (1978). *Four Critical Years.* San Francisco: Jossey-Bass.

Bagg, Lyman Hotchkiss. (1871). *Four Years at Yale: By a Graduate '69.* New Haven, CT: Charles C. Chatfield.

Bail, Hamilton Vaughn. (1958). Harvard fiction: some critical and bibliographical notes. *The Proceedings of the American Antiquarian Society.* 69: 211–347.

Barnes, James. (1896). *A Princetonian.* New York: G. P. Putnam's Sons.

Benchley, Robert. (1927). What college did for me. *The Early Worm.* New York: Harper & Brothers.

Bentinck-Smith, William, ed. (1953). *The Harvard Book: Selections from Three Centuries.* Cambridge: Harvard University Press.

Bernstein, Allen. (1986). *1987 Tax Guide for College Teachers and Other College Personnel.* Washington, DC: Academic Information Service.

Biemiller, Lawrence. (1983). The secret life of Sarah Lawrence controversy spreads. *The Chronicle of Higher Education,* 25 May, p. 3.

Blackburn, Robert T. (1983). *Education G609: The College and University Professor.* Ann Arbor: University of Michigan course syllabus.

Boys, Richard C. (1946). The American college in fiction. *College English* 7(7): 379–387.

Brown, Rollo Walter. (1935). *The Hillikin.* New York: Coward McCann.

Buchan, Perdita. (1966). *A Girl with a Zebra.* New York: Scribner's.

Burn, W. L. (1964). *The Age of Equipoise.* New York: Norton.

Cain, James. (1927). The man Merriwell. *The Saturday Evening Post,* 11 June, p. 129.

Canby, Henry Seidel. (1936). *Alma Mater: The Gothic Age of the American College.* New York: Farrar & Rinehart.

Canfield, Dorothy. (1922). *Rough-Hewn.* New York: Harcourt Brace.

Carpenter, Frederic I. (1960). Fiction and the American college. *American Quarterly* 12(4): 443–456.

Carrick, Gertrude. (1941). *Consider the Daisies.* New York: Lippincott.

Carrier, Warren. (1986). *Death of a Chancellor.* New York: Dodd, Mead.

Champagne, Marion G. (1944). *The Cauliflower Heart.* New York: Dial.

Cheit, Earl F. (1974). *The Useful Arts and the Liberal Tradition.* New York: McGraw-Hill.

Clark, Burton R., and Trow, Martin. (1967). *Determinants of Student Subcultures.* Berkeley: University of California Center for Research and Development in Higher Education.

Clark, Burton R. (1960a). The "cooling out" function in higher education. *American Journal of Sociology* 65: 565–576.

Clark, Burton R. (1960b). *The Open Door College: A Case Study.* New York: McGraw-Hill.

Clifford, Geraldine Joncich. (1983). *The College and University Novel: Syllabus.* Berkeley: University of California.

Conroy, Pat. (1982). *The Lords of Discipline.* Boston: Houghton Mifflin.

Crane, Clarkson. (1916). *The Western Shore.* New York: Harcourt Brace.

Davies, John. (1966). *The Legend of Hobey Baker.* Boston: Little, Brown.

DeMott, Benjamin. (1962). How to write a college novel. *Hudson Review* 15(2): 243–252.

Dunton, James. (1925). *Wild Asses.* Boston: Small, Maynard.

Earnest, Earnest P. (1953). *Academic Procession: An Informal History of the American College.* New York: Bobbs-Merrill.

Erskine, John. (1933). *Bachelor—of Arts.* Indianapolis: Bobbs-Merrill.

Farrell, James T. (1943). *My Days of Anger.* New York: Vanguard.

Farrell, James T. (1963). *The Silence of History.* Garden City, NY: Doubleday.

Fitzgerald, F. Scott. (1920). *This Side of Paradise.* New York: Charles Scribner's Sons.

Flandrau, Charles Macomb. (1901). *The Diary of a Freshman.* New York: Doubleday, Page.

Friedman, Bruce Jay. (1964). *A Mother's Kisses.* New York: Simon & Schuster.

Gilman, Mildred Evans. (1925). *Fig Leaves.* New York: Siebel Publishing.

Gwynn, Frederick L. (1949). The education of Epes Todd. *Harvard Alumni Bulletin.* 51: 388.

Halberstam, Michael J. (1969). The revolving bookstand: Stover at the barricades. *The American Scholar.* 1969: 470–476.

Hall, Holworthy. (1915). *Pepper.* New York: Century.

Hall, Oakey. (1953). *The Corpus of Joe Bailey.* New York: Viking.

Hall, Theodore. (1931). Harvard in fiction: a short anthology. *The Harvard Graduates Magazine* 40: 30–54.

Heller, Scott. (1986). Author! author! shouts a college town that is out for ex-chancellor's blood. *The Chronicle of Higher Education,* 26 November, pp. 1, 15.

Hirschorn, Michael W. (1987). The Citadel, trying hard to shed Old-South image, set back by "the incident." *The Chronicle of Higher Education,* 4 February, pp. 24–26.

Hodgkinson, Harold L. (1967). The impact of the American college on student values. *Education, Interaction, and Social Change.* Englewood Cliffs, NJ: Prentice-Hall.

Holbrook, Richard Thayer. (1900). *Boys and Men: A Story of Life at Yale.* New York: Charles Scribner's Sons.

Holland, Rupert Sargent. (1906). *The Court at Harvard.* Boston: L. C. Page.

Horton, John. (1986). "Spy" novels: intelligence failures: where do these writers get this stuff? *Washington Post,* 31 August, p. B2.

Howard, Joseph. (1979). *Breaking Away.* New York: Warner Books.

Hudson, Helen (pseudonym). (1966). *Tell the Time to None.* New York: Dutton.

Jencks, Christopher, and Riesman, David. (1968). *The Academic Revolution.* Garden City, NY: Doubleday Anchor.

Jensen, Oliver. (1974). *A College Album: Or, Rah, Rah, Yesterday.* New York: American Heritage.

Johnson, Nora. (1961). *A Step Beyond Innocence.* Boston: Little, Brown.

Johnson, Owen. (1912). *Stover at Yale.* New York: Frederick A. Stokes.

Johnson, Shirley Everton. (1902). *The Cult of the Purple Rose.* Boston: Richard C. Badger.

Kaufman, Reginald. (1901). *Jarvis of Harvard.* Boston: L. C. Page.

Knowles, John. (1971). *The Paragon.* New York: Random House.

Kramer, John. (1979). Images of sociology and sociologists in fiction. *Contemporary Sociology.* 8: 356–376.

Kramer, John. (1981). College and university presidents in fiction. *The Journal of Higher Education.* 52(1): 81–95.

Kramer, John E., Jr. (1981). *The American College Novel: An Annotated Bibliography.* New York: Garland.

Leggett, John Ward. (1969). *Who Took the Gold Away.* New York: Random House.

Lehman, B. H. (1925). *Wild Marriage.* New York: Harper & Brothers.

Loring, Frederick Wadsworth. (1871). *Two College Friends.* Boston: Loring.

Lyons, John O. (1962). *The College Novel in America.* Carbondale, IL: Southern Illinois University Press.

Marks, Percy. (1924). *The Plastic Age.* New York: Century Company.

Marquand, John P. (1940). *H. M. Pulham, Esq.* Boston: Little, Brown.

Mellow, James R. (1974): *Charmed Circle: Gertrude Stein and Company.* New York: Praeger.

Minnigerode, Meade. (1921). *The Big Year.* New York: G. P. Putnam's Sons.

Nathan, Robert. (1920). *Peter Kindred.* New York: Duffield.

O'Donnell, Richard. (1969). America's most popular character. *National Retired Teachers Association Journal,* November–December, p. 61.

Osborn, John Jay, Jr. (1971). *The Paper Chase.* Boston: Houghton Mifflin.

Pittman, Von V., Jr., and Theilmann, John M. (1986). The administrator in fiction: portrayals of higher education. *The Educational Forum.* 50(4): 405–418.

Randel, William. (1947). Nostalgia for the ivy. *Saturday Review of Literature* 30(48): 9–11, 39.

Rohrberger, Mary, Woods, Samuel H., and Dukore, Bernard F. (1968). The critical approaches to literature. *An Introduction to Literature.* New York: Random House.

Rose, Louise Blecher. (1974). *The Launching of Barbara Fabrikant.* New York: David McKay.

Rose, Louise Blecher. (1983). The secret life of Sarah Lawrence. *Commentary* 64 (May): 52–56.

Sanford, Nevitt, ed. (1962). *The American College: A Psychological and Social Interpretation of the Higher Learning.* New York: Wiley.

Santayana, George. (1936). *The Last Puritan.* New York: Charles Scribner's Sons.

Segal, Erich. (1970). *Love Story.* New York: Harper & Row.

Shulman, Max. (1943). *Barefoot Boy with Cheek.* Garden City, NY: Doubleday, Doran.

Snyder, Benson. (1971). *The Hidden Curriculum.* New York: Knopf.

Spectorsky, A. C., ed. (1958). *The College Years.* New York: Hawthorn.

Stone, Lawrence. (1971). The ninnyversity? *New York Review of Books,* 28 January, pp. 20–29.

Sullivan, Scott. (1962). *The Shortest, Gladdest Years.* New York: Simon & Schuster.

Thelin, John R. (1976a). Beyond the "factory model": new strategies for institutional evaluation. *College and University* 51(2): 161–164.

Thelin, John R. (1976b). *The Cultivation of Ivy: A Saga of the College in America.* Cambridge, MA: Schenkman.

Thelin, John R. (1979). Tales out of school: exposes of elite education. *Educational Studies* 9(3): 295–298.

Thelin, John R. (1982). *Higher Education and Its Useful Past: Applied History in Research and Planning*. Cambridge, MA: Schenkman.

Thelin, John R. (1983). Cry, the beloved campus: autobiographies of institutions. *The Review of Higher Education* 6(3): 233–238.

Thompson, Charles. (1957). *Halfway Down the Stairs*. New York: Harper & Brothers.

Thurber, James. (1933). University days. In A. C. Spectorsky (1958). *The College Years*. New York: Hawthorn.

Toth, Susan Allen. (1984). *Ivy Days: Making My Way Out East*. Boston: Little, Brown.

Tunis, John R. (1936). *Was College Worthwhile?* New York: Harcourt, Brace.

Turow, Scott. (1978). *One L*. New York: Penguin.

Veysey, Laurence R. (1965). *The Emergence of the American University*. Chicago: University of Chicago Press.

Webb, Eugene, Campbell, Donald T., Schwartz, R. D., and Sechrest, L. (1966). *Unobtrusive Measures: Non-Reactive Research in the Social Sciences*. New York: Rand McNally.

Weller, George Anthony. (1933). *Not to Eat, Not for Love*. New York: Smith & Haas.

Wells, Lewis. (1939). *They Still Say No*. New York: Farrar & Rinehart.

White, Barbara A. (1985). *Growing Up Female: Adolescent Girlhood in American Fiction*. Westport, CN: Greenwood.

White, Milton. (1966). *A Yale Man*. Garden City, NY: Doubleday.

Wiley, John. (1924). *The Education of Peter*. New York: Frederick A. Stokes.

Williams, Jesse Lynch. (1899). *The Adventures of a Freshman*. New York: Charles Scribner's Sons.

Winthur, Sophus Keith. (1947). *Beyond the Golden Gate*. New York: Macmillan.

Wister, Owen. (1903). *Philosophy 4*. New York: Macmillan.

Wolfe, Tom. (1976). The new journalism exposed. *New York Magazine*, Feb. 14, p. 1.

Strategy and Resources: Economic Issues in Strategic Planning and Management in Higher Education

James C. Hearn
University of Minnesota

The current era of economic, political, and demographic challenges to U.S. higher education has brought increased attention to the notion of "organizational strategy" (see Cope, 1981; Keller, 1983; Miller, 1983). Although the term has been variously defined, the strategic planning and management literature has usually stressed the interplay of organizational mission, environment, and values, and the necessity for aggressive action by institutions to shape their futures in difficult times (Cope, 1981; Peterson, 1980). The strategic approach has been initiated at many institutions because of resource concerns, and arguably owes whatever successes it has had at least in part to the resolution of vexing financing issues (Chaffee, 1983b, 1984). Although the theme is not usually stressed in the literature, one can even legitimately argue that strategic planning and management are fundamental economic activities themselves. The strategy literature stresses that strategic planning and management are primarily aimed toward helping institutions make more effectively rational decisions regarding programmatic changes, a goal which may be easily translated into helping them to make more effectively rational resource allocation decisions. Unfortunately, however, writings on the topic of strategic planning and management have only rarely been based in economic ideas, approaches, or data.

Because of the lack of extensive theoretical and empirical work on the topic, this chapter employs a somewhat nontraditional format. Rather than presenting a review of dominant theory, then a review of relevant empirical research, then a revised theoretical model, then some suggested topics for further analysis, the first three of these activities are blended. First, some of the leading theoretical and empirical writings on institutional and system strategy in higher education are examined, with particular attention to their connections to economic concerns. Then, on the basis of this overview, a conceptual framework for thinking about the issues of strategy and finance is proposed. Next, nine major aspects of the economics of strategy in higher education are discussed, with attention to evidence and thinking regarding these topics in the literature. Because of their special relevance, the demands of decline and crisis are considered next, with emphasis on the strategic economic issues involved. In the closing section, a critical summary of the field is presented and some possibly productive directions for further inquiry are proposed.

THE NOTION OF STRATEGY
IN THE HIGHER EDUCATION LITERATURE

"Strategic" management and planning seem so much in full flower on American campuses that Miller (1983) has termed them part of a "movement" rather than simply an approach to management and leadership. Regardless of problems of definition, application, and measurement (Cope, 1981; Chaffee, 1985; Mason, 1985), strategy seems important. This latest management approach to win the hearts of higher education leadership has often been praised as not only revolutionary but also critical to the survival of institutions in the era of decline and challenge (e.g., Keller, 1983). Some authorities have revealed doubts, however. For example, in reviewing strategic planning and other newer resource distribution approaches, Leslie (1984) notes that their "advocates . . . possess the righteous zeal of a fundamentalist preacher and the persuasiveness of an old-time flim-flam man" (p. 87). Similarly, James Miller (1983) suggests that the leaders of American higher education need answers, and such "answer books" as Keller's, however flawed, have been employed to fill the void. While he was not speaking solely of strategic planning, Peterson (1986) has added to the cautions, arguing that in higher education leaders, in borrowing many of their planning ideas from other settings, have too often become overzealous in their application (also see Baldridge and Okimi, 1982).

There is reason for a cautious stance toward "the revolution." Unfortunately, despite the myriad prescriptive writings on the topic, the higher education strategy literature has only rarely been based in theory, or in empirical research. Indeed, the strategic planning literature for colleges is similar to that for corporations and other sectors (Mintzberg, 1981) in that it has been more frequently hortatory and prescriptive than analytic, and more frequently conceptual than empirical. Cope has stated regarding higher education strategy that, "Little empirical research is available now and, considering the difficulty of studying real behavior in real colleges, little more is expected soon" (1981, p. 26). Ellen Earle Chaffee has suggested in her review of the topic that, "Writers on higher education have not yet looked deeply and widely into their own experience for a model that is inherent to their setting. Instead, most writers have typically offered suggestions based on their own logic or experience as to how strategy may be modified to suit higher education settings" (1985, p. 138). It has now been several years since Chaffee's excellent review, and several years more since Cope's comments on the topic, but their respective words still ring true, despite impressive recent contributions by Kim Cameron, Richard Clugston, James Morrison, David Whetten, and Raymond Zammuto, and Ellen Chaffee herself.

The literature problem is especially severe in the domain of the connections between strategy and resources. These connections have usually been considered in the literature only in passing and only in general terms. Instead, attention has been largely paid to managerial process, rather than to the often complex links between the process of strategic choice and the actual financial workings of institutions. There is, therefore, a special, and troubling, irony in what are perhaps the most familiar words of the strategic planning "movement" in higher education, those which begin George Keller's best-selling book *Academic Strategy:* "A specter is haunting higher education; the specter of decline and bankruptcy" (1983, p. 1). Resources may indeed be the problem, and strategy may indeed be the answer, but we are moving only slowly to replace speculation with knowledge and understanding.

The Strategic Concept

There is no reason to review here the origins of the strategic management and planning viewpoint, since Ellen Earle Chaffee did such an extensive review of this kind in Volume I of this *Handbook* (1985). There Chaffee discussed thoroughly not only the possible potential benefits of transferring the strategic idea from the general business literature to higher education settings but also the difficulties encountered by higher education researchers and administrators alike in applying those ideas. Instead, it is best to begin here by reviewing briefly some of the more prominent considerations of the topic in the higher education literature, paying particular attention to the resource issues these writings highlight.

George Keller's *Academic Strategy* has been called by J. L. Miller (1983) the "call to action" of the strategic planning movement. Keller's book is part journalistic description of "strategic" activities at various campuses and part stirring managerial prescription for a better future for colleges and universities. Keller used a rather global definition of strategic planning and management, stressing the need to integrate the future-thinking staff functions of planning and forecasting into the activities of the top leadership in institutions. This book represents more an action agenda than a research report, but his core tenets are clearly strategic in their emphasis on the interplay of institutional purpose and the external environment. Keller suggests that the most central contribution of the strategic perspective is the importance placed on "keeping the institution in step with the changing environment (p. 143)."

When one considers the literature from the perspective of theoretical and empirical scholarship, the very popular and very accessible Keller book does not stand out as pioneering or central work on strategy. On that criterion, attention should be focused instead on literature which is theoretically grounded and sensitive to earlier contributions in the literature. Over the past ten years, such work has been rare. Only a small group of scholars, including prominently Robert Cope, Marvin Peterson, and Ellen Earle Chaffee, have consistently met those standards. Because the contributions of many others have been rooted in ideas initially broached in the writings of these three cautious proponents of strategic approaches, much of the strategy review that follows is indebted to their work.

Robert Cope's 1981 monograph introduces the origins and basic tenets of strategic thinking in higher education. His review of the relevant research on the topic is skillfully done, although becoming dated. He argues that strategic planning is difficult to define but "can be understood intuitively." Among the themes stressed in Cope's 1981 work and his more recent essay (1985) are environmental sensitivity, open systems thinking, wide participation in planning processes, qualitative data, and a focus on process rather than products (i.e., plans).

Whereas Cope concentrates mainly on strategic ideas in their own right, Marvin Peterson (1980, 1981, 1986) has typically focused more inclusively on recent developments in higher education planning as a whole. In recent years, Peterson has stressed the emergence of a planning style that is more modest than before regarding the potentials of highly rationalized, quantifiable models, more accepting of qualitative approaches, more attentive to environmental constraints, more oriented to governance and planning at the institutional level, more integrative of academic, physical, and fiscal planning concerns, and more "strategic" in orientation. Peterson's chronology parallels that of Richard Heydinger (1980, 1983), who has suggested that there have been four phases in higher education planning: (1) planning as part of budgeting, an approach which faltered in Heydinger's judgment because of an inordinate focus on finances; (2) specification of goals and objectives, in which precomputing analyses provided the most orderly perspective administrators could find to guide their activities; (3) forecasting, an approach which faltered on the uncertainty of the world; and (4) strategic planning, the latest and most advanced approach, which focuses on the future, is data-based and oriented to rational decision making, and is focused more on process than product.

Peterson (1980, 1986) has been among the few authors stressing the notion of contingency in planning, i.e., the use of different kinds of planning for different kinds of situations. Accordingly, Peterson's work often views strategic thinking as a useful tool in certain circumstances. In his most recent writings (e.g., 1986), Peterson has suggested that administrators are learning to vary their planning approaches and techniques for selective use in different situations. Good leaders,

Peterson's work suggests, should be capable of varying their planning repertoire by issue, by kind of unit interdependencies, by tradition, and by environmental condition. In the 1980s, Peterson (1986) says, institutions' problems and needs have focused on decline, uncertainty, and effectiveness, and planning has therefore been aimed toward institutional renewal. In a return to a recurring theme in the literature on higher education planning in recent years, Peterson (1986) argues that this environment means planning activities must move away from concentrating solely on physical or financial matters. Instead, he suggests greater attention to academic planning and the pursuit of a more proactive stance that is oriented to the future, to developing planning behavior in individual leaders as well as in organizations, and to "strategic choice." On the latter, he says that

> Strategic choices are those that a) deal broadly with an institution's mission or structure, b) deal with relationships between the institution and its resource environment, c) affect the institution or many of its participants, d) often do not allow even small-scale pilot programs, e) are not easily reversible, and f) often require risk-taking and commitment to make them work. Clearly [the important planning issues of the next few years] involve strategic choices. Because of constrained resources they will require reallocation. More important, they are not objective problems to be solved but value choices which affect many constituents. Dealing with value-laden strategic choices will involve planning that is more qualitative and closely linked with governance and will require major priority, investment, and commitment decisions—something our informal governance processes do not handle well. Clearly we have the rational techniques to address these issues. We also recognize their political character, but need to formalize that strategic choice process. (ibid., p. 14)

Like Peterson and Cope, Ellen Earle Chaffee (1983, 1984, 1985) has noted the many conceptual and practical problems inherent in definitions of "strategic" approaches. Chaffee has been particularly attentive to the limitations of a strict interpretation of strategic planning. Citing the preference of some for the more inclusive term "strategic management" (see Ansoff, Declerck, and Hayes, 1976; Mintzberg, 1978), Chaffee suggests caution before adopting too constrained a vision of strategy. In this chapter, an attempt is made to view strategy from the perspective of its dominant interpreters. For this reason, Chaffee's cautionary note will be heeded. Strategic planning will be taken to include those managerial activities sometimes referred to more broadly as strategic management, including "operational management of the organization's competitive mode ('planning'), the entrepreneurial management of the organization's entrepreneurial mode ('adapting'), and the integrative management of both modes ('planned learning')" (Chaffee, 1985, pp. 134–135).

Chaffee's work (1983, 1984, 1985) has often been chastening for the more wide-eyed proponents of strategic approaches. In her exhaustive review of literature on higher education strategy (1985), she reminds her readers of the familiar cycle following higher education's importing of tools and tactics from other settings: enthusiasm, adoption, study, boredom, forgetting. Should anyone miss the point, she makes special reference to PPBS, MBO, and other prominent but largely misused and disused management innovations of the 1970s. Strategic management runs the same risks, she suggests.

Chaffee also cautions that the nature of the beast the academy has imported is not altogether clear. Perhaps the most innovative and influential contribution of Chaffee's excellent review is her discerning of three distinct models of strategy in the literature: "linear strategy," "adaptive strategy," and "interpretive strategy." Linear strategy, Chaffee argues, involves movement from determining long-term goals to adoption of actions and parallel allocation of resources for achieving the goals. This school of thought in the literature contains many writings on goals, rational planning, priority setting, program review, master planning, and forecasting (e.g., see Chandler, 1962; Conrad, 1974; Dickmeyer, 1982; Fenske, 1980). Adaptive strategy, Chaffee suggests, focuses upon the development of a viable match between risks and opportunities in the external environment and the organization's capabilities and resources. This school of thought in the literature contains much of the marketing, competitiveness, and effectiveness literature (e.g., see Miles and Cameron, 1982; Shirley, 1983; Cope, 1981; Peterson, 1980; Keller, 1983; Kotler and Murphy, 1982; Baldridge, 1983; Baldridge and Okimi, 1982; Cameron, 1982). Finally, Chaffee's interpretive strategy centers around the use of "orienting metaphors to motivate behavior expected to produce favorable organizational results" (Chaffee, 1985, p. 146). This school of thought pays particular attention to organizational symbols, meanings, cultures, legitimacy, and rituals (e.g., see Chaffee, 1984; Pettigrew, 1977). In closing her introduction to the three models, Chaffee notes that most writers on higher education strategy follow the adaptive model, although there are overtones of all three models in many writings.

The Principles and Process of Strategy

The selective review above reveals some of the disparate ways in which the term "strategy" is used in higher education. Similar confusion besets the more general term "planning" itself. Its meaning is far from clearly agreed upon among prominent organization theorists, some of whom have a hard time distinguishing it from other managerial activities (see, for example, Mintzberg, 1981). When one considers these twin confusions, the difficulties of writing critically on the topic of "strategic planning" come into sharp focus. Although popular and familiar, it is a doubly obscure notion.

One might even argue triply obscure, since the complexities of the notion of strategic planning are compounded by the extraordinary diversity of the higher education enterprise. Institutions differ greatly in their organizational features and needs (Baldridge et al., 1978; Peterson, 1980, 1986). The varying messages of the prescriptive chapters in Jedamus and Peterson (1980) on institutional planning in different kinds of institutions are upheld by the disparate findings of research on strategic planning in different settings. What Clugston (1987) found for strategic planning in a large research university does not fully parallel what Chaffee (1984), Anderson (1978), or Jonsen (1984) found for strategic planning in small colleges. The diversity is not solely a matter of institutional type: Finkelstein, Farrar, and Pfnister, (1984) note the extreme variations possible in the environments and "sociological set" of typologically similar institutions.

Nevertheless, the well-known writings on strategic planning do suggest some broad, minimal outlines of the topic, in the form of five principles stressed by the most prominent proponents of strategy. These principles will be outlined below, then evaluated as to their congruence with the nature of organizational life in higher education.

Core Principles

Principle 1 is that *strategic planning is wholistic, in that it is focused on broad organizational goals, purposes, values, and mission.* Strategic planning is not focused on tactics, execution, or parochial issues within the institution. In this way, Cope (1981) believes, strategic thinking is oriented to the basic character and the core competencies of institutions. Two issues are raised by this principle. First, it challenges decision traditions. Cope suggests that the wholism ideal may pose strategic planning's most difficult task: inculcating in institutional personnel the value of thinking of the organization as a whole, rather than in terms of its parts. The wholism principle implies a decision style which is participative and integrative, with inclusion of the faculty and staff of entire institutions (Cope, 1981, p. 3).

The second issue raised by the wholism principle is more fundamental: the match between core values of institutions and emerging environmental conditions is often awkward. Cope (1981), Peterson (1980), and Keller (1983) each pay central attention to dealing with this challenge. Empirical research by Chaffee (1983, 1985) has suggested that inattention to institutionwide values and mission, and the pursuit instead of rapid opportunistic change away from fundamental, historically rooted ideas about a school's role, may be harmful. Although the idea that organizations should not stray too far from their distinctive competencies is well-rooted in the general organization literature (e.g., see various chapters in Pennings et al., 1985), the constraints posed by distinctive cultures and traditions have been less considered in that literature. These constraints may be especially significant in research universities: academic culture and disciplinary cultures alike may resist the wholistic impulse of strategic planning, since their traditional norms are those of accommodation to individual and department-level discretion and adaptation (Clark, 1983; Dill, 1982; Thelin, 1985).

Principle 2 is that *strategic planning is medium-term in orientation, although it is executed in the short term via priority setting, program evaluations, budgets, and so forth.* This is a point stressed by virtually every author on the topic (e.g., see Cope, 1981; Uhl, 1983; Morrison, Renfro, and Boucher, 1984), although their definition of medium-term varies. Generally, medium-term seems to imply a time horizon of two to five years. The contrast has frequently been drawn between this approach and the very long time horizon of traditional long-range planning and the short time horizon of budget planning efforts (Cope, 1981). A statement defending the strategic value of the medium-term planning perspective comes from one of Kemerer, Baldridge, and Green's (1982) interviewees, a provost at a large university: "I am more than happy to let my enemies run the long-range planning committees. [While] they are off in a corner . . . making up their master plans . . . I am doing the unimportant stuff, at least from their point of view. I am setting the budgets, selecting the key people, and funding key programs. In the long run I am positive that I will have more influence over this institution's future" (p. 137).

Principle 3 is that *strategic planning is both externally and internally focused, and seeks actively to be both at once.* The matching of the proximate environment and the characteristics of an institution (specifically, its internal resources) has been identified as a major strategic goal for higher education institutions (Kotler, 1982; Kotler and Murphy, 1981; Collier, 1980, 1981). The external environment is a special concern in the early writings of Cope (1981) and Peterson (1980). For Cope (1981), strategic planning is external in perspective and open in its systems view, two characteristics that contrast it dramatically with older, internally focused styles of long-range planning. Baldridge and Okimi (1982) note that the focus of strategy is on "flexibility and quick response to changes in the outside environment," a point echoed by Miller (1983). Similarly, Richardson and Gardner (1985) note that much planning is external in focus, and comment on the external as a newly dominant focus: "Until very recently, most universities have been content to let an internal vision of the future shape their institution. Now there are forces in the external environment which threaten that vision and, accordingly, must be considered in the planning process" (p. 10). Zammuto and Cameron (1985) give especially detailed consideration to conceptualizing environmental concerns. They outline two kinds of environmental threats, one in which the level of activity for an institution or program is less environmentally supported than before, and a second in which the type of activity pursued is less environmentally supported than before. These authors argue that problems of level call for more efficiency, whereas problems of type call for program cuts, recasting, and innovations.

The subtleties involved in making balanced, informed judgments regarding external conditions and internal resources have been reflected in the emerging literature on organizational effectiveness in higher education. Cope (1981) argues strongly that strategic management and planning involve doing the right thing, rather than simply doing things right. This perspective is often stressed in the literature as an example of replacing a narrow "efficiency" orientation with a broader-minded "effectiveness" orientation (also see Baldridge and Okimi, 1982; Keller, 1983, pp. 142–3; Peterson, 1986). Among the most well-known authors contributing to research on effectiveness is Kim Cameron (1978, 1981). The notion of effectiveness is a challenging and difficult concept, and it has provided the rubric for a wide variety of strategic approaches ranging from a Darwinian focus on precise adaptation to external environments to a purely internal focus on educational production processes.

Arguing that strategic planning involves blending an external and internal focus, Cope (1981) was among the first authors to link higher education strategy explicitly to the business literature on market portfolio analysis, as a way to refine the traditional educational activity of program review. In the years since the earliest writing on the topic in the late 1970s, institutions have moved far beyond the lockstep application of relatively primitive and questionably appropriate business-originated approaches, such as the Boston Consulting Group's market portfolio analysis described by Keller (1983). In place of a simple two-by-two table of programs, placed in cells on the basis of their quality (high or low) and their demand characteristics (high or low), institutions have moved increasingly toward multiway breakdowns of program characteristics and environmental factors.

Principle 4 is that *strategic planning is ongoing, not simply a one-time planning effort.* This principle is reflected in Cope's argument (1981, p. 3) that strategic planning is "an iterative, continuing learning process" whose "emphasis is on change, review, reexamination. It is not static." Cope stresses that strategy's results are in the form of a process rather than a blueprint, and a stream of decisions rather than a plan (ibid.). In its emphasis on strategy as involving more than a periodic mechanical application of certain technical approaches, the Cope (1981) perspective parallels that of Marvin Peterson (1980, 1986). Both authors stress the connections between strategy and governance, and emphasize the importance of attention to democratic process.

An emphasis on the process of planning rather than its products is somewhat revolutionary for colleges and universities, and is central to other writings on the topic beside those of Cope and Peterson (see Baldridge and Okimi, 1982). Such an emphasis may be caricatured as favoring a kind of "know-nothing" approach and, not surprisingly, is far from being fully accepted. In a biting and provocative essay, Miller (1983) suggests the belittling of plans, "planners," quantification, and modeling is endemic to the writing on strategy. Perhaps the best light to put on this tendency, argues the admitted traditionalist Miller, is simply to assume that the strategic advocates wish only to blend the "rational" and nonrational in planning. A passage from Miller's text suggests his worries are greater than that, however:

"Strategic planning focuses on process," Cope says, adding that "with strategic planning, the institution will not print, bind, and distribute long-range plans . . . instead there may only be annual reviews of the institution's . . . direction of movement." The intent of the statement is positive, but another reading suggests the possibility that changes in institutional "direction" might be known only after the fact. Similarly, Cope reassuringly states that with strategic planning "less attention is given to computer models that project internal staffing requirements and internal resource requirements . . . instead more attention is given to changes outside the institution in what people value, what political institutions seek, and what competing institutions are likely to do." Hopefully, *someone will tally* the staffing and resource requirements—and remember to keep the check writing machine. The old cliche about being only a number on a card which should not be bent, stapled, or spindled was effective because it was simultaneously simplistic and salient. The same simplistic criticism of "rational" organizational planning and analysis is found in much of the strategic planning literature, along with assurances that with strategic planning those days will be over." (Ibid., pp. 43–44)

Other authors besides Miller have also found fault with the attention to process so frequently espoused in the strategic literature. For example, Morgan (1984) has quoted Wildavsky (1973): "When planning is placed in the context of continuous adjustment, it becomes hard to distinguish from any other process of decision" (p. 155), and Mintzberg (1981) has also raised some reservations. Nevertheless, the process orientation is imbedded deeply in the current strategic movement, and must be part of any evaluation of its relevance to resource distribution.

Principle 5 is that *strategic planning pursues a blend of qualitative and quantitative approaches.* In their orientation, both Cope (1981) and Peterson (1980, 1986) emphasize qualitative processes and information rather than processes and data attending strictly to the measurable facets of higher education's clients, resources, processes, and outcomes.

In summary, these five principles—concentrating upon the fundamental purposes and values of the organization as a whole, focusing on the medium term future, attending jointly to external conditions and internal resources, developing ongoing planning processes, and blending the qualitative and quantitative— appear to form the foundation for strategic behavior, as described in the literature. For the purposes of this chapter, literature on activities simultaneously involving these principles will be assumed to be literature on strategic planning and management, regardless of whether or not those precise terms are used.

Critical Steps in the Strategic Process

From a variety of sources (Chaffee, 1985; Cope, 1981; Uhl, 1983; Heydinger, 1983; Peterson, 1980), there emerges a rough concensus regarding the process of strategic planning and management. This process may be portrayed as a series of steps in an ongoing cycle.

Step 1 is to *catalogue current mission, goals, values, products, services, and activities*. This step represents the standard starting point in both the general organization literature and the literature on higher education strategy. Products, services, and activities may easily be listed or described, but mission, goals, and values are both more difficult and more fundamental. Yet the literature argues that it is critical that any strategy proposed must integrate all of these factors (Peterson, 1986; Collier, 1981; Chaffee, 1985; and many others). In particular, products, services, and activities must be made to fit well with the institution's preexisting values, saga, and culture (Clark, 1970).

Step 2 is to *assess constraints facing the institution in its strategy development*. Any institution must develop its own list of constraints, but some are so frequently encountered in nonprofit organizations that they constitute a general-purpose list. Kotler (1982, pp. 8–9) has listed four distinctive constraints on nonprofit organizations' strategic marketing: multiple publics, multiple objectives, the offering of services rather than physical goods, and public scrutiny. To this familiar list Anthony and Herzlinger (1975) have added legal constraints on services to be offered and the dominant presence of professionals in such organizations, often in tension with administrators. Not noted by those authors but overarching each of these constraints are the special financial constraints associated with nonprofit status. These will form an important focus in later parts of this chapter.

Step 3 is to *initiate two interfacing aspects of strategic planning: internal and external*. This step corresponds to the blended focus on the internal and external cited above as Principle 3 in strategic planning. The first aspect of this step is systematic environmental analysis. The respected organizational analyst James Thompson (1967) was among the first to note the need for environmental scanning that is both opportunistic and problem-centered. Aguilar (1967) was among the first to address this need in some detail. In the general organizational literature, representative investigations of this approach have come from Hambrick (1982) and Dutton and Jackson (1987). In both articles, the authors assess the nature of strategic issues in the environment and their relevance to planned change. In higher education, Cope (1981), Renfro and Morrison (1983b,c), Morrison et al. (1984), and Hearn and Heydinger (1985) have examined the typical techniques, which include assessment of threats and opportunities, development of probability/impact matrices, and impact network analyses. In her studies of strategy, Chaffee (1985) has viewed such activities as efforts at "anticipatory adapting."

The second, interrelated aspect of this step is a systematic internal resource audit. Kotler (1982) describes this process in a way that resembles a blend of Chaffee's (1985) "linear" approach (with overtones of traditional market portfolio analysis in business) and her "symbolic" approach. Among the "linear" resource ingredients to be considered are the human and material components of the institution. Among the symbolic resource ingredients to be considered are the cultural and symbolic aspects of the institution. The linear aspects of the internal resource audit connect clearly to the program review literature in higher education, particularly its attention to such program "portfolio" features as centrality, connectedness, quality, demand, comparative advantage, and cost. Mims (1980), Heydinger (1980, 1982, 1983), and Keller (1983) each provide examples of variants and refinements of portfolio models at such schools as S.U.N.Y., Buffalo; Ohio State; Illinois; and Minnesota. Regardless of differences in perspective on the details of this step's blend of environmental and internal analyses, the literature consistently suggests that it is fundamental to the development of strategy, and to the development of a strategic perspective from which all in an institution may draw inspiration and direction.

Step 4 is to *implement the developed strategic vision*. This step involves moving to modify goals, initiate programmatic and structural changes, and accommodate needed changes in organizational values. The final stage in the process is perhaps the most difficult. Step 5 is to *design and initiate the ongoing planning process*. Heydinger (1980, 1982, 1983), Peterson (1980, 1986), and many others stress the importance of activities as specifying information needs; scheduling rounds and cycles; evaluating results for consistency with the external environment and consistency with internal resources; and adjusting the process as necessary. Hatten (1982) provides an excellent overview of such efforts in a variety of colleges.

THE ECONOMICS OF STRATEGY IN HIGHER EDUCATION

The above review highlights the basic principles and steps of strategic planning and management in colleges and universities, as portrayed by its proponents and primary conceptualizers in the literature. What can be concluded about the connections of the approach to economic efficiency and effectiveness? Unfortunately, very little may be said at present on this question. The absence of extensive theoretical and empirical work on the topic, beyond the few pioneering contributions, is striking. There is a particularly troubling contrast between the lack of treatment of economic issues in the literature on higher education strategy and the more extensive treatment of those issues in the general organizations literature on strategy. In higher education, the economic aspects of the topic are among the least-explored strategic concerns.

Cope (1981), for example, pays little attention to resource issues. He does suggest (p. 27) that "restraints on time and money" may influence the strategic decision-making process and therefore may importantly affect the nature of strategic decisions. He also suggests that the costs and benefits of strategic planning are a significant topic for further research. It was left more to others, however, to consider these concerns in some depth. Peterson (1980, 1981) was among the first of a handful of authors to address resource issues in higher education strategy. Noting the novelty of this approach, Peterson (1981) characterizes the historical tendencies in financial planning as being primarily internal; limited to revenue and expense patterns; mostly responsive to environmental conditions, rather than proactive; mainly oriented to forecasts and modeling; taking place in a context of institutional budgeting; and either short-term or extremely long-term in orientation. Prior to the emerging attention to strategy, he argues, the focus was on techniques rather than strategy, and planning activities were dominated by administrative staff, with limited involvement by others (1981, p. 20).

Despite Peterson's sense that old concerns in financial planning are being replaced by strategic thinking, however, there is still a dearth of material on the topic. It is striking to note that in the many studies of business strategy reviewed by Chaffee (1985), the focal outcome for assessing strategic success was usually based in some indicator of resources, such as profit, ratio of income to assets, return on investment, cash flow, return on assets, return on equity, sales growth, or even the Fortune 500 rating of the corporation. In the higher education strategy studies, however, the focal outcomes were more often enrollment or quality driven, or were even more basic (e.g., survival versus closing). Only the Anderson (1978) analysis attended in detail to financial indicators. Since the Chaffee essay, Clugston (1987) has conducted an analysis of the budgeting implications of strategic efforts at a large university, but there has been little other focus on the financial implications of strategy in higher education. One obvious reason for this continuing avoidance of the topic, of course, is the attention to nonmonetary effectiveness criteria in nonprofit organizations. Colleges and universities, nevertheless, do not exist in an economic vacuum. Resources are essential for the kinds of success sought by higher education institutions. What is more, knowledgability about resources is critical to any conceivably successful model of strategy formation.

The battle cry of much of the preceding twenty years in the planning literature has been that we should move more toward integration of the fiscal, academic, and physical sides of planning (Micek, 1980; Chaffee, 1983a). Historically, these processes have gone on somewhat independently of each other, according to many of the chapters of Jedamus and Peterson's valuable 1980 edited volume, *Improving Academic Management*. This movement toward planning integration fits nicely with the strategic orientation. Empirically, very little research has been done from this perspective, however. Instead, a variety of sources, including Green, Nayyar, and Ruch (1979), Morgan (1984), and Merson and Qualls (1979), have employed inclusive strategic perspectives in largely descriptive, prescriptive, and atheoretical work. In each of these works, new planning approaches in higher education are catalogued and their respective strengths and weaknesses assessed. Green et al. suggest an integrated system linking planning and budgeting and based in zero-based budget analysis, principles of budgeting, and MBO. Much of their text contains strategic thinking, as defined by Cope (1981). In a similar vein, Morgan describes strategic planning and management as a new descendant of the well-known goals/rational approaches to higher education planning, as exemplified by PPBS and MBO. Finally, Merson and Qualls (1979) take an exhaustive financial approach to strategy. As Cope suggests regarding the first and third of these sources, however, none of these otherwise excellent works deals systematically with the external environment or with the general notion of strategy as explicated in the business literature. They are much more "micro" (single office) in approach and hence more limited in scope.

Of more direct relevance, several authors (e.g., Chaffee, 1985; Cope, 1981) have noted that the important 1974 book by Balderston also contains many ideas and insights regarding the strategy and resources link, even though it does not overtly use the terms of strategic planning and management. In particular, Balderston provides a masterful recounting of strategic resource issues involved in the merger of Case Institute and Western Reserve and similar issues involved in the termination of the Slavic Languages and Literature program at Princeton. Because of its centrality to our topic, the Balderston work will be referred to often in later portions of the chapter. This work is representative of a pattern in the literature: to the extent strategy has been linked to resources in the literature, the focus has been on medium to long-term capital investment choices. Targeted investments in chosen areas of institutions, and targeted cuts in other areas, are usually seen as preferable from the strategic perspective to a more passive, and perhaps more traditional, reliance on yearly across-the-board cuts and increments. Accordingly, one might argue that budgeting is to capital investment as short-term problem management is to strategic management and planning. In a sense, then, the question of the economics of strategy is simply a medium-term version of the familiar question of public economy: How should decision makers allocate limited resources among a variety of "good" public activities?

The strategic approach to this classic political problem is nicely addressed by Milter (1986):

A resource allocation problem is "strategic" to the extent that it involves a set of decisions which is typically unstructured, complex, and open-ended (Mintzberg and others, 1976). The elements of the decision process are interdependent (Mitroff and Emshoff, 1976), and decision making becomes "a critical tool for achieving important organizational changes" (Chaffee, 1983, p. 402). Nevertheless, it is virtually impossible for administrators to use to the fullest all available relevant information and to assess every internal and external organizational need. Even if all such information were to be incorporated into the budgeting process, competing priorities would make difficult a final allocation of scarce resources that would satisfy all those in the institution who have stake in the outcome. (p. 80)

Milter goes on to recommend certain emerging decision support systems [DSS] for dealing with the complexity. While there are clear practical merits in such an approach, the research question of resources and strategy demands a broader conceptualization.

A Conceptualization

Any conceptualization of the issues in the economics of strategy should begin by considering the fundamental concepts of the economics of the firm: scarcity, effectiveness and efficiency, constraints, price, incentives, supply, demand, productivity, unit costs, capital costs, capital structure, environmental support for organizational goals, time, uncertainty, risk, information seeking behavior, rates of return, preference functions, and utility (e.g., see Wernerfelt, 1984; Dutton and Jackson, 1987; and Barton and Gordon, 1987). For considerations of the microeconomics of colleges and universities, see Daniere (1964), Dickmeyer (1982), and Mortimer and Taylor (1984). The latter authors present an unusually insightful discussion of the two most fundamental concepts, scarcity and environmental uncertainty, as they apply in higher education decision making.

Using the core economic concepts as background, one can initiate exploration of the economics of strategy by considering the ways in which higher education strategy is likely to resemble and not resemble strategy in other settings. In Figure 1, an attempt is made to portray conceptually the economic conditions assumed to affect strategy in higher education, and to contrast those conditions with the economic conditions affecting strategy in a more typical or more nearly "ideal-type" strategic context, such as that portrayed in literature on the for-profit sector. Figure 1 may be viewed as a summary of the problems likely to be encountered in bridging the gap between economically based strategy research in other settings and the beginnings of such research in higher education. Among the many sources contributing to this conceptualization are Cyert (1978), Leslie and Johnson (1974), Kotler (1982), Wildavsky (1984), and Chaffee (1985). Of course, Figure 1 is an oversimplification: none of the characteristics associated with either side of the figure are always present.

The figure suggests that there are nine central aspects of the economics of strategy: the external environment, revenue sources, structural integration, the

FIG. 1. The economics of strategy in the ideal-type and higher education contexts.

	Ideal-type organizational context	The organizational context of higher education institutions
External environment	An enterprise charge: freedom to diversify portfolios, cut old products, initiate new products, "position" products in the marketplace	A societal charge: limits on freedom to diversify, cut, initiate, and "position"
	Norms of competition	Mixed norms of cooperation and competition
	Geographic mobility	Geographic immobility
	Mix of developing and mature product lines, threatened and unthreatened niches	Mix of mature and declining product lines, with multiple threatened niches
	A clearly bounded and relatively "knowable" external environment	A set of penetrating and vaguely defined external environments
Revenue sources	Passive resource providers and customers	Active resource providers, clients, and constituents
Structural integration	Goal clarity and consensus	Goal ambiguity and conflict
	Leadership discretion	Shared governance
	Private control	Mixed public and/or private control
Locus of authority	Hierarchical	Diffuse
Pricing decisions	Price discretion, subject to market conditions	Limited price discretion, subject to many constraints
Economics of innovation and change	Material incentives	Mixed incentives
	Slack resources	Minimal organizational slack
Production: Human resources	Flexible human capital	Inflexible human capital
Production: Technology	Discrete functions	Integrated functions
	Tight coupling of production elements	Loose coupling of production elements
	Economies of scale	Limited economies of scale
	Understood technology	Poorly understood technology
Production: Performance evaluation	Strong quality control, due to tangibility of products	Weak quality control, due to intangibility of services
	Clear returns on investment, often immediate	Unclear returns on investment, often over longer term

locus of authority, pricing decisions, the economics of innovation and change, the human resources aspect of production, the technological aspect of production, and the performance evaluation aspect of production. It is argued here that college and university strategy is shaped fundamentally by contextual differences from more familiar strategic conditions, and that these differences may be presented in terms of the nine aspects noted in the figure. In the section that follows, these aspects are presented in more detail and are explored in the higher education context.

NINE ASPECTS OF THE ECONOMICS OF STRATEGY

The External Environment

As Figure 1 suggests, the economic perspective of strategic planning in the for-profit sector assumes an enterprise charge, meaning that the larger legal, economic, political, and societal context provides for-profit organizations the freedom to diversify their portfolios, cut old products, initiate new products, and "position" products in the marketplace. All of these activities are aimed at inducing resource contributions from the external environment to increase returns to shareholders. For-profit organizations are assumed to operate under norms of competition, to enjoy the possibility of geographic mobility, subject only to the constraints of resources, to possess a mix of developing and mature product lines, to operate in a variety of competitive resource contexts, and to face a clearly defined and knowable external environment. In contrast, higher education institutions operate under a societal charge which limits their freedom to diversify portfolios, eliminate old products, initiate new ones, and "position" themselves in the economic marketplace (see Leslie and Johnson, 1974). What is more, colleges and universities usually operate under historic norms disfavoring intense competition among institutions, are allowed very little geographic mobility, control a mix of mostly mature or declining products in threatened niches, and face external environments which are difficult to "know" and which penetrate into the core of the institution in innumerable ways (Clark, 1983).

Perhaps the most formidable fact of economic life for nonprofit postsecondary institutions is the constraints posed by their distinctive role in society. Having a charge from society to educate, inculcate values, and develop new knowledge implies a distinctive environmental condition (Meyer and Rowan, 1978). Institutional portfolios of services are somewhat inflexible, due to public expectations that they maintain an English department, for example, regardless of its inherent quality. From a strategic perspective, exit from certain "markets" (e.g., offering of freshman-level English) is prohibited, as is entry into others (e.g., the offering of interstate trucking services, or the development of a chain of fast-food restaurants). What is more, the nature of some products, and their pricing, are often required to remain relatively stable.

Market flexibility is at the heart of the contrast of this situation to the classic model of strategic positioning. When one examines the literature on the economics of strategy in for-profit settings (e.g., see Wernerfelt, 1984; Teece, 1985; Camerer, 1985), the issue of entry and exit barriers is fundamentally seen as one of competitive advantage. Inflexibilities do exist in such settings, of course. The sunk costs and fixed costs of long-term investment in a particular profitable product line can make a firm's pricing and general competitive position in that arena unassailable (i.e., can pose a relatively impenetrable entry barrier to other firms interested in the arena). In addition, as Camerer (1987) cautions, the high levels of ongoing fixed costs for production of that product can also make exit difficult, should prospects for the product decline (witness the U.S. steel industry's dilemmas of recent times). Nevertheless, inflexibilities seem greater in higher education, where marketplace logic operates in only limited fashion. The nature of fixed costs does discourage exit from certain markets, especially when one considers tenured faculty salaries as a kind of fixed cost, but a variety of other noneconomic factors (e.g., accreditation standards, funding source expectations, public attitudes) also present exit barriers. Similarly, entry barriers can be formidable. Businesses can, and increasingly do, seek legislative redress when colleges and universities enter certain markets in which they can use tax-exempt status and other advantages to undercut prices (e.g., book sales, computer sales; see Jaschik, 1987). In addition, the nature of the labor pool and production technology, in universities in particular, can limit their ability to penetrate successfully new markets in which other competitors have long ago recovered their development costs and other entry costs.

Transaction-cost approaches to understanding organizational form and functioning have recently been employed in an attempt to fit strategic reasoning into an economic framework. Robins (1987) suggests that there are some ways to employ the transaction-costs (TC) approach productively to better understand the ways organizations contingently match their structures to the environmental conditions surrounding them. Robins' article represents a breakthrough of potential use for higher education research in that, unlike other examples of the TC approach, this piece deals with the pervasiveness of imperfect markets, such as those characterizing the nonprofit sector. Robins explores the ways in which firms adapt organizational structures which do not meet the standard criteria of economic efficiency (the usual "engine" for TC models) but which still are rational. In an unusual interdisciplinary gesture, he focuses especially on the work of Meyer and Rowan (1978) on the nonefficient adaptations of educational organizations, suggesting these adaptations are made in order to meet the environmentally imposed necessity for legitimated organizational forms, which in turn open access to critical resource flows for schools and colleges.

A subtle, yet important, aspect of colleges' and universities' economic environments is the degree of prestige they possess in their various services (e.g., undergraduate education, research capability, etc). In any sensible accounting, prestige is an environmental resource for an institution (Mingle et al., 1982). Strategically, it creates entry barriers for other prospective competitors, and to an extent buffers services from inspection. Although prestige is a primary competitive resource in higher education, it is difficult to value and difficult to buy. It is based in public perceptions which build up over long time periods, resist change, and tend to overflow across programs and activities within a single institution. For example, all programs at elite universities tend to be perceived as having high quality, despite the inevitable variability in their "actual" quality levels (Clark, 1983).

Prestige is closely akin to the notion of "good will" in standard accounting methods for business valuation. There is a major difference between the two concepts, however: the difficulty, and generally perceived unattractiveness, of attaching financial value to prestige and its resource correlates. How does one attach value to a "deep" admissions pool (more applicants than available spaces for students), to high levels of alumni loyalty, or to the legitimacy that leads news reporters to seek out a school's faculty as authorities on social and scientific issues?[1] All schools have historically operated in a special zone of consumer attitudes, a zone to which a "logic of good faith" is attached (Meyer and Rowan, 1978). In that zone, the marketplace's usual hard-nosed, dollar-based questions have been avoided. Although recent developments in the "excellence movement" may temper that protection, and although some schools have always lacked the necessary levels of public confidence, the most prestigious colleges and universities may be expected to continue to operate in markets in which their competitive position is largely unassailable.

Perhaps the most noteworthy examples of the power and material indefinability of prestige came in the supreme era of "strategic choice" in American higher education: the late 1800s, when wealthy industrialists were engaged in determined efforts at institution-building. Although there are numerous anecdotes regarding these men's uncomfortable experiences bumping up against the powerfully entrenched prestige hierarchy in higher education, the most telling (although perhaps now enlarged and reshaped by repeated retelling) may be those of the Duke brothers, who built their fortune in the tobacco industry, and Jane and Leland Stanford, who wished to use Leland's massive earnings from building the Western railroad system to begin a great university in honor of their recently deceased son. In each case, the founders visited elite Eastern universities, prominently including Harvard and Princeton, and are said to have inquired discreetly regarding the possible sale price of these institutions. These early "takeover" attempts were, of course, rebuffed as ludicrous intrusions by the sullied world of business into the sublime world of learning. It would no doubt seem deeply ironic to Thorstein Veblen, Charles Eliot, H. L. Mencken, and the others who ridiculed such efforts that the Stanfords and Dukes did successfully use their wealth to build prestigious institutions, although success required much more time than originally planned.

A number of authors have attempted to construct schemas to portray the degree of strategic flexibility organizations have within their external environments. At the heart of the models of Cameron (1984) and Clugston (1987) lies a notion of environmental dependence: the degree to which organizational resource flows are constrained by environmental conditions. An organization benefits from low environmental dependence to the extent that it draws its resources from multiple sources within a resource-rich environment which is stable over time and relatively insensitive to changes in institutional directions. Cameron suggests that strategic choice exists most clearly in organizations with low environmental dependence and high managerial influence (1984, p. 125). In other words, very high dependence on difficult external environments may crimp discretion of managers even beyond the constraints posed by the internal structures and dynamics of their organizations. Ironically, as Keller (1983) and others have noted, the very environmental conditions mentioned by him and others as contributing to the strategic planning "movement" may in fact contribute to its limitations. Scarcity in the external and internal climates may frustrate the kind of whole-hearted, time-consuming, democratic planning effort envisioned by strategic management and planning adherents. In such conditions, the absence of organizational slack and institutional loyalty may preclude faculty and staff (the key figures necessary for the success of the strategic approach) from energetically adopting strategic perspectives.

The issue of uncertainty regarding the external environment has led to research in noneducational settings on the control of strategy under conditions of ambiguity (see Schreyogg and Steinmann, 1987). Similar research in higher education appears lacking. It may be that the external environment of complex institutions of higher education is as well known or better known at the department and discipline levels as at the central level; such is the argument of many opposing a centralized environmental scanning approach (see Hearn and Heydinger, 1985). Nevertheless, the limited accuracy of forecasts concerning enrollment and other resource factors in recent years argues for strategic attention to dealing with uncertainty in environments within higher education as well. If, as Frances (1980) has argued, the enterprise has performed an about-face, moving from ignoring environmental prospects in the 1960s to surrendering to them in the 1980s, then corrections may be in order.

Along those lines, Peterson (1981) has argued that financial planning, in particular, needs to become more externally oriented, and has suggested that the increasing demands of external environments will require approaches other than quantitative modeling performed by limited numbers of administrative staff.

More scanning of the outside world, and more involvement by expert faculty, are needed, he suggests. To not do so, Peterson hinted in later work (1986), is to ignore the two primary environmental threats of the day: the demographic threat of declining traditional-age cohort sizes and the financial threat of limited state and federal fiscal support for higher education. He notes that, "despite lower inflation and improved GNP, there is little evidence that fiscal support for higher education will improve markedly . . ." (ibid., p. 11). To counter such conditions, Peterson argues that support for "institutional programs and investments will have to come from reallocation or more creative but risky debt financing" (ibid.). Similar points regarding the power of external environments and the emerging significance of monitoring them have been raised by Mason (1985) and by Mortimer and Tierney (1979).

The political aspects of external environments may merit special attention. Richardson and Gardner (1985) suggest that dealings with state legislators involve difficult strategic binds for public institutions. While the presence of crisis implies planning is essential, it also makes external relations harder. They suggest that, "The limited appeal of formal planning procedures in good times is better understood than the dubious benefit of planning for something that hopefully won't happen. If directed by the Governor's Office to plan for budget reduction of ten percent, is it better to demonstrate competency in planning by producing a neatly detailed scheme for making reductions without harming the educational program, or does it make more sense to cut where it is most visible while describing the catastrophic results to anyone who will listen?" (Richardson and Gardner, p. 10). Cast this way, the threats of environmental resource depletion may invoke two potentially opposed but arguably "strategic" behaviors: the rationally targeted approach to resource allocation, and efforts to construct an appropriate strategic "face" for external funders.

Revenue Sources

In the for-profit sector, resource providers tend to be relatively passive. For example, stockholders routinely elect leadership from board-approved slates and ratify board-backed initiatives, and customers are generally disorganized (i.e., not tied together into some functioning whole) and unknown to each other. In the higher education sector, students are similarly passive in regard to most core policy issues, but are, in contrast, actively involved resource-providing clients in the educational "production process," in that they shape the way they are treated through their classroom performance and behaviors. Even more critically, outside agencies (especially legislators and governors) increasingly demand evidence of the success of that production process, via accountability procedures. Such procedures are involved in grant performance reviews, in accreditation reviews, and in legislative reviews of performance. In strategic terms, these distinctive features of higher education have contrasting benefits and costs. From the benefit side, it is hard for institutions to avoid being "close to the customer" in certain ways. Peters and Waterman (1982) would likely be pleased: cues are heard when services are failing. On the cost side, procedures and organizational directions are contingent and often necessarily *ad hoc*. March and Simon (1958), Thompson (1967), and others have noted what might be termed an axiom of the economics of organization: nonroutinized procedures are likely to be higher in cost, higher in price, more subject to quality variations (the professionalism of faculty notwithstanding), and potentially more vulnerable to competition. Because central revenue providers in higher education are relatively active and often present at hand, institutions are prevented from pursuing full routinization of some of their core activities.

Structural Integration

In the ideal-type business setting, there exist goal clarity and consensus, high levels of executive leadership discretion in decision making, and relatively clear-cut (albeit often passive) private control, via the stockholders. The higher education sector is more noted for goal ambiguity and conflict, shared governance, and a mixture of public and private control (Cohen and March, 1974; Baldridge et al., 1978). In the terms of organization theory, the integrative mechanisms of the organization are more complex and problematic, especially in the multipurpose research university (Perrow, 1979; Clark, 1983).

A very fundamental aspect of the structural issue in strategy involves the appropriate levels of strategic planning and management. Although much of the literature on this question is based in program review considerations, this literature applies to strategic planning in that internal program review is a basic element of the strategic process (see Step 3, described earlier). The question arising here is the familiar one of the level at which decisions regarding program funding should be made (see Mortimer, Bagshaw, and Masland, 1985). Balderston (1974) has written on the well-known view in academic and fiscal planning that budgets should be driven by a "profit center" idea, in which "every tub has its own bottom," and has worried that the usual decentralization of position control in higher education leads inevitably to trouble for those seeking central direction and consistency. When strategic responsibility lies at the department level, rather than ultimately lying at the institution level, slowness of the central planning process is likely, Balderston suggests.

A number of structural tensions are likely to result from strategic planning in higher education, owing to its effective tightening of loosely coupled systems (Weick, 1978, 1982). Where, in the past, processes of instruction, research, and service continued largely unobserved by outside parties (Meyer and Rowan,

1978), strategic planning is one of a number of new activities intended to crack through the well-established buffers in educational organizations. Other emerging threats to the historic "logic of good faith" in educational organizations are outcomes assessment, stepped-up program review processes, and performance-based budgeting. In resource terms, strategic planning may represent the harbinger of lessened financial discretion at the local departmental level. In particular, assessing the strategic "centrality" of a program within the context of overall institutional purposes (Heydinger, 1982; Keller, 1983) may lead to termination of programs which are able to operate internal economies with defensible logic and returns at the micro (departmental) level but which have indefensible structural connections to the institutional whole.

At heart, the notion of centrality is ambiguous in the higher education context (Mingle and Norris, 1982, p. 58). Clark (1983) and others have argued that a noncentralized "disorderliness" is among the most effective features of American higher education, in that the absence of central authority, or even centralized definitions of goals, can foster the pursuit of quality at the level of the individual unit, where the relevant experts work. The strategic values of goal statements, instructional cohesiveness, and program centrality can come into conflict with the contrasting values of localized (departmental) quality. These value conflicts may erupt in the decisive reallocative steps of strategic planning processes, and may cause particular pain in eras of decline and challenge.

Some analysts have argued that innovation in higher education settings, particularly in the research universities, occurs mainly at the departmental level, rather than centrally (Clark, 1983; Weick, 1978). Much of that change occurs in ways unnoticed and uncontrolled by central administrations, as external professional and disciplinary environments, research developments, student enrollment patterns, and a variety of other externally driven factors shape the resource context of institutions (Hearn and Heydinger, 1985). In settings so effectively interpenetrated on multiple levels by their external environments, centrally directed change can potentially be as destructive as it is economically appealing (Clark, 1983). Relatedly, the nature of the research enterprise does not always correspond to the nature of central administrations' budgetary and planning categories. As Peterson (1981) has suggested, there is a need for planners to recognize the interrelationship of various resources on campuses: the fiscal sides of planning questions cannot always be compartmentalized as easily as some program review authorities suggest.

Much of the issue of level may be subsumed under the familiar debate over marketplace versus central approaches to planning and allocation systems in higher education (see Breneman, 1982; Morgan, 1984; Leslie, 1984). As Breneman points out, marketplace allocation schemes work best when information is complete or at least adequate, prices are based on marginal costs, or at least full costs or average costs, subsidies are equitably distributed, and organizational goals are clearcut. Since such conditions do not usually hold in American higher education, traditional economic reasoning might suggest reliance on central authority to offset market imperfections. Strategic systems are central systems, in that they invoke central planning efforts to exploit markets and achieve ends. Strategic systems are also partly market systems, however, in that they rely on competition and competitive position within and across institutions to determine, at least in part, the fate of individual academic programs.

The question of strategy and resources involves the differences between market-driven rationality, which is driven by behaviors and decisions at the level of buyer and seller (or client and service provider), and politically based decision systems, which are driven primarily by values, behaviors, and decisions at the central level. The tension of rational and "political" considerations in planning and budgeting is a theme common to the theoretical and prescriptive writings of Peterson (1980, 1981, 1986), Hoenack (1977, 1983), and Chaffee (1983a, 1985). Several of the chapters in Micek (1980) focus on this issue, as do Richardson and Gardner (1985), who stress the tension between planning as a rational process and planning as a political process, and suggest that the criteria for the two may be different. The same point was noted by Cope in his strategic planning and management monograph (1981), but he has stressed it more strongly recently. In fact, in his more recent consideration of the issue, Cope (1985) advised against any global endorsement of the concept of strategy, noting that greater attention to contextual issues, including the political environment, is necessary for both practice and research in higher education. It is an indicator of Cope's emerging, more contextual view of strategy that only in the final step of his 1985 "process" model of strategy does he consider 3–5 year goals and objectives, and the questions of "how we get there from here": rational, market-oriented notions of mission and fundamental purpose seem to occupy a less primary, less central role than in his earlier considerations of the topic.

Interestingly, the empirical research on the determinants of planning outcomes is sometimes conflicting (Milter, 1986). Chaffee (1983a) examined the relative roles of rationality and politics in university budgeting among university departments; she found aspects of both operating, but found rationality to be the dominant force (see also Rubin, 1977, 1979; Cameron, 1983). Pfeffer and Salancik (1974) and Pfeffer and Moore (1980) found department power more critical, however, in somewhat similar research. The results for changes over time in the dominant forces in planning outcomes are also rather contradictory. In times of stress, Cameron (1983) suggests, objectively rational criteria become more critical. According to a variety of other sources, however, political considerations become more critical at these times (Pfeffer and Moore, 1980; Baldridge et al., 1978; Breneman, 1982). Whenever an organization's resources are threatened by decline or external challenge, control over those resources tends to float to the top in the organization. Central planning is encouraged, and the market model displaced. A centralization process does not necessarily fully thwart economic rationality, but it does lend a political aspect to allocation procedures that involve other criteria than the efficiency, effectiveness, and equity concerns of economics (also see Schick, 1985).

Studies of state-level decision processes tend to support the notion that strategic resource distribution is more politicized at higher levels of the organization. Leslie (1984), reacting to Morgan (1984), suggests that state-level resource decisions resemble a political model, with interest groups, mobilization of forces, and so forth, but that "as one moves down the organizational structure, elements of the rational calculation model will prove more useful because incentive systems tend to become less political and more rational (p. 88). He suggests the president occupies a "no-man's land" between "the political and rational decision systems" (p. 89). In similar fashion, Leslie and Felix (1980) comment upon the tensions between political concerns at state level (such as historical legitimacy, contemporary fashion, and issues' relative degrees of controversy) and economic ("scientific") concerns at the institutional level, such as effectiveness (does the strategy accomplish what it set out to accomplish?), efficiency (does the strategy accomplish its goals within a specified constraining limit on resources?), and equity (to what extent are taxpayers treated fairly, and to what extent are users/beneficiaries sharing equally in costs?). Morgan (1984) and Leslie (1984) view both models as having merits, as well as some inevitability, and therefore focus upon the need to blend the two models in higher education decisions, since higher education places such high value on pursuing the rational, yet exists in an externally political context.

Of course, strategic control can exist too high to affect importantly an organization's future. Smartt (1984) suggests that efforts to have program review and performance budgeting control placed at the state level usually have failed to affect traditional core-type budget processes: "a state-level tie between program evaluation and budgeting is difficult because of conceptual and political problems (p. 46)." Smartt says instead that the real impact of program reviews (which are a facet of a strategic approach) has been at the institution level, and in departments and colleges inside institutions. At the state level, tradition and political factors have intruded to thwart the effectiveness of such efforts. A familiar example is the difficulty states have faced in pursuing institutional closings on the basis of cost, quality, and demand considerations.

One solution to the problems of market versus central planning schemes that seems to be pursued increasingly by universities and state systems is a differentiated one, in which parts of an institution or system may operate in a market economy whereas others operate in a centrally planned economy. Often, programs on the periphery of the academic enterprise on a campus (e.g., professional programs or continuing education programs) are asked to defend themselves via the marketplace route, whereas those nearer the core of the enterprise (e.g., English and physics departments' programs) are allowed protection from market forces. This reasoning is behind the idea of making professional schools charge something near to full market prices for their courses and programs while allowing heavy subsidies of core liberal arts and sciences courses and programs (Anthony and Herzlinger, 1975). This "profit·center" approach is in effect a modification of the familiar "every tub its own bottom" (ETIOB) philosophy commonly associated with Harvard University and some other research universities (Balderston, 1974). The revised notion may be stated as STTOB: "some tubs their own bottoms, but not all of them." Interestingly, according to Balderston (1975), Harvard itself does not pursue the ETIOB policy most often associated with it, but instead pursues something like the STTOB approach.

There are good reasons for pursuing an ETIOB approach, including the development of decentralized awareness of resource limits and difficult budgetary choices. There are also additional good reasons for pursuing an STTOB approach, including the offering of a pricing and subsidy system which appropriately treats programs providing primarily individual returns differently from programs providing substantial social returns. Nevertheless, as Balderston has suggested, such approaches can easily fail as institutional strategy. Market and funding signals provide inadequate bases for determining educational directions in an institution; program change cannot occur as rapidly as such signals change; new programs can be stifled by such "bottom line" criteria for allocations; and the interdisciplinary nature of many programs cannot easily be fit into such an accounts-driven system. In sum, the strategic value of the ETIOB and STTOB approaches is also their Achilles heel: institutions willing to live by the marketplace determination of policy must also be willing to suffer by that policy.

Some central themes emerge from the literature regarding structural factors affecting strategic resource allocation decisions. First, structural flexibility is important for successful reallocation efforts. Mims (1980) infers that organizational flexibility was critical to reallocation successes at Oklahoma State and Michigan, arguing that the ways funds are categorized have to be amenable to shifts at state levels, institution levels, etc. Second, there are overtones of the organizational notion of "buffers" in the literature on higher education strategy. For example, the comments above regarding the president as "middle man" or "middle woman" remind one of Thompson's (1967) point that there is a middle point between technical rationality and longer term political/external rationality in organizations, and often the central level of hierarchy in organizations (e.g., foremen, middle managers) must work as "translators" of one of the two perspectives to those holding the other perspective. Third, it is possible to think of strategic planning in higher education as involving an elaborate economic game, in which various forms of reasoning compete for a limited pool of resources disbursed by a wide variety of powerful, external, authorities (legislators, prospective students, donors, research agencies, etc.). The decisive external authorities are usually audiences for, rather than active participants in, the game, but command sufficient resources to dramatically shape the nature and outcomes of the planning process.

The Locus of Authority

Authority in for-profit settings tends to be clearly hierarchical. Officials at the top level are expected to be those most expert in affairs of the firm, and strategic direction is assumed to emanate from their offices and the board. This perspective of the firm and its decisions and directions has its roots in Weberian theory of social organization (Perrow, 1979), but is paralleled in microeconomic theory (Ferguson and Kreps, 1965; Teece, 1985; Barton and Gordon, 1987). It is such a viewpoint that allows organizational analysts to make such statements as the following, by Miles and Cameron (1982, p. 249): "This temporal space made it possible for the Big Six [tobacco firms] . . . to develop cigarette products that in several respects were responsive to the smoking-and-health challenge." In contrast, in higher education, authority tends to be relatively diffuse (Cohen and March, 1974; Blau, 1973). Many strategic decisions may be made, or avoided, at the departmental, committee, and individual levels, with only indirect central oversight and sanctions. For resource distribution, such a system of local autonomy, often supplemented by external review by accrediting agencies or research funding agencies, has been viewed as a primary strength of American higher education (Clark, 1983), since funds and accountability sources are so closely linked, without the middle levels of nondisciplinary-based administrative authority.

Pricing Decisions

The corporate sector generally enjoys discretion in setting the prices for its products, subject largely only to market conditions. In higher education, however, a variety of other factors impinge upon such discretion, including state boards, legislatures, and system authorities, as well as federal legislators via student aid and research funding policies (Chen, 1986). Because of the myriad public subsidies, noncompetitive pockets, and imperfections in the market, pricing in higher education tends not to resemble the familiar market model of economic pricing theory, which is often used to support strategic pricing policies (Daniere, 1964; Hoenack, 1977, 1983; Skolnik, 1980).

The distinctive qualities of higher education pricing make it a difficult challenge for leadership. Yet, in some respects, pricing is the central issue in the economics of strategy in higher education. Pricing lies at the intersection of supply and demand, and therefore provides the major signal involved in an institution's invitations (inducements) to its external environments to contribute resources. The pricing of education at the undergraduate level is primary in most institution's revenue flows, and therefore is a central strategic issue in those institutions (Litten, 1984a; Chen, 1986). As Murphy (1984, p. 88) has indicated, pricing is serious business in the current climate in higher education: "Administrators must constantly wrestle with the problem of offering a high-quality educational product at a reasonable price while adequately compensating faculty and staff and spending necessary amounts on improvements." Unfortunately, pricing is little researched and little considered in planning efforts (Litten, 1984c).

A variety of authors have written on the special issues involved in higher education pricing. At the most basic level is the question of full cost pricing. A number of authors (Daniere, 1964; Hoenack, 1977) have argued strongly for the pursuit of tuition levels which more accurately reflect the costs associated with delivering the educational services provided. Since higher education does not exist in a true market economy, dislocations will occur in the absence of pricing closely tied to costs. The logic of full cost pricing has been outlined by Daniere (1964): as long as pricing is set at below cost, consumers will excessively allocate resources to that service rather than to a service of comparable cost but higher price. Limited resources are therefore misallocated in the economy. In free markets, the marketplace will take care of inappropriate pricing. In industries where competition fails (is imperfect) or the profit motive is absent, the full cost pricing rule is needed, Daniere argues. In the case of those people with special needs, public subsidies to individuals can be used to lower the net prices they face. In higher education, full-cost pricing is the rare exception rather than the rule, even in the private sector, and in the public sector, prices remain well below the cost of education (Bowen, 1981).

General economic price theory and research (see Rusk and Leslie, 1978) suggests that the price of a product is affected not only by the costs of producing the product (assuming competition in the market and the absence of any public subsidies), but also by the marketplace demand for the product, the price of comparable products, the existence of competitors and their productive characteristics (e.g., scale), the net resources of potential buyers, the quality of the product, and the supply of the product (a little considered factor in higher education). In U.S. higher education in the late 1970s, research by Rusk and Leslie (1978) suggests, public institutions' tuition levels seemed to be more a result of evolutionary processes than systematic planning. In the absence of clear state policies, states seem to be setting levels either incrementally, in an unplanned fashion bordering on a "herd instinct," or in a direct attempt to maintain certain public/private and four-year/two-year price relationships. In a more hopeful close to their analysis, Rusk and Leslie suggest that in the late

1970s some states were beginning to examine tuition-setting in more thoughtful ways, and to consider the fundamental social values and economic philosophies underlying this increasingly important feature of institutional economies. Nevertheless, more recent case studies of Yale University and the public institutions in Washington State by Gilmour and Suttle (1984) suggest that incremental and politically driven processes are still the major forces at work in tuition-setting in both the public and private settings.

Shaman and Zemsky (1984) suggest that pricing in higher education has faltered on the conundrum of all educational cost analysis: "who is to determine what is to be charged to whom?" (p. 9). They suggest that progress in determining the costs for delivering educational products to students in complex institutions has been extraordinarily limited. The difficulty in determining costs of delivering products is paralleled by some difficulty in measuring and forecasting price responsiveness among students (see Leslie, 1987; Weiler, 1984). Relatedly, as Litten (1984b) has argued, college and university pricing involves joint production processes, many of which are shared by internal actors (faculty and staff) and the consumer (student). In such a context, different cost streams are occurring simultaneously and in difficult-to-measure fashion. For example, students' various activities in educating themselves accumulate nonfinancial costs (time and effort) jointly with the costs directly associated with the institutionally provided experience, and, in turn, those costs help determine other students' institutional experiences. Complexities like these make for difficulties in responding to the need for systematic, policy-driven price setting in strategic planning and management.

Since strategies for pricing in higher education cannot be driven by clearcut goals of profit maximization, and true (financial and nonfinancial) cost calculations are difficult, strategic pricing in higher education is problematic. Murphy (1984) tackles the issue from a pure marketing perspective, suggesting that there are several possible alternative strategies for pricing. Psychological strategies, such as the development of prestige or the offering of multiple price lines (differentiated tuition, for example) approach the issue from the perspective of consumer attitudes. Interestingly, consumers seem to associate higher prices with higher quality, a fact known and acted upon by many institutions, Murphy (1984) says. A second approach, multiple pricing, involves providing a variety of offsets to a single listed price. In higher education, student financial aid is a major approach to multiple pricing as a strategy. A case study of the use of such strategies and others is provided by Greenberg and Winterbauer (1986), who outline the central role of pricing in developing a strategy for improving quality at Rutgers. Whatever approach an institution takes, Murphy states, it should be aware that its prices also raise risks in consumers' minds, and these risks should be acknowledged and dealt with appropriately in marketing procedures.

Other authors have also dealt with possible prescriptions for the challenges of higher education pricing. Hoenack et al. (1974), Hoenack (1977), and Hoenack and Berg (1980) highlight ways in which prices can be used more effectively internally and externally to shape incentives in colleges and universities, relating their work to the special values of market-oriented planning models. Tierney (1981) discusses the uses of pricing and costing techniques in institutional priority setting, management information systems, and reallocation efforts. Chen (1986) suggests that institutions have difficulty in setting prices because many of the critical events are outside of their control: prices set by other institutions, institutional costs, economic conditions, etc. In addition, it is difficult to predict the short- and long-range effects of a given rise in tuition levels, since tuition levels affect other institutional variables in a complex series of causal relationships. In response to these difficulties, she suggests a systems dynamics modeling approach for aiding in the price decision process.

Anthony and Herzlinger (1975) suggest that colleges and universities resemble most nonprofit organizations in that they give very little thought to pricing policies. These authors suggest a number of fundamental principles of pricing which are often violated in higher education and other nonprofit settings. First, in order to facilitate output measurement, client motivation, and manager motivation, services should be sold rather than given away. Second, prices should affect consumer actions, giving them a sense of what is least and most expensive to provide and least and most capable of paying returns later. Third, price should generally be set equal to full cost, with subsidies given only to those with financial need. Exceptions should be granted only in cases where market-based pricing is preferable or where certain incentives or penalties are desired from a policy perspective. Such an approach fits the criteria of equity and efficiency, in that funds are not wasted and appropriate signals are sent to consumers. Fourth, the unit of service that is priced should be narrowly defined, to more closely match revenues, activities, and costs. This approach implies a need for universities and colleges to consider differentiating tuition in ways more closely tied to program costs (see Litten, 1984a). Fifth, prospective pricing (prices set prior to the performance of the service) is preferable to unit cost-reimbursement pricing.

Most of the sources above ignore the specific questions of "strategy" as they have been formulated in the 1980s. Yet pricing is so central to strategy that this work is reviewed here, if only to highlight some of the constraints on the strategic process outlined earlier. Very little has been written on the special place of pricing in strategic planning and management efforts in higher education, and that lack of attention detracts from the practical value of the prescriptive literature. We have much information on the problems of price-setting in higher education in general. We have very little information on pricing approaches to pursue in support of strategic efforts.

The Economics of Innovation and Change

The corporate sector is notable for its reliance upon material incentives for inducing internal change. It is also capable of rapid deployment of "slack" resources in the service of innovative strategic directions (Cyert and March, 1963; Whetten, 1981). In contrast, colleges and universities offer mixed incentives to staff and, from the perspective of central leadership, seem to enjoy very minimal levels of deployable organizational slack.[2] Non-deployable slack certainly exists, but these resources are more available to departmental leadership in typical institutions. The issues of incentives and slack differentiate the economics of strategy in ideal settings from that in higher education settings, as do the persistence of routine, the attention to financial risk, the costs of planning, and the special nature of costs in higher education. These concerns will be dealt with in turn.

On the matter of *incentives,* the funding pressures of the 1980s in most colleges and universities and the dominance therein of professionally based incentive systems (e.g., peer respect and scholarly perquisites as motivators) make achieving commitment to strategic planning more complex than organizations in profit-oriented sectors in economically healthy eras. Weick (1978, 1982) and Clark (1983) have noted the decentralized, loosely coupled nature of the enterprise and the divided loyalties that characterize many faculty. In such a context, the "normal" conditions for centralized strategic planning efforts do not so clearly hold. In politicized institutions in times of scarce resources, disincentives may exist for cooperating in the effort, at least for those in vulnerable units.

It would, of course, be naive to assume that material incentives comprise the only incentive system at work in for-profit firms. In the for-profit setting, it is realized increasingly that firms may operate on material incentives and focus organizational and individual performance evaluations along fiscal lines, but that they do not always seek pure profit maximization alone. The financial choices they make therefore should be interpreted from a more complex point of view. As Barton and Gordon have put it:

> Success is not assured solely by attainment of shareholder wealth maximization, but through the alignment by management of major factors that have an impact on the firm (i.e., management values and aspirations, environmental threats and opportunities, internal corporate strengths and weaknesses, and values imposed by society at large). . . . Consistent with this, the firm-level capital structure decision is a product of numerous factors reflecting the contextual nature of the firm as well as managerial values and choice. As a result, the decision is better understood when studied from the managerial perspective of the strategy paradigm, as opposed to the more global financial market perspective of the finance paradigm. (1987, p. 70)

Barton and Gordon (ibid.) propose several testable ideas regarding capital structure, suggesting that the nature of debt obligations will be a function of such behavioral and attitudinal factors as managerial risk-taking propensity, manage-rial goals for the firm (other than profit), managers' desire to avoid seeking funds outside the firm or from new stockholders, the attention by potential creditors to the risk-taking propensities of managers, and the constraints on financial choice imposed by the specific behavioral characteristics of the firm's managers. Several of the ideas advanced by Barton and Gordon, and the similar perspective earlier proposed by Cyert and March (1963), run against the grain of strict financing theory, for these authors are seeking an "open systems" understanding of some of the most putatively mechanistic and rationalized aspects of the firm. The ideas are suggestive of possible research efforts for higher education, efforts which would explore the nature of capital structure as a strategically chosen outcome subject to the same kind of calculations, debate, and values analysis as the strategic choice concerning product and service lines.

The issue of the incentive structure of higher education as an element in strategic planning has been covered before. Hoenack et al. (1974) and Hoenack and Berg (1980) propose planning models which are decentralized and market driven, being built around the idea of revising the incentive structures of universities. Tierney (1977, 1981) also has dealt with the sometimes perverse and paradoxical effects of current incentive structures, as they relate to management information systems, budgeting, and allocation procedures. While none of these authors deals extensively with the notion of strategic planning, their work directly informs the suggestion of Cope (1981) and others that the participation of a wide range of faculty and staff in the effort is essential to its success.

The rewards provided to those who participate, and those who feel the effects of strategic planning, need not be solely economic. In fact, one aspect of successful planning might be attention to the needs of those whose commitment is essential over periods of institutional change. Mortimer et al. note that institutions "can provide a number of low-cost/high-payoff nonmonetary re-wards to sustain successful faculty" (1985, p. 85). Some examples of such rewards are provided by Chait and Ford:

> New faculty slots to build a critical mass of colleagues; authorization for a new course, program, or degree; research assistants; teaching assistants; more clerical support; additional laboratory or computer equipment; an increased library budget; a reduced course load; smaller (or larger) classes; better students; a more compact schedule; a sabbatical; travel funds, research funds, or funds for a colloquium; and additional space for an honors or tutorial program. Any and all of these "payoffs" create conditions conducive to effective performance . . . (1982, p. 209)

Such reasoning could also be made to apply to the incentives facing professional nonacademic staff in the institution.

Organizational slack is the next of the economic factors affecting strategic innovation and change to be profiled here. Slack is defined by organization theorists (e.g., see Perrow, 1979; Pfeffer, 1981) as the excess of available resources over those necessary for meeting the resource outlay obligations of a firm. Slack may be differently distributed and more scarce in higher education in the 1980s than in settings more traditionally associated with strategic efforts. Cyert and March (1963) portray traditional microeconomic theory as suggesting that organizational slack will be zero in conditions of perfect competition, i.e., there will be no excess of resources on hand beyond those necessary for the firm's various resource obligations. In their own contrasting, more behavioral model of the firm, they suggest that slack will indeed typically exist in for-profit firms, and will aid managers by providing an additional form of compensation to leaders beyond that required simply for maintaining the organization.

Strategic planning and management seem to require some degree of slack in order to support robust amounts of managerial choice and attention to the social and psychological needs of members of the organization (Cope, 1981). This observation would seem to indicate that colleges and universities may be quite limited in their capability to undertake serious strategic efforts, especially in the initial, noninstitutionalized and time-consuming stage of the process. There is disagreement over whether organizations in threatened industries, such as higher education, will be hampered by low levels of slack, however. Cyert and March (1963) argue that the degree of slack is known to decline in times of environmental stress, making strategic approaches more difficult when most needed. Miles and Cameron (1982) have suggested otherwise: strategic theorists, they say, differ from natural-selection theorists and environmental determinists in their refusal to believe that powerful environments create powerless organizations with little organizational slack available for coping with environmental threats.

Miles and Cameron found that the Big Six tobacco firms did indeed have several forms of slack available for coping with the crisis imposed by the U.S. Surgeon General's report on smoking and health. Although the firms possessed managerial and political slack, owing to declining resistance to change in a time of crisis, the most significant kind of slack for higher education analogies may be the economic slack the tobacco firms possessed. Economic slack can derive from liquid financial assets and generalizable capital assets, such as that provided by adaptable plant capacity and technology not being utilized. The tobacco firms had very little capital-based slack, owing to the specialized nature of cigarette production machinery and plants, but did possess substantial monetary slack. It was this slack that was used to finance the ambitious efforts of several of the firms to fight their external threat, including joint political ventures, research efforts, advertising budgets in new markets, product development, overseas market development, and the acquisition of new businesses for their portfolios. In this sense, then, it was this financial slack that allowed the aggressive firms

to become well-known examples of the efficacy of strategic choice by environmentally threatened organizations.

Unfortunately, it may be an absence of that same slack which prevents
struggling higher education institutions from making similarly dramatic turn-
arounds. Organizational slack may be necessary for setting up planning, for
dealing with uncertain futures (via a reserve of slack), and for planning itself (for
similar ideas, see Thompson, 1967). If slack is not present, the often overlooked
benefits of "organized anarchy" may disappear, and strategy may be hurt by the
absence of resources to support reflection, foresight, "foolishness," and so forth
(Cohen and March, 1974). Alternatively, one might argue that the absence of
slack may strengthen the weak means/ends connections of higher education's
many organizational "garbage cans" of directionless debate and help to target
strategy more effectively. The expenses, and perhaps slack, required for
worthwhile strategic planning for enrollment threats and other challenges are
apparent from the work of several authors. Hearn and Heydinger (1985) note that
an experimental environmental scanning effort at one institution became extraordinarily time-consuming in the absence of actual staff assignments to, and
funding for, the task. Eventually, the team's efforts dwindled away in the face
of other pressing demands on staff time. Noting the likelihood of such
disappointing results for nascent strategic efforts, Baldridge, Kemerer, and
Green state that:

> To prepare for an uncertain future requires planning. And to back up the inevitable
> failures at planning requires built-in institutional resiliency, flexibility, and capacity.
> We cannot build brittle, understaffed institutions locked into a single image of the
> future. Instead, we must make our day-to-day, middle-range decisions so that a
> healthy, responsive institution can adapt to a rapidly changing future. Building that
> institutional capacity requires attention to planning, to staffing, to governance, and to
> student services.

The absence of slack in higher education may imbed strategic planning
activities in a climate of ongoing conflict. Pfeffer (1981) argues that slack or
excess resources in an organization can reduce the use of power and politics in
that organization in two ways. First, slack reduces the amount of interdependence among subunits, and thereby lessens one of the primary contributors to
conflict. In effect, slack helps to separate the potentially conflicting parties.
Second, slack means there is a climate of abundance in sectors of the
organization, and that climate reduces the potential for resource conflict, since
scarcity is a primary contributor to conflict. As Pfeffer notes, in the absence of
slack, power and politics became more salient and potentially disruptive aspects
of institutional life.

The next relevant aspect of the economics of innovation and change in higher
education is the persistence of *routine,* an element in what has been viewed as a

strong resistance to centrally imposed change in colleges and universities (especially the latter), due to their decentralized, professional staff, their democratic governance norms, their poorly understood technology, and their tendency to inconsistent, politically motivated participation in central affairs (Cohen and March, 1974; Baldridge et al., 1977, 1978). One outcome of these characteristics is likely to be an allegiance to routine possibly surpassing that of many other kinds of organizations.

The "bounded rationality" school of thought (Simon, 1979; March and Simon, 1958; Allison, 1971) is applicable to this aspect of the nexus of strategy and resources. This kind of thinking regarding organizations has been applied particularly to the higher education setting in recent years, by Cohen and March (1974), Manns and March (1978), Chaffee (1983a), Hackman (1983), and others (see the reviews of this literature by March, 1981, 1982, and Peterson, 1985). The perspective suggests that people and organizations are so limited in intelligence, reasoning, information, time, and value priorities that they tend to seize the first acceptable alternative; they rarely change unless things are dire; they limit their search for new information to well-trod paths, ideas, and sources; and they become preoccupied with routine. Clearly, under the especially constraining conditions of "organized anarchy" in universities, such tendencies could block or deter strategic planning hopelessly. In fact, they could act to make it a change effort which is both expensive and ineffective, given the multiple individual agendas that are liable to be placed in the "garbage can" of planning exercises such as the mission definition stage of strategy formation (Cohen and March, 1974). It is in this waste of scarce resources that the relevance of the bounded rationality literature to this chapter are most clear.

Even in an organizational context more amenable to the strategic paradigm, other economic factors may help to deter significant strategic change. For example, the difficulties of adapting to rapidly changing labor market considerations may encourage resistance to strategic change. Mortimer et al. (1985) suggest that it is extremely hard to reallocate funds fast enough to handle the enrollment shifts of students, and note that the "built-in rigidities of the faculty personnel system work against the rapid deployment of faculty resources" into needy areas (p. 74). The same authors also suggest that decremental budget systems are difficult to implement over time, since it is inevitable that conditions change, contingencies arise, and priorities shift. Accordingly, they argue, the familiar notion of starving problems and feeding opportunities (SPFO) requires extraordinary long-term commitment to succeed.

A number of authors have noted the appeal to administrators of avoiding the tough decisions associated with internal program review in strategic planning. Zammuto (1986) notes that one method of resorting instead to routine, the pursuit of across-the-board cuts of programs and expenses, has much visceral and political appeal but raises many problems. The chapter by Poulton (in

Jedamus and Peterson, 1980) provides an excellent discussion on the reasons behind the unfortunate divorce of decisive strategy from resource allocation techniques in most schools, and perceptive articles by Mortimer and Taylor (1984) and Bowen and Glenny (1981) also discuss the issue. Ironically for those who believe conflict can be avoided by the seemingly benign, hold-harmless approach of across-the-board cuts, such cuts may make planning take on something of crisis tone, since all programs are hurt (Glenny, 1982) and the slack resources useful for building strategically favored programs are hurt just as much as other, less primary resources (Bowen and Glenny, 1981).[3]

In place of such efforts, the proponents of strategy argue that strategic success means maintaining program variety but also requires market attentiveness and a willingness to cut programs that are unsuccessful (Balderston, 1974; Anderson, 1978; Bowen and Glenny, 1981; Chaffee, 1983b,c, 1984). Along those lines, Kotler (1982) argues that mission targeting is the key to dealing with constraint, and to the extent missions and programs can be cut, resources can be better spent on focal strategies. In a context of possible cutbacks, a determined push for efficiency and productivity is a major part of strategic success (Chaffee, 1983c). Balderston (1974) suggests that nothing is more painful than the priority setting approach to budgeting, but nothing is equally effective, either. Selective approaches have several difficult essential ingredients, however, Balderston suggests: a capability to analyze costs accurately, a way to blend academic judgment and fiscal information, a fair institutional process, and a quality and range of leadership that can succeed and endure in a challenging climate.

A further economic area relevant to changing the strategy/resources connection in higher education is the financial *risk* inherent in taking on new strategic direction. Dickmeyer (1982) urges college administrators to move toward the levels of attention to financial risk notable in the for-profit sector, arguing that strategic planning will work best when it is thoughtfully integrated with financial management. Dickmeyer argues that, although decisions in each domain of financial management (e.g., tuition rises, debt financing, capital investment) may be made separately with certain natural objectives for that domain in mind, it is also important that the various domains be considered jointly. Each decision in one financial domain will affect the other domains, to a greater or lesser degree. Each element of risk in a decision (the probability that an event with negative consequences may occur, the degree to which such an event will harm the institution monetarily, and the degree to which the event will harm the institution nonmonetarily) is therefore linked to decisions in the other financial domains.

Ideally, Dickmeyer suggests, the institution should take strategic risks up to the point that its core enterprises will be jeopardized: "An institution may deplete its reserves, tenure its faculty, and raise tuition only up to the point where a significant probability of revenue decline exists, especially when this decline would impinge on core academic programs'' (1982, p. 54). He suggests that defining core and noncore activities is a major practical task of strategic planning. Once that difficult task is done, Dickmeyer suggests, institutions should pursue a variety of ways to buffer core activities financially against risks. Active buffers are those which allow unplanned revenue and expenditure fluctuations to be absorbed directly by reducing expenditure or increasing revenues (e.g., hiring nontenured part-time faculty who can be released easily, or cutting out noncore programs). Passive buffers, Dickmeyer says, are those which can be used without altering revenues or expenditures. Employing reserves for contingencies, borrowing, expanding gift resources, and pursuing fiscal and strategic conservatism are familiar examples.

Dickmeyer believes institutions, in their strategic thinking, have insufficiently considered their risk expectations, risk tolerance, and the need for effective risk preparation. On the latter, he suggests first that they build buffers such as reserves. He also notes, in a passage reminiscent of Cyert and March (1963) regarding organizational slack, that building up discretionary expenditures patterns provides an element of expenditures and resources which can be cut when times become hard. Second, Dickmeyer suggests that institutions should reduce their financial exposure by diversification, such as seeking greater research funding, new clientele, and so forth (this strategy resembles the ''domain creation'' strategy Miles and Cameron noted among successful tobacco firms). Third, Dickmeyer argues that institutions should reduce their financial exposure by increasing their flexibility, reducing long-term commitments wherever possible. Involved here would be cutting back on granting of tenure, on new construction and its attendant long-term debt service, and increasing the use of part-time faculty. Without such balancing of strategic risks and financial buffers to meet those risks, institutions are likely to underestimate their vulnerability to environmental change and decline.

Apparent by now are the *significant costs associated with strategic reconsideration and change*. As noted before, the calculation of strategic planning's costs and benefits has been cited as a major area for future research in higher education (Cope, 1981). The process of strategic planning may be shaped by resource constraints. Cope (1981, p. 27) suggests that ''restraints on time and money'' may influence the strategic decision making process and therefore may importantly affect the nature of strategic decisions. In addition, a number of authors (Bean and Kuh, 1984; Richardson and Gardner, 1985) have begun in recent years to consider critically and from a broader perspective the costs of serious strategically focused planning. When is it worthwhile to pursue? How does one calculate its cost/effectiveness? As outlined in earlier sections of this paper, an institution pursuing the strategic approach will need to gather and organize information on internal and external contexts, and will need to analyze that information (see Armijo et al., 1980; Gonyea, 1980; Mims, 1980). In addition, the participation and deliberation required for the true strategic style (see Cope, 1981) involve major commitments of human resources. All told, these efforts can mean a nontrivial expense. In some cases, that expense may not "pay off." For example, Anderson's (1978) analysis suggests that strategic innovation may not always be financially worthwhile for threatened small private colleges, a result also suggested by Chaffee's (1983c) work in similar settings (see Chaffee, 1985, for a thoughtful review of this issue).

Of particular concern in the cost arena is the possibility that recommendations based in extensive rational planning efforts will be overturned by the intrusion of political decision agendas and styles. Richardson and Gardner (1985) propose a design for cost-effective planning process that effectively combines rational and political models. They suggest that administrators should concentrate their rational planning efforts only where change is visibly necessary, since political realities suggest that what does not exist is unlikely to be initiated and what does exist is unlikely to be ended. This suggestion reflects the importance of focusing on impending needs to reduce programs; on needs to change faculty behaviors, priorities, attitudes; and on the shared desire to prevent or moderate conflict via planning process. Richardson and Gardner also argue that leaders should concentrate on activities where planning will make a difference in events, should try hard to limit the number of events focused upon, and should always let purpose determine the scope and nature of the planning activity. They caution particularly against the temptation to over- or underexpend for planning projects and activities.

The final topic to be considered under the economics of strategic innovation and change is the *special nature of costs in higher education*. Higher education institutions seek no profits (at least in the usual sense), operate at least in part for the greater public good, and usually employ public subsidies in support of that purpose. These facts of life make the control of costs, and the determination of appropriate units for cost calculations, problematic. Institutions and policy makers confront a conundrum of sorting out "purpose," "goods," "quality," "missions," and dollars. As Bowen's (1981) "revenue theory of higher education costs" suggests, all else equal, costs will rise and be spent on expanded offerings of goods or services. There is always room for more dollars to be spent, all in the service of better education. The point at which spending should cease is undetermined in the absence of an effective marketplace mechanism.

Such a situation puts special pressure on strategic planning and management efforts. As Balderston has noted:

> Institutions often behave as if they were seeking to maximize expenditures—the larger the budget, the better. Many of the indicia of quality and vitality—high faculty salaries, generous allocations to the library, ease of funding new academic ventures—are associated with a high and rising expenditure rate. But this puts all the more premium

on a careful assessment of revenues and the planning of revenue growth to support such a pattern of intended expenditures. (1974, p. 219)

Strategic approaches will take place in a climate in which the familiar "dogs" and "cows" of market portfolio analysis are difficult to distinguish, and all are generally considered worthy in their own right. Monetary costs may be clear, but opportunity costs and contributions to institutional effectiveness, as a proxy for returns, usually are not. In sum, the special nature of costs creates a climate in which thoughtful and persistent administrative leadership is imperative.

Many organization theorists, e.g. Pfeffer and Salancik (1974), Pfeffer and Moore (1980), Pfeffer (1981), Babcock (1981, 1982), Hackman (1985), and Tolbert (1985), adopt a "resource dependency" perspective on organizational action, arguing that behaviors are shaped by the dictates of the primary resource providers within and outside organizations. The vagueness of cost evaluation in higher education may make it particularly susceptible to this influence pattern. In an environment where the relative "goodness" of specific costs and revenue flows is debatable, strategic planning may be especially likely to be shaped and reshaped by providers of major sources of funds, or the outcomes of important external resource requests, such as was the case in the funding campaign described by Greenberg and Winterbauer (1986).

Production and Human Resources

The for-profit sector may be viewed as potentially enjoying great flexibility in its deployment of human capital: staff may be fired, hired, retrained, and transferred rather easily, compared to the inflexibilities imposed by tenure, professionalism, specialization, and demographic conditions in higher education. The inflexibility of budgets, resource distributions, and staffing has been the focus of a number of planning studies (e.g., see Mortimer et al., 1985). Chaffee notes in her case study of "Enterprise College" that the worst consequences of poor planning can be escaped when the planning is not capital-based (1983c, p. 48). To the extent planning leads to major long-term investments, the risks of planning failures grow. Considering that much of higher education's growth in the 1960s was associated with development of human capital and physical plant resources, the source of the much-lamented inflexibilities of the current era are apparent.

Several studies have focused on the unchanging nature of most higher education budgets. In essays on the topic, Fincher (1983) discusses budgets as unexamined traditions, and Caruthers and Orwig (1979) recount the many barriers to using budgets effectively in change efforts. In empirical studies of changes in budgetary allocations among departments at research universities, Clugston (1987) studied the persistence of certain funding patterns in the face of strategic change efforts, Chaffee (1983a) assessed the roles of rationality and politics, Babcock (1982) assessed budgetary responses of two very differently situated colleges in one university, and Pfeffer and colleagues (Pfeffer and Salancik, 1974; Pfeffer and Moore, 1980) examined the role of power and internal and external resource conditions. In a related analysis, Hackman (1985) traced budget patterns in a multiinstitution sample. In each study, institutions and their units showed some responsiveness to external and internal threats, but the overall levels of change in budget patterns were rather small.

The roots of this stability over time lie in the human resources sector, and are dug deeper by the resilience and tenacity of individual academic programs built by, and staffed around, tenured faculty (Gray, 1982; Dougherty, 1982; Kotler, 1982; Kotler and Murphy, 1981). Chaffee (1985) argues that the autonomy of departments creates a real constraint on leadership in higher education, forming an internal strategic context quite distinct from that in other organizational sectors (for similar arguments, see Rubin, 1977, 1979). Only in rare conditions, Chaffee (1985) argues, is the loose coupling in higher education a favorable condition for fostering strategically chosen change.

The potential human barriers to effective strategic change are also discussed by Peterson (1981, 1986) in separate essays on the financial and academic sides of planning. Peterson notes in both essays the many resource constraints on higher education in the mid-1980s, some external (demographic and economic) and some internal. Somewhat surprisingly, he suggests that the constraint perhaps most critical is that of a weakened "institutional climate": "Faculty salaries continue to lag; reductions and reallocations continue to be threatening; academic support services and equipment . . . are scarce. In some fields, faculty are 'stuck,' and in others good faculty are hard to keep" (1986, p. 11). The internal climate, Peterson suggests (1981, 1986), is presently characterized by economically and externally driven constraint: declining economic welfare, increased workload, decreased control of programs and job conditions, stronger faculty and staff organizations, and unchanged professional and career expectations. With these conditions has come an "internal press" characterized by "uncertainty, fear, loss of morale, resistance to change, protective and divisive stances, administrator/faculty tensions, and antipathy to planning and management" (Peterson, 1981, p. 24). Peterson suggests that, in such conditions, financial planning (and implicitly, planning in general) must exhibit "confidence, commitment, willingness to ask, cooperative effort, mutual respect, credibility, and legitimacy" (ibid.).

A number of analyses share the concern of Peterson over the difficult balance between meeting financial demands for retrenchment and flexibility and maintaining productive human resources. Mortimer et al. (1985) note that the usual tactic of moving toward part-time, nontenure track faculty or fixed-term contracts may buy flexibility at the cost of appreciably higher administrative costs in hiring, supervising, and evaluating such personnel. As an example of the new costs imposed, they report that the turnover in such ranks is significantly higher than under a more traditional personnel system (see also Chait and Ford, 1982; Leslie, Kellams, and Gunne, 1982). An additional problem with such an approach is that it may indirectly raise costs by threatening accreditation in some programs, according to Mortimer and colleagues.

As a response to the problems of planning in the face of difficult-to-change human resource contexts, Mortimer et al. suggest that personnel and fiscal affairs must be linked. They note, with Chait and Ford (1982), Mitchell (1981), and Patton (1979), that the opportunity and carrying costs of early retirement and faculty retooling plans are often difficult to assess, due to labor market conditions, state laws, faculty attitudes regarding retirement and retraining, replacement strategies, faculty education and salary levels, and so forth. In some cases, the costs of such efforts may simply be too high, thus precluding some of the more popular techniques of strategic adaptation.

Production and Technology

In the for-profit sector, production functions tend to be discrete (i.e., separable from each other). Engine assembly represents a separate function from fender attachment in the production processes for automobiles. Production elements tend to be tightly coupled, however (e.g., many subassembly units are linked sequentially and dependently). Clear-cut economies of scale exist, since the components of products and the definition of an acceptable product are clear-cut themselves. Relatedly, the core production processes in a firm are themselves clearly understood. The ways a firm constructs a videocassette recorder or a bicycle are standardized.

In the technology of higher education, quite different conditions prevail. Production functions tend to be closely integrated and production elements tend to be loosely coupled (Weick, 1978, 1982). For example, a graduate with certain expected reasoning and writing abilities is produced via a mixture of course and other experiences, yet the content of these experiences is not always known, consistent, coupled, sequenced, or supervised across the school. The point was made ably by Allan M. Cartter (1964), referring to production differences both within and across institutions:

> The theory of the firm is traditionally two-dimensional, dealing with quantity and cost (or price assuming either a standardized product or a clearly differentiated one with a separate identifiable demand). Higher education pretends to produce certain standardized commodities (e.g., B.A.'s, M.A.'s, Ph.d.'s), but in fact qualitatively exhibits wide range and variety. (p. 13)

Because quality variations preclude clearly defining the educational product and impose related barriers to assessing an institution's productive capacity, economies of scale in higher education tend to be limited and somewhat fuzzy (Brinkman and Leslie, 1985). It is such observations that have led many theorists to observe that the technology of production processes in higher education is only poorly understood (Cohen and March, 1974; Meyer and Rowan, 1978).

Part of the question of unclear technology derives from the unique nature of the educational client: he or she is both a product and a customer. In the higher education sector, clients (students) tend to be active in the educational "production process," and increasingly so. They are allowed great discretion in the ways they are "processed," via major area, course, and adviser selection, extracurricular activity, and so forth. Even if their "voice" is mainly expressed through their feet (i.e., their educational choice behaviors), students demand attention to their needs and encourage alterations in the ways they are being treated. In this sense, the specifics of the production process are not, and cannot be, set in advance.

These problematic aspects of technology constrain the strategic choice process in several ways. For one thing, elements of the "product line" are difficult to lop off at will. While one person might argue that veterinary medicine is peripheral to a school's mission, another might argue it is central, thereby confusing the debate over changes in program offerings (see Heydinger, 1982). In addition, the absence of full control over production, due to heavy client involvement, precludes the unhindered adoption of changes in modes of delivery and the pursuit of economies which might go unnoticed by final customers in other settings.

Production and Performance Evaluation

In the for-profit sector, particularly in the manufacturing sector, quality control tends to be relatively strong, due to the tangibility of products. The clarity of the "scorecard" in that sector (usually in dollar terms) also suggests that returns on investment generally will be clearly known, for better or worse, and that those returns will often be immediate. In contrast, in higher education, quality control tends to be weak, due to the intangibility of educational services. In addition, returns on investment are often over the longer term and can be extraordinarily unclear (witness the complexity of assessing colleges' short and long-term impacts on students, much less on society or the economy as a whole; see Bowen, 1977).

Problematic performance evaluation has direct implications for strategic analysis and management. The absence of the familiar monetary scorecard for assessing markets and products, or any quantitative scorecard of general acceptability, is compounded by the dangers of the nonquantitative approaches recommended by adapters of the strategic paradigm for higher education (e.g., see Cope, 1981). Milter (1986, page 75) has focused on this problem in higher education's efforts at strategic planning and management, observing that,

> Due to the "messy" nature of strategic decisions . . . and the fact that they typically involve more than one person, it is thought wise to be wary of using conventional

computer-based techniques that may force an unrealistic simplification of the problem, conflict with the learning and problem solving of those involved, or exclude important political considerations. The complexity of strategic problems is such that purely empirical and rational approaches to their resolution often seem incomplete in the scope of analysis and likely to result in unsatisfactory outcomes. . . . On the other hand, an approach to strategic problems that is dominated by subjective beliefs and ignores available information is likely to be equally inadequate. (1986, p. 75)

The problem is two-sided. There is first a need to identify the current quality and other characteristics of an institution's existing programs and services. It is here, in Kotler's (1982) internal resource audit, that the question of finding a widely acceptable definition of quality first arises. The second aspect of the problem arises later in time, and involves the need to have a workable measure of strategic success: did the institution achieve its intended goals in a strategic initiative? These two aspects of the performance evaluation issue will be discussed in turn.

In higher education, the nature of quality (sometimes cast in terms of productivity) has been debated for years (Balderston, 1974; Buchtel, 1980; Tierney, 1981; Conrad and Blackburn, 1985). Clearly, quality in this context is complex and multidimensional. For most institutions, there is no unanimity on standards for quality, since they have no unanimity on mission, goals, or ways to meet them (Baldridge et al., 1978). Jones suggests:

it is quite common for faculty to view quality in terms of prestige, for administrators to view it in terms of resources they command, for students to view it in terms of access to resources and the personal and academic growth they have achieved, and for other client groups to view it as a matter of the institution's contribution to the economic development of that region. However, it is not uncommon for behavior to belie the underlying diversity. Funds are often requested—and provided—for improvement to quality without further definition of intended consequences. It is unlikely, however, that such an arrangement will have the desired effects. There will be an increasing need to address the questions, What do you mean by quality? and How do you know quality when you see it? If the answers to these questions are ambiguous, the likelihood of embarrassment increases when the moment of accountability arrives—as it most certainly will. (1984, p. 18)

A number of efforts have been made to integrate considerations of quality with financial considerations. In the original, most straightforward adaptations of the strategic portfolio analysis model to higher education, cost and quality were portrayed as the two fundamental aspects of program review. A valuable program was not only high in quality but also had a favorable cost/volume profile. Difficulties in adapting budget data for strategic use were among several factors which hampered taking such a dichotomous approach, however. As Powers (1982), Young (1984), and Mingle and Norris (1982) have suggested, it is especially difficult to measure program-level cost. Do we compare a program on campus to the same programs on other campuses, to other programs on the same campus, or what? What are the intangible costs? The lost income? Mingle and Norris suggest that data-sharing across institutions is critical to assessing costs well, but realize the noncomparability of much of the data.

The work of Ellen Earle Chaffee and others cautions strategic planners to remember the differences between "budget logic," "program logic," and "strategic logic." The inseparability of services and programs (i.e., their overlaps) in higher education (see Chaffee, 1985) may make the determination of success doubly difficult. Products are not discrete, and programs and products do not always coincide. What is more, research funding, service funding, and student-based funding are difficult to disentangle, and strategic initiatives (e.g., new programs in "cognitive science") may be impossible to evaluate, particularly in research institutions. The accounting styles of the "three logics" do not always coincide. The strategy/budget link is particularly unclear, since strategy focuses on assessing initial resources (both "hard" and "soft") and pursuing appropriate subsequent processes over an undetermined period, whereas budgeting focuses on assessing finite "hard" resources on a year-to-year basis. It follows that administrators should be careful not to rely too heavily on performance funding as an aspect of strategic development, if it simply tends to reward the strong while punishing the enduringly weak. On the other hand, there are clear dangers to ignoring the possible strategic incentives created by intelligently designed performance-oriented systems.

In the area of cost/effectiveness and cost/benefit analysis to support strategic planning's program reviews, higher education analysts might want to take advantage of previous considerations of the topic in other nonprofit settings. Hirschleifer and Shapiro (1970) assess in detail approaches to evaluating costs and benefits in nonprofit public agencies. Similarly, Anthony and Herzlinger (1975) discuss the difficulties of joint evaluations of social costs, private costs, social returns, and private returns.

One primary similarity of higher education to other nonprofit settings is its multiple constituencies (the general public, legislators, alumni, students, and so forth), which imply multiple environmental resource dependencies, and thus multiple, and often conflicting, ways of "scoring" program cost effectiveness. At a land-grant institution, one board member's scorecard for a low-demand, high cost, moderate quality dental school might be low, whereas another might see such a profile as attractive, on balance. Economists would see this as a problem of resolving competing utilities or preference functions. Using that notion as background, Lewis and Wasescha (1986) present an unusual attempt to employ cost effectiveness analysis for program review by addressing the utility (preference) functions of various decision makers in the academic setting.

However one deals with the complexity of the enterprise of internal review, it is clear that strategic thinking requires multidimensional decision making. Some would argue that the constraints are too great for such an intendedly rational approach. Morgan (1984), for example, suggests that a major weakness of the strategic approach is its "assumption of knowledge" regarding both internal and external conditions and its assumption that such "knowledge" can be used in coherent fashion. Others are more sanguine. Working from both the strategic and the program review paradigms, Heydinger (1982), Young (1984), Mims (1980), Cope (1981), Keller (1983), and others have stressed both the need and the practical possibility of considering such interrelated program criteria as centrality to the institution, connectedness to other programs, comparative advantage, academic quality, environmental demand, and cost. The value of these in program review for academic planning is clear, but how is one to separate them? A number of authors have attempted to address this question (e.g., Mingle and Norris, 1982; Young, 1984), some via more formal and rationalized approaches and others via more subjective and potentially political approaches.

In this context of complexity, the important followup question of "how do we know when we get there?" becomes more challenging (see Buchtel, 1980). The assessment of the success of any decision-based process in higher education, much less of strategic planning in particular, is especially difficult, argue Cohen and March (1974), whose research found that the ambiguity of "success" in decisions haunts leaders in higher education, and characterizes the limits on planning and planning assessment in higher education. Chaffee (1985) reviews the variety of definitions of success in the business literature, finding most to be profit-based. Because of the association of quality and success in higher education with higher spending, however, Peterson (1986) suggests that the evaluation of planning is likely to be affected by increasingly frequent debates in higher education over quality and its tensions with cost-containment concerns.

The tensions of success evaluation range even wider than that, however. Issues of the appropriate time range and the appropriate organizational reference point for evaluations have been raised by Chaffee (1985) and Anderson (1978) in separate studies of small colleges' responses to environmental threats. In her case study of "Prophet College," Chaffee (1983c, pp. 68–70) notes that the college succeeded in meeting the threat to its survival but suffered from its "deferred maintenance on human capital." In other words, success of one kind may be achieved only at a cost to other kinds of success. Similar conclusions may be drawn from the research by Anderson: strategically successful colleges had leaders who shared authority with their faculty but "also were more inclined to take decisive and painful personnel actions. When compared to officers [of declining institutions], they were more likely to block promotions, fire faculty, and generally become involved in personnel matters" (1978, p. 45). Although these two studies differ somewhat in design and results, they both reveal the tradeoffs inherent in success, and the dependence of definitions of success on the choice of indicators.

A number of writers have argued that there is a need to employ wide-ranging information skillfully in evaluating success in strategic-style planning (Balderston, 1974; Clugston, 1987), but the conditions for doing so are difficult. The dominant costing approaches in higher education do not always allow easy measurement of performance, according to a major study by an accounting association (Gambino, 1979). Institutions' long-standing, deeply ingrained, and highly routinized attention to budgets provides a possible invitation for strategic error. Historically, budgets have been viewed as the foundation to which critical decisions are coupled in higher education. As Caruthers and Orwig (1979) note, however, many factors preclude the integration of budget information and outcomes assessment as it relates to important programmatic or strategic goals. Instead of viewing budgets as frameworks for accountability, Jones (1984) argues that "it is useful to think of budgets as *post facto* mirror images of planning" (p. 19). When accountability measures are framed in purely financial terms, he suggests,

> managers are held responsible for spending funds in accordance with the way allocations were determined (so much for instruction, so much for libraries) or in accordance with budget line items. Without additional measures, the allocation algorithm becomes a spending plan, and procedure becomes a surrogate for policy. Questions regarding accountability shift from, Did you accomplish what was agreed upon? to, Did you use your resources as planned? (Ibid.)

Jones concludes that the easy route to assessment (using the budget process to promote academic quality) leads administrators generally to focus on "the enhancement of assets rather than outcomes and the value-added aspects of academic quality" (ibid., p. 27).

The question of returns on investment (or more generically, cost-benefit analysis) may be seen as offensive by traditionalists in the educational setting. Such a perspective may, nevertheless, not only be necessary for, but also implicit in, successful strategic program review. Specially adapted definitions of the base level of investment may be necessary, however. A large proportion of funds in education are attached to particular individuals or programs, and are therefore relatively untouchable. Trusts and endowments are often unbreachable preserves, as are categorical grants and contracts. In similar fashion, tight regulations for the protection of tenure effectively lock into place long-term labor costs. Institutions therefore may find it useful to do for higher education what Weidenbaum (1970) did for the federal government; that is, to provide estimates of total controllable resources and maps of their location in sectors and functions of the organization. In the end, such efforts may help in attempts to estimate true returns.

Attempts at institutional rationality in higher education strategy assessment inevitably must confront the politics of scarce resources, however (Baldridge,

1983; Baldridge et al., 1977; Baldridge and Deal, 1983). Using the framework of politics and power as driving forces in higher education resource allocations, Jeffrey Pfeffer (1981) has found in his empirical research that objective criteria are used selectively in higher education when resource decisions are planned. Department heads argue for central allocation philosophies which reinforce the internal economies of their departments. In the genteel norms of the academy, he suggests, power bids are best done unobtrusively rather than bluntly. If arguments for institutional adoption of certain "objective" criteria for resource allocation can be made to seem neutral and universalistic, they may be accepted more easily than raw bids for increased funds on the basis of the specific character of one's own department. Pfeffer goes on to argue that such behavior is in keeping with the elevation of planning and rationality to the virtual status of religion in formal organizations. The intentions of actors in this context are to seek and use power unobtrusively, in order to make a political decision process "appear to conform to widely shared social values of rationality and justice" (p. 194).

The power perspective informs consideration of the assessment of strategic planning because the environmental threats of the 1980s and 1990s make it increasingly appropriate. Pfeffer (1981) notes that institutions have a very great preference for growth, since it implies more positions and more budget resources to allocate each year, and reduces the troubling presence of raw power conflicts. Facing instead a climate of decline, institutions will try hard to avoid political difficulties. For example, he notes (ibid., p. 90) that the proliferation of administrative positions in universities has increased as institutions have confronted more and more resource scarcity. This result suggests that strategic planning which seeks to avoid conflict by simply repositioning less valued individuals and programs does not represent an effective response to resource difficulties. On one level, such an approach might be deemed successful due to its termination of unsuccessful programs, but on another it may be seen as failed due to its inattention to fundamental resource and efficiency questions.

CRISIS: THE SPECIAL CASE

The generally threatening environmental conditions in higher education in the current era are well known. The central question of the 1980s in higher education may be how institutions confronting these trying economic and demographic circumstances can plan for and respond to decline in ways that will be consonant with their basic educational goals (Mingle et al., 1982, p. 1). Not all institutions are in crisis, or even under the threat of decline, of course. Many institutions have adapted and thereby avoided crises, through such tactics as program review, selective retrenchment, reallocation, and strategic planning, and the closings have been fewer in number than forecast in the dire writings of the

1970s. Some institutions continue to face very real threats to their continued health and survival, however. This section considers institutions in crisis and decline, and the special context they pose for strategic efforts. For many such institutions, the need for change in the face of environmental difficulties is becoming more manifest yearly, as the early 1990s (with their shrunken eighteen-year-old population cohorts) grow nearer. According to many proponents of strategy, it is in schools in crisis or under threat of decline that strategic planning and management may perhaps be most fruitfully applied, assuming the necessary resources and time are available.

A variety of analysts (e.g., see Milter, 1986; Young, 1984) have explored the view that crisis can potentially provide leaders with appealing strategic opportunities. Unfortunately, that potential, if it indeed exists, is not always realized. Whetten (1981) has argued persuasively that administrators tend to take a closed-system, efficiency-oriented perspective in time of crisis, rather than an open-system, effectiveness-oriented perspective. He argues that there are at least six responses to scarcity in the external environment which foster a conservative, piecemeal approach by leadership: the desire to limit and avoid stress, the unfamiliarity of administrators with nongrowth conditions, the innovation resistant structure of educational organizations, the tendency to solve problems using efficiency-oriented data and avoiding more complex and difficult-to-collect information on the external environment, the tendency of the most qualified staff to exit the organization first, and the tendency to resort to traditional values in the face of crisis (for similar conclusions, see Pfeffer and Salancik, 1974; Pfeffer and Moore, 1980; Rubin, 1977; Pfeffer, 1981). Referring to the differences in responses of educational organizations and those of other organizations, Whetten concludes:

> In the private sector it is assumed that businesses generate resources during times of slack resources and then focus primarily on increasing efficiency in periods of scarcity. The latter is the time to live off the organization's fat and not waste precious resources experimenting with new ideas. However, as has been noted earlier, the absence of a strong competitive market in education reduces the applicability of this model for educational organizations. Because they have little incentive to innovate during periods of resource abundance, educational organizations typically use additional resources to do "more of the same." *Therefore, the key to enhancing the adaptive potential of these organizations is utilizing the pressure of scarcity to spur innovation.* (p. 92) [italics in the original]

Taking a similar perspective on public-sector organizations in general, John Bryson (1981) views crisis as potentially opening up "opportunity spaces" for strategic planners, i.e., providing conditions in which dramatic and effective strategic changes can be undertaken. In his case-study research on metropolitan planning, Bryson found several managerial factors associated with effective use of crisis for strategic opportunity. First, effective managers realize that crises can be predicted. Second, they take full advantage of opportunity spaces opening up due to crises, since they soon close up as the precrisis state resumes. Third, they weigh resource opportunities in their thoughts as heavily as resource threats and dangers. Fourth, in order to assure stability after crisis, they work to make their chosen solutions (implemented plans) reflect the "normal" organizational relationships in place in precrisis or noncrisis times.

As suggested in an earlier section of this chapter, the question of administrators making selective cuts versus making across-the-board cuts becomes especially crucial in times of crisis. Howard Bowen (1982) has argued that campus morale is fragile in difficult times, and is hurt by selective strategic cuts. As a consequence, he maintains, selective approaches should be undertaken very cautiously. Bowen acknowledges that selectively cutting programs in order to augment resources to survivors is "consistent with accepted economic reasoning," but believes that in higher education such strategies may in the end decrease institutional effectiveness overall. Bowen goes on to stress "that there are many ways to retrench, and each institution should find the least destructive combination . . . restraint in the use of the selective approach is advisable" (ibid., p. 10). Bowen's cautious view about this popular approach fits with the findings of Chaffee (1983c) and Anderson (1978) of some troubling, although perhaps unavoidable, side effects of tough-minded strategic reallocation and retrenchment efforts.

Opposed to Bowen's view are those who believe that across-the-board freezes are popular but misguided approaches to decline. Among the opponents favoring more selective, strategic approaches are Frank Bowen and Lyman Glenny (Bowen and Glenny, 1981; Glenny, 1982), as well as Frank Newman (1982). Each of these analysts recognizes the inevitable negative effects associated with selective retrenchment, but favors the approach nonetheless. Arguments advanced for that view are the position that across-the-board cuts make institutional planning and the institutional climate take on an overwhelmingly negative tone, since all programs are equally hurt and the spare resources useful for building programs are hurt just as severely as other resources.

The blend of pain and necessity inevitable with selective cuts is well reflected in the empirical work conducted by Mortimer and Taylor (1984). Their analysis reveals the extent to which using selective strategies to deal with crisis conditions (budget cuts and reallocations) can sometimes create tensions in academic and nonacademic areas; can put great pressure on existing data, systems, formulas; can encourage the strategically losing programs to turn to legislators and other outsiders; can be hard to implement over time unless blended with other fiscal approaches and targets; and can fail to save money unless people are terminated. They also note that there can be problems in pursuing a philosophy of starving problems and feeding opportunities (SPFO), when institutions are unable to persist with consistent definitions of problems and opportunities. Because of its incrementalism and tenuous stability, Mortimer and Taylor (1984) argue that an SPFO philosophy is an inherently nonstrategic form of selective cuts. They also agree with Bowen (1982) on the dangers to campus morale, suggesting that there is potential for trouble if faculty are asked to review individual colleagues rather than focus on methods and criteria for retrenchment. Having enumerated these many potentials for trouble in selective cuts, particularly when undertaken in nonstrategic ways, these authors still conclude that taking selective approaches in a threatening context can focus attention in new ways on priorities and needs for funds, and can make decisions rise appropriately in the system to levels at which relative priorities can be reviewed and determined. In the end, Mortimer and Taylor note that a selective approach should be pursued with "modest expectations" for strategic choice, stressing the many constraints on true strategy in higher education (p. 83).

Specifically financial strategies for confronting and overcoming crisis and decline have been a popular topic in the literature for nearly two decades. In the early 1970s, prior to higher education's heavy retrenchments, Earl Cheit (1971) wrote that institutions adapt to financial decline in several general ways: postponing expenditures, belt-tightening, marginal reallocation of resources, increasing income, planning, or worrying. Much of the literature since Cheit's observation has focused upon reallocation approaches of different kinds, especially strategic planning and management (e.g., Mims, 1980; Heydinger, 1980). Nevertheless, many institutions have avoided the hard choices required by such approaches (Whetten, 1981; Chaffee, 1985). The reasons are not all easily attributed to weak management and governance. As discussed earlier, the financial slack necessary to support effective planning is hardest to come by in times of threat, yet planning is perhaps most critical then (recall that Miles and Cameron, 1982, found that financial slack played a critical role in certain tobacco companies' turnaround in face of environmental threat).

It would be foolhardy, though, to let the absence of financial strength deter any effort at response. There are numerous stories of successful financial adaptation within threatened small-college contexts (see Anderson, 1978; Chaffee, 1983c). In the university context, Mims' work (1980) suggests that the successful University of Michigan and Oklahoma State reallocation efforts shared the following features: both were based in multiyear "taxes" on budgets; both were linked to planning conceptually and operationally; both led to monetary shifts of various kinds; and both were fair but depended on central administration leadership for final decisions. What is more, the "tax" imposed was in both cases big enough to make a measurable difference in activity, to prevent simple down-sizing, and to improve other programs with measurable results. Mims' results studying these two cases convinced her that (1) a one-shot, one-year effort is inadequate to the task of serious reallocation; (2) people are central to success—leaders, managers, and other staff; (3) for crisis planning to succeed, real objectives must be clear and there must be a recognition in the reallocation effort that there is a financial "problem" and/or "opportunity" which calls for a differential, not across-the-board response; and (4) information and analysis are keys to success, but can comprise a "nontrivial" expense in planning. Mims closes her discussion of these two success stories with an obvious but necessary caveat, however: systems which will effectively cover all possible needs and events cannot be designed.

In the same cautious tone, a variety of analysts have discussed the merits of multicomponent reallocation efforts. Mortimer et al. (1985) have argued that administrators should realize and deal effectively with the fact that selective budget cuts put great pressure on traditional systems of allocating resources within institutions, and are felt across academic and nonacademic units regardless of targeting efforts. Similarly, Mingle and Norris (1982) stress that no single strategy should be relied upon as adequate for achieving needed reductions in spending. Instead, there is a pressing need to respond creatively and humanely to the human and material constraints on unilateral financial action. In that vein, Heydinger (1982), Young (1984), Powers (1982), Mingle and Norris (1982), and many others have written thoughtfully on such ideas as creative early retirement packages and contracts not based in tenure considerations.

The strategic approach to crisis and decline is somewhat more broad-based than any purely internal reallocation approach, however. The environment is more fully considered, and short- and long-term factors blended. Mortimer and Tierney (1979) say strategies for reallocation must be linked to achieving long-term financial equilibrium, as well as short-term crisis resolution. In other words, institutions must balance the budget, but also connect productively with the long-term economic conditions affecting the school. In an even more specific application of strategic ideas, Mortimer et al. (1985) suggest that the strategic approach to reallocation relies upon selective decrements and increments based on three possible tacks: the imposition of standard budget targets on each unit with reallocation to highest priority units, the imposition of variable targets to create a reallocation fund (sometimes called a fund for excellence), and reallocations that arise from and follow priorities that have been identified through a comprehensive program review process. They argue that the institutional context is critical for the imposition of such approaches to reallocation, citing Leslie's observation that:

> In the early stages of decline, institutional actions are highly political; above all, they seem to be aimed at keeping interest group reactivity at a low level. However, as fiscal conditions worsen, more traditionally rational approaches begin to appear, and by the time the crisis truly arrives, rational strategies of high reactivity are commonplace. It seems clear that highly rational reactive strategies become politically feasible when conditions are desperate, but not much before. (1984, p. 94)

Whatever the degree of threat to an institution, the literature regarding strategic approaches to decline (Whetten, 1981, 1986; Mingle and Norris, 1982; Cameron, 1983, 1984; Chaffee, 1985) is unequivocal on one point: precious time (a key resource) can be lost in an institution debating the likelihood of decline, so boldness and strong leadership are essential.

CONCLUSIONS

What are we left to conclude regarding the performance and prospects for strategic planning and management in higher education? The answer to that must be deferred. The foregoing review has been based in a literature that is far from mature. The review has imported many studies and theories from noneducational settings to inform its arguments, due to the absence of specifically strategic analysis of higher education settings. As Chaffee (1985) and Peterson (1985) have suggested, there is a real need for theory-driven research, hypotheses, and dependent and independent variables in higher education strategy research in general. That need is especially clear in the subarea of the economics of higher education strategy.

Evaluating the Economic Effects of Strategy

Although the field is undeveloped, some important first steps toward evaluating the economic effects of strategic approaches in small colleges have already been taken (see Anderson, 1978; Chaffee, 1983b,c, 1984). Work has also been done on strategic behaviors in large institutions (Mims, 1980; Clugston, 1987), although it has not been so directly focused on strategy alone. In general, the results of these evaluative studies have suggested that certain kinds of strategic activities undertaken in certain kinds of internal and external contexts are likely to produce measurable effects, in the desired direction, on resource distributions and institutional health. Four cautions must be stressed, however. First, the beneficial effects discovered are usually not large. Second, it is not always clear from these studies that the strategic activity itself accounted for the benefits; other factors also were influential. Third, strategic efforts are not panaceas: strong environmental pressures or entrenched institutional resistance to change may thwart even the best-designed strategies. Fourth, the planning activities labeled "strategic" by their administrative champions sometimes did not incorporate all of the principles and steps of the approach, as outlined in the literature and in an earlier part of this chapter; such efforts therefore do not provide for an adequate evaluation of the full model.

Some examples can help to develop these four cautions regarding positive evaluations of the strategic approach. The early empirical work of Mortimer et al. (1985) on strategic effectiveness suggests that the key to success in strategic planning is realistic expectations: strategic systems operate "on the margin" of institutional economies and usually cannot deliver quick, major change. They argue that, even in the promising context provided by a pervasively felt need for change (as in times of impending crisis), success is far from guaranteed. These themes are echoed in another, more recent study by Clugston (1987). He found in his analysis of resource distributions at a large public research university over a ten year period that the strategic targeting of certain programs for reduction and certain programs for growth explained an additional three percent of the variance in regression equations for programs' budgetary distributions, beyond the considerable portion (over ninety percent) of variance explained by the preexisting generic trend in budgetary allocations to those programs. Intriguingly, Clugston also found that the planning process at that university was perhaps inappropriately labeled "strategic," since there was very little evidence of systematic attention to the external environment. Thus far, there is no evidence in the literature of a clear evaluation of a truly "strategic" effort at a large, complex institution.

Some analysts might argue that a truly "strategic" effort is itself impossible in most American universities, and that evaluations will always be forced to deal with incompletely realized processes. Along those lines, any evaluation of strategic efforts must deal with a structural tension discussed several times in this paper: that between strategic planning and management as a centrally controlled or directed activity and as a democratic, participatory process dominated by professionals at the department level. If, as its proponents have argued, the process (1) is centrally initiated and managed; (2) involves everyone, including the autonomy-minded professionals; and (3) deals with explicit, differential evaluations of the centrality, quality, and value of various programs, then conflict and interest group mobilization seem certain on any campus seeking to use strategy to confront emerging financial difficulties.

Under such circumstances, the politicization of strategy can be avoided only if one or more of the three defining conditions above is dropped. For example, if conditions (1) and (3) are dropped, then strategic planning and management would be reduced to something resembling simply the traditional collegial model at the departmental level. Without centrally directed strategic efforts, institutions would be left to hope that what is good strategy for individual departments may eventually "add up" in some fashion to good fortune for the institution as a whole. Such an argument is not too far from that advanced in different forms by Weick (1978), Clark (1983), Boulding (1975), and other observers. As these authors have argued, there are certain benefits to "inefficiency" that may outweigh those to be gained by the zealous centralized application of quantified comparisons across programs. Planning that is decoupled from central administrations may indeed be more environmentally responsive and better attuned to faculty and student needs, and organizational adaptation may indeed be best done inefficiently, slowly, and haltingly, but it would be difficult to term such an approach "strategic." On the other hand, if condition (2) is dropped, as may have been more the case in the various recent applications of strategic approaches in American higher education, the acceptance of the process by all parties on campus would be doubtful except in times of true wealth. The nature of the "participation" resulting from such a centralized approach would differ from that ideally associated with the strategic approach in that it would be more confrontational and *ad hoc* than democratic in nature. In sum, because it is meant to encompass all three of the conditions, the process of strategy formation and execution is fraught with practical difficulties in complex institutions.

The centralization problems potentially associated with the strategic approach in higher education have been discussed thoughtfully in recent work by Cope (1985), Heydinger (1982), and others, but are rooted in concerns which are both older and more general. In a now classic treatment of the problems of central government budgetary systems, Wildavsky (1984, 4th ed.) discussed the problems inherent in attempting to direct and improve organizational outcomes using programmatic evaluation conducted from a centralized base. Although Wildavsky was referring to the problems of the PPBS approach (Planning, Programming, and Budgeting Systems) being used to deal with federal-level resource distribution issues, his points ring equally true for the strategic approach now being used to deal with overarching institutional issues in higher education. Like PPBS, strategic planning and management was imported into nonprofit government and higher education settings from other sectors. Like PPBS, it features attention to programs (in this case academic programs) and to the evaluation of those programs by way of data regarding their performance along several centrally determined dimensions (the "internal audit," as outlined by Kotler, 1982, and Keller, 1983).

According to Wildavsky, PPBS suffered from troubles with its objectivity, its centralization, and its political content. Regarding objectivity, he stressed that programs are not divinely ordained. They are interdependent and, to some extent, arbitrary creations, touched by all the messiness and subjectivity of human affairs. Regarding centralization, he notes that the centralization versus decentralization debate is equivalent to debate regarding who will rule. Responsibility for programs is scattered across a variety of government bureaus, and the disparate contexts of programs inevitably affect the ways they are implemented. Pursuing across-program evaluations (i.e., evaluations which pit programs against one another on centrally determined indicators) requires centralization. It not only removes authority from the program level, where core subject matter and organizational expertise is located, but betrays a distrust of truly widespread participation in decision making. Finally, regarding politics, Wildavsky notes that there are three kinds of politics: policy politics (which policy will be adopted?), partisan politics (which political party will win office?), and system politics (how will decision structures be set up?). Wildavsky argues that the thrust of program budgeting makes it an integral part of system politics. As such, PPBS entails certain hidden economic effects: "The literature of economics usually treats organizations and institutions as if they were costless entities. The standard procedure is to consider rival alternatives (in consideration of price policy or other criteria), calculate the differences in cost and achievement among them, and show that one is more or less efficient than another. This way of thinking is insufficient. If the costs include getting an agency to change its policies or procedures, then these organizational costs should be taken into account" (p. 193).

Translating these persuasive comments into the world of strategy in higher education, one might argue that strategic approaches suffer from virtually identical problems. Just as at the federal level, it is extraordinarily difficult to define operationally the programs, products, costs, and benefits of higher education and to act upon them. To the extent strategic approaches seek to take program distinctions as unassailable givens for the strategic analysis, seek to centralize legitimately decentralized decisions, and ignore or underestimate the nonmonetary costs of programmatic recisions and changes, they may fall victim to the same inadequacies that doomed PPBS as a workable management system for colleges and universities. Ultimately, strategic action may be as difficult to implement effectively as PPBS, which is now widely regarded as an outright failure in nonprofit settings. Perhaps, as Wildavsky argued regarding PPBS, the defects of strategic planning and management are defects in principle, not in execution.

For now, however, the case remains open. There is very little evidence that strategic planning and management results in major economic benefits outweighing the costly human effort associated with it. On the other hand, there is evidence of some net benefits at the margin, and that positive hint is enough to argue against abandonment of the approach. That the approach suffers more from a lack of much useful evidence on effectiveness than from an accumulation of nonsupportive evidence may indicate a basic difficulty in ever really judging it on more than circumstantial terms. If it is indeed to be ongoing (Cope, 1981; Keller, 1983), and indeed to involve matters of interpretation and gloss in addition to matters of measurable behaviors (Chaffee, 1985), then judgments regarding success may necessarily be relative and highly sensitive to context. Strategy may be everything its proponents claim, or it may be simply the latest in a long line of ostensibly rational but ultimately impractical approaches imported into higher education from other, more hospitable settings. The evidence, one way or the other, is elusive.

DIRECTIONS FOR FURTHER RESEARCH

New techniques and new contexts for strategic planning and management are possible areas of investigation worthy of research attention. There is a special need for evaluation of techniques to facilitate resource distribution under strategic planning. Milter (1986) has argued that decision support systems (DSS) may be helpful in helping blend the "softness" and subjectivity of strategic planning with the hard numbers of budgets and reallocation needs. In the arena of pricing, Chen (1986) has argued in favor of systems dynamics modeling as a potential aid to institutions in dealing with the complexities of pricing decisions. There is little evidence regarding how these approaches might help or hinder strategic processes and outcomes.

It would be remiss here not to mention also the emerging demographic context as a possible focus for research on strategic choice. Involved is a question of the quality of human resources, but also of the depth of financial and managerial resources, as salaries and benefits are potentially freed up and flexibility increased by the coming retirements of large numbers of senior faculty. For researchers, these changing conditions point to alterations in the modal levels of organizational slack in the system, a factor arguably central to strategic success.

There is also little previous work on the precise nature of strategic change. As Chaffee (1985) has emphasized, this is one aspect of the broader question of the nature of organizational change in higher education. Chaffee (1985) suggests researchers take the perspective of organizational change theory more often, and this appears to be good advice, given the rich literature which already exists. Although most of the research on organizational change in education reported in Baldridge and Deal (1983), for example, is not on strategic change per se, it has much to recommend it to those exploring the initiating conditions and results of strategic efforts in higher education. Similarly, the work of Louis (1984) on decline in state agencies seems relevant albeit not overtly strategic. The March 1984 issue of the *Journal of Higher Education* also contains a number of studies of adaptation which can inform strategic research. Especially relevant is the work reported there by Cameron (1984) on institutional adaptation. Finally, interested analysts might also wish to review the provocative work by Cameron and Whetten (1983) on applying organizational life cycle models to higher education research.

Is there a symbolic side to strategic planning, management, and resource distribution, in that the efforts are conducted as an exercise of demonstrated rationality for the benefit of significant third parties not directly involved (legislators, trustees, the public, and so forth)? A rich variety of potential research topics springs from this question. Some research hints that strategic resource redistribution can often end up producing zero change over time, as priorities change. From some perspectives, one might ask whether this pattern is by definition an indictment of the process. Leslie (1984) and Morgan (1984) are among many who have commented on the symbolic political maneuvering related to strategic planning. In this vein, Nutt (1984) has coined the phrase "gesture" strategies, to convey the idea that strategies sometimes exist in which actions are taken with no focus on improving quality, no focus on winning acceptance on rational grounds, and no focus on producing successful innovations. Instead, such strategies are pursued solely as a performance for outside parties.

In a more directly educational context, Richardson and Gardner (1985) have highlighted the need for politically sensitive dealings with legislators in times of threat. Administrators should ask, they suggest, what symbolic messages they are sending regarding their requests for resources, and should consider the relative merits of direct and somewhat indirect recountings of need to legislatures. Perhaps the earliest consideration of the symbolic side of planning was that of Cohen and March (1974), whose research results seemed to reveal that planning served several purposes on campuses, and few of those purposes were stressed in the classic rational literature on the topic. Specifically, Cohen and March found plans operating as symbols, advertisements, games, and excuses for interaction. From their perspective, strategic planning may simply be the latest favored symbolic activity conducted by administration for parties outside and inside the university, in their determinedly visible pursuit of fairness and rationality (see March, 1981; Pfeffer, 1981).

One need not equate the symbolic side of strategic planning and management with political maneuvering, of course. Ellen Chaffee's ground-breaking work on interpretive strategy (1983b, 1985) reiterated Burton Clark's (1970) emphasis on the symbolic side of higher education as central to the continuation and health of the enterprise. The relative importance of symbols, interpretive styles, and traditions in the success of strategic planning seems a fruitful avenue for future inquiry.

The need for attention to the interpretive side of planning, and its significance for resource redistribution and ultimate financial health, is part of a broader need for attention that might be paid to processes of strategy formation and their relation to resource issues. Work in general management studies has suggested that strategies are often "emergent" rather than "deliberate" (Mintzberg and Waters, 1985). Process-oriented research along the lines Mintzberg and Waters suggest seems particularly appropriate, since decisions in higher education are probably less often deliberately chosen than in other sectors (Cohen and March, 1974). It may be that financing seems divorced from strategy in much previous research because we cannot find strategy working under the blinders of the "deliberate action" assumption. Mintzberg and Waters (p. 257) suggest that "since strategy has almost inevitably been conceived [by researchers] in terms of what the leaders of organizations 'plan' to do in the future, strategic formation has, not surprisingly, tended to be treated as an analytic process for establishing goals and action plans for an organization; that is, as one of formulation followed by implementation. As important as this emphasis may be, we would argue that it is seriously limited, that the process needs to be viewed from a wider perspective.'' We may have paid too much attention to the notion of deliberate process, too little attention to the actual process followed (deliberate or emergent), and too little attention to the results of whatever process was followed. One area of process that could bear much closer scrutiny is perhaps the most basic: the nature and extent of specific resource redistributions under emergent strategies.

Several areas of potentially productive investigation relate closely to the economics of higher education markets and resources. First, one may argue that, in a sense, the focus in higher education strategic research has been on processes and dynamics (see Cope, 1981), rather than on states or conditions, in the terms of econometric analysis. Yet the fundamental building blocks of strategy in economic terms are assets, stocks, and portfolio analysis (Wernerfelt, 1984). What may be needed is attention to both, in an interactive sense; i.e., attention to acts of strategic decision making, but also to the economic results of acts. There is a void between strategic research in higher education and asset enhancement, yet the latter is a usual primary focus of discretionary budgeting approaches (see Jones, 1984, p. 27).

Second, there is a need to explore new perspectives on effectiveness, given the absence of the clear-cut financial indicators of success used in business settings. It may be worthwhile to explore the possibility of assessing strategic outcomes via some variant of the economist's production function analysis. One might operationalize the goals of individual units or programs on a campus, then develop criteria by which achievement of those goals might be measured (e.g., percentage of market penetration).

Third, Wernerfelt's (1984) work on the economic theory of strategy in the for-profit firm points the way to some potentially innovative research using economic notions of market entry, exit and resource barriers. In the usual economic analysis of strategy, the pre-existence of a program on a campus creates a barrier to others considering entry into a field of offerings (entry barrier), and having a strong program also creates a barrier to others in the area (ongoing resource barrier). In this sense, strategic resources can include customer loyalty, production skills, scale economies, contacts locally, contacts nationally, and so forth. Also of potential interest from this economic view is the potential strategic advantage of using one kind of existing resource (e.g., faculty skills in sociology) for other purposes (e.g., starting up programs in new areas of management studies). If an institution can use faculty in this flexible across-program fashion, it faces a cheaper cost of entry than other schools with no such resources.

Fourth, an especially productive resource issue for further research involves the place of information in strategy. Information is a critical resource in the process, but its use is little examined (Balderston, 1974; Mims, 1980; Tierney,

1977, 1981; Hearn and Corcoran, 1988; Clugston, 1987). At the very least, it is a strange resource, clearly different from monetary resources in that it is capable of being recast, reinterpreted, disputed as to value, and shared without loss to the original owner. Pfeffer (1981) has examined information as a source of power in for-profit organizations, but little work has been done on this issue in higher education. Clearly, good information is essential to effective evaluation of internal resources and external conditions (the cornerstone activities of strategy), but also essential is a sophisticated understanding of its limits.

Fifth, much research is beginning to be conducted now on the match between external environments, particularly market structures, and the decentralization patterns of firms, from a transactions-cost perspective (Robins, 1987). This research could be carried into higher education productively, since the enterprise is notable for such high levels of decentralization and loose coupling (Clark, 1983; Weick, 1978). This could be a form of contingency analysis that would productively blend theoretical perspectives from economics (e.g., see Teece, 1985; Camerer, 1985; Robins, 1987) and sociology (e.g., see Meyer and Rowan, 1978; Perrow, 1979; Pfeffer, 1981). In research on the finances of strategy, such attention to the notion of contingency seems essential. There are different kinds of postsecondary institutions, different kinds of environments and dependencies facing those institutions, different kinds of strategy in those institutions, and different kinds of resource implications to these strategies. As just one example, the gentle, mannered strategic dance of Nutt's (1984) ''gesture'' approach (see above) should not be confused by researchers or others with the substantive, purposeful organizational movement pursued by some of Chaffee's (1983c, 1984) small colleges. Perhaps the most direct and provocative attempt to tackle the issue of contingency in strategy is that of Peterson (1980). Focusing on variations in the nature of institutional resource dependencies, he argues for different kinds of planning to match different kinds of situations. Later, Peterson (1986) suggests that administrators are learning better to vary their planning approach or technique in different situations, by issue, by unit interdependence, by tradition, and by environmental condition. No evidence is provided, however. Research from an organizational behavior perspective on the actual abilities of administrators to identify varying environmental resource conditions and act upon them seems a promising venture.

Peterson (1981) has suggested that there is a need for financial planning in higher education to become more strategic: more open, more involving of faculty, staff, and others, more receptive to environmental assessment, more comprehensive and more integrative of a variety of aspects of campus life, especially the priority-setting process. In concluding this review, it may be noted that there is a corresponding need for strategic research to pay more attention to financial and resource conditions within and outside colleges and universities, with an aim toward building understanding of the role of these factors in strategic direction.

Acknowledgments. The author appreciates the helpful suggestions and comments of Carl Adams, Melissa Anderson, David Berg, Richard Clugston, Richard Heydinger, and Larry Leslie. They are blameless for its remaining defects, however.

NOTES

1. Prestige is certainly reflected in the level of tuition charged by institutions. The nation's highest priced schools (e.g., Harvard, Stanford) are also among its most prestigious schools (Clark, 1983). Nevertheless, the variety of market economies in higher education blurs the relationship. Most private four-year colleges charge substantially more than Berkeley or Wisconsin, yet few are able to compete with those schools in prestige. To the extent internally consistent economic sectors exist, however, the cost/prestige connection may indeed hold. For example, within the public sector of a state system, the research university is generally able to compete effectively for undergraduates despite higher tuition charges and unclear curricular superiority.
2. Unfortunately, empirical evidence on this observation is scarce.
3. Larry L. Leslie (personal communication) has argued, however, that initial across-the-board cuts, although generally somewhat risky, can serve as a politically effective prelude to necessary selective cuts at a later time. He suggests that all units have on hand some degree of slack prior to retrenchment, and thus can weather this early round of indiscriminant cuts without undue damage.

REFERENCES

Aguilar, F. J. (1967). *Scanning the Business Environment.* New York: Macmillan.

Allison, G. T. (1971). *Essence of Decision: Explaining the Cuban Missile Crisis.* Boston: Little-Brown.

Alpert, D. (1985). Performance and paralysis: The organizational context of the American research university. *Journal of Higher Education,* 56(3): 241–281.

Anderson, R. E. (1978). A financial and environmental analysis of strategic policy change at small private colleges. *Journal of Higher Education* 49: 30–46.

Andrews, K. R. (1980). *The Concept of Corporate Strategy.* Homewood, IL: Irwin.

Ansoff, H. I., Declerck, R. P., and Hayes, R. L., eds. (1976). *From Strategic Planning to Strategic Management.* New York: Wiley.

Ansoff, H. I., and Hayes, R. L. (1976). Introduction. In H. I. Ansoff, R. P. Declerck, and R. L. Hayes (eds.), *From Strategic Planning to Strategic Management.* New York: Wiley.

Anthony, R. N., and Herzlinger, R. E. (1975). *Management Control in Nonprofit Organizations.* Homewood, IL: Irwin.

Armijo, F., Hall, R. S., Lenning, O., Jonas, S., Cherin, E. H., and Harrington, C. (1980). *Comprehensive Institutional Planning: Studies in Implementation.* Boulder, CO: National Center for Higher Education Management Systems.

Babcock, J. A. (1981). Organizational responses to problematic resources: A comparative model of adaptation and modification. Paper presented at the annual meeting of the Academy of Management, San Diego, August.

Babcock, J. A. (1982). Budgetary responses to declining and growing resource trends. Paper presented at the annual meeting of the Eastern Academy of Management, Baltimore, May.

Balderston, F. E. (1974). *Managing Today's University*. San Francisco: Jossey-Bass.

Baldridge, J. V. (1983). Strategic planning in higher education: Does the emperor have any clothes? In Baldridge and Deal, *The Dynamics of Organizational Change in Education*.

Baldridge, J. V., Curtis, D. V., Ecker, G. P., and Riley, G. L. (1977). Alternative models of governance in higher education. In G. L. Riley and J. V. Baldridge (eds.), *Governing Academic Organizations*, pp. 1–25. Berkeley: McCutchan.

Baldridge, J. V., Curtis, D. V., Ecker, G. P., and Riley, G. L. (1978). *Policy Making and Effective Leadership*. San Francisco: Jossey-Bass.

Baldridge, J. V., and Deal, T. (1983). *The Dynamics of Organizational Change in Education*. Berkeley, CA: McCutchan Publishing.

Baldridge, J. V., Kemerer, F. R., and Green, K. C. (1982). *The Enrollment Crisis: Factors, Actors, and Impacts*. AAHE-ERIC/Higher Education Research Report No. 3 Washington, D.C.: AAHE.

Baldridge, J. V., and Okimi, P. H. (1982). Strategic planning in higher education: New tool—or gimmick? *AAHE Bulletin* 35: 6–18.

Barton, S. L., and Gordon, P. J. (1987). Corporate strategy: Useful perspective for the study of capital structure? *Academy of Management Review* 12: 1, 67–75.

Bean, J. P., and Kuh, G. D. (1984). A typology of planning problems. *Journal of Higher Education* 55(1): 35–55.

Birnbaum, R. (1983). *Maintaining Diversity in Higher Education*. San Francisco: Jossey-Bass.

Blau, P. (1973). *The Organization of Academic Work*. New York: Wiley.

Bleau, B. L. (1981). Planning models in higher education. *Higher Education* 10(2): 153–168.

Boulding, K. (1975). The management of decline. *Change* 7: 8–9.

Bowen, F. M., and Glenny, L. A. (1981). The California Study. In Leslie, L. L. and Hyatt, J. (eds.), *Higher Education Financing Policies: States, Institutions, and Their Interactions*. Tucson: Center for the Study of Higher Education, University of Arizona.

Bowen, H. R. (1977). *Investment in Learning*. San Francisco: Jossey-Bass.

Bowen, H. R. (1981). *The Costs of Higher Education*. San Francisco: Jossey-Bass.

Bowen, H. R. (1982). Sharing the effects: The art of retrenchment. *AAHE Bulletin*, Sept., 10–13.

Breneman, D. W. (1982). Strategies for the 1980s. In Mingle et al., *Challenges of Retrenchment*.

Brinkman, P. T., and Leslie, L. L. (1985). Economies of scale in higher education: Fifty years of research. Paper presented at the annual meeting of the Association for the Study of Higher Education, Chicago, March.

Bryson, J. M. (1981). A perspective on planning and crises in the public sector. *Strategic Management Journal* 2(2): 181–196.

Buchtel, F. S. (1980). Approaches of medium-sized universities. In Jedamus et al., *Improving Academic Management*, pp. 602–625.

Camerer, C. (1985). Thinking economically about strategy. In Pennings et al., *Organizational Strategy and Change*, pp. 64–75.

Cameron, K. (1978). Measuring organizational effectiveness in institutions of higher education. *Administrative Science Quarterly* 23: 604–632.

Cameron, K. (1981). Domains of organizational effectiveness in colleges and universities. *Academy of Management Journal* 24: 25–48.

Cameron, K. (1983). Strategic responses to conditions of decline: Higher education and the private sector. *Journal of Higher Education* 54: 359–380.

Cameron, K. (1984). Organizational adaptation and higher education. *Journal of Higher Education* 55(2): 122–144.

Cameron K., and Whetten, D. A. (1983). Models of the organizational life cycle: Applications to higher education. *Review of Higher Education* 6: 269–290.

Cartter, A. M. (1964). Economics of the university. Paper presented to the Annual Meeting of the American Economics Association, December.

Caruthers, J. K. (1981). Strategic master plans. In N. Poulton (ed.), *New Directions for Institutional Research: Evaluation of Management and Planning Systems, No. 31.*

Caruthers, J. K., and Orwig, M. (1979). *Budgeting in Higher Education.* ERIC/AAHE Research Report Number 3, 1977. Washington, D.C.: American Association for Higher Education.

Chaffee, E. E. (1983a). The role of rationality in university budgeting. *Research in Higher Education* 19: 387–406.

Chaffee, E. E. (1983b). Turnaround management strategies: The adaptive model and the constructive model. Unpublished manuscript, National Center for Higher Education Management Systems, Boulder, CO.

Chaffee, E. E. (1983c). *Case Studies in College Strategy.* With D. A. Whetten and K. Cameron. Boulder, CO: National Center for Higher Education Management Systems.

Chaffee, E. E. (1984). Successful strategic management in small private colleges. *Journal of Higher Education,* 55(2): 212–241.

Chaffee, E. E. (1985). The concept of strategy: From business to higher education. In J. C. Smart (ed.), *Higher Education: Handbook of Theory and Research,* Vol. I, pp. 133–172. New York: Agathon Press.

Chait, R. P., and Ford, A. T. (1982). *Beyond Traditional Tenure: A Guide to Sound Policies and Practices.* San Francisco: Jossey-Bass.

Chandler, A. D. Jr. (1962). *Strategy and Structure.* Cambridge, MA: MIT Press.

Cheit, E. F. (1971). *The New Depression in Higher Education.* New York: McGraw-Hill.

Chen, F. (1986). Systems dynamics models and institutional pricing decisions. In J. Rohrbaugh and A. T. McCartt (eds.), *New Directions for Institutional Research: Applying Decision Support Systems in Higher Education, No. 49,* 93–106.

Chronicle of Higher Education (1985). Too much information, too few questions for campus reviews? October 2, p. 26.

Clark, B. R. (1970). *The Distinctive College: Antioch, Reed, and Swarthmore.* Chicago: Aldine.

Clark, B. (1983). *The Higher Education System: Academic Organization in Cross-National Perspective.* Berkeley: U. of California Press.

Clark, D. L. (1981). In consideration of goal-free planning: The failure of traditional planning systems in education. *Educational Administration Quarterly* 18(3): 42–60.

Clugston, R. M. (1987). Strategic adaptation in an organized anarchy: The case of a liberal arts college of a large public university. Unpublished doctoral dissertation, University of Minnesota.

Cohen, M., and March, J. (1974). *Leadership and Ambiguity: The American College President.* New York: McGraw-Hill.

Collier, D. (1980). Strategic planning for colleges and universities: The strategic academic unit approach. Unpublished paper, cited in Cope (1981). Boulder, CO: National Center for Higher Education Management Systems.

Collier, D. (1981). The applicability of the strategic planning concept to colleges and universities. Unpublished paper, cited in Cope (1981). Boulder, CO: National Center for Higher Education Management Systems.

Conrad, C. (1974). University goals. *Journal of Higher Education* 7: 504–516.

Conrad, C. F., and Blackburn, R. T. (1985). Program quality in higher education: A review and critique of literature and research. In J. C. Smart (ed.), *Higher Education: Handbook of Theory and Research,* Vol. I, pp. 283–308. New York: Agathon Press.

Cope, R. G. (1981). *Strategic Planning, Management, and Decision-Making.* AAHE-ERIC/Higher Education Research Report No. 9.

Cope, R. G. (1985). A contextual model to encompass the strategic planning concept: Introducing a newer paradigm. *Planning for Higher Education* 13:(3): 13–20.

Corson, J. J. (1960). The university—a contrast in administrative process. *Public Administration Review* 20: 2–9.

Cyert, R. M. (1978). The management of universities of constant or decreasing size. *Public Administration Review* 38: 344–349.

Cyert, R. M. and March, J. G. (1963). *A Behavioral Theory of the Firm.* Englewood Cliffs, NJ: Prentice-Hall.

Daniere, Andre. (1964). *Higher Education in the American Economy.* New York: Random House.

Deal, T., and Wiske, M. (1983). Planning, plotting and playing in education's era of decline. In Baldridge and Deal, *The Dynamics of Organizational Change in Education.*

Dickmeyer, N. (1982). Financial management and strategic planning. In C. Frances (ed.), *New Directions for Higher Education: Successful Responses to Financial Difficulty, No. 38,* 51–60.

Dickmeyer, N. (1983). *Financial Conditions of Colleges and Universities.* Washington, D.C.: American Council on Education and the National Association of College and University Business Officers.

Dill, D. (1982). The management of academic culture: Notes on the management of meaning and social integration. *Higher Education* 11: 303–320.

Dougherty, E. A. (1982). Evaluating and discontinuing programs. In Mingle et al., *Challenges of Retrenchment,* pp. 69–87.

Dutton, J. E., and Jackson, S. E. (1987). Categorizing strategic issues: Links to organizational action. *Academy of Management Review* 12(1): 76–90.

Fenske, R. H. (1980). Setting institutional goals and objectives. In Jedamus et al., *Improving Academic Management,* pp. 177–199.

Ferguson, C. C., and Kreps, J. M. (1965). *Principles of Economics* (2nd ed.). New York: Holt, Rinehart, and Winston.

Fincher, C. (1983). Budgeting myths and fictions: The implications for evaluation. In R. A. Wilson (ed.), *Survival in the 1980s: Quality, Mission, and Financing Options.* Tucson: Center for the Study of Higher Education, University of Arizona.

Finkelstein, M. J., Farrar, D., and Pfnister, A. O. (1984). The adaptation of liberal arts colleges to the 1970s: An analysis of critical events. *Journal of Higher Education* 55(2): 242–268.

Firestone, W. A., and Herriot, R. E. (1981). Images of organization and the promotion of educational change. In A. C. Kerckhoff (ed.), *Research in Sociology of Education and Socialization* 2: 221–260.

Frances, C. (1980). Apocalyptic vs. strategic planning. *Change* 12: 19–44.

Gambino, A. J. (1979). *Planning and Control in Higher Education.* New York: National Association of Accountants.

Gilmour, J. E., and Suttle, J. L. (1984). The politics and practicalities of pricing in academe. In Litten, L. H. (ed.), *New Directions in Institutional Research: Issues in Pricing Undergraduate Education, No. 42,* 47–62.

Glenny, L. A. (1982). The concept of short-run decision making. In R. Wilson (ed.),

Responses to Fiscal Stress in Higher Education. Tucson: The Center for the Study of Higher Education, University of Arizona.

Gonyea, M. A. (1980). Determining academic staff needs, allocation, and utilization. In Jedamus et al., *Improving Academic Management,* pp. 364–372.

Goodman, P., Brazerman, M., and Conlon, E. (1980). Institutionalization of planned organizational change. *Research in Organizational Beahavior* 2: 215–246.

Gray, J. A. (1982). Legal constraints on faculty cutbacks. In Mingle et al., *Challenges of Retrenchment,* pp. 171–193.

Green, J. L. Nayyar, D., and Ruch, R. (1979). *Strategic Planning and Budgeting for Higher Education.* La Jolla, CA: J. L. Green and Associates.

Greenberg, M. W., and Winterbauer, N. S. (1986). Developing a financial strategy for academic distinction. *Planning for Higher Education* 14(4): 30–34.

Hackman, J. D. (1983). Seven maxims for institutional researchers: Applying cognitive theory and research. *Research in Higher Education* 18(2): 195–208.

Hackman, J. D. (1985). Power and centrality in the allocation of resources in colleges and universities. *Administrative Science Quarterly* 30: 61–77.

Hambrick, D. C. (1982). Environmental scanning and organizational strategy. *Strategic Management Journal* 3: 159–174.

Hatten, M. C. (1982). Strategic management for not-for-profit organizations. *Strategic Management Journal* 3(2): 89–104.

Hearn, J. C., and Corcoran, M. (1988). Factors behind the proliferation of the institutional research enterprise. *Journal of Higher Education,* forthcoming.

Hearn, J. C., and Heydinger, R. B. (1985). Scanning the external environment of a university: Objectives, constraints, and possibilities. *Journal of Higher Education* 56(4): 419–445.

Heydinger, R. B. (1980). Introduction: Academic program planning in perspective. In R. B. Heydinger (ed.), *New Directions in Institutional Research: Academic Planning for the 1980s, No. 28,* 1–8.

Heydinger, R. B. (1982). Using program priorities to make retrenchment decisions: The case of the University of Minnesota. Atlanta: Southern Regional Education Board.

Heydinger, R. B. (1983). Institutional research and planning: Is futures research the next step? In Morrison, J. L., Renfro, W. L., and Boucher, W. I. (eds.), *New Directions in Institutional Research: Applying Methods and Techniques of Futures Research, No. 39,* 85–98.

Hirschleifer, J., and Shapiro, D. L. (1970). The treatment of risk and uncertainty. In R. H. Haveman and J. Margolis (eds.), *Public Expenditures and Policy Analysis,* pp. 291–313. Chicago: Markham.

Hoenack, S. A. (1977). Direct and incentive planning within a university. *Socioeconomic Planning Sciences* 11: 191–204.

Hoenack, S. A. (1983). *Economic Behavior Within Organizations.* Cambridge: Cambridge University Press.

Hoenack, S. A., and Berg, D. L. (1980). The role of incentives in academic planning. In R. B. Heydinger (ed.), *Academic Planning for the 1980s. New Directions in Institutional Research, No. 28,* 73–95.

Hoenack, S. A., Meagher, P. D., Weiler, W. C., and Zillgitt, R. A. (1974). University planning, decentralization, and resource allocation. *Socio-economic Planning Sciences* 8: 257–272.

Hofer, C. W. (1976). Research on strategic planning: A survey of past studies and suggestions for future efforts. *Journal of Economics and Business* 28: 261–286.

Hopkins, D. S. P., and Massy, W. F. (1981). *Planning Models for Colleges and Universities*. Palo Alto, CA: Stanford University Press.

Ikenberry, S. O. (1972). The organizational dilemma. *Journal of Higher Education* 43(1): 23–34.

Jaschik, S. (1987). Angry congressmen upbraid colleges over businesses. *Chronicle of Higher Education*, July 1, pp. 1, 14.

Jedamus, P., Peterson, M. W., and associates, eds. (1980). *Improving Academic Management: A Handbook of Planning and Institutional Research*. San Francisco: Jossey-Bass.

Jones, D. (1984). Budgeting for academic quality: Structures and strategies. In J. Folger (ed.), *New Directions in Institutional Research: Financial Incentives for Academic Quality, No. 48*, 15–28.

Jonsen, R. W. (1984). Small colleges cope with the eighties: Sharp eye on the horizon, strong hand on the tiller. *Journal of Higher Education* 55(2): 171–183.

Keller, G. (1983). *Academic Strategy: The Management Revolution in American Higher Education*. Washington, D.C.: American Association for Higher Education.

Kemerer, F. R., Baldridge, J. V., and Green, K. C. (1982). *Strategies for Effective Enrollment Management*. Washington D.C.: American Association of State Colleges and Universities.

Kotler, P. (1982). *Marketing for Nonprofit Organizations* (2nd ed.). New York: Prentice-Hall.

Kotler, P., and Murphy, P. E. (1981). Strategic planning for higher education. *Journal of Higher Education* 52: 470–489.

Leslie, D. W., Kellams, S. E., and Gunne, M. G. (1982). *Part-Time Faculty in American Higher Education*. New York: Praeger.

Leslie, L. L. (1984). Bringing the issues together. In L. L. Leslie (ed.), *New Directions in Institutional Research: Responding to New Realities and Funding, No. 43*, 87–99.

Leslie, L. L., and Brinkman, P. T. (1987). Student price response in higher education: The student demand studies. *Journal of Higher Education* 58(3): 181–204.

Leslie, L. L., and Felix, F. J. (1980). Alternatives for financing higher education facilities. *Planning for Higher Education* 8(3): 15–22.

Leslie, L. L., and Johnson, G. P. (1974). The market model and higher education. *Journal of Higher Education* 45(1): 1–20.

Lewis, D., and Wasescha, A. (1986). Costs and benefits of assessment in post-secondary education. Paper presented at the Conference on Assessment in Higher Education. The University of Minnesota, Minneapolis.

Lindblom, C. (1959). The science of muddling through. *Public Administration Review* 19: 79–88.

Litten, L. H., ed. (1984a). *New Directions in Institutional Research: Issues in Pricing Undergraduate Education, No. 42*. San Francisco: Jossey-Bass.

Litten, L. H. (1984b). Editor's notes. In Litten, *Issues in Pricing Undergraduate Education*, pp. 1–6.

Litten, L. H. (1984c). Advancing the research agenda on undergraduate pricing. In Litten, *Issues in Pricing Undergraduate Education*, pp. 91–98.

Louis, K. S. (1984). Organizational decline: How state agencies adapt. *Education and Urban Society* 16(2): 165–188.

Manns, C. L., and March, J. G. (1978). Financial adversity, internal competition, and curriculum change in a university. *Administrative Science Quarterly* 23: 541–552.

March, J. G. (1981). Footnotes to organizational change. *Administrative Science Quarterly* 26: 563–577.

March, J. G. (1982). Emerging developments in the study of organizations. *Review of Higher Education* 6(1): 1–18.

March, J. G., and Simon, H. A. (1958). *Organizations*. New York: Wiley.

Mason, R. O., and Mitroff, I. (1981). *Challenging Strategic Planning Assumptions*. New York: Wiley.

Mason, T. R. (1985). The search for quality in the face of retrenchment: Planning for program consolidation within resource capacities. *Planning for Higher Education* 13(4): 18–30.

Merson, J., and Qualls, R. (1979). *Strategic Planning for Colleges and Universities*. San Antonio, TX: Trinity University Press.

Meyer, J. W., and Rowan, B. (1978). The structure of educational organizations. In M. W. Meyer (ed.), *Environments and Organizations*. San Francisco: Jossey-Bass.

Micek, S. S., ed. (1980). *Integrating Academic Planning and Budgeting in a Rapidly Changing Environment: Process and Technical Issues*. Boulder, CO: National Center for Higher Education Management Systems.

Miles, R. H., and Cameron, K. S. (1982). *Coffin Nails and Corporate Strategies*. Englewood Cliffs, N.J.: Prentice-Hall.

Miller, J. L. (1983). Strategic planning as pragmatic adaptation. *Planning for Higher Education* 12(1): 41–47.

Milter, R. G. (1986). Resource allocation models and the budgeting process. In J. Rohrbaugh and A. T. McCartt (eds.), *New Directions for Institutional Research: Applying Decision Support Systems in Higher Education, No. 49*, 75–91.

Mims, R. S. (1980). Resource allocation: Stopgap or support for academic planning? In R. B. Heydinger (ed.), *New Directions in Institutional Research: Academic Planning for the 1980s, No. 28*, 57–72.

Mingle, J. R., and associates (1982). *Challenges of Retrenchment*. San Francisco: Jossey-Bass.

Mingle, J. R., and Norris, D. M. (1982). Institutional strategies for responding to decline. In Mingle et al., *Challenges of Retrenchment*, pp. 47–68.

Mintzberg, H. (1978). Patterns in strategy formation. *Management Science*, 24(9): 934–948.

Mintzberg, H. (1981). What is planning anyway? *Strategic Management Journal* 2: 319–324.

Mintzberg, H., Raisinghani, D., and Theoret, A. (1976). The structure of "unstructured" decision processes. *Administrative Science Quarterly* 21: 246–275.

Mintzberg, H., and Waters, J. A. (1985). Of strategies, deliberate and emergent. *Strategic Management Journal* 6(3): 257–282.

Mitchell, B. A. (1981). Faculty early retirement: A planning and budgeting issue in higher education. In M. Christal (ed.), *Higher Education Planning and Budgeting: Ideas for the 80s*. Boulder, CO: National Center for Higher Education Management Systems.

Mitroff, I. I., and Emshoff, J. R. (1979). On strategic assumption-making: A dialectical approach to policy and planning. *Academy of Management Review* 4(1): 1–12.

Morgan, A. W. (1984). The new strategies: Roots, context, and overview. In L. L. Leslie (ed.), *New Directions in Institutional Research: Responding to New Realities and Funding, No. 43*, 5–19.

Morgan, A. W., and Mitchell, B. L. (1985). The quest for excellence: Underlying policy issues. In J. C. Smart (ed.), *Higher Education: Handbook of Theory and Research*, Vol. I, pp. 309–348. New York: Agathon Press.

Morrison, J. L., Renfro, W. L., and Boucher, W. I., eds. (1983). *New Directions for*

Instructional Research: Applying Methods and Techniques of Futures Research, No. 39. San Francisco: Jossey-Bass.

Morrison, J. L., Renfro, W. L., and Boucher, W. I. (1984). Futures research and the strategic planning process: implications for higher education. ASHE/ERIC Research Report 9. Washington, D.C.: Association for the Study of Higher Education.

Mortimer, K. P., Bagshaw, M., and Masland, A. T. (1985). Flexibility in academic staffing: effective policies and practices. ASHE/ERIC Research Report Number 1, 1985. Washington, D.C.: Association for the Study of Higher Education.

Mortimer, K. P., and Taylor, B. E. (1984). Budgeting strategies under conditions of decline. In L. L. Leslie (ed.), *New Directions in Institutional Research: Responding to New Realities and Funding, No. 43,* 67–86.

Mortimer, K. P., and Tierney, M. (1979). The three R's of the eighties: reduction, retrenchment, and reallocation. AAHE/ERIC Research Report No. 4. Washington, D.C.: American Association for Higher Education.

Murphy, P. E. (1984). Pricing in higher education: A marketing perspective. In Litten, L. H. (ed.), *New Directions in Institutional Research: Issues in Pricing Undergraduate Education, No. 42,* 77–90.

Newman, F. (1982). Selecting the effects: The priorities of retrenchment. *AAHE Bulletin,* Sept. 11–13.

Newman, W. H., and Wallender, H. W. (1978). Managing not-for-profit enterprises. *Academy of Management Review* 3: 24–31.

Nutt, P. C. (1984). A strategic planning network for non-profit organizations. *Strategic Management Journal* 5(1): 57–85.

Patton, C. V. (1975). Budgeting under crisis: The Confederacy as a poor country. *Administrative Science Quarterly* 20: 355–370.

Patton, C. V. (1979). *Academia in Transition: Mid-Career or Early Retirement.* Cambridge, MA: Abt.

Pennings, J. M., and associates (1985). *Organizational Strategy and Change.* San Francisco: Jossey-Bass.

Perrow, C. (1979). *Complex Organizations: A Critical Essay* (2nd ed.). Glenview, IL: Scott, Foresman.

Peters, T. J. (1984). Strategy follows structure: Developing distinctive skills. *California Management Review* 26(3): 111–125.

Peters, T. J., and Waterman, R. H. (1982). *In Search of Excellence.* New York: Harper & Row.

Peterson, M. W. (1980). Analyzing alternative approaches to planning. In Jedamus et al., *Improving Academic Management.*

Peterson, M. W. (1981). Financial planning for the 1980's: A response to reality and competition. *Planning for Higher Education* 9(4): 19–28.

Peterson, M. W. (1985). Emerging developments in postsecondary organization theory and research: Fragmentation or integration. *Educational Researcher,* March, 5–12.

Peterson, M. W. (1986). Continuity, challenge, and change: An organizational perspective on planning past and future. *Planning for Higher Education* 14(3): 6–15.

Pettigrew, A. M. (1977). Strategy formulation as a political process. *International Studies of Management and Organization* 7(2): 78–87.

Pfeffer, J. (1981). *Power in Organizations.* Boston: Pitman.

Pfeffer, J., and Moore, W. L. (1980). Power in university budgeting: A replication and extension. *Administrative Science Quarterly* 25: 637–653.

Pfeffer, J., and Salancik, G. R. (1974). Organizational decision making as a political process: The case of a university budget. *Administrative Science Quarterly* 19: 135–151.

Powers, D. R. (1982). Reducing the pain of retrenchment. *Educational Record*, 8–12.

Prinsky, L. E. (1978). Public vs. private: Organizational control as a determinant of administrative size. *Sociology and Social Research* 62(3): 401–413.

Quinn, J. B. (1980). *Strategies for Change: Logical Incrementalism*. Homewood, IL: Irwin.

Renfro, W. L., and Morrison, J. L. (1983a). The scanning process: Getting started. In Morrison, J. L., Renfro, W. L., and Boucher, W. I. (eds.), *New Directions in Institutional Research: Applying Methods and Techniques of Futures Research, No. 39*, 5–20.

Renfro, W. L., and Morrison, J. L. (1983b). The scanning process: Methods and uses. In Morrison, J. L., Renfro, W. L., and Boucher, W. I. (eds.), *New Directions in Institutional Research: Applying Methods and Techniques of Futures Research, No. 39*, 21–38.

Richardson, R. C., and Gardner, D. E. (1985). Designing a cost-effective planning process. *Planning for Higher Education* 13(2): 10–13.

Robins, J. A. (1987). Organizational economics: Notes on the use of transaction-cost theory in the study of organizations. *Administrative Science Quarterly* 32: 68–86.

Rubin, I. (1977). Universities in stress: Decision making under conditions of reduced resources. *Social Science Quarterly* 58: 242–254.

Rubin, I. (1979). Retrenchment, loose structure, and adaptability in the university. *Sociology of Education* 52: 211–222.

Rusk, J. J., and Leslie, L. L. (1978). The setting of tuition in public higher education. *Journal of Higher Education* 49(6): 531–547.

Schick, A. G. (1985). University budgeting: Administrator perspective, budget structure, and budget process. *Academy of Management Review* 10(4): 794–802.

Schmidtlein, F. (1985). Changing governance and management strategies. In M. W. Peterson and M. Corcoran (eds.), *New Directions in Institutional Research: Institutional Research in Transition, No. 46*, 59–79.

Schreyogg, G., and Steinmann, H. (1987). Strategic control: A new perspective. *Academy of Management Review* 12(1): 91–103.

Scott, W., and Meyer, J. (1984). Environmental linkages and organizational complexity: Public and private schools. Project Report No. 84-A16, Institute for Research on Educational Finance and Governance, Stanford University School of Education.

Shaman, S., and Zemsky, R. M. (1984). Perspectives on pricing. In Litten, *Issues in Pricing Undergraduate Education*, pp. 7–18.

Shirley, R. C. (1982). Limiting the scope of strategy: A decision-based approach. *Academy of Management Review* 7: 262–268.

Shirley, R.C. (1983). Identifying the levels of strategy for a college or university. *Long Range Planning* 16: 92–98.

Shirley, R. C., and Volkwein, J. F. (1978). Establishing academic program priorities. *Journal of Higher Education* 49: 472–488.

Simon, H. (1979). Rational decision making in business organizations. *American Economic Review* 69: 493–513.

Skolnik, M. L. (1980). Pricing as an element in university planning: Some principles and problems. *Planning for Higher Education* 9(1): 18–24.

Smart, J. C., and McLaughlin, G. W. (1978). Reward structures of academic disciplines. *Research in Higher Education* 8: 39–55.

Smartt, S. (1984). Linking program reviews to the budget. In J. Folger (ed.), *New Directions in Institutional Research: Financial Incentives for Academic Quality, No. 48*, 43–56.

Teece, D. J. (1985). Applying concepts of economic analysis to strategic management. In Pennings et al., *Organizational Strategy and Change,* pp. 35–63. San Francisco: Jossey-Bass.

Tetlow, W. L. (1983). The pragmatic imperative of institutional research. In J. W. Firnberg and W. F. Lasher (eds.), *New Directions for Institutional Research: The Politics and Pragmatics of Institutional Research, No. 38,* 3–9.

Thelin, J. R. (1985). Beyond background music: Historical research on admissions and access in higher education. In J. C. Smart (ed.), *Higher Education: Handbook of Theory and Research,* Vol. I, pp. 349–380. New York: Agathon Press.

Thomas, D. R. E. (1978). Strategy is different in service businesses. *Harvard Business Review* 56: 158–165.

Thomas, R. (1980). Corporate strategic planning in a university. *Long Range Planning* 13: 70–78.

Thompson, J. D. (1967). *Organizations in Action.* New York: McGraw-Hill.

Tierney, M. (1977). Administration: The impact of management information systems on governance. In G. L. Riley and J. V. Baldridge (eds.), *Governing Academic Organizations,* pp. 211–227. Berkeley: McCutchan.

Tierney, M. (1981). Priority setting and resource allocation. In N. Poulton (ed.), *New Directions for Institutional Research: Evaluation of Management and Planning Systems, No. 31,* 29–43.

Tolbert, P. S. (1985). Institutional environments and resource dependence: Sources of administrative structure in institutions of higher education. *Administrative Science Quarterly* 30: 1–13.

Uhl, N. P. (1983). Editor's introduction: Institutional research and strategic planning. In N. P. Uhl (ed.), *New Directions in Institutional Research: Using Research for Strategic Planning, No. 37,* 1–6.

Weick, K. (1978). Educational organizations as loosely coupled systems. *Administrative Science Quarterly* 23: 541–52.

Weick, K. (1982). Management of organizational change among loosely coupled elements. In Paul S. Goodman and associates (eds.), *Change in Organizations,* pp. 375–408. San Francisco: Jossey-Bass.

Weidenbaum, M. L. (1970). Institutional obstacles to reallocating government expenditures. In R. H. Haveman and J. Margolis (eds.), *Public Expenditures and Policy Analysis,* pp. 232–245. Chicago: Markham.

Weiler, W. C. (1984). Using enrollment demand models in institutional pricing decisions. In Litten, *Issues in Pricing Undergraduate Education,* pp. 19–34.

Wernerfelt, B. (1984). A resource-based view of the firm. *Strategic Management Journal* 5(2): 171–180.

Whetten, D. A. (1981). Organizational responses to scarcity: Exploring the obstacles to innovative approaches to retrenchment in education. *Educational Administration Quarterly* 17: 80–97.

Wildavsky, A. (1973). If planning is everything, then maybe it's nothing. *Policy Sciences* 4: 127–153.

Wildavsky, A. (1980). The self-evaluating organization. In D. Nachmias (ed.), *The Practice of Policy Evaluation,* pp. 441–460. New York: St. Martin's Press.

Wildavsky, A. (1984). *The Politics of the Budgetary Process* (4th ed.) Boston: Little-Brown.

Wilensky, H. (1969). *Organizational Intelligence: Knowledge and Power in Government and Industry.* New York: Basic Books.

Young, C. A. (1984). Using the instructional budget to maintain quality. In D. G. Brown (ed.), *New Directions for Higher Education: Leadership Roles for Chief Academic Officers, No. 47,* 49–62.

Zammuto, R. F. (1986). Managing decline in American higher education. In J. C. Smart (ed.), *Higher Education: Handbook of Theory and Research,* Vol. II, pp. 43–84. New York: Agathon Press.

Zammuto, R. F., and Cameron, K. S. (1985). Environmental decline and organizational response. *Research in Organizational Behavior* 7: 223–262.

Faculty Vitality:
Context, Concerns, and Prospects

Shirley M. Clark

and

Darrell R. Lewis
University of Minnesota

Since the late 1970s, scholars and popular appraisers of the status and condition of American higher education have argued that faculty members are, in effect, victims of larger social forces and considerable benign neglect. Significant demographic, economic, and political changes in society have affected the academic profession, institutional environments, and faculty careers adversely, resulting in a perceived current and increasingly problematic decline in faculty vitality.

Although the social forces and environmental conditions affecting higher education have received considerable attention and need not be fully explicated here, it may be helpful to note briefly several shifts or conditions that are commonly implicated in causal ways in faculty vitality issues. First, student enrollment projections range from no growth to significant declines in the traditional college age group with little prospect of doing more than staying even, even if older, part-time, and minority students might be aggressively recruited (National Center for Educational Statistics, 1985). Finances of institutions are formulaically tied very closely to enrollments. Consequently, faculty position replacement demands are estimated to be only a modest proportion of all new doctorates in this decade (e.g., Carnegie Council on Policy Studies in Higher Education, 1980; National Science Foundation Advisory Council, 1978).

Second, enrollments within institutions have shifted away from the humanities and the social sciences and into technical and professional areas, while tenured faculty members have stayed behind in their disciplinary specialities (Carnegie Foundation for the Advancement of Teaching, 1985). In addition, the annual turnover rate in tenure track positions has been slowing since the 1960s and is currently estimated at less than 2% per year (Hellweg and Churchman, 1981). Concomitantly, proportions of full-time faculty who are tenured are estimated to be much higher than in the past and possibly as high as 75% or more, according to Bowen and Schuster (1986) based on data provided by the National Center for Education Statistics.

Third, after the early 1970s and continuing into the mid-1980s, real earnings of the faculty have fallen significantly (and more than those of most other occupational groups) even as the work environment has become less satisfactory in other respects (Hansen, 1985; Bowen and Schuster, 1986).

Fourth, changing birthrates, expanded access patterns, and changing high school curricula have allegedly contributed to the phenomenon on many campuses of the underprepared student whose needs for compensatory education challenge and tax the kind of teaching for which most doctoral-level faculty have traditionally been prepared (Baldwin, 1982; Edgerton, 1980; Watkins, 1982).

Fifth, since 1985, a spate of reports, all critical of the current situation in undergraduate education and advocating curricular reforms, have made demands for quality and effectiveness in higher education a national and state issue (cf. Education Commission of the States, 1986; National Endowment for the Humanities, 1984; National Institute of Education, 1984). Yet the response is often for greater accountability, tighter controls on budgets, hyperrationalized review procedures, and increased coordination of higher education at state and federal levels (Peterson and Blackburn, 1985).

A sixth development (or possibly a result of the foregoing complex of forces and issues) affecting assumptions about faculty vitality is the contention that fewer highly able and talented persons are choosing to prepare for the academic careers that will be possible in a decade or so when retirements will create numerous positions for new faculty members (Bowen and Schuster, 1986; National Center for Educational Statistics, 1985).

In sum, social forces and environmental conditions have contributed to an institutional scenario that includes deterioration in the conditions of academic work brought about by declines in enrollment and associated financial support, changes in the character of student bodies, shifts in demands for fields of study, declines in research sponsorship, and the increasing average age of the faculty. The individual scenario includes "graying" faculty members who are experiencing a decline in esprit and morale and who appear to be unable to respond to the new demands and to adapt to the changes currently taking place in higher education. In addition, the age and opportunity structures of science and academe may be unable to accommodate the forward thrust of new groups such as women and minorities.

Accordingly, this chapter will focus on how the problem of vitality for mid-career and older professionals, especially faculty members, is perceived; how individual career vitality and organizational vitality are interrelated; how morale, obsolescence, and vitality are also interrelated and conceptualized; and how simplistic assumptions about the effects of aging on work do not describe adequately or accurately the life experience of most professionals.

GENERAL PERCEPTIONS OF VITALITY
IN PROFESSIONAL CAREERS

Vitality, as a problematic issue for individuals, is often viewed as a life-course phenomenon. It is most generally understood to arise in life as we pass from youth to the point where we come to realize that there are increasing limits to our physical capabilities and to our abilities to tackle challenges. As Sarason (1977) says, it is a matter of "growing up and running down" (p. 257). The trajectory of life is metaphorically upward, with the value of growth expressed in continuing and higher educational attainments and organized personal growth experiences (e.g., personal growth seminars and contracts, self-actualization, and exploiting one's human potential). Emphasizing growth may be the antithesis of a deliberate concern with aging and death. According to Sarason (1977), emerging values since World War II have emphasized that "personal growth as a value is a litmus test by which all major areas of living (work, sex, friendship, marriage, parenthood) are tested" (p. 261). These values were reflected in the significance attached to education when the theme of lifelong education as liberation from various problems began to emerge and to receive social and political support.

As we look around us, we see everywhere—in the arts, in education, in science, in politics—individuals who, like Pablo Picasso, Howard Bowen, Clark Kerr, Margaret Mead, Barbara McClintock, Jessie Bernard, Robert Havighurst, Ronald Reagan, and Deng Xiaoping, go on in their seventies and eighties to new challenges of body and mind. In a purely physiological sense, there are typically gradual declines in capabilities, but these are relatively limited in their meaning for most people until the decade of the seventies. More serious and limiting is the sense people develop that they lack the possibility of tackling something new, that it may be beyond them, that in some sense the world is passing them by. The problem of vitality in midlife and beyond is not and need not be an inevitable one. For some people, it is not a serious issue, and for others, it may be a problem of social forces and powerful cultural expectancies as much as of individual conditions.

How is the career vitality problem perceived? Several alternative perspectives have conventionally been presented relating to perceived relationships between aging and productivity, status, career blockage, and morale.

Aging and Productivity

One widespread perspective incorporates a linear assumption about aging and productivity, especially in the more codified sciences. The imagery of science as the territory of the young (e.g., "science is a young man's game") is linked to the fact that formal education is typically confined to the early decades of life and that, at any given time, older people are generally disadvantaged, with respect to the knowledge transmitted, relative to younger ones. Science is a special case of the rapidly changing content of formal preparation, a situation which may produce problems of career obsolescence for scientists as they move through their careers (Zuckerman and Merton, 1972). It is believed that the age structure of scientific groups affects their productivity, but few good data are available on this point. This belief also appears to be generally held with respect to the "seniorization" of the professoriate, with assumed concomitant declines in productivity regardless of the paradigmatic natures of the many disciplines.

This perspective on career vitality problems draws attention to employment policies that effectively screen out applicants in their fifties and sixties for new employment positions. Although this is less of an issue for some professionals than for others, it seems to be the case that the mid-career professional (e.g., faculty member, administrator, or engineer) who works in organizational settings finds relocation increasingly difficult as he or she gets older. Assumptions on the one hand that they may not be as well trained, productive, adaptable, and flexible as younger professional cohorts and, on the other, that they are more expensive seem to account for this loss of mobility.

Aging and Cultural Devaluation

A second perspective recognizes the widespread stereotyping and cultural devaluing of older people (Levine, 1980). As Rosow (1974) argues, older people in modern affluent societies, as compared to simpler societies, occupy a problematic institutional position. Their power and status, based traditionally on property ownership, strategic knowledge, productivity, mutual dependence, tradition and religion, kinship, and community life, are diluted. Consequently older people are devalued, stereotyped categorically with various negative characteristics attributed to them, excluded from social participation, and deprived through role loss and ambiguity. By contrast, a more socially approved current image is that of the Yuppie on the fast track (e.g., the ambitious, well-educated, newly skilled young person who invests almost exclusively in self-development and career advancement). The mid-career worker whose life is a balance of occupational and family roles, and whose goals have been reevaluated in light of the work situation and self-assessment, probably stands between these polar images (Clausen, 1972).

One Life–One Career

A third perspective on vitality is commonly represented by Sarason's "one-life–one-career imperative" for professionals (1977). According to this imperative, the developmental task of the individual is to decide on a single linear career. The force of culture leaves unquestioned in the individual's mind that no matter how dysfunctional this choice may seem to be later on, the individual *should* remain committed to the occupation. The immutability of the choice is reinforced by the investment in extended training, by aspects of the occupational socialization process, and by occupational identity and lifestyle. If catastrophe strikes, it may be very difficult for the individual affected by this potent imperative to contemplate a career change. Faculty members and scientists are often referenced as good examples of this imperative because they generally exit their professions only through death or reluctant retirement.

Relating to this perspective is the notion of "stuckness" in mid-career that has been presented by Kanter (1977) and specifically addressed to persons in higher education (1979). Stuck people have low ceilings in their jobs or are blocked from promotion in a system where vertical hierarchical movement spells success. Stuckness is apparently not an unusual experience for faculty members at some point in their lives. How and how well the problem is resolved is viewed as an indicator of the self-renewal capabilities of the individual, and as an important aspect of vitality (Corcoran and Clark, 1985).

Diminished Rewards and Morale
Associated with Workplace Changes

A fourth perspective on professional career vitality as it relates to workplace changes is best represented by Schuster and Bowen's concern for the "weakening of faculty morale" (1985). According to this perspective, the social and demographic forces noted earlier have caused declining compensation, a deteriorating work environment, and a tightening labor market, which, in turn, have contributed to "shaky faculty morale" and less effective performance. These authors have argued that campus reward systems have "indiscriminately triggered a substantial shift in values" so that the old rules under which older faculty were hired no longer apply (p. 15). It is argued that anxiety and stress predominate in the professional lives of existing faculty, and that such perceived stress and morale problems, along with declining rewards, are making academic careers less productive for existing faculty and less attractive to new recruits. Further, this weakening of faculty esprit has contributed to a more segmented, dispirited faculty, and its consequences are likely to be most profound within liberal arts faculty. Although we do not develop the idea here, workplace changes of a negative sort arguably affect the morale and performance of various other professional groups as well (e.g., physicians and engineers).

Underlying these several perspectives on the vitality problem, whether viewed as a potential national crisis or as a problem of individual career stagnation, are assumptions about the ability of individuals to perform effectively in a professional environment of changing expectations. These assumptions reflect a value system that idealizes youth and devalues older people. For individuals themselves, there may be problems of declining productivity, such as an inability to keep up with output expectations (e.g., students taught, patients treated, cases handled, or publications produced), or with demands bought about by changes in the profession (e.g., greater usage of computers in every field and technical advances in medicine). A sense of obsolescence may develop, accompanied by a feeling that the basic values of the profession which had been its attraction in the beginning have been undermined. Sarason (1977), for example, writes of midlife physicians who entered medicine after World War II, picturing a future of autonomy, service, and satisfaction, only to find themselves "dethroned" by armies of new professionals, changing governmental regulations, and self-doubts about the quality of their work. From the standpoint of the employer, there may be dissatisfaction with the professional, leading to removal from positions of power rather than outright dismissal. There may also be a loss of respect from colleagues and associates, inevitably leading to loss of a personal sense of status and esteem.

The circular effects of these experiences, the loss of status and rewards fostering still further declines in energetic and active involvement in work, present an unattractive prospect for those coming up the professional ladder as they encounter the inevitable problems of the middle and later stages of their careers. However, this rather depressing picture puts the worst face on the mid-career and older professional worker's situation. It may not be the typical one. But as is often the case, inquiries tend to be focused on the problems. Our analysis thus begins with further delineation of the conceptualizations of vitality and an attempt to assess the seriousness of professional career vitality problems. We examine institutional success and faculty morale as possible indicators (or symptoms) of such vitality. After that, the relationships between vitality and obsolescence and aging are examined. Then, drawing from the career development literature, vitality is examined in the context of career aspirations and career blockage. How individuals and institutions respond is also explored. Implications for policy and further research are presented; a number of possible strategies for dealing with vitality issues are discussed from an institutional perspective on human resource development.

CONCEPTUALIZING AND MEASURING VITALITY

The concept of vitality is difficult to define and even more difficult to measure and differentiate from related concepts. It is a widely used but seldom specified construct. It shares this difficulty with some other important, but nonetheless primitive, imprecise concepts. In the following quotation, what Cameron (1985) says of "effectiveness" could be said of "vitality":

> effectiveness is extremely difficult to define and measure in colleges and universities. Indicators of effectiveness are not obvious, principles for improving and maintaining effectiveness have not been developed, no standards exist against which to judge

effectiveness, and ambiguity persists regarding the meaning of the word and its relationship to other similar concepts. . . . It cannot be pinpointed, counted, or observed since it is primarily a sensemaking device used to interpret reality. (pp. 1, 2)

As far as can be determined from reviewing the literature, there is no "theory" of faculty career vitality, at least not in any strict sense of the term. Nor have many attempted to define *vitality* (or related terms such as *renewal, revitalization,* or *productivity*). Contemporary writers may assume agreement with respect to the concept, but that assumption is open to question.

Nevertheless, the concept of vitality may be useful as a heuristic concept for describing a complex phenomenon in the professions, including higher education. Although it is difficult to say just what vitality *is,* what we can do is ask two questions: First, to what phenomena does the concept of vitality sensitize us? And second, what more concrete phenomena or ideas can we attempt to specify or measure that are derived from the concept of vitality?

Several writers who have pondered the meaning of vitality as it applies to late-twentieth-century higher education credit John W. Gardner with stimulating their thinking (Centra, 1985; Clark, Boyer, and Corcoran, 1985; Maher, 1982; Peterson and Loye, 1967). In two of his popular works, Gardner presents the reader with several kinds of theoretical statements or hypotheses about the capacities of individuals, institutions, and societies for adaptation and change. In *Self-Renewal* (1963), for example, the following ideas emerge:

> Continuous renewal depends upon conditions that encourage fulfillment of the individual. (p. 2)

> Too often in the past we have designed systems to meet all kinds of exacting requirements except the requirement that they contribute to the fulfillment and growth of the participants. . . . It is essential that in the years ahead we undertake intensive analysis of the impact of the organization on the individual. (pp. 63–64)

In a later book, *Morale* (1978), Gardner provides some synonyms for vitality, and some further statements of meaning:

> regeneration. (p. 13)

> physical drive and durability. (p. 59)

> enthusiasm . . . zest . . . sense of curiosity . . . care about things . . . reach out . . . enjoy . . . risk failure. (p. 62)

> A society concerned for its own continued vitality will be interested in the growth and fulfillment of individual human beings—the release of human potentialities. (p. 73)

Institutional Success as a Vitality Indicator

In his introduction to *Conversations Toward a Definition of Institutional Vitality* (Peterson and Loye, 1967), Peterson acknowledges the creative stimulation provided by Gardner's ideas to the development of an inventory for measuring institutional functioning and success. Peterson and his colleagues struggled to define both institutional vitality and an idealized institution of higher learning. Discussants suggested that the definitions should be multidimensional, should include the idea that the vitality of institutions comes from the vitality of the people in it, should not be elitist but open to a diversity of institutional types, and should allow for the notion of dynamic vitality.

This early work by scholars at the Educational Testing Service predated the systematic attempts in the 1970s to undertake curricular reviews and reforms, to initiate and institutionalize faculty development, to improve and evaluate instruction, and to experiment with organizational and administrative development activities. However, conditions and issues in academe continued to change throughout the 1970s, and while they seem to have intensified concern for faculty and institutional vitality, they have also added to the complexity of the matter. A more recent statement of institutional vitality by Maher (1982) reflects this:

> In essence, then the quest for vitality might be said to focus on the capacity of the college or university to create and sustain the organizational strategies that support the continuing investment of energy by faculty both in their own career and in the realization of the institution's mission. (p. 7)

The intertwining or interaction of institutional and faculty vitality is an important theme. Ideal types of faculty will differ according to institutional type and mission. Thus, for example, at a large, land-grant, research-oriented institution such as the University of Minnesota, where the mission is tripartite (i.e., teaching, research, and service), a position paper on planning strategies contains the following definition of faculty vitality:

> A faculty is vital if it exhibits sustained productivity in its teaching, its research, and its service activities . . . if it is continually creating important, new knowledge and expanding our understanding of the world in which we live . . . if the instructional programs of the University are continually being monitored and developed . . . if it is responding to the needs of the state, the nation, and the world of new knowledge. Perhaps most important a faculty is vital if its members find their work stimulating, enjoyable, and satisfying. (Planning Council, University of Minnesota, 11 February 1980, p. 4)

From his recent comparative studies of the intellectual enterprise, Burton Clark (1985) has concluded that the academic profession today "stands as a plethora of disciplines, a widening array of subject affiliations, a host of subcultures that speak in strange tongues" (p. 36). And this is but half the fragmentation of the professoriate. Academics are dispersed among many types of institutions in a system that is large, diverse, extremely decentralized, influenced by norms and traditions prevailing in the prestigious research-oriented colleges and universities, and highly competitive. Therefore, disaggregation is necessary, according to B. Clark, when generalizing about "the faculty."

It is well known that a division of labor exists between "teaching" and "research" institutions in higher education. Even within these kinds of institutions, value-laden definitions of faculty vitality will differ in their emphases for, say, two-year community colleges, liberal arts colleges, and universities with greater or lesser research orientation. As suggested by Fulton and Trow (1974), ideal types of academic roles include the expectation of continuing research activity in some universities and colleges, but not in others; in yet other institutions, teaching is emphasized and research is not a normal expectation. Prevailing ideal types of faculty roles affect patterns of recruitment and socialization for faculty members. Reflected and reaffirmed in the reward structures, these ideal types may be linked with personal preferences, social origins, and other variables about which relatively little is known.

Satisfaction and Morale as Vitality Indicators

As noted earlier, it is well documented that the conditions of academic work have deteriorated or declined in recent years. This is an objective, tangible, measurable organizational reality. However, it is the faculty's perceptions of their circumstances that drive their responses to their environment and affect their vitality, satisfaction and morale.

Satisfaction and morale of faculty are related but different phenomena according to Austin and Gamson (1983). *Satisfaction* refers to personal contentment and a sense of well-being, whereas *morale* relates to one's relationship to the employing organization: "Morale is based on such factors as pride in the organization and its goals, faith in its leadership, and a sense of shared purpose with and loyalty to others in the organization" (p. 43). While it is plausible to assume that under some circumstances the satisfaction level may vary in an inverse direction from morale, it seems likely that faculty morale is affected by some of the same factors that diminish satisfaction.

Satisfaction of faculty has been given more attention by research than has morale. Studies of faculty have frequently emphasized the importance of motivational factors intrinsic in a faculty member's work in contrast to extrinsic factors, such as salary. For example, in a series of studies of faculty in Minnesota's higher education institutions initiated by Eckert and Stecklein (1961), the most frequently identified sources of satisfaction have been those intrinsic in the career, including opportunity to work with students, stimulating colleagues, the intellectual atmosphere of the campus, and autonomy in the form of freedom to plan one's time. The most recent update in this series of studies produced the finding that the large majority of faculty (85%) continued to be satisfied or very satisfied, although some declines were noted in the satisfaction of faculty in the four-year institutions (Willie and Stecklein, 1982). Frequently mentioned dissatisfactions were working conditions such as the number of meetings, salary, and administrative attitudes. Relating these and other similar findings to faculty productivity, McKeachie (1982) concluded:

> Peer support, a feeling of autonomy and control over one's work, a sense of stimulation from one's students and colleagues, and an administration that encourages rather than restricts faculty initiative—all of these contribute to higher levels of motivation and investment on the part of faculty members. (p. 462)

That extrinsic factors such as salary and administrative leadership may be more important determinants of job *dis*satisfaction for most faculty was noted by Finkelstein (1978) in his synthesis of the studies to date. He further notes that the research does not explain why this observation is so, nor does it adequately address the question of the relationship between satisfaction and productivity. Possibly, he suggests, satisfaction and dissatisfaction may be two constructs rather than one, as is commonly supposed.

Several major and some more limited-scope studies in the 1970s and 1980s have investigated faculty morale and satisfaction in the context of the new set of problematic conditions in academe and with explicit (if general) concern for faculty vitality and productivity issues.

In two national surveys, Baldridge et al. (1978) and Anderson (1983) studied faculty morale using quantitative survey approaches. Baldridge and colleagues collected their data in the early 1970s, prior to the period of financial stress of the early 1980s. Using as their indicators of high morale faculty members' trust of administrators, satisfaction with working conditions, strong identification with their employing institutions, and the tendency to take less than strident positions on critical issues, Baldridge et al. found faculty members in research-oriented institutions to have relatively high morale. This high morale was explained by the advantageous status and the favorable working conditions of faculty in these kinds of institutions. Somewhat later, Anderson (1983) approached faculty morale via item indicators of "institutional esprit." He also asked respondents directly to estimate their level of faculty morale. The finding was that morale had declined from the 1960s to 1981, and that the extent of the decline was related to the extent of faculty "voice" in institutional governance, with more involved faculty estimating less of a decrease in morale. A more recent national study by Williams, Olswang, and Hargett (1986) leads to cautions about assumptions of simple associations between faculty involvement in decision making and the level of faculty morale. In the Williams et al. survey of a sample of institutions belonging to the Association of American Universities on the relationship between faculty involvement in budget reduction decision-making and changes in faculty morale, it was found that as budget reduction decisions reached more difficult levels (e.g., toward the termination of faculty), faculty involvement increased. However, and contrary to expectations, under these conditions, levels of faculty morale decreased in spite of increased participation.

Another recent national survey of 5,000 faculty by the Carnegie Foundation produced decidedly more negative results than earlier studies relative to assessments of faculty satisfaction and morale in two- and four-year institutions (1985). For example, suggestive of a decline in satisfaction, 40% of all faculty members said they were less enthusiastic about their work now than when their careers began; almost one-third of the faculty at two- and four-year institutions indicated a feeling of professional entrapment and an interest in considering another profession. Nearly 40% said they might leave academe within the next five years. In a majority of cases, they were displeased with their compensation packages. Morale in their departments was considered worse than five years before by 40% of all respondents. And if they had to do it over again, one-fifth would not have become college teachers. Over one-third of the Carnegie respondents agreed that abolition of tenure would improve American higher education.

A national interview-based study of a diverse (although nonrepresentative) sample of 38 campuses and 532 faculty and administrators was conducted by Bowen and Schuster (1986) between November 1983 and May 1984 to illuminate the condition of the American professoriate. Seemingly mindful of Burton Clark's (1983, 1985) admonition about fragmentation of the profession and divisions within the academic enterprise, Bowen and Schuster included five types of campuses within their study: research universities, doctorate-granting institutions, comprehensives, liberal arts colleges, and community colleges. Their findings are organized into four overarching themes: the faculty dispirited, the faculty fragmented, the faculty devalued, and the faculty dedicated. Morale was found to vary considerably, with no easily discernible institutional pattern apparent, and, interestingly, faculty thought their morale was worse than did administrators. Morale appeared to be the product of numerous factors: perceptions of campus leadership, the perceived role of external agencies, the level of compensation, the adequacy of working conditions, improved institutional financial stability, shifting values and the demand for published scholarship, and finally, the self-perceptions of stuckness, that is, perceived immobility. "Middling morale" was the norm, with many nervous, apprehensive faculty:

> All in all, the faculty mood was glum. Making allowances for the varied circumstances of the thirty-eight campuses in our sample, we found that faculty members tended to be apprehensive and discontent. The common view was that faculty life had once upon a time been better and that conditions could very well get worse, maybe a lot worse, in the foreseeable future. Our overall sense was that faculty were frustrated and dispirited. (p. 146)

The Bowen and Schuster (1986) report noted that increased faculty fragmentation attributed to continuing and unabated specialization, the growing heterogeneity of the faculty, and the increasing diversity of the higher education system had occurred. They were "surprised and disturbed" (p. 146) to find isolated junior faculty who were pressured intensely to produce and publish, mid-career faculty who felt threatened by the new emphasis on research, and senior faculty who were faced with a shifting reward structure. Campus aspirations, they say, have spiraled upward and are being pursued with single-minded, uncritical determination.

Although evidence mounts that compensation has declined and that working conditions are deteriorating (the faculty-devalued theme), faculty members were found to be coping with adversity in a variety of ways, including engagement in consulting and moonlighting forms of entrepreneurial activities.

Finally, a larger proportion of the sample in the Bowen and Schuster study than of the Carnegie study indicated that they would choose the academic profession if they were starting over again. In spite of several years or a decade of early exit plans for selective early retirement or severance, "genuine voluntary attrition— that is, among tenured faculty—is almost invisible" (Bowen and Schuster, 1986, p. 159). On the surface, faculty appear to be committed to their institutions, disciplines, and lifestyles. Just below the surface is evidence of dissatisfaction and low or mixed morale. Bowen and Schuster conclude, "The satisfactions and frustrations of faculty life appear to hang in uneasy balance" (p. 162).

Work in process by Burton Clark (1985) from a guided interview-based study of over 170 academics in six fields of study in 16 institutions, should shed more light on both the forces of fragmentation and the avenues of integration in the profession, and from there on satisfaction, morale, and vitality in highly divergent circumstances. In a preliminary report of analyses and impressions, Clark writes of the different worlds of research and teaching in the three major sectors of American higher education (e.g., leading universities, state colleges, and community colleges) relative to sources of vitality and psychic gratification. While some may look for strong centripetal forces toward integration in academe, others, like Clark, look to the integration that comes "not from commonness, but from overlapping connections among differences" (p. 43), a fish-scale model of integration. For the future, the process of developing subcultures in academe continues, fragmentation continues, and even multidisciplinary efforts become new specialties and subcultures. If someday we understand better what the differences and similarities are up and down the institutional chain, academic satisfaction, morale, and productivity will be better understood from the perspectives of faculty members in the vastly different sets of circumstances.

Other recent types of studies of satisfaction, morale, and vitality include institutional case studies in research universities and surveys and site visits focused on small, independent colleges (with the latter now under way on a national scale by the Council of Independent Colleges in Washington, D.C.).

Prototypical institutional case studies, such as the qualitative study conducted at the University of Minnesota by Clark and Corcoran (1983, 1985, 1986) proceed from the assumption that faculty vitality seems to have a situational, contextual dimension that makes the concept difficult without taking institutional type and mission into account. These case studies, which are both convenient and problematic when researchers select their own institutions as the sample site, are sometimes used for professional social inquiry into problem solving, particularly with respect to the policy value of designing inquiry to facilitate the social learning required to change attitudes and dispositions (Lindblom and Cohen, 1979). Such policy-oriented inquiry proceeds in a manner that recognizes the attitudes and positions of potential decision-makers and the faculty members themselves, and it suggests directions that could inform and broaden these attitudes and dispositions.

The Clark and Corcoran study, for example, was designed to assess various dimensions of faculty vitality of three samples of tenured faculty (i.e., highly active, representative, and promotion-delayed) in four major field areas. The assessment included questions about career choice and socialization, work interests and preferences, dimensions of productivity and success, stuckness, morale and satisfaction, and assessment of the academic career today. On almost all of the vitality assessment indicator items, the highly active group responded in the more vital direction, suggesting that self-ratings, career blockage experience, and changes in morale and productivity are all potentially useful indicators of vitality. Changes (declines) in morale were more often reported by faculty in the delayed promotion group (e.g., 64% versus less than half of the respondents in the other two groups). Faculty members expressed considerably more specific satisfactions than dissatisfactions. Half of the faculty cited work with students, especially graduate students, as satisfying. The opportunity to work with ideas and, particularly for the highly active group, work freedom (e.g., freedom to set one's own schedule, to select one's own focus of interest, and to be one's own boss) was considered very important. Other satisfactions concerned collegial relationships and teaching experiences. The major source of dissatisfaction was the time required for routine bureaucratic tasks and committees. When the samples were divided into generational cohorts, some interesting and disquieting differences relative to vitality assessments emerged; more recent cohorts were more dissatisfied with financial rewards (and within the highly active group felt less supported by the system to take risks in their work) and also indicated that they would be less likely than their older peers to choose an academic career if they were starting over today (Corcoran and Clark, 1984).

In response to the call to study faculty vitality issues in a variety of institutional contexts in order to extend understanding of this complex phenomenon, Baldwin (1987) has an interview-based study of highly active (vital) faculty in small, independent liberal arts colleges under way. His goal is to compare how vital professors in small colleges parallel university professors and to determine how their attributes, perceptions and experiences differ in significant ways. Preliminary analyses suggest interesting similarities and contrasts. For example, faculty in both types of institutions express a great deal of agreement that environmental conditions and relationships facilitate their success; however, the content of these conditions and relationships differs. As expected, faculty respondents have highly differing orientations and work preferences relative to the balance of research and teaching in research universities and small colleges. Vital professors in both settings were long-hours people and, on average, had careers that were characterized by continuous momentum and opportunity.

These definitions of vitality refer to those essential, yet intangible, positive qualities of individuals and institutions that enable purposeful production. Just as performance and vitality are associated, so are individual and institutional vitality intermeshed and mutually reinforcing. In sum, most notions of faculty vitality seem to have a contextual dimension that makes defining the concept difficult at best without taking into account institutional type and mission. Doing so leads to consideration of institutions as the settings in which faculty members pursue careers as scholars, teachers, and researchers, and as organizations that shape these careers. The literature needs more inquiry of the type which links these organizational characteristics with the developmental nature of faculty careers.

Obsolescence as a Vitality Indicator

Although the construct is infrequently used in discussions of faculty vitality, the idea of obsolescence as an indicator of vitality is not new. According to Miller (1977),

> Human obsolescence was first identified when the onrush of technological change outstripped the education of engineers and scientists. Thus it was seen as "knowledge obsolescence." In some cases, it represented a failure to add new knowledge. In this era, we discovered the so-called half-life of an engineering education. We discovered that the content of an undergraduate education was changing by 50 percent in about seven years. Change rate caused the problem. At the core of the problem also was our concept of careers. It was believed that preparation for a career took place early in life and would last for life. (p. 29)

The professional's expert knowledge, originally obtained during formal educational preparation, is strengthened and extended in the performance of the professional work role. However, the professional whose expertise is based on scientific or technical knowledge is continually confronted with knowledge obsolescence (Taylor, 1968). Perrucci and Rothman (1969) have conceptualized obsolescence as a dual process involving both deterioration or depreciation of knowledge and the professional's failure to acquire new knowledge in the field.

Kaufman (1974) observed that it has been difficult for behavioral and organizational scientists to arrive at a clear-cut definition of obsolescence. His own synthesized definition is "Obsolescence is the degree to which organizational professionals lack the up-to-date knowledge or skills necessary to maintain effective performance in either their current or future work roles" (p. 23). In contrast to Kaufman's "deficiencies" emphasis, Fossum et al. (1986) incorporate two elements, the job and the person, as follows:

> Obsolescence occurs when the person requirements of a job which are demanded by its tasks, duties, and responsibilities become incongruent with the stock of knowledge, skills and abilities currently possessed by the individual; given that the knowledge, skills, and abilities were previously congruent with job demands. (p. 364)

Thus, any efforts to remedy obsolescence must attend to both the nature and degree of changes in jobs and the rate of growth, decline, or change in workers' knowledge, skills, and abilities (i.e., the workers' human capital).

In writing about the causes of depreciation in human capital, Machlup (1984) distinguishes among four major categories. The first is one in which elimination or termination of the carrier of knowledge as participant in the production process takes place; the second is the deterioration of the carrier's mental or physical capacities; the third is a decline in the scarcity value of the knowledge in question; and the fourth is obsolescence of the knowledge in question. Obsolescence in cases of knowledge embodied in individuals is treated as different from cases in which knowledge is embodied in machines and material goods and is clearly related to the nature of the occupation or profession and to events in the organization and society.

A number of other economists have struggled with this conceptual and empirical issue of obsolescence of human knowledge carriers in their estimates for various groups of lifetime productivity and earnings resulting from education (Graham and Webb, 1979; Moreh, 1973; Rosen, 1972, 1975, 1983). Both Machlup (1984) and Rosen (1975) agree that obsolescence is obviously related to some concept of "vintage" (i.e., period of education or training), although "no a priori grounds seem to favor any one of these (rates of obsolescence in human capital); and no empirical evidence has been mustered to support one of them more strongly than others" (Machlup, 1984, p. 568).

Rapid obsolescence of professional competence is a phenomenon of our times (Lindsay, Morrison, and Kelley, 1974; Shearer and Steger, 1975). The accelerating pace of information generation, rapid advances in technology, and changes in various societal institutions have made it difficult for professionals (indeed, for all) to keep abreast of developments. Among professionals, engineers have been especially concerned with conditions thought to be obsolescence-inducing. Kaufman (1979) has identified four broad factors and studied their effects on several hundred engineers in a major high technology organization. He notes rapid environmental change, such as advances in technical knowledge, the organizational climate and reward system in which engineers work, the nature of technical work to which engineers are assigned, and individual characteristics (cognitive, motivational, and personality) of the engineer as important factors leading to obsolescence. Interestingly, no evidence was found to support the widespread belief that older engineers are more obsolete than young ones; obsolescence was determined to be a consequence of organizational practices and policies, including the nature of the work assigned.

The relationship between the process of obsolescence and the career patterns of engineers was also examined by Rothman and Perrucci (1970). Four career options of four cohorts of engineers were selected for study: breadth of technical complexity and responsibility, technical versus administrative involvement, research and development, and stable versus dynamic industries. The findings lent support to the contention that technical obsolescence and career patterns are interrelated. Conducive to weakening of professional expertise were positions involving narrow technical activities, extensive administrative responsibilities, application rather than research, and organizational situations involving stable technologies. The authors speculated that these positions neither required nor stimulated the maintenance of expertise. These positions also offered the less knowledgeable an acceptable career adaptation to the pressures produced by obsolescence.

The rate of obsolescence or depreciation of knowledge may also be affected by the paradigmatic status of the field. Zuckerman and Merton (1972) reviewed the characteristics of highly codified "hard" fields and less codified "soft" fields, suggesting that the more highly codified fields tend to "obliterate the original versions of past contributions by incorporating their essentials into newer formulations" (p. 303). Evidence from a study of career interruptions of academic women supports the idea the obsolescence is field-related (McDowell, 1982). Choice of field significantly affected the consequences of career inter-ruption, with more negative effects upon careers in fields with less durable knowledge (the physical sciences) than in fields with more durable knowledge (the humanities).

A recent study of faculty by Willis and Tosti-Vasey (1986) sought to assess the relationship between knowledge obsolescence, as measured by knowledge of changes that had occurred in the material taught in the introductory course in the discipline over the past ten years, and personality characteristics and scholarly productivity. Among other findings, more up-to-date faculty rated higher on a physical-psychological energy dimension than less up-to-date peers, reported working more hours per week, and related opportunities to interact with experts as significantly more useful. As well, they exhibited a higher rate of scholarly productivity. The two groups did not differ on age-related characteristics.

From this preliminary review of the obsolescence dimension of career vitality, it seems evident that both constructs, vitality and obsolescence, suffer from imprecision of conceptualization and lack of a well-developed guiding model to suggest important variables. In the next section, the relationship between working and aging will be explored with a focus on vitality concerns.

Aging as a Vitality Indicator

In earlier sections of this chapter, we characterized vitality problems of mid-career and older professionals, including faculty, as not unlikely but highly variable in their effects upon individuals and institutional concerns. In the preceding section, it became apparent that individual career obsolescence or vitality, in the case of faculty members and some other professionals, is related to organizational structures, expectations, practices, and policies, as well as to individual characteristics. In this section, we wish to deal more directly with the widespread belief that age represents a reasonably good proxy variable for work productivity. But first, a contextual comment is in order.

American society is in the midst of a demographic revolution that, when concluded in the middle of the next century, will have squared the population pyramid with respect to relative proportions of younger and older people. By the year 2035, possibly every fourth American will be sixty-five or over, and life expectancy will be pressing toward one hundred (Pifer and Bronte, 1986). Without a doubt we are an aging society, as are most other developed countries of the world. Increasingly, we are called upon to examine emerging issues regarding extended longevity and work. In the course of this century, people have more and more concentrated their economic activity in the early and middle adult years; their labor force participation has been eroding.

The age composition of the work force will change dramatically as those born immediately after World War II grow older. U.S. Bureau of the Census data presented by Doering, Rhodes, and Schuster (1983) document this dramatic shift. According to their analyses, during the 1970s, the average worker was just entering the work force. In contrast, the work force of the 1980s is characterized by 25- to 34-year-olds. Persons of early middle years (34–44 years) will characterize the 1990s, and the average age of the worker of the first two decades of the next century is projected to be 45 and over. While it is hoped that attitudes will change, "there has been a pervasive belief in this country that all older workers should retire because they are no longer productive and that longevity simply prolongs their uselessness" (Riley and Riley, 1986, p. 59).

Beliefs about the effects of aging almost always convey directionality: increased age is associated with lower productivity. As expressed by Blackburn and Lawrence (1986) in the case of the professoriate, indeed, "the observed and predicted increase in the average faculty age is viewed . . . as a problem, that is, a situation that has numerous negative consequences and few, if any, positive outcomes" (p. 265). The list of the believed deficiencies of older faculty is long; it includes lower productivity, less creativity, less adaptability to changed conditions, less effectiveness as teachers and researchers, and many more. Furthermore, older faculty members cost more in higher salaries. Specific assumptions about obsolescence are sometimes commingled with beliefs about the declining productivity of older faculty. Shin and Putman (1982), for example, assert that "older scientists tend to lose touch with the developing heart of their discipline, their knowledge becomes obsolete, and they are less likely to achieve the innovative theory or influential breakthrough than younger colleagues" (p. 222). With such beliefs and perceptions commonplace, it is important to determine whether a basis exists for a tight coupling between age and age-related factors, on the one hand, and professional worker performance, on the other.

There are many theories of aging and work, most of which can be classified as biological-physiological, psychological, sociological, or economic. From each of these theoretical streams, central research findings can be drawn regarding performance and aging.

Biological-Physiological Theories of Aging

The focus of biological-physiological theories of aging is on losses of responsiveness, sight, hearing, coordination, taste, smell, and other physiological functioning which accompanies aging. However, age seems to be a poor proxy for physical, mental, or emotional status. Comprehensive surveys of medical and psychological evidence dating from the past forty years and cited in gerontological literature on a wide variety of occupations (Butler, 1975; Levine, 1980; Meier and Kerr, 1976) conclude that the competence and work performance of older workers are, by any general measures, at least equal to those of younger workers. The evidence clearly establishes the continued productivity of workers who are sixty-five years of age or older. Furthermore, Meier and Kerr (1976) have concluded that the physical demands of most jobs today are well below the capabilities of healthy aging personnel. Properly placed, older workers function effectively, steadily, and loyally.

As for findings in this domain, one would not expect to find any significant reduction in professional workers' ability to perform up to the age of normal retirement. (This overall finding would need to be modified for those professionals, such as surgeons, whose work would be affected by slowed reaction time or decreased physical strength.) While the official age of retirement for faculty members is now set at seventy years, some faculty members—and certainly many physicians and lawyers—continue to work at professional tasks well into their seventh and eighth decades. Studies by Havighurst (1980, 1985) of male social scientist faculty and academic administrators support the continuity principle. That is, "there is continuity or stability of life-style from middle age through the age period from 60–75, with little or no change caused by retirement, mandatory or voluntary" (1985, p. 106). High and low publishers among the social scientists continued their principal concerns. Of the four definable subgroups among administrators, only one, consisting of people who radically changed their lifestyles, was sharply discontinuous from previously established roles. Work time may be lost due to health, but "reduced mental acuity and physical performance are not 'normal' aging consequences" (Blackburn and Lawrence, 1985, p. 5).

Psychological Theories of Aging

Psychological approaches to aging include attention to intelligence, learning, and memory, and to adult development stages. There is a variety of opinion and thought on relations between age and creativity (discoveries and path-breaking work) in the various academic disciplines (Reskin, 1985). Suffice it to say that different disciplines show different patterns possibly related to the paradigmatic nature of the fields. Two broad categories of intellectual performance studied by Horn and Cattell (1967) in relation to aging are categorized as crystallized and fluid intelligence. Crystallized intelligence is the collective societal intelligence (word meanings, mechanical knowledge, fluency of ideas, general information, and arithmetic ability). Fluid intelligence (inductive reasoning, figure matching, and perceptual speed) is thought to be more directly dependent upon the physiological structure of the organism. It is therefore more subject to decline after middle age than is crystallized intelligence, although many older adults compensate by taking more time with certain tasks. In sum, crystallized intelligence continues to grow slowly during the adult years, and even after age sixty if the person is intellectually active. Fluid intelligence declines slowly with age, but compensations are possible and even typical.

As for the life-span psychological theories which serve as the underpinnings of adult and career development frameworks and of the faculty development movement, Dannefer (1984) has argued that these theories demonstrate the fallacies of both a biologistic and psychologistic reductionism. Instead of positing a fixed universal sequence of life and career stages (which will be explored further in a subsequent section), Dannefer prefers a more sociogenic paradigm that includes greater attention to environmental effects on humans who are malleable throughout their lives.

Like the findings from biological theories, the general principle drawn from psychological evidence is that while there are some losses with aging, they are rather minor when compensatory behaviors are taken into consideration. With good health and exercising of psychological functions, there is little basis for positing loss over the normal worklife span.

Sociological Theories of Aging

Sociological theories of aging include concerns with age stratification, age stereotyping, intergenerational rivalry, cultural devaluing, role disengagement, organizational demography, and more. The most current and inclusive statement of sociological vision on the emergent field of aging is found in the 1986 Presidential Address to the American Sociological Association by Matilda White Riley (1987), where she claims that the sociology of aging involves substantive integration across many disciplines:

> While recognizing that aging is in certain aspects the proper subject matter of both biology and psychology, it denies frequent imperialist claims of these disciplines. . . . aging refers to a person's social interactions and relationships, but aging also involves an interplay of social processes with genetic predispositions; changes in immune, endocrine, neural, and other physiological systems; and changes in perceptual, cognitive, emotional, and othe psychological processes. Cohort flow is linking to history. . . . The understanding of dynamic age structures is buttressed by alliances of sociology with economics, political science, and anthropology. (p. 10)

Within the discipline, sociologists of science, in particular, have long been interested in the relationship between aging and scientific productivity, that is, the quality and quantity of discoveries and contributions. Reskin (1985) presents a summary and a methodological critique of recent major studies of scientists serving as faculty members in academic departments. She reviewed several models of the relationship between age and the research productivity of faculty members. These models included linear or cumulative growth; the declining rate of increase, which reflects the notion that performance tapers off over time; the leveling out or plateauing function due to aging; the obsolescence function, a parabolic function in which performance rises and then declines; the spurt function, a bimodal distribution that combines the expected effects of the academic reward system and the effects of aging to produce two peaks—one early in the career and the second about a decade or so later; and finally, a spurt-obsolescence function bimodal distribution, in which the second peak is followed by a performance decline. Reskin then applied these models to several fields on which age and productivity data are available, including physics, astronomy, mathematics, chemistry, chemical engineering, biochemistry, biology, earth sciences, geology, psychology, economics, and sociology. Her conclusions are that some regularities do occur across disciplines. First, in no case did research productivity show a simple, negative relationship with age. Generally, a simple linear model of cumulative growth was inadequate, too. Second, the results by discipline suggest that linear models are inadequate and that spurt-obsolescence models are generally better; market, generational, and selective attrition effects seem to be overlaid with any effects of aging. And third, any simple effects of aging seem to be small.

Blackburn (1985) has used faculty productivity data plotted against career age from major studies as evidence in his search for a theory of career development. He examined some existing relevant theories, such as the Levinson adult development stage theory, demographic theory, and socialization theory, and he overlaid the age and productivity grids on the theoretical career stages, events, activities, and processes. In this confrontation of evidence with theory, Blackburn found that psychological stage theory did not fit the productivity evidence particularly well. A better fit was obtained when a career events (degrees and professional ranks earned) line was added to the grid.

With respect to teaching and aging, the data are even more inadequate. Methodologically, there are several problems. The studies are cross-sectional, and with regard to assessments of effectiveness of teaching, the assessment measure is effectiveness as judged by students. Institutions neither collect longitudinal data on the effectiveness of the same teachers, nor is there consistency in the instruments across the institutions or through time (Blackburn and Lawrence, 1986). There is some evidence that interest in teaching increases with age (Fulton and Trow, 1974), although it may not be the case that more attention is devoted to it. Several studies over a thirty-year period find low-order positive correlations between teaching effectiveness and academic rank; but since rank of full professor covers roughly the age span of 40- to 70-year-olds, one must be careful in inferring a positive relationship with aging (Blackburn and Lawrence, 1986). Centra and Zinn's (1976) cross-sectional study of aging and teaching performance found lower ratings for older faculty. As Blackburn (1982) summarized the situation in an earlier essay, "The conclusion from direct evidence, then, is that there are not career phases in the motivation to teach. On the other hand, in the absence of a purposeful test of this proposition, one is reluctant to close the books" (p. 96).

Economic Theories of Aging

Although not directly expressed as an "economic theory of aging," economists have long been concerned with age-earning profiles as they have concentrated on rates of return to education and the development of a theory of human capital. In this theory of human capital, it is clearly assumed that earnings reflect productivity in the workplace. Following Jacob Mincer's (1974) early work at the National Bureau of Economic Research, economic researchers today try to separate the returns to schooling per se from the returns to experience (net of deterioration and obsolescence) as the individual ages in the workplace.

The typical characteristics of these age-earnings profiles are that earnings rise with age to a single peak and then flatten or fall until retirement age; the profiles are steeper for higher educated individuals than for those with less education; and the higher the level of education, the later the age at which earnings reach their peak. An important feature of this work is the fact that earnings are determined not only by a worker's educational level, but also by the effects of age and experience on his or her productivity. Earnings reflect, of course, other forms of investment in human capital (including on-the-job training), as well as the worker's natural ability, personal characteristics (such as attitudes, motivation, social class, family background, sex, race, and place of work), and other variables that influence earning capacity. However, the point here is that it has been generally accepted in the human capital literature that productivity and average earnings increase with age and work experiences (Fase, 1970; Machlup, 1984; Mincer, 1974, 1979; Rosen, 1987; Rosenzweig, 1976). Mincer (1974) and Rosenzweig (1976) have even attempted to relate these theoretical economic effects of aging in the context of biological theory relating to deterioration. Although none of this work has been done specific to faculty, there is no reason to believe that such findings from the general population and other professions are not generalizable to higher education as well.

In summary, each of the four major approaches sheds some light on the relationships between working and aging. There is little basis for decline in professional performance in middle and later years due to the biology and physiology of the aging process. Psychologically, the same conclusion is supported, although the expectancies created by assumptions of a fixed sequence of adult development stages could affect individuals' behaviors and the social response to them, as in the example of the "midlife crisis." Sociological theories suggest that faculty members must be considered in the general context of roles in social institutions and organizations, in culture and society. And economic theories relating to human capital and rates of return over the worklife of individuals further support the enhanced quantity and quality of productivity in the workplace as a result of experience. The specific contexts of workers must also be considered, as different disciplines or fields involve particular socialization processes, expectations, and rewards that structure and give meaning to aging as the individual moves through the work career.

Career Development as a Vitality Indicator

Several years ago, many of us recognized that universities had begun to face serious problems in academic personnel planning. But we were not at all sure that what was being identified as a problem of faculty vitality and what was being proposed to solve it matched very well with the conditions of faculty life. We were also concerned that recommendations for faculty and career development were typically designed to change the individual but ignored the organizational and institutional contexts that shape and structure careers. All too often in the employment of faculty development schemes, there was evidence of overgeneralization. Problems of obsolescence, for example, particular to engineering and the sciences were assumed to apply to faculties at large, despite different rates of change in various fields, and despite quite different responsibilities of faculties in undergraduate and graduate institutions.

Adult and Career Development

Adult development theory received much attention in the 1970s (e.g., Sheehy, 1974; Levinson et al., 1978; Gould, 1978), and it has often been proposed as the foundation for understanding and resolving faculty vitality issues in the 1980s. As indicated in the earlier section on psychological theories of aging, the paradigm that underlies the dominant approach to adult development is psychological and ontogenetic; that is, the individual is treated primarily as a self-contained organism that develops according to a predetermined sequence (Jung, 1933; Erikson, 1950; Erikson and Erikson, 1981). In Erikson's scheme, each development stage is defined by a dichotomy. For example, middle adulthood is characterized by the generativity/self-absorption dichotomy, and older adulthood is characterized by the integrity/despair dichotomy. Levinson et al. (1978), Gould (1978), Valliant (1977), and Valliant and Milofsky (1980) identified similar stages and focused on the long period of adulthood. Levinson et al.'s stages, which are associated with chronological age, correspond roughly to the career development stages identified by Super and Bachrach (1957), Hall and Nougaim (1968), Baldwin (1979), and London (1983). Baldwin, for example, attempted to link formulations of adult development and academic career development by creating two parallel charts. His conceptualization of faculty development uses academic rank structure: two stages for assistant professors, one for associate professors, and two for full professors.

The stage-theory work of Levinson et al., Gould, and Valliant is based on intensive, semiclinical interviews. In their study of forty midlife males living in one region of the United States between 1968 and 1970, Levinson et al. claim to have found a common and universal human pattern of sequential stability and transitional change. Like Erikson (1950), they have made much of the issues of the middle adulthood stage: generativity versus stagnation, the midlife crisis, a time of potential upheaval and turmoil. Other studies focusing on this stage have examined the restructuring of one's orientation (e.g., Dubin, 1973; Hill and Miller, 1981; London, 1983; Neugarten, 1968; Sonnenfeld, 1978; Sonnenfeld and Kotter, 1982) and biographies of mid-career changes (Sarason, 1977).

Career development theory, as noted above, is compatible with other development and life-cycle theories. The basic assumption of most career development models is that an occupation proceeds through a series of stages that present different challenges or tasks and require different responses. Hall (1976), for example, describes five career stages that are compatible with life-cycle stages: growth, exploration, establishment, maintenance, and decline. Brooks and German (1983) summarize this confluence of theories:

Between the ages of 25 and 45, the objectives are establishment and advancement in the field chosen. By middle adulthood, white collar careers usually are reaching the end of the establishment stage. Just as the generativity stage is critical to the future of the individual, the maintenance stage can be critical to the future of the career. Some individuals continue to grow in mid-career; others begin to decline. Finally, as cues are received indicating that the limit of advancement has been reached, the need to compete decreases. This reduction in competitive drive often results in reduced productivity and career commitment. (p. 16).

In this quotation, there is some suggestion of interplay between individual maturation sequences and career progression, of a normative career disengagement and decline, and of a loose connection between chronological age and individual maturation and the career course.

In a timely critique of adult development theory, life-span developmental psychology, and dialectical life-span psychology, Dannefer (1984) argues that Levinson et al.'s ontogenetic paradigm represents a universal human sequence and inadequately considers environmental and organizational effects on behavior. For example, Levinson et al. (1978) hypothesized that

this sequence of eras and periods exists in all societies . . . at the present stage of human evolution. The eras and periods are grounded in the nature of man as a biological, psychological and social organism. (p. 322)

This claim of universality has been challenged by Brim (1976), Riley (1978), and Rossi (1980). Van West (1982) has questioned its application to faculty, and Cytrynbaum, Lee, and Wadner (1982) have questioned its application to female faculty and dual-career couples. Efforts to operationalize the stages have not been particularly fruitful. Stumpf and Rabinowitz (1981) and Baldwin (1979) have had some qualified success in associating faculty performance and career satisfaction with career stages and academic ranks. Rush, Peacock, and Milkovich (1980), Entrekin and Everett (1981), and Van West (1982) were unable to find career stage and age linkages, universal progression through a hypothesized sequence, close association between generalized career-stage models and a specific academic career-stage model, or agreement between faculty's perception of their career development and the career stages described in the professional literature. Braskamp, Fowler, and Ory (1984), using academic ranks in combination with a life-cycle scheme, concluded that a conceptual framework of alternating stages of transition and structure has "sufficient heuristic value for describing and interpreting the career development of faculty members" (p. 219). They note, however, that there are differences between faculty and that these differences can probably be attributed to academic disciplines and to the experiences of cohorts. Braskamp et al. also note that in contrast to faculty at liberal arts colleges (cf. Baldwin, 1979), the faculty at the research university they studied did not indicate that their preference for teaching increased over time. Corcoran and Clark (1984) and Blackburn and Lawrence (1985) have used demographic-cohort schemes linked to differential patterns of early socialization to account for sources of variance in faculty members' research behavior, career satisfaction and dissatisfaction, and perceptions of risks and rewards.

Mid-Career Stuckness

The notion of stuckness in careers in one that has received particular attention because of Rosabeth Moss Kanter's much-quoted works (1977, 1979), and it is increasingly being noted in the management sciences literature (Ference, Stoner, and Warren, 1977; Hill and Miller, 1981; London, 1983; Near, 1985). Kanter uses the term *stuckness* primarily to refer to individuals who reach a dead end in opportunity in industry. These are people who have "low ceilings in their jobs," who are blocked from movement, and who lack opportunity in a system where mobility above all means success. In this context, awareness of stuckness involves a low promotion rate, a ceiling on one's opportunities for promotion, and getting old in one's job. Although it is clear that academics do not necessarily view promotion in the administrative hierarchy as opportunity, they certainly look at rank promotion, tenure, and economic rewards as significant. Kanter's ideas with respect to the experiences and reactions of stuck individuals can be reflected in the careers of many individuals in higher education today (Clark and Corcoran, 1985). These ideas also inform us about "successful" faculty who view themselves as good but not at the "top of the ladder." As Kanter notes, the most vital and active individuals may well be those who feel most dissatisfied with their jobs because of their sense of frustration in realizing their career goals.

Nature of the Stuck Experience

It has been suggested that most faculty members will at some time in their careers feel that they are in some sense stuck or blocked from moving ahead in their work. In recent research reported by Clark and Corcoran (1985), it was noted that most faculty members reporting career blocks spoke about blocks in their research or scholarly work. These blocks took several forms: (1) consistently productive researchers who thought they were on a plateau; (2) faculty whose research had been set aside for administrative work at some point and who subsequently found it hard to resume this aspect of their career; (3) faculty who preferred a line of research that was "out of favor" with funding agencies; (4) some faculty who saw their research interest as lacking value in the eyes of their colleagues (e.g., because it was not experimental in an experimentally domi-nated area, or because it dealt with the pedagogy of the field); (5) faculty whose line of research was exceptionally costly in time and travel or, for other reasons was unusually difficult to bring to maturity; and (6) cases where the shift from the first line of work to another was particularly problematic (e.g., the case of the second book in history, the first book being based on the dissertation).

These situations, presented as representative rather than exhaustive, indicated the dominant inclination to attribute blockage to situational circumstances, including those related to funding, lack of collegial support, lack of graduate student interest, lack of career mobility opportunity, and a general sense that opportunities for advancement were tightening up.

Resolution of Career Blocks

As we have seen, faculty career blockage experiences vary in their scope: some focus on one highly salient career function (research), while others are broadly pervasive, involving a total career outlook. They also vary in attribution. Some involve an inward orientation to individual life circumstances, while others are oriented outward toward contemporary conditions of academic life. These variations in specificity and attribution are reflected in the approaches that faculty members use in addressing blockage experiences. Quite a number have been successful in shifting to a new research or teaching area. Some have contemplated—and a few have made—a career change to a nonuniversity position, such as a move to an industrial laboratory or a different profession (Patton and Palmer, 1985). Many others have stayed in academe and are still trying to come to terms with a life stage with which they were unprepared to deal. A few may be resigned to living out their careers by satisfying minimal teaching requirements and seeking satisfactions elsewhere.

Among the conclusions drawn from studies of the vitality of faculty groups is that stuckness or blockage is not an unusual experience (Clark and Corcoran, 1983, 1985; Bowen and Schuster, 1986; B. Clark, 1985). It is likely to happen at some point during most academic careers. While some blockages are related to "midlife crises," others occur earlier or later. Most frequently, blockages are contextual or situational in origin. Faculty who are experiencing delays in promotion are more likely to report stuckness or problems. Finally, most often, faculty resolve their own blockages with little help forthcoming from colleagues or institutional sources. Their career socialization, maturity, and problem-solving orientation contribute to effective problem resolution.

IMPLICATIONS FOR
POLICY AND RESEARCH DIRECTIONS

In this chapter, we have considered how the problem of the vitality of mid-career and older professionals, especially faculty members, is perceived; how individual career vitality and organizational vitality are interrelated; how morale, obsolescence, and vitality are also interrelated and conceptualized; and how simplistic assumptions about the effects of aging on work do not describe the experience of professionals adequately or accurately. Further, we have examined the career blockage experience of stuckness as a vitality issue thought to be associated with mid-career or older professional workers.

To keep faculty or older professionals among the "moving" rather than the "stuck" will require the development and maintenance of an opportunity and power structure that opens career paths, provides developmental activities, facilitates lateral or vertical movement to ensure stimulation, involves people in organizational decision-making processes, deliberately builds sponsorship ("old-hand–newcomer") relationships within the organization, and recognizes good performance in a variety of ways. Consequently, continuing research attention needs to be given to those organizational factors and policies which can facilitate these processes.

Most human resource development perspectives today reflect the idea that individual and institutional vitality are interrelated and interactive. Miller (1977) poses the question directly in asking, "What is a human resources strategy and how can it impact vitality and overcome obsolescence?" (p. 30). The organization which invests in training, retraining and education, and facilitative organizational policy, and that advances its own employees is operating with a strategy that humans are enhanceable. Such a strategy

> supports and enhances vitality because individuals sense the security necessary for taking risks of individual growth. It also supports vitality because it provides for job changes which stimulate both productivity and personal development. Lastly, it supports vitality because employees sense that the organization puts a high value on its human resources. (p. 30)

Institutional or corporate perspectives on human resource development are being bolstered and enriched by the studies of organizational cultures and climates and their effects on the behavior of managers and workers in a wide variety of organizations, including colleges and universities (Masland, 1985). However, to date, little of a systematic nature has been developed to assist policy making and personnel management in the matter of vitality enhancement.

When human obsolescence was first identified as knowledge obsolescence in the era of rapid technological change, which resulted in the so-called half-life of professional and technical education, the first solutions to the problem were continuing education and reeducation. These solutions continue in favor; however, the extent to which education offsets obsolescence and maintains vitality is not clear and has not been demonstrated empirically. Historically, adult learning has been voluntary, and many are concerned that "mandated" adult education in the form of continuing education is coercive and not really a guarantee of permanent adequacy. According to Cross (1981), almost all of the states now require continuing education in some form for licensed professionals, varying from optometrists to nursing-home administrators. In Iowa, in the late seventies, the legislature passed a bill requiring all twenty-three professional licensing boards in the state to establish continuing education requirements for relicensure. Most other states have mandatory continuing education required of certain groups. Adult educators are divided on the issue of the efficacy or the wisdom of mandatory requirements, and they are aware that professional associations desire to protect the integrity of their fields themselves through monitoring, didactic, and informal educational activities. Presumably, this policy area will continue to be filled with jurisdictional conflicts, tensions, and developments (Houle, 1980). Without a doubt, this area also will receive greater attention relative to matters of obsolescence in higher education as well.

Traditional approaches to encouraging "anti-obsolescence" in professionals, especially in highly technical fields, have included self-assessment (introspective evaluation and soul searching), seminars, workshops, courses, and self-study (Kaufman, 1979; Sonner, 1983). Many professionals are learning effective use of the microcomputer via a combination of these methods. Another way of keeping up to date is to move from positions concentrating on theory and research to those focusing on practice and application and back again. Illustrative of this approach is faculty consulting work and summer or part-time employment in applied fields related to professional and disciplinary expertise (Boyer and Lewis, 1985).

Earlier we had remarked that the general condition of academe in terms of projected institutional and faculty vitality is mixed, and that the long-term solutions to the problems appear to be limited. Institutions, of course, can attempt to alter the rate and composition of new faculty entering their employ, or to alter the rate and composition of faculty leaving academe in order to achieve a more optimal age and human capital structure. Much has been written about these two strategies in recent years. Possibly the best known of the proposals to increase the number of new young faculty members ("fresh blood" or "hiring against the grain") involves the petitioning of federal agencies or philanthropic foundations for support of young doctorates in regular institutional positions to the point of tenure, when the institutions themselves take over fiscal responsibilities for their support (Radner and Kuh, 1978; Schuster, 1986). The costs of these programs have been high, and the number of them funded to the present has undoubtedly been low. Nevertheless, we need follow-up information as to both the efficacy and the efficiency of such efforts to date.

The second strategy for changing the faculty age distribution involves altering the rate and composition of the faculty leaving academe. At least in part, this strategy is predicated on conventional notions of aging and productivity that we have argued are open to question. However, a substantial minority of faculty members may not be happy with their careers; they may feel blocked, stuck, demoralized, or highly dissatisfied with intrinsic and extrinsic rewards (Carnegie Foundation for the Advancement of Teaching, 1985; Schuster and Bowen, 1985). Under favorable circumstances, some of these individuals have shown themselves willing to consider voluntary mid-career options, or phased or early retirement. Patton and Palmer (1985), Hansen (1985), and Holden (1985) have analyzed these options and the conditions under which they seem to work best. Cautionary reminders are given with the variability of individual and institutional needs in mind. For example, age composition differs greatly from institution to institution; early retirement incentives are very costly, and phased retirement programs may have the unanticipated consequence of later retirements than might have been the case otherwise, or more productive people may opt for phased or early retirement in order to pursue other options. Normally, only a one-time effect on the institution's demography is obtained (Hansen, 1985).

While these strategies may result in a modest degree of change in the near future, it is a certainty that most regular faculty members, like other professional employees, will stay put for the rest of their careers. The question remains: "What might be done to enhance the vitality of existing faculty in whom resources have been invested and to whom institutional commitments have been made?" (Clark, Corcoran, and Lewis, 1986). Strategies that are premised on shared individual and organizational responsibility for vitality enhancement are clearly the most realistic, feasible, and compatible with the professional ethos. There is some urgency attending analysis of these issues and the formulation of policies to enhance vitality, and some have asserted that neither the academic profession, the disciplines, nor the institutions have given sufficient attention to the development of incentives and rewards for their staffs (Lewis and Becker, 1979; Toombs, 1985). As Schuster and Bowen (1985) state, on the basis of their thirty-eight-institution study,

> Alas, educational leaders must also ask themselves what can be done *now* when resources are scarce and may become scarcer. . . . One thing they could do is to improve the quality of interpersonal relations between administrators and faculty and among faculty members. It is our contention that an unfortunate paradox exists: on the one hand, our colleges and universities are unquestionably the leading repositories of knowledge about enlightened human relations. Yet we find that many colleges and universities do a relatively poor job in paying attention to the human needs of their instruction staff. (p. 21)

A relatively recent response to human resource development needs in higher education is faculty development programs. According to Centra (1978), by 1976, 756 American colleges and universities had reported that they were providing some form of faculty development program. A recent survey of the literature on faculty development strategies of the past twenty years by Bland and Schmitz (1988) produced a bibliography of several hundred sources and thirty-five categories of strategies. Bland and Schmitz found that "individual-level strategies were discussed eight times more frequently than department-level strategies, and five and a half times more frequently than institution-level strategies" (p. 192). Faculty development strategies have focused traditionally and almost exclusively on improving individual instructional competence; but they have not been targeted to faculty whose needs for assistance even in that domain are greatest. Moreover, they appear to have been reduced with retrenchments even while the higher education literature is arguing their importance. Reviews of faculty development programs of the 1970s conclude that levels of faculty participation and results achieved were less than impressive. As Bassis (1986) put it, "When a problem is attributed to the failure of individuals, individuals naturally avoid any identification with the problem. Faculty, like nations, do not appreciate being perceived as 'underdeveloped'" (p. 4). In addition, fewer sabbaticals are being awarded (and many eligibles feel that they cannot afford to take them because income is reduced), research funds are scarce and more competitive, and less money is available to support participation in conferences of professional associations which provide opportunities for antiobsolescence activities and networking. These commonplace observations seem to be related to faculty malaise, immobilization, reduced opportunity, and perceptions of stuckness, which we discussed earlier.

From an institutional perspective with concern for fostering the long-term vitality of existing faculty, particularly those productive and engaged faculty who are not potential candidates for the early exit strategies, several suggestive substrategies have emerged from consultation with faculty members themselves (Baldwin, 1985; Bowen and Schuster, 1986; Clark, Corcoran, and Lewis, 1986; B. Clark, 1985; Rice, 1985). The first is the importance of administrative leadership behavior and attitudes which reflect scholarly professional concerns, which recognize the full range of accomplishments, and which encourage the development of an intellectually stimulating group of colleagues who have a psychological sense of community. The second strategy focuses on supporting, functionally and symbolically, important professional values of the faculty: freedom of inquiry; interest in scholarly research activities and adequate, concentrated time in which to do their work; provision of "seed" money to initiate new studies and new instructional activities; and, of course, adequate facilities for the work to be done. For faculty members in research-oriented institutions, concerns about the quality of, and the support for, graduate students also enter this substrategy. The third area includes targeted assistance to meet the vitality needs of individual faculty, such as those whose research interests have run dry, those whose research is not currently attractive to the programmatic orientations of funding agencies, those whose teaching areas are weak in student and programmatic demand, those who experience discontinuities between role and performance expectations and the reward system, and those who confront the high productivity standards now set for probationary faculty in a time of uncertain rewards. Schuster (1985) has combined these strategies into two, sometimes indistinguishable, groups of factors, which he calls the tangibles, that bear directly on faculty working conditions and require monetary resources to ensure their availability, and the intangibles, "not so much concrete dimensions of the work place as they are reflections of attitudes toward the faculty" (p. 25).

Regardless of the human resource principles and policies of an organization, and of the enlightened and informed quality of the administrative leaders and managers, individual vitality is also a personal responsibility. Problem solving is an important part of the occupational role socialization of faculty members, physicians, engineers, lawyers, and others. Those of us in higher education expect to define and, in the main, to be the key actors in solving our own problems. But there is little to be gained in treating a complex systemic issue simply by exhorting individuals to resocialize, retrain, and remotivate. Research needs to be targeted on interactions between the life-course development of faculty members in their careers and the environmental conditions affecting individual performance. The problem of faculty vitality inheres not only in personal characteristics but also in situations, structures, and relationships. Strategies for problem analysis, research, and policy formulation in addressing faculty vitality issues must be multifaceted.

REFERENCES

Anderson, R. E. (1983). *Finance and Effectiveness: A Study of College Environments.* Princeton, NJ: Educational Testing Service.

Austin, A., and Gamson, Z. (1983). *Academic Workplace: New Demands, Heightened Tensions.* (ASHE-ERIC Higher Education Research Report 10.) Washington, DC: Association for the Study of Higher Education.

Baldridge, J. V., Curtis D. V., Acker, G., and Riley, G. L. (1978). *Policy Making and Effective Leadership.* San Francisco: Jossey-Bass.

Baldwin, Roger G. (1985). *Incentives for Faculty Vitality.* (New Directions for Higher Education, Vol. 13, No. 3.) San Francisco: Jossey-Bass.

Baldwin, Roger G. (1987). Faculty vitality: a "primitive concept" in the liberal arts college context. Paper presented at the annual meeting of the Association for the Study of Higher Education, San Diego, California.

Baldwin, Roger G. (1982). Fostering faculty vitality: options for institutions and administrators. *Administrator's Update* 4: 1–5.

Baldwin, Roger G. (1979). Adult and career development: what are the implications for faculty? *Current Issues in Higher Education* 2: 13–20.

Baldwin, Roger G., and Krotseng, M. V. (1985). Incentives in the academy: issues and options. In R. G. Baldwin (ed.), *Incentives for Faculty Vitality.* (New Directions for Higher Education, Vol. 13, No. 3.) San Francisco: Jossey-Bass.

Bassis, M. (1986). The quality of undergraduate education: toward an agenda for inquiry and action. *Teaching Sociology* 14: 1–11.

Blackburn, R. T. (1979). Academic careers: patterns and possibilities. *Current Issues in Higher Education* 2: 25–27.

Blackburn, R. T. (1982). Career phases and their influence on faculty motivation. In J. Bess (ed.), *Motivating Professors to Teach Effectively*. (New Directions for Teaching and Learning.) San Francisco: Jossey-Bass.

Blackburn, R. T. (1985). Faculty career development: theory and practice. In Clark and Lewis, *Faculty Vitality and Institutional Productivity*.

Blackburn, R. T., and Baldwin, R. G. (1983). Faculty as human resources: reality and potential. In R. G. Baldwin and R. T. Blackburn (eds.), *College Faculty: Versatile Human Resources in a Period of Constraint*. (New Directions for Research, No. 40.) San Francisco: Jossey-Bass.

Blackburn, R. T., and Lawrence, J. (1985). Aging and faculty job performance. Paper presented at the annual meeting of the American Educational Research Association, Chicago.

Blackburn, R. T., and Lawrence, J. (1986). Aging and the quality of faculty job performance. *Review of Educational Research* 56: 265–290.

Bland, C., and Schmitz, C. (1986). Faculty vitality on review: retrospect and prospect. *Journal of Higher Education* 59: 190–224.

Bowen, H. R., and Schuster, J. H. (1986). *American Professors: A National Resource Imperiled*. New York: Oxford University Press.

Boyer, C., and Lewis, D. (1985). *And on the Seventh Day: Faculty Consulting and Supplemental Income*. (ASHE-ERIC Higher Education Research Report 3.) Washington, DC: Association for the Study of Higher Education.

Braskamp, L. A., Fowler, D. L., and Ory, J. C. (1984). Faculty development and achievement: a faculty's view. *Review of Higher Education* 7: 205–222.

Brim, O. (1976). Theories of male mid-life crisis. In N. K. Schlossberg and A. D. Entive (eds.), *Counseling Adults*. Monterey, CA: Brooks/Cole.

Brooks, M., and German, K. (1983). *Meeting the Challenges: Developing Faculty Careers*. ASHE-ERIC Higher Education Research Report 3. Washington, DC: Association for the Study of Higher Education.

Butler, R. (1975). *Why Survive? Being Old in America*. New York: Harper & Row.

Cameron, K. (1985). Institutional effectiveness in higher education, an Introduction. *Review of Higher Education* 9: 1–4.

Carnegie Council on Policy Studies in Higher Education. (1980). *Three Thousand Futures: The Next Twenty Years for Higher Education*. San Francisco: Jossey-Bass.

Carnegie Foundation for the Advancement of Teaching. (1985). The faculty: deeply troubled. *Change* 17: 31–34.

Centra, J. (1978). Types of faculty development programs. *Journal of Higher Education* 49: 151–162.

Centra, J. (1985). Maintaining faculty vitality through faculty development. In Clark and Lewis, *Faculty Vitality and Institutional Productivity*.

Centra, J., and Zinn, R. I. (1976). Student points of view in ratings of college instruction. *Educational and Psychological Measurement* 36: 693–703.

Clark, Burton R. (1983). *The Higher Education System*. Berkeley: University of California Press.

Clark, Burton R. (1985). Listening to the professoriate. *Change* 17: 36–43.

Clark, S., Boyer, C., and Corcoran, M. (1985). Faculty and institutional vitality in higher education. In S. Clark and D. Lewis (eds.), *Faculty Vitality and Institutional Productivity*.

Clark, S., and Corcoran, M. (1983). Professional socialization and faculty career vitality. Paper presented at the annual meeting of the American Educational Research Association, Montreal.

Clark, S., and Corcoran, M. (1985). Individual and organizational contributions to faculty vitality: an institutional case study. In Clark and Lewis, *Faculty Vitality and Institutional Productivity*.

Clark, S., and Corcoran, M. (1986). Perspectives on the professional socialization of women faculty: a case of accumulative disadvantage? *Journal of Higher Education* 57: 20–43.

Clark, S., Corcoran, M., and Lewis, D. (1986). The case for an institutional perspective on faculty development. *Journal of Higher Education* 57: 176–195.

Clark, S., and Lewis, D., eds. (1985). *Faculty Vitality and Institutional Productivity: Critical Perspectives for Higher Education*. New York: Teachers College Press.

Clausen, J. (1972). The life course of individuals. In M. W. Riley, M. Johnson, and A. Foner (eds.), *Aging and Society. Volume 3: A Sociology of Age Stratification*. New York: Russell Sage Foundation.

Corcoran, M., and Clark, S. (1984). Professional socialization and contemporary career attitudes of three faculty generations. *Research in Higher Education* 20: 131–153.

Corcoran, M., and Clark, S. (1985). The "stuck" professor: insights into an aspect of the faculty vitality issue. In C. Watson (ed.), *The Professoriate: Occupation in Crisis*. Toronto: Ontario Institute for Studies in Higher Education.

Cross, K. P. (1981). *Adults as Learners*. San Francisco: Jossey-Bass.

Cytrynbaum, S., Lee, S., and Wadner, D. (1982). Faculty development through the life course. *Journal of Instructional Development* 5: 11–12.

Dannefer, D. (1984). Adult development and social theory: a paradigmatic reappraisal. *American Sociological Review* 49: 100–116.

Doering, M., Rhodes, S. R., and Schuster, M. (1983). *The Aging Worker: Research and Recommendations*. Beverly Hills, CA: Sage Publications.

Dubin, S. S. (1973). Updating and mid-career development and change. Paper presented at the annual meeting of the American Psychological Association, Montreal.

Eckert, R. E., and Stecklein, J. E. (1961). *Job Motivations and Satisfactions of College Teachers: A Study of Faculty Members in Minnesota Colleges*. Washington, DC: U.S. Government Printing Office.

Edgerton, R. (1980). Perspectives on faculty. Keynote address to the Kansas Conference on Postsecondary Education, Topeka.

Education Commission of the States. (1986). *Transforming the State Role in Undergraduate Education*. Denver: Educational Commission of the States.

Entrekin, L. V., and Everett, J. E. (1981). Age and mid-career crisis: an empirical study of academics. *Journal of Vocational Behavior* 19: 84–97.

Erikson, E. (1950). *Childhood and Society*. New York: Norton.

Erikson, E., and Erikson, J. (1981). On generativity and identity: from a conversation with Erik and Joan Erikson. *Harvard Educational Review* 51: 249–269.

Fase, M. (1970). *An Econometric Model of Age-Income Profiles*. Rotterdam: Rotterdam University Press.

Ference, T. P., Stoner, J. A., and Warren, E. K. (1977). Managing the career plateau. *Academy of Management Review* 2: 602–612.

Finkelstein, M. J. (1984). *The American Academic Profession*. Columbus: Ohio State University Press.

Finkelstein, M. J. (1978). Three decades of research on American academics: a descriptive portrait and synthesis of findings. Ph.D. dissertation, State University of New York, Buffalo.

Fossum, J., Arvey, R., Paradise, C., and Robbins, N. (1986). Modeling the skills obsolescence process: a psychological/economic integration. *Academy of Management Review* 11: 362–374.

Fulton, O., and ·Trow, M. (1974). Research activity in American higher education. *Sociology of Education* 47: 29–73.

Gardner, J. (1963). *Self-Renewal*. New York: Harper & Row.

Gardner, J. (1978). *Morale*. New York: Norton.

Gould, R. L. (1978). *Transformations: Growth and Change in Adult Life*. New York: Simon & Schuster.

Graham, John W., and Webb, R. H. (1979). Stocks and depreciation of human capital: new evidence from a present-value perspective. *Review of Income and Wealth* 25: 200–224.

Hall, D. T. (1976). *Careers in Organizations*. Santa Monica, CA: Goodyear.

Hall, D. T., and Nougaim, K. (1968). An examination of Maslow's need hierarchy in an organizational setting. *Organizational Behavior and Human Performance* 3: 12–35.

Hansen, W. L. (1985). Changing demography of faculty in higher education. In Clark and Lewis, *Faculty Vitality and Institutional Productivity*.

Havighurst, R. (1980). The life course of college professors and administrators. In K. W. Back (ed.), *Life Course: Integrative Theories and Exemplary Populations*. Boulder, CO: Westview Press.

Havighurst, R. (1985). Aging and productivity: the case of older faculty. In Clark and Lewis, *Faculty Vitality and Institutional Productivity*.

Hellweg, S. A., and Churchman, D. A. (1981). The academic tenure system: unplanned obsolescence in an era of retrenchment. *Planning for Higher Education* 10: 16–18.

Hill, R. E., and Miller, E. L. (1981). Job change and the middle seasons of a man's life. *Academy of Management Review* 24: 114–127.

Holden, K. (1985). Maintaining faculty vitality through early retirement options. In Clark and Lewis, *Faculty Vitality and Institutional Productivity*.

Horn, J. L., and Cattell, R. B. (1967). Age differences in fluid and crystallized intelligence. *Acta Psychologica* 26: 107–129.

Houle, C. (1980). *Continuing Learning in the Professions*. San Francisco: Jossey-Bass.

Jung, C. G. (1933). *Man in Search of a Soul*. New York: Harcourt Brace.

Kanter, R. (1977). *Men and Women of the Corporation*. New York: Basic Books.

Kanter, R. (1979). Changing the shape of work: reform in academe. *Current Issues in Higher Education* 1: 3–9.

Kaufman, H. G. (1979). Technical obsolescence: work and organizations are the key. *Engineering Education* 69: 826–830.

Kaufman, H. G. (1974). *Obsolescence and Professional Career Development*. New York: American Management Association.

Levine, M. (1980). Four models for age/work policy research. *The Gerontologist* 20: 561–574.

Levinson, D. C., Darrow, C., Klein, E., Levinson, M., and McKee, B. (1978). *The Seasons of a Man's Life*. New York: Knopf.

Lewis, D. R., and Becker, W. E. (1979). *Academic Rewards in Higher Education*. Cambridge: Ballinger.

Lindblom, C. E., and Cohen, D. K. (1979). *Usable Knowledge: Social Science and Social Problem Solving*. New Haven: Yale University Press.

Lindsay, C., Morrison, J., and Kelley, E. J. (1974). Professional obsolescence: implications for continuing professional education. *Adult Education* 25: 3–22.

London, M. (1983). Toward a theory of career motivation. *Academy of Management Review* 8: 620–630.

Machlup, Fritz. (1984). *The Economics of Information and Human Capital*, Vol. 3. Princeton: Princeton University Press.

Maher, J. (1982). Institutional vitality in higher education. *AAHE Bulletin* 34: 10.

Masland, A. (1985). Organizational culture in the study of higher education. *Review of Higher Education* 8: 157–168.

McDowell, J. (1982). Obsolescence of knowledge and career publication profiles: some evidence of differences among fields in costs of interrupted careers. *American Economic Review* 72: 752–768.

McKeachie, W. J. (1982). Enhancing productivity in postsecondary education. *Journal of Higher Education* 53: 460–464.

Meier, E., and Kerr, E. (1976). Capabilities of middle-aged and older workers: a survey of the literature. *Industrial Gerontology* 3: 147–156.

Miller, D. (1977). Counteracting obsolescence in employees and organizations. *Professional Engineer* 49: 29–31.

Mincer, J. (1974). *Schooling, Experience and Earnings*. Washington, DC: National Bureau of Economic Research.

Mincer, J. (1979). Human capital and earnings. In D. M. Windham (ed.), *Economic Dimensions of Education*. Washington, DC: National Academy of Education.

Moreh, Jacob. (1973). Human capital: deterioration and net investment. *Review of Income and Wealth* 19: 279–302.

National Center for Educational Statistics. (1985). *The Condition of Education*. Washington, DC: U.S. Department of Education.

National Endowment for the Humanities. (1984). *To Reclaim a Legacy: Report of the Study Group on Humanities in Education*. Washington, DC: National Endowment for the Humanities.

National Institute of Education. (1984). *Involvement in Learning: Realizing the Potential of American Higher Education*. Washington, DC: National Institute of Education.

National Science Foundation Advisory Council. (1978). *Report of Task Group #1: Continued Viability of Universities as Centers for Basic Research*. Washington, DC: National Science Foundation.

Near, J. P. (1985). A discriminant analysis of plateaued versus non plateaued managers. *Journal of Vocational Behavior* 26: 177–188.

Neugarten, B. L. (1968). *Middle Age and Aging*. Chicago: University of Chicago Press.

Patton, C., and Palmer, D. (1985). Maintaining faculty vitality through midcareer change options. In Clark and Lewis, *Faculty Vitality and Institutional Productivity*.

Perrucci, R., and Rothman, R. (1969). Obsolescence of knowledge and the professional career. In R. Perrucci and J. Gerstl (eds.), *The Engineers and the Social System*. New York: Wiley.

Peterson, R., and Blackburn, R. (1985). Faculty effectiveness: meeting institutional needs and expectations. *The Review of Higher Education* 9: 21–34.

Peterson, R., and Loye, D. (1967). *Conversations Toward a Definition of Institutional Vitality*. Princeton, NJ: Educational Testing Service.

Pifer, A., and Bronte, D. L. (1986). Introduction: squaring the pyramid. *Daedalus* 115: 1–11.

Planning Council. (1980). A proposal for a study on "The Future Vitality of the Faculties of the University." Memorandum to President C. Peter Magrath, University of Minnesota, Minneapolis.

Radner, T., and Kuh, C. (1978). Preserving a lost generation: policies to assure a steady flow of young scholars until the year 2000. Report and recommendation to the Carnegie Council on Policy Studies in Higher Education.

Reskin, B. (1985). Aging and productivity: careers and results. In Clark and Lewis, *Faculty Vitality and Institutional Productivity*.

Rice, R. Eugene. (1985). *Faculty Lives: Vitality and Change (A Study of the Foundation's Grants in Faculty Development, 1979–1984)*. St. Paul: Northwest Area Foundation.

Riley, Matilda White. (1987). On the significance of age in sociology. *American Sociological Review* 52: 1–14.

Riley, Matilda White. (1978). Aging, social change and the power of ideas. *Daedalus* 107: 39–52.

Riley, M. W., and Riley, J. W. (1986). Longevity and social structure: the added years. *Daedalus* 115: 51–75.

Rosen, Sherwin. (1972). Learning and experience in the labor market. *Journal of Human Resources* 7: 326–342.

Rosen, Sherwin. (1975). Measuring the obsolescence of knowledge. In F. T. Juster (ed.), *Education, Income, and Human Behavior*. New York: McGraw-Hill.

Rosen, Sherwin. (1983). Specialization and human capital. *Journal of Labor Economics* 1: 43–49.

Rosen, Sherwin. (1987). Vintage effects and education. In G. Psacharapoulos (ed.), *Economics of Education Research and Studies*. New York: Pergamon Press.

Rosenzweig, M. R. (1976). Nonlinear earnings functions, age and experience: a non-dogmatic reply and some additional evidence. *Journal of Human Resources*, Winter.

Rosow, J. (1974). *Socialization to Old Age*. Berkeley: University of California Press.

Rossi, A. S. (1980). Life-span theory and women's lives. *Signs: Journal of Women in Culture and Society* 6: 4–32.

Rothman, R., and Perrucci, R. (1970). Organizational careers and professional expertise. *Administrative Science Quarterly* 15: 282–293.

Rush, J., Peacock, A. C., and Milkovich, G. T. (1980). Career stages: a partial test of Levinson's model of life/career stages. *Journal of Vocational Behavior* 16: 347–359.

Sarason, S. B. (1977). *Work, Aging, and Social Change: Professionals and the One Life-One Career Imperative*. New York: Free Press.

Schuster, J. (1985). Faculty vitality: observations from the field. In R. Baldwin (ed.), *Incentives for Faculty Vitality*. (New Directions for Higher Education, Vol. 13, No. 3.) San Francisco: Jossey-Bass.

Schuster, J. (1986). Transformational leadership for enhancing faculty effectiveness. In M. Waggoner, R. Alfred, M. Francis, and M. Peterson (eds.), *Academic Effectiveness: Transforming Colleges and Universities for the 1990s*. Ann Arbor, University of Michigan.

Schuster, J., and Bowen, H. (1985). The faculty at risk. *Change* 17: 13–21.

Shearer, R. L., and Steger, J. A. (1975). Manpower obsolescence: a new definition and empirical investigation of personal variables. *Academy of Management Journal* 18: 263–275.

Sheehy, G. (1974). *Passages: Predictable Crises of Adult Life*. New York: Dutton.

Shin, K., and Putman, R. (1982). Age and academic-professional honors. *Journal of Gerontology* 37: 220–229.

Sonnenfeld, J. (1978). Dealing with an aging workforce. *Harvard Business Review* 56: 81–92.

Sonnenfeld, J., and Kotter, J. P. (1982). The maturation of career theory. *Human Relations* 35: 19–46.

Sonner, J. (1983). Combating technical obsolescence in ET faculty. *Engineering Education* 73: 803–804.

Stumpf, S. A., and Rabinowitz, S. (1981). Career stage as a moderator of performance relationships with facets of job satisfaction and role perception. *Journal of Vocational Behavior* 18: 202–218.

Super, D. E., and Bachrach, P. B. (1957). *Scientific Careers and Vocational Development Theory*. New York: Teachers College Press.

Taylor, L. (1968). *Occupational Sociology*. New York: Oxford.

Toombs, W. (1985). Faculty vitality: the professional context. In R. Baldwin (ed.), *Incentives for Faculty Vitality*. (New Directions of Higher Education, Vol. 13, No. 3.) San Francisco: Jossey-Bass.

Valliant, G. (1977). *Adaptation to Life*. Boston: Little, Brown.

Valliant, G., and Milofsky, E. (1980). Natural history of male psychological health: empirical evidence for Erikson's model of the life cycle. *American Journal of Psychiatry* 137: 1348–1359.

Van West, P. (1982). The greying professoriate: theories, perceptions and policies. Mimeographed. Normal: Center for Higher Education, Illinois State University.

Watkins, B. T. (1982). A new academic disease: faculty burnout. *Chronicle of Higher Education* (24 March): 1, 8.

Williams, D., Olswang, S. G., and Hargett, G. (1986). A matter of degree: faculty morale as a function of involvement in institutional decisions during times of financial distress. *Review of Higher Education* 9: 287–301.

Willie, R., and Stecklein, J. (1982). A three-decade comparison of college faculty characteristics, satisfactions, activities, and attitudes. *Research in Higher Education* 16: 81–93.

Willis, S. L., and Tosti-Vasey, J. L. (1986). Professional obsolescence in mid-career college faculty. Paper presented at the annual meeting of the Eastern Psychological Association, New York.

Zuckerman, H., and Merton, R. (1972). Age, aging and age structure in science. In M. W. Riley, M. Johnson, and A. Foner (eds.), *Aging and Society. Volume 3: A Society of Age Stratification*. New York: Russell Sage Foundation.

Faculty Participation
in Strategic Policy Making

David D. Dill
University of North Carolina at Chapel Hill
and
Karen Peterson Helm
North Carolina State University

Turning and turning in the widening gyre
The falcon cannot hear the falconer;
Things fall apart; the center cannot hold;
Mere anarchy is loosed upon the world,
The blood-dimmed tide is loosed, and everywhere
The ceremony of innocence is drowned;
The best lack all conviction, while the worst
Are full of passionate intensity

William Butler Yeats

A strong case has been made that institutions of higher education in the United States are confronted not simply with increased competition due to declines in enrollment and economic support, but with a fundamental transformation in the nature of their environments (Cameron and Ulrich, 1986). This transformed context will, in turn, require academic decision-makers to think in more fundamental terms about essential programs and processes, emphasizing a strategic perspective sensitive to positioning academic institutions among the shifting sands of opportunities and constraints (Keller, 1983). This entrepreneurial view of academic decision-making—distinctively and characteristically American, one should add—is at odds with the European and more recent American tradition of faculty control and gradual incremental change in academic institutions (Jencks and Riesman, 1977). Thus, the advocates of ''strategic management'' in academic settings pose unsettling questions about the pace of academic change, about the most efficacious means of governing colleges and universities in turbulent times, and about the internal balance of power within academic institutions. What, for example, is the apropriate faculty role in "strategic" decision-making? Are traditional conceptions of "shared authority" obsolete? What are the effective mechanisms for sustaining faculty involvement? Finally, are traditional conceptions of faculty authority and participation valid in an environment in which capital investment decisions, fund raising, and student recruitment play such a critical role? Like Yeats's vision of impending revolution, our faith in traditional forms of academic authority is challenged, we are no longer certain as to the appropriateness of existing forms of governance, let alone the new forms to be desired.

Assuming that these transformational conditions and the corresponding demands upon existing governance and decision-making processes are a reality, what has been written about the appropriate form of faculty participation during this new period? Surprisingly, very little. Our review of the major bibliographic indices, leading journals of higher education, and the most recent review of the literature of the field (Floyd, 1985) reveals that the literature on faculty participation per se and on governance, which was such a rich field as recently as 1978 (Millett, 1978; Mortimer and McConnell, 1978), has essentially dried up. Even though there have been some surveys suggesting declines in faculty involvement in decision making (Anderson, 1983), there has been little research on or serious analysis of the issues confronting academic governance during the last ten years.

In this chapter, we will assay the nature of faculty participation in strategic policy-making. First, we will briefly review the history of faculty participation in academic governance in the United States. Second, we will clarify what we mean by strategic policy-making. Third, we will explore the increasing differentiation of the American system of higher education. This differentiation, well established in the research literature, suggests that the ideal of faculty involvement in decision making is a reality for only a small proportion of academic institutions, and that current forces suggest this reality will not change. Fourth, we will review a set of useful guidelines for designing joint participation processes developed from the literature and test these guidelines against six contemporary case studies of faculty participation in strategic policy-making. Finally, we will conclude with an analysis of the current logic for faculty participation in academic governance, and we will compare this view with the insights to be gained from the traditional basis for faculty authority and control.

There is ample theoretical and empirical support for the proposition that as the environmental context of an organization shifts, there is pressure for change within the organization, including the structure of authority and the decision-making process (Aldrich, 1979; Katz and Kahn, 1978; Zammuto, 1986). It is important, however, to stress at the outset that any discussion of the authority structure of an organization cannot be easily and simply separated from the organization's basic values. Satow (1975) has suggested that organizations dominated by professionals, such as academic organizations, are "value-rational'' organizations, in which members of the organization have an absolute belief in the values of the enterprise for their own sake, independent of the institution's prospects for success. Satow further suggests that value-rational organizations such as academic institutions are not only identified by their values but bound together by them. As Wolff (1969) similarly argued, reflecting on the student disruptions of the 1960s, the structure of authority in an academic organization is inextricably linked to the types of values and goals the institution pursues. Thus, the nature of the academic enterprise, both its pattern of authority and its basic techniques of social organization, is dependent upon its core values or culture (Dill, 1982).

Therefore, as this essay will suggest, a study of faculty participation in decision making is not simply an inquiry into the various forms or processes of decision making, but an inquiry into the nature of the academic enterprise itself.

THE THREE PERIODS OF FACULTY PARTICIPATION

The evolution of American higher education in the twentieth century has been reflected in three different periods of faculty participation in decision making. These three periods will be termed *faculty control, democratic participation,* and *strategic policy-making.*

The history and development of academic governance in the United States has been carefully chronicled by Hofstadter and Metzger (1955). The conception of *faculty control* and authority which informs the 1966 ''Statement on Government of Colleges and Universities'' is a direct descendant of the medieval university, which operated as a guild of academic men who controlled their own activities. The rituals of the guildlike model are still visible in the direct control of Oxford and Cambridge colleges by English dons, but this romantic image disguises an important conversion in the English and European universities. The evolution of church control into state control over the universities in England and Europe made academics government employees. Thus the state assumed the role of providing the necessary capital and operating funds and delegated to the faculty the control of the institution.

While the founding of Harvard and William and Mary in the seventeenth century followed the English model of faculty control, there were numerous forces which quickly eroded this model: an insufficient number of experienced professors, sectarian control of the institutions, and limited crown, colonial, and, later, state support. These unique American conditions led to the evolution of institutional governing boards composed of laymen, principally sectarian representatives, who provided the legitimating authority for the institution, which in Europe was provided by the state. The legality of this American model was affirmed in the Dartmouth College case which established that these boards of control were ''corporations'' independent of the control of the state. Thus the

American model of academic governance throughout the eighteenth and most of the nineteenth century was of small colleges (i.e., an average of 10 faculty and 92 students in 1870), with a young teaching staff ruled by a president and a board of trustees. The development of the research universities in the late nineteenth century, with their conception of the faculty member as scholar, changed the nature of the faculty and helped to recover the concept of faculty control and authority. Thus, as Jencks and Riesman (1977) argued, an "academic revolution" occurred throughout the twentieth century, in which the faculty came to possess primary influence over governance, at least in the elite academic institutions. The appearance of the 1966 "Statement on Government of Colleges and Universities," however, suggests that this period was the high-water mark for faculty control and also reveals that even at high tide, there were large numbers and varieties of institutions untouched by the waters.

During the late 1950s, the rapid growth of enrollments, the changing composition of student bodies, and a volatile political climate combined to raise a fundamental question regarding the integrity of the academy (Millett, 1978). During this period, there were intense debates concerning the representativeness of existing governance mechanisms and an interest in experimenting with forms of institutional decision-making which emphasized *democratic participation*. Particularly at the most prestigious colleges and universities where faculty controlled the governance process, the dominant coalition of faculty members and administrators was confronted by demands to democratize the governance process and to include students and other disaffected constituencies in traditional faculty senates (Dill, 1971; Hodgkinson, 1974). Less noted during this period was the growing power exercised by administrators and legislators in new and rapidly growing community colleges, state colleges, and private colleges where faculty control had never flowered (Mortimer and McConnell, 1978). In the late 1960s and the 1970s, this issue came to the fore with the development of collective bargaining. While certain prestigious colleges flirted with or endorsed collective bargaining (cf. Oberlin College and New York University), principally because of a movement toward *too* democratic a process and/or administrative usurpation, the primary location for collective bargaining in higher education was in those community colleges, state colleges, and small private colleges which had never experienced a period of faculty control (Baldridge et al., 1981; Carnegie Council on Policy Studies in Higher Education, 1977). Ironically, collective bargaining extended the concept of democratic participation to the faculties of these institutions, since the process presented in a legal context some of the same issues of influence of a disaffected constituency lacking formal authority which were addressed by student demands for participation. Also, many collective bargaining contracts democratized the governance process of their institution because nontraditional constituencies such as counselors, librarians, and research personnel were defined as part of the bargaining units which subsequently negotiated policies on the terms and conditions of work. Thus the period of democratic participation included demands for the extension of participation to new groups as well as to those faculties which had never gained faculty control. This period spawned a rich literature on participation and governance (Floyd, 1985).

The period of democratic participation has ended, however. The beginnings of the sea change were detectable in the early 1970s as the strong economic support experienced by higher education since World War II was eroded by inflation and energy costs. Faculty members on all campuses fought for greater influence over decisions on the allocation of financial resources, with particular concern for faculty salaries. By the late 1970s, a series of trends coincided to presage a genuinely new environment for higher education (Mortimer and Tierney, 1979). At the end of the decade, four resource flows critical to institutions of higher education had stabilized or were in actual decline: student enrollments, federal support for research and development, federal support for student financial aid, and real family discretionary income (Leslie, 1980; Zammuto and Cameron, 1985). The effect of this environmental change was to lay bare the underlying market competition among colleges and universities for students, faculty members, revenues, and, ultimately, prestige. This competitive market has existed throughout American history but was rendered practically invisible by the remarkable and continuing growth in market demand for higher education which existed from the founding of Harvard College until the late 1970s. This increasing demand was made possible by the continual growth in the size of the college-age cohort and the proportion of the age cohort attending college, by growth in federal and state allocations, and by a rising standard of living for the population as a whole. These growth conditions in enrollment and economic support have now shifted to an invironment of decline (Zammuto, 1986).

The proposed institutional response to this new environment of higher education is *strategic policy-making* designed to help administrators evaluate their institutional strengths and weaknesses in the light of environmental conditions and to allocate resources accordingly (Keller, 1983). These transformational conditions are likely both to continue and to intensify through this century, as colleges and universities confront profit-making, degree-granting agencies with superior new technologies which compete effectively with the traditional functions of teaching, research, and service (Cameron and Ulrich, 1986). Unlike the earlier periods of faculty control and democratic participation, it can now be argued that the *substance* of governance has changed. Institutions will not be faced primarily with maintenance decisions, such as the allocation of incremental budgets, the administration of traditional curricula and programs, and the governing of student behavior. The governance issues of the last ten years and for the foreseeable future will involve policy issues affecting the nature of the enterprise: the types of research, teaching, and service programs to be offered; developing priorities among these programs; and allocating (or reallocating) resources to the highest priority programs (Shirley, 1983).

The tenets, respectively, of faculty control and democratic participation, while different, were articulated during a period of growth and general prosperity for American higher education. The current environment of scarcity and competition is thus strange to both governance perspectives. Therefore, the values and the structural mechanisms of the period of growth are now being applied in a new period of strategic policy-making in which academic decision-makers must confront the most substantive and divisive issues faced by institutions of higher education.

STRATEGIC POLICY-MAKING

The concept of strategic policy-making emerges in direct response to the environment of decline now influencing higher education (Zammuto, 1986). Three types of internal institutional strategies have been articulated to deal with decline: (1) *domain offense* involves more effort being put into existing operations to improve effectiveness and to protect market share; (2) *domain consolidation* is a variant of domain offense which involves cutting back in some operations, and reallocating, to improve efficiency; and (3) *domain creation and substitution* require eliminating weak programs and adding new, more "profitable" programs.

There is substantial debate in the literature as to whether all, or even the majority of, institutions will need to address the strategic turnaround strategies of domain creation and substitution (Cameron and Ulrich, 1986) or whether the operating changes of domain offense and consolidation are of principal importance (Chaffee, 1984; Hardy, 1987). We anticipate that the choice of strategy will necessarily vary by type of institution. The types of policy issues in higher education, however, will very likely be the same from institution to institution (Hardy et al., 1983). These policy choices include (1) the elaboration of the basic mission into specific programs and services offered the public; (2) the character of critical inputs such as the type of academic staff, the nature of student enrollments, and the programs for external fund-raising; (3) the academic infrastructure necessary to accomplish the mission, for example, the types of buildings and facilities to construct, the major research equipment to be purchased, and the development of computer systems and libraries; and (4) the structure and forms of academic governance, including the design of the committee system, and the regulations concerning promotion and tenure.

How are faculties to participate in these types of policy choices? The joint AAUP/ACE/AGB "Statement on Government of Colleges and Universities" (1966) has generally served as the standard reference for an *ideal* policy on academic governance. The document assumes three spheres of decision making.

The faculty has primary responsibility for curriculum, subject matter and methods of instruction, research, faculty status, and those aspects of student life which relate to the educational process. The governing board and administration have primary responsibility for maintaining the endowment and obtaining the needed capital and operating funds. Shared responsibility and authority exist in areas such as the framing of long-range plans, deciding on buildings and other facilities, allocating financial resources, and determining short- and long-range priorities. A comparison of this document with the strategic decisions outlined by Hardy et al. (1983) suggests that the majority of strategic policy issues fall within the sphere of governance labeled as *shared authority*. From this perspective, the types of decisions confronting colleges and universities in the years ahead should logically require *more* consultation and sharing of authority between administrators and faculty than may have been characteristic of the incremental growth conditions of previous periods of academic governance.

In fact, the research suggests that faculty participation and shared authority is declining during this period of strategic policy-making (Anderson, 1983; Bowen and Glenny, 1980), and that the existing mechanisms and policies seem inadequate to the task (Floyd, 1985). In a study of representative universities, state colleges, liberal arts colleges, and community colleges, Anderson (1983) discovered a constant decline in faculty perceptions of "democratic governance" between 1970 and 1981. Faculty members toward the end of the decade perceived that control, power, and decision making were more closely held by administrators; that "wide faculty involvement" in important decisions about how the institution would be governed was less characteristic; and that the concept of shared authority (faculty and administrators jointly deciding) was not as evident in campus governance. These results are somewhat predictable in that studies in a variety of organizations suggest that as competition, conflict, and demands for survival increase in an organization, decision making tends to become centralized and less participatory (Zammuto, 1986). Anderson (1983), however, asserts that while administrators of the most "effective" institutions were not shy in exercising authority when needed, particularly in personnel decisions, the most effective institutions were more characterized by shared authority than were the less effective institutions.

THE REALITIES AND POSSIBILITIES
OF SHARED AUTHORITY

While shared authority and joint participation have remained ideal types for the governance of all academic institutions, one of the most consistent discoveries of research on academic institutions is the variation among institutions in the American system on faculty participation and control (Baldridge et al., 1978; Kenen and Kenen, 1978; Mortimer, Gunne, and Leslie, 1976; Ross, 1977). A national survey by Baldridge et al. (1978) presented substantial evidence as to the differentiation between academic institutions in the nature of their environments (e.g., public control versus private flexibility), the nature of the professional task (e.g., the quality of students and the faculty's involvement in research), and institutional size and complexity. On the specific issue of faculty involvement in governance, there were substantial differences between types of institutions. Utilizing a revised version of the typology developed by the Carnegie Commission on Higher Education, Baldridge et al. (1978) suggested that faculty primacy over academic matters and participation in strategic planning and budgeting issues was most likely at research universities and elite liberal arts colleges. The faculty's autonomy and control over their own work, and particularly faculty participation in what we have termed here *strategic policy issues,* declined steadily as one climbed down the pecking order of academic prestige, through public comprehensive colleges, public colleges, and private liberal arts colleges (especially sectarian institutions), and it was least evident in community colleges and private junior colleges. In a comparable analysis of national data collected by T. Parsons and G. Platt, Ross (1977) concluded that faculty's perceptions of their influence on general educational policy and faculty personnel issues were greater in those institutions with higher faculty qualifications as measured by possession of a Ph.D. and scholarly productivity. Similar institutional differences in faculty influence were also identified by Mortimer et al. (1976) and by Kenen and Kenen (1978), who emphasize the primacy of administrators in the governance of community colleges and sectarian colleges. While the concentration of faculty autonomy and shared authority in the research universities and elite liberal arts colleges is clear in each of these studies, the research also consistently reports the obvious control of administration and trustees over financial policy (Finkelstein, 1984).

The most recent study of authority patterns in American higher education confirms the survey reports of Anderson (1983). Faculty control and shared authority, while still in existence, has retreated even further into the ranks of elite research universities and liberal arts colleges; the differentiation between types of institutions is increasing, not decreasing (Clark, 1987). Clark (1987) has suggested the term *authority environments* to describe the general understandings, ground rules, and frames of governance which characterize academic organizations. The research university is characterized by collegial control of major academic decision-making, faculty criteria for key administrative appointments, and a process of department-based, bottom-up governance. At the other end of the spectrum, the community college authority environment is characterized by a more bureaucratic decision-making process on faculty hiring and curriculum, by more centralized procedures bearing the imprint of school administration, and by contractual obligations detailed in collective bargaining agreements:

Interviews in institutions situated between the extremes of research universities and community colleges demonstrated that as one moves up the status hierarchy, one encounters more professional control, and as one moves down, one observes more administrative dominance and even autocracy. (Clark, 1987, p. 268)

There are gray areas in such a hierarchy. For example, Baldridge et al. (1978) argued that many liberal arts colleges may closely approximate the collegial ideal of shared authority on institutionwide decisions, because of a weak departmental structure and small size. Similarly, Finkelstein and Pfinister (1984), in a study of liberal arts colleges drawn from Carnegie Classifications I and II, discovered an increase in faculty participation in collegewide decision-making, budgetary planning, and promotion and tenure based upon data through 1978. These authors attributed these changes to an increase in faculty expertise and sophistication in these settings brought about by the increased market supply of Ph.D.'s.

Research on collective bargaining confirms the argument for a differentiated system of higher education. The majority of bargaining units have been formed in that stratum of higher education which already possessed little faculty autonomy or participation (Baldridge et al., 1981). Further, the focus of collective bargaining has been limited to the terms and conditions of contracts (Begin, 1978). To the extent that the relationship between collective bargaining and strategic policy-making has been subject to research, it suggests that collective negotiation has led to greater administrative centralization on strategic issues outside of the terms and conditions of employment (Floyd, 1985).

This consistent pattern of research suggests that while the concept of shared authority and faculty participation in decision making is an "ideal type" for all academic institutions, it has consistently occurred only within a limited stratum of American higher education (Baldridge, 1982). Furthermore, as recent research indicates, the "authority environments" conducive to faculty participation are becoming more rare, being eroded by state and federal legislation, and by entrepreneurial or autocratic executive decision-making. The tradition of faculty authority and control is increasingly restricted to a certain class of institutions: elite research universities and liberal arts colleges.

THE PROCESS APPROACH TO
FACULTY PARTICIPATION

The limited contemporary research on governance suggests that neither the traditional forms of faculty control (e.g., departmental autonomy and faculty senates) nor the structures of democratic participation (e.g., unicameral senates and collective bargaining) appear to be useful models for faculty participation during the evolving period of strategic policy-making (Powers and Powers, 1984). Instead, a focus on process, on consultative decision-making and the means of involving and utilizing faculty experience and expertise, is advocated as likely to be a more fruitful and more generalizable approach (Hardy et al., 1983; Mortimer and McConnell, 1978; Powers and Powers, 1983). Although the models vary, six general stages of consultation can be detected.

1. *Early consultation*. It is critical that the individuals or groups to be involved in decision making have the opportunity to consider the phrasing of issues as well as the formulation of alternatives well before choices are made. We do not judge as consultation informing faculty groups of decisions after they are made and asking for assistance in implementation. Early consultation also involves the effective use of experience and expertise. The forming of committees based upon political representation without regard to the professional experience or expertise of the members lessens the potential for creative and strategically valuable contributions (Bradford and Bradford, 1981). Finally, early consultation does not stifle but encourages managerial initiative in the phrasing of issues and alternatives. A good example of this technique was the leadership of Clark Kerr, who as chancellor at Berkeley regularly would draft a report for the discussion of a major issue, discuss it at length with a faculty committee, and then revise it in light of their comments (McConnell and Mortimer, 1971). Similarly, Powers and Powers (1983) advocate initiating consultation processes through the circulation of a "white paper."

2. *Joint formulation of procedures*. A characteristic of a successful strategic policy-making process is *a priori* joint consultation over the procedures to be followed in the consultation process itself. This, of course, is a characteristic of the collective bargaining process, but as Hardy et al. (1983) indicate, the design of the processes to be utilized for decision making is itself one of the critical strategic policy issues to be considered.

3. *Time to formulate responses*. Timing is often used by administrators as a device for avoiding participation, for example, scheduling key student-related decisions over the summer months. Involvement of faculty expertise and perspective requires adequate time for consideration and response. However, some administrators err by not setting explicit timetables for consultation and adhering to them.

4. *Availability of information*. Within obvious limits, such as confidential personnel files, faculty engaged in consultation should have access to the information they need. One characteristic of successful faculty committee work is that the committee is often assigned a staff member from a related administrative office (e.g., finance or institutional research) to help provide data and the interpretation of data.

5. *Adequate feedback*. Following the rendering of advice, those participating in the consultation deserve an adequate response. While there is an obvious reluctance to provide written responses on critical personnel issues, the provision of a basis for the modification or the rejection of a committee report is critical to

preventing the type of alienation which often exists between faculty and administrators (Austin and Gamson, 1983).

6. *Communication of decision.* How a decision is to be implemented or communicated is a fair issue for discussion during the consultation process. Implementation is a stage where many decisions founder precisely because inadequate time has been given to examining the acceptability and adoption of the decision (Vroom, 1984). Given the unique organization of colleges and universities, in which "professional judgment" controls so many of the operating procedures of the institution, implementation is a much more critical step than in the "top-down" hierarchy of corporate settings.

While these six processes appear unexceptional, there has been little research or study of the application of this model in the new period of strategic policy-making. What type of process works in the critical areas of program review and evaluation, priority setting, and budgetary allocation or reallocation? How is faculty expertise utilized in this process? What is the appropriate balance and relationship between *ad hoc* advisory groups and ongoing structures? How is "shared authority" achieved? In the section which follows, we will analyze several case studies to gain some insight into the utility of this model of consultative strategic policy-making. We will then review the implications of these cases for our understanding of the process and bases of faculty participation in policy making and turn to implications for research.

MODES OF FACULTY PARTICIPATION IN STRATEGIC DECISION-MAKING

A review of leading research journals, popular administrative journals, monographs available from the National Center for Higher Education Management Systems, and a small sample of conference presentations and institutional documents produced only a handful of case studies describing a strategic decision-policy process in which the pattern of faculty involvement could be clearly identified (see Table 1). In this section, we will examine some of the patterns observed among these case studies in an effort to highlight the more common modes of faculty participation. Then, we will look more closely at six of the cases which best illustrate these modes and evaluate them according to the six stages of consultation described in the model above.

Faculty are involved in strategic policy-making in a variety of functional areas, which are well described by Zammuto's (1986) three categories. Among the processes normally resulting in domain offense strategies are program review, curriculum reform, reorganization, and revision of promotion and tenure policies. Among the processes normally resulting in domain consolidation strategies are planning and budgeting. Among the processes resulting in domain creation and substitution strategies are retrenchment and related policies governing the declaration of fiscal exigency and releasing tenured faculty.

TABLE 1. Strategic Domains and Modes of Participation by Institutional Type[a]

Type (see below)	Number	Strategic domains			Modes of participation			
		Domain offense	Domain consolidation	Domain substitution/ creation	Ad hoc coms.	Standing coms.	Joint coms.	Separate coms.
R/Us	10	1	5	4	6	4	4	6
D/Gs	4	2	1	1	3	1	2	2
C/Us	5	2	3	0	2	3	4	1
L/As	5	3	2	0	2	3	3	2
C/Cs	1	0	1	0	0	1	0	1
Total:	25	8	12	5	13	12	13	12

R/Us (Research Universities): Berkeley (Trow, 1983); Duke (Franklin, 1982; Peterson, 1985); Emory (Teel, 1981); Michigan State (Crawley, 1981); NCSU (Peterson and Moazed, 1986); Princeton (Herring et al., 1979); Stanford (Chaffee, 1983); SUNY–Albany (Caruthers and Lott, 1981); West Virginia (Kieft, 1978; Poulton, 1980); Univ. of Minnesota (Heydinger, 1982).

D/Gs (Doctoral Granting Universities): Bowling Green Univ. (Moore, 1978); Ohio Univ. (Armijo et al., 1980); Old Dominion (Darby et al., 1979); Univ. of Vermont (Tashman, Carlson and Parke, 1984).

C/Us (Comprehensive Universities): King's College (Farmer, 1983); Mt. St. Mary's (Campbell, 1983); Univ. of Richmond (Vulgamore, 1981); Univ. of Toledo (Reid, 1982); Western Washington Univ. (Kieft, 1978).

L/As (Liberal Arts Colleges): Birmingham–Southern (Berte and O'Neil, 1980); Curry College (Hill, 1985); Lewis and Clark (Arch and Kirschner, 1984); Villa Maria (Kieft, 1978); Willamette Univ. (Armijo et al., 1980).

C/Cs (Community Colleges): Lorain County Community College (Armijo et al., 1980).

[a]Based upon *The Carnegie Classification of Higher Education* (Carnegie Foundation, 1987).

Strategic policy-making processes differ not only according to functional area, but also according to two characteristics describing the modes of faculty participation: duration of involvement and degree of integration with administrative decision-making. First, in some cases, faculty are involved permanently in ongoing processes through representation on *standing committees*, such as faculty senate committees or budget and planning committees. In others, faculty are consulted temporarily on episodic issues through *ad hoc committees* charged, for example, with retrenchment planning, reorganization, or mission review. Second, faculty in some cases serve on *joint committees* as equal voting partners with administrators, for example, in recommending priorities among budget

TABLE 2. Strategic Domains by Modes of Faculty Participation

	Ad hoc com.	Standing com.	Joint com.	Separate com.
I. Domain offense	7	1	2	6
II. Domain consolidation	1	11	10	2
III. Domain substitution	5	—	1	4
Total ($N = 25$)	13	12	13	12

requests. In other cases, the administration seeks faculty opinion by consulting a *separate committee,* as a distinct stage in the decision-making process.

Among the case studies in our small, certainly unscientific sample, the mode of faculty participation as described by these two characteristics did not vary according to class of institutions. Research universities, comprehensive universities, and liberal arts colleges seem to involve faculty in similar ways. Instead, the mode of faculty participation varied according to functional area (Table 2).

In processes involving domain offense (for example, program review, curriculum review, and reorganization), the mode of faculty participation is generally through separate *ad hoc* committees. Policies in these particular areas need be established only on a periodic basis and are quite dependent on the faculty's disciplinary expertise. Frequently, such processes involve faculty from a given set of disciplines or fields, rather than representatives from the institution as a whole.

In processes involving domain consolidation (for example, planning and budgeting), the mode of faculty participation is generally through joint standing committees. In contrast to program evaluation efforts, these decisions require institutionwide processes and are not discipline-specific. Here, faculty represent the general interests of critical stakeholders, much as trustees.

In processes involving domain creation and substitution (for example, retrenchment and fiscal exigency policies), the mode of faculty participation is through separate *ad hoc* committees. The reason for such committees to have only a temporary life is obvious; however, the rationale for separating faculty from administrative deliberations on such pivotal decisions deserves closer scrutiny, and we will return to this issue later.

Now we will examine in greater detail six case studies which provided sufficient information on faculty participation to permit analysis of the process of faculty involvement. Not surprisingly, these six institutions reflect our earlier point regarding the limited group of institutions whose authority environments can be characterized as *shared authority.* Four of the cases describe strategic policy-making in Research I universities, one case a Research II university, and one case a Liberal Arts I college (Carnegie Foundation for the Advancement of Teaching, 1987). We conclude with the latter case, a negative instance, because it summarizes a number of the themes we wish to explore in the final sections.

THE UNIVERSITY OF CALIFORNIA AT BERKELEY

The extensive review and reorganization of the biological sciences undertaken by the University of California at Berkeley in the late 1970s and early 1980s (Trow, 1983) is an example of a domain offense strategy employing, initially, a separate *ad hoc* faculty committee. The committee's deliberations resulted in a strategic policy to secure and invest new resources in redefined program emphases in an effort to protect the university's high national rankings in those fields.

At Berkeley, as elsewhere, the biological disciplines and hence the academic departments were originally defined according to categories of living things, for example, zoology, botany, bacteriology, and entymology. As a consequence of developments in molecular theory, biochemistry, and advanced research technologies, biologists have in this century turned to the study of underlying similarities in the composition of all living organisms. Molecular genetics, cell biology, and other new disciplines emerged, each overlapping the more traditional disciplines and crossing departmental lines. At Berkeley, the result was nineteen or twenty different departments in the biological sciences located in five schools, most of which had developed a full complement of faculty representing the same range of "new" disciplines.

Administrators' awareness of the need to reorganize the biological sciences was precipitated by the poor condition and the growing obsolescence of the university's research and teaching laboratories. Departments began having difficulty competing successfully for the best young faculty, and a national assessment of graduate programs showed Berkeley's rank falling in several fields at once. An external review committee reported that graduate programs had not developed fully in spite of outstanding individual faculty members; the lack of an effective means for coordination and interchange in the newer, interdisciplinary subject areas limited development in several emerging fields.

There was widespread agreement that a new building and vast improvements in laboratory facilities were necessary to attract desirable faculty and to regain Berkeley's standing. In order to evaluate exactly what kinds of faculties were needed, the administration conducted an inventory of all biological research on campus and organized the information according to areas of research rather than by department. As expected, the inventory highlighted the expected organizational issues. In response, the administration appointed an *ad hoc* faculty Internal Biological Sciences Review Committee to evaluate all programs and to analyze space needs. Four subcommittees were organized around the four interdepartmental research areas that had emerged during the inventory stage.

The committee's final report outlined the rationale for recommended changes based on the evolution of the biological sciences; recommended specific research areas deserving of special attention; assessed the space needs for all biological fields, regardless of department; recommended the establishment of interdepartmental "affinity groups"; and recommended that laboratory facilities in the new building be organized in a way that would permit researchers from different departments to focus on similar problems in a common work environment. The committee considered but declined a recommendation to reorganize all biological departments into a single college with internal divisions more closely allied with emerging research areas than with traditional disciplines. Instead, the committee recommended the establishment of a new standing committee, an Advisory Council on Biology, which would advise the deans and the chancellor on strengthening the biological sciences and on the distribution of faculty positions and the composition of faculty search committees.

The report and each of its recommendations were approved by the chancellor, who has been successful in obtaining support for the new building from the system administration, the legislature, and private donors. Until the time when major reorganization becomes appropriate, the Advisory Committee will function as a means of tapping faculty expertise regarding the development of resources in areas where Berkeley can make the most significant contributions to the fields of biology.

WEST VIRGINIA UNIVERSITY

West Virginia University (WVU) is the state's land-grant and major research university with an enrollment of approximately 21,000. Since the late 1960s, WVU has developed an integrated, comprehensive planning process that translates academic goals into the annual operating budget and influences facilities management (Poulton, 1980; Kieft, 1978). This domain consolidation strategy utilizes a standing committee comprised jointly of faculty members, administrators, and students.

The rationale for faculty participation in the annual planning and budgeting process is based on the beliefs that an academic plan ought to provide the cornerstone for planning in other functional areas, including the budget, and that faculty ought to play a key role in describing the future of academic programs, within situational constraints and parameters. Participation is effected at two levels. At the institutional level, a University Council on Planning advises the president on the formulation of planning assumptions and reviews the plans and budget proposals submitted by group activity centers (i.e., academic departments, divisions, and centers). Its membership includes 9 faculty members, 3 students, and 3 *ex officio* administrators, including the provost for planning, who sits in the chair.

At the program level, faculty participate in the development of local planning assumptions and of annual plans. By 1977–1978, 30 of 45 group activity centers had appointed planning councils whose membership and responsibilities are similar to the University Council on Planning.

The annual planning and budgeting process at WVU includes the following steps. The University Council on Planning develops a set of institutional planning assumptions for a given period of time, which are then used by group activity centers to develop planning assumptions for their own units, according to local planning processes. The group activity centers then prepare plans according to a common outline, which requires that all proposals for new programs be ranked in priority order, be justified according to local and university planning assumptions, and detail budget requirements.

The first level of review by the president's office includes oral presentations by the dean or director of each group activity center. Then, the university's annual plan and operating budget request is prepared using the planning assumptions prepared by the University Council on Planning as criteria for evaluating program proposals and identifying priorities among competing claims for resources.

A few months after the university's annual plan and budget request are submitted to the Board of Regents, each group activity center has the opportunity to alter its priorities and to suggest new proposals based on information and needs that may have come to light since the process was initiated. Again, each change is justified and evaluated on the basis of stated objectives and the decision criteria identified earlier. Once funds are allocated by the Board of Regents, the preliminary plan and budget requests are translated into operating plans for the coming year.

Throughout the year, group activity centers may submit to the president's office requests to alter their plans and to shift resources accordingly. All requests are reviewed against the same decision criteria used throughout the planning process.

At West Virginia University, this planning and budgeting process is the means of coordinating and prioritizing the allocation of resources according to an academic plan that outlines programmatic goals and objectives. The budget is, in a sense, program goals translated into dollars (Kieft, 1978). Faculty play a critical advisory role through standing committees that develop planning assumptions and that review program proposals at both the local and the institutional levels.

PRINCETON UNIVERSITY

A mature university, with an enrollment of around 6,000 and a high degree of shared values and interests, Princeton University has employed a standing joint faculty, student, and administrative committee to advise the president on the allocation of resources for more than fifteen years (Herring et. al., 1979). As at West Virginia University, this planning and budgeting process illustrates a domain consolidation strategy.

The charge to the Priorities Committee is to make recommendations on matters affecting the annual budget for the following year, including both income projections and broad priorities among possible expenditures, and to make recommendations on matters affecting longer range plans for resource allocation. The committee's membership includes six faculty members, including one from each of the four main divisions of the university; four undergraduates; two graduate students; and three *ex officio* administrators: the provost (the chairman), the dean of the faculty, and the financial vice-president and treasurer.

The Priorities Committee concentrates its work in about three months, from mid-October to mid-January. For six to eight weeks, it reviews budget requests from academic and administrative units and reports on major budgetary concerns, such as salaries and auxiliary income. The administrative head of each unit also makes an oral presentation to the committee, at which time questions may be asked about the rationale or the impact of a budget reduction or a modification of priorities.

After listening to all requests, the committee reviews all income and expenditure items not under the university's direct control, such as endowment earnings. Then, based on the committee's overall income projections and the total of all budget requests, the controller's office assembles a budget showing, of course, a large deficit. The committee then sets about reducing that deficit by increasing income or reducing expenditures.

Before the holidays, the committee produces a tentative budget package, which is reported to the larger university community. During the holidays, the staff draft a final report which summarizes the proposed budget and analyzes its implications for future budgets. The committee makes whatever changes it wishes and reports to the president in early January. After consultation with the committee and members of the larger university, the president forwards a budget to the Board of Trustees.

Throughout the committee's deliberations, regular reports are made to the university community through the campus newspapers, and all budget requests are made available to anyone who wishes to review them. Although working sessions are closed, the committee holds a public hearing wherein faculty, staff, and students may express their views with respect to the university's financial situation and future priorities. In the mid-1970s, a ground swell rose among students to argue against increases in tuition and fees and reduction in certain services, and general interest in the budgeting process has increased over time. Although increased interest may threaten the process by reducing rationality and politicizing the process, it has also improved the committee's understanding of the views of its public and vice versa.

That the priorities committee has played a critical role in the development of Princeton's budget for many years, and that its membership and charge have remained essentially unchanged demonstrate its effectiveness as a means of universitywide review of institutional goals as they are translated into the budget. During some periods, such as the energy crisis of 1974, the committee has been challenged to reduce expenditures in order to eliminate a sizable deficit. In other periods, the committee has selectively recommended increases and new initiatives.

DUKE UNIVERSITY

During the 1970s, Duke University faculty and administrators shared the belief that the university had considerable potential for significantly improving its national reputation as a research university. A growing endowment and an application pool increasing in size and quality contributed to rising expectations for the university, whose enrollment was approaching 10,000 and whose eight schools included a large medical center. However, the challenges shared by higher education during this period—increasing costs and competition for students—began to threaten the financial base on which the community could build to compete successfully with institutions in the top rung of American universities. Duke's attempts to address this environment illustrate aspects of a domain creation and substitution strategy, utilizing a separate *ad hoc* faculty committee.

The chancellor believed that the regular budgeting process, which normally provided incremental increases, would not result in strategic reallocations to the programs with the greatest potential for reaching or maintaining a high ranking nationally (Peterson, 1985; Franklin, 1982). In 1977, he assembled an *ad hoc* Long Range Planning Committee (LRPC), consisting of ten faculty, eight of whom were nominated by the primary faculty representative body (the Academic Council) and, in fact, were the current leaders of that body. After consulting with this group privately for eighteen months, the chancellor recommended to the board of trustees that the university undertake a planning process that would reduce the scope of its activities and concentrate its resources on fewer programs. His report, which he drafted on the basis of his conversations with the LRPC, provided a rationale for retrenchment, the criteria for discontinuance, and a planning calendar recommending at least eighteen months for consideration by the entire university community. No programs were identified as potential targets; the report recommended only the details of a planning process. The Board of Trustees approved the report in December 1978.

No actions were taken by the administration for eight months, while the university community mulled over the retrenchment process. After minimal debate about whether the faculty, not the Board of Trustees, had the authority to eliminate degree programs, the Academic Council recommended that the LRPC continue to represent the faculty, that its membership be expanded to include two additional council members, and that the LRPC be permitted to advise the administration directly, without requiring full review first by the council as a whole. The chancellor stated that if the LRPC did not agree with his final recommendations, the committee would be invited to address the board of trustees.

In August 1979, the chancellor issued a second report, in which he identified six programs to be considered for discontinuance and proposed a process for reviewing each of these programs according to the criteria identified in the earlier report. The LRPC was divided into six subcommittees, each of which was supplemented with another member of the general faculty and was responsible for reviewing one of the six programs. Based on its own analysis of institutional data, consultation with the affected program administrators, and the reports of external reviewers, each subcommittee made a recommendation for retrenchment, reorganization, or continuance to the full committee, which made its final recommendations to the chancellor in June 1980.

In September, the chancellor submitted the committee's recommendations, unaltered, to the Board of Trustees *for its information*. It was at this stage that the larger university community had the opportunity to react to the recommendations. The Academic Council listened to testimony from each of the affected units during the following three months and endorsed the recommendations in December. The Board of Trustees gave its approval immediately thereafter. One school and one degree program were discontinued; one school and one research laboratory were continued, contingent on further review; one department was reorganized; and one department remained intact.

YALE UNIVERSITY

In the late 1960s, Yale like many universities was deeply engaged in debates about the nature of the relationship between the university and the external society. A particular issue at Yale was university investments and relationships to corporations in which the university held securities. In 1969, President Kingman Brewster asked a group of faculty members to organize an interdisciplinary seminar to explore investor responsibility issues. One result of the seminar was a book, *The Ethical Investor: Universities and Corporate Responsibility* (Simon, Powers, and Gunnemann, 1972), which examined universities' ethical responsibilities in managing investments and outlined "Guidelines for the Consideration of Factors Other Than Maximum Return in the Management of the University's Investments." These guidelines, in reality a sample policy designed for adoption by colleges and universities, established criteria and procedures by which a university could respond to requests from members of its community that the university take into account values in addition to economic return when making investment decisions and when exercising its rights as a shareholder. In 1972, the Yale Corporation adopted a version of these guidelines as a formal policy, and the guidelines subsequently served as a blueprint for ethical investment policies adopted by other universities.

While Yale's ethical investment policy does not fit neatly into any of the strategic categories we have discussed thus far, we have included it as an example of faculty participation in a domain creation and substitution strategy for several specific reasons. First, the policy "repositions" Yale with regard to several key external constituencies, including donors, alumni, and corporations in which Yale invests. The university no longer takes a value-neutral position on investments, nor does it invest solely on the basis of maximum economic return. Rather, it has formally adopted a policy which includes the criterion of minimizing social injury from the activities of companies in which Yale holds securities. Thus the ethical investment policy significantly altered Yale's relationship with its environment, particularly in 1972, when a policy of this type was unique. Therefore the policy represents a strategic action of no minor consequence to a private university heavily dependent upon private funds. Second, the policy involves sharing authority over financially related issues that have traditionally fallen under the exclusive control of administration and trustees.

The Yale policy involved the creation of two standing committees, the Corporation Committee on Investor Responsibility (CCIR) and the Advisory Committee on Investor Responsibility (ACIR). The CCIR is composed exclusively of members of the corporation (Yale's trustees) and retains control over investment policy and all investment decisions. In discharging its responsibility, the CCIR is assisted by the ACIR, composed of two students, two alumni, two faculty, and two staff members, all of whom are appointed by the president of Yale. The ACIR performs the practical work of policy implementation for the CCIR. Two of its principal tasks are to advise on the voting of corporate proxies dealing with ethical issues and to communicate with companies regarding compliance with Yale policy.

The dynamics of this policy and process have varied over the last fifteen years. During the first six years, several hundred issues were raised and resolved through this mechanism. More recently, the major issue under study has been divestment from South Africa. The establishment of the policy and process has not necessarily led to preemptory action; as of the spring of 1988, Yale had not totally divested its holdings in companies doing business with South Africa. The existence of the dual committees, particularly the ACIR, has been perceived to be of value in providing a campus-based forum to focus discussion and analysis of ethical investment issues before submission to the corporation.

There are several interesting elements of this example of shared authority on strategic policy. First, a draft policy and supporting philosophy were developed by a group of faculty and students with relevant expertise (i.e., law, philosophy, ethics, economics, and religious studies) who worked together over the course of a year and sought broad-ranging criticism. Second, the policy as implemented by the corporation retains trustee control over the policy and over final decisions on investments. This not only maintains the tradition of administrative (trustee) primacy on financial issues but also places the locus of decision making in the hands of individuals formally separated from the academic community, thus helping to limit the politicization of the academic community itself. Third, the creation of the ACIR puts into place a group of individuals from the academic community who can provide advice and analysis to the corporation committee. While this is not an unusual device, the Yale policy explicitly calls for individuals to be named to the ACIR who have knowledge of the subject-matter areas in which investment questions are likely to occur and/or who have training in one of the various disciplines pertinent to the resolution of the questions which are likely to arise. This concern with "expertise," as opposed to representation of plural interests, is an usual aspect of the Yale policy. The concept was explicitly outlined by Simon et al. (1972), who made a strong case that certain professional, scientific, and analytical skills on policy questions of this type exist within the academic community and should be brought to bear on strategic policy issues. The stress on expertise extended to the provision of financial staff to the ACIR as a means of assisting in the assessment of corporate issues. To provide more thorough and efficient research and analysis of ethical investment issues, Yale joined with other universities and foundations in establishing the Investor Responsibility Research Center (IRRC) in 1972. An independent, not-for-profit clearinghouse, the IRRC conducts research and publishes impartial reports on contemporary social and public policy issues and the impact of those issues on major corporations and institutional investors.

While the Yale ethical investment policy does not deal exclusively with faculty participation (other constituencies are also involved), it provides an interesting example of a process and a structure for faculty participation in strategic policy issues.

ANTIOCH COLLEGE

Following World War II, Antioch College held a reputation as one of the most distinctive liberal arts colleges of quality in the United States (Clark, 1970). The college was particularly well known for its collegial form of governance and, in the 1960s, helped to articulate an early position statement on shared governance (Keeton, 1971). Since that time, Antioch has gone through a marked decline, culminating in the suspension of pay to all employees in 1979. While Antioch continues as a viable institution, its rapid decline serves as a negative case of strategic policy-making in the context of a liberal arts college (Wilson, 1985).

Indeed, the case of Antioch College serves as a microcosm for many of the points made in this essay. During the last twenty years, the college was confronting a changing environment of opportunities and threats as represented by differing cohorts of new faculty, students, and administrators; the emergence of active social movements with strong attractions to Antioch; changes in federal student funding with substantial impact upon a campus fully committed to a work-study program; and the changing agendas of prominent foundations. Liberal arts colleges, particularly those with innovative traditions such as Antioch, have boundaries which are quite permeable to changing social and cultural intrusions. Therefore a critical function of strategic policy-making is to identify those intrusions that promote the institution's purpose and those which do not, and to devise mechanisms to capitalize on the former and to minimize the latter.

In the case of Antioch, several strategic policies were chosen which led to its decline. The first was the development of a laissez-faire first-year program with credit automatically awarded, partially funded by grants from the Danforth and Exxon Foundations. The second was the active recruitment in 1968–1973 of urban ghetto black students, unfamiliar and uncomfortable with the academic traditions of a liberal arts college. This program was supported by the Rockefeller Foundation. The third, and most significant, policy was the creation of the Network, a program of satellite campuses designed to empower through education Vietnam veterans, prisoners, urban ethnic groups, and the rural poor of Appalachia. The programs of these satellite campuses were heterogeneous and the sites widely scattered; the rapid growth of the network was supported by funds from the Ford Foundation. Ultimately, the president's office was relocated from the traditional Yellow Springs campus, and Antioch was renamed a university, with the attendant problems of loss of control over faculty recruitment, admissions, quality control, and financial resources by the Yellow Springs faculty, as well as increasing demands for local autonomy by the satellite campuses.

While much of this change was fostered by a single president, it is reasonable to ask why faculty authority and governance were not influential in altering those strategic policies which threatened the institution's integrity and led to its decline. Wilson (1985) suggests several currents of the external culture which had a profound impact at Antioch. First, the value of equality which was influential on many institutions during the governance period of democratic participation made a substantial impact upon the governance process at Antioch, possibly because of a strong Quaker tradition of community rather than collegial government. Distinctions between staff members, even the appropriateness of differentiating the role and unique skill of faculty members, came to be seen as invidious. Individual faculty selection came to be based upon a rough equality of potential, and work was judged by universal criteria. Teachers, administrators, and persons involved in job placement were equally faculty: at one point, the longtime headwaiter at the Tea Room was made an honorary faculty member. Once the classification *faculty* was diluted, it had a profound effect on governance, since the title of faculty member conferred an equal vote in shaping organization policy and practice. Furthermore, the commitment to equality, at least in this setting, led to an antagonism to evaluation. Hence, there was little incentive to assess the relative effectiveness of various products, procedures, or "processors."

A second valued characteristic of the larger society was pluralism, interpreted as a celebration of diversity, tolerance, and the open marketplace of ideas. Wilson suggests that pluralism can also lead to an indifference to the public costs of private aggrandizement. In the absence of shared beliefs, groups will rationally act in their own self-interest, because investment in the community's welfare provides an insufficient return to the individual or group. The assumption that the welfare of the larger academic community will be maintained by an "invisible hand" through the competing interests of rival groups therefore proved false in the Antioch case. The demands of interest groups, constitutencies internal to the traditional campus or the new sattelite campuses themselves, had no limits and tended to outrun the potential resources. Lacking the common value commitment of faculty members to the maintenance of an academic enterprise, the centrifugal forces of the interest groups caused the continuing organization to fly apart.

The net effect of these collective forces appears to be one of devolving the governance process at Antioch from a collegial structure, involving the formal agencies of administration and the tenured faculty with a long-term commitment, to informal pressure groups of students and others with a transient interest in the community. Consequently, the changes in the institution's environment, moderated by adaptations in the institution's governance process, were influential in the college's decline.

EFFECTIVENESS OF CONSULTATION STRATEGIES

The six stages of consultation listed earlier provide a useful basis for the analysis of these six case studies. A major point of variation is the nature of the consultation, whether faculty participation is through an *ad hoc* process to study a particular strategic issue, or through a standing committee with oversight responsibility. The cases reported here represent the practice as illustrated in the larger literature. Standing committees are most typically employed in the domain consolidation strategy of ongoing planning and budgeting processes, as at Princeton and West Virginia. *Ad hoc* committees are most typically employed in domain offense or domain creation and substitution strategies, such as program review and retrenchment, as at Berkeley and Duke.

The distinction between *ad hoc* and standing committees is useful for examining the process of *early consultation*. As a step in a consultative process, early consultation is most critical for *ad hoc* committees and task forces, since by definition they often represent initial attempts to grapple with a problem or issue. In the two cases of Berkeley and Duke, consultation with *ad hoc* committees seemed to play a very important role in defining the issue. Before naming the Internal Biological Sciences Review Committee, the responsible vice-chancellor at Berkeley had numerous discussions with faculty and administrators and had commissioned a study of the situation, which was widely circulated before the committee was named. At Duke University, the chancellor spent eight full months discussing the situation and considering alternative approaches with the Long Range Planning Committee (which represented the faculty leadership) before proposing a possible planning process for the university community's consideration. In both situations, the faculty's opportunity to shape the agenda was largely through informal discussions rather than through formal negotiations. As Reid (1982) suggested in an analysis of administrative evaluation at the University of Toledo, if *ad hoc* faculty participation is to be effective it must occur early, at the point of the development of general policy, such as evaluation criteria and procedures.

In the case of ongoing standing committees, early consultation is common but is structured in a different manner. For example, as at Yale, where a faculty seminar was the basis for the initial thinking on a possible policy for ethical investment, standing committees are often themselves the product of initial *ad hoc* committees or task forces which develop a recommendation for the president and/or the trustees. Thus the alternative forms and procedures for ongoing strategic policy-making in these institutions are often set in place through early consultation with faculty-dominated committees. Even with well-established standing committees on planning and budgeting, such as those at Princeton and West Virginia, faculty input in the annual cycle is emphasized *early,* usually at the stage of generating planning assumptions and budgetary criteria, rather than attempting to involve faculty members in the frequently frantic last moments of budgetary allocations.

As illustrated in these cases, the *joint formulation of procedures* occurs, but usually not in a joint committee structure. As at Berkeley, Duke, and Yale, the administration anticipates an area of strategic action such as retrenchment or ethical investment and then turns first to *ad hoc* faculty groups to outline the policies, procedures, and criteria by which these strategic policies should be implemented. Based upon our review of the literature, *ad hoc* committees in program review and retrenchment are frequently composed exclusively of faculty members, as at Berkeley and Duke, for the purpose of maintaining the integrity of faculty primacy in academic programs and procedure. The joint formulations of procedures for strategic policy-making usually begin with the administration's setting the agenda by charging an *ad hoc* task force, and by circulating background papers. A period of bargaining then follows in which administrators negotiate with faculty committees over subsequent recommendations. What is distinctive about the Antioch College case is the apparent bypassing of the faculty for a communitywide constituency for defining and deciding strategic policy questions.

In contrast to these largely *ad hoc* processes of joint formulation, the more familiar "joint committee" procedure is visible in the planning and budgeting committees at Princeton and West Virginia. In those cases, standing committees are composed of senior members of the faculty, the chief academic and financial officers of the institution, and other members of the academic community. In the case of Yale, the use of hierarchically related committees (the CCIR, with ultimate responsibility for policy decisions, and the campus-based ACIR, which carries out the function of issue identification and analysis) provides a joint process of decision making. While standing-committee structures emphasize joint deliberation, their effectiveness is greatest when the values and processes by which they work are firmly established by earlier consultation, by previous iterations of the same committee, or by well-understood institutional traditions.

Sufficient *time to formulate responses* is always relative, but critical is the care and seriousness with which responses are sought. Berkeley, for example, set in motion an extended process involving an internal committee, an external visiting committee, and several studies prior to the implementation of programmatic decisions. Yale's establishment of a standing advisory committee on ethical investment with analytical support and opportunity for submissions by members of the academic community suggests a commitment to seeking responses. The Duke University case provides an excellent example of how a decision-making process can be designed to give both the committee and all constituencies at large the opportunity and time to consider questions of process and to generate alternative recommendations. It is not clear to what degree the Long Range Planning Committee supported the determination that retrenchment was necessary, and certain avenues of participation were not offered by the administration. However, once the Board of Trustees had approved the general concept of retrenchment, the faculty had several months to consider how the process should be undertaken and what the roles of the committee and the Academic Council should be. Before any potential targets were named, there was widespread support for the criteria and procedures that would be used to make the decision. In addition, after the administration made its recommendations to the trustees, three months were allotted for widespread consideration of the recommendations before final action was taken.

In all five positive cases, the administration provided healthy staff support and made relevant *information available* to assist the committees in making their recommendations. Special studies were made, and presentations or hearings were organized at all five institutions. The reports of external reviewers were employed at Berkeley and Duke. The two standing committees at West Virginia and Princeton utilized budgetary data and planning submissions which have become standard in their deliberations.

Yale's use of a faculty seminar involving expertise from law, ethics, and economics was a unique and academically appropriate means of developing alternatives and criteria in an extremely contentious area. The university also committed financial staff to analyzing corporate practices and eventually joined with other nonprofit entities to found the Investor Responsibility Research Center, which now provides analytical investment services to many organizations. In this context, it is appropriate to note Wilson's (1985) observation that a critical weakness of the Antioch community was an opposition to the evaluation of different procedures and processes. Critical to the wise selection of strategic opportunities and to the evidence of inappropriate ones, Wilson argues, is effective organizational intelligence, or research and development, on the dynamic connection between organizational procedures and product.

The best context for *adequate feedback* and the *communication of decisions* is one in which it is very clear before the consultation process is initiated exactly how the results will be used. In five of the six cases, the planning assumptions, budget priorities, retrenchment recommendations, and ethical criteria fit neatly into a larger decision-making process to which the administration was fully committed and which *required* the results of faculty deliberation in order to move forward. Because the faculty's recommendation had a critical role to play, information was freely provided, and feedback came in the satisfying form of subsequent, even immediate, action. For example, in the Berkeley case, Trow (1983) reports that the vice-chancellor began implementing some of the recommendations even before the committee had completed its work. In the other four positive-case instances, committee recommendations were carried to the next level of decision making almost immediately, which requires that one assume adequate informal consultation between committee and administration throughout the process.

This ongoing informal consultation was characteristic of several processes. Informal discussions were held between the Duke chancellor and the Program Review Committee. Hearings were used in the Duke, Princeton, and West Virginia instances because they promote both the opportunity for in-person representation and immediate feedback. Princeton's budget and planning committee regularly distributed reports of its activities through the campus newspaper to inform the larger community. Also, by virtue of their joint composition and involvement in the budgeting cycle, the faculty and student members of the Princeton and West Virginia committees are continually apprised of administrative reactions to their proposals. Within the parallel structure at Yale University, the ACIR formulates and presents recommendations to the CCIR directly and thereby is assured of immediate feedback.

In contrast to these various feedback mechanisms, the communication of decisions *appears* straightforward. Decisions are made, the academic community is thus notified. The size, complexity, and variety of constituencies within colleges and universities gives the lie to this simple assumption. At Princeton and West Virginia, the implementation of the budget clearly signals the decisions made, but at Duke and Berkeley, the administration was cognizant of the importance of communicating not only the decisions made about academic programs but also the values behind the decisions and the processes used. Given the structure of academic communities, strategic policies offer an important opportunity to communicate the basic culture and values of an institution, particularly those that represent strategic shifts from previous traditions (Feldman and March, 1981). For this reason, extensive written analyses are often a hallmark of communicating decisions. The leadership at Yale, for example, felt it necessary to distribute to all members of the community a detailed broadsheet, "Yale University Investments in South Africa" (1986), explaining the institution's position on South African investments and its relationship to the existing ethical investment policy. Perhaps the best known and most effective use of communicating strategic policies in a way that builds and maintains community values is Stanford's annual report on its operating budget (Chaffee, 1983). Distributed annually to all members of the academic community, this document articulates the issues confronting Stanford, the priorities to be implemented through the upcoming budget, and the allocation of the operating budget to achieve the stated ends. Thus, the members of the academic community are not required to seek out what decisions have been made, or to try to interpret the purpose of decisions; rather, the logic of decisions and their relationship to the community's values and norms are presented to each participant, each year.

EXPERTISE: THE MISSING ELEMENT OF FACULTY PARTICIPATION

The six cases just reviewed also suggest some dimensions of faculty participation in strategic decision-making which are not emphasized in recent writings on the subject (Floyd, 1985; Mortimer and McConnell, 1978; Powers and Powers, 1983). The most notable is the dimension of faculty experience and expertise. For example, in the Berkeley case, an internal team of respected scholars evaluated the quality of faculty research in the multiple departments of the biological sciences on the campus. Partially as a result of their findings, the various departments were placed in a form of receivership, and all future personnel decisions of each department were to be screened by a campus committee of distinguished biologists. Similarly, in the Yale case, a strong argument was made that members of the Advisory Committee on Investor Responsibility should be selected not simply to represent various constituencies of the academic community, but at least partly by the criteria of expertise, that is, with regard to their professional knowledge of relevant policy issues (e.g., environmental pollution) and/or basic fields of knowledge (e.g., economics or ethics). In their analysis of the concept of ethical investment, Simon et al. (1972) explicitly argue that the university community possesses professional, scientific, and analytical skills which should be brought to bear on the policy issues confronting universities. In both cases, there appears to be recognition that certain strategic questions posed to contemporary colleges and universities require not representative opinion, but expert academic opinion.

This represents an apparent shift in the bases for authority and participation, from those commonly articulated during the period of democratic participation. During that period, the templates of "representative democracies" (McConnell and Mortimer, 1971) and of "oligarchies" (Eckert and Hanson, 1973) were laid against the prevailing models of faculty senates, and the senates were found wanting in the first instance and predictably flawed in the second. Even as late as 1978, Mortimer and McConnell criticized the composition of the Committee on Budget and Interdepartmental Relations at Berkeley, which appraises qualifications for merit salary increases and for appointment, tenure, and promotion. Mortimer and McConnell report that "only senior scholars with records of superior research productivity were appointed to the Budget Committee. *The definition of superior research productivity was so restrictive as to exclude all but a small number of Berkeley's faculty members*" (p. 39; italics added). It is ironic to examine this criticism of the distribution of faculty authority at Berkeley in 1978, in the light of the current effort to reorganize the biological sciences at the campus.

The attention to experience and expertise also represents a different perspective from the current organizational involvement model (Austin and Gamson, 1983; Floyd, 1985). In this perspective, the contemporary arguments of organizational theory and Japanese management are introduced as a rationale for faculty (and staff) participation in increasingly centralized strategic decisions (Lawler, 1986). The lack of participation, particularly among highly educated professionals, is assumed to promote faculty alienation, dissatisfaction, and lowered commitment to the organization. A sense of individual satisfaction and involvement requires building a "corporate" vision or culture, which can be achieved only through participative mechanisms and joint decision-making.

These studies provide useful insights into the possible causes for low morale, low satisfaction, and faculty turnover. But similar to the arguments for democratic participation, they diminish academic organizations to the category of organizations committed to political or economic purposes. While the proponents of democratic participation adopt a political perspective which leads to equal representation in decision making (Wilson, 1985), the proponents of "involvement" adopt a therapeutic perspective which similarly leads to a need to involve all parties. Neither model is attentive to the changing *content* of academic decision-making. The net effect is to lessen the centrality of faculty expertise and authority in the determination of the core processes and procedures of academic organizations.

Both the proponents of democratic participation and the contemporary proponents of faculty and staff involvement ignore the traditional argument for faculty participation: the notion of a self-governing guild or community of scholars, who controlled the judgments necessary for maintaining the community because they *possessed the knowledge and expertise necessary for the decisions* (Clark, 1963). Furthermore, research on organizations in changing environments suggests that it is precisely in these conditions that professional experience and expertise become critical, because of the need to make strategic policy choices concerning core programs, technologies, and processes (Cameron and Ulrich, 1986; Katz, 1974; Wilson, 1985). Academic organizations reverse the hierarchy of business organizations in that faculty members possess the "line" expertise necessary to evaluate the feasibility of strategic proposals brought forward by administrative staff relating to academic programs, research, and the supporting infrastructure (Etzioni, 1964). But under the pressure of transformational environments, college and university administrators may usurp strategic policy-making because the emerging policy issues transcend the traditional departmental locus of faculty authority (e.g., policies on universitywide computer systems), and/or because the collegial norms and controls which support shared authority have eroded (Clark, 1983). We would argue, therefore, that the philosophical basis for faculty participation in strategic policy-making ironically rests in a renewed appreciation of traditional forms of faculty authority and control.

THE GUILD MODEL AND STRATEGIC POLICY-MAKING

Clark (1983) has argued that "guild authority," characteristic of traditional academic organizations, is composed of personal authority, which is grounded in functionally based expertise, and collegial authority, which is collective control by a body of peers through norms congenial to the expression of expert judgment. The concept of a guild is conventionally seen as archaic, if not oppressive, perhaps because guild systems of masters can act to retard or repress creativity or innovation among "journeymen" (cf. the view that tenure and promotion decisions in academia act to promote conventional ideologies). Marx (1965) argued that guild systems would disappear in a capitalist society as the patriarchical relationship between master and journeyman came to be replaced by the monetary relationship between capitalist and worker. This replacement has largely occurred in modern society and is part of the reason for the current orientation toward participation and involvement as a means of diminishing the alienation which has supposedly ensued (Lawler, 1986). The guild model has persisted, however, particularly in elite research universities and liberal arts colleges, where collegial forms of governance dominated by senior academics selected on merit still exist.

The fundamental conflict between the traditional guild model and democratic participation was articulated by Wolff (1969). He suggested, similarly to Wilson (1985), that the portrayal of a university as a "multiversity" (Kerr, 1963), composed of equal but competing subcommunities, leads to the adoption of the American model of democratic pluralism as a model for internal governance (see, e.g., Baldridge, 1971). Wolff (1969) argues that reliance on the pressure-group politics of pluralistic democracy leaves the institution unable to distinguish between good and bad pressures, or between legitimate and illegitimate policy choices (cf. the Antioch College case). Second, pluralism provides no collegial standards for decisions regarding the allocation of scarce resources; hence the resort to internal competitive markets, or "every tub on its own bottom," as a basis for the allocation of goods (Zemsky, Porter, and Oedel, 1978). Finally, Wolff questions whether the art of compromise characteristic of a pluralistic democracy, which makes sense when "interests" conflict, still makes sense when principals or central values conflict (e.g., in the Yale investment policy).

Instead, because of his view of the purpose of the university as educational excellence, Wolff (1969) called for a distribution of authority based upon demonstrated competence. Thus (1) standards of competence should be set by members of the profession who have demonstrated their own competence; (2) the relative superiority of competence should be acknowledged within the profession; (3) final authority should rest in the hands of the masters of each field, whose proven competence equips them to pass judgment; (4) the preponderance of authority belongs by right to the ablest members of the profession (regardless of age!); and (5) the administration ought to be a servant of the faculty, for as administration it *lacks the knowledge to define or enforce professional standards in a university.*

Viewed simply as a rhetorical device, Wolff's argument is helpful in highlighting the distinctions between the respective models of faculty control and democratic participation. But it can also be viewed as a contemporary rearticulation of the guild model of governance, in which masters, by virtue of individual authority vested in their academic expertise, act collegially to set the fundamental conditions for the practice of the profession.

From this perspective, the observed behaviors in our six case studies can be reviewed. First, faculty participation in strategic policy-making appears most effective when faculty "masters" articulate the collegial norms whereby subsequent decisions are to be made and interpreted. In this manner, the collegial norms which help to sustain the guild and to control the behavior of overly entrepreneurial or independent administrators can be maintained. These collegial norms, or policies, include, for example, the criteria and process for closing programs at Duke, *not* the programs to be closed; and the priorities and criteria for university investment decisions at West Virginia and Princeton, *not* the budgetary allocations themselves. Second, on academically strategic or policy-initiating issues, the faculty masters should initially act independently in order to maintain and sustain the reality of faculty authority (e.g., as at Duke, Berkeley, and Yale and, as a negative example, Antioch). Third, in establishing faculty committees, *competence* should take precedence over interest group representation. The primacy of competence in the case of the Berkeley review is remarkable, and it illustrates in part the reaction against the model of democratic participation and pluralism in the current transformational environment. However, in many strategic decisions (for example, the type of computer infrastructure in which the university should invest), the *nature* of the appropriate competence is not always obvious. Here Yale's argument for expertise in policy-related areas (e.g., a faculty member with acknowledged experience with large-scale computerized data bases) or for knowledge in a substantively related field (e.g., an electrical engineer) may be relevant to committee composition. In this sense, as strategic policies become increasingly technical and related to fundamental academic processes, such as the design of research facilities, the maintenance of the democratic participation governance model can become destructive to the effectiveness of the institution.

In sum, we would argue that the effective employment of faculty participation in strategic policy-making can be interpreted as the reassertion of a guild tradition of faculty authority over the recent models of democratic participation and pluralism. Fundamental to this development is attention to the primacy of academic expertise in the establishment of collegial norms to govern strategic decisions.

CONCLUSION

The contemporary environmental pressures for strategic policy-making can lead to an alteration in the structure of authority within academic institutions. In its most dysfunctional form, this change in structure can result in administrative centralization or autocracy. But in the cases of faculty participation reviewed here, the response to strategic change appears in the most effective instances to have led to a reassertion of academic meritocracy over pluralism and democratic participation.

We have argued that the critical importance of expertise in strategic policy-making provides some guidance to the issue of the distribution of authority and the role of faculty participation. Hardy et al. (1983) have suggested that the strategic decisions of institutions of higher education introduced previously can be partitioned into those of administrative fiat (comparable to administrative primacy), professional judgment (comparable to faculty primacy), and collective judgment (comparable to shared authority). Administrators possess the expertise to make strategic decisions regarding financial investments, buying and selling property, embarking on fund-raising campaigns, and a number of support services clearly under administrative control, such as alumni and public relations, athletics and archives, accounting and payroll, printing, and building services and physical plant. In all of these areas, the professional expertise for making decisions of domain creation and substitution, domain offense, or consolidation is most likely to rest in administrative hands. Professional judgment, by contrast, clearly controls what matters to research and teaching. But because of the potential for the research activity or teaching interests of a single faculty member to evolve into a unique new program, Hardy et al. (1983) rightly note that the exercise of professional judgment by individual faculty members can often produce strategic consequences such as a whole new product or activity for an institution. In contrast, overt strategic policies need to be articulated by a process of collective choice utilizing a variety of interactive processes involving faculty members and administrators. These policies include (1) the definition, creation, design, and discontinuation of programs, departments, and research centers; (2) promotion, tenure and hiring decisions; (3) budgeting priorities; and (4) the design of critical academic support services, such as libraries and computers. Thus both the traditional ''Statement on Government of Colleges and Universities'' (1966) and the analysis of organizational theorists (Hardy et al., 1983) reach similar conclusions about the types of decisions which need to be arrived at through shared authority or collective choice.

Our review of the contemporary literature on strategic decision-making suggests a number of different mechanisms of participation whereby faculty knowledge and expertise are brought to bear on strategic policy issues. In addition, we have raised a number of related questions, which might help to guide and reinvigorate research on academic governance.

1. Research on academic governance must be more attentive to the variance in authority environments among institutions of higher education which exists and appears to be increasing. More systematic analyses of the dynamics of collective bargaining in community and junior colleges, of the process of collegial decision-making in liberal arts colleges, and of mechanisms for the collective exercise of faculty expertise in research universities are needed to increase our understanding. In each of these instances, an attention to the *process* of decision making is critical. In contrast, models or analyses of faculty governance which sample institutions without sensitivity to existing variations within institutions are of little value.

2. Mechanisms to promote what Wilson (1985) has termed *centripetal*

forces—and what we would term *collegial norms*—are of critical importance to academic institutions, given their inevitable tendency toward differentiation and specialization. In this sense, the communication of decisions is an understudied and potentially critical component of the maintenance of collegial forms of governance. As Feldman and March (1981) have suggested, academic decision-making is itself a symbolic representation of the academic community's belief in the pursuit of truth. Therefore, the process for reaching those decisions and communicating them offers a critical opportunity for maintaining an institution's core culture. The communication and implementation stage of academic decision-making has received very little attention, possibly because of a bias toward political models of participation.

3. The relationship between academic governance and the quality and nature of information available for decision making is an interesting and growing area of importance. As Wilson (1985) suggests, traditional models of academic authority are difficult to sustain, particularly in times of change, without careful "research and development" on the relationships between processes and products. It might even be asserted, that in the absence of some concrete institutional "screening mechanism" to identify the characteristics of a college or university's products, it is spurious to argue that any common institutional goals exist (Dill, 1988). In this sense, the current concern with measuring "academic outcomes" (see Ewell, this volume) represents another example of the fundamental change occurring in the nature of the policy choices confronting contemporary colleges and universities. The relationship between institutional efforts toward serious research and development (e.g., background research and professional staffing of faculty committees, or investment in outcomes assessment) and the maintenance of faculty authority and control is a topic of significant importance for the decades ahead.

4. We have suggested that the environmental factors affecting colleges and universities are changing and that market forces will lead to increasing differentiation among types of institutions of higher education. One model which could be usefully applied in understanding the dynamics of this process and its implications for the distribution of authority within academic institutions is the ecological model of organizations (Aldrich, 1979; Birnbaum, 1983).

At the outset, we argued that because academic organizations are "value-rational" organizations, an inquiry into the bases of authority of these institutions constitutes an inquiry into their core values as well. The application of "political models" to academic institutions (Baldridge, 1971; Kerr, 1963) can thereby be seen as not simply a descriptive exercise, but a normative one as well, with profound implications for our conceptions of academic institutions. The significance of this shift in orientation and tone is only now being examined (Wilson, 1985), although the larger debate between pluralism and community is now active in our society (Bellah et al., 1985; Bloom, 1987; MacIntyre, 1981).

Perhaps the most fundamental and needed scholarship is that which examines the changing models and underlying values which inform our study of academic governance.

REFERENCES

Aldrich, H. E. (1979). *Organizations and Environments*. Englewood Cliffs, NJ: Prentice-Hall.

Anderson, R. E. (1983). *Finance and Effectiveness: A Study of College Environments*. Princeton, NJ: Educational Testing Service.

Arch, E., and Kirschner, S. (1984). Lewis and Clark College: gender balancing as a catalyst for institutional change. *Educational Record* 65: 48–52.

Armijo, F., Hall, R. S., Lenning, O. T., Jonas, S., Cherin, E., and Harrington, C. (1980). *Comprehensive Institutional Planning: Studies in Implementation*. Boulder, CO: National Center for Higher Education Management Systems.

Austin, A. E., and Gamson, Z. F. (1983). *Academic Workplace: New Demands, Heightened Tensions*. (ASHE-ERIC/Higher Education Research Report No. 10.) Washington, DC: Association for the Study of Higher Education.

Baldridge, J. V. (1971). *Power and Conflict in the University: Research in the Sociology of Complex Organizations*. New York: Wiley.

Baldridge, J. V. (1982). Shared governance: a fable about the lost magic kingdom. *Academe* 68: 12–15.

Baldridge, J. V., Curtis, D.V., Ecker, G., and Riley, G. L. (1978). *Policy Making and Effective Leadership*. San Francisco: Jossey-Bass.

Baldridge, J. V., Kemerer, F. R., and associates. (1981). *Assessing the Impact of Faculty Collective Bargaining*. (AAHE-ERIC/Higher Education Research Report No. 8.) Washington, DC: American Association for Higher Education.

Begin, J. P. (1978). Statutory definitions of the scope of negotiations: the implications for traditional faculty governance. *Journal of Higher Education* 49: 247–260.

Bellah, R. N., Madsen, R., Sullivan, W. M., Swidler, A., and Tipton, S. M. (1985). *Habits of the Heart: Individualism and Commitment in American Life*. Berkeley: University of California Press.

Berte, N. R., and O'Neil, E. H. (1980). Managing the liberal arts institution: a case study. *Educational Record* 61: 25–33.

Birnbaum, R. (1983). *Maintaining Diversity in Higher Education*. San Francisco: Jossey-Bass.

Bloom, A. (1987). *The Closing of the American Mind*. New York: Simon & Schuster.

Bowen, F. M., and Glenny, L. A. (1980). *Uncertainty in Public Higher Education: Responses to Stress at Ten California Colleges and Universities*. Sacramento: California Postsecondary Education Commission.

Bradford, D. L., and Bradford, L. P. (1981). Temporary committees as ad hoc groups. In R. Payne and C. Cooper (eds.), *Groups at Work*. London: Wiley.

Cameron, K. S., and Ulrich, D. O. (1986). Transformational leadership in colleges and universities. In J. C. Smart (ed.), *Higher Education: Handbook of Theory and Research*, Vol. 2. New York: Agathon Press.

Campbell, J. W. (1983). Mount St. Mary's College: how one small liberal arts college involved the faculty in core curriculum revision. *Educational Record* 64: 57–60.

Carnegie Council on Policy Studies in Higher Education. (1977). *Faculty Bargaining in Public Higher Education*. San Francisco: Jossey-Bass.

Carnegie Foundation for the Advancement of Teaching. (1987). *The Carnegie Classification of Higher Education.* Princeton, NJ: Princeton University Press.

Caruthers, J. K., and Lott, G. B. (1981). *Mission Review: Foundation for Strategic Planning.* Boulder, CO: National Center for Higher Education Management Systems.

Chaffee, E. E. (1983). The role of rationality in university budgeting. *Research in Higher Education* 19: 387–406.

Chaffee, E. E. (1984). Successful strategic management in small private colleges. *Journal of Higher Education* 55: 212–241.

Clark, B. R. (1963). Faculty organization and authority. In T. F. Lunsford (ed.), *The Study of Academic Administration.* Boulder, CO: Western Interstate Commission for Higher Education.

Clark, B. R. (1970). *The Distinctive College: Antioch, Reed, and Swarthmore.* Chicago: Aldine Press.

Clark, B. R. (1983). *The Higher Education System.* Berkeley: The University of California Press.

Clark, B. R. (1987). *The Academic Life: Small Worlds, Different Worlds.* Princeton: Carnegie Foundation for the Advancement of Teaching.

Crawley, N. (1981). A tight budget forces Michigan State to make hard decisions. *Change* 13: 44–45.

Darby, D. A., Robinson, J. E., and Lick, D. W. (1979). A faculty-managed approach to instructional development. *Educational Record* 60: 87–92.

Dill, D. D. (1971). *Case Studies in University Governance.* Washington, DC: National Association of State Universities and Land-Grant Colleges.

Dill, D. D. (1982). The management of academic culture: notes on the management of meaning and social integration. *Higher Education* 11: 303–320.

Dill, D. D. (1988). Toward a system of educational quality control: national achievement tests and the "theory of screening." In R. Haskins and D. MacRae, Jr. (eds.), *Policies for America's Public Schools.* Norwood, NJ: Ablex.

Eckert, R. E., and Hanson, M. S. (1973). *The University Senate and Its Committees: An Analysis and Critique.* Minneapolis: College of Education, University of Minnesota.

Etzioni, A. (1964). *Modern Organizations.* Englewood Cliffs, NJ: Prentice-Hall.

Farmer, D. W. (1983). Developing a collegial approach to integrated planning at a small college: communication, understanding, and cooperation. *Planning for Higher Education* 11: 18–24.

Feldman, M., and March, J. G. (1981). Information in organizations as signal and symbol. *Administrative Science Quarterly* 16: 171–186.

Finkelstein, M. J. (1984). *The American Academic Profession: A Synthesis of Social Scientific Inquiry since World War II.* Columbus: Ohio State University Press.

Finkelstein, M., and Pfinister, A. O. (1984). The diminishing role of faculty in institutional governance: liberal arts colleges as the negative case. Paper presented at the annual meeting of the Association for the Study of Higher Education, Chicago, IL.

Floyd, C. E. (1985). *Faculty Participation in Decision-Making.* (ASHE-ERIC Higher Education Report No. 8.) Washington, DC: Association for the Study of Higher Education.

Franklin, P. (1982). Duke University: retrenchment can be accomplished without alienating the university community from its administration. *Educational Record* 63: 34–38.

Hardy, C. (1987). Turnaround strategies in universities. *Planning for Higher Education* 16: 9–23.

Hardy, C., Langley, A., Mintzberg, H., and Rose, J. (1983). Strategy formation in the university setting. *Review of Higher Education* 6: 407–433.

Herring, C. P., Lemonick, A., McCrudden, C., Schafer, C., and Spies, R. R. (1979). *Budgeting and Resource Allocation at Princeton University: Report of a Demonstration Project Supported by the Ford Foundation,* Vol. 2. Princeton, NJ: Princeton University Press.

Heydinger, R. B. (1982). *Using Program Priorities to Make Retrenchment Decisions: The Case of the University of Minnesota.* Atlanta: South Regional Education Board.

Hill, J. E. (1985). On a roll: term contracts at Curry College. *Educational Record* 66: 52–56.

Hodgkinson, H. L. (1974). *The Campus Senate: Experiment in Campus Democracy.* Berkeley: Center for Research and Development in Higher Education, University of California.

Hofstadter, R., and Metzger, W. P. (1955). The development of academic freedom in the United States. New York: Columbia University Press.

Jencks, C., and Riesman, D. (1977). *The Academic Revolution.* Chicago: University of Chicago Press.

Katz, D., and Kahn, R. L. (1978). *The Social Psychology of Organizations* (2nd ed.). New York: Wiley.

Katz, R. L. (1974). Skills of an effective administrator. *Harvard Business Review.* (September–October): 90–102.

Keeton, M. (1971). *Shared Authority on Campus.* Washington, DC: American Association for Higher Education.

Keller, G. (1983). *Academic Strategy: The Management Revolution in American Higher Education.* Baltimore: Johns Hopkins.

Kenen, P. B., and Kenen, R. H. (1978). Who thinks who's in charge here: faculty perceptions of influence and power in the university. *Sociology of Education* 51: 113–23.

Kerr, C. (1963). *The Uses of the University.* New York: Harper & Row.

Kieft, R. N. (1978). *Academic Planning: Four Institutional Case Studies.* Boulder, CO: National Center for Higher Education Management Systems.

Lawler, E. E., III (1986). *High-Involvement Management.* San Francisco: Jossey-Bass.

Leslie, L. L. (1980). The financial prospects for higher education in the 1980's. *Journal of Education* 51: 1–17.

MacIntyre, A. (1981). *After Virtue: A Study in Moral Theory.* Notre Dame: University of Notre Dame Press.

Marx, K. (1965). *Pre-Capitalist Economic Formations.* New York: International Publishers.

McConnell, T. R., and Mortimer, K. P. (1971). *The Faculty in University Governance.* Berkeley: Center for Research and Development in Higher Education, University of California.

Millett, J. C. (1978). *New Structures of Campus Power: Success and Failures of Emerging Forms of Institutional Governance.* San Francisco: Jossey-Bass.

Moore, M. A. (1978). On launching into exigency planning. *Journal of Higher Education* 49: 620–638.

Mortimer, K. P., Gunne, M. G., and Leslie, D. W. (1976). Perceived legitimacy of decision making and academic governance patterns in higher education: a comparative analysis. *Research in Higher Education* 4: 273–90.

Mortimer, K. P., and McConnell, T. R. (1978). *Sharing Authority Effectively.* San Francisco: Jossey-Bass.

Mortimer, K. P., and Tierney, M. L. (1979). *The Three ''R's'' of the Eighties:*

Reduction, Reallocation, and Retrenchment. (AAHE-ERIC/Higher Education Research Report No. 4.) Washington, DC: American Association for Higher Education.

Peterson, K. R. (1985). Constraints on faculty participation in university governance: politics of retrenchment. Unpublished paper, North Carolina State University.

Peterson, K. R., and Moazed, K. L. (1986). Effective faculty participation in planning and decision-making. Paper presented at the annual meeting of the Society for College and University Planning, San Diego.

Poulton, N. L. (1980). Strategies of large universities. In P. Jedamus and M. W. Peterson (eds.), *Improving Academic Management.* San Francisco: Jossey-Bass.

Powers, D. R., and Powers, M. F. (1983). *Making Participatory Management Work.* San Francisco: Jossey-Bass.

Powers, D. R., and Powers, M. F. (1984). How to orchestrate participatory strategic planning without sacrificing momentum. *Educational Record* 65: 48–52.

Reid, J. Y. (1982). Politics and quality in administrator evaluation. *Research in Higher Education* 16: 27–39.

Ross, R. D. (1977). Faculty qualifications and collegiality: the role of influence in university decision making. *Research in Higher Education* 6: 201–214.

Satow, R. L. (1975). Value-rational authority and professional organizations: Weber's missing type. *Administrative Science Quarterly* 20: 526–531.

Shirley, R. C. (1983). Identifying the levels of strategy for a college or university. *Long Range Planning* 16: 10–15.

Simon, J. G., Powers, C. W., and Gunneman, J. P. (1972). *The Ethical Investor: Universities and Corporate Responsibility.* New Haven: Yale University Press.

Statement on government of colleges and universities. (1966). (Statement of the AAUP, ACE, and AGB). *AAUP Bulletin* 52: 375–379.

Tashman, L. J., Carlson, R., and Parke, E. L. (1984). A management lesson in curricular development. *Educational Record* 65: 54–56.

Teel, L. R. (1981). A coke and a smile: Emory University decides how to allot. *Change* 13: 12–21.

Trow, M. A. (1983). Organizing the biological sciences at Berkeley. *Change* 15: 28–53.

Vroom, V. H. (1984). Leaders and leadership in academe. In J. L. Bess (ed.), *College and University Organization: Insights from the Behaviorial Sciences.* New York: New York University Press.

Vulgamore, M. L. (1981). Planning: the University of Richmond experience. *Educational Record* 62: 55–57.

Wilson, E. K. (1985). What counts in the death or transformation of an organization. *Social Forces* 64: 259–280.

Wolff, R. P. (1969). *The Ideal of the University.* Boston: The Beacon Press.

Yale University investments and South Africa. (1986). Office of the Vice President for Finance and Treasurer, Yale University.

Zammuto, R. F. (1986). Managing decline in American higher education. In J. C. Smart (ed.), *Higher Education: Handbook of Theory and Research,* Vol. 2. New York: Agathon Press.

Zammuto, R. F., and Cameron, K. S. (1985). Environmental decline and organizational response. *Research in Organizational Behavior* 7: 223–262.

Zemsky, R., Porter, R., and Oedel, L. P. (1978). Decentralized planning: to share responsibility. *Educational Record* 59: 229–53.

The Conceptual Foundations
of
Organizational Culture

Kim S. Cameron

and

Deborah R. Ettington
The University of Michigan

Reviewing the development of theory and research in organizational studies reveals a continual tension between rational, empirical, explicit approaches and nonrational, qualitative, implicit approaches. At various times, each of these paradigms has taken center stage in academic work, and each has led to important insights and contributions not available from the other. For example, the early rationalistic scientific management principles of Fredrick Taylor (1911) in the early part of the 1900s and the administrative principles of Gulick and Urwick (1937) gave way to an emphasis on informal, nonrational group norms (Whyte, 1943) and the "Hawthorne effect" in the 1940s and 1950s (Roethlisberger and Dickson 1939; Homans, 1950). The 1960s brought back empirical multivariate analyses of organizational structure, technology, and size (Pugh et al., 1969; Blau and Scott, 1962). But the late 1970s and the 1980s are being dominated by an emphasis on culture and symbol—a return to the nonrational aspects of organizations (*Administrative Science Quarterly*, 1983).

Methods of investigation have also shifted back and forth between empirical measurement studies and case studies or ethnographies as each intellectual paradigm has emerged as the predominant approach. Currently, ethnographic research and qualitative methods command a great deal of attention in the published literature, although the central place of the computer in quantitative analysis has guaranteed that empirical measurement will never be superseded entirely. Calls for "thick description" of organizational phenomena have been influential in changing the methods used by many researchers in their investigations, however.

At the center of this emphasis on ethnographic research lies the concept of culture. Whereas sociologists and anthropologists have studied societal and community culture for several decades, only recently has organizational culture emerged as a focus of attention. It has become integrally associated with qualitative methods and an emphasis on nonrational phenomena, not because these methods are required to investigate culture, but because organizational culture is usually equated with phenomena that are not easily observable or quantifiable.

The centrality of organizational culture in the literature is highlighted by two of its champions:

> the study of organizational culture has become one of the major domains of organizational research, and some might even argue that it has become the single most active arena, eclipsing studies of formal structure, or organization-environment research, and of bureaucracy. (Ouchi and Wilkins, 1985, p. 458)

At least two concerns are associated with this dominance of the concept of culture in organizational and higher education literature. One concern is that organizational culture will become no more than a passing fad. This concern is pertinent because, as is typical in most new research areas, the culture literature is uneven in quality and, to a large extent, noncumulative. The development of a systematic body of knowledge on this subject is hindered not only by the confused status of the theoretical literature but also by the paucity of empirical research, especially comparative investigations. The importance of new research areas is often overstated and seldom justified, and this criticism seems characteristic of organizational culture.

A second concern is the lack of a precise definition of the concept and its separation from other related concepts. Some confusion exists, for example, between the concepts of organizational culture and organizational climate. Some authors use them synonymously, some independently. Without a precise definition, the development of a well-conceived nomological network that forms the basis for a theory of organizational culture is unlikely. So far, a consensual definition has not been forthcoming.

Our purpose in this chapter is to address these two concerns directly. We do so first by reviewing the literature associated with organizational culture. Our purpose is to identify the theoretical foundations of organizational culture, to clarify the definition of the concept, and to identify important dimensions of culture that may be most fruitful in future research. Additionally, we report our own empirical investigation of organizational culture and its association with organizational effectiveness in colleges and universities. This is done in order to illustrate some of the critical dimensions of culture and to introduce a theoretical model of culture that provides a conceptual grounding for this concept. Finally, we summarize the major findings gleaned from our literature survey in a form that produces testable hypotheses for future research on culture in higher education.

ORGANIZATIONAL CULTURE

As mentioned previously, the conceptual boundaries of organizational culture are neither precise nor consensual. While this is similar to the status of many other concepts in the social sciences (e.g., effectiveness, adaptability, and environment), it contributes to the faddishness of organizational culture studies, and to the lack of theoretical development. This imprecision and diversity, however, are not without justification. Substantial variation exists in the perspectives of writers on organizational culture (see reviews and critiques of the culture literature by Burrell and Morgan, 1979; Sanday, 1979; Gregory, 1983; Louis, 1983; Morgan et al., 1983; Smircich, 1983; Ouchi and Wilkins, 1985; Roberts, 1970; Bhagat and McQuaid, 1982). Part of this diversity is due to the two separate disciplines from which the concept itself emerged; cultural anthropology and sociology. Within each of these two disciplines, moreover, two divergent perspectives have developed.

INTELLECTUAL FOUNDATIONS

Most of the current popular work on organizational culture has focused on business organizations, and it has relied upon the "functionalist" tradition in anthropology. This tradition (e.g., Radcliffe-Brown, 1952; Malinowski, 1961) focuses on the group, the organization, or the society as a whole and considers how the practices, beliefs, and values embedded in that unit function to maintain social control. The researcher is the central figure in interpreting phenomena that are observed in organizational functions, events, and activities. The researcher's job is to construct a meaning for the organizational phenomena and to identify and label certain patterns. For example, published descriptions of the aggressiveness of Pepsico's, AT&T's, and General Electric's corporate cultures, or the innovativeness of Hewlett Packard's and Digital Equipment Company's cultures (Deal and Kennedy, 1982), exemplify this functionalist foundation. Such descriptions are based on the activities and strategies implemented in these firms, and the interpretation of these firms' cultural patterns are generated by the researcher.

A second school of thought in anthropology, the "semiotic" tradition, has had a major impact on a substantial amount of the scholarly (nonpopularized) literature of the last two decades or so. This tradition is represented by Geertz (1973) and Goodenough (1971), in which obtaining the "native's point of view" and "thick description" predominate. Language, symbols, and rituals are the principle artifacts by which the native's point of view is discerned, and intuition and immersion by researchers in the phenomena of study are required. The researcher's job in this tradition, in contrast, is to obtain interpretations from "locals." Complete immersion in the culture is required through participant observation so that the researcher himself or herself can actually experience the native's point of view. Van Maanen's (1979) participant observation of police organizations and

Barley's (1983c) detailed look at the restorative domain of funeral work are examples of organizational culture analyses in the semiotic tradition.

These two traditions differ primarily in whose point of view is legitimate (researchers' or natives') and in the level of analysis (organization versus individual cognitions). The functionalist tradition views culture as a component of the social system and assumes that it is manifested in organizational behaviors; the semiotic tradition views culture as residing in the minds of individuals. The former relies on researcher-based data; the latter on the natives' data.

Authors influenced by the functionalist tradition include Ouchi (1981), Pascale and Athos (1981), Deal and Kennedy (1982), Peters and Waterman (1982), Schein (1983), and Kilmann, Saxton, and Serpa (1985). The semiotic tradition is represented by Pondy (1978), Smircich (1983), Gregory (1983), Barley (1983a), Evered (1983), and Van Maanen (1979), and Frost and Morgan (1983). One of the best recent discussions of the historical and intellectual roots of the culture concept in anthropology is found in Allaire and Firsirotu (1984).

In sociology, Durkheim's (1893) early emphasis on ritual and myth, along with Weber's (1947) and Toennies's (1957) distinctions between implicit and explicit features of social life, gave rise to a focus on the nonrational aspects of organizations in this discipline. Whereas empiricism dominated sociology for several decades, the banner of cultural analysis was raised by influential publications such as Goffman's (1959) analysis of face-saving devices, Berger and Luckmann's (1966) focus on sense-making and interpretation systems, and the symbolic interactionist perspective (Blumer, 1969), which reinforced the social construction of reality. These authors represent a tradition in sociology that views culture as comprised of the individual's cognitive framework—similar to the semiotic tradition in anthropology. These authors developed interpretations and frameworks of social life through the eyes of the participants in those phenomena, not through their own eyes.

On the other hand, another group of contributors had influence in developing an alternative cultural perspective in sociology, including Selznick's (1949) analysis of the Tennessee Valley Authority, Whyte's (1943) analysis of gang behavior in Chicago slums, Stinchcombe's (1959) analysis of construction firms, Kanter's (1968) work on utopian communities, Spradley's (1970) skid-row community analyses, and Clark's (1970) analysis of colleges. This second group of sociological researchers resemble the functionalist tradition in anthropology. Culture is analyzed as an integral part of social (not individual) activity and behavior, and the interpretive schema is generated by the researcher.

Despite similarities between the sociological and the anthropological perspectives on culture, an important difference exists as well. The sociological emphasis more often than not considers the concept to be an *independent* variable for explaining organizational structure, performance, or activity. The anthropological tradition was more likely to treat it as a *dependent* variable, that is, the

FIG. 1. Distinctions in the traditional approaches to organizational culture.

Anthropological	Sociological
● focus on *behavior*	● focus on *behavior*
● *researchers* interpret data	● *researchers* interpret data
● *outside observation* by investigators	● *outside observation* by investigators
● treated as a *dependent* variable	● treated as an *independent* variable
● assumption: culture *is* something	● assumption: culture *for* something
● organizations *are* cultures	● organizations *have* cultures
● focus on *cognitions*	● focus on *cognitions*
● *natives* interpret data	● *natives* interpret data
● *immersion* required of investigators	● *immersion* required of investigators
● treated as a *dependent* variable	● treated as an *independent* variable
● assumption: culture *is* something	● assumption: culture *for* something
● organizations *are* cultures	● organizations *have* cultures

object of explanation. In sociology, in other words, culture is often used as a predictor of behavior or performance (cf. Clark, 1970; Kanter, 1968). In anthropology, culture is usually considered the object of prediction or explanation (cf. Durkheim, 1893; Goffman, 1959). One of the best recent discussions of the sociological foundations of culture is by Ouchi and Wilkins (1985).

A second distinction that emerged from an analysis of these two traditions is that anthropological literature tends to view culture as something an organization *is;* sociological literature tends to view culture as something an organization *has.* In the former tradition, culture is treated as a metaphor for organizations in the same way that *open system, loosely coupled system,* or *force field* is a metaphor used for describing organizations. The latter tradition treats culture as one attribute in a complex of attributes possessed by organizations that help explain effective organizational performance. The former treats culture *as* something, the latter treats culture *for* something. Figure 1 summarizes these two points of view. More will be said of these two perspectives later in connection with methods of studying cultures. For now, we turn to the different kinds of definitions of culture that have emerged from these different perspectives.

DEFINITIONS AND DIMENSIONS OF CULTURE

The lack of precision and consensus regarding the definition of organizational culture has a long tradition. Ambiguity has existed in the fields of anthropology and sociology for several decades (and continues to exist). A representative sample of the definitions of culture used by different authors in the recent published literature illustrates the variety in the approaches taken. For example, culture is variously defined to be:

A shared appreciation system and a set of beliefs that help distinguish aspects of situations from one another. (Sapienza, 1985)

The amalgam of shared values, behavior patterns, mores, symbols, attitudes, and normative ways of conducting business that differentiate one organization from all others. (Tunstall, 1985)

The taken-for-granted and shared meanings that people assign to their social surroundings. (Wilkins, 1983)

Distinct and locally shared social knowledge. (Wilkins and Ouchi, 1983)

The pattern of basic assumptions that a group has invented, discovered, or developed in learning to cope with its problems of external adaptation and internal integration. (Schein, 1984)

A set of commonly held attitudes, values, and beliefs that guide the behavior of an organization's members. (Martin, 1985)

Informal values, understandings, and expectations indicated through symbolic structures, myths, heroes, and precedents. (Leitko, 1984)

The shared philosophies, ideologies, values, assumptions, beliefs, expectations, attitudes, and norms that knit a community together. (Kilmann et al., 1985)

A system of property rights or economic and social relations that define the position of each individual with respect to others regarding the use of resources. (Jones, 1983)

An integrative framework for sensemaking, both a product and a process, the shaper of interaction and an outcome of it, continually being created and recreated through these interactions. (Jelinek, Smircich, and Hirsch, 1983)

A common set of ideas shared by group members; a theory held by individuals of what their fellows know, believe, and mean. (Jaeger, 1986; Keesing, 1974)

The shared beliefs, ideologies, and norms that influence organizational action manifested through overriding ideologies and established patterns of behavior. (Fiol and Lyles, 1985)

A core set of assumptions, understandings, and implicit rules that govern day-to-day behavior in the workplace. (Deal and Kennedy, 1982)

A set of taken-for-granted assumptions, expectations, or rules for being in the world, often referred to as a paradigm, map, frame of reference, interpretive schema, or shared understanding. (Adler and Jelinek, 1986)

Collectively held and sanctioned definitions of the situation. (Bate, 1984)

A relatively enduring, interdependent symbolic system of values, beliefs, and assumptions evolving from interacting organization members that allow them to explain and evaluate behavior and ascribe common meanings to it. (Schall, 1983)

What is directly describable about members of a community. (Ashforth, 1985; Sathe, 1983)

The way we do things around here. (Arnold and Capella, 1985; and others)

A close look at these definitions highlights the view that culture is something the organization has (not is), and that the definitions are dominated by the anthropological functionalist paradigm. In general, they can be categorized as one of three types: (1) social interpretation definitions; (2) behavioral control definitions; and (3) organizational adaptation definitions. Social interpretation definitions focus on the interpretation schemas, meanings, or frames of references of individuals as indicators and components of culture (cf. Wilkins, 1983). Behavioral control definitions focus on patterns of interaction or activities that define shared organization behavior (cf. Tunstall, 1985). Organizational adaptation definitions emphasize habituated solutions to commonly encountered organizational problems (e.g., integration and adaptation problems) (cf. Jones, 1983; Schein, 1984).

It is also instructive to note that a majority of these definitions focus on attributes of culture that are enduring and are centered on values, beliefs, and assumptions. These attributes distinguish the concept of culture from the concept of climate, which, although sometimes used synonymously in the literature, centers on individual attitudes and perceptions. This difference explains why organizational climate may change much more quickly than organizational culture.

In addition to variation in the definitions of culture, authors have identified (often implicitly) a variety of dimensions that help organize the core attributes of the concept. The importance of dimensions is that they serve as a groundwork upon which a theory of organizational culture may be built in the future. As yet, no such theory exists, but by specifying the core dimensions, researchers and theorists have begun identifying both the phenomena to measure and the relationships among the components of culture.

Several authors have attempted to develop frameworks of important dimensions of culture, but in most cases, they are not based on a theoretical and empirical foundation but are merely commonsense propositions or long lists of itemized factors. A sample of these frameworks will help illuminate the diversity of approaches proposed.

Sathe (1983), Schall (1983), and Schein (1984) are among the many authors who argue that cultural strength and cultural congruence are the main dimensions of interest. Strength is usually defined as the power of the culture to enforce conformity, while congruence refers to the fit and similarity among the various cultural elements. The general argument is that strength and congruence are associated with high organizational effectiveness. Albert and Whetten (1985) identified a holographic versus an ideographic dimension as being critical in studying culture. Holographic culture exists when all organizational units share a common culture or identity in addition to their unique culture. Ideographic culture exists when each unit possesses only its own specialized culture. Holographic cultures are hypothesized to be better at executing strategies, whereas ideographic cultures are hypothesized to be better at maintaining adaptability to diverse environmental conditions.

Arnold and Capella (1985) proposed a two-by-two matrix of cultures based on a strong-weak dimension and an internal-external focus dimension. The best cultures, they claimed, were strong, externally focused cultures. Deal and Kennedy (1983) proposed another two-by-two typology of cultures based on a speed-of-feedback dimension (high speed to low speed) and a degree-of-risk dimension (high to low). The four emerging types of cultures, each of which is argued to be appropriate under a different environmental condition, are (1) tough-guy/macho (high speed, high risk); (2) work hard/play hard (high speed, low risk); (3) bet your company (low speed, high risk); and (4) process (low speed, low risk). Ernest's (1985) two-by-two model used a people orientation (participative-nonparticipative) and response to the environment (reactive-proactive) to develop four types of cultures: interactive (participative-reactive), integrated (participative-proactive), systematized (nonparticipative-reactive), and entrepreneurial (nonparticipative-proactive). He argued that no one culture type is best, but that organizations in the same industry should have similar cultures. Riley (1983) proposed that culture is best analyzed by two main factors: structures and symbols. The most important structural dimensions, according to Riley, are (1) means of achieving significance; (2) means of acquiring legitimacy; and (3) means of achieving dominance. The most important symbol dimensions are (1) verbal; (2) action; and (3) material. The intersection among each type of symbol and structure identifies a factor that helps diagnose corporate culture.

Bate (1984) analyzed language patterns, stories, and rituals in three organizations and proposed six dimensions of culture that helped organize patterns in his findings: unemotionality, depersonalization, subordination, conservatism, isolationism, and antipathy. Gordon (1985) assessed "management climate," which he later relabeled "corporate culture," based on a Hay Associates questionnaire administered over several years. The items clustered into 11 dimensions of culture: clarity and direction, organizational reach, integration, top management contact, encouragement of individual initiative, conflict resolution, performance clarity, performance emphasis, action orientation, compensation, and human resource development. Hofstede (1980) has a well-known set of dimensions for differentiating national or societal cultures, and several authors have made attempts to apply them to corporate cultures (e.g., Jaeger, 1986). These dimensions are power distance, uncertainty avoidance, individualism, and masculinity.

Martin et al. (1983) identified seven common themes in the stories that people tell to reflect their culture. Most organizations project their cultural values through some sort of unique stories; yet those stories are characterized by certain common themes or questions: How will the organization deal with obstacles? How will the boss react to mistakes? Will the organization help me if I have to move? Will I get fired? Can the little person rise to the top? Is the big boss human? What happens when I break rules? Each story relates to conflicts between organizational needs and members' values. Jones (1983) argued that culture is a product of institutional arrangements to regulate transactions and exchanges among individuals, and that five characteristics describe those transactions. These characteristics define "property rights": vested in person or position, length of contract, degree of preciseness in specifying rights, degree of inclusiveness of facets of employment, and configuration of rights in the organization. Strong property rights indicate a strong culture, that is, rights vested in persons, precise, inclusive, and enduring.

Kets de Vries and Miller (1986) focus on dysfunctional organizational cultures arising from pathological strategies and structures. They identify paranoid, avoidant, charismatic, bureaucratic, and politicized types of cultures. Trice and Beyer (1984) concentrate on rituals or rites as the main indicator of cultural forms. They suggest that these performances are the most appropriate way to capture the complexity of an organization's culture. The six rituals identified are rites of passage, rites of degradation, rites of enhancement, rites of renewal, rites of conflict reduction, and rites of integration.

The dimensions of culture reviewed above differ from one another in that some emphasize underlying organizing factors for cultural phenomena, and others emphasize typologies of cultures. The long lists of factors identified by authors such as Trice and Beyer, Bate, Gordon, and Kets de Vries and Miller tend to be enumerations of attributes of cultures. The two-by-two matrices, on the other hand, proposed by Deal and Kennedy, Arnold and Capella, and Ernest, tend to identify ways of organizing these factors into typologies of cultures.

Our review of the empirical and the theoretical work on culture suggests to us that the following seem to be the most frequently cited, or at least the most potentially fruitful, conceptual dimensions used in culture research: (1) cultural strength (the power to control behavior); (2) cultural congruence (the fit or homogeneity among cultural elements); (3) cultural type (the focus on certain dominant themes); (4) cultural continuity (the extent to which consistency in culture has been maintained over time); (5) cultural distinctiveness (the uniqueness of the culture); and (6) cultural clarity (the extent to which the culture is unambiguously defined, understood, and presented).

Of these dimensions, most authors have identified strength of culture and cultural congruence as the most critical. They are certainly the most frequently mentioned. A strong and congruent culture (i.e., a culture that supports the structure and strategies of the organization) is more effective than a weak and incongruent or disconnected culture, it is argued. For example, Peters and Waterman (1982), Deal and Kennedy (1982), O'Reilly and Moses (1984), and others have asserted that a strong culture is associated with organizational excellence: "a strong culture has almost always been the driving force behind continuing success in American business" (Deal and Kennedy, 1982, p. 5). Galbraith and Kazanjian (1986), Tichy (1982), Broms and Gahmberg (1983), Wilkins and Ouchi (1983), and others have argued that a culture supportive of organizational strategies leads to high performance: "to be successful, a company's culture needs to support the kind of business the organization is in and its strategy for handling that business" (Tichy, 1982, p. 71). This cultural "fit" or congruence theme is also espoused by Nadler and Tushman (1980), Quinn and Hall (1983), Kotter (1980), and others, who have suggested that a variety of cultural attributes must be aligned to produce effectiveness: "Other things being equal, the greater the total degree of congruence or fit between the various components, the more effective will be organizational behavior at multiple levels" (Nadler and Tushman, 1980, p. 275). We will return to an examination of these important dimensions of organizational culture in a later section as we describe an empirical investigation of three such dimensions. A discussion of alternative approaches to investigating culture, however, is necessary first.

APPROACHES TO INVESTIGATING CULTURE

As mentioned before, culture is generally treated by authors in one of two ways: as something the organization *is,* or as something the organization *has.* The definitions and dimensions just discussed largely focus on the latter. It is necessary to discuss briefly the former perspective, however, in order to highlight the basis for the differences among three main methods used by investigators to assess organizational culture.

Treating culture as something that an organization *is* presupposes that culture is a metaphor in the same way that "open-system," "bureaucracy," "organized-anarchy," or "machine" metaphors are used to describe the nature of organizations. The purpose of a metaphor for describing organizations is simply to highlight and uncover aspects of the organization that are ordinarily ignored by observers—in this case, the nonrational, taken-for-granted, underlying assumptions that drive organizational behavior and the shared interpretive schemas of organizational members. Treating culture as a metaphor goes beyond the instrumental view of those who treat culture as a variable in organizations. Instead, it defines culture as the "shared knowledge," the "shared meaning," and the "unconscious mental operation" of organizational members (Smircich, 1983; Goodenough, 1971; Agar, 1982; Hollowell, 1955; Geertz, 1973; Rossi and O'Higgins, 1980). This implies that culture cannot be observed directly but exists only in the heads of those associated with the organization. An outsider can never truly understand the culture, only those immersed in it. Approaches ranging from psychoanalytic procedures to story or linguistic analysis characterize the research in this tradition (e.g., Chomsky, 1972; Mitroff, 1983b; Pfeffer, 1981; Pondy, 1983).

This use of culture as a root metaphor highlights the continuing controversy regarding how culture should best be assessed. Some authors argue that quantitative techniques have no place in empirical studies of culture; others assert that multiple methods—including quantitative and qualitative methods—are appropriate (see Van Maanen, 1979; Ouchi and Wilkins, 1985; Louis, 1984, for examples). Thus far, three main approaches have been taken in investigations of organizational culture, but little integration among them has occurred in the literature. The three are (1) holistic studies through participant observation; (2) metaphorical or language studies; and (3) quantitative studies mainly relying on survey research or experimental manipulation (see Ouchi and Wilkins, 1985).

Holistic Studies

An emphasis on the whole organization and its culture (i.e., organizations as cultures) typifies these studies. Important examples in this category include Rohlen's (1974) participant observation of a Japanese bank, Krieger's (1979) portrait of a San Francisco rock music station, Van Maanen's (1973) description of the socialization of police recruits, Manning's (1979) study of the world of detectives, Dyer's (1982) description of a computer company, Wilkins's (1983) study of subcultures in an electronics company, Trice and Beyer's (1985) study of the routinization of organizational founders, and Barley's (1983b) study of role evolution in the introduction of CAT scanning equipment in two hospitals. Most of these studies relied on field observation for 6–20 months, although a few used quantitative techniques such as content analysis of organizational documents or communications (e.g., Martin et al., 1983). Archival and historical documents have been substituted for direct observations by authors such as Clark (1970), Boje (1983), Kanter (1968), and Martin and Siehl (1983), thus permitting a longitudinal perspective not possible with participant observation.

By and large, investigators are required to immerse themselves in a culture in order to study it—to become natives themselves. In fact, the argument is that true natives who have not experienced any other culture cannot articulate, and often are not even aware of, many cultural attributes and assumptions because they have no point of contrast. Only outside investigators who become insiders can really study culture in a holistic way.

Metaphorical Studies

A focus on language and metaphor characterizes these studies, as exemplified by Gregory's (1983) study of the language of Silicon Valley professionals in a rapidly changing environment, Barley's (1983a) study of the language of funeral directors, Pondy's (1983) study of the role of metaphor in Communist China and in an African tribe (the Nuer), Huff's (1983) study of the language of different subgroups within a graduate school of management, and Pondy and Huff's (1983) study of the language of public documents in public schools.

Investigators in these studies analyze the outward manifestations of cultural effects. Just as individuals possess unique finger prints, voice prints, and word prints in writing, it is assumed that unique organizational prints can also be detected by studying language patterns in organizations. This is done by analyzing official reports, documents, and written communications as well as informal rituals, stories, and conversations. The intent is to understand and describe the culture, not to predict other behaviors or performances based on the cultural manifestations.

Quantitative Studies

Like studies of organizational climate, quantitative studies of culture mainly rely on survey methodology and statistical data analysis. For example, Ouchi and Johnson (1978) used questionnaires to differentiate the cultures of two different firms. O'Reilly (1983) surveyed employees in high-tech firms in Silicon Valley to test the association between strong culture and employee identification with the firm. Bowditch, Buono, and Lewis (1983) compared climate and culture surveys in the merger activity of two banks. Beck and Moore (1983, 1984) reported studies using projective measures to assess norms and culture in Canadian banks. Meyer (1982) used questionnaires and content analysis of interview data to examine shared values. And Martin and Powers (1983) compared information from stories with quantitative information in assessing their vividness and persuasive impact on employees.

Investigators in these studies have been criticized most for assessing not really culture, but climate. That is, attitudes and feelings (the basis for organizational climate) are rather easily assessed by means of questionnaires, but core values and assumptions (the basis for organizational culture) are difficult to assess via questionnaires. Some investigators have handled this problem by denying that any difference exists between the concepts of culture and climate (Denison, 1984; Glick, 1985), and they have simply labeled their data cultural regardless of their source. Others have attempted to overcome this liability by asking directly for values and assumptions in their questions, hoping that they can obtain more than mere surface attitudes. In general, quantitative methods remain controversial in the study of culture. An alternative quantitative method designed to overcome some of the difficulties of standard survey methodology is explained in the next section.

These three different approaches to the study of culture are associated with the different perspectives discussed in previous sections. Holistic studies generally treat culture as an independent variable, manipulable by managers. Various books and articles offering practical advice to managers in organizations have emerged from this view, for example, Peters and Waterman (1982), Ouchi (1981), and Deal and Kennedy (1983). These and other works suggest manipulating the organization's mission (Clark, 1970), ideologies (Harrison, 1972), ceremonies (Trice and Beyer, 1985), myths (Boje, Fedor, and Reinwand, 1982), and stories (Mitroff and Kilmann, 1976) in order to manage culture and to improve organizational effectiveness.

Metaphorical studies, on the other hand, are more likely to treat culture as a dependent variable. It is assumed that organizational culture emerges from an overall societal culture (Hofstede, 1980; Jaeger, 1986) and is a product of historical events and activities that are not manipulable by management. The primary intent in this research is to discover and describe an organization's culture, not to determine how it can be modified to enhance effectiveness.

Quantitative approaches occupy the middle ground in that they are used in both independent-variable and dependent-variable studies. Some quantitative studies have attempted to identify and validate dimensions of culture or to develop typologies and thus have treated culture as a dependent variable (e.g., Albert and Whetten, 1985; Allaire and Firsirotu, 1984; Adler and Jelinek, 1986). Other studies have tried to find relationships between culture and other individual or organizational outcomes and thus have treated culture as an independent variable (e.g., Arnold and Capella, 1985; Bate, 1984; Bresser and Dunbar, 1986).

INVESTIGATING THE DIMENSIONS
AND FRAMEWORKS OF CULTURE

Thus far in this chapter, we have pointed out that a wide variety of perspectives, dimensions, definitions, and methods of assessment are associated with organizational culture. Simplifying this variety is one of the major challenges of organizational scholars, since such variety and disagreement inhibit theoretical development and practical application of this concept. In this section, we review a study conducted by Cameron (1985a) in which a comparison was made among the major dimensions of organizational culture to assess which was the most powerful in accounting for effectiveness in colleges and universities. We also introduce a theoretically based model which identifies four types of organizational cultures. Our intent in summarizing this study is to address directly some of the continuing ambiguities associated with cultural dimensions and assessment techniques, especially in higher education institutions, and to introduce a framework that may be helpful in future culture investigations. Following the description of this study, we summarize the major findings of this and other studies as they relate to colleges and universities.

The study we summarize here was undertaken to investigate the relationships between the congruence and strength of organizations' cultures and the effectiveness of those organizations. The intent was to explore the linkages between culture and effectiveness in a variety of higher education institutions to determine the extent to which the assumptions of past authors, that the dimensions of strength and congruence are the most important dimensions in assessing culture, could be supported. In addition, the intent was to address directly the dearth of theoretical models in the culture literature.

The approach taken in this study was to make no prior assumption about whether culture is something an organization *has* or *is,* but to investigate that proposition directly. Also, the study took the middle ground between the holistic and the metaphorical approaches to assessment. That is, organizational culture was treated as both a dependent variable and an independent variable.

THE PSYCHOLOGICAL UNDERSTRUCTURE OF CULTURE

The culture of an organization is grounded in the taken-for-granted, shared assumptions of individuals in the organization. These preconscious, shared assumptions have been the focus of investigations by a number of psychologists. These authors assert that "axes of bias" (Jones, 1961) or "psychological archetypes" (Jung, 1973) organize individuals' interpretations of reality into a limited number of categories. These categories help identify the different frameworks used by individuals to organize underlying assumptions, interpretations, and values. Consequently, these categories also can be used to identify types of cultures in organizations, since cultures are based on the same assumptions and interpretations (see Mitroff, 1983a; Newmann, 1955, 1970; Jaynes, 1976; Quinn, 1988).

One conclusion emerging from research on psychological archetypes is the commonality that is typical of the underlying axes of bias used to interpret and categorize information. That is, similar categorical schemas have been found to exist in the minds of individuals across a wide variety of circumstances. Mitroff writes:

> The more that one examines the great diversity of world cultures, the more one finds that at the symbolic level there is an astounding amount of agreement between various

archetypal images. People may disagree and fight one another by day but at night they show the most profound similarity in their dreams and myths. The agreement is too profound to be produced by chance alone. It is therefore attributed to a similarity of the psyche at the deepest layers of the unconscious. These similar appearing symbolic images are termed archetypes. (1983a, p. 85)

Psychological archetypes serve to organize the underlying assumptions and understandings that emerge among individuals in organizations which become labeled cultures. They establish "patterns of vision in the consciousness, ordering the psychic material into symbolic images" (Neumann, 1955, p. 6).

A variety of frameworks have been proposed for conceptualizing these underlying archetypes of axes of bias, but one of the most well known and widely researched was developed by Jung (1923). The appeal of the Jungian framework is that substantial amounts of research exist to support its validity, and that the dimensions of the framework have been directly related to managerial and organizational styles (Myers, 1980; Keen, 1981; Mason and Mitroff, 1973; Wade, 1981). Even though the Jungian dimensions were originally posited to identify personality types, "the Jungian framework can be used to shed light on organizational and institutional differences" (Mitroff, 1983a, p. 59).

The Jungian framework focuses primarily on the manner in which individuals gather and evaluate information. It has been used in psychological studies, such as the development and refinement of the Myers-Briggs Type Indicator (Myers and Briggs, 1962), and in a substantial amount of research by the Educational Testing Service and other social science researchers on cognitive and behavioral differences among individuals and groups (for example, Center for Applications of Psychological Type, 1980; McCaulley, 1977; Myers, 1980; Churchman, 1964, 1971; Mason and Mitroff, 1973; Henderson and Nutt, 1980). It has also been applied on the organizational level, such as in Quinn and Rohrbaugh (1981) and Carrier and Quinn (1985), who independently derived the same dimensions as those upon which the Jungian framework is based in analyses of organizational effectiveness criteria and of leadership styles. These dimensions accounted for approximately 90% of the variance in differences among the models of effectiveness in one study and in leadership types in another. In addition, Driver (1979, 1983) found evidence for individual decision or information-processing styles that match the Jungian framework and that help explain the differences in person-organization fit. Mitroff and Kilmann (1975, 1976, 1978) studied managerial behavior and found a fit between the Jungian framework and important management style differences. Mason and Mitroff (1973) found differences in the types of organizational stories told by managers to describe their organizational cultures. These story types were organized on the basis of the Jungian dimensions. McKenney and Keen (1974) found different types of problem-solving styles in three studies of MBA students at Harvard. The differences among the students were interpreted on the basis of the Jungian typology, and predictive validity was established. Slocum (1978) found clear differences in change agent strategies as a result of their cognitive styles. The cognitive style differences were based on the Jungian framework. Keen (1981) argued for the validity of the Jungian framework in a review of research based on the Myers-Briggs Type Indicator by pointing out supportive evidence for conceptual validity, construct validity, convergent validity, discriminant validity, predictive validity, and nomological validity.

In sum, the Jungian framework is a frequently used and highly reliable model for organizing the shared underlying assumptions and interpretations (i.e., psychological archetypes) used by individuals that subsequently become manifest as organizational cultures. Mason and Mitroff (1973) and Mitroff and Kilmann (1976) found, for example, that organizations attract individuals who emphasize different psychological archetypes (based on the Jungian dimensions), and that cultures in organizations are described in a manner consistent with the Jungian typology. Because cultural information in organizations is interpreted by individuals in the context of their underlying archetypes, the manner in which culture is experienced and transmitted can also be conceptualized on the basis of the Jungian dimensions. Four ideal types of culture emerging from these dimensions are described in Figure 2.

The framework in Figure 2 is consistent with research by Quinn and Rohrbaugh (1981) in which a categorical schema for criteria of organizational effectiveness was derived. The model developed by those authors was called the *competing values model,* since it identified characteristics of effectiveness that seemingly were opposite from one another. The Jungian dimensions were discovered to lie at the heart of that model. Subsequently, studies by Quinn and Cameron (1983), Quinn and Rohrbaugh (1983), Lewin and Minton (1986), and others helped develop and elaborate this framework. They pointed out that organizational culture can be meaningfully organized on the basis of this same Jungian-based model.

One problem with labeling the dimensions in the Jungian framework is that no single word or phrase captures their complexity. Those who interpret the Jungian framework often use multiple descriptors for each dimension and long explanations of the meaning of each quadrant (cf. Mitroff and Kilmann, 1975, 1976; Myers, 1980). To illustrate, the vertical dimension in Figure 2 is grounded on one end by an emphasis on flexibility, individuality, and spontaneity, and on the other end by an emphasis on stability, control, and predictability. This dimension identifies the distinction in organizations between soft, human concerns and hard, control concerns. It also identifies a dynamism-stability distinction. The horizontal dimension is grounded on one end by an organizational emphasis on internal maintenance, short-term orientation, and smoothing activities (e.g., eliminating strain). The other end is characterized by an organizational emphasis

FIG. 2. A model of cultural congruence for organizations.

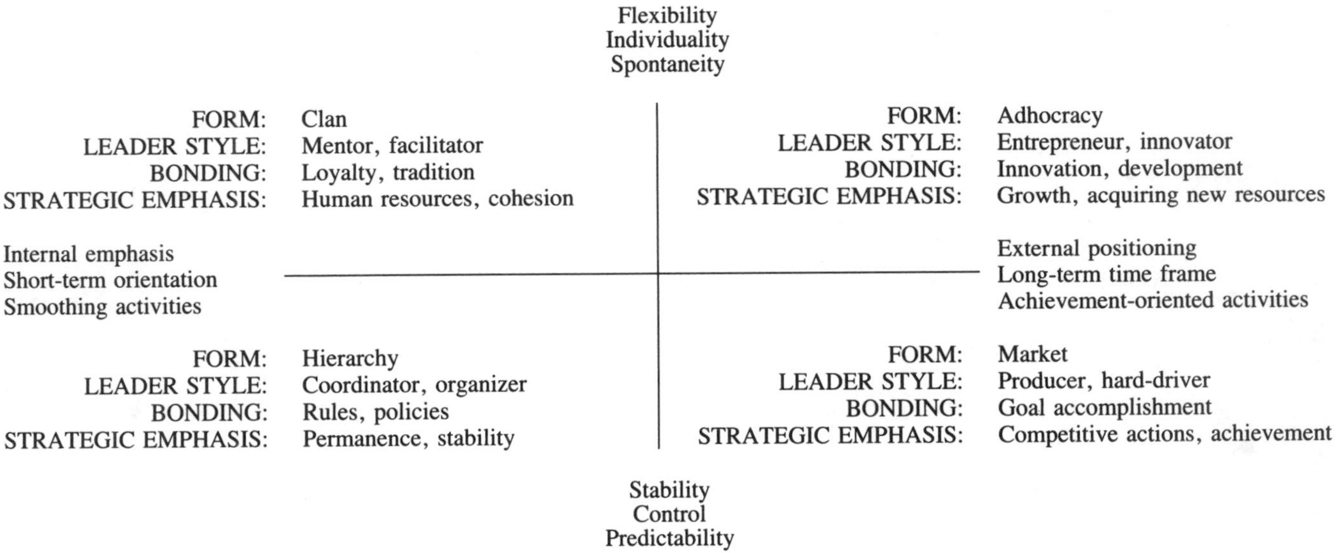

Flexibility
Individuality
Spontaneity

FORM: Clan		**FORM:** Adhocracy
LEADER STYLE: Mentor, facilitator		**LEADER STYLE:** Entrepreneur, innovator
BONDING: Loyalty, tradition		**BONDING:** Innovation, development
STRATEGIC EMPHASIS: Human resources, cohesion		**STRATEGIC EMPHASIS:** Growth, acquiring new resources

Internal emphasis
Short-term orientation
Smoothing activities

External positioning
Long-term time frame
Achievement-oriented activities

FORM: Hierarchy		**FORM:** Market
LEADER STYLE: Coordinator, organizer		**LEADER STYLE:** Producer, hard-driver
BONDING: Rules, policies		**BONDING:** Goal accomplishment
STRATEGIC EMPHASIS: Permanence, stability		**STRATEGIC EMPHASIS:** Competitive actions, achievement

Stability
Control
Predictability

on external positioning, long-term time frames, and achievement-oriented activities (e.g., competitive actions). The main emphasis in this dimension is separating an internal orientation from an external orientation.

The four types of cultures that emerge from this framework are labeled *clan, hierarchy, adhocracy,* and *market.* Mitroff and Kilmann (1975, 1976) used the Jungian symbols to label the culture quadrants and called them simply ST, NF, SF, and NT type cultures. The labels used in Cameron's study were selected because they are consistent not only with the Jungian dimensions, but also with the descriptions of Williamson (1975), Ouchi (1980), Weber (1947), Mintzberg (1979), Wilkins and Ouchi (1983), and others of the characteristics possessed by clan, hierarchy, market, and adhocracy type organizations.

Specifically, the lower left quadrant—the hierarchy culture—emphasizes order, rules and regulations, clear lines of authority, uniformity, and efficiency. Transactions are under the control of surveillance, evaluation, and direction (Ouchi, 1980). The lower right quadrant—the market culture—emphasizes competitiveness, goal accomplishment and production, environmental interaction, and customer orientation. Transactions are governed by equitable exchange and market mechanisms (Ouchi, 1980). The upper left quadrant is the clan culture, which emphasizes shared values and goals, participativeness, individuality, and a sense of family. Transactions are controlled by congruence of beliefs and consensual objectives (Ouchi, 1980). The upper right quadrant is not identified by Ouchi as a major type of organization. However, Bennis (1973), Toffler (1980), Mintzberg (1979), and Hedberg, Nystrom, and Starbuck (1976) use the term *adhocracy* to describe this type of culture. It emphasizes entrepreneurship, creativity, adaptability, and dynamism. Transactions are governed by flexibility and tolerance, development and growth, and a commitment to innovation (Mintzberg, 1979).

The relative placement of these four cultural types in the figure illustrates the relationship each holds to the others. Consistent with the competing values model of organizational effectiveness and the Jungian framework of cognitive types, each culture possesses opposite characteristics from the diagonal culture in the figure but shares some characteristics with the two cultures in the adjacent quadrants. For example, hierarchies are opposite from adhocracies in characteristics but share some characteristics of internal orientation with clans and some characteristics of control and order with markets. Few organizations are likely to be characterized by only one culture, since each culture in the model is an ideal or pure type. Most organizations have attributes of more than one of the cultures, and paradoxical cultures often characterize organizations.

CULTURAL CONGRUENCE

Figure 2 identifies characteristics of each cultural type that have appeared in the literature. Specifically, the work of Wilkins and Ouchi (1983), Quinn (1984),

Quinn and Cameron (1983), Quinn and McGrath (1984), Smircich (1983), Deal and Kennedy (1982), Lundberg (1984), Sathe (1983), Mason and Mitroff (1973), and Mitroff and Kilmann (1975) was used to identify the particular attributes of each culture that represented congruency or fit. The dominant type of leadership, the bases for bonding or coupling, and the strategic emphases present in the organization are among the important attributes that must be aligned with cultural type to produce cultural congruency, and they were selected for consideration in this study. More specifically, associated with each cultural type is a particular style of leadership that best enforces and shares its values. The research of Mitroff and Kilmann (1975, 1976), for example, found that certain types of managers are reinforced by and share the values of certain types of organizations. Quinn (1984) elaborated this fit between leader style and cultural type in a review of the leadership literature. In brief, he found that the coordinator, organizer, and administrator roles are most consistent with the characteristics of the hierarchy culture. This cultural type reinforces the style of leadership that Mitroff and Kilmann called the ST leader. The opposite style of leader, the entrepreneur, innovator, or risk taker (Mitroff and Kilmann's NF leader), is most consistent with the adhocracy or emergent system form, since the culture emphasizes change and growth. A leader style emphasizing competitiveness, production, and achievement best fits with the market form (Mitroff and Kilmann's NT leader), whereas the clan reinforces a participative mentor, facilitator, or parent-figure style (Mitroff and Kilmann's SF leader). In each case, authors hypothesize that the appropriate leader style in each organizational type leads to a condition of minimum conflict and maximum efficiency. Congruent cultures are characterized by fit with leadership style. Incongruent cultures are characterized by lack of fit.

Other cultural characteristics enumerated in Figure 2 refer to the nature of bonding or coupling in each culture and the strategic emphases that characterize organizational action. Hierarchies rely on formal rules and policies for bonding; adhocracies on a commitment to risk, innovation, and development; markets on an emphasis on task accomplishment, customer satisfaction, and marketplace competitiveness; and clans on loyalty and tradition. The strategic emphases in hierarchies focus mainly on maintaining stability, predictability, and smooth operations; in adhocracies, mainly on prospecting, acquiring new resources, and enterpreneurship; in markets, mainly on competitive actions and achievement; and in clans, mainly on human resource development and maintaining cohesion and morale (see Quinn and Cameron, 1983; Miles and Snow, 1978; Cameron and Whetten, 1983).

In sum, because so many authors have argued that congruency among these major elements of organizational culture is associated with effective performance, and that strength in these cultural types also has a positive relationship with effectiveness, this study was designed to investigate the relationship of congruence, strength, and types of culture with organizational effectiveness. The two research questions guiding the study were: *Are organizations with congruent cultures or with "strong" cultures more effective than those with incongruent cultures or with "weak" cultures? And what is the relationship between culture type and effectiveness?*

THE STUDY'S METHODOLOGY

In a previous section, we summarized some of the drawbacks of questionnaire methodology in assessing organizational culture. We did not review, however, any shortcomings of qualitative methods. An important drawback of qualitative methods is the number of organizations that can be included in an investigation. When in-depth interviews and participant observation are the means of obtaining information on culture, cost and time constraints make multiple organizational observations prohibitive. That is why virtually all qualitative analyses of organizational culture focus on only one or a very few organizations. On the other hand, to investigate questions of cultural congruence and strength, comparisons must be made among multiple organizations. *Congruence* and *strength,* like *effectiveness,* are terms that have meaning only in relation to other referents. Therefore, in-depth qualitative analyses in one organization must be traded off against the need for multiple, comparative observations by means of questionnaire analyses.

One way to obtain the benefits of each type of method—questionnaire and qualitative—is to replace Likert-type attitude questions with written descriptions of cultural attributes, or scenarios. In qualitative methodologies, respondents are stimulated to report underlying cultural assumptions and values by responding to probing interview questions or by telling stories. Another way to obtain the same result is to write scenarios describing certain types of organizational cultures and to have individuals rate the extent to which each scenario is similar to their own organization. In this way, cultural information can be obtained from multiple perspectives and on multiple organizations. The key is to stimulate individuals to make an interpretation of their organization's culture in more than a superficial way. This is done by constructing word pictures for respondents that they can use as reflections of cultural attributes. These word pictures help respondents to convey not just the extent to which they are satisfied or dissatisfied with their organization (climate) but the core values and orientations that characterize it (its culture). Table 1 provides the scenarios used to obtain the organizational culture data.

THE INSTITUTIONAL SAMPLE USED IN THE STUDY

The 334 colleges and universities in the United States selected for inclusion in this study were representative of the entire population of four-year higher education institutions in America. No known bias existed in the sample of institutions or respondents (see Cameron, 1985a, for a sample description).

At each of the 334 schools, individuals were identified who could provide an

TABLE 1. An Instrument for Assessing Organizational Culture

These questions relate to the type of organization that your institution is most like. Each of these items contains four descriptions of institutions of higher education. Please distribute 100 points among the four descriptions depending on how similar the description is to your school. None of the descriptions is any better than the others; they are just different. **For each question, please use all 100 points.**

FOR EXAMPLE:
In question 1, if institution A seems very similar to mine, B seems somewhat similar, and C and D do not seem similar at all, I might give 70 points to A and the remaining 30 points to B.

1. **Institutional Characteristics (Please distribute 100 points)**_____

_____ points for A   Institution A is a very personal place. It is like an extended family. People seem to share a lot of themselves.

_____ points for B   Institution B is a very dynamic and entrepreneurial place. People are willing to stick their necks out and take risks.

_____ points for C   Institution C is a very formalized and structured place. Bureaucratic procedures generally govern what people do.

_____ points for D   Institution D is very production oriented. A major concern is with getting the job done. People aren't personally involved.

2. **Institutional Leader (Please distribute 100 points)** _____

_____ points for A   The head of institution A is generally considered to be a mentor, a sage, or a father or mother figure.

_____ points for B   The head of institution B is generally considered to be an entrepreneur, an innovator, or a risk taker.

_____ points for C   The head of institution C is generally considered to be a coordinator, an organizer, or an administrator.

_____ points for D   The head of institution D is generally considered to be a producer, a technician, or a hard driver.

3. **Institutional "Glue" (Please distribute 100 points)**_____

_____ points for A   The glue that holds institution A together is loyalty and tradition. Commitment to this school runs high.

_____ points for B   The glue that holds institution B together is a commitment to innovation and development. There is an emphasis on being first.

_____ points for C   The glue that holds institution C together is formal rules and policies. Maintaining a smooth-running institution is important here.

_____ points for D   The glue that holds institution D together is the emphasis on tasks and goal accomplishment. A production orientation is commonly shared.

4. **Institutional Emphases (Please distribute 100 points)**_____

_____ points for A   Institution A emphasizes human resources. High cohesion and morale in the school are important.

_____ points for B   Institution B emphasizes growth and acquiring new resources. Readiness to meet new challenges is important.

_____ points for C   Institution C emphasizes permanence and stability. Efficient, smooth operations are important.

_____ points for D   Institution D emphasizes competitive actions and achievement. Measurable goals are important.

overall institutional perspective, that is, who had a view of the overall institution's culture and not just a small subunit perspective. These respondents constituted the internal dominant coalition for each institution and consisted of presidents; chief academic, finance, student affairs, external affairs, and institutional research officers; selected faculty department heads; and selected members of the board of trustees. Of the 3,406 individuals participating in the study (55% of the total receiving a questionnaire), 1,317 were administrators (39% of the sample); 1,162 were department heads (34% of the sample); and 927 were trustees (27% of the sample).

ASSESSING ORGANIZATIONAL CULTURE IN THE STUDY

Brief scenarios were constructed that described the dominant characteristics of each of the four cultural types in Figure 2. The four types were all present as alternatives in each question. Respondents divided 100 points among the four alternatives in the question depending on how similar they thought their own organization was to the scenario. This gave them the opportunity to indicate both the type of culture(s) that characterized the organization and the strength of the culture (i.e., the more points given, the stronger, or more dominant, the cultural type). As mentioned before, the rationale for this type of question was that underlying assumptions about organizational culture were more likely to emerge from questions that asked respondents to react to already-constructed organizational descriptions than from asking respondents to generate the descriptions themselves. The questions were intended to serve essentially as mirrors, where respondents rated their familiarity with each different reflection. One question assessed the general cultural characteristics, a second assessed leader style, a third assessed institutional bonding or coupling, and a fourth assessed strategic emphases.

When respondents gave the highest number of points to cultural attributes representing the same quadrant of Figure 2, the institution was identified as having a congruent culture. For example, if a respondent gave the most points to the scenario indicating a clan-type culture, identified the leader as a facilitator or mentor, and indicated that bonding occurred on the basis of loyalty, and that strategic emphases focused on human resource development—all upper-left-quadrant attributes—then the organization was labeled a congruent culture. On the other hand, it was also possible to identify incongruent cultures if the highest number of points represented a different quadrant for each of the four cultural attributes (e.g., a clan [upper left] was led by an entrepreneur [upper right], bonded together by formal rules [lower left], and strategically emphasized competitive actions [lower right]). Different amounts of congruence were represented by having two or three of the quadrants receive the highest number of points, so that a continuum of congruence could be derived from the instrument ranging from complete *incongruence* (when a different quadrant was dominant in each question) to complete *congruence* of the culture (when the same quadrant was dominant in each of the four questions).

In addition, it was possible to determine the *strength* of the culture based on the number of points given to the attributes. When respondents gave, say, 70 points to an attribute rather than, say, 40 points, that attribute was considered to be stronger, or more dominant, in the culture. *Type* of culture was also determined in the questions by examining organizations with congruent cultures and determining which of the four types of culture was dominant. A clan culture was indicated by congruence among the four attributes in the upper left quadrant (i.e., a personal place, like a family; led by a mentor, facilitator, or parent figure; bonded together by loyalty and tradition; and emphasizing human resources). An adhocracy was indicated by congruence among the four attributes in the upper right quadrant (i.e., a dynamic, entrepreneurial place; led by an entrepreneur or innovator; held together by a commitment to innovation and development; and emphasizing growth and acquiring new resources). A hierarchy was indicated by congruence in the lower-left-hand quadrant (i.e., a formalized, structured place; led by a coordinator or organizer; held together by formal rules and policies; and emphasizing permanence and stability). A market was indicated by congruence in the lower right quadrant (i.e., a production-oriented place; led by a hard driver or producer; held together by an emphasis on task and goal accomplishment; and emphasizing competitive actions and achievement).

The points given by respondents to each attribute in each institution were averaged to produce an organization score for each attribute in each type of culture (e.g., a leader style score was produced for each of the four cultural types). These scores were used first to investigate the validity of the four culture types and to compare the organizational effectiveness of congruent and incongruent cultures, strong and weak cultures, and the different types of cultures on the basis of institutional mean scores.

IDENTIFICATION OF CULTURES IN THE STUDY

Table 2 presents a summary of the descriptive data analyses. No institution was characterized totally by only one culture (i.e., none received all 100 points on an attribute), but dominant cultures were clearly evident in some of the schools. For example, 47 institutions (14%) were classified as having congruent cultures, with 11 more added (3%) if tie scores were included. (That is, 11 organizations gave equal points to at least two different quadrants, one of which was the congruent quadrant.) Thirty-two organizations (10%) had completely incongruent cultures. The largest number of organizations had congruence in three of the quadrants (124, or 37%) with 55 more added (16%) if those with one tie were included. Sixty-six organizations (20%) were congruent in only two of the quadrants.

**TABLE 2. Description of the Cultures of 334 Colleges
and Universities**

Number of congruent quadrants		Number of organizations	
4		47	
4 with ties		11	
3		124	
3 with ties		55	
2		66	
1		32	
Type of culture	Congruent	Incongruent	Strong culture
Clan	25		21
Adhocracy	9		4
Hierarchy	12		3
Market	1		0
Total	47	32	28

Clans were the most numerous type of culture in the sample. Of the organizations, 25 had congruent clan cultures (7% of the total sample), 9 were adhocracies (3%), 12 were hierarchies (4%), and only 1 was a market. Strong culture was defined by at least 50 points being given to a particular attribute. If an organization was a congruent clan, for example, and all the clan attributes received at least 50 points, it was classified as a strong culture. Of the congruent organizations, 28 (57%) had strong cultures: 21 were clans, 4 were adhocracies, and 3 were hierarchies.

INVESTIGATING THE VALIDITY
OF CULTURAL TYPES IN THE STUDY

The first analysis was an investigation of the organizational characteristics associated with each culture type. For validity purposes, it was of interest to determine if each culture type was associated with traits consistent with the theoretical framework. That is, clan cultures should be associated with different kinds of organizational structures and processes than, say, markets if the proposed model is to be considered valid. Table 3 reports the results of discriminant analyses in which a large number of organizational attributes and strategies were used as discriminators. These variables were all based in the organizational literature as important descriptors of cultures and were assessed in

TABLE 3. The Most Powerful Discriminators Among the Four Organizational Cultures

Function	Eigenvalue	Canonical Correlation	Wilks' Lambda	Chi Square	D.F.	Significance
1	8.999	.949	.013	157.760	45	.0000
2	2.994	.866	.133	73.717	28	.0000
3	.887	.686	.530	23.174	13	.0396

	I		II		III	
Variables	A^a	B^b	A	B	A	B
Distinctive purpose (saga)	.754	.524***	-.558	-.012	-.148	-.171
Mission agreement (saga)	.057	.449***	.930	.337**	.274	-.124
Increasing innovation	-.413	.438***	-.840	-.447**	-.686	.080
Increasing morale	.101	.349***	.289	-.037	.735	.204
Absence of slack	-.386	-.437***	.205	.156	.316	.135
Higher leader credibility	-.911	.210	-.592	-.193	-1.208	-.291*
Increasing boundary spanning	.524	.586***	.027	-.169	.305	.111
Prospector strategy	.377	.370**	-.304	-.619***	.942	.590***
Increasing administrator quality	.716	.552***	.187	-.074	-.306	.061
Emphasizing revenue initiatives	.364	.414***	-.455	-.459***	-.155	-.054
Anarchy (decision style)	1.533	.150	.178	.012	-.343	-.171
Collegial (decision style)	.374	.385***	.548	.302**	-.136	.008
Rational (decision style)	1.474	.365**	.406	.064	.192	.063
Student personal development	.222	.391***	.388	.456***	.086	-.258*
System openness	.667	.490***	.022	-.031	.010	.031

Group	Centroid 1	Centroid 2	Centroid 3	Percent correctly classified
Clan culture	1.617	.949	-.435	
Adhocracy culture	2.179	-2.565	1.004	100
Hierarchy culture	-4.513	.499	.534	
Market culture	-5.873	-6.636	-4.569	

^{a}A = discriminant coefficient. ^{b}B = correlation with the discriminant score. *p < .05; **p < .01; ***p < .001.

each of the 334 institutions via the questionnaire. Strategy, structure, decision-making style, leadership style, and organizational processes were among the types of variables assessed. (See Cameron, 1985a, for explanations and justifications of these variables and for a detailed description of the statistical procedures used.)

Three discriminant functions were produced with this analysis, resulting in 100% of the institutions being correctly classified in the appropriate culture after knowing their scores on the organizational attributes. This indicates that the discriminating variables were very powerful and that the cultures differed significantly from one another.

The results supported the validity of the theoretical framework. Institutions with clan cultures were characterized by variables such as high morale and collegial decision-making. Institutions with adhocracy cultures were characterized by variables such as innovative strategies and boundary spanning. Institutions with hierarchy cultures were characterized by variables such as mechanistic structures and an absence of slack resources. Institutions with market cultures were characterized by variables such as market initiative and proactivity. These results suggested that, in general, the four types of cultures are linked to organizational attributes that are consistent with their conceptual rationale and with the underlying Jungian framework. Moreover, the results help support the view that culture may be used as *either* something the organization *has* or something the organization *is*. Organizations may be thought of as clans, hierarchies, adhocracies, or markets—something the organization is—since this framework helps organize cultural and organizational attributes (e.g., Ouchi, 1980; Williamson, 1975). Or they may be thought of as entities with cultural types that predict other attributes of organizations, such as performance or effectiveness. Using the latter approach, the study investigated the relationship between major cultural dimensions and effectiveness.

COMPARISONS AMONG CULTURES IN THE STUDY

In order to investigate the assumed congruence hypothesis (i.e., that congruent cultures are more effective than incongruent cultures), it was necessary to assess the organizational effectiveness of the institutions in the study. This was done using the nine dimensions of effectiveness developed by Cameron (1978, 1981, 1986), which were found to be both valid and reliable indicators of the effectiveness of colleges and universities. Long-term viability of institutions, as well as current levels of high performance in colleges, is strongly associated with scores on those dimensions of effectiveness. Those dimensions are:

1. Student educational satisfaction

2. Student academic development

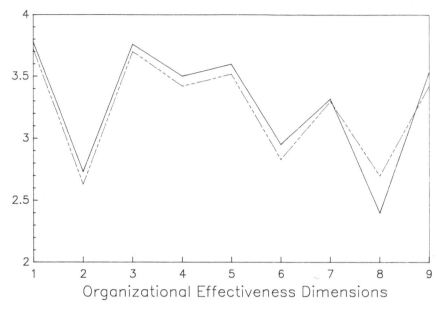

FIG. 3. A comparison of congruent and incongruent cultures.
Solid line: congruent. Dashed line: incongruent.

3. Student career development

4. Student personal development

5. Faculty and administrator employment satisfaction

6. Professional development and quality of the faculty

7. System openness and community interaction

8. Ability to acquire resources

9. Organizational health

Mean scores on each of the effectiveness dimensions were computed for each institution, and comparisons were made between congruent and incongruent cultures and between strong and weak cultures. Figures 3, 4, and 5 summarize the results. No significant differences were found between the means of organizations possessing a congruent culture and those possessing an incongruent culture on any dimension of effectiveness (Figure 3). Even when five different levels of congruence were used, no differences appeared (Figure 4). The same was true of the comparisons between strong and weak cultures (Figure 5).

On the other hand, comparisons made among the four types of cultures—clan,

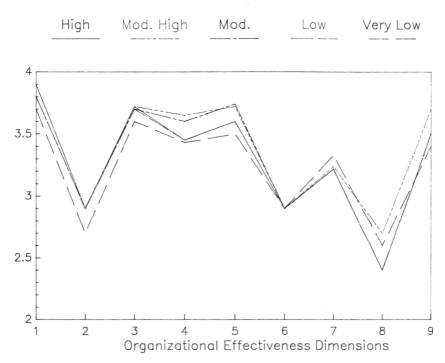

FIG. 4. A comparison among five levels of cultural congruence.

adhocracy, hierarchy, and market—along with the incongruent culture on the nine dimensions of effectiveness revealed significant differences among the groups' mean effectiveness scores on five of the nine dimensions (Figure 6). Clan cultures scored highest on four of the dimensions, adhocracy cultures scored highest on four of the nine dimensions, and the market culture scored highest on the remaining dimension. On no dimension did the incongruent group score lowest. At least one congruent culture group scored lowest on each of the effectiveness dimensions.

What these results point out is that cultural congruence and cultural strength do not predict effectiveness in colleges and universities. Rather, the type of culture present has a much stronger association with effectiveness on certain dimensions than the other two attributes of culture. In fact, an interesting finding was the discovery of the consistency between the dimensions of effectiveness on which the various cultures scored highest and their primary cultural attributes.

Past research has found that the nine dimensions of effectiveness used in this

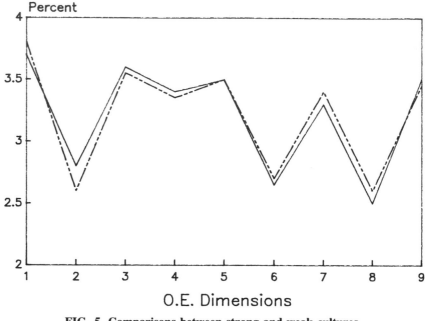

FIG. 5. Comparisons between strong and weak cultures.
Solid line: strong. Dashed line: weak.

study are associated with three major domains of activity in colleges and universities (see Cameron, 1981, for an explanation of effectiveness domains in higher education). Table 4 (see p. 386) gives the domains with which each effectiveness dimension is associated and matches each dimension and domain with the culture that scored highest.

For example, clans scored highest on the four dimensions of effectiveness associated with the morale domain in colleges and universities. This is consistent with the attributes of the clan culture, with its emphasis on human resources, consensus, and cohesion. The adhocracy culture, with its emphasis on innovation, creativity, and entrepreneurship, scored highest on the two dimensions comprising the external adaptation domain, which is consistent with the conceptual rationale, and on two dimensions comprising the academic domain. This latter finding also appears to be consistent with the emphases present in an adhocracy—freedom and individual discretion, creativity, growth, and development—all of which form the core of the values of scholarship and academics. The market culture scored highest on the ability to acquire resources, which is consistent with the orientation of market organizations. With an emphasis on

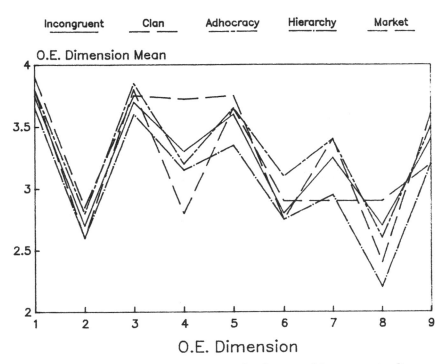

FIG. 6. Comparisons among four types of cultures and incongruent cultures.

competitive actions and achievements, and with an orientation toward external (rather than internal) resources, it is not surprising that the market culture was most effective in acquiring resources from the environment. (Adhocracies scored next highest, a finding also consistent with expectations.)

This study revealed, then, that the effectiveness of institutions is more closely associated with the *type* of culture present than with the *congruence* or the *strength* of that culture. The major attributes and emphases of a culture tend to be associated with high effectiveness in comparable domains. Probably a more important contribution of the study, however, is that it introduces and helps develop a theoretically based framework of organizational culture. The evidence supporting the framework's validity in higher education institutions is strong and should help provide a stimulus for others to investigate further the properties of that framework.

SUMMARY OF PROPOSITIONS FOR INSTITUTIONS OF HIGHER EDUCATION

The summary of Cameron's (1985a) study and the review of the culture literature at the beginning of the chapter have now prepared us to identify some

TABLE 4. A Summary of Which Culture Scored Highest on Which Dimension of Organizational Effectiveness

Dimensions of effectiveness	Domain (Cameron, 1981)	Culture scoring highest[a]
1. Student educational satisfaction	Morale	Clan
2. Student academic development	Academic	Adhocracy
3. Student career development	External adaptation	Adhocracy
4. Student personal development	Morale	Clan
5. Faculty and administrator employment satisfaction	Morale	Clan
6. Professional development and quality of the faculty	Academic	Adhocracy
7. System openness and community interaction	External adaptation	Adhocracy
8. Ability to acquire resources	Academic	Market
9. Organizational health	Morale	Clan

[a]The highest scoring culture was significantly higher ($p \leq .05$) than at least one other culture on each dimension of effectiveness.

propositions regarding the relationship between organizational culture and institutions of higher education. In so doing, our purpose is to use this summary to advance testable hypotheses for future investigators of organizational culture in higher education. We do not intend to suggest that these propositions summarize all we know about organizational culture. Instead, our purpose is to identify some theoretically based and commonly assumed relationships between culture and other higher education outcomes. Investigating these propositions and hypotheses may help researchers progress toward a more integrated and cumulative literature. Up to now, lack of theory and definitional ambiguity threaten to perpetuate a faddishness in organizational culture research. We hope this chapter provides a step in helping to overcome that tendency.

Because few studies of organizational culture have been conducted in multiple institution sites in higher education, many of these summary propositions are based on studies in other organizational sectors (e.g., business organizations). Whereas it is not uncommon for higher education researchers to borrow from business research, we should not assume that the applicability is direct in all cases. Therefore, whereas these 20 propositions all have supporting evidence available from some investigation, the extent to which they are indicative of colleges and universities is still somewhat questionable:

1. No single type of culture is best in all environmental conditions (Cameron, 1985a; Ernest, 1985). A match must exist between culture and environment (Deal and Kennedy, 1983).

2. The changing demographic composition of institutions of higher education (e.g., nationality and age) may lead to a change in the culture of these organizations (Adler and Jelinek, 1986). A shift from clans to markets is a likely change (Cameron and Ulrich, 1986).

3. Cultures shift as institutions develop over time, especially when growth or decline occurs. Different leaders and different criteria of success become valued at different times (Quinn and Cameron, 1983; Cameron, Whetten, and Kim 1987).

4. All institutions have attributes of all four culture types, and a majority of institutions are not characterized by one dominant type. Most institutions do not have a congruent culture (Cameron, 1985a).

5. The clan culture in institutions is usually inherently stronger (i.e., has more impact on an individual's behavior) than the cultures of markets and hierarchies (Wilkins and Ouchi, 1983).

6. Strong cultures that are also externally oriented (i.e., adhocracies and markets) are more successful in turbulent, competitive environments (such as typify current conditions) than weak, internally oriented cultures (Arnold and Capella, 1985).

7. Certain types of cultures better foster organizational learning and therefore are better able to avoid stagnation and "groupthink," mainly markets and adhocracies (Fiol and Lyles, 1985; Bennis and Nanus, 1985).

8. A certain amount of nonconformity must be permitted in the organization's culture in order to prevent stagnation (i.e., some emphasis must exist in the adhocracy quadrant) (Sathe, 1983).

9. Holographic cultures are less adaptive than ideographic cultures in organizations (Albert and Whetten, 1985). Diverse subcultures with a weak overall culture may be most adaptive in changing environments (Schein, 1984).

10. A changing culture requires that other major aspects of an organization change also, such as strategy, structure, relevant skills of personnel, and the human resource system (i.e., rewards, selection, appraisal, and development systems) (Waterman, Peters, and Philips, 1980; Kilmann, Saxton, and Serpa, 1985). Culture change assumes broad-scale systems change.

11. Cultures lead to effectiveness when the organization's leader articulates a consistent vision that is clearly understood by organizational members (Gordon, 1985; Cameron and Ulrich, 1986; Tichy and Devanna, 1986).

12. Socialization practices for new employees that utilize the following characteristics lead to a strong culture and, presumably, to organizational effectiveness (Pascale, 1985; Martin and Siehl, 1983; Louis, 1980; Trice, 1983):

a. Conscious use of rhetoric oriented toward establishing a sense of community.
b. Convincing new members that the organization has their best interests at heart.
c. Cultivating jokes, stories, and sagas and communicating them frequently to new employees.
d. Utilizing off-site training experiences for new employees.
e. Designing rites of passage that are communicated and rewarded.
f. Carefully selecting entry-level candidates.
g. Inducing humility, or generating a desire to adopt the new culture in new employees.
h. Training new members "in the trenches" with meaningful, responsible jobs.
i. Reward and control systems reinforcing the desired behaviors that are consistent with the corporate culture.
j. Requiring personal sacrifices to enter the institution.
k. Developing mentoring relationships.
l. Leaders providing constant and consistent role models.

13. The greater the discrepancy between private organizational identity and public identity (i.e., incongruence), the lower the organizational effectiveness (Albert and Whetten, 1985).

14. Strong cultures are more apt to lead to organizational effectiveness than weak cultures, especially in environments that challenge or threaten the survival of the institution (Lofland, 1971; Deal and Kennedy, 1982; Ashforth, 1985).

15. Participative cultures have more impact on effectiveness than strong and congruent cultures (Denison, 1984; Heller and Guastello, 1982).

16. Clarity of culture leads to effectiveness and arises from clear communication from the leader (Albrecht and Zemke, 1985).

17. Organizational size decreases the utility of culture for controlling behavior (Jones, 1983).

18. A well-organized work environment (i.e., a consistent culture) leads to organizational effectiveness (Denison, 1984).

19. Employees are more committed to organizations where cultures are richer and stronger (i.e., have more stories told about them) (Wilkins, 1979).

20. Cultural change in organizations requires the conscious destruction of old processes and structures, as well as the institutionalization of new processes and structures. Symbolic or interpretation changes are at least as important as substantive or strategic changes (Miles and Cameron, 1982; Cameron and Ulrich, 1986; Chaffee, 1984).

Acknowledgments. The authors gratefully acknowledge the financial support of the National Center for the Improvement of Teaching and Learning through contract number G008690010 with the U.S. Office of Educational Research.

REFERENCES

Adler, N. J., and Jelinek, M. (1986). Is "organizational culture" culture bound? *Human Resource Management* 25: 73–90.

Administrative Science Quarterly, Special issue on Organizational Culture. (1983). 28: 331–502.

Agar, M. H. (1982). Whatever happened to cognitive anthropology: a partial review. *Human Organization* 11: 83–86.

Albert, S., and Whetten, D. A. (1985). Organizational identity. *Research in Organizational Behavior* 7: 263–502.

Albrecht, K., and Zemke, R. (1985). Instilling a service mentality: like teaching an elephant to dance. *International Management* 40(11): 61–67.

Allaire, Y., and Firsirotu, M. E. (1984). Theories of organizational culture. *Organization Studies* 5: 193–226.

Arnold, D. R., and Capella, L. M. (1985). Corporate culture and the marketing concept: a diagnostic instrument for utilities. *Public Utilities Fortnightly* 116(8): 32–38.

Ashforth, B. E. (1985). Climate formation: issues and extensions. *Academy of Management Review* 10: 837–847.

Barley, S. R. (1983a). Semiotics and the study of occupational and organizational cultures. *Administrative Science Quarterly* 28: 393–413.

Barley, S. R. (1983b). The evolution of roles in technological subculture: a case from CAT scanning. Presented at the conference on Interpretative Approaches to Study of Organizations, Alta, Utah.

Barley, S. R. (1983c). Codes of the dead. *Urban Life* 12(1).

Bate, P. (1984). The impact of organizational culture on approaches to organizational problem-solving. *Organization Studies* 5: 43–66.

Beck, B., and Moore, L. (1984). Linking the host culture to organizational variables. Presented at the Conference on Organizational Culture and Meaning of Life in the Workplace, Vancouver, Canada.

Beck, B., and Moore, L. (1983). Influence of corporate image on manager's styles: the example of five Canadian banks. Presented at the Conference on Organizational Folklore, Santa Monica, CA.

Bennis, W. G. (1973). *The Leaning Ivory Tower.* San Francisco: Jossey-Bass.

Bennis, W., and Nanus, B. (1985). Organizational learning: the management of the collective self. *New Management* 3(1): 6–13.

Berger, P. L., and Luckmann, T. (1966). *The Social Construction of Reality: A Treatise in the Sociology of Knowledge.* New York: Anchor.

Bhagat, R. S., and McQuaid, S. J. (1982). Role of subjective culture in organizations: a review and reflections for future research. *Journal of Applied Psychology Monograph* 67(5): 653–685.

Blau, P. M., and Scott, W. R. (1962). *Formal Organizations.* San Francisco: Chandler.

Blumer, H. (1969). *Symbolic Interactionism: Perspective and Method.* Englewood Cliffs, NJ: Prentice-Hall.

Boje, D. (1983). The fraternal spirit and folklore of the commercial printer. UCLA Graduate School of Management, Working Paper No. 83–27.

Boje, D. M., Fedor, D. B., and Reinwand, K. M. (1982). Mythmaking: a qualitative step in OD intervention. *Journal of Applied Behavioral Science* 18: 17–28.

Bowditch, J., Buono, A., and Lewis, J., III (1983). When cultures collide: the anatomy of a merger. Presented at the Academy of Management Meetings, Dallas.

Bresser, R. K., and Dunbar, R. L. M. (1986). Context, structure, and academic effectiveness: evidence from West Germany. *Organization Studies* 7: 1–24.

Broms, H., and Gahmberg, H. (1983). Communication to self in organizations and cultures. *Administrative Science Quarterly* 28: 482–495.

Burrell, G., and Morgan, G. (1979). *Sociological Paradigms and Organizational Analysis.* London: Heineman.

Cameron, K. S. (1978). Measuring organizational effectiveness in institutions of higher education. *Administrative Science Quarterly* 23(4): 604–632.

Cameron, K. S. (1981). Domains of organizational effectiveness in colleges and universities. *Academy of Management Journal* 24: 25–47.

Cameron, K. S. (1985a). Cultural congruence, strength, and type: relationships to effectiveness. Unpublished working paper, the University of Michigan Business School.

Cameron, K. S. (1985b). The paradox in institutional renewal. In R. Davis (ed.), *New Directions in Higher Education.* San Francisco: Jossey-Bass.

Cameron, K. S. (1986). A study of organizational effectiveness and its predictors. *Management Science* 32: 87–112.

Cameron, K. S., and Ulrich, D. (1986). Transformational leadership in colleges and universities. In J. Smart (ed.), *Higher Education: Handbook of Theory and Research,* Vol. 2. New York: Agathon.

Cameron, K. S., and Whetten, D. A. (1983). Models of the organizational life cycle: applications to higher education. *Review of Higher Education* 6: 269–299.

Cameron, K. S., Whetten, D. A., and Kim, M. U. (1987). Organizational dysfunctions of decline. *Academy of Management Journal.* 30(1): 126–138.

Carrier, H. D., and Quinn, R. E. (1985). The understructure of social theory: an empirical examination of the competing values leadership model. Working paper, Rockefeller College, SUNY-Albany.

Center for Applications of Psychological Type. (1980). Gainesville, Florida.

Chaffee, E. E. (1984). Successful strategic management in small private colleges. *Journal of Higher Education* 55: 212–241.

Chomsky, N. (1972). *Language and Mind.* New York: Harcourt Brace Jovanovich.

Churchman, C. W. (1971). *The Design on Inquiry System.* New York: Basic Books.

Churchman, C. W. (1964). Managerial acceptance of scientific recommendations. *California Management Review* 7: 31–38.

Clark, B. R. (1970). *The Distinctive College: Antioch, Reed and Swarthmore.* Chicago: Aldine.

Deal, T. E., and Kennedy, A. A. (1982). *Corporate Cultures: The Rights and Rituals of Corporate Life.* Reading, MA: Addison-Wesley.

Deal, T. E., and Kennedy, A. A. (1983). Culture: a new look through old lenses. *Journal of Applied Behavioral Science* 19(4).

Denison, D. R. (1984). Bringing corporate culture to the bottom line. *Organizational Dynamics* 13(2): 4–22.

Driver, M. (1979). Individual decision making and creativity. In S. Kerr (Ed.), *Organizational Behavior.* Columbus, OH: Grid Press.

Driver, M. (1983). Decision style and organizational behavior: Implications for academia. *Review of Higher Education* 6: 149–168.

Durkheim, E. (1893): *The Division of Labor in Society.* (Transl. G. Simpson, 1933.) New York: Fill.

Dyer, W. G., Jr. (1982). Culture in organizations: a case study. MIT Sloan School of Management, working paper.

Ernest, R. C. (1985). Corporate cultures and effective planning: an introduction to the organizational culture grid. *Personnel Administrator* 30(3): 49–60.

Evered, R. (1983). The language of organizations: The case of the Navy. In Pondy et al., *Organizational Symbolism*, pp. 125–144.

Fiol, C. M., and Lyles, M. A. (1985). Organizational learning. *Academy of Management Review* 10: 803–813.

Frost, P., and Morgan, G. (1983). Symbols and sensemaking: The realization of a framework. In Pondy et al., *Organizational Symbolism*, pp. 207–236.

Galbraith, J. R., and Kazanjian, R. K. (1986). *Strategy Implementation: Structure, Systems, and Process*. St. Paul, MN: West.

Geertz, C. (1973). *The Interpretation of Cultures*. New York: Basic Books.

Glick, W. H. (1985). Conceptualizing and measuring organizational and psychological climate: pitfalls in multilevel research. *Academy of Management Review* 10: 601–616.

Goffman, E. (1959). *The Presentation of Self in Everyday Life*. New York: Doubleday.

Goodenough, W. (1971). *Culture, Language, and Society*. Reading, MA: Addison-Wesley Modular Publ., No. 7.

Gordon, G. G. (1985). The relationship of corporate culture to industry sector and corporate performance. In R. H. Kilmann, M. J. Saxton, R. Serpa, and Associates (eds.), *Gaining Control of the Corporate Culture*, pp. 103–125. San Francisco: Jossey-Bass.

Gregory, K. (1983). Native-view paradigms: multiple cultures and culture conflicts in organizations. *Administrative Science Quarterly* 28: 359–376.

Gulick, L., and Urwick, L. (1937). *Papers on the Science of Administration*. New York: Institute of Public Administration, Columbia University.

Harrison, R. (1972). Understanding your organization's character. *Harvard Business Review* 5: 119–128.

Hedberg, B. L. T., Nystrom, P. C., and Starbuck, W. H. (1976). Camping on seesaws. *Administrative Science Quarterly* 21: 41–65.

Heller, R. M., and Guastello, S. J. (1982). Convergent and discriminant validity of psychological and objective indices of organizational climate. *Psychological Reports* 51: 183–195.

Henderson, J. C., and Nutt, P. C. (1980). The influence of decision style on decision making behavior. *Management Science* 26: 371–386.

Hofstede, G. (1980). *Culture's Consequences: International Differences in Work-Related Values*. Beverly Hills, CA: Sage Publications.

Hollowell, A. I. (1955). *Cultures and Experience*. Philadelphia: University of Pennsylvania Press.

Homans, G. (1950). *The Human Group*. New York: Harcourt, Brace, and World.

Huff, A. (1983). A rhetorical examination of strategic change. In Pondy et al., *Organizational Symbolism*.

Jaeger, A. M. (1986). Organization development and national culture: where's the fit? *Academy of Management Review* 11: 178–190.

Jaynes, J. (1976). *The Origin of Consciousness in the Breakdown of the Bicameral Mind*. Boston: Houghton Mifflin.

Jelinek, M., Smircich, L., and Hirsch, P. (1983). Introduction (to ASQ special issue): a code of many colors. *Administrative Science Quarterly* 28: 331–338.

Jones, G. R. (1983). Transaction costs, property rights, and organizational culture: an exchange perspective. *Administrative Science Quarterly* 28: 454–467.

Jones, W. T. (1961). *The Romantic Syndrome: Towards a New Method in Cultural Anthropology and the History of Ideas*. The Hague: Martinus Wijhaff.

Jung, C. G. (1973). *Four Archetypes, Mother/Rebirth/Spirit/Trickster*. Princeton, NJ: Princeton University Press.

Jung, C. G. (1923). *Psychological Types*. London: Routledge & Kegan Paul.

Kanter, R. (1968). Commitment and social organization: A study of commitment mechanisms in utopian communities. *American Sociological Review* 33: 499–517.

Keen, P. G. W. (1981). Cognitive style research: a perspective for integration. Proceedings of the Second International Conference on Information Systems, Cambridge, MA.

Keesing, R. (1974). Theories of culture. *Annual Review of Anthropology* 3: 73–97.

Kets de Vries, M. F. R., and Miller, D. (1986). Personality, culture, and organization. *Academy of Management Review* 11: 266–279.

Kilmann, R. H., Saxton, M. J., and Serpa, R. (1985). Introduction: five key issues in understanding and changing culture. In R. H. Kilmann, M. J. Saxton, R. Serpa, and Associates (eds.), *Gaining Control of the Corporate Culture*, pp. 1–16. San Francisco: Jossey-Bass.

Kotter, J. P. (1980). An integrative model of organizational dynamics. In E. E. Lawler, D. A. Nadler, and C. Cammann (eds.), *Organizational Assessment: Perspectives on the Measurement of Organizational Behavior and the Quality of Working Life*. New York: Wiley.

Krieger, S. (1979). *Hip Capitalism*. Beverly Hills: Sage.

Leitko, T. A. (1984). Organizational culture change: theme appreciation in a university. *Sociological Practice* 5(1): 37–64.

Lewin, A. Y., and Minton, J. W. (1986). Determining organizational effectiveness—another look, and an agenda for research. *Management Science* 32(5): 514–538.

Lofland, J. (1971). *Analyzing Social Settings*. Belmont, CA: Wadsworth.

Louis, M. R. (1984). An investigators guide to workplace culture: assumptions, choice points, and alternatives. Presented at the Conference on Organizational Culture and Meaning of Life in the Workplace, Vancouver, Canada.

Louis, M. R. (1983). Organizations as culture-bearing milieux. In Pondy et al., *Organizational Symbolism*, pp. 39–54.

Louis, M. R. (1980). Surprise and sense making—what newcomers experience in entering unfamiliar organizational settings. *Administrative Science Quarterly* 25: 226–251.

Lundberg, C. (1984). In J. R. Kimberly and R. E. Quinn (eds.), *The Management of Organizational Transitions*. Homewood, IL: Irwin.

Malinowski, B. (1961). *Argonauts of the Western Pacific*. London: Routledge, Kegan Paul.

Manning, P. (1979). Metaphors of the field: varieties of organizational discourse. *Administrative Science Quarterly* 24: 660–671.

Martin, H. J. (1985). Managing specialized corporate cultures. In R. H. Kilmann, M. J. Saxton, R. Serpa, and Associates (eds.), *Gaining Control of the Corporate Culture*, pp. 148–162. San Francisco: Jossey-Bass.

Martin, J., and Powers, M. (1983). Truth or corporate propaganda: the value of a good war story. In Pondy et al. (eds.), *Organizational Symbolism*, pp. 93–108.

Martin, J., and Siehl, C. (1983). Organizational culture and counter-culture: an uneasy symbiosis. *Organizational Dynamics* 12(2): 52–64.

Martin, J., Feldman, M. S., Hatch, M., and Sitkin, S. B. (1983). The uniqueness paradox in organizational stories. *Administrative Science Quarterly* 28: 438–453.

Mason, R. O., and Mitroff, I. I. (1973). A program for research in management. *Management Science* 19.

McCaulley, M. H. (1977). The Myers longitudinal medical study. Center for the applications of psychological type, Monograph 2, Gainesville, FL.

McKenney, J. L., and Keen, P. G. W. (1974). How managers minds work. *Harvard Business Review* 51: 79–90.

Meyer, A. (1982). How ideologies supplant formal structures and shape responses to environments. *Journal of Management Studies* 19(1): 45–61.

Miles, R. E., and Snow, C. C. (1978). *Organizational Strategy, Structure, and Process.* New York: McGraw-Hill.

Miles, R. H., and Cameron, K. S. (1982). *Coffin Nails and Corporate Strategies.* Englewood Cliffs, NJ: Prentice-Hall.

Mintzberg, H. (1979). *The Structuring of Organizations.* Englewood Cliffs, NJ: Prentice-Hall.

Mitroff, I. (1983a). *Stakeholders of the Organizational Mind.* San Francisco: Jossey-Bass.

Mitroff, I. (1983b). Archetypal social systems analysis: on the deeper structure of human systems. *Academy of Management Review* 8: 387–397.

Mitroff, I., and Kilmann, R. (1978). *Methodological Approaches to Social Science: Integrating Divergent Concepts and Theories.* San Francisco: Jossey-Bass.

Mitroff, I. I., and Kilmann, R. H. (1976). On organizational stories: an approach to the design and analysis of organization through myths and stories. In R. H. Kilmann, L. R. Pondy, and D. F. Slevin (eds.), *The Management of Organization Design,* Vol. 2, pp. 189–207. New York: Elsevier North-Holland.

Mitroff, I. I., and Kilmann, R. H. (1975). Stories managers tell: a new tool for organizational problem solving. *Management Review* 64: 18–28.

Morgan, G., Frost, P., and Pondy, L. (1983). Organizational symbolism. In Pondy et al., *Organizational Symbolism.*

Myers, I. B. (1980). *Introduction to Type.* Palo Alto, CA: Consulting Psychologists Press.

Myers, I. B., and Briggs, K. C. (1962). *The Myers-Briggs Type Indicator.* Princeton: Educational Testing Service.

Nadler, D. A., and Tushman, M. L. (1980). A congruence model for organizational assessment. In E. E. Lawler, D. A. Nadler, and C. Cammann (eds.), *Organizational Assessment: Perspectives on the Measurement of Organizational Behavior and the Quality of Working Life.* New York: Wiley.

Newmann, E. (1970). *The Origins and History of Consciousness.* (trans. R. F. C. Hull). Princeton: Princeton University Press.

Newmann, E. (1955). *The Great Mother: An Analysis of Archetype.* Princeton: Princeton University Press.

O'Reilly, C. (1983). Corporations, cults and organizational culture: lessons from Silicon Valley firms. Presented at the Academy of Management Meetings, Dallas, Texas.

O'Reilly, C., and Moses, M. (1984). Corporations, cults, and organizational culture: lessons from Silicon Valley companies. Paper presented at the Conference on Organizational Culture and Meaning of Life in the Workplace, Vancouver.

Ouchi, W. G. (1981). *Theory Z: How American Business Can Meet the Japanese Challenge.* Reading, MA: Addison-Wesley.

Ouchi, W. G. (1980). Markets, bureaucracies, and clans. *Administrative Science Quarterly* 25: 129–141.

Ouchi, W. G., and Johnson J. (1978). Types of organizational control and their relationship to emotional well-being. *Administrative Science Quarterly* 23: 293–317.

Ouchi, W. G., and Wilkins, A. L. (1985). Organizational culture. *Annual Review of Sociology* 11: 457–83.

Pascale, R. (1985). The paradox of "corporate culture": reconciling ourselves to socialization. *California Management Review* 27(2): 26–41.

Pascale, R. T., and Athos, A. G. (1981). *The Art of Japanese Management*. New York: Warner.

Peters, T. J., and Waterman, R. H. (1982). *In Search of Excellence: Lessons from America's Best-Run Companies*. New York: Harper & Row.

Pfeffer, J. (1981). Management as symbolic action: the creation and maintenance of organizational paradigms. In L. Cummings and B. Staw (eds.), *Research in Organizational Behavior* 3: 1–51.

Pondy, L. R. (1983). The role of metaphors and myths in organization and in the facilitation of change. In Pondy et al. (eds.), *Organizational Symbolism*.

Pondy, L. R. (1978). Leadership is a language game. In M. McCall and M. Lombardo (eds.), *Leadership: Where Else Can We Go?* Greensboro, NC: Duke University Press.

Pondy, L. R., and Huff, A. (1983). Achieving routine. University of Illinois, Department of Business Administration. working paper.

Pondy, L. R., Frost, P. M., Morgan, G., and Dandridge, T. C., eds. (1983). *Organizational Symbolism*. Greenwich, CT: JAI.

Pugh, D. S., Hickson, D. J., and Hinings, C. R. (1969). The context of organizational structures. *Administrative Science Quarterly* 14: 91–114.

Quinn, R. E. (1988). *Beyond Rational Management*. San Francisco: Jossey-Bass.

Quinn, R. E. (1984). Applying the competing values approach to leadership. In J. G. Hunt, R. Stewart, C. A. Schreisheim, and D. Hosking (eds.), *Managerial Work and Leadership: International Perspectives*. New York: Pergamon.

Quinn, R. E., and Cameron, K. S. (1983). Organizational life cycles and shifting criteria of effectiveness: some preliminary evidence. *Management Science* 29: 33–51.

Quinn, R. E., and Hall, R. H. (1983). Environments, organizations, and policymakers: toward an integrative framework. In R. H. Hall and R. E. Quinn (eds.), *Organizational Theory and Public Policy*. Beverly Hills, CA: Sage.

Quinn, R. E., and McGrath, M. R. (1984). The transformation of organizational cultures: a competing values perspective. Paper presented at the Conference on Organizational Culture and Meaning of Life in the Workplace, Vancouver.

Quinn, R. E., and Rohrbaugh, J. (1983). A spatial model of effectiveness criteria: towards a competing values approach to organizational analysis. *Management Science* 29: 363–377.

Quinn, R. E., and Rohrbaugh, J. (1981). A competing values approach to organizational effectiveness. *Public Productivity Review* 5: 122–140.

Radcliffe-Brown, A. (1952). *Structure and Function in Primitive Society*. London: Oxford University Press.

Riley, P. (1983). A structurationist account of political culture. *Administrative Science Quarterly* 28: 414–437.

Roberts, K. H. (1970). On looking at an elephant: an evaluation of cross-cultural research related to organizations. *Psychological Bulletin* 74: 327–350.

Roethlisberger, F. J., and Dickson, W. J. (1939). *Management and the Worker*. Cambridge, MA: Harvard University Press.

Rohlen, T. (1974). *For Harmony and Strength: Japanese White-collar Organization in Anthropological Perspective*. Berkeley: University of California Press.

Rossi, I., and O'Higgins, E. (1980). The development of theories of culture. In Ino Rossi (ed.), *People in Culture*, pp 31–78. New York: Praeger.

Sanday, P. (1979). The ethnographic paradigm(s). *Administrative Science Quarterly* 24: 527–538.

Sapienza, A. M. (1985). Believing is seeing: how culture influences the decisions top managers make. In R. H. Kilmann, M. J. Saxton, R. Serpa, and Associates (eds.), *Gaining Control of the Corporate Culture*. San Francisco: Jossey-Bass.

Sathe, V. (1983). Implications of corporate culture: a manager's guide to action. *Organizational Dynamics* 12(2): 5–23.

Schall, M. S. (1983). A communication-rules approach to organizational culture. *Administrative Science Quarterly* 28: 557–581.

Schein, E. H. (1985). *Organizational Culture and Leadership*. San Francisco: Jossey-Bass.

Schein, E. H. (1984). Coming to a new awareness of organizational culture. *Sloan Management Review* 25(2): 3–16.

Schein, E. H. (1983). Organizational culture. *Organizational Dynamics* 12: 13–28.

Selznick, P. (1949). *T.V.A. and the Grass Roots*. Berkeley, CA: University of California Press.

Slocum, J. W. (1978). Does cognitive style affect diagnosis and intervention strategies of change agents? *Group and Organization Studies* 3: 199–210.

Smircich, L. (1983). Concepts of culture and organizational analysis. *Administrative Science Quarterly* 28: 339–358.

Spradley, J. (1970). *You Owe Yourself a Drunk: An Ethnography of Urban Nomads*. Boston: Little, Brown.

Stinchcombe, A. (1959). Bureaucratic and craft administration of production. *Administrative Science Quarterly* 4: 168–187.

Taylor, F. W. (1911). *The Principles of Scientific Management*. New York: Harper.

Tichy, N. M. (1982). Managing change strategically: the technical, political, and cultural keys. *Organizational Dynamics* 11: 59–80.

Tichy, N. M., and Devanna, M. A. (1986). The transformational leader. *Training and Development Journal*, July 27–32.

Toennies, F. (1957). *Community and Society* (transl. C. P. Loomis). East Lansing, MI: Michigan State University Press.

Toffler, A. (1980). *The Third Wave*. New York: Morrow.

Trice, H. (1983). Rites and ceremonials in organizational culture. In S. Bacharach and S. Mitchell (eds.), *Perspectives in Organizational Sociology: Theory and Research*, Vol. 4. Greenwich, CT: JAI.

Trice, H., and Beyer, J. (1985). The routinization of charisma in two social movement organizations. In B. Staw and L. Cummings (eds.), *Research in Organizational Behavior*, Vol. 7. Greenwich, CT: JAI.

Trice, H. M., and Beyer, J. M. (1984). Studying organizational cultures through rites and ceremonials. *Academy of Management Review* 9: 653–669.

Tunstall, W. B. (1985). Breakup of the Bell system: a case study in cultural transformation. In R. H. Kilmann, M. J. Saxton, R. Serpa, and Associates (eds.), *Gaining Control of the Corporate Culture*, pp. 44–65. San Francisco: Jossey-Bass.

Van Maanen, J. (1979). The fact of fiction in organizational ethnography. *Administrative Science Quarterly* 24: 539–550.

Van Maanen, J. (1973). Observations on the making of policemen. *Human Organization* 32: 407–418.

Wade, P. F. (1981). Some factors affecting problem solving effectiveness in business: a study of management consultants. Unpublished Ph.D. dissertation, McGill University.

Waterman, R. H., Peters, T. J., and Phillips, J. R. (1980). Structure is not organization. *Business Horizons* 23(3): 14–26.

Weber, M. (1947). *The Theory of Social and Economic Organization*. New York: Free Press.

Whyte, W. F. (1943). *Street Corner Society*. Chicago: University of Chicago Press.

Wilkins, A. L. (1983). The culture audit: a tool for understanding organizations. *Organizational Dynamics* 12(2): 24–38.

Wilkins, A. L. (1979). Organizational stories as an expression of management philosophy. Unpublished dissertation, Stanford University.

Wilkins, A. L., and Ouchi, W. G. (1983). Efficient cultures: exploring the relationship between culture and organizational performance. *Administrative Science Quarterly* 28: 468–481.

Williamson, O. E. (1975). *Markets and Hierarchies: Analysis and Antitrust Implications*. New York: Free Press.

Graduate Education as an Area of Research in the Field of Higher Education

Gary D. Malaney
University of Massachusetts at Amherst

The purpose of this chapter is to look at graduate education as a subfield of study within the general field of higher education. In any area of study, research is of major importance, and graduate education is no exception. While research related to graduate education in the United States has existed almost since the inception of graduate study in this country in the 1800s, there has been no common effort or direction, and no theories to drive any effort. The bulk of the research related to graduate education is relatively recent, pertains to students, and coincides with the explosion of student interest in graduate study since 1960.

The emphasis of this chapter is on the review of literature devoted to research studies on various topics in graduate education since 1976, which marks the publication of the most recent books devoted solely to research on graduate education (Cartter, 1976; Katz and Hartnett, 1976; Solmon, 1976; National Board on Graduate Education, 1976). Those books represent significant contributions to research in this area, and they can be viewed as a culmination of the intense interest in graduate study that developed in the 1960s and continued into the early 1970s. It was reported recently that interest in research on graduate students dropped between 1969 and 1983 (Kuh et al., 1986).

While it is not the purpose of this chapter to provide a history of the development of graduate education, some background is necessary to set the stage. Thus, what immediately follows is a brief background from the beginning of graduate education in the United States to 1976. After the background information, the focus shifts to a discussion of the recent research literature which has been conducted on all aspects of graduate education, with the exception of program quality and departmental rankings, topics which were discussed in Volume I of this handbook. The review is generally limited to scholarly articles that have appeared in academic journals. The chapter concludes with some recommendations for future research in the area of graduate education.

BACKGROUND

Graduate study in the United States began fairly early in the nineteenth century, with Harvard having "resident graduates" as early as 1826 and Princeton following suit in 1829 (Walters, 1965). That system of study was very informal, however, and it was not until 1847 at Yale that a formal structure for graduate study was developed. Storr (1953) stated that in 1847 the Yale Corporation approved the formation of a Department of Philosophy and the Arts to "offer advanced work in the arts and sciences not already being taught and their application to the arts" (p. 55). The first Ph.D. degree was awarded at Yale University in 1861. Harvard announced in 1872 that it would offer formal graduate work, and Harvard's first Ph.D. was awarded in 1873. Graduate study was a primary concern at Cornell University as soon as it was founded in 1868.

Despite the above facts, many historical accounts of the origin of graduate education in the United States attribute the "official" beginning to the founding of Johns Hopkins University in 1876 (Berelson, 1960; Griggs, 1965; Hartnett and Katz, 1976). The reasoning behind that thinking seemed to be that Johns Hopkins was founded solely for the purpose of providing graduate instruction. Griggs (1965) indicated that the German concept of graduate-only institutions was criticized, and Johns Hopkins had to alter its thinking to include undergraduate instruction as well. Thus, the comprehensive research universities in this country had a mixture of German and English influence. And as Hartnett and Katz (1976) indicated, the combination has produced a strain that has characterized American higher education.

The growth in graduate education in the past century has been astronomical. One measure of that growth is the number of degrees that have been awarded. By 1900, approximately 500 graduate degrees had been awarded (Griggs, 1965), and of that number, 239 were Ph.D.'s (Harmon and Soldz, 1963). There were 382 earned doctorates in 1900, 615 in 1920, and 3,290 in 1940 (Walters, 1965). In 1960, there were 9,733 earned doctorates, and the number rose dramatically each year throughout the 1960s, ending with 29,498 doctorates being awarded in 1970 (National Research Council, 1986). The number of earned doctorates peaked in 1973 at 33,755, and it has since leveled out at around 31,000 per year. The number of master's degrees awarded is far greater, currently exceeding 300,000 per year.

It was not long before graduate education became a major component of higher education, and accordingly, scholars soon became interested in writing about graduate education. One of the early outlets of such writings was the journal *School and Society*. And while the majority of the articles were essays pertaining to the value of graduate education, in 1915 the journal published a research study related to the proportion of undergraduates who go on to graduate study at the same institutions that awarded their undergraduate degrees (Walcott,

1915). Walcott conducted that study by simply collecting data that were available in college catalogs in the Columbia University library, a practice which, as he admitted, limited his choice of the institutions to be studied.

Walcott's study was hardly an elaborate or highly scientific study, but it was typical of some of the early efforts in this area. For instance, Burg (1917) conducted a study which analyzed the fact that seven institutions consistently accounted for half of the doctorates that were awarded each year. Like Walcott's study, Burg's study also involved simply an accounting process based on institutional records.

Because graduate study had become such an important component of higher education, in the mid-1950s a few scholars, led by W. Gordon Whaley, who was the dean of the graduate school at the University of Texas, initiated the publication of a journal entitled *The Graduate Journal*. As indicated on the inside title page, the journal was "Designed to facilitate communication in graduate education and research." The major vehicle of communication in this journal was the scholarly essay, and virtually no research on issues dealing with graduate education was presented.

As the journal matured, the articles became less specifically related to the happenings of formal graduate education, and in fact, such articles became rare. It appeared that almost from the journal's inception, the advisory board had often debated the journal's contents as they related to the title of the journal. In fact, as early as 1960, the phrase "Designed to facilitate communication in graduate education and research" was dropped from the title page. Devoting a portion of the second issue of Volume 7 to the policies and processes of formal graduate education, Whaley (1966) presented some of the arguments concerning the continuing debate regarding the content of the journal:

> The *Journal* has come, over time, to owe its allegiance only to expressing man's intellectual creativity and how this creativity changes the order of things and is itself shaped by the existing order. We shall not change the *Journal's* title, partly because we like the way it looks on the cover, but more importantly because we have become acutely aware of the narrowness of the modern definition of advanced education and the compelling need for redefinition in terms of ideas, innovation, and adventure. We shall simply assume that a graduate journal is appropriately titled for anyone who has been graduated from anything, and we shall continue to deal with as broad a spectrum of the thinking and affairs of modern man as we can. These concerns include graduate education as it is formally understood. We shall occasionally, as we have in the past, deal with it. (p. 281)

Articles pertaining to issues related to graduate education in general became the exception rather than the norm. *The Graduate Journal* ceased publication in 1975 for reasons about which one can only speculate. But given the lack of clear direction for content and the lack of dedication to the purpose of writing solely about graduate education, its demise can be understood. Still, it should be noted that the journal had been originally intended as a project of only a few years anyway.

One cannot help but wonder if the journal could have survived if research on issues pertaining to graduate education had been encouraged. And perhaps the time is now right for the renewal of such a journal, which combines both philosophical essays and research related to graduate education. Currently, there exists no single outlet for research and/or thought pertaining solely to graduate education. Instead, such articles can be found from time to time in most of the major journals which deal with issues in higher education. The creation or revitalization of a journal devoted to graduate education could serve to increase the current interest in this important subfield of the study of higher education.

THE LITERATURE

As mentioned previously, the focus of this review is on the research literature on graduate education which has been produced since 1976, and the primary emphasis is on articles that have been published in academic journals. In an effort to locate such articles, three separate search methods were employed: (1) an automated reference search; (2) a hand search of the *Education Index;* and (3) a hand search of the journals that publish research related to higher education in general.

While this search was very thorough, undoubtedly a few articles were inadvertently overlooked. All nonresearch articles pertaining to graduate education and some research articles that were very discipline-specific were not included in the group to be reviewed. Examples of this latter group include several articles that have been published in the *Journal of Education for Social Work* and that pertain specifically to the area of social work and an entire issue of *Communication Education* (Vol. 28, No. 4), which emphasized the field of communication.

The search produced 112 articles which were located in 22 different journals. Table 1 provides a breakdown of the journals by topic of research. Only the 12 journals that contained more than one article are listed individually in the table. The vast majority (81%) of the articles are contained in the following eight journals: *Research in Higher Education, College Student Journal, Educational and Psychological Measurement, Journal of College Student Personnel, Journal of Higher Education, College and University, American Educational Research Journal*, and *Improving College and University Teaching.* Clearly, the most popular vehicle of research on graduate education has been *Research in Higher Education,* which has published almost twice as many articles as the second leading source, *College Student Journal.*

While most of the leading journals published articles covering a large variety of topics, two journals have been quite limited in their scope. Virtually all of the

TABLE 1. Types of Graduate Education Research Articles and the Journals in which They Appear

Type of research	Academic Journals (see *Note*)													
	RHE	CSJ	EPM	JCSP	JHE	C&U	AERJ	ICUT	NAW DAC	Appl Psyc	Educ Psyc	PDK	Other	Total
Students														
Matriculation	8	1	1	1		7		1		2		1	2	24
Predicting success, performance	2	2	8				1				2		1	16
Gender differences, women	5	2		1	2				2				1	13
Graduate assistants	1	2		1	2		1	1		1				9
Standardized tests			5		1							1		7
Employment, career	1	1		2										4
Minorities				1	1		1						1	4
Stress and anxiety		2		1							1			4
Attitudes toward research	1			1									1	3
Impact of marriage, family									1				1	2
Attrition, retention		1						1						2
Miscellaneous	2	2		2										6
Faculty-student interaction														
Evaluation of faculty and programs	2	1												3
Mentoring		1					1							2
Social power							1							1
Faculty and administrators														
Administration, structure, function	2							2					1	5
Departmental characteristics, degrees	1				1							1	1	4
Miscellaneous	3													3
Total	28	15	14	10	7	7	5	5	3	3	3	2	10	112

Note: RHE = *Research in Higher Education*
CSJ = *College Student Journal*
EPM = *Educational and Psychological Measurement*
JCSP = *Journal of College Student Personnel*
JHE = *Journal of Higher Education*
C&U = *College and University*

AERJ = *American Educational Research Journal*
ICUT = *Improving College and University Teaching*
NAWDAC = *National Association of Women Deans, Administrators and Counselors Journal*
Appl Psyc = *Journal of Applied Psychology*
Educ Psyc = *Journal of Educational Psychology*
PDK = *Phi Delta Kappan*

Other = *Journal of Educational Technology Systems, Teaching of Psychology, Journal of Experimental Education, Journal of College Admissions, Education, Journal of Student Financial Aid, Journal of College Science Teaching, Journal of Negro Education, Sociology of Education, Lifelong Learning.*

articles that have appeared in *Educational and Psychological Measurement* have pertained to standardized tests and the prediction of success and performance. All of the articles in *College and University* have pertained to the matriculation area. Both of these results are understandable given the nature of the journals and their respective audiences.

As indicated in Table 1, students have been the major focus of research, with 84% of the articles devoted solely to the study of students and an additional 5% on the interaction among students and faculty. Only 11% of the articles placed no emphasis on students. The most popular area of student research has been the area of matriculation, which includes recruitment, admissions, and student characteristics. The second most popular area has been the prediction of student performance. A somewhat surprising finding is the lack of research on minority students, which appears to be a slightly more popular topic at the undergraduate level (Kuh et al., 1986).

Each of the topics in Table 1 is discussed in some detail in the following review of the literature. The review is organized and presented generally in the same order as the listing in Table 1, and it basically presents a brief description of each article. There is some overlap of topics in some of the articles, but the classification is an attempt to categorize the primary topic of each article. While each article is not discussed in detail, all are at least cited for the benefit of the reader.

Students

Matriculation

This topic is actually quite broad and encompasses five identifiable subtopics which could arguably be treated as individual topics. But since there is considerable overlap among the subtopics and it would be difficult to discuss one of the subtopics without others coming into play, they have been collapsed here into one topic. Below is a breakdown of the 24 articles by subtopic with the number in parentheses representing the number of articles having that particular subtopic as the primary emphasis: recruitment (3), admissions (8), selection of institution or field of study (7), financial aid (2), and student characteristics and expectations (4).

Recruitment. The area of student recruitment has long been the domain of undergraduate education. As Turcotte (1983) noted:

> Graduate education as an entity is perceived to be far behind the undergraduate in establishing a body of knowledge regarding admission characteristics and activities of

students; methods of recruitment; utilization of available technology; centralization of effort and funding; enrollment management and modeling. (p. 28)

Malaney (1984) discussed the extant literature on graduate student recruitment, and he indicated that the previous literature on this subject had been limited to an emphasis on "special" students, such as women and minority groups (Atelsek and Gomberg, 1978; Henry, 1980; Brooks and Miyares, 1977) or nonspecial students in specific departments (Czinkota, 1980; Malaney, 1983; McClain, Vance, and Wood, 1984). In an effort to expand the base of literature in this area, Malaney (1984) studied the entire population of new graduate students at a single institution within the context of the impact of financial aid on recruitment. He also studied graduate departments in order to determine the types of recruiting practices used both before and after students express interest in the programs (Malaney, 1987a).

This latter article emphasized an important difference between undergraduate and graduate recruitment activities. While undergraduate activities are primarily centralized within an institution's admission or enrollment management office, recruitment activities at the graduate level can be centralized only superficially because of the very discipline-specific nature of graduate education (Malaney, 1987c). The primary impetus must come from the individual academic departments, which Malaney (1987a) has shown to vary greatly in the number and type of recruitment activities used.

Turcotte (1983) voiced an opposing opinion concerning centralization. "Believing that enrollment management at the graduate level is not only possible but an indispensable requirement" (p. 25), he surveyed all graduate schools in the United States. When asked what they were doing now in the recruitment, admissions, and enrollment areas, popular responses dealt with the lack of money. He also indicated that a popular response was "The Graduate Admissions Office and Administration must become more and more involved in general publication and recruitment, etc. The days are over when only departments publicize their own programs" (p. 26). It is questionable whether departmental faculty and administrators would have views similar to the graduate school administrators surveyed in this study.

Turcotte's results are difficult to interpret because only 35% of the graduate schools responded, and the only demographic variable provided was a public-private breakdown. It would have been helpful to know demographics on such variables as the size and type of institutions and the highest degree offered. Without these demographics, one cannot be sure of the representativeness of the sample, which makes interpretation of the data difficult.

Admissions. The admissions process itself has been the focus of eight articles, and some of those articles overlap with predicting academic performance because the purpose of the admissions process is to select students who will succeed in a program. The eight articles represent a wide range of issues in admissions. Millimet and Flume (1982) tried to determine which factors actually led to positive admission decisions. Their interest was prompted by the fact that "publicized minimum criteria for graduate school admission are rarely sufficient to gain entrance to the school of one's choice" (p. 125). The authors collected data from 76 institutions in order to determine the "effective" admission standards in the field of psychology. They found that effective admission standards vary according to the national ranking of the program, with the higher ranked programs having the highest effective standards and the lower ranked programs having the lowest effective standards. They also found that GRE scores, followed by undergraduate grade-point averages, were the most important factors in admission decisions.

McClain et al. (1984) and Remus and Isa (1983) also looked at factors related to successful admission decisions, but they were primarily concerned with predicting the proportion of admittees who decided to enroll. Two of the articles looked at actual models of admission decisions (Wallace and Schwab, 1976; Youngblood and Martin, 1982). Williams (1978) discovered that students serving on admissions committees were not as successful as faculty members in predicting the eventual success of the applicants they rated.

Logan (1980) studied sex bias in the admissions process of all graduate programs at a single institution, and while some evidence of bias in some programs was found, most disappeared when he made adjustments for quality differences between male and female applicants. And finally, the value of letters of recommendation in the admissions process has also been studied (Baxter et al., 1981). The authors determined that one recommender generally used the same descriptors for two different students and two recommenders seldom shared descriptors for the same student.

Selection of Institution or Field of Study. The decision to attend graduate school and the selection of an institution and a field of study have been dealt with periodically since Baird's (1976a) thorough treatment. Not surprisingly, Baird found that higher undergraduate grades increased the likelihood of attending graduate school. He also discovered that "students from wealthier homes generally are more likely to attend graduate or professional school, whatever their grades" (p. 33).

In his analysis of factors leading to the decision to enter graduate and professional schools, Baird compared student responses based on whether students were entering arts and humanities, biological and physical sciences, social sciences, law school, or medical school. He found greater differences between students entering graduate programs versus professional schools, but he also discovered differences depending upon the field of graduate study.

Another large and sophisticated study on this topic was conducted by Ethington and Smart (1985). The data were drawn from a longitudinal, multi-institutional study where college freshmen were surveyed in 1970 and again in a follow-up survey in 1980. Restricting their sample to 6,242 individuals, the authors proposed and tested a causal model regarding the decision to enter graduate school. They found that variables measuring background characteristics, institutional characteristics, undergraduate experiences, degree completion, and receipt of graduate financial aid accounted for 35.4% and 31.6% of the variance for men and women, respectively.

While undergraduate degree completion and offers of financial aid for graduate school had the greatest impact on graduate school attendance, other factors were also important and especially interesting when broken down by gender. For instance, men attending more selective undergraduate institutions were more likely to attend graduate school, while for women, it was the size of the institution, not its selectivity, that was influential. For men, academic integration in the undergraduate institution was nearly three times as important as social integration in determining graduate school attendance, but for women, the two sets of variables had nearly the same impact.

Olson and King (1985) studied all domestic graduate students at a single institution. They sent questionnaires to a random sample, which was stratified by the level of the degree being pursued and by major. The sample consisted of 750 students out of a total population of approximately 3,350, and 303 usable questionnaires were returned. One of the foci of that study was on the factors influencing the initial consideration of an institution, and they found that the following four factors pertaining to that issue showed significant differences among the academic colleges which housed the students' fields of study: (1) whether a student had earned a previous degree from the university; (2) the cost of education; (3) the amount of assistantship stipend; and (4) the influence of the undergraduate adviser. They also found that the three following factors pertaining to the ultimate decision to enroll at the university differed significantly depending upon the academic college: (1) previous undergraduate attendance at the university; (2) employment in the community or area at the time of the enrollment decision; and (3) the speed of acceptance into the program. Unfortunately, the authors did not detail how these factors were differentiated among fields.

Another problem with the study involves the authors' decision to sample from all graduate students instead of just new graduate students. The varied length of time that students had been in residence at the institution might have confounded the data. While this problem could have been discounted by comparing opinions by number of years of attendance, no such analysis was offered. Indeed, there was no mention that length of attendance was even considered as one of the strata in sampling, so it is unknown whether there would have been enough cases in each year of attendance to make such an analysis meaningful. The authors also offered no analysis by demographic variables.

Malaney (1987c) studied why students went to graduate school and why they applied to a specific school. He found that the most important reasons for wanting to go to graduate school were the desire to learn and personal satisfaction. Also, reasons related to getting a job were often mentioned. Regarding why the specific school in the study was selected, respondents indicated most importantly that they perceived their departments as having good academic reputations. The two next important reasons were finances and location. Malaney investigated the variation of reasons across six demographic characteristics of the respondents and discovered several differences.

For instance, women were more likely than men to go to graduate school because a friend was going or for personal satisfaction. Younger students were more likely to go to graduate school because they had nothing else to do or felt their job prospects would be better, while older students were more likely to say they wanted an advanced degree for professional reasons. White students were more likely than nonwhite students to apply to a specific school because of location. Students with higher undergraduate grades were more likely than students with lower grades to apply to a specific school because of departmental reputation and financial concerns.

Malaney (1986d) also studied the characteristics of students in relation to their chosen areas of study, as defined by the three dimensions developed by Biglan (1973a,b) to classify academic departments. Using discriminant function analysis, Malaney showed that the GRE quantitative score had the most impact on determining placement in the hard and soft science departments, as students with higher scores were more likely to be in the hard areas. Citizenship and the GRE verbal score had the most impact on the life and nonlife dimension, as domestic students and students with lower GRE verbal scores were more likely to be in the life areas of study. The GRE verbal score, the degree level, and the undergraduate grade-point average had the most impact on the pure and applied research dimension, as students having higher scores and grade-point averages and students pursuing Ph.D.'s were more likely to be in the pure research areas.

In their work on student perceptions of the importance of graduate admission factors, Powers and Lehman (1983) offered a profile of prospective students and their intended fields of graduate study. They looked at three demographic variables (age, ethnic group, and gender), and at five areas of graduate study (biological sciences, education, humanities, physical sciences, and social sciences). The authors found that black students were more likely than white students to choose social sciences, and that white students were more likely to choose biological sciences, humanities, and physical sciences. Women were more likely than men to choose biological sciences and education, and men were more likely to choose physical sciences. Older students (over 30) were more likely than younger students to choose education, and younger students were more likely to choose biological and physical sciences.

Lang (1984) used national studies from 1969 and 1975 to analyze the influence of students' undergraduate achievement, gender, and ethnicity on the rank of graduate school attended, and he found that undergraduate achievement was the strongest influence. Drory (1980) applied expectancy theory to analyze the motivation behind the decision of Israeli students to seek graduate study in their home country or to elect to travel abroad for their advanced study, and he discovered that the decisions were more intrinsically than extrinsically motivated.

Financial Aid. Turning to the importance of financial aid in student matriculation, Turcotte (1983) suggested that ambiguity exists related to this issue. In analyzing his data from graduate school administrators, he stated:

> It is interesting to note that financial concerns, that is the level of support to students provided by an institution, is not perceived as an influential factor in students applying or enrolling. However, financial considerations are ranked second and third as the perceived reasons why accepted applicants ultimately go to *another institution*. (p. 26)

In Malaney's (1984) survey of new students, he found that departmental reputation was clearly the most important factor in choice of institution, but the second most important factor was financial. He also surveyed departmental administrators for that study and discovered that almost two-thirds of those administrators indicated that they felt they were not losing students because of the level of assistantship stipends. But slightly over two-thirds indicated that they felt they were losing students because they did not have enough assistantships to offer.

Another issue related to financial aid is that the increased indebtedness of undergraduates may begin to dissuade them from pursuing advanced degrees (Hauptman, 1986). Smith (1985) noted that students in the arts and sciences may have already been discouraged because of their large undergraduate debts. Snyder (1985) indicated that decreased assistantship support from the federal government has compounded the problem.

Compounding the problem of trying to understand issues related to financial aid is the serious lack of information regarding who receives financial support. Recognizing the "embarrassing lack of current and comprehensive information on what types of students enroll in graduate and professional schools and how they pay for their education," the Association of American Universities asked for and received funding from the Ford Foundation to review the various sources of data and make recommendations "for how both the quality and the amount of data collected might be improved" (Hauptman, 1986, p. ix). Hauptman's book is an excellent resource on the various current national data-collection efforts related to graduate students in general and to funding specifically. Organizations included in these efforts are the National Center for Educational Statistics, the National Research Council, the Graduate Record Examination Board, the Council of Graduate Schools, the Graduate and Professional Student Financial Aid Service, and the Consortium of Financing Higher Education. A bibliography of studies associated with these organizations is also included in Hauptman's book. Most of the research results are in the form of reports from the organizations and have not been published in academic journals or books.

Baird (1976a) and Hauptman (1986) offered data concerning the characteristics of students who receive funding. Baird discovered that the undergraduate grades of recipients of fellowships and scholarships were clearly superior to those of nonrecipients. Proportionally, there were just as many women among the recipients as among the nonrecipients, and recipients tended to be slightly younger than nonrecipients. He also discovered that there were proportionally more minorities among the recipients of fellowships and scholarships than among the nonrecipients.

Hauptman addressed the issue of foreign students and financial support. He noted that foreign students were less likely than domestic students to receive American-based fellowships, but foreign students received teaching and research assistantships in the same proportion as domestic students.

Both Baird and Hauptman also discussed differences in funding for graduate students based on different fields of study. Hauptman found that among doctoral students, those in the social sciences, the arts and humanities, and education were much more likely to borrow money than those in physical and life sciences and engineering. He also indicated that the students in the physical and life sciences and in engineering were much more likely to hold research assistantships, while students in the arts and humanities and the physical sciences were much more likely to hold teaching assistantships. Baird noted that students in biological and physical sciences were the most likely to be able to obtain research assistantships.

The two studies by Baird and Hauptman are based on national data and do not necessarily reflect the situation at individual institutions. Interestingly, this is the reverse of most research related to students, which generally involves an overabundance of institutional studies and very few national studies. Malaney (1987b) conducted an institutional study related to who receives financial support, and his findings supported the results of both Hauptman and Baird.

Student Characteristics and Expectations. While characteristics of students have been discussed throughout this section on matriculation, the subtopic dealing with characteristics and expectations was added for those articles that did not fit elsewhere. Three of the four articles are quite discipline-specific but were included as examples of research that has most likely been done in a variety of fields outside the search parameters of this study. McCarthy et al. (1979) studied the characteristics and attitudes of doctoral students in educational administration, Kuh, Greenlee, and Lardy (1978) investigated the characteristics of graduate students in college student personnel, and Blanchard (1977) focused on master's students in several areas of education.

Baird's (1978) article is more general, since it uses some of the same national data as his previous study (Baird, 1976a), and focuses on the following four areas of advanced education: graduate study in the arts and sciences, graduate study in education, professional study in law, and professional study in medicine. He compared the expectations of students before entering their chosen fields with their perceptions of the reality after one year of study. He found that

> over a third of the sample said that their expectations of what graduate or professional school would be like were not fulfilled, and that approximately 40 per cent said they would strongly consider changing to another program if they could do so without losing ground. (Baird, 1978, p. 72)

Clearly, Baird's data show a large discrepancy between students' expectations and their actual experiences. Baird suggested that prospective students need more accurate information about fields of study from professional organizations and about individual programs from the departments and institutions themselves.

McCarthy et al. (1979) offered a profile of the typical educational administration doctoral student. The student is a married male about 37 years old with one or two children. He has taught for about six years and has served as a building administrator for several years. He most likely reads *Phi Delta Kappan,* and his immediate career objective is to become either a central office administrator or a college professor.

Kuh et al. (1978) found that graduate students in college student personnel were generally younger than the education administration students, but most of the students in student personnel were master's students, as opposed to doctoral students, who were found to be significantly older. The authors also discovered that the doctoral students were more likely than the master's students to be males. Respondents were most likely to read the *Journal of College Student Personnel,* and they were generally satisfied with their preparatory programs.

Blanchard's (1977) study epitomizes the problem associated with many studies dealing with master's students. He focused on a single degree, a single field, and a single institution, as he offered a profile of the typical DePaul University School of Education master's degree graduate, who is a woman, was born in Chicago, resides in Illinois, has a bachelor's degree from DePaul, began the master's program at the age of 32, and took seven years to earn her degree.

Predicting Success, Performance

There are 16 articles in this section, all of which have the primary purpose of predicting the performance of graduate students. Eleven of the articles have very similar purposes and approaches, and they are referred to as *standard studies*. While the approaches vary in each study, there is a certain commonality in those 11 articles. That commonality involves the use of fairly standard demographic predictor variables (e.g., gender, age, undergraduate grade-point average, and standardized test scores) and common measures of performance (e.g., graduate grade-point average and completion of degree). About half of the standard studies employed correlational and/or regression analyses, and about half utilized some twists (e.g., path analysis, canonical correlation, discriminant analysis, matched pair sampling, and differential predictability).

The five studies that were not included in the standard group have been labeled *nonstandard studies* because they used either different approaches or different types of variables from the studies in the standard group. For instance, three of the studies in the nonstandard group used personality-related variables as predictors.

Standard Studies. The standard studies have a few other things in common in their approaches to this issue. Each of these studies investigated only one institution, and only one article looked at more than one field of study. The fields of most interest were education and business, and the studies dealing with the latter field are reviewed first.

The first study (Hendel and Doyle, 1978) dealt with the differences between students whose primary language was English and those whose primary language was other than English as they related to measures of predictability of success in an MBA program. The study used 7 performance variables and 11 predictor variables, more variables than any other study discussed. The authors found that of the 77 bivariate correlations, 24 were significant for the English-speaking group and only 7 were significant for the non-English-speaking group. Based on these data and regressions for each group, the authors indicate that success for these two groups would be differentially predictable.

Messmer and Solomon (1979) used differential predictability procedures to predict for males and females their graduate grade-point averages in an MBA program:

> Differential predictability occurs when a variable moderates the relationship between a predictor and a criterion so that the predictor(s) work differently for two or more groups of applicants. (p. 860)

For predictors, Messmer and Solomon used scores from the Graduate Management Admissions Test (GMAT) and the SAT and undergraduate grade-point averages. While the authors determined that the predictors did significantly predict graduate grade-point average in a pooled regression model, their test of differential validity did not suggest the need for separate regression models for males and females.

Breaugh and Mann (1981) had moderate success using discriminant analysis to discriminate graduates and nongraduates of an MBA program. They found that age and the quantitative scores from the GMAT were both significant contributors in discriminating the two groups. As mentioned previously, an interesting point here is that older students were more likely to graduate, which is a finding counter to those in other studies in which age has been found to be a significant predictor of success.

Sobol (1984) studied the impact of undergraduate grade-point averages and GMAT scores on the graduate grade point averages of MBA students, and the author noted significant effects with both. A 12-point scale related to the students' backgrounds, activities, and personal qualities was developed, and the author found that using the scale "in conjunction with UGPA and GMAT scores shows that it is a significant help in the prediction of academic success as measured by graduate grade point average" (p. 87).

Cook and Swanson (1978), Pristo (1979), and Vacc and Picot (1984) all studied doctoral degree completion in the field of education. Cook and Swanson (1978) were interested in predicting the probability of graduation from doctoral programs. They used two sets of predictor variables: (1) factors available to the selection committee and (2) factors that emerged after admission. The former set consisted of age, gender, citizenship, part-time or full-time enrollment status, undergraduate grade-point average, and graduate admission test scores. The latter set consisted of graduate grade-point average, whether students held assistantships, whether they had programs of study accepted, and whether they had dissertation proposals accepted. Path analysis was employed in this study, and the results indicated that while there were several indirect effects of selection variables through program variables on graduation, the only direct effects were produced by two program variables: having programs of study and dissertation proposals accepted.

Knowing that accepted programs of study and dissertation proposals increase the likelihood of graduation is of questionable value, since a student generally cannot progess in a program without having an accepted program of study or dissertation proposal. However, the fact that the path analysis allows one to see the indirect effects of such variables as grades and holding assistantships is very useful.

As a side note, one admission variable (age) was shown to have a relatively strong, indirect negative effect on graduation. This is interesting because Breaugh and Mann (1981) found a strong positive effect related to the completion of the MBA degree.

Pristo (1979) studied two performance variables and 13 predictors and employed canonical correlation as the analytical technique. The two dependent performance variables were degree completion and cumulative graduate grade-point average. The following eight predictors made a significant contribution to the analysis: years since undergraduate degree, years since master's degree, master's grade-point average, type of master's institution, graduate hours earned, number of institutions attended, age, and gender. The significant canonical correlation disappeared under cross-validation, but that may have been due to the disparity in sample sizes between the standard sample ($N = 65$) and the cross-validation sample ($N = 21$).

Vacc and Picot (1984) studied students who had completed or withdrawn from doctoral programs, and the performance criterion variable was whether or not a student completed the degree. The following variables were used as predictors: undergraduate grade-point average, graduate grade-point average, scores from the Miller Analogies Test, time lapse between master's degree and entrance into the doctoral program, doctoral major, age, gender, marital status, and ethnicity. In a regression analysis, only graduate grade-point average had a significant effect. The authors also had limited success using discriminant analysis to discriminate between successful and unsuccessful students, but that may have been due in part to the sample size, which for the discriminant run entailed only 11 unsuccessful students.

The only other doctoral study in this area was conducted by Pogrow (1977), who collected data for doctoral students in all fields at Stanford University. While he did look at all fields, the sample was not large enough for him to analyze relationships by field of study. His primary concern was the effect of age on performance, and he determined that age did not adversely affect the attitudes and performance (grade-point average) of first-year students. The unique point about his study relative to the others is that it employed a matched-pairs sampling procedure.

The studies by Omizo and Michael (1979) and Kirnan and Geisinger (1981) focused on predicting performance on master's comprehensive examinations in counselor education and psychology, respectively. Both used GRE scores and undergraduate grade-point averages as predictors. Omizo and Michael found that undergraduate grade-point average was the major predictor, while Kirnan and Geisinger discovered the GRE verbal score to be the major predictor. These studies highlight a point made by Pristo (1979), who indicated that "procedures which effectively predict success in one school will not necessarily work somewhere else, and that variables selected for one study may be valid predictors in one environment but not in another" (pp. 932–933). Also, different fields of study must be considered.

Leonardson (1979) tried to predict the graduate grade-point averages of students enrolled in a master's program in education. He used undergraduate grade-point average and scores on the Ohio State Psychological Examination and the Cooperative English Test as his predictor variables. In a regression analysis, undergraduate grade-point average was the only variable that had any significant impact on graduate grade-point average.

Nonstandard Studies. Dole and Baggaley (1979) used standard predictor variables in their study, but their performance variables were unique relative to the above studies. The performance variable consisted of rankings on two dimensions: scholarship and professionalism. In collecting the data, the researchers asked faculty members to rank the 81 students who received doctoral degrees in education at one institution. The authors found several significant predictors. Undergraduate and graduate grade-point averages had positive impacts and age had a negative impact on both performance variables, while the selectivity of the undergraduate institution and the GRE verbal score had positive impacts on scholarship, as well. Scholarship and professionalism were strongly correlated (.73).

Garett and Wulf (1978) used standard performance variables (graduate grade-point average and number of units completed), but they used unique predictor variables relative to the standard studies. For their predictor variables, they used scores on selected personality scales from the Minnesota Multiphasic Personality Inventory and scores related to critical thinking skills from the Cornell Critical Thinking Test. Their analysis of education graduate students in one institution showed that for both males and females, critical thinking ability was predictive of success in graduate school.

Two of the studies in this group dealt with personality traits as predictor variables and examination performance in education courses as measures of success. King et al. (1976) studied the hypothesis that anxiety-proneness influences the intensity and frequency of anxiety manifestation, which influences achievement, and the findings suggested that anxiety-proneness had a direct causal influence on both anxiety manifestation and achievement, as well as influencing achievement through anxiety manifestation. Griffore (1977) investigated fears of success and failure in relation to performance and discovered that while the factors are highly related, neither had much impact on examination performance.

The final article (Reilly, 1976) in this section is the most unusual of all, because the purpose of the study was not to actually predict performance but to determine factors that faculty use to evaluate student performance. Faculty members were surveyed in three academic fields: chemistry, English, and psychology. The three corresponding factor analyses resulted in fairly similar item loadings and the production of eight identifiable factors, which were labeled "independence and initiative, conscientiousness, critical facility, enthusiasm, research and experimentation, communication, teaching skills, and persistence" (p. 125).

Attrition, Retention

This area is closely related to predicting success and performance, but subtly different in that the issue of withdrawals from programs is of primary concern here. While the problem of graduate student retention has been discussed for decades, there has been very little systematic research conducted on this topic, partly because of the difficulties involved in the design of such studies (Girves and Wemmerus, 1986; Girves, Wemmerus, and Rice, 1986). While the studies initiated by Girves represent some of the best work to date on the retention of graduate students, the papers are currently being revised for publication and therefore are not ready for review at this time. While the two articles to be reviewed in this section are much less sophisticated, they do present some interesting findings.

In his study of doctoral students in business, Pogrow (1978) found a nonlinear relationship between standardized test scores and degree completion. Both lower scorers and extremely high scorers were less likely to finish. He discovered a disproportionate number of younger students with the highest test scores, and he found that older students were more likely than younger students to finish. The older students not only scored lower on the standardized admissions test, they also received less financial aid.

Jacks et al. (1983) were concerned with the infamous ABDs, students who had completed all degree requirements but their dissertations. The researchers conducted a telephone survey which involved approximately 40-minute interviews with 25 such individuals who had been out of school for about 10 years. The individuals were from six different fields, 18 different departments, and 15 different universities. The study was presented in a qualitative nature, or as the authors indicate, a "narrative portrait" or "collective biography." It would probably be worthwhile to follow up the study with more subjects so that statistical analyses could be conducted to compare the various fields, departments, and institutions, especially in light of Pogrow's (1978) observation that

> the nature and causes of attrition varies [*sic*] between organizational units. Indeed they may even vary in a given department over time, or in the same disciplines in different institutions; depending on the type of program which exists. (p. 348)

At any rate, Jacks et al. did discover some interesting findings. All of the students gave multiple reasons for leaving their programs. Almost half of the students indicated that they left because of financial difficulties, and almost half identified poor working relationships with the adviser or committee. Also, 36% identified substantive problems with the dissertation research, and 36% identified personal or emotional problems. These authors did find some differences by discipline. For instance, all of the psychologists ($N = 8$) cited problems with their advisers or committees, while all but one of the sociologists ($N = 6$) had good relations with their advisers and committees, but many of them had problems with their dissertion research. Unfortunately, given the variations in departments and universities for each group, no specific conclusions can be drawn. If this study were conducted with more respondents and perhaps fewer institutions, more systematic conclusions might be drawn.

Gender Differences

While differences between males and females have been discussed in several of the above research studies, gender differences were not the primary focus of those studies. In the studies to be discussed in this section, an analysis of gender differences was the major purpose of the research.

The most extensive study on gender differences of graduate students was published in a book by Solmon (1976), who designed a three-phase national study which (1) analyzed graduate school catalogs; (2) analyzed discrimination studies which had been undertaken by individual institutions; and (3) surveyed graduate school deans. While specific results are cited later, Solmon did generally conclude that "Those who charge blatant, malevolent discrimination by graduate institutions in the United States apparently are basing their accusations on weak evidence" (p. 105). That is not to say that no discriminatory evidence was found by Solmon, but clearly, he felt that most of the evidence was not discriminatory.

There are two major concerns about Solmon's study. The first, which he also noted, is that the data pertain to only those individuals who have completed their degrees, so the problems encountered by women who dropped out are not known. The second concern is that the data are based on institutional records provided by institutional publications or by the offices of graduate school deans, which means that individual student attitudes and concerns are not known. Many of the studies reviewed in this section have eliminated those problems.

In addition to Solmon's book, another source of useful information is Vartuli's (1982) collection of writings dealing with the experiences of women pursuing Ph.D.'s; however, since the observations are primarily anecdotal, the book is not reviewed in this chapter. The 13 articles which are discussed here have been divided into subtopics and are discussed in the following order: matriculation, sexual harassment, and employment and careers.

Matriculation. Most of the articles that have focused on gender differences have been related to matriculation and student characteristics. On the positive side, the proportion of women earning degrees in all aspects of higher education has increased, with the most pronounced increases being in professional and doctoral degrees (Roemer, 1983). While women still have a long way to go to be equal with men in terms of the number of earned professional and doctoral degrees, women are now virtually equal with men in terms of the number of earned bachelor's and master's degrees (Roemer, 1983).

Other positive findings for women include that they scored slightly higher (not significantly) than men on the verbal portion of the GRE, and that they have higher grade-point averages (Solmon, 1976). Solmon also found that the majority (71%) of the 84 doctoral institutions that he studied admitted proportionally more women than men. Regarding financial aid, Berg and Ferber (1983) found that women and men were equally successful in being funded. Berg and Ferber and Solmon agree that most of the prior literature indicates that women are less likely to complete their highest degree of choice, but the authors agree that "this conclusion may be erroneous" (Berg and Ferber, 1983, p. 630).

Turning to the negative side, Solmon (1976) found that women scored significantly lower on the quantitative portion of the GRE. Ethington and Wolfle (1986) and Nielsen (1980) also found lower quantitative skills for women than for men. Solmon reported that women are more conservative than men in choosing an institution and that they are more likely to opt for a secondary choice of school in order to receive funding. He also found that they are less likely to borrow money to support their education. Women are more likely to pursue master's degrees than doctorates (Berg and Ferber, 1983). Women are more likely to receive teaching assistantships, while men are more likely to receive research assistantships, which, according to Solmon, appear to be more important in professional development. Men are reported to be more self-confident than women (Adler, 1976). Women in more traditional sex roles need more external support from family and friends, while women in nontraditional sex roles believe they exercise more control over their lives (Brown, 1983).

Other gender differences that have been observed in studies include women students being less likely to be married and less likely to have children than men students (Adler, 1976; Berg and Ferber, 1983). Women were reported as being older than men when they began their studies (Solmon, 1976), but that point was disputed by Berg and Ferber (1983). Special concerns for women over 30 have been reported (Kaplan, 1982).

Hartnett (1981) and Hite (1985) reported finding differences between men and women according to field of study. For instance, Hartnett found that women students in psychology reported greater satisfaction with the learning environment, greater faculty concern for them, and a higher quality of assistantship experience than women students in history. Among her findings, Hite noted that both men and women in traditional female fields perceived more faculty support and less peer support than students in other fields.

Two trend studies (Rice, 1977; Roemer, 1983) indicate that things have been getting better in recent years, but progess has been slow to come. For instance, Rice studied graduates at two time periods, 1971 and 1975, and found that "less than a fourth of either sample of women reported positively on access to financial aid information or faculty encouragement for doctoral study" (p. 33). And Roemer's (1983) study of degree selection among women from 1970 to 1978 shows the continuing low proportion of women pursuing doctorates. "Apparently, the effects of affirmative action programs, policies and changes in the interim period have been in raising awareness and consciousness rather that in changing actual experience'' (Rice, 1977, p. 36).

Sexual Harassment. Recently, a growing area of concern related to women graduate students has been sexual harassment by faculty members (Dziech and Weiner, 1984). Schneider (1987) did an excellent job of reviewing the literature on this topic in addition to completing her own study at one particular institution. She found that 60% of the women reported experiencing at least one incident of ''everyday harassment,'' which she defined as including stares, jokes, physical contact, passes, and sexual propositions. Nine percent (31 women) reported experiencing either coercive pressure to date or to engage in sexual activity.

The behaviors of women students and the direct consequences of their interactions with faculty members were discussed by Schneider. The reactions of women students to sexual harassment and their actual dating of faculty members could have a negative impact on their graduate careers and on immediate employment, especially since the recommendations of faculty members are so crucial to the employment process, at least in the area of faculty employment. Clearly, such problems exist, and Schneider offered suggestions to help control the problems.

Employment and Careers. As the two studies in this subtopic show, women already have enough disadvantages in the job market. Even though women have experienced some recent advantages over men in admissions and financial aid, women have achieved less career progress (Stark et al., 1985), and new women Ph.D.'s face higher unemployment than new male Ph.D.'s (Tuckman and Tuckman, 1984).

Stark, Lowther, and Austin (1985) reported that opportunities for women in male-dominated fields have appeared to improve, so these researchers turned their interest to the female-dominated field of education. Studying two groups of doctoral recipients, one of which received degrees between 1964 and 1970 and the other between 1974 and 1980, these authors found little evidence of institutional discrimination against women in either group. However, in both groups, men have made greater upward career advancement. The situation has not improved over time, as women in the 1960s cohort group have shown greater advances relative to men in their group than the women the 1970s cohort group have shown relative to the men in their group. The authors found that the strongest predictor of career progress for both genders was work experience prior to doctoral study.

Wertheim, Widom, and Wortzel (1978) studied first-year graduate students in four different professional fields: business, education, law, and social work. They studied personality, aptitude, achievement, and demographics in an attempt to see if differences across fields were greater than differences between men and women in regard to professional career choices. They found that this was indeed the case, as sex differences were primarily limited to psychological masculinity/femininity and sex-role attitudes, but men and women who had chosen the same field of career had similar aptitude, achievement, and demographic profiles.

Graduate Assistants

Despite the lengthy and pervasive existence of the "graduate assistantship," little effort appears to have been made to describe it functionally and to assess its value and potential as a purposeful, integrated, practical and supervised component within graduate professional education preparation programs. (Thompson and Ellis, 1984, p. 78)

While the above quote was made in reference to assistantships within the field of education, the observation is relevant to assistantships in all fields of graduate study. The pervasiveness of assistantships can be seen by looking at some figures by Hauptman (1986). He reported that of all 1983 doctorate recipients, nearly 40% had received research assistantships and nearly 50% had received teaching assistantships at some time while they were graduate students. And these figures are even greater in certain fields. For instance, nearly 70% of students in the physical sciences and in engineering have held research assistantships, and nearly 70% of students in the physical sciences and the arts and humanities have held teaching assistantships. Given the number of students who are affected by assistantships, it is somewhat surprising that more research has not been conducted on this topic.

This section looks at the few existing studies pertaining to assistantships. Most of the research has been related to teaching assistants, and those articles are discussed in the first subtopic. Other types of assistantships are discussed in a second subtopic.

Teaching Assistantships. Carroll (1980) provided a review of the research prior to 1977 on the effects of training programs for teaching assistants. He found very fragmented approaches to developing training programs and noted several issues to be considered by program developers: size of program, extent of training, characteristics of trainers, and whether to centralize the administration of programs. He emphasized that faculty interest and participation are crucial to a program's success.

More recently, Jackson and Simpson (1983) attempted to discover the most popular methods of improving the effectiveness of teaching assistants. The authors conducted a study of the graduate deans at the 59 institutions that produced the largest number of Ph.D.'s during the preceding 10 years. Of the 56 institutions that responded, 64% indicated that efforts to improve the effectiveness of teaching assistants had improved in the past 5 years. Handbooks and awards for teaching assistants were the most common universitywide services provided for teaching assistants, with 39% of the institutions providing each. In addition, 32% of the institutions provided in-service workshops, 30% provided coursework for teaching improvement, and 27% offered preservice workshops.

The authors also found that 30% of the institutions restricted the types of courses that teaching assistants could teach to low-level survey courses, and another 23% indicated restrictions to undergraduate courses only. Of the respondent institutions 21% required prior teaching experience from teaching assistants, and 11% required admission to doctoral candidacy. Finally, it should be noted that the methods and restrictions discussed were institutionwide, but many graduate schools noted that responsibilities were left up to individual departments.

Rippetoe and Peters (1979) were also interested in effectiveness as they looked at the common lecture and discussion format, in which undergraduate students attended lectures (taught by a lecturer) twice per week and discussion (taught by a teaching assistant) once per week. The purpose was to analyze the relationship between satisfaction with the discussion and the teaching assistant and (1) the lectures and the lecturer and (2) the course as a whole. The authors found that (1) students who were satisfied with the discussion reported greater satisfaction with the lectures; (2) students who were dissatisfied with the discussion reported greater dissatisfaction with the lectures; and (3) students considered the discussion sections to be unimportant to the course as a whole.

Nevill, Ware, and Smith (1978) compared undergraduates' evaluations of teaching assistants and full-time faculty. The authors studied 799 undergraduates in 36 sections of analytic geometry and calculus at the University of Florida. In this study, 16 teaching assistants and 19 faculty members were evaluated. The authors found no significant differences in the way the undergraduates rated the teaching assistants and the faculty members. The results showed similar rating scores and similar conceptual frameworks within which students made their judgments.

The other two studies on this subtopic had somewhat unique purposes. Vecchio and Costin (1977) studied admission variables and graduate grade-point average in an effort to predict the effectiveness of graduate teaching assistants, as measured by student achievement and student satisfaction. They found that a teaching assistant's GRE advanced score and the number of psychology courses taken as an undergraduate were the best predictors of the achievement of students taught by the teaching assistant in an introductory psychology course. The authors also found that a teaching assistant's GRE verbal score was the best predictor of student satisfaction with the teaching assistant.

Shymansky and Penick (1979) studied gender-bias behaviors exhibited by teaching assistants in laboratory classes. They did find differences in some behaviors of male and female teaching assistants but could not conclude that blatant gender bias or sex-role stereotyping existed. They did find that compared to males, female teaching assistants asked more short-answer and extended-thought questions, appeared to be better listeners, and provided more assistance in obtaining materials and lab equipment for students. Both male and female teaching assistants were found to do more observation of but less interaction with mixed-gender lab partnerships.

Other Assistantships. While most of the research on assistantships has focused on teaching assistantships, most of the funding, at least in terms of dollars, has been focused on research assistantships (Hauptman, 1986). And while both faculty and students believe that in general all assistantships are relevant to educational goals, programs, and career development (Thompson and Ellis, 1984), the only article in this study related to career development pertains to the research assistantship (Roaden and Worthen, 1976).

In the late 1960s, Roaden and Worthen (1976) conducted a nationwide study of all members of the American Educational Research Association "to elicit information about their research assistantship experience and their subsequent participation in educational research" (p. 143). Of the 3,963 respondents who returned a questionnaire, 1,710 were identified as having a genuine research assistantship, which meant that "assisting in the conduct of research is the primary activity" (p. 143). In addition to this first phase of data collection, the 50 most productive (obtaining research publications or grants) former research assistants and a random sample of 50 nonproductive former research assistants were asked to respond to another questionnaire.

The authors found many differences between the high producers and the nonproducers on a variety of structural, experiential, perceptual, and supervisor-assistant interaction variables. For instance, being assigned to an individual faculty member and having adequate access to data analysis equipment led to more productivity. Research assistants who designed studies, wrote proposals, wrote articles, presented research papers, and used a variety of statistical techniques became more productive than their counterparts who did not do those things. Having intense professional interaction with the supervisor led to greater productivity. Research assistants who thought their supervisors viewed them as highly competent went on to be productive. While the study is impressive, unfortunately the data are now at least 20 years old.

It should be noted that graduate assistantships are not just teaching- and research-oriented. In fact, Roaden and Worthen had to eliminate many of the respondents who claimed to have research assistantships but performed primarily administrative tasks. At some institutions, the graduate administrative assistant-ship is an actual title, and while no research studies were found to relate to that title in general, one specific type of administrative assistantship was researched. Winston, Ullom, and Werring (1983) conducted a study of 147 "housing graduate assistants" in the designated top five housing programs in the country. They reported that the vast majority of the assistants were single and pursuing master's degrees, and that slightly over half were in student personnel or counseling programs.

Standardized Tests

Standardized tests such as the Graduate Record Examination (GRE), the Miller Analogies Test (MAT), the Law School Admissions Test (LSAT), the Medical College Admissions Test (MCAT), the Graduate Management Admissions Test (GMAT), and the Test of English as a Foreign Language (TOEFL) are used heavily in the admission process of graduate and professional schools. As a result, the articles in this section have some overlap with the previously discussed area of matriculation. Also, since standardized test scores are also used as a popular criterion to predict performance, there is some overlap with that previously discussed area. The particular articles were placed in this category as opposed to other categories because the primary emphasis of the articles in this section is the standardized tests themselves. While matriculation and predicting performance are used as subtopics in this section, one subtopic which does not overlap with other topical areas is the equivalencing of standardized tests.

Matriculation. Oltman and Hartnett (1985) produced an excellent study on the role of the GRE in admissions. The researchers surveyed department chairpersons in eight academic disciplines across institutions to determine (1) which programs required or recommended that students submit scores; (2) how the scores were used; (3) how important the users judged the scores to be; and (4) the reasons for not recommending scores. The authors also collected data from *The Graduate Programs and Admissions Manual.*

The authors found that more than half of the 7,000 master's programs and more than three-fourths of the doctoral programs at least recommended that students submit GRE scores, and the percentage of programs with that policy ranged greatly both among and within disciplines. Most of the programs indicated that when an applicant's other credentials were strong, the GRE scores were unimportant in admissions decisions. The GRE scores were not as important as undergraduate performance and recommendations. The primary reason that was given for not using the scores was that the departments were getting along fine without them, and that the scores would add no useful information.

Baird (1976b) conducted a study of the relationship between student characteristics and low and high scores on three standardized admission tests: the GRE, the LSAT, and the MCAT. By looking at the same characteristics for each of the three examinations, he also provided for some comparison among the tests. For instance, on all examinations, compared to the lower scorers, the higher scorers obtained higher undergraduate grades, had more self-confidence in their academic abilities, had considered advanced study at a younger age, had higher degree aspirations, and had been accepted to more advanced schools.

There were also some notable differences among the tests. For instance, (1) males tended to score higher than females on the quantitative portion of the GRE; (2) higher scorers on the GRE verbal and the LSAT came from more affluent backgrounds; and (3) higher scorers on the LSAT and the MCAT more often had Jewish religious orientations.

Predicting Performance. Herbert and Holmes (1979) conducted a study in the same vein as those on performance previously discussed, but their approach was much simpler in that the scores on the separate sections of the GRE were their only predictor variables, and graduate grade-point average was the only measure of success. These authors studied the records of 67 master of education students at one institution and found that the verbal section of the GRE was a significant predictor of graduate grade-point average. There is no information in this study that is not contained in other more sophisticated studies.

Additional information is contained in the study by Ayers and Peters (1977), who looked at the predictive power of the TOEFL for Asian students who had graduated from engineering, chemistry, and mathematics programs at one institution. They found that the TOEFL and the verbal portion of the GRE were useful predictors in determining the successful completion of degree programs.

Equivalencing Tests. Three articles in this subtopic deal with comparing the GRE and the MAT. Furst and Roelfs (1979) studied doctoral students in one education program in order to determine which standardized test was a better predictor of success. Success was measured by grades in two specific courses and ratings on an analytical exercise which involved the writing of an essay. The authors found that a composite score on the GRE verbal, the GRE quantitative, and the GRE advanced portions was the best predictor, followed by the GRE verbal, the GRE advanced, the GRE quantitative, and the MAT. The MAT was not a strong predictor compared to the GRE.

Stock, Kagan, and Van Wagenen (1980) and Kagan and Stock (1980) developed and tested methods of actually equating the scales of the GRE and the MAT. In the former article, the authors examined the following four methods of equivalencing the scores of doctoral students on the two examinations: linear transformation, linear regression, column means, and equipercentiling. They found that only the first two methods were adequate. In the latter article, Kagan and Stock tested the two adequate methods with scores from master's students.

They discovered that "standard deviations of regression equivalence scores were consistently smaller than those actually obtained in the sample, whereas standard deviations of linear equivalence scores were the same as those in the sample. Means did not differ" (p. 34).

Employment, Career

While Ph.D.'s are not the most common by-product of graduate education, they seem to have drawn the most research interest, and the area of employment is no exception. Two of the most extensive research studies on graduate education in the past 15 years have been on this topic and have been published in two books which are very good references on this topic (Cartter, 1976; Bowen and Schuster, 1986). Both of these works highlight the overproduction of Ph.D.'s relative to the demand, and they question the value of such overproduction.

Turning to the four articles in this section, the most recent and comprehensive study was conducted by Clark and Centra (1985). They studied Ph.D. recipients in six different fields 3, 5, and 13 years after receiving their degrees. These authors actually conducted two different studies, one comparing chemistry, history, and psychology, and the other comparing the physical sciences, the biological sciences, and the social sciences. The purpose was to determine the academic and personal characteristics which explain career accomplishments. The academic characteristics included GRE scores, grades, and the quality of the graduate program. The personal characteristics included age, gender, the number of years since the Ph.D. had been awarded, and the type of employment (e.g., research/teaching/administrative and academic/private). Career accomplishments were defined by income and the number of publications and presentations.

The authors projected a causal model to depict the relationship among the variables. They found that academic ability generally did not directly affect productivity or income, but that it did have an indirect effect through its influence on the quality of the program that had awarded the Ph.D., which influenced job setting and responsibilities. Specific findings were that (1) individuals in research-oriented positions had more publications; (2) people in administrative or private research positions had higher incomes than people in academic teaching or research positions; and (3) women had lower incomes than men. One important note regarding the last finding is that income was defined as including all professionally related income, not just salary. The authors indicated that perhaps men had more opportunities for outside income; thus, the figures might not reflect actual salary bias. Even so, it appears just as likely that salary bias would have been found also.

Two of the remaining three studies in this topic area were fairly simplistic in their design. Both dealt with the field of education at single institutions. Through the use of a telephone survey, which was rarely used in any of the research related to graduate education, Thompson and Layne (1980) surveyed 323 subjects who were randomly sampled from over 6,500 master of education graduates during a 10-year period. The purpose was simply to determine their current professional status and future educational goals. The researchers found that over 80% of the graduates held positions in education, and that males were more likely than females to be in administration. Job satisfaction was quite high, and about 25% were pursuing or planning to pursue advanced degrees.

Holmes, Verrier, and Chisholm (1983) limited their study to the field of student affairs, and they were most interested in attrition in the field. Unlike their teacher-education counterparts in the above study, these individuals were moving out of their profession at alarming rates. Almost 90% of the graduates had positions in higher education in the first year after graduation, but gradual attrition each year resulted in only 39% employment in the field by the sixth year.

The final study employed a more sophisticated design than the previous two studies. McCaffrey, Miller, and Winston (1984) used both freshman and senior undergraduates as well as graduate students in various fields of study to examine and compare their "career maturity." The authors refer to career maturity as a point on a continuum of career development where a student progresses through types of behaviors related to coping with decisions and the activities necessary for career choice and progression. They found significant differences between freshmen and seniors and between freshmen and graduate students, but not between seniors and graduate students. They found no significant differences between men and women. Unfortunately, the authors did not discriminate on length of time in graduate school or degree level for the graduate students. Indeed, these factors were not mentioned at all, so the information is unknown. One might expect the number of years in graduate school and the level of degree being pursued to have an impact on career maturity.

Minorities

In 1976, there was a noticeable lack of literature on minority graduate experiences (Duncan, 1976; National Board on Graduate Education, 1976), and more than a decade later, this is still the case. Even though differences in ethnic groups have been discussed in other research topics in this chapter, it was surprising to see only four articles with ethnicity as the primary focus of the study. The issue of gender differences was also discussed in several articles where those differences were not the primary topic, yet there were still 13 additional articles in which gender differences were the primary focus of the research. Since the discussion of ethnic and gender differences often appears in the same articles, it seems reasonable to assume that there would be equal interest in the topics on an independent level. The evidence here does not support that assumption, but perhaps on the undergraduate level, the topics are treated more equally.

A repeated observation in the review of research on graduate students is the effort of the researchers associated with the Educational Testing Service. Having at their disposal hundreds of thousands of prospective graduate students taking the Graduate Record Examination certainly had a positive impact on their studies, and this is especially evident in the first study to be reviewed in this section. Because of the large number of records available (223,582), Centra (1980) was able to identify enough subjects from eight different ethnic groups to compare attitudes pertaining to degree aspirations in three large aggregate areas of study.

Centra defined degree aspirations as the simple dichotomous variable of whether a student planned to obtain a master's or a doctoral degree. As predictor variables, he used four student characteristics and six characteristics of the students' undergraduate institutions. The student characteristics were gender, GRE verbal and quantitative scores, and grade-point average for the last two years. The institutional characteristics were predominant race and gender composition, selectivity, affluence, enrollment, and the percentage of seniors who pursued advanced degrees. Centra found that the student characteristics were much better predictors than the institutional characteristics. Generally, he found that undergraduate grades, test scores, and gender were the best predictor variables. Higher GRE verbal scores and grades were the most consistent predictors of doctoral degree aspirations across fields and ethnic groups. One other fairly consistent result across fields and ethnic groups was that males were more likely than females to aspire to doctoral degrees.

The importance that the Graduate Record Examination plays in graduate admissions and performance prediction has been observed throughout this chapter. However, the question of how much importance it should actually play has been discussed only casually. Admissions committees commonly believe that higher scores are good indicators of potential positive performances, although there has been a great deal of debate about that issue recently, especially in regard to the examination's possible bias against minorities.

Scott and Shaw (1985) add to that debate with the results of their study. They examined the relationship between GRE scores and performance, which was based on first-year graduate grade-point averages, in order to see if there were differences between black and white students. A matched-sampling procedure was used so that the two groups of students would be matched by department, gender, age, and amount of time in the department. While the authors noted that correlations between GRE scores and grade-point averages do vary by institution, the results found at the institution used for their study, the University of Florida, were particularly surprising. For blacks and whites, Scott and Shaw discovered opposite relationships between GRE scores and grade-point averages.

For whites, grade-point averages increased as GRE scores increased, but for blacks, grade-point averages decreased as GRE scores increased. As one possible explanation of the results, the authors suggested motivational differences among blacks, meaning that blacks with low GRE scores worked harder to compensate for deficiencies and that blacks with higher scores worked less. Thus the study implied that the university which implemented affirmative action policies in its admission of blacks by lowering acceptable GRE scores did not sacrifice its scholarly standards. This study warrants further investigation at other institutions.

Anderson and Hrabowski (1977) were also interested in the performance of black graduate students, but their comparison was between black students who as undergraduates attended traditionally black institutions and black students who as undergraduates attended historically white institutions. The authors found positive correlations between undergraduate and graduate grade-point averages for both groups, but they did not find significant differences between the groups on graduate grade-point average, retention rate, or graduation rate.

Carrington and Sedlacek (1977) were concerned about the attitudes of black graduate students in predominantly white institutions, and they conducted a study at the University of Maryland to ascertain the students' feelings and reactions to both the academic and the nonacademic environments. The findings offered evidence of perceived racism and desires for more black faculty as role models.

Stress and Anxiety

"Graduate students in general, but notably doctoral candidates, seem to display more neuroticism than ever" (Topp, 1977, p. 105). The experiences of graduate education can produce high levels of stress and anxiety in many students as they proceed through the various stages of development (Lange, 1980). The ability to stay in school might actually be related more to the types of situations encountered and to coping styles and strategies than to academic abilities (Kjerulff and Wiggins, 1976). The four articles in this section discuss research related to the stress and anxiety experienced by graduate students and the students' abilities to cope.

Both Valdez (1982) and Williams, Gallas, and Quiriconi (1984) used modified versions of the Holmes and Rahe (1967) Social Readjustment Rating Scale to measure the total Life Change Units, which are any experiences that result in a change in behavior in order to adapt or cope. Both studies involved small samples within the field of social work: 11 subjects in the Williams study and 33 in the Valdez study. The purpose of the Valdez study was to determine the level of crisis being experienced by first-year doctoral students in a specific program. He found that 48% of the students were experiencing "major crisis," which meant that they were in a high-risk category for illness.

Valdez found very little illness among the students, and he accredited that fact to their ability to cope. While that may, in fact, be the case, it also may be that the rating instrument designed for a general population is not valid for doctoral students, a point to which Valdez does allude. Regarding the number of Life Change Units, Valdez found no significant differences based on gender, ethnicity; the area reared in, relocation, professional goals, or the number of years out of school before beginning doctoral studies.

While Valdez did not discuss coping behaviors, the purpose of the Kjerulff and Wiggins (1976) study was to analyze how students responded to stressful situations. After collecting data on stressful situations and employing a three-mode factor analysis, two types of graduate students emerged: less competent and more competent. Among many findings, the authors noted that when faced with an academic failure situation, the first type felt responsible for the problem and the latter did not. Both felt anxious and depressed in that type of situation.

Being concerned about the stress and anxiety facing graduate students, Rimmer, Lammert, and McClain (1982) conducted a needs assessment study of 82 students in one institution in order to find out their concerns. The greatest needs included departmental orientation programs, a graduate student newsletter, a centralized location for information and social activities, and workshops for professional development and career planning and placement. Women students had additional concerns about personal growth counseling and child care. Minority students were interested in support groups. Single students wanted time management workshops.

Several authors have offered suggestions to help alleviate stress. Both Williams, et al. and Valdez suggested a "buddy" or student-support system, where current students in a program are assigned to help new students even before the new students arrive on campus. Lange (1980) developed a model of student anxiety and faculty support that could be shared by faculty and students to help them realize what to expect in terms of anxiety and support as students progress through their degree programs. For doctoral programs, Topp (1977) had several specific recommendations: (1) to eliminate any foreign language require-ment; (2) to match students and advisers so that they relate well to each other; and (3) to provide more structure.

Impact of Marriage, Family

Marriage and family can be strongly related to stress and anxiety, which are prominent among graduate students. Spouses and family members can play important roles in both creating stress and providing support systems for graduate students. While it is not unusual for half of the graduate students in a given department or institution to be married (Feldman, 1974), there has been very little research relating marriage and education, in general, and especially marriage and graduate education (McKeon and Piercy, 1980). Works before 1977 were reviewed by Gilbert (1982), who concluded that graduate school is potentially destructive to family life, especially for married female students. Only two research articles since then were discovered for review here.

Lewis (1983) interviewed 30 married women graduate students and their husbands, all of whom had been together from the beginning of the wife's studies through the current stage of writing her dissertation. The purpose was to determine if a pattern of marital adjustment existed. Four stages were identified: preenrollment; introductory, which was the first two terms of enrollment; preliminary, when most of the coursework was completed and preparation for the comprehensive examination was under way; and candidate, when the comprehensive examination had been completed and the dissertation was under way. The findings showed that the relationships were most vulnerable during the second and third stages. There was a decrease in adjustment for both spouses during these stages, but at the candidate stage, the wives made very strong increases in adjustment, while the husbands did not make similar recoveries.

Lewis tested the relationship of several demographic variables to marital adjustment but found a significant relationship with only length of time before candidacy. She found that marital adjustment was lower when the wife proceeded quickly (2 to 3 years) to candidacy, and adjustment was highest when the wife took 6 to 9 years. She reported that the educational level of the husband did not make a difference, although one would think that if the husband had already obtained a doctorate or perhaps even a master's degree, he would be more prepared for his wife's ordeals. Unfortunately, Lewis did not indicate the demographic breakdowns for any of the variables, so the reader remains uniformed about the actual level of education of the husbands in her sample.

Related to the above point, the purpose of McKeon and Piercy's (1980) study was to determine if marital adjustment was higher when both spouses were students or when only one spouse was a student. The authors collected data from 49 married graduate students by using the Locke and Wallace (1959) Short Marital Adjustment Test. They found that "the marital adjustment of students whose partners were also engaged in studies was significantly higher than that of students whose partners were not engaged in studies" (p. 40). The authors did not indicate whether the study was at the master's or doctoral level, so an interesting research study would be to compare marital adjustment across levels of study for spouses. Actually, there is much room for further research related to marriage and graduate study, and since it has been reported that as many as 69% of all male and 55% of all female graduate students are married (Feldman, 1974), the issue takes on added importance. While there is no study available to provide current figures on the marital status of graduate students, Gilbert (1982) suggested that there is evidence for the period 1962 to 1974 of "stability in student composition for this variable" (p. 129).

Attitudes Toward Research

"Relationships between graduate education and academic research are intuitively accepted, but have been given limited examination" (Toombs, 1977, p. 43). The knowledge and practice of research is an important part of graduate education, especially for Ph.D. students in nonapplied fields, but very little is known about how students feel about research, how much they know about existing research studies, or what drives their own research studies. The three articles in this section address these topics.

Perl and Kahn (1983) conducted a national study of psychology graduate students to assess their attitudes about research. From 39 universities, 1,839 respondents returned completed questionnaires, and 97% of them were pursuing Ph.D.'s. For analysis, the respondents were divided into three groups according to their specialty: clinical, nonclinical applied, and nonclinical nonapplied. Generally, all three groups had positive attitudes toward research and graduate training in research, but there were some expected differences. Actually, the first two groups had similar attitudes, but some important differences were observed in the third group.

The nonapplied students were more interested in doing research in graduate school, and they reported actually doing more research than the other groups. They also reported that they were making greater progress on their dissertations. They were more likely to have published articles and presented papers at conferences. They were simply more enthusiastic about research, but this is to be expected, given the differences in the general orientation of applied and nonapplied areas of study.

Toombs (1977) was concerned about the levels of awareness of and the use of academic research by doctoral students, and to investigate these issues, he collected data from 470 students from a total of 18 departments in one university. He found a high level of awareness, measured by recognition of current departmental research projects and by whether research projects were linked to the dissertation. He also found a high level of usefulness of campus research in the student's own work, with the major uses being theoretical leads and basic data sources.

Based on the data from their study on 310 dissertation topics in the fields of higher education, counseling, and student personnel from 28 different institutions, Aronson et al. (1985) hinted that individual programs and faculty members might be providing too much influence on the nature of dissertation topics. Several institutions had high percentages of dissertations in only one or two topic areas. The fear of the authors seemed to be that faculty preferences, as opposed to student preferences, were driving the selection of research topics.

In addition to a discussion of topic areas, the authors also provided a breakdown by the populations studied and whether a theoretical, descriptive, or attitudinal orientation was employed. While this study is interesting in its approach, the authors definitely attempted to draw too many conclusions from their data. One simply is incapable of determining the major emphases of a dissertation by analyzing titles alone. The authors should have at least incorporated the use of *Dissertation Abstracts International* to assist them in speculating on the nature of the dissertations.

Miscellaneous

The six articles in this section cover a wide range of issues and could not be placed easily in any of the other topics. The first study deals with a group of students that is growing in number but that has been virtually disregarded in the literature: the part-time commuter student (Reisman et al., 1983). While the undergraduate part-time commuter has been dealt with at some length (Chickering, 1974), the graduate part-time commuter has been ignored. This is especially important since these students are actually a majority in many departments.

Reisman was concerned about this group of students because 99% of all students, both graduate and undergraduate, at her institution were commuters, and about 40% were part-time evening students. She and her coauthors indicated that these students have special needs, and they designed a study to get more information about those needs. Of the 146 respondents to a survey, 60% indicated that they did not spend time on campus after class for the following reasons: family obligations, commuting time, employment, and no place to spend it. Almost two-thirds of the students indicated that they would use a graduate student lounge if their department had one. About 60% were interested in meeting on a regular basis with other students. Almost all students were interested in having a newsletter. Over half of the students were interested in having planned social activities for students. The authors concluded that there was clearly a need for some type of community and belonging for these students.

In the second article, Vidler and Wood (1981) compared the curiosity and motivational levels of undergraduate and graduate students. To measure academic and intellectual curiosity and intrinsic motivation, they administered a 45-item questionnaire called the Academic Curiosity Scale to 21 sophomores, 22 juniors, 20 seniors, and 25 graduate students. They followed up with personal interviews about a month later in order to derive more information. They found almost identical scores among the undergraduate groups on a scale of curiosity, but the graduate students had a significantly higher level of curiosity compared to the composite of undergraduate students. The authors also found that the graduate students indicated a wider range of motivational factors and a greater tendency toward intrinsic motivations. The authors did not indicate whether the graduate students were pursuing master's degrees or doctorates, and it would be interesting to see if there are differences between these two groups. There also might be some value in using the scale as a predictor of success in graduate school.

The third study presents research related to the ageless question of whether students are more interested in getting a degree or in getting an education. Stodt and Thielens (1985) conducted 27 exploratory interviews with medical students and with graduate students in three fields: business administration, higher education administration, and psychology. The purpose of those initial interviews was to explore the meanings that students attached to credentials, getting an education, and acquiring competence. This information was then used to create a questionnaire, which was administered to over a thousand students distributed across the four fields.

The authors found that the major components of credentials were perceived as the degree, graduation from a prestigious school, high grades, recommendations, sponsorship by an influential professor, and honors and awards. The perceived components of competence included a knowledge of basic theory, the ability to perform the necessary technical skills, skills in oral and written communication, the ability to work with people, leadership skills, and knowledge of the latest developments. The students were asked to indicate the relative importance of gaining credentials and competence in their decisions to attend graduate school. In all but one field, "the students attributed great significance to obtaining *both* credentials and competence" (p. 260). The exception was the medical field, where the students valued competence much more than credentials. Based on the data, the authors concluded that there were few students who were primarily concerned with obtaining just credentials.

The fourth study, conducted by Kuh and Thomas (1983), dealt with the application of adult development theories to graduate students. The authors' purpose was to determine if graduate students go through developmental transitions or tasks that correspond to the chronological age periods discussed in popular adult development theories. The researchers conducted personal interviews with a sample of 40 students who had been divided equally by gender and two age groups, younger (22–28 years) and older (33–40 years). The results indicated statistically significant differences between the two age groups on 11 of the 16 questions which had been asked in the interviews. The authors concluded that "adult developmental theory processes identified in the literature were found to be generally applicable to graduate students" (p. 19).

In the fifth study in this section, Bess (1978) was concerned with the question of how to find more student-oriented teachers. He wondered whether students being admitted to graduate schools were losing their student orientations somewhere in the process of becoming faculty members, or perhaps they had simply never had such orientations at the time of admission. In a previous study, Bess (1976) had administered a 320-item survey to 800 faculty members from six institutions. The survey asked faculty to assume that their pay and status reward system was prompted by how they performed on tasks they liked, and thus to evaluate 320 task descriptions on a 5-point scale as to their intrinsic satisfaction in performing the tasks. In the more recent study, he asked admitted graduate students, before they arrived on campus, at a single institution to respond to the same survey. For analysis, he selected only those students who expressed the desire to teach in college, and he compared their responses to those of younger faculty (under 30) and older faculty (over 35).

Bess noted that while pregraduate students do have slightly more concern about undergraduate student development, they actually "differ relatively little from faculty members. They are quite similar to younger faculty and only slightly less different from older faculty" (p. 312). He indicated that this finding contradicts previous literature on graduate student socialization, which showed graduate school as a socializing process. He also noted that "there is little likelihood that those [students] presently applying to graduate school will become faculty with significantly different dispositions from those already there" (p. 313), and he expressed the hope that this situation would be changed through different admissions policies. It is questionable that a majority of faculty share his sentiments regarding the need for new faculty with different attitudes.

In the final study, Smart (in press) investigated graduate student satisfaction with academic programs. He tested the students' level of satisfaction based on the similarity of their undergraduate and graduate environments (academic programs) as defined by Holland's (1973; 1985) hexagonal model of environments. Smart found that satisfaction increased as similarity between undergraduate and graduate environments increased. He noted that 37% of the students in his sample were pursuing graduate degrees in fields that were dissimilar from their undergraduate programs; thus, as he stated, many such students stand to benefit from early identification of the dissimilarity in programs and from special counseling that could be arranged to discuss the potential adjustment problems they are likely to face as a result of the dissimilarity.

Faculty-Student Interaction

Graduate students and faculty interact in a variety of ways both within and outside the classroom. Within the classroom is the ever-present and controversial evaluation processes: the teacher evaluating the students, and the students evaluating the teacher. Three articles in the first section to follow discuss the evaluation of either instructors or programs.

The second section deals with interaction outside the classroom. Two articles discuss the process and the importance of mentoring in graduate education, a process which highlights the often very close relationships that some faculty and graduate students share.

The final section respresents a return to classroom interaction. The one article, by Rouse (1983), looks at classroom interaction within the context of social power.

Evaluation of Faculty and Programs

Trent and Johnson (1977) noted that student evaluation of faculty began as a feedback mechanism for the instructors, but with increased student demands for accountability, many administrators began using the evaluations as evidence of teaching effectiveness. Both Trent and Johnson (1977) and Patalano (1978) questioned whether such evaluations are valid measures and thus worthy of such administrative use.

Trent and Johnson investigated the extent to which students' values and attitudes played a role in their decisions regarding the worth of a course or an instructor. The authors studied 65 graduate students enrolled in four sections of a course in adult learning at North Carolina State University. Data were collected on the students' values, educational attitudes, and evaluations of the course and the instructor through the use of the Rokeach (1973) Value Survey, Hadley's (1975) Educational Orientation Questionnaire, and the department's Course and Instructor Evaluation Survey, respectively. Regression and path analyses determined that there was no significant relationship between values and evaluations, but that there was a significant relationship between attitudes and evaluations. The combination of attitudes and values explained 27.7% of the variance in student evaluations, which led the authors to conclude that instructors must take into account the values and attitudes of the students in the interpretation of evaluations, and that administrators, who generally have less intimate knowledge of the evaluators, need to recognize the limitations of such evaluations.

Patalano (1978) was concerned as to whether student judgment of teaching effectiveness was influenced more by a faculty member's professional skills or personality characteristics. He studied 40 graduate students in a school psychology program and determined that a significant proportion of the sample emphasized personality over professional skills for both effective and ineffective instructors. The only two groups that did not follow this pattern were female students and students who had grade-point averages higher that 3.5, and these groups appeared to be interrelated. So, the results of that study also provide evidence of the need for caution in interpreting evaluations. As noted in that study, students placed more emphasis on an instructor's sense of humor, friendliness, warmth, and empathy than on knowledge of the subject, intellectual ability, lecturing ability, and class preparation.

The final article in this section looked at evaluation from a broader perspective. Freeman and Loadman (1985) surveyed alumni from the education Ph.D. programs at two major research universities, Michigan State University and Ohio

State University, in order to compare alumni perceptions of guidance committee activities, course work, comprehensive examinations, and dissertations. Identical surveys were used, and the mailings resulted in 57% and 58% response rates and 365 and 311 respondents, respectively.

The authors found fairly consistent ratings for the two institutions. Generally, survey participants were satisfied with the assistance they had received from their faculty committees, except in the area of finding jobs. They were generally satisfied with the number of courses taken in each of 36 curricular areas, although between 17% and 25% of the alumni from both institutions desired more course work in an area related to research design, evaluation, and statistics.

Some differences between the institutions were also observed. For instance, regarding comprehensive examinations, 94% of the alumni from one institution reported taking both written and oral examinations, while only 16% from the other institution reported a similar process. Also, the former group spent longer studying for exams (5.6 weeks compared to 4.6 weeks). While the two groups of alumni were similar in having published at least one article (31% and 29%), they were strikingly different in having published an article from their dissertations (40% and 23%). The authors indicate that this latter finding suggests "a clear difference in normative expectations regarding the publication of dissertation findings" (p. 345). The authors concluded the article by making several recommendations for doctoral guidance committees.

Mentoring

Most of the mentoring research has dealt with business and industry, although there has been an increase in interest in the study of mentoring in education, especially in graduate education where the mentoring process is most likely to occur. A problem with research related to mentoring has been in the definition of the term (Busch, 1985). And given the differences between industry and higher education, more problems related to the definition of mentoring are to be expected in higher education.

Typically, mentoring is viewed as a one-way street, where the more experienced "teacher" assists the less experienced "student" in learning about an environment in order to be better able to succeed. In her study on mentoring, Busch utilized O'Neil's (1981) definition, which looked at mentoring as a two-way street with benefits for both the mentor and the mentee.

Busch (1985) studied mentoring from the mentor's perspective. In the field of education, she selected a nationwide sample of 1,088 associate or full professors, of whom an equal number were men and women. Of that sample, 537 completed and returned a demographic questionnaire, and of that group, 238 reported currently having mentees. One mentee for each faculty member was targeted, and a mentoring questionnaire was sent to each faculty member with directions to respond in regard to the relationship with the targeted mentee. Eighty-nine percent of the faculty returned a completed questionnaire.

Busch found that the mentors felt that they had received many benefits from the mentoring experience, which is evidence of the two-way street hypothesis. In addition to collaborating on research, there were reports of fulfillment in seeing a mentee develop professionally. In her demographic analysis, Busch did find a significant relationship between age and mentoring. She found that younger mentors reported more "mutuality," which included such items as having a "close relationship" and the mentee's encouraging the mentor when the mentor was discouraged. On the other hand, she found that the older mentors reported more "comprehensiveness," which included such items as the mentor's discussing professional dilemmas with the mentee and the mentee's discussing personal problems with the mentor. Busch indicated that she planned to do a follow-up mentee project to see how the perceptions of mentor and mentee compared.

LeCluyse, Tollefsen, and Borgers (1985) studied mentoring from the mentee's perspective and specifically, that of the female mentee. They studied 228 graduate students who were enrolled in either education or the liberal arts and sciences at one institution. The purpose was to examine the extent of mentoring and to compare the professional activities, grade-point averages, and self-acceptance of students who were mentored and those who were not.

The researchers found that 76% of the students reported having a mentor. They found no difference between the mentored and nonmentored students relative to grade-point averages or self-acceptance scores. However, there were differences relative to professional involvement. The mentored women reported a significantly higher level of professional involvement, but this relationship is not necessarily causal. It would be interesting to see how personality variables might affect these relationships.

Social Power

While the classroom has been reported as being the beginning of many mentoring relationships (LeCluyse et al., 1985), it is also the source of a very different kind of relationship between students and faculty. The last article in this section discusses the classroom interaction between faculty and students in terms of social power. Rouse (1983) studied the manipulation of resources (e.g., expertise, rewards, and authority) by faculty members as a measure of power, and she looked at the impact of that manipulation on the mood and morale of graduate students.

Rouse distributed questionnaires to both faculty and student samples in 10 academic departments at one institution. The faculty response rate was 73.2% and yielded 41 usable questionnaires. The student response rate was 51.5% and produced 238 usable questionnaires. Regression and factor analyses led Rouse to conclude that faculty use of power did affect the mood and morale of graduate students. She found that more manipulation of punishing and negative resources led to lower student satisfaction and morale and a less positive mood. On the other hand, the use of rewarding resources had the opposite effect. While these results are not surprising, they may "help advance understanding of how the relationship between teacher and student influences classroom outcomes, including student satisfaction, at all levels of education" (p. 382). Future studies might show relationships between power and mentoring as well.

Faculty and Administrators

The previous discussion in this chapter has focused on research related to students in graduate education. While research on issues in graduate education that do not specifically pertain to students is limited, there have been several studies since 1976. The range in topics of these studies is quite broad, which makes categorization difficult, but two distinct categories have been identified for this section. The first involves research related to the administration, structure, and function of graduate education in general. The second involves departmental characteristics and degrees. Articles that did not fit into either of these categories have been included in a miscellaneous category.

Administration, Structure, Function

Wiant et al. (1978) conducted a national study of institutions involved in graduate education in order to determine whether there existed "grades of membership on the graduate faculty" and, if so, how they were determined. Grading systems could include a variety of classifications, but the authors did not elaborate on the different systems. A simple schema would be one that distinguishes between faculty who could advise only master's students and faculty who could advise both doctoral and master's students.

Questionnaires were sent to almost every institution having graduate programs, and 204 graduate school deans (or equivalents) responded. Most of the institutions (60.8%) did not have grades of membership on their graduate faculties; 44.4% of the state-supported schools did, and only 11.1% of the private schools did. Schools that had such systems were more likely to feel that the systems were desirable. Faculty productivity, not academic rank, was the most important criterion for membership grades. The authors concluded that "Generally, private schools and those offering only master's work have somewhat less stringent requirements for membership" (p. 142).

Baldwin (1977) was concerned about the general function of doctoral programs, specifically whether programs should be training researchers or teachers. He felt that the primary emphasis of programs was on research, yet most of the Ph.D. graduates went on to emphasize teaching in their careers; thus, they were underprepared for those careers. He surveyed 243 departmental chairpersons and 450 graduates in a variety of academic areas. He found that few graduates had had prior teaching experience before taking their first job upon graduation, and that few programs offered preparation in teaching methods in their curricula. This study led Baldwin to conclude that "it is time to swallow former differences and provide constructive and worthwhile courses to meet this end" (p. 84).

The next two studies (Malaney, 1986a,b) were based on the same research project which was designed to gather information about the need for and the potential use of a computerized data base to monitor graduate education, a data base which is described in detail elsewhere (Malaney, 1986c). In the first article, Malaney (1986a) reported on his survey of all college deans, department chairpersons, and graduate study committee chairpersons at one institution. A variety of dependent and independent variables were discussed, but the most important result was that the support for the development of the proposed data base was very strong.

In the second article, Malaney (1986b) discussed the development of the data base in relation to theories of differentiation and integration (see Lawrence and Lorsch, 1967a,b; Blau, 1973). The data base was proposed as an integrating device in an organization differentiated by size of academic unit and field of study, as defined by Biglan (1973a,b). The purpose was to determine the specific areas of support of the data base, and Malaney concluded that the size of the academic unit was a stronger determinant of support than any of the Biglan dimensions.

In the final study in this category, Quarles and Roney (1986) discussed their research on the preparation, style, and format of doctoral dissertations. In a nationwide study of graduate deans or chief executive officers at institutions of higher education offering doctoral degrees, the authors surveyed the same 194 institutions which had been surveyed 10 years previously. They reported on the various requirements specific to the preparation of the dissertations, such as the number of copies required, the type of paper used, and the acceptable page margins. They also reported on the use of technological advancements; for instance, 68% of the respondents reported that at least 70% of their students used computers to produce the final version of their dissertations. The authors reported that institutions still placed a high value on the dissertation as the culminating academic requirement for their highest degree.

Departmental Characteristics, Degrees

In this category, two articles deal with departmental characteristics and the production of Ph.D.'s. One article deals with the attitudes of chief administrators toward external doctoral degrees. And a fourth article is concerned with the teaching-related doctor of arts degree.

Both Hargens (1983) and Moffat (1978) were concerned with Ph.D. production in the disciplines of chemistry and physics, respectively. Moffat utilized data from secondary sources to produce a data set with the unit of analysis being the graduate physics departments in 112 institutions. The dependent variable of interest was annual Ph.D. output, and the independent variables included changes in federal funding for the sciences, faculty growth rates, graduate student enrollment levels, and the prestige ranking of the department. Moffat found that enrollment levels, the prestige of the department, and departmental research funds had the greatest impacts on explaining Ph.D. production among departments. Hargens discovered that the production of new Ph.D. recipients had a moderate positive association with measures of the recognition and eminence of the faculty who trained those new Ph.D. recipients.

In a short article, Mayall (1979) presented some of the major conclusions of his dissertation regarding the attitudes of college and university presidents and school superintendents toward external doctoral degrees. Unfortunately, he presented only conclusions and recommendations in the article. There was no methodological section, so it is difficult for a reader to determine the value of the research. He did indicate that the respondents, in general, were favorable toward external degrees, provided that the quality of the doctoral programs and the granting institutions was high.

Dressel and Thompson (1978) investigated the history and development of the doctor of arts (D.A.) degree, which was initiated in 1967 as a teaching-oriented alternative to the Ph.D. While the differences between the D.A. and the Ph.D. are dependent upon the institution, generally the D.A. places more emphasis on teaching-related courses and practice, such as an internship. Also, there is less emphasis on "pure" research. The authors reported that as of June 1977, 23 institutions had D.A. programs in a total of at least 18 fields of study. There had been 482 D.A.'s awarded, and at least 740 students were actively pursuing the degree. The authors concluded that after 10 years, the D.A. "has attained a character reasonably well defined, but still in a formative state, and has become acceptable as a meritorious degree in its own right" (p. 335).

Miscellaneous

Three articles have been included in this category, and only the first has the explicit purpose of studying an issue directly related to graduate education. In that article, Khoury (1977) studied 422 Ph.D.'s who held faculty positions in sociology. His purpose was to study the geographic mobility of individuals from the region of the country where the doctorate was earned to the region where the individual was currently employed. He discovered that "the largest proportion of Ph.D. recipients from all regions tends to adopt the region of their doctorate training for employment" (p. 158), and he noted that this observation was strongest in the South, with 64% staying, and lowest in the northcentral region, with 48% staying. He found a "moderately strong" relationship between the academic quality of the Ph.D. region and the current job region. He also found that the "most brilliant and gifted" Ph.D. recipients, defined as receiving the Ph.D. before age 28, were disproportionately employed in the region of their doctorate training compared to other regions.

The next two articles are related in that the second is a critical analysis of the first, provides a reanalysis of the data, and draws new conclusions. The issue in both articles is an analysis of predictors of external funding for research among members of the American Association of State Colleges and Universities. The link to graduate education lies in the claim that an institution's increased emphasis on graduate education leads to increased external funding.

In the first article, Muffo and Coccari (1982) conducted a stepwise regression in order to determine the impact of 22 independent variables on the level of outside funding. They discovered several significant effects, but in the second article, Wolfle (1982) criticized their method of analysis. He indicated that they had incorrectly employed a stepwise regression procedure in light of the high degree of multicollinearity among the independent variables. He also indicated that several of the independent variables were measuring the same dimensions. Wolfle reanalyzed the data by creating four latent theoretical variables based on several of the prior 22 independent variables, and he tested his model using LISREL. His analysis then showed that the only significant predictors of external funding were past success in obtaining funds and an emphasis on graduate education. The reason that an emphasis on graduate education is important is the close link between graduate study and research.

DIRECTIONS FOR FUTURE RESEARCH

Since the research related to graduate education has been so limited, there are a number of directions for future research. This section looks at the general areas of student-related research and research related to the administration of graduate education. Some general observations are made about prior research, especially in the student-related area, and some specific directions for future research are suggested.

Students

General Observations

As has been noted, students are the primary focus of 94 of the 112 articles in this review. Before offering any recommendations for specific types of future studies related to students, some general observations are in order. These general observations are discussed in terms of two analyses: (1) the methods of data collection that have been utilized in the studies and (2) the foci of the research designs in terms of the field(s) of study, the number of institutions, and the level of degree pursued.

Table 2 provides information related to the first analysis. Surveys have been the dominant means of obtaining data in student-related research studies, with 63% of the reported data collection methods being surveys. Within the survey typology, mail surveys have been the most popular method of obtaining data, which probably comes as no surprise to most readers; however, a somewhat surprising finding was the very low number of personal interviews. Of course, mail surveys are far easier and less time-consuming to conduct than personal interviews, but the type of extensive data gained from personal interviews is often desired for particular studies and by particular researchers.

Any data collection method is, of course, dependent upon the purpose of a particular research idea. For instance, surveys have been popular because they are most appropriate for the attitudinal research which has been so popular. Institutional records have been used primarily for research related to admissions, performance, and standardized tests, because they provide the most reliable data related to these topics. There has been a lack of interest in the qualitative research methods such as personal interviewing, mentioned above, and observational techniques, of which only one incident was reported.

The one incident of an observational approach dealt with the interaction between students and faculty. This approach could also be useful in looking at relationships among students or evaluations of departmental climate in general. Such research might be useful on a variety of established topics, such as stress and anxiety, performance, and retention.

The method of data collection is only one aspect of a total research design. Other important aspects related to research on graduate students are included in the second analysis, which refers to the following three variables: (1) the degree level of the students studied, either master's or doctoral; (2) whether single or multiple fields of study were investigated, and (3) whether single or multiple institutions were studied. Such knowledge is important in terms of the generalizability of a study, as well as in indicating gaps in the literature.

Table 3 provides information on the 94 student-related research studies in terms of the three foci mentioned above. Several points are obvious based on the table. First, there has been a fairly even distribution of studies between single and multiple fields of study; 46 and 48, respectively. While on the surface this may appear as a positive venture into multiple-field studies, the figure is misleading. The problem lies in the fact that almost half of the multiple-field studies (22 of 48) do not actually specify individual fields. They are simply studies of students in all fields, and no analysis was done to distinguish separate fields. However, because graduate education is such a discipline-specific

TABLE 2. Research Methods for the 94 Student-Related Studies

Research method		N
Surveys		65
Mail	(37)	
Hand-distributed	(12)	
On-site administered	(8)	
Questionnaire on GRE	(4)	
Personal interview	(3)	
Telephone interview	(2)	
Institutional records		27
Analysis of documents		4
Quasi experiment		3
Special task		2
Literature review analysis		1
Observation		1
Total[a]		104

[a]Total does not equal 94 because some studies employed more than one method.

endeavor, investigating differences among fields is quite important, as evidenced by some of the 26 studies that have analyzed data by fields.

Another obvious point seen in Table 3 is the fairly even distribution of the types of students studied: 20 master's studies and 21 doctorate studies. The not-so-obvious point pertains to the nature of the studies that fall in the nonspecific/both category. Unfortunately, 43 of the 53 studies in this category are nonspecific, which means that the reader either does not know whether the students were at the master's or doctoral level or that only demographic counts were provided, with no analysis by level of student. Some previous studies have shown that differences do exist between master's and doctoral students on certain issues, so future researchers must be cautious as to the nature of the particular issues under investigation and as to whether the degree level may have an impact on the analysis of a specific issue.

The most interesting observation pertaining to research related to master's students is that none of the studies employed a multiple-institution design. In fact, all of the master's-only studies utilized fairly simplistic designs. Only 2 of the 20 master's-only studies looked at more than one field. These findings add evidence to the long-standing criticisms by several individuals that not enough research has been devoted to master's education. Hauptman (1986) made the

TABLE 3. Number of Student-Related Research Studies in Each of Three Foci

Type of student	Single institution		Multiple institutions		Total
	Single field	Multiple field	Single field	Multiple field	
Master's	18	2	0	0	20
Doctorate	9	4	4	4	21
Nonspecific/both	12	22	3	16	53
Total	39	28	7	20	94

following point: "master's degree students are virtually an unknown quantity despite the fact that those students represent by far the largest component of advanced degree enrollments" (p. xiii). More research in this area is definitely warranted.

Looking at a more general breakdown of single and multiple-institution studies, Table 3 indicates that only 27 of the 94 studies utilized more than one institution. While the proportion of multiple-institution studies is already low, there is also the fact that only one of those 27 studies aggregated institutions for comparative purposes. Granted, comparing graduate student opinions by institutions was not a purpose of any of these studies, but such an analysis is needed. Differences among graduate institutions do exist, and it is likely that differences among students at various institutions would be found if such studies were conducted. In fact, Malaney (1987c) mentioned this point in the comparison of his results to those of another study conducted at a different institution.

Specific Directions

While the above discussion alludes to various areas where improvements could be made in the general design of research related to graduate students, there are also several specific topics that warrant further research. Some of these topics were mentioned earlier but are elaborated here, while other suggestions have not been mentioned previously.

First, pertaining to the studies on predicting success in graduate school, most of the previous research has focused on such predictors as standardized test scores, grades, and other academic measures, but a large part of success in graduate school seems to involve traits not related to academics. More work needs to be done relating personality variables such as stamina or perseverance, willpower, and motivation to success in graduate school. Given the extraordinary amounts of work and the time demands placed on students, organizational ability might also prove to be an important predictor of success. The ability to interact positively with others, especially faculty, could also be an important factor.

Regarding financial concerns, a major point in Hauptman's (1986) book deals with the lack of information on how graduate and professional students finance their advanced studies. He suggested that surveys of currently enrolled graduate and professional students be taken periodically to determine exactly how they finance their studies. He also suggested that additional surveys concentrate on undergraduate borrowers to study the impact of debt on various issues, including the desire to pursue advanced study.

There has also been very little theory-based or theory-generating research. The study by Kuh and Thomas (1983) on adult development theory was intriguing because of the attempt to apply existing theories to a graduate student population. While graduate students may have certain similarities to the general population, they are also different in many respects. In fact, a theory on graduate student development is probably in order. The various transitions that graduate students must endure can be perceived as developmental. It is likely that behavioral modifications do occur over time due to the graduate experiences. This is most likely true of doctoral students, who often take many years to complete their degrees. In order to study such developmental processes, some type of longitudinal design would be ideal.

There clearly has not been enough research on minorities in graduate education. With the current trend of the decreasing enrollment of blacks in graduate school, this issue becomes more crucial for that population. One can speculate that much of the problem of decreasing enrollments is due primarily to financial concerns, but research is needed to verify this speculation. Another potential reason may be related to the perceived value of advanced degrees.

Another area of concern regarding minority graduate students is the quality of life they experience in academic departments and universities as a whole. Minority graduate students are virtually nonexistent in some fields, as are minority faculty members to serve as role models. The particular concerns of these students must be understood, especially in order to increase their retention rates. Research along these lines is needed desperately.

One possible reason for a lack of research on minority students could be simply the low number of students in particular fields and institutions. The low numbers are especially dissuasive of the quantitative analytical techniques which have become so dominant in higher education research in general, but the low numbers do not prohibit qualitative research. In fact, methods such as ethnography should be particularly appealing for trying to understand the general climate for minority students and their experiences in trying to pursue graduate education in certain fields of study and in certain institutions. Such research techniques have been overlooked in graduate education research, and in some cases, they may be the best techniques to utilize. The complex issue of minority graduate education appears to be such a case.

Administration of Graduate Education

Turning from the student-based research, there has been very little research related to the administration of graduate education. The following four quasi-related potential research topics are discussed here: (1) rules and regulations pertaining to graduate education; (2) the organizational structure of graduate education; (3) decision making in graduate education; and (4) the power of academic departments relative to the graduate school.

Rules and Regulations

Two recent studies which were discussed previously in this chapter looked at some of the rules and processes of graduate education. In a national study, Quarles and Roney (1986) looked at the style and format requirements for the preparation of dissertations. Freeman and Loadman (1985) looked at some of the requirements for the doctoral comprehensive examination in the field of education at two institutions. But these two studies touch only the surface of all of the various rules and regulations that pertain to graduate study. For instance, there are residency requirements, credit hour requirements, time deadlines, and rules of examination processes. A more thorough study would provide more knowledge about the meaning of an earned graduate degree across institutions.

A fairly complete study of the centralized rules of graduate schools could probably be conducted by simply reviewing graduate school catalogs and other related documents. Since individual academic departments are likely to have additional rules, a researcher might also want to investigate the rules in particular disciplines. One could compare institutions, perhaps using the Carnegie classifications, to determine if, for instance, the doctoral programs in a specific field have similar standards and requirements across institutional type. Such research might prove useful not only for faculty and administrators in the given fields, but for the potential graduate students in those fields.

Structure, Decision Making, and Power

Regarding the organizational structure of graduate education, very little has been written about the placement of a graduate school in the overall university organizational structure. Some graduate school deans are in charge of research and report to the provost, while others report to a vice-president who is in charge of both research and graduate studies. While a variety of organizational structures exist, little is known about their composition or their relative organizational effectiveness. A study designed to investigate the organizational placement of graduate schools within the central administration and the effectiveness of the various structures could prove quite valuable to university administrators.

Regarding decision making, many graduate schools have decision-making bodies, sometimes referred to as graduate councils, which are comprised of faculty and student representatives from the academic departments within an institution. These councils create the policies by which the academic departments guide their graduate programs. The councils can also set the tone of interaction between the graduate school and the academic departments. Virtually nothing is known about these decision-making bodies and the interactions that occur among a council, the graduate school dean, and the departments.

The interactions that do occur often pertain to some type of power situation. Departments often want something from the graduate school, such as money or a special dispensation from rules. Some departments get what they want, while others do not. This leads to an important potential research question: What is the relative power of individual departments compared to the power of the graduate school dean and/or the graduate council on matters of graduate education? Of course, part of the answer involves the strength of leadership and the management style of the dean, but the relative power of an individual department might also be attributed to such factors as its size in terms of the number of faculty and students, its national rank and prestige, its amount of external funding, and its political influence on campus. One could hypothesize that the power of a graduate school dean is inversely proportional to a department's score on each of these variables.

A study designed to address this question of power, as well as organizational structure and decision making, would add to the understanding of graduate education and would be an addition to the higher education literature on organization and administration. If such a study were also to include an investigation of the effectiveness of various organizational structures and decision-making processes of graduate education, the information could serve as a structural guide for university administrators. Too often, one sees new university presidents reorganize existing structures simply because of past familiarity with the structures and without the benefit of any research findings on the effectiveness of the structures.

Unfortunately, such a study would not be easy to conduct. A two-phase research design would appear to be appropriate, the first phase being simply to survey graduate schools to ascertain information relative to the structure and function of graduate education at each institution. The member institutions of the Council of Graduate Schools could serve as a population for the study. The second phase of the study would be more time-consuming, as it would entail site visits to selected institutions in order to talk to graduate faculty and administrators and to actually observe the processes in action. But given the complexity of the issues involved in such a study, it would be most difficult to obtain meaningful data in any other way. Regardless of the method of research, a major study of these topics is long overdue.

CONCLUSIONS

There is a strong need for ongoing national, longitudinal data related to a variety of factors in graduate education, especially students. Such research would add information to several topics discussed in this review, from recruitment to retention to employment. In fact, some topics, such as retention, are desperately in need of longitudinal designs. While the need exists, the vehicle for such research is still a mystery. While the new Center for Research in Graduate Education at the University of Rochester may be such a vehicle in the future, its focus is to be directed toward the top research universities in the country, so the data may not be representative of graduate students in general. Hauptman (1986) has suggested that the annual survey conducted by the Council of Graduate Schools and the GRE Board "should be revamped and expanded to become the reliable national data source on graduate student enrollments" (p. xiv). Whether this suggestion is viable is dependent upon the two organizations themselves, but it seems like a good recommendation.

Clearly, there are many more directions that future research on graduate education can take, but first there is also another question to consider: How does one stimulate such research? One possible answer was mentioned at the beginning of this chapter, namely, a new academic journal for research on graduate education. Of course, a new academic journal can exist only if there is enough quality research to fill the pages. Based on the research studies that were reviewed in this chapter, a potential editor may have cause for concern. Another potential problem for the field of higher education, as a whole, is that a new journal would very likely attract articles that are currently being published in existing higher education journals, which may need those articles for their own survival. Regardless of the costs, an academic journal devoted solely to issues and research in graduate education could be valuable in stimulating new research and attracting new researchers to this area.

Acknowledgments. I would like to thank Roy Koenigsknecht, Dean of the Graduate School at The Ohio State University, who provided me with both the time and opportunity to conduct the research and write this chapter.

REFERENCES

Adler, N. E. (1976). Women students. In J. Katz and R. T. Hartnett (eds.), *Scholars in the Making: The Development of Graduate and Professional Students*, pp. 197–225. Cambridge, MA: Ballinger.

Anderson, E. F., and Hrabowski, F. A. (1977). Graduate school success of black students from white and black colleges. *Journal of Higher Education* 58(3): 294–303.

Aronson, J. A., Bennett, D., Moore, L. V., and Stoll, N. C. (1985). Student personnel dissertation topics, 1979 to 1983. *Journal of College Student Personnel* 26: 262–264.

Atelsek, F. J., and Gomberg, I. L. (1978). Special programs for female and minority graduate students. Higher Education Panel Report, No. 41.

Ayers, J. B., and Peters, R. M. (1977). Predictive validity of the Test of English as a Foreign Language for Asian graduate students in engineering, chemistry, or mathematics. *Educational and Psychological Measurement* 37(2): 461–463.

Baird, L. L. (1976a). Who goes to graduate school and how they get there. In J. Katz and R. T. Hartnett (eds.), *Scholars in the Making: The Development of Graduate and Professional Students,* pp. 19–48. Cambridge, MA: Ballinger.

Baird, L. L. (1976b). Biographical and educational correlates of graduate and professional school admissions test scores. *Educational and Psychological Measurement* 36: 415–420.

Baird, L. L. (1978). Students' expectations and the realities of graduate and professional schools. *College and University* 54(1): 68–73.

Baldwin, T. R. (1977). The function of today's doctoral programs. *Improving College and University Teaching* 25(1): 83–84.

Baxter, J. C., Brock, B., Hill, P. C., and Rozelle, R. M. (1981). Letters of recommendation: a question of value. *Journal of Applied Psychology* 66(3): 296–301.

Berelson, B. (1960). *Graduate Education in the United States.* New York: McGraw-Hill.

Berg, H. M., and Ferber, M. A. (1983). Men and women graduate students: Who succeeds and why? *Journal of Higher Education* 54(6): 629–648.

Bess, J. L. (1976). Organizational implications of faculty role/activity preferences. Paper presented at the annual meeting of the American Educational Research Association. San Francisco. (ERIC Document Reproduction Service No. ED 134 089.)

Bess, J. L. (1978). Anticipatory socialization of graduate students. *Research in Higher Education* 8(4): 289–317.

Biglan, A. (1973a). The characteristics of subject matter in different academic areas. *Journal of Applied Psychology* 57(3): 195–203.

Biglan, A. (1973b). Relationship between subject matter characteristics and the structure and output of university departments. *Journal of Applied Psychology* 57(3): 204–213.

Blanchard, B. E. (1977). A four-year survey of master degree graduates. *Improving College and University Teaching* 25(2): 93–96, 99.

Blau, P. M. (1973). *The Organization of Academic Work.* New York: Wiley.

Bowen, H. R., and Schuster, J. H. (1986). *American Professors: A National Resource Imperiled.* New York: Oxford University Press.

Breaugh, J. A., and Mann, R. B. (1981). The utility of discriminant analysis for predicting graduation from a master of business administration program. *Educational and Psychological Measurement* 41(2): 495–501.

Brooks, G. C., and Miyares, J. (1977). Assessment of recruitment strategies for other-race, first-time, full-time graduate and professional students of University of Maryland. ERIC-RIE No. ED158687.

Brown, R. (1983). Locus of control and sex role orientation of women graduate students. *College Student Journal* 17(1): 10–12.

Burg, J. C. (1917). The doctorates of philosophy conferred by American universities. *School and Society* 5(110): 145–149.

Busch, J. W. (1985). Mentoring in graduate schools of education: mentors' perceptions. *American Educational Research Journal* 22(2): 257–265.

Carrington, C. H., and Sedlacek, W. E. (1977). Attitudes and characteristics of black graduate students. *Journal of College Student Personnel* 18(6): 467–471.

Carroll, J. G. (1980). Effects of training programs for university teaching assistants: a review of empirical research. *Journal of Higher Education* 51(2): 166–183.

Cartter, A. M. (1976). *Ph.D.'s and the Academic Labor Market*. New York: McGraw-Hill.

Centra, J. A. (1980). Graduate degree aspirations of ethnic student groups. *American Educational Research Journal* 17(4): 459–478.

Chickering, A. W. (1974). *Commuting Versus Resident Students*. San Francisco: Jossey-Bass.

Clark, M. J., and Centra, J. A. (1985). Influences on the career accomplishments of Ph.D.'s. *Research in Higher Education* 23(3): 256–269.

Cook, M. M., and Swanson, A. (1978). The interaction of student and program variables for the purpose of developing a model for predicting graduation from graduate programs over a 10-year period. *Research in Higher Education* 8: 83–91.

Czinkota, M. R. (1980). Medicine and marketing: the case of a graduate medical education. *Journal of Medical Education* 55: 906–911.

Dole, A. A., and Baggaley, A. R. (1979). Prediction of performance in a doctoral education program by the Graduate Record Examinations and other measures. *Educational and Psychological Measurement* 39(2): 421–427.

Dressel, P. L., and Thompson, M. M. (1978). The doctor of arts: a decade of development, 1967–77. *Journal of Higher Education* 49(4): 329–336.

Drory, A. (1980). Expectancy theory prediction of students' choice of graduate studies. *Research in Higher Education* 13(3): 213–223.

Duncan, B. L. (1976). Minority students. In J. Katz and R. T. Hartnett (eds.), *Scholars in the Making: The Development of Graduate and Professional Students*, pp. 227–242. Cambridge, MA: Ballinger.

Dziech, B. W., and Weiner, L. (1984). *The Lecherous Professor: Sexual Harassment on Campus*. Boston: Beacon.

Ethington, C. A., and Smart, J. C. (1985). Persistence to graduate education. *Research in Higher Education* 24(3): 287–303.

Ethington, C. A., and Wolfle, L. M. (1986). Sex differences in quantitative and analytical GRE performance: an exploratory study. *Research in Higher Education* 25(1): 55–67.

Feldman, S. D. (1974). *Escape from the Doll's House: Women in Graduate and Professional School Education*. New York: McGraw-Hill.

Freeman, D. J., and Loadman, W. E. (1985). Advice to doctoral guidance committees from alumni at two universities. *Research in Higher Education* 22(4): 335–346.

Furst, E. J., and Roelfs, P. J. (1979). Validation of the Graduate Record Examinations and the Miller Analogies Test in a doctoral program in education. *Educational and Psychological Measurement* 39(1): 147–151.

Garett, K., and Wulf, K. (1978). The relationship of a measure of critical thinking ability to personality variables and to indicators of academic achievement. *Educational and Psychological Measurement* 38(4): 1181–1187.

Gilbert, M. G. (1982). The impact of graduate school on the family: a systems view. *Journal of College Student Personnel* 23: 128–135.

Girves, J. E., and Wemmerus, V. (1986). Developing a model of graduate student degree progress. Paper presented at the annual meeting of the Association for the Study of Higher Education, San Antonio, February.

Girves, J. E., Wemmerus, V., and Rice, J. (1986). Financial support and graduate student degree progress. Paper presented at the annual meeting of the Association for Institutional Research, Orlando, June.

Griffore, R. J. (1977). Fear of success and task difficulty: effects on graduate students' final exam performance. *Journal of Educational Psychology* 69(5): 556–563.

Griggs, C. M. (1965). *Graduate Education*. New York: Center for Applied Research in Education.

Hadley, H. N. (1975). Development of an instrument to determine adult educators' orientation: androgogical or pedagogical. Unpublished doctoral dissertation, Boston University.

Hargens, L. L. (1983). The production of Ph.D.'s in chemistry. *Research in Higher Education* 19(3): 259–276.

Harmon, L. R., and Soldz, H. (1963). *Doctorate Production in United States Universities 1920–1962*. Publication No. 1142. Washington, D.C.: National Academy of Sciences, National Research Council.

Hartnett, R. T. (1981). Sex differences in the environments of graduate students and faculty. *Research in Higher Education* 14(3): 211–227.

Hartnett, R. T., and Katz, J. (1976). Past and present. In J. Katz and R. T. Hartnett (eds.), *Scholars in the Making,* pp. 3–15. Cambridge, MA: Ballinger.

Hauptman, A. M. (1986). *Students in Graduate and Professional Education: What We Know and Need to Know*. Washington, DC: Association of American Universities.

Hendel, D. D., and Doyle, K. O., Jr. (1978). Predicting success for graduate study in business for English-speaking and non-English-speaking students. *Educational and Psychological Measurement* 38(2): 411–414.

Henry, J. L. (1980). Increasing recruitment and retention of minority students in health programs—dentistry. *Journal of Dental Education* 44: 191–194.

Herbert, D. J., and Holmes, A. F. (1979). Graduate Record Examinations aptitude test scores as a predictor of graduate grade point average. *Educational and Psychological Measurement* 39(2): 415–420.

Hite, L. M. (1985). Female doctoral students: their perceptions and concerns. *Journal of College Student Personnel* 26: 18–22.

Holland, J. L. (1973/1985). *Making Vocational Choices*. Englewood Cliffs, NJ: Prentice-Hall. (First edition, 1973; 2nd ed., 1985.)

Holmes, D., Verrier, D., and Chisholm, P. (1983). *Journal of College Student Personnel* 24: 438–443.

Holmes, T. H., and Rahe, R. H. (1967). The social readjustment rating scale. *Journal of Psychosomatic Research* 11: 213–218.

Jacks, P., Chubin, D. E., Porter, A. L., and Connolly, T. (1983). The ABCs of ABDs: a study of incomplete doctorates. *Improving College and University Teaching* 31(2): 74–81.

Jackson, W. K., and Simpson, R. D. (1983). A survey of graduate teaching assistant instructional improvement programs. *College Student Journal* 17(3): 220–224.

Kagan, D. M., and Stock, W. A. (1980). Equivalencing MAT and GRE scores using simple linear transformation and regression methods. *Journal of Experimental Education* 49(1): 34–37.

Kaplan, S. R. (1982). A feminist cinderella tale: women over thirty in graduate and professional school. *Journal of NAWDAC* 45(2): 9–15.

Katz, J., and Hartnett, R. T. (1976). *Scholars in the Making: The Development of Graduate and Professional Students*. Cambridge, MA: Ballinger.

Khoury, R. M. (1977). The geographic mobility of academic talent: some evidence from sociology. *Research in Higher Education* 7: 155–165.

King, F. J., Heinrich, D. L., Stephenson, R. S., and Spielberger, C. D. (1976). An investigation of the causal influence of trait and state anxiety on academic achievement. *Journal of Educational Psychology* 68(3): 330–334.

Kirnan, J. P., and Geisinger, K. F. (1981). The prediction of graduate school success in psychology. *Educational and Psychological Measurement* 41(3): 815–820.

Kjerulff, K., and Wiggins, N. H. (1976). Graduate student styles of coping with stressful situations. *Journal of Educational Psychology* 68(3): 247–254.

Kuh, G. D., Bean, J. P., Bradley, R. K., Coomes, M. D., and Hunter, D. E. (1986). Changes in research on college students published in selected journals between 1969 and 1983, *The Review of Higher Education* 9(2): 177–192.

Kuh, G. D., Greenlee, F. E., and Lardy, B. A. (1978). A profile of graduate students in college student personnel. *Journal of College Student Personnel* 19(6): 531–537.

Kuh, G. D., and Thomas, M. L. (1983). The use of adult development theory with graduate students. *Journal of College Student Personnel* 24: 12–19.

Lang, D. (1984). Education, stratification, and the academic hierarchy. *Research in Higher Education* 21(3): 329–352.

Lange, S. (1980). An anxiety-support model for graduate education. *Journal of College Student Personnel* 21: 146–150.

Lawrence, P. R., and Lorsch J. W. (1967a). Differentiation and integration in complex organizations. *Administrative Science Quarterly* 12(1): 1–47.

Lawrence, P. R., and Lorsch J. W. (1967b). *Organization and Environment: Managing Differentiation and Integration.* Boston: Graduate School of Business Administration, Harvard University.

LeCluyse, E. E., Tollefson, N., and Borgers, S. B. (1985). Differences in female graduate students in relation to mentoring. *College Student Journal* 19(4): 411–415.

Leonardson, G. R. (1979). The contribution of academic factors in predicting graduate school success. *College Student Journal* 13(1): 21–24.

Lewis, L. H. (1983). Coping with change: married women in graduate school. *Lifelong Learning* 7(1): 8–9, 28, 31.

Locke, H. J., and Wallace, K. M. (1959). Short marital-adjustment and prediction tests: their reliability and validity. *Marriage and Family Living* 21: 251–255.

Logan, S. H. (1980). Testing for sex bias in graduate school admissions. *College and University* 55(2): 156–170.

Malaney, G. D. (1983). Graduate student recruitment in professional public administration programs: a low-cost method of projecting potential student markets. *College and University* 58: 260–269.

Malaney, G. D. (1984). An analysis of financial aid in the recruitment of graduate students at The Ohio State University. *Journal of Student Financial Aid* 14: 11–19.

Malaney, G. D. (1986a). Use of a computerized data base for monitoring graduate education: an analysis of faculty and administrative support, *Journal of Educational Technology Systems* 14(3): 239–260.

Malaney, G. D. (1986b). Differentiation in graduate education, *Research in Higher Education* 25(1): 82–96.

Malaney, G. D. (1986c). Microcomputers in graduate school administration: the design and implementation of a computerized relational data base system for monitoring graduate education. *Journal of Educational Technology Systems* 15(1): 91–114.

Malaney, G. D. (1986d). Characteristics of graduate students in Biglan areas of study. *Research in Higher Education* 25(4): 328–341.

Malaney, G. D. (1987a). Efforts to recruit graduate students: an analysis of departmental recruiting practices. *College and University* 62(1): 126–136.

Malaney, G. D. (1987b). Who receives financial aid to pursue graduate study? *Research in Higher Education* 26: 85–98.

Malaney, G. D. (1987c). Why students purse graduate education, how they find out about a program, and why they apply to a specific school? *College and University* 62: 247–258.

Mayall, M. M. (1979). Attitudes of chief administrators toward external doctoral degrees. *Phi Delta Kappan* 60(8): 610.

McCaffrey, S. S., Miller, T. K., and Winston, R. B., Jr. (1984). Comparison of career maturity among graduate students and undergraduates. *Journal of College Student Personnel* 25: 127–132.

McCarthy, M. M., Kuh, G. D., and Beckman, J. M. (1979). Characteristics and attitudes of doctoral students in educational administration. *Phi Delta Kappan* 61(3): 200–203.

McClain, D., Vance, B., and Wood, E. (1984). Understanding and predicting the yield in the MBA admissions process. *Research in Higher Education* 20: 55–76.

McKeon, D. M., and Piercy, F. P. (1980). Factors in marital adjustment of graduate students. *National Association of Women Deans, Administrators and Counselors Journal* 43: 40–43.

Messmer, D. J., and Solomon, R. J. (1979). Differential predictability in a selection model for graduate students: implications for validity testing. *Educational and Psychological Measurement* 39(4): 859–866.

Millimet, C. R., and Flume, M. E. (1982). Estimating graduate admission standards in psychology. *Research in Higher Education* 17(2): 125–137.

Moffat, L. K. (1978). Departmental characteristics and physics Ph.D. production 1968–1973. *Sociology of Education* 51(2): 124–132.

Muffo, J. A., and Coccari, R. L. (1982). Predictors of outside funding for research among AASCU institutions. *Research in Higher Education* 16(1): 71–80.

National Board on Graduate Education. (1976). *Minority Group Participation in Graduate Education*. Washington, DC: National Academy of Sciences.

National Research Council. (1986). *Summary Report 1984 Doctorate Recipients from United States Universities*. Washington, DC: National Academy Press.

Nevill, D. D., Ware, W. B., and Smith, A. B. (1978). A comparison of student ratings of teaching assistants and faculty members. *American Educational Research Journal* 15(1): 25–37.

Nielsen, L. (1980). Feminism and factoral analyses: alleviating students' statistics anxieties. *College Student Journal* 13(1): 51–56.

Olson, C., and King, M. A. (1985). A preliminary analysis of the decision process of graduate students in college choice. *College and University* 60: 304–315.

Oltman, P. K., and Hartnett, R. T. (1985). The role of the Graduate Record Examinations in graduate admissions. *Journal of Higher Education* 56(5): 523–537.

Omizo, M. M., and Michael, W. B. (1979). The prediction of performance in a counselor education master's degree program. *Educational and Psychological Measurement* 39(2): 433–437.

O'Neil, J. M. (1981). Toward a theory and practice of mentoring in psychology. In J. M. O'Neil and L. S. Wrightsman (Chairs), Mentoring: Psychological, personal, and career implications. Symposium presented at the annual meeting of the American Psychological Association, Los Angeles, August.

Patalano, F. (1978). School psychology graduate students' perceptions of effective and ineffective teachers. *College Student Journal* 12(4): 360–363.

Perl, K. G., and Kahn, M. W. (1983). Psychology graduate students' attitudes toward research: a national survey. *Teaching of Psychology* 10(3): 139–143.

Pogrow, S. (1977). The effect of age on the attitude and performance of doctoral students at Stanford University. *Education* 98(1): 78–81.

Pogrow, S. (1978). Program characteristics and the use of student data to predict attrition from doctoral programs. *College Student Journal* 12(4): 348–353.

Powers, D. E., and Lehman, J. (1983). GRE Candidates' Perceptions of the Importance Graduate Admissions Factors. *Research in Higher Education* 19(2): 231–249.

Pristo, L. J. (1979). The prediction of graduate school success by the canonical correlation. *Educational and Psychological Measurement* 39(4): 929–933.

Quarles, D. R., and Roney, R. K. (1986). Preparation, style, and format of doctoral dissertations in U.S. colleges and universities. *Research in Higher Education* 25(1): 97–108.

Reilly, R. R. (1976). Factors in graduate student performance. *American Educational Research Journal* 13(2): 125–138.

Reisman, B. L., Lawless, M., Robinson, R., and Beckett, J. (1983). Urban graduate students: a need for community. *College Student Journal* 17(1): 48–50.

Remus, W., and Isa, D. (1983). Predicting actual university enrollments. *College Student Journal* 17(2): 137–140.

Rice, J. K. (1977). Perceptions of males and females concerning their graduate education experience in counseling. *Journal of NAWDAC* 41(1): 32–37.

Rimmer, S. M., Lammert, M., and McClain, P. (1982). An assessment of graduate student needs. *College Student Journal* 16(2): 187–192.

Rippetoe, J. K., and Peters, G. R. (1979). Introductory courses and the teaching assistant. *Improving College and University Teaching* 27(1): 20–24.

Roaden, A. L., and Worthen, B. R. (1976). Research assistantship experiences and subsequent research productivity. *Research in Higher Education* 5: 141–158.

Roemer, R. E. (1983). Changing patterns of degree selection among women: 1970–78. *Research in Higher Education* 18(2): 435–454.

Rokeach, M. (1973). *The Nature of Human Values*. New York: Free Press.

Rouse, L. P. (1983). Social power in the college classroom: the impact of instructor resource manipulation and student dependence on graduate students' mood and morale. *American Educational Research Journal* 20(3): 375–383.

Schneider, B. E. (1987). Graduate women, sexual harassment and university policy. *Journal of Higher Education* 58(1): 46–65.

Scott, R. R., and Shaw, M. E. (1985). Black and white performance in graduate school and policy implications of the use of Graduate Record Examination scores in admissions. *Journal of Negro Education* 54(1): 14–23.

Shymansky, J. A., and Penick, J. E. (1979). Do laboratory teaching assistants exhibit sex bias? *Journal of College Science Teaching* 8(4): 223–225.

Smart, J. C. (1987). Satisfaction with graduate education. *Journal of College Student Personnel*. 28: 218–222.

Smith, B. L. R. (1985). Graduate education in the United States. In B. L. R. Smith (ed.), *The State of Graduate Education*, pp. 1–30. Washington, DC: Brookings Institution.

Snyder, R. G. (1985). Some indicators of the condition of graduate education in the sciences. In B. L. R. Smith (ed.), *The State of Graduate Education*, pp. 31–55. Washington, DC: Brookings Institution.

Sobol, M. G. (1984). GPA, GMAT, and SCALE: a method for quantification of admissions criteria. *Research in Higher Education* 20(1): 77–88.

Solmon, L. C. (1976). *Male and Female Graduate Students: The Question of Equal Opportunity*. New York: Praeger.

Stark, J. S., Lowther, M. A., and Austin, A. E. (1985). Comparative career accomplishments of two decades of women and men doctoral graduates in education. *Research in Higher Education* 22(3): 219–249.

Stock, W. A., Kagan, D. M., and Van Wagenen, R. K. (1980). Graduate Record Examination and Miller Analogies Test scores: examining four methods of equivalencing. *Educational and Psychological Measurement* 40(4): 829–834.

Stodt, M. M., and Thielens, W., Jr. (1985). Credentialism among graduate students. *Research in Higher Education* 22(3): 251–272.

Storr, R. J. (1953). *The Beginnings of Graduate Education in America.* Chicago: University of Chicago Press.

Thompson, D. N., and Layne, B. H. (1980). The employment status of M.Ed. graduates Georgia State University. *College Student Journal* 14(3): 260–263.

Thompson, M. L., and Ellis, J. R. (1984). A study of graduate assistantships in American schools of education. *College Student Journal* 18(1): 78–86.

Toombs, W. (1977). Awareness and use of academic research by doctoral students. *Research in Higher Education* 7: 43–65.

Topp, R. F. (1977). The neurotic graduate student of our time. *Improving College and University Teaching* 25(2): 105, 107.

Trent, C., and Johnson, J. F. (1977). The influence of students' values and educational attitudes on their evaluation of faculty. *Research in Higher Education* 7: 117–125.

Tuckman, B. H., and Tuckman, H. P. (1984). Unemployment among graduating Ph.D.'s: do economic conditions matter? *Research in Higher Education* 20(4): 385–398.

Turcotte, R. B. (1983). Enrollment management at the graduate level. *The Journal of College Admissions* 27: 24–28.

Vacc, N. N., and Picot, R. (1984). Predicting success in doctoral study. *College Student Journal* 18(2): 113–116.

Valdez, R. (1982). First year doctoral students and stress. *College Student Journal* 16(1): 30–37.

Vartuli, S. (1982). *The Ph.D. Experience: A Woman's Point of View.* New York: Praeger.

Vecchio, R., and Costin, F. (1977). Predicting teacher effectiveness from graduate admissions predictors. *American Educational Research Journal* 14(2): 169–176.

Vidler, D. C., and Wood, P. H. (1981). Differences in curiosity level between undergraduate and graduate students. *College Student Journal* 15(2): 153–155.

Walcott, G. D. (1915). Statistical study of doctor of philosophy men. *School and Society* 1(2): 66–71.

Wallace, M. J., Jr., and Schwab, D. P. (1976). A cross-validated comparison of five models used to predict graduate admissions committee decisions. *Journal of Applied Psychology* 61(5): 559–563.

Walters, E. (1965). The rise of graduate education. In E. Walters (ed.), *Graduate Education Today,* pp. 1–29. Washington, DC: American Council on Education.

Wertheim, E. G., Widom, C. S., and Wortzel, L. H. (1978). Multivariate analysis of male and female professional career choice correlates. *Journal of Applied Psychology* 63(20): 234–242.

Whaley, W. G. (1966). In place of slogans. *The Graduate Journal* 7(2): 281–299.

Wiant, H. V., Jr., Nourbon, W. T., Somberg, S. I., and Young, W. T. (1978). Structure of graduate faculties in the United States Today. *Improving College and University Teaching* 26(2): 141–142.

Williams, E. E., Gallas, J. A., and Quiriconi, S. (1984). Addressing the problem of dropouts among graduate students. *Journal of College Student Personnel* 25: 173–174.

Williams, M. (1978). Faculty and students as admissions raters: a comparison of the validity of their predictions. *College and University* 53(2): 172–182.

Winston, R. B., Jr., Ullom, M., and Werring, C. J. (1983). The housing graduate assistantship: factors that affect choice and perceived satisfaction. *Journal of College Student Personnel* 24: 225–230.

Wolfle, L. M. (1982). Predictors of outside funding for research among AASCU institutions: a reanalysis. *Research in Higher Education* 17(2): 99–104.

Youngblood, S. A., and Martin, B. J. (1982). Ability testing and graduate admissions: decisions process modeling and validation. *Educational and Psychological Measurement* 42(4): 1153–1162.

Author Index

455

Subject Index

A

Academic alienation, 25
Academic governance, 320, 350-352. *See also* Policy-making, faculty participation in
Academic improvement, *see* Outcomes
Academic policy, 82-83. *See also* Policy-making, faculty participation in
ACPU (Assessment of the Performance of Colleges and Universities) survey, 84-85
Action research, *see* Outcomes
Activities Index (AI), 3, 7
Adaptive strategy, 217
Ad hoc committees, 330, 332, 336, 341-343
Adhocracy, 372-373, 378-381, 383-387
Administration
  faculty participation in, *see* Policy-making, faculty participation in
  graduate education, 436-438, 444-446
  strategic planning, *see* Strategic planning
Affective outcomes, 61-62
Aging
  biological-physiological theories of, 299-300
  and cultural devaluation, 285
  economic theories of, 302-303
  and productivity, 283-285, 299
  psychological theories of, 300
  sociological theories of, 301-302
  as vitality indicator, 298-303
AI (Activities Index), 3, 7
Alienation, academic, 25
Alpha press, 3
Alverno College, 62-63, 68, 87, 95
Anthropological approach to organizational culture, 358-360
Antioch College, 339-341, 343-344, 348-349
Anti-Semitism, 188-189, 204
Anxiety, graduate education research on, 401, 426-427
Assessment, *see* Outcomes

Assessment of the Performance of Colleges and Universities (ACPU) survey, 84-85
Assistants, graduate, 401, 418-421
Athletics, 190-191
Attrition, 1-2, 401, 413-415. *See also* Enrollment
Australia, 116
Austria, 109, 127, 131, 133, 135, 138
Authority
  environments, 326
  guild, 347-349
  locus of, 238
  shared, 325-237

B

Barnard College, 186
Behavioral approaches to environmental study, 2
Belgium, 168
Bennington College, 4
Berkeley, University of California at, 15, 332-333, 341-345, 349
Beta press, 3
"Big Six" tobacco firms, 238, 244, 248, 261
Biological-physiological theories of aging, 299-300
Bloom taxonomy, 56-57
Britain, *see* United Kingdom
Brown University, 188
Budgeting, 225, 233-235. *See also* Resources

C

California Institute of Technology, 15
Cambridge University, 321
Canada, 18, 116
Careers and employment
  in Europe, *see* Europe, employment and education in
  faculty development, 286, 303-307
  graduate students in U.S., 401, 417-418, 423